MODERN
AFGHANISTAN

MODERN AFGHANISTAN
THE IMPACT OF 40 YEARS OF WAR

EDITED BY
M. NAZIF SHAHRANI

INDIANA UNIVERSITY PRESS

This book is a publication of

Indiana University Press
Office of Scholarly Publishing
Herman B Wells Library 350
1320 East 10th Street
Bloomington, Indiana 47405 USA

iupress.indiana.edu

© 2018 by Indiana University Press

All rights reserved
No part of this book may be reproduced or utilized in any form or by any means, electronic or mechanical, including photocopying and recording, or by any information storage and retrieval system, without permission in writing from the publisher. The Association of American University Presses' Resolution on Permissions constitutes the only exception to this prohibition. The paper used in this publication meets the minimum requirements of the American National Standard for Information Sciences—Permanence of Paper for Printed Library Materials, ANSI Z39.48-1992.

Manufactured in the United States of America

Library of Congress Cataloging-in-Publication Data

Names: Shahrani, M. Nazif Mohib, 1945- editor.
Title: Modern Afghanistan : the impact of 40 years of war / edited by M. Nazif Shahrani.
Description: Bloomington, Indiana : Indiana University Press, 2018. | Includes bibliographical references and index.
Identifiers: LCCN 2018004320 (print) | LCCN 2017056689 (ebook) | ISBN 9780253030269 (e-book) | ISBN 9780253029775 | ISBN 9780253029775q(hardback :qalk. paper) | ISBN 9780253030054q(pbk. :qalk. paper)
Subjects: LCSH: Afghanistan—Social conditions—20th century. | Afghanistan—Social conditions—21st century. | Violence—Afghanistan. | Political stability—Afghanistan. | Afghanistan—Politics and government—20th century. | Afghanistan—Politics and government—21st century.
Classification: LCC HN670.6.A8 (print) | LCC HN670.6.A8 M63 2018 (ebook) | DDC 306.09581—dc23
LC record available at https://lccn.loc.gov/2018004320

1 2 3 4 5 23   22 21 20 19 18

DEDICATION

For Maha Noureldin and our sons (Samad, Abdurahim, and Noorhadi), who desire peace and opportunities for the peoples of Afghanistan as much as I and the vast majority of the peoples of Afghanistan do. May all of us soon witness the end of wars and violence in Afghanistan and beyond.

CONTENTS

Preface — ix
Acknowledgments — xv
Maps — xvii

Introduction: The Impact of Four Decades of War and Violence on Afghan Society and Political Culture / M. Nazif Shahrani — 1

Part I: Technologies of Power—Competing Discourses on National Identity, Statehood, and State Stability — 19

1. Afghanistan: A Turbulent State in Transition / Amin Saikal — 21

2. Afghanistan's "Traditional" Islam in Transition: The Deep Roots of Taliban Extremism / Bashir Ahmad Ansari — 37

3. Language, Poetry, and Identity in Afghanistan: Poetic Texts, Changing Contexts / Mohammad Omar Sharifi — 56

4. Lineages of the Urban State: Locating Continuity and Change in Post-2001 Kabul / Khalid Homayun Nadiri and M. Farshid Alemi Hakimyar — 77

5. Webs and Spiders: Four Decades of Violence, Intervention, and Statehood in Afghanistan (1978–2016) / Timor Sharan — 102

6. Merchant-Warlords: Changing Forms of Leadership in Afghanistan's Unstable Political Economy / Noah Coburn — 121

7. Borders, Access to Strategic Resources, and Challenges to State Stability / Ahmad Shayeq Qassem — 133

8. Brought to You by Foreigners, Warlords, and Local Activists: TV and the Afghan Culture Wars / Wazhmah Osman — 149

Part II: Personal and Collective Identities, Gender Relations, and the Trust Deficit — 177

9. "The War Destroyed Our Society": Masculinity, Violence, and Shifting Cultural Idioms among Afghan Pashtuns / Andrea Chiovenda — 179

10. Engendering the Taliban / Sonia Ahsan — 200

11. Anticipating Discontinuous Change: Afghanistan in Retrospect and Prospect / Robert L. Canfield and Fahim Masoud — 213

Part III: Adapting to a New Political Ecology of Uncertainties at the Margins — 227

12. Badakhshanis since the Saur Revolution: Struggle, Triumph, Hope, and Uncertainty / M. Nazif Shahrani — 229

13. Hazara Civil Society Activists and Local, National, and International Political Institutions / Melissa Kerr Chiovenda — 251

14. Adapting to Three Decades of Uncertainty: The Flexibility of Social Institutions among Baloch Groups in Afghanistan / Just Boedeker — 271

15. Party Institutionalization Meets Women's Empowerment? Acquiring Power and Influence in Afghanistan / Anna Larson — 290

Part IV: Violence, Social Services Delivery, and the Rising Trust Deficit — 311

16. Childbirth and Social Change in Afghanistan / Kylea Laina Liese — 313

17. Signatures of Distrust in Contemporary Afghanistan: More Than a Decade of Development Effort for Vulnerable Groups: The Case of Disability / Parul Bakhshi and Jean-Francois Trani — 327

Index — 353

PREFACE

IN THIS VOLUME, a new generation of Afghanistan studies scholars present systematic interdisciplinary assessments of the impact of almost four decades of war—from outside military invasions and interventions, resistance and rebellions against the center, pervasive internecine factional violence, and proxy wars. They also assess the impact of international political and economic reconstruction programs (since 2002) on the social institutions, personal and collective identities, and political culture of Afghanistan.[1] Unlike the security-centered studies that have predominated recent research and writing on Afghanistan, the aims of contributors to this volume are twofold: first, to offer detailed analyses and assessments of the impact of state failures and violence on the internal sociopolitical dynamics, gender, and intergroup relations (ethno-linguistic, tribal, sectarian, ideological, and regional group and community relations) from the various perspectives of the peoples of Afghanistan themselves; second, to explicate how experiences of war and violence have shaped and reshaped the social fabric, institutional norms, and governance practices in Afghanistan as well as the consequences of ongoing security challenges and poor governance within the country's troubled neighborhoods and beyond.

Early drafts of ten of the chapters in this volume were presented in two panels held at the 2012 Annual Meeting of the American Anthropological Association (AAA) in San Francisco.[2] Complemented by eight additional invited contributions from eleven scholars, the papers were then extensively discussed in the workshop held (April 18–21, 2014) at the Ostrom Workshop in Political Theory and Policy Analysis, Indiana University, Bloomington. In all, twenty-five scholars from Afghanistan, Europe, Australia, and the United States (half of them with deep personal roots in Afghanistan) participated in these fora.[3] These highly policy-relevant and timely essays make significant contributions to our knowledge and understanding, not only of consequences of the wars on Afghanistan society and political culture but they also point toward ways to best address pending challenges of governance, security, and instability in Afghanistan as well as in the wider region.

This book was conceived as a follow-up to two other panels organized over three decades ago by my colleague Robert L. Canfield (Washington University, St. Louis) and me at the 1980 Annual Meeting of the American Anthropological Association (AAA) in Washington, DC, involving eighteen scholars with extensive research on Afghanistan. That meeting was held at a dramatic moment in Central Asian history: Afghan communist "revolutionaries" had seized the reins of government with the intent to radically transform Afghan society and culture. A popular Islamic resistance movement or jihad was gathering strength, forcing the Soviets to militarily intervene in defense of their clients in Kabul.

The 1980 panelists, who had carried out extensive ethnographic field research covering different parts of the country during the 1960s and 1970s, presented authoritative reports and analyses of why and how various peoples of Afghanistan were reacting to the Soviet invasion and occupation of their Muslim homeland during the 1980s. They also discussed how the popular jihad resistance was likely to influence the course of events in Afghanistan and the region. No one, however, expected the conflict to continue for as long as it has, or to instigate the so called global war on terror at the dawn of the twenty-first century. Thirteen of the papers were coedited by Shahrani and Canfield as *Revolutions and Rebellions in Afghanistan: Anthropological Perspectives* and published (1984) by the Institute of International Studies (IIS) at the University of California, Berkeley.[4] This earlier volume stands as a testament to the collective anthropological knowledge and analysis of Afghanistan's social systems, institutional structures, and political culture at that critical moment in its tumultuous history.

The almost four decades of war and persistent violent conflicts have affected virtually all the peoples and social institutions of every tribal, ethnic, and sectarian group and region across the country and left the fabric of traditional Afghan society substantially altered. Since 2002, Afghanistan has been the object of considerable international collective attention for reconstruction and development, albeit with dubious results. The contributors to this volume were asked to consult the essays in the *Revolutions and Rebellions in Afghanistan* volume as the available ethnographic baseline data and analyses at the onset of the wars. They were urged to assess the impact of nearly four decades of chronic warfare and violence on the fabric of Afghan society, personal and social identities, and its political culture with special attention to enhancing state stability and effective governance in post-Taliban Afghanistan, especially in the period following interventions by the United States, NATO, and their non-NATO allies.

During the April 2014 workshop, we asked the participants to consider examining their data in light of the analytical utility of the institutional analysis and development (IAD) and social ecological systems (SES) frameworks developed at the

Ostrom Workshop in Political Theory and Policy Analysis on the campus of Indiana University.[5] Many of the authors found the concepts and analytical approaches of the IAD and SES useful, as reflected (explicitly and implicitly) in many chapters of this book. All participants at the workshop benefited greatly from the active engagement of many affiliated faculty of the Ostrom Workshop, who served as facilitators and discussants of particular sessions during the workshop.[6] Their feedback on the papers at the workshop and on some later cases, helped in the revisions of the chapters as well as the reorganization of the book in its current form.

More specifically, this volume examines continuities and changes in key aspects of Afghanistan's state-society relations and political culture. In part 1, shifts and continuities in technologies of power, especially of the political economy of the Afghan state, the emergence of contested discourses of sovereignties and national identity, the reaffirmation of the contested parts of the national borders and governance structures, and continued challenges to state stabilization are analyzed. Part 2 focuses on the analysis of the impact of war and violence on personal and collective identities, gender relations, and the crises in state-citizen trust. Part 3 considers adaptations to new political-economic opportunities and uncertainties in the peripheries of state and society. Part 4 explicates consequences of the pervasive culture of violence on the delivery of social services, especially to the most vulnerable, resulting in a growing trust deficit among the peoples of Afghanistan toward state officials and international institutions. The introductory chapter further elaborates on the organization of the book within the broader context of the changing nature of war during the last century, especially in the Muslim Middle East and Central Asia.

Notes

1. By political culture I mean the ideals, attitudes, beliefs, and sentiments as well as operating norms that give order and meaning to the political process. That is, political culture provides a model of and model for political reality within a society (see Pye [1968], Diamond [1993, 7–8], and Geertz [1973, 93–94], and for a brief review and a working definition and function of the concept, see Shahrani [2013]).

2. Robert L. Canfield (Washington University, St. Louis) and M. Nazif Shahrani (Indiana University, Bloomington coorganized and chaired the panels. Four of the participants in the AAA panels—Katja Mielke (ZEFa Bonn University), Elia Susanna I. Lopez (Universitat Autonoma de Barcelona), Gabriele Rasuly-Paleczek (University of Vienna, Austria), and Christopher Wenzel (Humboldt University)—were unable to contribute to this volume.

3. Professor Amin Saikal (Australian National University-ANU) was the ANU-IU Pan Asia Institute visiting Distinguished Scholar on our campus at Indiana University, Bloomington, and delivered the keynote address to the April 2014 Workshop. Bashir Ansari, Parul Bakhshi, Farshid Hakimyar, Ann Larson, Fahim Masoud, Khalid Naderi, Wazhmah Osman, Ahmad Shyeq Qassem, Omar Sharifi, and Jean-Francois Trani, who were not

participants at the AAA panels in 2012, presented their papers at the Indiana University workshop. Gabriele Rasuly-Paleczek and Elia Susanna I. Lopez also participated at the workshop, but Katja Mielke and Christopher Wenzel were unable to do so. The papers by the rest of 2012 AAA panelists—Sonia Ahsan, Just Boedeker, Robert L. Canfield, Andrea Chiovenda, Melissa Kerr Chiovenda, Noah Coburn, Kylea L. Liese, and M. Nazif Shahrani—were also discussed extensively at the 2014 Ostrom Workshop at IUB.

4. Long out of print but still in high demand, *Revolution and Rebellions in Afghanistan* is being republished concurrently with this volume by Indiana University Press, with permission of the previous publisher.

5. Elinor Ostrom, the only female Noble Laureate in economics (2009), and her husband, Vincent Ostrom, were founders and codirectors of the Workshop in Political Theory and Policy Analysis (famously known as the Workshop). In collaboration with many other scholars worldwide, the Ostroms began the work on the institutional analysis and development framework (IAD) in the early 1980s (Kiser and Ostrom 1982). It then led to the development of the social-ecological system (SES) framework (for details, see Ostrom [2007a, 2007b and 2010]; for its concise history and key concepts and principles see McGinnis [2010]; for an earlier attempted application of the frameworks in studying political culture in Afghanistan, see Shahrani [2013]). In this volume, the chapters by Just Boedeker, Ann Larson, and Robert L. Canfield and Fahim Masoud make explicit use of the IAD framework.

6. My esteemed colleagues, professors Catherine Tucker (then chair of Department of Anthropology at Indiana University), Eduardo Brondizio (anthropology), Anas Malik (Political Science Department, Xavier University, Cincinnati, Ohio), Tom Evans (geography department and then codirector of the Ostrom Workshop), Dan Cole (Maurer School of Law and School of Public and Environmental Affair-SPEA) and Michael McGinnis (political science) helped in running the Ostrom Workshop smoothly and productively. I am grateful to them all for their help.

Bibliography

Diamond, Larry, ed. 1993. *Political Culture and Democracy in Developing Countries.* Boulder, CO: Lynne Rienner

Geertz, Clifford. 1973. *Interpretations of Culture: Selected Essays.* New York: Basic Books.

Kiser, Larry, and Elinor Ostrom. 1982. "The Three Worlds of Action: A Metatheoretical Synthesis of Institutional Approaches." In *Strategies of Political Enquiry,* ed. Elinor Ostrom, 179–222. Beverly Hills, CA: Sage.

McGinnis, Michael D. 2011. "An Introduction to IAD and the Language of the Ostrom Workshop: A Simple Guide to a Complex Framework." *Policy Studies Journal* 39 (1): 169–83.

Ostrom, Elinor. 2007a. "A Diagnostic Approach for Going beyond Panacea." *Proceedings of the National Academy of Science* 104 (39): 15181–87.

———. 2007b. "Institutional Rational Choice: An Assessment of Institutional Analysis and Development Framework." In *Theories of Policy Process,* 2nd ed., ed. Paul A. Sabatier, 21–64. Boulder, CO: Westview Press.

———. 2010. "Beyond Markets and States: Polycentric Governance of Complex Economic Systems." *American Economic Review* 100 (3): 641–72.

Pye, Lucien. 1968. "Political Culture." In *International Encyclopedia of the Social Sciences*, vol. 12, ed. David L. Sills, 218–25. New York: Macmillan and Free Press.

Shahrani, M. Nazif. 2013. "Approaching Study of Political Culture in Afghanistan with Institutional Analysis and Development (IAD) and Social-Ecological Systems (SES) Frameworks." In *Sociocultural Systems: The Next Step in Army Cultural Capability* (ARI research Product 2013–02), ed. Beret E. Strong, LisaRe Brooks Babin, Michelle R. Zbylut, and Linda Roan, 169–92. Fort Belvoir, VA: U.S. Army Research Institute for the Behavioral and Social Sciences.

ACKNOWLEDGMENTS

A COLLABORATIVE EFFORT such as this could not have been possible without the cooperation of colleagues whose work is included in this volume as well as those who participated in other phases of this project. I am personally grateful to each and every one of them. I would also like to acknowledge the encouragement and support of my colleagues at the Ostrom Workshop, its then codirectors Tom Evans and Burney Fischer, who sponsored the proposal for holding the workshop on "Afghanistan: Assessing the Impact of 35 Years of Wars and Violence on Social Institutions" and offered initial seed money for the project. Tom also wrote letters of support for obtaining other funds from other sources on campus. At the workshop, I also enjoyed the wise counsel and support of other colleagues: especially Eduardo Brondizio, Dan Cole, Michael McGinnis, Catherine Tucker, and Anas Malik, and they have my gratitude for their help and assistance. Financial support from the following Indiana University units made convening the workshop possible: The Ostrom Workshop in Political Theory and Policy Analysis, College of Arts and Sciences Ostrom Faculty Grant Program, College Arts and Humanities Institute (CAHI), Office of the Vice President for International Affairs, Center for the Study of the Middle East, Russian and East European Institute, Inner Asian and Uralic National Resource Center, Pan Asia Institute, and the Department of Anthropology. Their generosity is gratefully acknowledged.

Piper O'Sullivan, now a PhD candidate in our Central Eurasian Studies department has helped tirelessly from the start of this project. She assisted with participants' travel and local hospitality, publicity about the workshop, and more importantly, took copious notes during the workshop that were shared with the authors when revising the papers. Piper also read all the papers at various stages and made extremely helpful corrections and suggestions on a few of them. She also helped me with keeping in touch with the contributors, easing my burden more than she can imagine. Piper also solicited the critical assistance of Ms. Theresa Quill, the Social Sciences Librarian (GIS/Maps) at the Wells Library,

Indiana University, who volunteered her valuable time in preparing all the maps used in this volume. I am grateful for Theresa's assistance and it has been a pleasure to know and work with her. Piper has been a marvelously diligent and hardworking graduate student assistant over several years and I am grateful for all she has done. Another PhD graduate student, Hamid Qeyam, in the Department of Near Eastern Languages and Cultures, also helped with logistical matters during the workshop, and his help is acknowledged with gratitude.

My acquisitions editor at Indiana University Press, Dr. Jennika Baines, has my gratitude for her enthusiasm from the outset for this project and her most constructive editorial suggestions and constant support. Her associates in this collective effort, Dr. Kate Schramm and Shannon S. Brown, have been most helpful in making the process smooth and a pleasure. I thank them all for their help and support. I am, however, solely responsible for any shortcomings.

M. Nazif Shahrani

MAPS

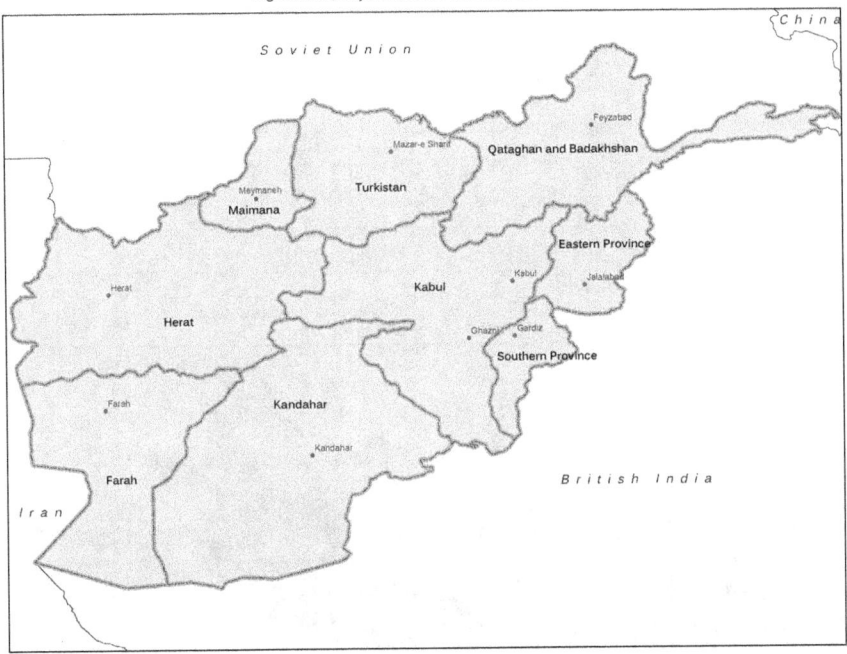

Map 0.1.

xviii | Maps

Map 0.2.

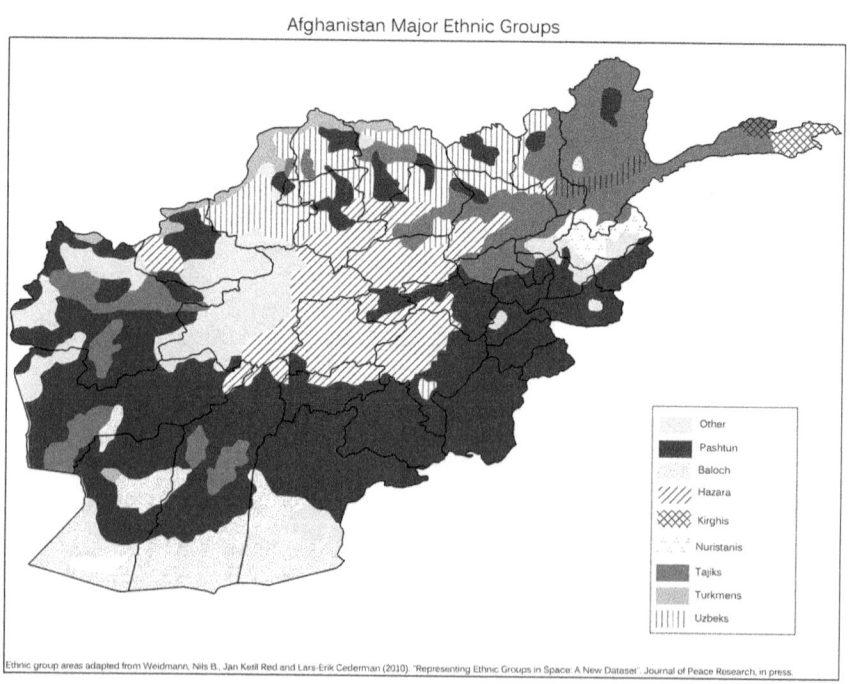

Map 0.3.

Maps | xix

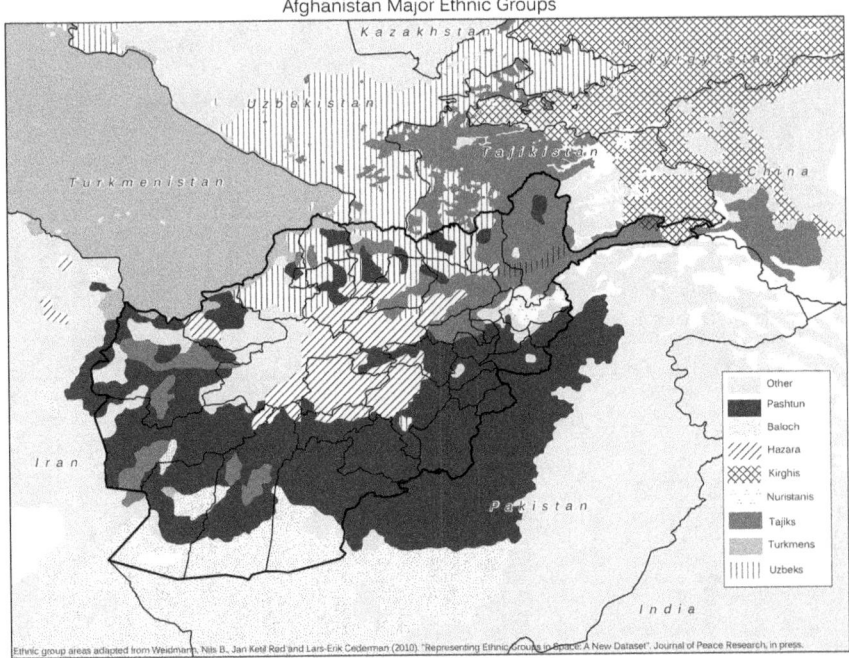

Map 0.4.

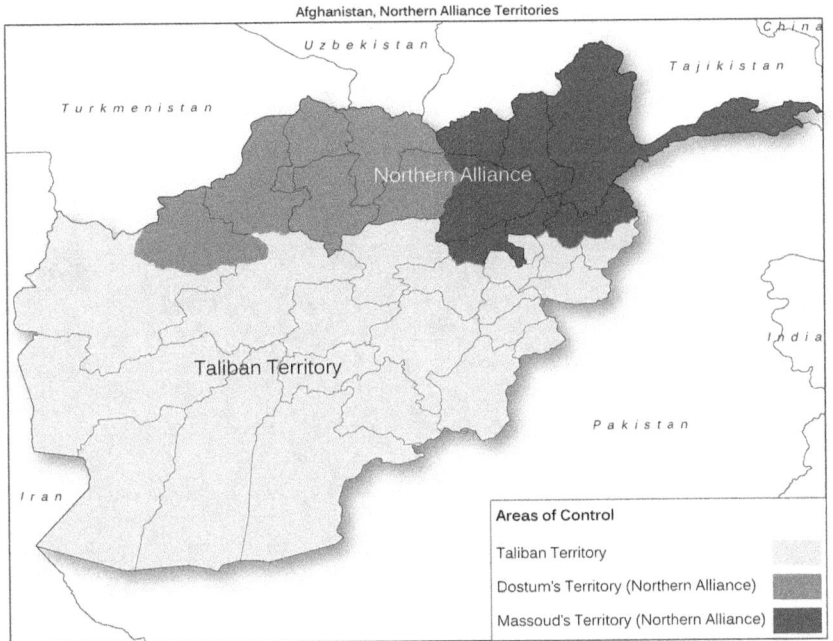

Map 0.5.

MODERN
AFGHANISTAN

INTRODUCTION: THE IMPACT OF FOUR DECADES OF WAR AND VIOLENCE ON AFGHAN SOCIETY AND POLITICAL CULTURE

M. Nazif Shahrani

Prefatory Words

This volume is a collaborative effort in studying the impact of war on society, identity, and political culture of Afghanistan by a group of interdisciplinary scholars, most of whom have carried out extensive ethnographic field research during ongoing violence and conflicts in the country. In an earlier coedited volume (Shahrani and Canfield 1984), the causes and context of the Soviet-inspired communist coup of April 1978, which led to the popular Islamic resistance and jihad of the 1980s, was explored. The militarily successful Afghan jihad against the invading Red Army of the former Union of Soviet Socialist Republics (USSR) (1979–1989) did not end in peace. Instead, the conflict morphed into more devastating proxy wars with unanticipated consequences for Afghanistan and its neighbors both near and far, and evolved into serious regional and global security threats.

The strengthening of state institutions, considered a dividend of nineteenth- and twentieth-century wars in Europe and America, has not been an outcome of the last four decades of war in Afghanistan either. Indeed, since 1978, wars have reversed the former articulation of state power structures, especially between Kabul and the provinces. Monopoly of power by foreign subsidized regimes in Kabul—monarchies by the British (1880–1978) and communist regimes by the former Soviet Union (1978–1992)—was shattered for the first time in the 1980s when multiple foreign-sponsored jihadi groups received weapons and cash in large quantities from diverse foreign sources to fight the Soviet-backed communist regime. By the time the United States and its NATO allies invaded Afghanistan in 2001, all major and some minor ethnic communities had their own well-armed and relatively wealthy jihadi *Qumandans* (commanders) lording over their ethnic territories. With the overthrow of Dr. Najeebullah's regime in 1992, and the victorious mujahideen's dismal failure to establish a viable central authority in Kabul, regional self-governments along ethno-linguistic and tribal cleavages dominated the landscape. Virtually all powerful *Qumandans* had participated in the destructive proxy wars of the 1990s against each other or opposing the Taliban. In order to finance their wars, most of them participated in drug running, smuggling contraband, and other criminal activities, and in considerable human rights violations during internecine bloodlettings, a reality widely experienced by multiethnic divided societies in postcolonial states fighting civil wars during the twentieth century in Asia, Africa, and Latin America. Contributors to this volume assess the impact on society and the identities and political culture of Afghanistan of the nearly four decades of brutal wars, conjoined with development and reconstruction efforts undertaken by the world's two major powers (the former Soviet Union and the United States) and their allies in the digital age of war on global terrorism.

Militarized US Foreign Policy and the Muslim Middle East

During the Cold War era, US policies and practices were rationalized by claims that they would stop the spread of communism and maintain stability in the Middle East. The Soviet invasion of Afghanistan (1979) and (covert) US promotion of a globalized jihad enabled Afghan mujahideen forces to defeat the Red Army, effecting their 1989 withdrawal. Collapse of the Soviet Union in 1991 together with the end of the Cold War radically shifted the global power ecology in favor of the United States. The declared victory of capitalism accrued considerable hubris and supported ambitions for greater militarization in US foreign policy. The launching of the first Gulf War in 1991 by the United States at the head of a military coalition against Saddam Hussein's invasion of Kuwait gave birth to Al Qaeda and related terror organizations who began targeting American interests in the region and beyond.[1] This was a development, which by 1996 culminated in a Taliban-dominated Afghanistan that became a safe haven and the launching pad for the September 11, 2001, attacks against mainland US targets. In retaliation, President George W. Bush led the NATO coalition to overthrow the Taliban regime in Afghanistan (2001), later forging the "coalition of the willing" to effect regime change in Iraq (2003) and launching the so-called global war on terror.

Indeed, as these words are being typed in August 2016, the Muslim Middle East and Southwestern Asia are ablaze with wars, violence, corruption, and domestic oppression from Kashmir, Pakistan, Afghanistan, Iraq, Syria, Palestine, Saudi Arabia, Bahrain, Yemen, Egypt, Tunisia, Libya, Turkey, and post-Soviet Central Asian republics. The physical destruction caused by wars in these countries occurs daily and is consistently visualized by all forms of electronic digital media. The impact of persistent conflicts, war, violence, and politics of rage on these societies, their social institutions, and political cultures, both short and long term, are not adequately studied or understood (see Shahrani 2016). By the time this book is in print, the peoples of Afghanistan will have endured four decades of war and conflict that began in 1978. Contributions in this volume are small, but we expect significantly more understanding about the effects of these four decades of war and violence on some key aspects of Afghan state, society, identity, and political culture to result.

Forty Years of War: State, Society, and Political Culture of Afghanistan

The peoples of Afghanistan, their state, society, and local communities, embattled as they have become at the dawn of the twenty-first century, cannot be understood except as part of the much larger struggles of the colonized non-Western societies, especially Muslim societies of the Middle East and Central Asia. Postcolonial and post-Soviet Muslim majority nations have been seriously damaged and deformed by their encounters with colonization during the nineteenth and twentieth centuries and deeply affected by their experiences of nation-state building during the twentieth century. Afghanistan's experiences with war and violence are by no means unique in the region. However, as the contributions in this volume will show, the troubled history of the country has left its unique imprint on key aspects of Afghanistan's state institutions, personal and collective identities, and political culture. The country's greatest challenge, like most others in this region since its birth as a buffer nation-state between the British Indian and tsarist Russian empires in the 1880s, has arguably been the failure to establish an effective modern state and governance system. Instead, external colonialism was simply replaced by imposition of an internal colonialism, which eventually led to communist revolution and subsequent wars. A largely failed state-building effort affected Afghanistan's social institutions and political culture; these are addressed by the contributors in Part I of this volume.

The creation of Afghanistan as a modern political entity under this name was the outcome of the Second Anglo-Afghan War of 1879–1880. The military invasion of the then Kingdom of Kabul was undertaken by British India, primarily in response to the tsarist Russian conquest of Tashkent in the mid-1860s, threatening other Central Asian Khanates, and by implication, the security of British India as part of the so-called Great Game of that time. Thus, the birth of the Kingdom of Afghanistan was midwifed by military invasion followed by generous provisions of British arms and money to Amir Abdur Rahman (r. 1800–1901), whom they crowned in August 1880. The British then withdrew their troops, leaving him in charge of securing the new Kingdom of Afghanistan for them.

The British choice of ruler, a princeling of the Muhammadzai clan of the Durrani Pashtuns that for a decade lived in self-exile in tsarist-controlled Samarkand, was deliberate and proved highly effective. The British firmly supported Amir Abdur Rahman, whom they later described as the "Iron Amir" because of his unprecedented cruelty in using the swords and guns they had provided to pacify the subjects of his new kingdom. He terrorized the recalcitrant heretofore self-governing tribes and ethno-linguistic and sectarian communities into submission to his absolute centralizing power from his capital, Kabul. His repressive and genocidal policies of war and destruction with modern British weapons, especially toward the Hazara Shi'as in the central mountain regions and to a lesser extent against his own Ghilzai Pashtun tribesmen, the Uzbeks and Tajiks of northern Afghanistan, are legendary and amply documented (see McChesney 2013).

It is also important to note that without Britain's delivery of modern guns and considerable financial subsidies to the Iron Amir to wage war against his subjects, the project of establishing a dynastic state lasting half a century (1880–1929) in Afghanistan could not have been possible. British weapons and financial subsidies continued to ensure the rule of his son and heir, Amir Habibullah (r. 1901–1919) at the cost of the permanent loss of Pashtun/Pathan/Pakhtun-inhabited territories to the east of the Durand Line (see Qaseem in this volume). Management of Afghanistan's foreign relations was surrendered to British India. Upon the declaration (in 1919) of independence by the grandson of the Iron Amir, Amanullah (r. 1919–1929), the British subsidies and technical support promptly ceased, which not only seriously impeded Amanullah's ambitious centralization, Pashtunization, and modernization programs but ultimately led to civil war and the violent end of his rule.

After nine months of turmoil when the Kabul throne was claimed by a Tajik from the Shamali plains just north of the capital, Amir Habibullah Kalakani (r. 1929), a collateral paternal relative of Shah Amanullah, and his former minister of war, General Nader Khan, a Barakzai Durrani Pashtun, secured arms and money from British India, thus putting an end to Kalakani's interregnum and establishing a new Barakzai Pashtun Musihiban dynasty, which lasted almost another half a century (1929–1978). This development once again firmly established the contingency of anyone aspiring access to the Afghan throne and their ability to secure money and weapons from the former European colonial masters. Indeed, Nadir Shah (r. 1929–1933) and his dynastic successors became quite skilled in feigning a discourse of "national independence" from outside powers to impress their own impoverished subjects, while relying heavily on foreign aid, coercive technologies of power, and development assistance from both Western and Soviet bloc countries to be able to rule. After World War II, Afghanistan's governing elites broadened and deepened the country's dependence even further by procuring large quantities of modern weapons and other technologies of war, including training of military and security officers, from its northern neighbor, the former Soviet Union.

Post–World War II expansion of Western economies and the rise of ideologically motivated American and Soviet empires of trust (also called empires by invitation), each country competing for clients and influence in the Third World, opened new possibilities for Afghan ruling elites as well as other postcolonial states in the region to seek "development" assistance (see Saikal's contribution in this volume).[2] This rather novel condition of joining with one of the opposing imperial giants or remaining neutral and trying to beg from both sides encouraged a further strengthening of politics and the economics of extraction and exclusion in Afghanistan and beyond. Afghanistan opted to remain nonaligned and tried for a time to extract rent from both the Western and the Eastern camps.

The ability to extract foreign assistance, acquire modern military hardware, and create a large conscripted military force offered the rulers some sense of security which, in turn, resulted in provisioning of some minimal social services such as education, health care, communication, and economic development projects to their subjects. Extension of such services in turn became occasions for discrimination against certain ethno-linguistic, tribal, regional, and sectarian groups thus further dividing the heterogeneous Afghan society. Increased spread of schooling during the decades of the 1950s to 1970s, in turn, introduced varieties of new and extra-Islamic political ideologies among both urban and rural youth studying in government-sponsored boarding vocational schools in the capital, Kabul. The repressive and biased state policies and practices favoring segments of the Pashtun tribesmen resulted in the rise of opposition movements to the ruling elites within the large urban environments, especially among high school and college student and graduates. Conflicting and hypocritical democratization policies after the liberal constitution of 1964 led to greater instability, especially in Kabul as Marxist and Islamist opposition groups agitated against the government as well as fought each other on university campuses and during street demonstrations.

Thus, a century of failed state-building efforts by Afghanistan's rulers culminated in the Soviet-inspired military coup of 1978, followed by the 1979 Soviet invasion—an event which set off a popular Islamic jihad resistance spanning almost forty years of wars, more outside invasions, domestic terror, and violence (see Shahrani 1986, Shahrani and Canfield 1984, Roy 1986, and Saikal 2012, and chap. 1 in this volume). The Soviets were forced to withdraw in 1989, and eventually both the Soviet Union and their client communist regime in Kabul collapsed, but Afghanistan continued to suffer a relentless series of calamities with unprecedented consequences for the peoples of Afghanistan, the Afghan state, society, and political culture. The triumphant Afghan mujahideen parties, with help from the globalized jahadis, could not establish a working government due to desperate struggles for factional dominance. The deadly bloodletting resulted not only in them wrecking their own capital city, Kabul (see the chapter by Nadiri and Hakimyar in this volume) but also subjected the country to more destructive proxy wars during the 1990s. An entirely new kind of coalition, the Pakistan-backed Taliban extremists, arose to drive the warring jihadist factions out of the capital, and themselves became hosts for another alien force, Al Qaeda, the global jihadist group formed and led by Osama Bin Laden.

The 9/11 attacks in New York City and Washington, DC, prompted the global war on terror by launching the United States–NATO coalition's invasion of Afghanistan to dislodge the Taliban, accompanied by grand promises associated with dividends of war—that is, state building, democratic stability, and prosperity in Afghanistan. However, this effort was quickly waylaid when President George W. Bush started the war in Iraq to get rid of Saddam Hussein. Afghanistan's neighbors (Pakistan and Iran), hosts to more than five million Afghan refugees, played a relentless game of duplicity, espousing public commitment to the war on terror while aiding and abetting Taliban resurgence in Afghanistan and providing a continued safe haven to Al Qaeda and Taliban terrorists.

President Obama in 2009 decided to "Afghanize" the war initially by increasing US troops and then announced an end to the US-NATO combat role in Afghanistan by the end of 2014 (later extended to the end of 2016) and withdrew all but a residual force of fewer than 10,000 US forces who remained to train and equip Afghanistan's security forces of more than 350,000 strong. However, the war in Afghanistan rages on with the emergence of even more violent militant extremists calling themselves the Khurasan branch of the Islamic State (ISK) or Daesh within the borders of Afghanistan, with considerable presence in eastern and especially northern Afghanistan along the former Soviet Central Asian republics, furthering the continued instability of Afghanistan and endangering the security of the entire region, extending as far as Russia, China, and the Indian subcontinent.

Because of these wars and persistent violent conflicts, virtually all the peoples and social institutions of every tribal, ethnic, and sectarian group across the country were affected, and the fabric of traditional Afghan society has been substantially altered. Millions of Afghans, both rural and urban, were displaced (internally, regionally, and globally), much of the former middle class devastated, infrastructures destroyed, traditional mechanisms of social control collapsed, and women's and girls' right to education, employment, and political participation denied or substantially curtailed, especially during the 1990s. New jihadi and Western-educated technocratic elites are empowered by the Americans and their coalition partners who have seriously mismanaged, misappropriated, and criminalized Afghanistan's common resources—that is, pasture, water, minerals, forests, state-owned lands, and more.

Since 2002, Afghanistan has also been the object of considerable international collective attention for reconstruction and development, albeit with dubious results. The Taliban and other terrorist groups' threat level remains high, while the large Afghan security force—poorly trained, ill equipped, and utterly dependent (financially and technologically) on US support—appears overstretched. The extraconstitutional National Unity Government (NUG), forced on the country by direct intervention of US secretary of state John Kerry following one of the most scandalously fraudulent elections (in 2014) in Afghan history, is notoriously corrupt, inept, and fragile. And now, it is faced with greater losses of territory to Taliban control, compounded by even greater violence by the resurgent Taliban, Al Qaeda, and now Daesh-IS fighters, who have posed an existential threat in mid-2016 to the Afghan state and society. So the question is: What has been the impact of the forty years of war, violence, and foreign interventions, including persistent "humanitarian wars" alongside the military invasions on the peoples of Afghanistan, the stability of their state institutions, their governance system, relations between the center and periphery, rural and urban dynamics, and on personal and collective identities, gender relations, and provision of social services, among others?

War, Violence, and Shifting Technologies of State Power

The decades of war and violence have effected shifts in technologies of power—material, ideological, and institutional—at the behest of changing power elites and their opponents. The producers, financiers, and managers of these wars, for the most part, were and are not the peoples of Afghanistan. Afghans have been mere consumers of wars orchestrated by others. Amin Saikal, in chapter 1, points out that the wars in Afghanistan have resulted in creating neither a stronger state nor much local wealth, at least not for the great majority of the peoples of Afghanistan.

Saikal says strategic location of the country is "a curse and an asset" inviting great powers' attention. Focusing on the latest military intervention by the US allied forces, he addresses four key interrelated issues: the United States' original goals and means for achieving them, the capability (or lack) of the US-created Afghan security forces in dealing with the Taliban-led insurgency, a comparison of the common variables that impeded US success in Vietnam and Soviet occupation of Afghanistan with the US experience in post-Taliban Afghanistan, and the possible future trajectories of the Afghan state in light of US and international communities' state-building efforts.

He argues that the Soviets and their Afghan communist allies shattered many Afghan traditional social and political institutions—for example, the ruling royal elite, the local strongmen (khans) with their clients, and the religious establishment (mullahs and Sufi *pirs* and their networks)—without replacing them with durable and functioning alternatives. As a consequence, Saikal, as well as Timor Sharan (chap. 5) and Noah Coburn (chap. 6) discuss the rise of a new breed of armed and wealthy jihadist power elites aspiring to rule (see also Baker 2009). Ethno-linguistic and sectarian differences have been, because of both past and present policies, transformed into articulated forms of social fragmentation inhibiting the forging of an enduring sense of national unity. The emergence of a small group of intelligentsia under all regimes was invariably suppressed or decimated by the succeeding ruling cliques, depriving Afghanistan of the very asset that it so badly needed to move it beyond stagnation and backwardness.

Producers of war in Europe and America have also produced and peddled modern political religions of the twentieth century—capitalism, communism, Nazism, nationalism, and fascism—to deploy in pursuit of their interests globally. Anticolonial wars in the Muslim majority areas, however, have led to greater politicization and nationalization of religion (Islam) as the most potent popular mobilization force, especially in Afghanistan. Bashir Ansari (chap. 2) examines significant shifts in religious discourses from piety-based "traditional" (pre-1978 era) Islam to the more radical Islamist ideologies of the mujahideen (in the 1980s) and Taliban (since 1994) within Afghanistan's political culture of resistance against outside invasions and occupations and internal corruption and exclusions. The most important shift has been from traditional Khorasani Sufi ideals and practices of popular piety, spirituality, ethical conduct, mutual respect, and tolerance among ordinary peoples of Afghanistan, toward greater political instrumentalization of Islam in Afghanistan, especially since 1978 (also see Roy 1986, Olesen 1995, Shahrani 2013). Ansari argues that strident forms of Islamic theological discourse found their way into the curricula of the Pakistani *madrassas* (Islamic seminaries or religious schools), ultimately influencing the political behavior of their students, the Taliban. The United States and its allies' support and encouragement of jihad against the Red Army in the 1980s led to globalization of jihad and ultimately the rise of radical jihadist movements (from Al Qaeda to the IS and Daesh) after the first Gulf War (1991). Ansari, also ponders the likelihood of redeploying traditional Khorasani Muslim ideals constructively for the restabilization of Afghanistan.

It is clear that military interventions and support for proxy wars have not resulted in stronger states or more effective governments in postcolonial societies. Instead, these wars have led to greater politicization of identities and dividing multiethnic Muslim states, including Afghanistan. The collapse of a centralized state and the resulting wars also created space for the production of considerable vernacular literature, especially resistance poetry during the 1980s and in the post-Taliban era. Indeed, the wars opened unprecedented space for contesting prewar politics and the economics of exclusion. In chapter 3, Omar Sharifi, explores the impact of wars and violence on Afghanistan's political culture by focusing on language policies and the poetics of identity. He examines policies and practices of the Pashtun-dominated central governments, especially since the 1930s, in undermining the role Afghanistan's lingua franca, Dari/Persian, and its literary heritage in favor of their own nationalized vernacular language, Pashto/Pashtu. By focusing on Persian poetry as a didactic means of political socialization in Afghanistan and the region as a whole, Sharifi explains why and how literary texts continue to function as the mirror of Afghanistan's political culture, especially during the recent decades of persistent societal upheavals.

Echoing Ansari (chap. 2), Sharifi argues that, until the early twentieth century, sociocultural identity in Afghanistan and the wider Persianate region was continuously articulated and transmitted by the didactic Islamic Persian textual tradition (also see Shahrani 1991). The rise of "Afghan," or more precisely, Pashtun nationalism, in the 1910s to the 1930s challenged the existing Persianate cultural practices and attempted to change the notions of national identity, personhood, and nationality through language policies favoring Pashto. Thus, language, and specifically Dari/Persian poetry, has increasingly become the center of cultural and political contestation. Indeed, being a poet or knowing particular genres of poetry has become the very essence of claiming one's heritage, establishing one's social position, and defining one's political and cultural life and perpetuity.

In the tortured politics of state building, Afghanistan's capital, Kabul, has played a prominent role. Khalid Nadiri and Farshid Hakimyar (chap. 4) explore the status of this historic city as the microcosm of the larger Afghan societal dynamics with a focus on its post-Taliban manifestations. They examine three interrelated aspects of urban life—social, political, and economic—unpacking the changing historical role of Kabul, its shifting demographics, and the effects of highly disorganized resource allocations on Kabul's built environment. Kabul has been a virtual barometer of national politics and economics (both domestic and international), and despite violent government turnover over the past four decades, the combination of social convergence and political competition for control of Kabul have characterized the capital city.

After the 9/11 attacks, when the United States and its allies were looking for local partners to oust the Taliban, they acted expediently. That is, reminiscent of their World War II choice of Stalin for a partner, the Americans made common cause with many of the local Afghan "devils"—what the Western media called the "warlords." Those who joined the Americans in their anti-Taliban and anti–Al Qaeda war soon became extremely wealthy, powerful, and influential new government officials. Timor Sharan (chap. 5) further pierces beneath the veneer of formal post-Taliban state institutions to reveal what he calls "networked politics" both at the national and subnational levels. Newly empowered members of ethnic and tribal cliques compete for influence by securing strategic appointments within the Afghan government and emergent civil society organizations created by the invaders. As such, Sharan contends an entirely novel form of a "networked state" has taken shape in post-Taliban Afghanistan. These networked political leaders with requisite religious and ethno-political claims are the power brokers and facilitators running the government while securing new outside resources for themselves and their cronies (also, see Mukhopadhyay 2014).

In another important manifestation of the impact of US-NATO intervention, Noah Coburn (chap. 6) examines the rise of "merchant-warlords." Using data gathered since 2005 from a range of sites across the country, particularly communities around Bagram Airbase in the Shomali Plain, he explores how emergent Afghan local leaders have worked carefully to bring nongovernmental organization (NGO) funds to their communities. He looks at how warlords have used internationally sponsored elections to solidify their patronage networks, and how all forms of aspiring leaders have become increasingly reliant on the international presence and international resources. Many of these entrepreneurs have become rich from either military contracts or development funds but continue to maintain local community ties.

A remarkable benefit of the US-led intervention, and a powerful addition to the technology of power, has been the unprecedented growth of media (radio, television, print, and rapidly expanding social media, especially mobile phones) in post-Taliban Afghanistan. Wazhmah Osman (chap. 8) assesses the impact of dozens of new television and radio stations and the influx of media imports from the surrounding countries (especially India, Iran, and Turkey). A development almost entirely funded by the international donor community, transnational media corporations as well as local merchant warlords politicians use their television stations as platforms for self-promotion. Osman suggests that the public service announcement (PSA) has become the favorite launching pad for much needed educational and informational campaigns by the international community. She cautions, however, that the transformative or repressive potential of media depends on factors such as censorship, access, and infrastructure.

Unlike wars in Europe and America that led to stability of borders and frontiers, the recent decades of war in Afghanistan have aggravated a long-standing border dispute with Pakistan. Ahmad Shayeq Qassem, (chap.7), examines the legacies of the British-imposed Durand Line and its impact not only on dividing the Pashtuns on both sides of the border between Afghanistan and Pakistan but also impeding access to strategic resources and posing a serious challenge to Afghanistan's territorial integrity and state stability. This long-standing dispute and acrimonious relations with Pakistan have not only profoundly affected Afghanistan's security and stability but as Qassem in his chapter indicates it has also made the "effective use of its natural resources and strategic location as a crossroad of overland commerce and interaction between Central Asia and South Asia" virtually impossible. He also points out that the Afghan leaders cannot expect the Pakistanis to help stabilize Afghanistan while Afghan (Pashtun) leaders are "effectively staking claim on more than half of [Pakistan's] ... territory and challenging their national sovereignty."

War, Identities, Gender Relations, and Trust Deficit

The impact of war on technologies of power, state institutions, and state instability in Afghanistan have been profound and multifaceted. The imposition of oppressive modern nation-state structures in the final decades of nineteenth century, without a doubt, have been the most significant force affecting the personal lives of both men and women, their collective identities, and interpersonal and intergroup relations in Afghanistan. The demise of the central government, together with decades of war, foreign intervention, proxy wars, and civil conflicts, has also induced significant changes in gender relations, notions of masculinity, and politicization of collective identities, producing a trust deficit between the state and its subjects.

Andrea Chiovenda (chap. 9), utilizing ethnographic field data from eastern Afghanistan, analyzes the impact of war and violence on the performance of masculinity among Pashtun men in the Nangarhar and Paktia provinces near the Pakistan frontier. Strictly sex-segregated Pukhtun/Pashtun communities, adhering to stern definitions of gender roles as codified in *Pakhtunwali* (male codes of honor), are challenged because of protracted wars, especially with the post-9/11 international intervention promoting a "Western" notion of personhood, individuality, and agency. Chiovenda suggests that, instead of a presumed single rigid model of masculinity among the Pashtun, several competing models (some new, some old) have become available.

The impact of various governments' policies during the decades of war on women, family, and gender relations is examined by Sonia Ahsan (chap. 10). Drawing on her ethnographic fieldwork at a *khanayee-amn* (safe house) established after the 2001 US-NATO intervention, in Kabul, she argues that the goals of the communist-era Ministry of Social Affairs (MOSA) and the post-Taliban Ministry of Women's Affairs (MOWA) under the Karzai regime differed drastically from those of the Taliban. That is, Ahsan states "the Taliban state preferred designating and dealing with total populations, rather than with individual cases. Women were targeted as total and homogenous populations rather than as particular individuals potentiating trouble." When the Taliban captured Kabul, they began targeting the private realm, which historically has been a world of women. The Taliban edict for protecting women, says Ahsan, has had significant effects in humiliating and shaming the fathers, husbands, and brothers whose daughters, wives, and sisters, extricated from their families by the Afghan state under the Karzai or Ghani-Abdullah regimes and taken to the women's shelter, *khanayee-amn*. The Taliban, Ahsan asserts, changed conceptions of the state by mystifying and transcendentalizing "honorable and dishonorable states of being."

In war-ravaged postcolonial societies, military invasions create not only massive displacements and chronic uncertainty about future, but the withdrawal of armies can also produce considerable anxiety. Robert L. Canfield and Fahim Masoud (chap. 11), investigate a consequence of the announced withdrawal of American combat forces from Afghanistan. Masoud had witnessed a riot on September 7, 2013, directed against the Iranian Consulate in the western city of Herat, resulting in the death of one person and leaving several injured. This violent event, Canfield and Msoud contend, highlights "the widespread sense of unease about the future" due to the announcement that the American and NATO forces were leaving by December of 2014. The most important question in the minds of those involved was: "Would civil war again break out, as it had several times in the previous three decades? What could keep the Taliban from coming to power?"

Canfield and Masoud argue that this sense of dread about the future affected the behavior of those who came to the Iranian Consulate on September 7, 2013. The fears that the country would return to internecine warfare and violence, they suggest, contributed to pervasive anxiety, riotous behavior, and alarm about the necessity of relocation to Iran again. The riots, therefore, are explained in terms of the local conventions of thought that informed them. Since the riots occurred adventitiously, Canfield and Masoud have considered them to be an example of how "discontinuous change" shapes behavior, especially in reference to the new institutional economic theory. Anticipating greater economic and political uncertainty, the Herati rioters were wishing to establish a beachhead under the safety of neighboring Iran. A collective concern and increased trust deficit about the future of the country manifested itself two years later, in 2016, into a major refugee problem for Turkey and the European Union plus a brain drain of younger educated individuals and their families from Afghanistan (as well as from war-torn Syria). Afghanistan lost the human capital they so desperately need to rebuild their country.

War and the Political Ecology of Uncertainties at the Margins

Wars waged by central governments, colonial or national, are intended to consolidate power over the peripheries and result in political integration. The impact of chronic warfare against the center in Afghanistan, however, has presented unprecedented opportunity to long-marginalized communities and groups to take control of their own communities or even the center, if temporarily. Nazif Shahrani (chap. 12) examines the changing fortunes of the Badakhshanis in the remote northeastern mountainous province bordering on Pakistan, China, and Tajikistan (a former Soviet republic). Historically marginal to the national politics, Badakhshan assumed a new strategic, political, and economic importance during the decade of jihad against Soviets, the period of mujahideen rule (1992–1996/2001), and the anti-Taliban fight by the Northern Alliance in the 1990s.[3] Most of the Sunni Tajik and Uzbek Badakhshanis rebelled against communist rule. Ismaili Shi'as along the Soviet border and a segment of educated youth from towns supported the communists. Burhanuddin Rabbani, a Badakhshani Tajik from the provincial capital, Faizabad, headed one of the largest non-Pashtun Islamist resistance parties, the Jamiati Islami Afghanistan, and became president of Afghanistan (1992–1996/2001). Badakhshan and the Panjsher valley north of Kabul gained fame for defying the Taliban and successfully resisting the conquest of their territories. After the US-led military intervention of 2001 and the establishment of a new recentralizing government, Badakhshan once again was relegated to its prewar political insignificance in the periphery, but with a growing potential geostrategic security role for Central Asia and beyond. Using longitudinal ethnographic data collected since the early 1970s, including recent field research (2002–2015), Shahrani explores the impact of the shifting significance of Badakhshan's geostrategic role in national politics at different phases of the more than three decades–long war and violence.

The effects of war on the Hazara Shi'as of central Afghanistan, is explored by Melissa Kerr Chiovenda (chap. 13). She discusses the Hazaras' own understanding of their historical marginality and subordination within the Afghan state, as well as their current and future status as "Afghans." On the basis of the ethnographic fieldwork in Bamyan, she highlights how the Hazaras remember past events in this periphery and tie them seamlessly into their narratives of suffering and marginality spanning the monarchy period, communist rule, civil war, and the Taliban era. In Bamyan, she asserts, the landscape itself plays a role in the narration of memories—that is, as sites of distant and recent violence by Mongol invaders in the thirteenth century and the most recent Taliban destruction of the Buddha statues and Yakawlang massacres—which are presented as evidence of Hazara suffering within the Afghan state, itself viewed as a corrupt and alien, externally imposed body (see Nadiri and Hakimyar, chap. 4). Therefore, she argues, for the Hazaras, the US-led military intervention of 2001 is seen as a possible break from their prolonged marginality, and as such, she considers the presence of international organizations a force for good. Hazaras have taken advantage of new opportunities for education and employment that were not previously available to them, while at the same time, they are frustrated by the slow progress of development in their region, evidenced through a lack of basic infrastructure in the province.

Ethnographer Just Boedeker (chap. 14) turns to the plight of the Baloch in southwestern Afghanistan, who reside in three countries—Afghanistan, Iran, and Pakistan. Drawing on extensive multisited field research, Boedeker explores the dynamism of Baloch social institutions' response to instability and changing political conditions such as the nationalities policy of the Soviet occupation (in the 1980s), the rise of the mujahideen resistance parties, and the imposition of Taliban rule on Baloch tribesmen. He illustrates how *kaum/qawm*—a context-dependent polysemic concept signifying social belonging in smaller kin-based or territorial units and tribal or religious groups to the Baloch nation—was deployed by Baloch individuals and groups to adapt relatively easily to the social upheavals of the last decades.

The effects of wars have not been limited to only spatially peripheral groups in the country. Anna Larson (chap. 15) examines the tribulations of ideologically based political parties and how they have fared during these decades of war in Afghanistan. Utilizing conversations and interviews with party leaders and members over some eight years, Larson examines how "party institutionalization meets women's empowerment" and explores how, without having ever been assigned a political role in government, political parties in Afghanistan have been repeatedly pushed to the fringes by successive regimes in Kabul. More significantly, she points out that political parties have come to be associated with extremism, war, and violence in the minds of many Afghans.

War, Violence, Social Services Delivery, and Disappointment

Afghanistan ranks among the worst in the world on several basic health indexes, including child, infant, and maternal mortality. The ouster of the Taliban regime and establishment of the Karzai administration was accompanied by a considerable influx of international funds to establish and rebuild a basic public health delivery system. Because of decades of conflict, Afghanistan lacked the infrastructure, organization, and technical expertise to provide even the most basic health services. Post-Taliban efforts have been further hampered by the challenges of topography, climate, ongoing insurgencies, and political instabilities. Drawing on ethnographic data collected in Badakhshan (2005–2008), an evaluation of a community midwifery program in the three northeastern provinces of Kunduz, Takhar, and Badakhshan (in 2010), and her work as a midwife trainer in Kabul in 2011, Kylea Liese (chap. 16), discusses extremely high maternal mortality in the context of ongoing wars. More specifically, she explores how Afghan women negotiate the biological and social risks they face in childbirth within the chronic environment of war.

In addition, the recent major international development and reconstruction efforts in Afghanistan have not bridged social inequalities, according to Parul Bakhshi and Jean-Francois Trani (chap. 17). Instead, they argue that international assistance programs have either worsened social inequalities or sustained them. They point out that the current pattern of Afghanistan's dependency on international assistance mimics the prewar situation. That is, major beneficiaries of development aid were and still are urban political elites, who continue to leave rural masses devoid of any improvements in their living conditions. a situation which makes the most vulnerable and destitute—that is, persons with disabilities, women and children disabled at birth, or people with learning, intellectual, or mental disability—dependent exclusively on their own impoverished social networks for help.

One third of Afghanistan's population (about nine million people) still live in extreme poverty. But, reconstruction and development efforts since 2002 have not so far been focused on meeting the basic needs of the population. Instead, the pattern of expenditures shows that security trumps investment in poverty reduction, health, education, and employment support programs. This has been so, despite the fact that the United States alone has spent over $100 billion in nonmilitary aid (during 2002–2012). Much of the international assistance funds have been wasted, resulting in disappointment and "the loss of trust of local populations in development actors and foreign aid." Warning of the daunting challenges facing the peoples of Afghanistan after the US-NATO withdrawal of forces and the concomitant reduction of support for the country, they assert that the erosion of trust by the peoples of Afghanistan remains the most critical future challenge.

Conclusions

The expected dividends of almost four decades of war and chaos in Afghanistan have not been anywhere near comparable to the effects of nineteenth- and twentieth-century wars for Europe and America. Because, in the wars in postcolonial societies, lethal powers have been controlled asymmetrically by the industrialized and largely Western imperial great powers. These wars have further fragmented already fractured multiethnic states and societies. Postcolonial states have often been the cause of increased death by violence, not a factor in reducing them as theorized by Ian Morris (2014), for these states have indulged in repeated ethnocide and genocide against their own subjects. Wars in postcolonial societies, especially in the Muslim Middle East and post-Soviet Central Asia have not resulted in transformation of subjects into empowered citizens, as has been the case in the West (see Shahrani 2009). Indeed, in many instances, including Afghanistan, extensions of citizenship rights, especially constitutional gender equality and political inclusion of women and minorities, when insisted on by foreign patrons of wars or local regimes, have remained on paper, discursive, and for the most part rhetorical rather than substantive.

These proxy wars have rarely produced genuine heroes with well-articulated national visions, plans, or programs. They have resulted in huge displacements of populations and the flight of national capital, natural and intellectual resources, generally, to countries that have instigated those conflicts. Poverty, backwardness, criminality, warlordism, inequalities, and long-term dependency on foreign assistance and uncertainties have deepened, while prospects for attaining peace, national freedom, liberty, and self-reliance sunk beyond reach.[4] This was a depressing and hopeless realization which apparently came to Babrak Karmal, the Soviet-installed communist leader of Afghanistan (1980–1986) and head of the People's Democratic Party of Afghanistan (PDPA), only a year before his death in 1996. During his internal exile in the port town of Termiz, on the Amu Darya near Mazar-i Sharif, he lamented to the Soviet journalist, Vladimir Sangriev, saying: "The greatest lesson learned from my life experiences is this: *No country can ever attain freedom, independence, and progress by relying on foreign powers. One must respect the will of the people and defend nation's independence. Every nation must try to stand on its own feet by itself*" (Danish 2004, emphasis added). Sadly, this is a luxury which is unlikely to avail itself to war-torn postcolonial states and societies such as Afghanistan anytime soon, unless, of course, one adheres to these words describing Ahmed Shah Massoud: "He turned reflections about past errors into a new force that dwelt within him and gave him added strength. ... [He also believed] that one should never give up, that the battle is never lost so long as one has courage, conviction, and ideals" (Ponfilly 2015:155). We hope that the peoples of Afghanistan and their leaders will master the requisite courage, conviction, and wisdom to keep the dream of enabling their nation to stand on its own feet.

Notes

Professors Amin Saikal, Anas Malik, and Robert L. Canfield were extremely kind and helpful in reading an earlier draft of this introduction and making very helpful suggestions for improving my arguments. I gratefully acknowledge my gratitude for their most precious time and shared wisdom. I am, however, solely responsible for all shortcomings.

1. For a recent summary of the consequences of the 1991 Gulf War, see Fradkin and Libby (2015).
2. For elaboration of the rise of these new and more pernicious forms of post–World War II empires, see Shahrani (2016).
3. This term was coined by the Inter Service Intelligence (ISI) and Pakistani media to further their claim that the Pashtun in the south did not support them, but in fact, a number of Pashtun jihadi groups such as Abdur Rabb Rasul Sayyaf's group as well as other smaller Pashtun groups were part of the Northern Alliance in their opposition to the Taliban.
4. For a detailed report, see Special Inspector General for Afghanistan Reconstruction (SIGAR). (2016).

Bibliography

Baker, Aryn, 2009. "The Warlords of Afghanistan." *Time* 173, February 23, 41.
Danish, Mustafa. 2004. *Khatirati az Akharin Deedar ba Babrak Karmal* (Recollection from my last meeting with Babrak Karmal in 1995). BBC Persian site. Accessed July 1, 2016. http://www.bbc.com/persian/afghanistan/story/2004/12/041220_aa_mdanesh.shtml.
Fradkin, Hillel, and Lewis Libby. 2015. "The First Gulf War and Its Aftermath." *InFocus Quarterly*. Hudson Institute, October 14. Accessed September 17, 2016. http://www.hudson.org/research/11787-the-first-gulf-war-and-its-aftermath.
McChesney, Robert D. 2013. *The History of Afghanistan: Fayz Muhammad Katib Hazarah's Siraj al-Tawarikh*. Translation, introduction, notes and index by R. D. McChesney, vols. 1–4. Leiden: Brill.
Morris, Ian. 2014. *War! What Is It Good for? Conflict and Progress of Civilization from Primates to Robots*. New York: Farrar, Straus, and Giroux.
Mukhopadhyay, Dipali. 2014. *Warlords, Strongman Governors, and the State in Afghanistan*. New York: Cambridge University Press.

Olesen, Asta. 1995. *Islam and Politics in Afghanistan*. London: Routledge.
Ponfilly, Christophe de. 2015. (2001). "Ahmad Shah Massoud: The Man behind the Legend.". Reprinted in *Afghanistan: Identity, Society and Politics since 1980*, ed. Micheline Centlivres-Demont. London: I. B. Tauris, 154–55.
Roy, Olivier. 1986. *Islam and Resistance in Afghanistan*. Cambridge, UK: Cambridge University Press.
Saikal, Amin. 2012. *Modern Afghanistan: A History of Struggle and Survival*. London: I. B. Tauris.
Shahrani, M. Nazif. 1986. "State Building and Social Fragmentation in Afghanistan: A Historical Perspective." In *The State, Religion, and Ethnic Politics: Afghanistan, Iran, and Pakistan*, ed. Ali Banuazizi and Myron Weiner, 23–74. Syracuse, NY: Syracuse University Press.
———. 1991. "Local Knowledge of Islam and Social Discourse in Afghanistan and Turkistan in the Modern Period." In *Turko-Persia in Historical Perspective*, ed. Robert L. Canfield, 161–88. Cambridge, UK: Cambridge University Press.
———. 2009. *Afghanistan's Alternatives for Peace, Governance and Development: Transforming Subjects to Citizens & Rulers to Civil Servants*. Afghanistan Papers No. 2 (August 2009). Ottawa, Canada: Center for International Policy Studies (CIPS) & The Center for International Governance Innovations (CIGI). Available at cigionline.org.
———. 2013 "Islam and the State in Afghanistan." In *The Oxford Handbook of Islam and Politics*, ed. John Esposito and Emad El-Din Shahin, 453–74. Oxford: Oxford University Press.
———. 2016. "Why Muslim Sectarian Politics of Rage in the Age of 'Empires of Trust?'" *Journal of Islamic and Muslim Studies* 1 (1): 28–46.
Shahrani, M. Nazif, and Robert Canfield, eds. 1984. *Revolutions and Rebellions in Afghanistan: Anthropological Perspectives*. Berkeley: Institute of International Studies, University of California.
Special Inspector General for Afghanistan Reconstruction (SIGAR). 2016. *Corruption in Conflict: Lessons from the U.S. Experience in Afghanistan*. Accessed September 17, 2016. https://www.sigar.mil/pdf/lessonslearned/SIGAR-16-58-LL.pdf.

PART I:
TECHNOLOGIES OF POWER—COMPETING DISCOURSES ON NATIONAL IDENTITY, STATEHOOD, AND STATE STABILITY

1

AFGHANISTAN: A TURBULENT STATE IN TRANSITION

Amin Saikal

AFGHANISTAN IS THE only country in the world with the dubious reputation of having been invaded by all three major powers—Great Britain, the Soviet Union, and the United States—over the last one-and-a-half centuries. Yet, all these powers have failed to tame the country and to shape it according to their ideological and geopolitical preferences. At the close of 2014, the United States and its allies withdrew most of their troops from Afghanistan, leaving only limited contingents for two years, although President Donald Trump decided to increase the number of American troops, with an emphasis on 'killing terrorists' and enhancing pressure on Pakistan to halt its support for insurgent Taliban and their affiliates. Afghanistan was once again placed in the throes of a major political, economic, and security transition. At the time of the withdrawal, the country remained domestically fragile and externally vulnerable, with the Taliban-led insurgency maintaining a robust posture. As such, it was not clear where this transition would eventually take the country. Many questions remained about the fate of Afghanistan and the impact that the ongoing conflict has had on the country's socially divided and multifaceted society since the communist coup of April 1978.

The US invasion of Afghanistan has not been the first attempt by an international superpower to steer the course of Afghanistan's future. Yet it has given rise to a cluster of problems that need to be considered both in their specific context and in comparison with other modern military interventions. After providing the necessary historical background to the US-led intervention in Afghanistan, this chapter focuses on the contemporary set of problems in Afghanistan, mainly until the advent of the National Unity Government in September 2014 through four major interrelated issues. The first is the intervention's original goals and its conduct. The second is the capability of the Afghan security forces to deal with the Taliban-led insurgency. The third is the set of common variables that impeded success in the US involvement in Vietnam, the Soviet occupation of Afghanistan, and finally, the US experience in Afghanistan. The fourth is possible directions that the Afghan situation may take in the coming years.

Background

Landlocked Afghanistan is often described as a country important largely because of its strategic location, as it is sensitively situated at the crossroads of Central, South, and West Asia, as well as the Far East. This location has proved to be both an asset and a curse for the country. It has led scholars to describe Afghanistan as a potential "hub of connectivity," part of "the heartland of Eurasia," a "geographical pivot of history," a "highway of conquest," and at the same time, "unconquerable" and a "graveyard" for those powers that have sought to dominate it.[1] Beyond its geostrategic value, the country has historically had little to offer to the outside world in terms of either human or natural resources. However, this situation may change with Afghanistan's recent claim that it possesses US$1 trillion worth of valuable minerals buried deep under its harsh and treacherous terrain (Risen 2010).

Afghanistan has indeed lived up to all of these descriptions at different moments since its consolidation as a state in 1747. Neither the two British imperial expeditions in the country (1839–1842, 1878–1880) nor the Russians' counter-efforts to subdue Afghanistan as part of what Rudyard Kipling popularized as the "Great Game" between the two imperial powers for domination in Central Asia, came to any good for the imperial predators (Kipling 1901). Nor did the Soviet occupation of Afghanistan in the 1980s succeed in transforming the country into a stable socialist state, as had been desired. If anything, the Soviet adventure was a major disaster for both the Afghan people and the Soviets.[2] It shattered many Afghan traditional social institutions and formations without replacing them with durable alternatives. The invasion also enabled the Soviets' adversaries, the United States in particular, to give back to the Soviet Union what they had helped to inflict on the United States in Vietnam a decade earlier—a humiliating defeat. The United States' support of the Afghan Islamic resistance forces, the mujahideen, was instrumental in defeating Afghanistan's Soviet-sponsored communist government. Yet, it also resulted in the empowerment of a new breed of armed and wealthy strongmen who have popularly become known as warlords, endowed with protection, dispensation, and patronage capabilities. These figures effectively eclipsed the influence of the traditional power holders in Afghan society, who derived their prowess from landed and conservative religious and social structures, and operated either in alliance with an almost perpetually weak central government, or in cahoots with one another.

The Soviet departure, and the concomitant US claim of the triumph of liberalism over communism and of capitalism over socialism, was accompanied by the superpowers' abandonment of postcommunist war-torn Afghanistan. Left to their own devices and at the mercy of their neighbors, especially Pakistan, the Afghans were in a fractious state. The result was internecine conflict between various mujahideen groups, as well as Pakistan's "creeping invasion" of Afghanistan, which eventually empowered the medievalist Islamic Taliban and transformed Afghanistan into a hub for international terrorism. Had it not been for the September 11, 2001 Al Qaeda terrorist attacks on the United States, Afghanistan would likely have remained subject to the dark, Pakistan-backed rule of the Taliban for many more years.

These outside rivalries and interventions have historically interacted with the mosaic ethno-tribal and sectarian Afghan society, whose people have been mostly traditional, illiterate, and fiercely, although not radically, Muslim. In conjunction with the emergence of strongmen and royal polygamy—which caused intense interdynastical rivalries lasting at least until 1978—Afghanistan's social diversity has played a key role in holding the Afghans back from building strong domestic structures and institutions, and from forging an enduring national unity (Saikal 2012, chaps. 4, 6, 9). The country's internal fragility has, in turn, rendered it vulnerable to periodic domestic rebellions and external interventions. Rule by strongmen and the personalization instead of institutionalization of politics, interrupted by a few periods of relative peace and stability (especially from 1930 to 1978), became a dominant feature of the country. Afghanistan thus evolved as a weak state in dynamic relations with strong microsocieties that functioned in loose relationships with one another and the central authority in Kabul (see Shahrani 1986, 23–74).

The underlying institutions that could ensure the growth of a viable and enduring political order that would underpin stability and continuity as well as effective social and economic development, remained persistently unsolidified. In general, poor governance, patronage, corruption, human rights violations, dependence on foreign aid, and stunted social and economic reforms remained the hallmark of national life in Afghanistan. The progress achieved during the longest period of relative tranquility in modern Afghan history (1930–1978) was limited in scope and was managed within an informal triangular relationship between the ruling royal elite, the local strongmen, and the religious establishment, and in compliance with the political needs of those in positions of power and authority. The emergence of a small group of intelligentsia under any particular regime was invariably suppressed or decimated by the succeeding political and ideological cluster, depriving Afghanistan of the very asset that it badly needed to move it beyond stagnation and backwardness.

The US-Led Intervention

Against this historical backdrop, the United States launched its military campaign, with a seemingly promising start. The immediate goals of the campaign were to oust the Taliban, to destroy the Al Qaeda terrorist network, and to capture the latter's leader, Osama Bin Laden. The first goal was rapidly achieved. Al Qaeda's leadership and fighters were dispersed, potentially opening the way for building, as President George W. Bush put it, a new stable, secure, prosperous, and democratic Afghanistan, so that the country would never again be a hub for extremism and terrorism (Saikal 2013). An interelite Afghan settlement under the auspices of the United Nations (UN), without the Taliban's participation but with the determining influence of Washington and the cooperation of Tehran, was forged in Bonn by December 2001 (Saikal 2014b, chap. 3). This agreement delivered a coalition administration under the leadership of a little-known ethnic Pashtun with some appealing credentials, Hamid Karzai. It also legitimized the interventionist role of the UN as well as the United States and its allies in Afghanistan. Meanwhile, Washington prompted Pakistan's military ruler, General Pervez Musharraf, to declare Pakistan's support for the United States against its clients, the Taliban and Al Qaeda, and for what President Bush declared as America's wider war on terror.

While the United States quickly removed the Taliban from power, they did not succeed in defeating them or their supporters. This was in part due to the United States' inability to exert enough pressure on Pakistan to cut all its ties with the Taliban and restructure its Afghanistan policy in support of US efforts toward stabilization and reconstruction. The Taliban and their affiliates, most importantly Al Qaeda, simply melted away into the treacherous landscape of Afghanistan and across the border into Pakistan to fight another day. Islamabad ostensibly sided with America in return for massive economic and military aid, but ultimately found it expedient to keep its organic links with the Taliban as leverage to shape US involvement in Afghanistan in line with its own strategic interests. In addition, the United States remained too focused on fighting the so-called war on terror, a battle that soon became as elusive as its targets. At the same time, the Bush administration developed an obsession with toppling the regime of America's old foe in Iraq, Saddam Hussein, as a precondition to consolidating the objectives for which it had invaded Afghanistan.

Today, more than three thousand American and allied soldiers have been killed and thousands more injured and diseased in the theater of the war. US$1 trillion have been spent on military operations and some US$100 billion on Afghanistan's reconstruction, not to mention the incalculable loss of Afghan lives and property. Yet, Afghanistan is still far from reflecting America's original main objectives (Saikal 2014b, chap. 2). This is not to claim that certain infrastructural, telecommunications, and social and civil society developments have not taken place. On the contrary, Afghanistan today has a larger pool of young educated people, with greater political and social awareness who are capable of doing the heavy lifting for a better future, and who deserve to be given the necessary opportunity to do so. The country's smaller minorities, who belong to ethnic groups other than the largest Pashtun cluster, which comprises around 42 percent of the Afghan population and to whose rival tribes many members of the Afghan ruling elite and the Taliban belong, are empowered to play a greater role in their country than at any time previously.[3] Afghanistan has also been put on a very basic and shaky but nonetheless electoral process of governance. This was largely reflected in the April 2014 presidential election to replace Karzai, when some seven million Afghans out of the twelve million who had registered to vote cast their ballot for an electoral transfer of power for the first time in Afghan history. As flawed as that ballot may have been, it represented the wish of the Afghan people for the creation of a popularly sanctioned, credible government. In addition, Afghanistan has achieved possibly the highest level of freedom of expression and media in the region.

Yet, the country remains mired in instability, insecurity, poverty, patronage, corruption, national divisions, and a culture of drugs and deception, with the influence of strongmen pervasive throughout the country and electoral fraud continuing to plague the nation. While the first round of the 2014 presidential election was promising, with Abdullah Abdullah and Ashraf Ghani emerging as frontrunners with 45 percent and 32 percent, respectively, the runoff between the two was marred by widespread fraud. As Abdullah challenged the preliminary results of the runoff that favored Ghani by a large margin, a potentially devastating dispute began to loom. This prompted US secretary of state John Kerry to make an emergency visit to Kabul where he secured the agreement of Abdullah and Ghani to an audit of all the votes and to the formation of a "National Unity Government," irrespective of who won the election.[4]

Given the rising costs of the war and complexity of the Afghan situation, the United States and its allies found it expedient, as far back as 2009, to disentangle themselves from what had shaped up to be an "Afghan trap." The war had become the longest the United States had fought over the last century. The US government and allied partners no longer had the support of their domestic constituencies to continue the war, which proved to be a major drain on their resources at a time when they were facing serious financial and economic difficulties at home and escalating crises abroad. The Obama administration finally instigated a strategy whereby at first the United States and its allies would substantially scale down their military deployment by the end of 2014 and then fold it up altogether within two years. Under the US-Afghan Bilateral Security Agreement, which President Ashraf Ghani signed immediately after the inauguration of the National Unity Government on September 29, 2014, the United States committed to retain about ten thousand troops beyond 2014 for another year.

This commitment, which was matched by America's NATO allies, was all ostensibly for the purpose of training Afghan security forces and fighting terrorism but also for facilitating US drone attacks against militants across the border in Pakistan. The question at the time was about whether such a small force within a limited operational scope would be able to make a substantial difference to Afghanistan's security needs, and whether the Afghan security forces had reached the point whereby they could protect the country against the threat of a return to Taliban rule. This is an issue that requires a brief examination of the Afghan security forces as a critical determinant of the country's capacity to secure itself from both the Taliban and international terrorism, in line with what the United States had put forward as the goals of its invasion.

Afghan Security Forces

As part of the exit strategy, the United States and its allies focused, especially from late 2009, on two imperatives. The first was to accelerate their endeavors to empower the Afghan security forces to take over all security operations from foreign forces. By the close of 2014, the Afghan forces totaled more than 350,000, which the United States had funded, trained, and equipped at the cost of some $65 billion. However, many seasoned analysts of Afghanistan believe that these forces were not as yet coherent, equipped, disciplined, or strong enough to ensure Afghanistan's security without substantial support from US/NATO forces. Even a Pentagon report concluded in late 2012 that out of twenty-three divisions of the Afghan National Army (ANA), only one was ready to fight on its own (Bumiller 2012). The ANA reportedly suffered from a high desertion rate and a lack of internal cohesion and uniform training. It was inadequately equipped and lacked an effective air force, the building and maintenance of which would require long-term massive outside support, from the United States in particular. Since taking over increased operational responsibilities from mid-2012 in preparation for the foreign troop withdrawal, the ANA has taken an unsustainably high degree of casualties. For example, in 2014, it lost five thousand troops in fighting and fifteen thousand in desertion—something which has continued at an even higher rate since then. Relatively speaking, the same had proved to be the case with the national police force, which is also reported to be quite corrupt, although no more than recently created *arbaki or local militia forces in some parts of the country*. Only the Afghan "special forces" and the Directorate of National Intelligence, which are responsible for dealing with sporadic and isolated incidents, such as protests and terrorist attacks, appeared to be effective in certain cases.

The second imperative that the United States and its allies pursued was when, in 2010, they joined the Karzai government in an earnest desire to negotiate a political settlement with the Taliban as a necessary option for bringing the Afghan conflict to an end. This was despite having condemned the militia and its affiliated groups as terrorists for years. However, their efforts have so far failed to produce any tangible results, and they are unlikely to do so for as long as the insurgent groups feel that time is on their side. Although the founder and spiritual leader of the Taliban, Mullah Mohammad Omar, died in Pakistan in early 2013 (his death was revealed two years later) and his successor, Mullah Akhtar Mansour, was killed in an American drone strike in May 2016, none of these developments could cause a fatal blow to the ability of the Taliban and their affiliates, Pakistan's Inter-Services Intelligence (ISI)-linked Haqqani Network in particular, to pursue their violent opposition.

The Thwarting Variables: The "War on Terror" in Comparative Perspective

Ironically, the very variables that thwarted the United States' efforts during the Karzai era in Afghanistan are similar to those experienced by the United States in Vietnam and by the Soviets in Afghanistan. Four of these variables are worth mentioning as a common theme running through the US-Vietnam fiasco, the Soviet quagmire and retreat from Afghanistan, and what is now increasingly shaping up as the United States' debacle in Afghanistan.

The first factor concerns the outside powers' lack of understanding of the complexity of the society and regional context of the invaded countries and their failure to learn lessons from each other's invasion experiences. Former US secretary of state Robert Gates (2008–2013) captured this point well in his recent autobiography. Recalling America's role in countering the Soviet invasion of Afghanistan, he aptly observed, "Our lack of understanding of Afghanistan, its culture, its tribal and ethnic politics, its power brokers, and their relationships, was profound.... [T]wenty years later, I came to realize that in Afghanistan, as in Iraq, having decided to replace the regime, when it came to 'with what?', the American government had no idea what should follow. We had learned virtually nothing about the place in the twenty years since helping defeat the Soviets there" (Gates 2014, 336). This statement also applies to the US misapprehension of the Vietnam situation and the Soviet miscalculation of the Afghan situation.

The second variable is the inability of the intervening powers to secure a credible and effective partner within the invaded country, thereby to have the core mechanisms on the ground necessary for processes of stabilization and transformation. The United States could not achieve this goal in Vietnam, as the US-sponsored governments of Ngo Dinh Diem and its successors under Nguyen Cao Ky and Nguyen Van Thieu proved to be incompetent, dysfunctional, and corrupt (see Borer 1999, especially chap. 5). This was also precisely one of the key factors that bogged down the Soviets and contributed to their defeat in Afghanistan. Soviet efforts to harness a united and effective People's Democratic Party of Afghanistan (PDPA) government in Kabul produced no enduring results. They could not stop bitter factional fighting within the

PDPA, which continuously tore itself apart and which could not survive, even in a nominal form, without massive Soviet support. The Soviets' assassination of Hafizullah Amin in late December 1979, replacement of him with Babrak Karmal, and subsequent removal of Karmal in favor of Najibullah six years later did little to alleviate factional strife. Najibullah's government, for three years following the Soviet troop withdrawal in May 1989, survived primarily because of the disunity among the mujahideen and the Soviet supply of a lifeline to his government, which lasted until the disintegration of the Soviet Union at the end of 1991. After the Soviet Union's collapse, it was impossible for the PDPA rule to endure (Saikal 2012, chaps. 8–9).

The United States and its allies have faced a similar situation in Afghanistan. President Karzai did not prove to be an effective partner and state builder. Skilled in the art of political survival, he acted largely in the manner of a Pashtun tribal chief—the ethnic cluster that includes the rival Durrani and Ghalzai tribes, to which Karzai (and many of his cohorts), and the Taliban as well as Ashraf Ghani belong, respectively. He presided over a very dysfunctional and corrupt government, and relied largely on family, tribal, ethnic and factional connections, and patronage to maintain power, with limited writ over what has become a narco state, dependent on foreign aid and rentier economics for its survival. Karzai had a unique opportunity, especially after his election in 2004, to inaugurate a new phase in the historical evolution of the Afghan state and society. He enjoyed a degree of domestic and international support that none of his predecessors could ever have dreamed of and therefore was in an unprecedented position to engage in bold, visionary, and innovative policy actions. Instead, he resorted to traditional tactics of power maintenance, thus squandering a unique opportunity to chart a new course for Afghanistan's future.

Today, Afghanistan possesses no more than very fragile state institutions. By personalizing the presidency and its powers, Karzai essentially ignored the need for a strong parliament and judiciary. The underdevelopment of parliamentary powers in Afghanistan was exacerbated by US-backed postinvasion policies that implemented an American-style presidential system rather than the more decentralized parliamentary one, although the latter would have been a more appropriate choice in the mosaic Afghan context. Karzai manipulated both the Afghan parliament and its judiciary to support his own position and that of other self-centered, self-seeking, and poorly qualified political and ethnic entrepreneurs around him. No constructive relationship was nurtured between the three branches of government, and every effort was made to disable the legislature and judiciary from checking the excesses of the executive. When it came to his interests and those of his larger family, most importantly his brothers, Karzai rarely refrained from undermining the constitution and the legal system, which has delivered little justice to ordinary Afghans but which has been harnessed to benefit a small minority of the powerful and rich. Wittingly or unwittingly, he nurtured a Karzai "cartel" (Saikal 2014b, chap. 2).

Karzai also proved to be erratic and confusing in the conduct of his relations with his supporters and adversaries. He was unpredictable in his relations with the Afghan people, with no clear platform of state building. It was not clear whether he stood for an Islamic Afghanistan with a democratic face or vice versa. He frequently vacillated between praising the United States and NATO for their invaluable support and blaming them for his failures. Similarly, he condemned Pakistan as the force behind the Taliban on the one hand, while seeking its favors as a Muslim brother and neighbor on the other. He applied the same contradictory dictum to his approach to the Taliban and their affiliates. The United States and its NATO allies found him to be unreliable and contradictory, Pakistan regarded him as untrustworthy, and the Taliban castigated him as nothing more than a "Western puppet." In his final two years in office, Karzai focused more on a desire to be remembered as a nationalist as against a "Western stooge" rather than on what was best for Afghanistan's national interests. This explains his refusal to sign the Afghan-US Bilateral Security Agreement, as well as his support for Russia's annexation of Crimea, despite the Afghan people's bitter memory of the brutal Soviet occupation of their country.

The third variable common to these three cases is the inability of the invading powers to sell their invasions successfully to the invaded people, their own constituencies, and the international community. In much the same way that the United States was unable to market its invasion to a majority of the Vietnamese people and the international community, and that the Soviets were unable to enlist the support of the Afghan people and the outside world for its invasion, the United States could not be spared of this problem in regard to its Afghanistan adventure. Initially, a majority of the Afghans seemed happy with the US-led intervention, as they saw it as an act that would save them from the dreadful rule of the Taliban. However, they grew very disillusioned with what they viewed as the Americans' inability, or even unwillingness, to markedly improve the quality of their lives. This disillusionment was accompanied by an increasing perception within the international community as a whole that the United States and its allies had achieved only limited success in Afghanistan relative to their investment, in blood and money, in the country. The narrative of the Afghan War as the "good war" or "war of necessity" as distinct from the "bad war" or "war of choice," with which the Iraq War was labeled by many, including President Obama, rapidly lost its gloss.

The fourth variable is the invading powers' failure to halt outside support for resistance forces. Just as the United States could not contain outside assistance to North Vietnam, most significantly from the Soviet Union and China, and as an extension of this to the Viet Cong, and the Soviets could not prevent Western,

Arab, and Pakistani support to the mujahideen, the same has been true with the United States and its allies in Afghanistan. The United States failed to neutralize Pakistan's support for the Taliban and their affiliates and was unable to build a regional consensus on Afghanistan. Islamabad has continued to provide safe sanctuaries and logistical support for the Afghan insurgents, and to act very skillfully to position itself simultaneously as part of the problem and the solution in Afghanistan.

This was very much the case under the presidency of General Musharraf (1999–2008) and continued, in different shades, under his civilian successor, Asif Zardari (2008–2013). The Nawaz Sharif government initially promised more cooperation in order to stabilize Afghanistan, but Sharif could not fulfill that promise unless he had the full support of Pakistan's powerful military and military intelligence, the ISI, which have invested heavily in the Afghan insurgent groups for both domestic and wider regional purposes. The Afghanistan-Pakistan border has remained very volatile, with frequent cross-border military clashes between the two sides (Saikal 2014b, chap. 3). Indeed, in late 2014 to early 2015, there were some signs of improvement in bilateral relations, as President Ghani found it expedient to make strong overtures to Islamabad in order to entice the Taliban to negotiate with his government. While promising to take stronger steps in containing the Taliban, Islamabad did little in practice.

The underlying factors that have historically marred relations between the two sides remain unresolved. The most important of these are the border dispute and complicated cross-border ethnic Pashtun ties between the two countries, but other factors include the traditional Afghan-Indian friendship, Pakistani-Indian enmity, Pakistani-Iranian competition, Pakistani-Saudi strategic ties, and Iranian-Saudi rivalries, not to mention Iranian-American hostilities in pursuit of conflicting regional interests. It is only recently that the US-Iranian enmity has experienced a reduction. This has followed a resolution of the dispute over Iran's nuclear program, based on the signing of an agreement between Iran and the five permanent members of the UN Security Council plus Germany in July 2015 and the implementation of that agreement to large extent since then in return for the lifting of international sanctions against Iran. However, given President Trump's hostile attitude towards Iran, the nuclear agreement is now in serious jeopardy.

As India has provided Afghanistan noncombat military assistance, Pakistan has found it expedient to maintain its support for the Taliban and the Haqqani network, which Washington has listed as a terrorist group in one form or another. This, together with the US-Iranian adversarial relations and Tehran's dim view of Islamabad, has been instrumental in the persistent lack of a regional consensus on Afghanistan.

The Consequences of the Conflict

It is not surprising to see today an Afghanistan whose political and economic life and social fabric remain highly vulnerable to continued disruption and deprivation, with long-term structural disorder and insecurity characterizing the country's landscape. A small class of the nouveau riche, made up of mostly members of the Karzai family, senior government officials, former mujahideen commanders, drug traffickers, and criminal gangsters, has flourished at the cost of a majority of the Afghan people remaining impoverished. The 2011 International Monetary Fund's GDP per capita report listed Afghanistan as the twelfth-poorest country in the world, with an average GDP per capita of $956, an unemployment rate of 35 percent, and an extremely high poverty rate, with 42 percent of the population living on less than one dollar a day. Transparency International's annual list for 2013 named Afghanistan, North Korea, and Somalia as the world's three most corrupt countries. Although no new survey of the Afghan people's reflections on corruption is available, the extent of the problem is strongly indicated by the fact that during 2009, one Afghan out of every two had to pay kickbacks to public officials. In that year, Afghans paid $2.5 billion in bribes, accounting for an astronomical one-quarter of Afghanistan's GDP (United Nations Office on Drugs and Crime 2010, 4–5). There is no indication that this situation has changed much to date. The Afghans voted in the April 2014 election to close the gap between their rulers and the ruled, but the dichotomy between the two and ethnic and sectarian divisions have never been greater.

A host of social issues plague Afghan society. Given the high rate of violent incidents affecting civilians, hundreds and thousands of Afghans continue to remain internally displaced – a problem which is exacerbated by the return of more Afghan refugees from Pakistan and Iran. Displaced families face an uphill battle; coping mechanisms and support networks are disrupted and unreliable. In addition to this widespread problem of national insecurity, a majority of Afghans live under threat from security operations, suicide bomb attacks, and improvised explosive devices (IEDs). These constant difficulties are compounded by a chronic shortage of food, shelter, water, sanitation, and access to meaningful education. John Ging, director of operations for the UN Office for the Coordination of Humanitarian Affairs, illustrated the severity of the current situation when he pointed out that the level of malnutrition in Afghanistan stood at 59 percent as of June 2012 (United Nations Office for the Coordination of Humanitarian Affairs 2013, also see Chapter 16).

The continued plight of women in contemporary Afghanistan also disproves the self-aggrandizing rhetoric of Washington and government under Karzai. According to former first lady Laura Bush, as early as 2001, the US intervention had restored to the women of Afghanistan the "rights and dignity" taken from them by "terrorists" (Gerstenzang and Getter 2001). While some improvement can be claimed compared to women's status under the Taliban, this is not saying very much. Most Afghan women remain repressed by and shackled to traditional practices in the name of either Islam or cultural norms, or both. If there has been any change in their living conditions, it has been confined mostly to a select number of women in the main urban centers, Kabul in particular (for further details see Chapters 15 and 17 in this volume).

Many of the women's nongovernmental organizations (NGOs) operating in Afghanistan, such as the Afghanistan Women's Education Centre, the Afghanistan Women's Network, and the US-based Women for Afghan Women belong to what Thomas Carothers calls "advocacy NGOs" as opposed to "development" or "reconstruction" NGOs (see Carothers 1996). A 2008 report by Amnesty International, whose conclusions remain relevant today, found that "Afghan women and girls still face widespread discrimination from all segments of society, domestic violence, abduction, and rape by armed individuals, trafficking, forced marriages, including ever younger child marriages, and being traded in settlement of disputes and debts" (Amnesty International 2008). A study undertaken in the same year by Global Rights found that 58.8 percent of Afghan women were living in forced marriages, with around 40 percent reporting physical domestic violence at least once in the past year (Nijhowne and Oates 2008). There were more women and young girls in jails around the country for "moral crimes" in 2013 than ever before since the end of Taliban rule, with Human Rights Watch reporting a rise of over 50 percent since mid-2011 (Human Rights Watch 2013; also see Chapter 10 in this volume).

A presidential decree banning violence against women, child marriages, and forced marriages was issued in 2009. However, when the decree was put forward at the *Wolesi Jirga* (the Lower House of the Afghan parliament) in mid-May 2013 for legislative support, the debate was aborted by the conservative legislators to the disgust of all the female members and their supporters who had initiated the move.[5] Karzai's reluctance to undertake positive action in this direction was linked to his growing need to win over conservative factions, including the Taliban. The overall picture for women in Afghanistan, even after over a decade and half of international intervention, indeed remains exceedingly grim.

All this has constituted enormous challenges that the Ashraf-Abdullah National Unity Government is expected to overcome in the short to medium term. Without large-scale international support for structural, political, economic, and social reforms on the one hand, and for security enhancement on the other, this task will be an uphill battle. The withdrawal of most of the foreign forces has already resulted in a substantial reduction in outside support, leaving Afghanistan in a more vulnerable position. In its first visit to Washington in late March 2015, the National Unity Government leadership pitched strongly for a continuation of American financial, economic, and security assistance on a substantial scale, and President Obama promised not to leave Afghanistan in the lurch. Even so, there is little chance that the decline in foreign assistance can be arrested, unless Afghanistan is endowed with sources of substantial internal income in pursuit of self-sufficiency—a development whose prospects do not look bright at present.

The Future

Afghanistan faces an uncertain future. As the situation stands, it could go in one of four directions in the medium to long term. The first is the "Afghanization" of the conflict, which is already in progress. In this case, the Afghan security forces could be expected to hold out, with US logistical and air support, for some time until the insurgents and their supporters are exhausted and decide to settle for a negotiated settlement. The chances of such a scenario emerging, however, are slim, given that such an approach did not work in relation to the United States in Vietnam or the Soviets in Afghanistan.

The second is a possible power-sharing agreement between Kabul and the Taliban. However, such an agreement can only work if there is support from a cross section of the mosaic population of Afghanistan and if the Kabul government is strong enough not to allow the Taliban to prevail or dominate. At this stage, the Afghan government does not have the necessary strength, and the Taliban are convinced that they will emerge victorious. President Ghani's efforts to bring the Taliban to the negotiating table for a political settlement have already generated much concern among those elements of the Afghan society, including women's groups, who do not trust either the Taliban or Pakistan to act in good faith. The success of the so-called Islamic State (IS) in establishing a niche in Afghanistan has added to the overall complexity of the situation.

The third is a descent into an internecine conflict, with the country's neighbors scrambling for influence, similar to what was experienced during the mujahideen rule from 1992 to 1996, and, to a lesser extent, during Taliban rule. This scenario could eventuate if the Afghan leaders fail to forge a national consensus and work together amicably and constructively. The National Unity Government could implode, with different Afghan microsocieties fending for themselves against one another. This is a scenario that President Ghani and Chief Executive Abdullah as well as the international community, most importantly the United States and its NATO allies, want to avoid.

The fourth is that, with the persistent vigilance and support of the United States and its allies in particular, the Afghan leaders could finally embrace the idea that the only way they can salvage themselves and Afghanistan is to leave their personal, political, and social differences aside for the sake of national unity and reformation. In the process, they would need to avoid the pitfalls that marred Karzai's rule, and harness synergies from within for orderly change and development rather than looking for assistance to outsiders, who have sought to affect the evolution of Afghan politics and society for too long in one direction or another. It is very telling that since the early nineteenth century, Afghan leaders have rarely come to power or remained in power without the backing of an outside patron.

The possibility of this last scenario developing is not inconceivable, given that the Afghanistan of today is not the same as the one the United States invaded in 2001. The country has politically and socially changed: the people are more connected, and a new and younger generation of Afghans has emerged, free of the baggage of the generation that has been in power since the US-led intervention. This generation wants better and peaceful lives for themselves and their country, and can be expected to work actively toward this end, provided that they are given the necessary opportunity to play a central role in charting the destiny of their country.

If the last scenario emerges, it may not deliver democracy and total security to Afghanistan. But it will enable the new generation of Afghans to build a civil society, with liberty and political pluralism as the foundation for an eventual transition of Afghanistan into an appropriate form of democracy. The history of Afghanistan has been one of struggle and survival, and this may remain the case for the foreseeable future. The country has received severe blows. At the same time, however, its people have shown a resilience that has prevented the total collapse of the Afghan state and society.

AMIN SAIKAL is professor of Political Science, director of the Centre for Arab and Islamic Studies (the Middle East and Central Asia) and a public policy fellow at the Australian National University. His latest books include *Iran at the Crossroads*; *Modern Afghanistan: A History of Struggle and Survival*; and *The Rise and Fall of the Shah: Iran from Autocracy to Religious Rule*.

Notes

1. For a detailed discussion, see Saikal (2014a, 141–56), Mackinder (1904), Fletcher (1965), and Jones (2009).
2. Detailed treatments of the Afghanistan invasion from the perspective of Soviet foreign policy can be found in Collins (1986) and Freedman (1991).
3. For a figure of about 40 per cent in the 1990s, see Magnus and Naby (2002, 93) and Janata (1990, 64).
4. See Latifi and Bengali (2014).
5. For more detail, see International Crisis Group (2013).

Bibliography

Amnesty International. 2008. *Afghanistan: Women's Human Rights Defenders Continue to Struggle for Women's Rights*. March 7. Accessed March 19, 2017. https://www.amnesty.org/en/documents/asa11/003/2008/en/.
Borer, Douglas A. 1999. *Superpowers Defeated: Vietnam and Afghanistan Compared*. London: Frank Cass.
Bumiller, Elisabeth. 2012. "Pentagon Says Afghan Forces Still Need Assistance." *New York Times*, December 10.
Carothers, Thomas. 1996. *Assessing Democracy Assistance: The Case of Romania*. Washington, DC: Carnegie Endowment for International Peace.
Collins, Joseph J. 1986. *The Soviet Invasion of Afghanistan: A Study in the Use of Force in Soviet Foreign Policy*. Lanham, MD: Lexington Books.
Fletcher, Arnold. 1965. *Afghanistan: Highway of Conquest*. Ithaca, NY: Cornell University Press.
Freedman, Robert O. 1991. *Moscow and the Middle East: Soviet Policy since the Invasion of Afghanistan*. Cambridge, UK: Cambridge University Press.
Gates, Robert M. 2014. *Duty: Memoirs of a Secretary at War*. New York: Alfred A. Knopf.
Gerstenzang, James, and Lisa Getter. 2001. "Laura Bush Addresses State of Afghan Women." *Los Angeles Times*, November 18.
Haussegger, Virginia. 2011. "Prospects for Women: Gender and Social Justice." In *The Afghanistan Conflict and Australia's Role*, ed. Amin Saikal. Melbourne: Melbourne University Press.
Human Rights Watch. 2013. *Afghanistan: Surge in Women Jailed for "Moral Crimes."* May 21. Accessed March 19, 2017. http://www.hrw.org/news/2013/05/21/afghanistan-surge-women-jailed-moral-crimes.
International Crisis Group. 2013. "Women in Conflict in Afghanistan," Asia Report No. 252, October 14. Brussels: International Crisis Group. Accessed July 27, 2016. http://www.crisisgroup.org/~/media/Files/asia/south-asia/afghanistan/252-women-and-conflict-in-afghanistan.pdf.
Janata, Alfred. 1990. "Afghanistan: The Ethnic Dimension." In *The Cultural Basis of Afghan Nationalism*, ed. Ewan W. Anderson and Nancy Hatch Dupree. London: Pinter.
Jones, Seth G. 2009. *In the Graveyard of Empires: America's War in Afghanistan*. New York: W.W. Norton.
Kipling, Rudyard. *Kim*. [1901] 2008. Oxford: Oxford University Press.
Latifi, Ali M., and Shashank Bengali. 2014. "Afghan Rivals Sign Deal on Unity Government Ending Standoff." *Los Angeles Times*, September 21.
Mackinder, H. J. 1904. "The Geographical Pivot of History." *Geographical Journal* 23 (4): 421–37.
Magnus, Ralph H., and Eden Naby. 2002. *Afghanistan: Mullah, Marx and Mujahid*. Boulder, CO: Westview Press.
Nijhowne, Diya, and Lauren Oates. 2008. *Living with Violence: A National Report on Domestic Abuse in Afghanistan*. Washington, DC: Global Rights.
Risen, James. 2010. "U.S. Identifies Vast Mineral Riches in Afghanistan." *New York Times*, June 13.
Saikal, Amin. 2012. *Modern Afghanistan: A History of Struggle and Survival*. London: I. B. Tauris.

———. 2013. "Afghanistan's Uncertain Future." ABC News, November 11. Accessed July 27, 2014. http://www.abc.net.au/news/2013-11-12/saikal-afghanistans-uncertain-future/5083770.

———. 2014a. "Afghanistan's Geographic Possibilities." *Survival: Global Politics and Strategy* 56 (3): 141–56.

———. 2014b. *Zone of Crisis: Afghanistan, Pakistan, Iran and Iraq.* London: I. B. Tauris.

Shahrani, M. Nazif. 1986. "State Building and Social Fragmentation in Afghanistan: A Historical Perspective." In *The State, Religion, and Ethnic Politics: Afghanistan, Iran and Pakistan*, ed. Ali Banuanzizi and Myron Weiner, 23–74. Syracuse: Syracuse University Press.

United Nations Office for the Coordination of Humanitarian Affairs. 2013. "Afghanistan and Pakistan: Humanitarian Needs Must Not Be Neglected," Says OCHA's John Ging. June 6. Accessed March 19, 2017. http://www.unocha.org/top-stories/all-stories/afghanistan-and-pakistan-humanitarian-needs-must-not-be-neglected-says-ocha.

United Nations Office on Drugs and Crime. 2010. *Corruption in Afghanistan: Bribery as Reported by the Victims.* UNODC Statistics and Surveys Section, January.

2

AFGHANISTAN'S "TRADITIONAL" ISLAM IN TRANSITION: THE DEEP ROOTS OF TALIBAN EXTREMISM

Bashir Ahmad Ansari

Introduction

A deep and complex relationship between religion (Islam) and politics in Afghanistan is often assumed, and with a few exceptions (Roy 1990, 1998; Oleson 1995; Nawid 1999; Shahrani 2013; Wilber 1949), it has not yet been systematically investigated. Instrumental deployment of Islam, especially in times of political crisis in the country, has been persistent in the history of Afghanistan. What is new is the radical shift in favor of Islamic militancy and extremism since the 1970s. In this chapter, I will attempt, however briefly, to examine a significant cause of this radical shift from traditional Islam (pre-1970s) toward extremism during the last forty years of war and violence, and analyze discourses about Islam among the peoples of the larger region of Khorasan which encompasses modern Afghanistan.

More specifically, the chapter will discuss the pervasiveness of the traditional institutions of Khorasani Sufism as the dominant means for the expression of popular piety, spiritual purification, and ethical teaching in educational institutions. I will also briefly review how this traditional knowledge and practice of Islam which encouraged peaceful life with justice, compassion, and tolerance among the ordinary peoples of the region before the 1970s, was produced and reproduced in the vernacular languages of Afghanistan and perpetuated among the largely nonliterate peoples of Afghanistan. The chapter will then discuss how after the Soviet-inspired communist coup of 1978 and the subsequent four decades of war and violence, the emergent political elites in Afghanistan have increasingly relied on instrumental uses and abuses of Islamic militancy in pursuing their goals while disregarding the historically rooted and well-established Islamic moral and ethical values in their own personal lives as well as in their public conduct. In order to be able to resume peace and stability in the country, I will advocate for key changes in

Islamic education and in public discourse and why and how they should be incorporated in the Islamic religious education curriculum in the *madrassa* systems in Afghanistan and Pakistan. Let us begin with a brief review of traditional Islam in the Khorasan region before the onset of the recent wars.

The Decline of Khorasani Mysticism

When reaching the territories encompassing modern day Afghanistan, Islam incorporated or Islamized elements of local culture to give it a distinctive local Islamic flavor. As the result of this syncretism, the Khorasani or eastern mysticism took shape with important influences on society, culture, literature, and civilization of the region and beyond. This influence came to be manifest in the new rationalist philosophy of Abu 'Ali al-Husayn ibn Sina—better known in Europe by the Latinized name as Avicenna (980–1037)—a Khorasani who studied mysticism as part of philosophy.[1] One of Avicenna's contemporaries, Khawja Abdullah Al-Ansari (1006–1088), a Khorasani mystic whose shrine is an important pilgrimage site in the city of Herat, in western Afghanistan, and a notable Hanbali scholar, interpreted the Qur'an from a Sufi perspective (Maibud 2003). In his book, *Manazil al-Sairin* or the stations of Sufi paths, Ansari describes the *khuluq* or character and ethics of Sufism as follows:

> All speakers about this knowledge agreed that Sufism is nothing but ethics, and the core argument of [this path] is to make an effort for goodness and avoid harming others. This [goal] can be achieved through three things: knowledge, generosity, and patience, and it is being built on three levels: the first level is *maqam al-khalq* or knowing the position of created being, and that they are tied to their destiny bounded to their limited power and that they are not subjects of [your] judgment. This knowledge can benefit by three things; to let created being, even dogs, [be] safe and secure, love people and be savior of the creatures. (Abdullah al-Ansari 1966, 22).

The rationalist school of jurisprudence based in Iraq (represented by scholars who followed the path of Imam Abu Hanifa (699–767), whose interpretive tradition is adhered to in Afghanistan and wider Central Asia) together with the mystical teachings and understanding of Islam formed the two authentic pillars of Khorasani Muslim religious identity—i.e., closely adhering to *shari'a* (law and ethics) while practicing *tariqa* (mysticism). Indeed, Khorasani mysticism and its ethical universe covered a large geographic region—that is, from India and northwestern China (Xinjiang) to Afghanistan, Iran, the Indian subcontinent, Central Asia, Iraq, Turkey, and even Eastern Europe.

The moderate character of Islam in Afghanistan, which focused on people's harmonious relations with God, nature, humanity, and its embodiment within themselves, has been associated with mysticism, and it has been impressed on the Muslim to aspire for harmony, tolerance, compassion, peace, and moral uprightness. The Khorasani mystics believed in unity of God's existence, unity of religious truth, and viewed difference as a crucial part and parcel of a Creator God's design (Masroori 2010). The didactic poets and religious scholars of Khorasan, Rumi, Attar, and Sanaie, among others, make use of powerful key religious symbols of Khorasan in their writings expounding the valued lessons of tolerance and acceptance of others. One of the most popular literary figures, Sa'di Shirazi (1210–1291), who is considered to exemplify the heights of lyrical humanism in Persian literature, articulates the essence of a famous hadith (saying of the Prophet Muhammad) as follows:

Bani adam a'zaye yak deegar and…
Human beings are all part of a single organism
In creation, of one essence
If one organ is afflicted with pain
Other parts shall not be spared the pain

Sa'di also said:

To kaz mehnati deegaran beghami
Nashayad ki naamat nihand adami
If you are indifferent to others misfortune/suffering,
You are unworthy to be called a human

(Sa'di AH 1371, 128)

In yet another couplet, Sa'di, shares his gratitude for the blessings of this world to his Sustainer (*Rabb*) in this manner:

Ba jahan Khurram az anam ke jahan khurram az ost
Asheqam bar hama alam ke hama alam az ost
I am happy in the world, for it is fresh and green because of Him
I am in love with the whole world, because it belongs to Him

(Saadi AH 1371, 634)

Muhammad Jalaluddin Balkhi (1207–1273), widely known as Rumi in the West, is another great Khorasani humanist and mystic. The idea of religious tolerance, empathy, and love pervades every verse written by Rumi. He summarizes the main reason behind one of his major poetry collections, the *Mathnawi/Masnawi*, by saying: "Our *Mathnawi* is the store of unity (*wahdat*), whatever you see beside unity is idol worship" (Rumi AH 1379, 870). He also adds:

Munbasit bodim o yak gawhar hama
Bi sar o bi pa bodim an sar hama

Yak guhar bodim hamchoon aftab
Bi gereh bodim safi hamcho ab
In essence there is no division and numeration,
Nor is there diversity and separation,
In the beginning, we were all of the same infinite essence,
Without beginning, without any end;
Of one core we were, like the rays of sun
Like water were we, clear and unknotted

(Rumi AH 1379, 45)

Chonke bi rangi asiri rang shud
Mosawi ye ba Mosawi ye dar jang shud
Choon ba bi rangi rasi kan dashti
Mosawi o Fer'awn daashti aashti
When the colorless became imprisoned in colors
Jew started fighting Jews
When and if the colorless retuned to original colorlessness
Even Moses and Pharaoh will make peace.

(Rumi AH 1379, 114)

Traditional Islamic values, practice, and discipline during the last four decades took a different turn in the Khorasan region because of a few major transformative developments of the twentieth century. The first transformation was effected as the result of the fall of the Ottoman Empire. The Ottoman's Hanafi-based Muslim cultural heritage was a blend of rationalism and Shari'a-based Khorasani mysticism (Gamm 2011). The other significant change in the Muslim world in general and Central Asia in particular was the closure of the centers of religious learning (*madaaris*) in Turkestan following the colonization of the cities of Bukhara, Samarqand, and other centers of Islamic learning, first by the tsarist and later Soviet Russians. This area had been the cradle of Islamic education in the region, especially in the territories of modern day Afghanistan, for over a millennium. The Central Asian educational traditions, often referred to as schools of rationalism or *ra'y* (reasoning), were largely neglected during the tsarist Russian occupation, and their doors shut completely after the establishment of the Bukharan Soviet Socialist Republic (1921). Since that time, the fundamental tenets of Marxism and communism have been at odds with religions in general and with Islam in particular. Elimination of these pedagogic sites of higher Islamic learning have had very serious consequences for Muslims and especially for the peoples of Afghanistan.

Religious education in the region was also seriously affected by the British overthrow of Muslim rule and colonization of India. Moghul Muslim ruling dynasties were for the most part supporters and promoters of Islamic religious institutions in the Indian subcontinent. With their demise and the imposition of colonial rule, Islamic education was allowed to deteriorate into a marginalized institution in the service of colonialism, guaranteeing the political and ideological control of India (Cohn 1997). However, the ultimate transformative changes in the region were effected by the discovery and exploitation of hydrocarbon deposits of oil and gas in the Arabian Gulf. The growth of oil wealth enabled state sponsors of the radicalized forces from the Gulf region to spread the more radical Salafi ideologies of political Islam far beyond their own cloistered environments. These ideological incursions, as will be discussed, began to undermine the traditional rationalist or reason-based understanding of Islam which had long been integrated with indigenous *Urfan* or Khorasani shari'a-based mystic traditions in the region. The disastrous consequences of these socioeconomic, political, and ideological shifts reached their apex after World War II, with the onset of the Cold War and eventually the former Soviet Union's invasion of Afghanistan. It is to the brief examination of these brutal developments to which we will now turn.

Rise of Extremism in Afghanistan

To understand the relationship between Islam and its increasing instrumentalization as a political device by governments and their opponents during the last four decades in Afghanistan, one cannot ignore the impact of the changes in the geopolitical climate of the region more broadly. After taking power via a military coup in 1977, General Zia-ulHaq became the president of neighboring Pakistan. The following year, in April 1978, when the Afghan communists staged their own Soviet-inspired military coup to take over the government in Kabul, President Zia-ulHaq decided immediately to support Afghanistan's Islamist resistant groups, the Afghan mujahideen who rose up to oppose the communist regime. The Soviet Red Army's invasion of Afghanistan in December 1979 drew the support of the United States and its regional allies, especially Saudi Arabia, to the proxy war. Together, the United States and the Saudis provided billions of dollars in assistance to Pakistan for hosting both millions of Afghan refugees and providing safe spaces within Pakistan for the Afghan mujahideen to wage their jihad against the Afghan communist regimes and their Russian patrons. The success of the Iranian Islamic Revolution (1979) and the establishment of the Islamic Republic in predominantly Shi'a Iran by Ayatollah Khomeini began to further influence or expand the role of religion in the emergent political culture of the region. The fact that Afghanistan has a Shi'a population of its own and shares a common language (Persian/Dari), culture, and history with Iran added greater weight to the long-term impact of these novel regional developments, especially for Afghanistan.

These major external and local developments made Islam more central than ever to the politics of this region. The Soviet Russian invasion of Afghanistan, as it is well known, provoked serious reaction from the West and the Muslim world. The coming together of these events prepared the conditions for a combustive mixture of oil, politics, religious fanaticism, and tribalism in this region. The most detrimental consequence of the conjunction of these factors, I suggest, has been the weakening and subversion of the historically moderate traditions of Khorasani jurisprudence (*fiqh*) and humanistic/ethical mysticism.

The venomous processes of undermining traditional Islamic normative values and practices in Afghanistan began shortly after the declaration of jihad against the communist regime in Kabul and its Soviet Russian sponsors. The popular resistance movement, in defense of the nation and its religion as it was threatened by the Soviet atheistic empire, had a well-remembered precedent in Central Asia. Mobilizing for the cause of jihad against the proven enemy of Islam, communism and the Soviet Union, was very much within the tradition of the people of Afghanistan, Khorasan, and Turkistan. However, the jihad movement of the people of Afghanistan was quickly appropriated and misdirected by far more powerful forces beyond their control.

That is, Pakistan's General Zia-ul Haq opportunistically joined the chants of jihad and other Islamic slogans, and presented himself as the champion of jihad in Afghanistan. What at the time appeared to be a courageous move on President Zia's part procured hundreds of millions of dollars to Pakistan from Western and Arab countries. Therefore, while for Afghans, participating in jihad was a religious duty and an obligation to defend the country, for Pakistan's government and Zia-ul Haq, Islam and jihad became a convenient ideological weapon against the Soviet Union and its client regime in Kabul. As a result, Pakistan's Deobandi *madrassas*, a network of traditional schools of Islamic religious learning, were called on to serve the national interests of Pakistan, both politically and militarily.

Coincidentally, the recent victory of the Shi'a revolutionary clerics in Iran catapulted the Gulf sheikhdoms and Saudi Arabia to valorize and financially strengthen the conservative Sunni Deobandi *madrassas* in Pakistan. Huge sums of money poured into Pakistan from these oil-rich countries to help open additional *madrassas* in different parts of Pakistan, especially in the Northwest Frontier province (NWFP, now renamed as Pakhtunkhaw or Pashtun territory) and in Baluchistan, just south of the Afghanistan border. Within a few years after the Soviet occupation of Afghanistan, millions of Afghan families took refuge in Pakistan to escape imprisonment and the horrors of war. Since Pakistan denied Afghan refugee youth free access to their government-run secular school system, they were welcomed to enter the Deobandi *madrassas*, which also offered them free food and living accommodations to study. The Pakistan government encouraged the opening of many more *madrassas* with the Deobandi school curriculum in and near the refugee camps for Afghans located in the NWFP and Baluchistan provinces to accommodate displaced and desperate refugee youth.

In July 1979, President Jimmy Carter decided in favor of destabilizing Soviet Central Asia's Muslim republics by disseminating Islamic literature among them with the aim of persuading them to declare their own jihad against the Soviet Union. Michael J. Adamski (2009, 33), claims that, in order to further the strategic goals of the CIA and Pakistan's Inter-Services Intelligence (ISI) in Central Asia, they needed to recruit willing leaders of the Deobandi schools to promote their political aims. Therefore, after 1979, for the first time, a new enterprise, namely the "business of Madrasas and jihad" made its appearance in this strategic part of the world.

It was during these years that Osama bin Laden and his "Arab-Afghan" cohorts made their way to Peshawar, Pakistan. Bin Laden and company brought their Salafi doctrine to the fertile fields of Afghanistan in the 1980s. The spread of the radicalized teachings of the school of *Ahli-Hadith* (followers of the traditions of the Prophet) discouraged adherence to the living ideals and practices of the school of rationalism (*Ahli Ra'y*) and Khorasani mysticism.

With his Yemeni tribal roots, Bin Laden's move into the Pashtun tribal belt along the Afghanistan-Pakistan frontiers made the atmosphere ripe for a meeting of the minds, coexistence, and collaboration through the local Deobandi Pashtun tribal managers of *madrassas* and their wider Pakistani sponsors in Peshawar and Baluchistan. By 1989, when Bin Laden met Mullah Omar, the future leader of Afghan Taliban, the foundation for future cooperative relations between the two camps had been laid. According to Ayesha Jalal (2008), the historic encounter occurred in the Bnuria Masjid, a Deobandi stronghold in Karachi. In the environment of anticommunist jihad and encouragement of greater militancy by the United States and its Western and Middle Eastern allies (Gulf Sheikhdoms), Salafi ideology promoted by the firebrand Palestinian jihadist Sheikh Abdullah Azzam, who had also moved his operations to Peshawar, began to spread. The most systematic means of infiltration became the curriculum of the vastly enlarged Deobandi *madaaris* (Arabic plural for *madrassa*) in Pakistan. War, violence, and hatred filled the young minds of the *taliban* (*madrassa* pupils) dislodging the traditional sober and humane Islamic religious teachings in such seminaries. The impact of this shift in the Deobandi curriculum on the behavior of students and teachers cannot and should not be ignored. Therefore, let us turn to a brief discussion of the nature of these curricular changes and their impact on the future Taliban and their activities.

Deobandi Curriculum: Past and Present

A large network of pietistic Islamic religious seminaries popularly known as Deobandi *madaaris* across the Indian subcontinent used an instructional curriculum that focused on the literal interpretation of the Islamic sacred texts rather than focusing on the spiritual essence of Islam and its teachings.[2] The Taliban in Afghanistan and Pakistan consider themselves students of these schools. More specifically, the Deobandi *madaaris* follow a curriculum called Nizamia Nisab, which was prepared by a scholar named Mullah Nizam Uddin Sehalvi (1677–1748). The main characteristic of this curriculum was reliance on memorization of religious texts and their interpretations by earlier commentators without critical engagement with the texts and the specific time and place in which they were produced and without any regard to their intelligibility to the readers or hearers within their own times and context.

The eight-year-long course of study at Deobandi *madaaris* included taking the following: ten thematic courses on the subjects (*mazaamin*) of jurisprudence (*fiqh*), eight on hadith (collections of the sayings and reported deeds of the Prophet Muhammad), two on calligraphy, and just one on *akhlaq* or etiquette and ethics (see Deoband Online 2014). Significantly, the curriculum does not include anything about Sufism (Islamic mysticism) and its rich history or the history and politics of Muslim societies which produced such knowledge and civilization. Taqi Uddin Usmani, a prominent leader of the Deobandi movement, having noticed this inadequacy, wrote to the Deobandi schools and asked them to add the subject of mysticism to their curriculum and also to include Sufi themes in their studies (Ingram 2011), but Usmani's suggestion was apparently ignored by the administrators of the Deobandi *madaaris*.

Ironically, Mullah Nizam Uddin, founder of the Nizamia curriculum, according to Ingram (2011), taught mysticism in his home but neglected to include it explicitly in the school's instruction. According to Taqi Usmani, "Sufism and ethics (*akhlaq*) were not included in madrasa coursework [by Nizam Uddin] because the very environment of the madrasa trained one in ethics and the Sufi path, and for anything else attachment to a Sufi master would be sufficient." Usami also adds: "This may have been true of his [Nizam Uddin's] times, but nowadays it seems necessary that books on Sufism and ethics should be included into the foundations of madrasa coursework. To this end, [Usmani suggests] selected parts from Ghazali's *Bidaya al-Hidaya*, [beginning of guidance], *Arba'in* [forty principles of religion], and *Ihya al-'Ulum* [revival of religious science], Suhrawardi's *Awarif al-Ma'arif* [knowledge for encountering God] Thanawi's *Al-Takashshuf* [discovering as the mission of Sufism], and so on can be incorporated at different levels of coursework"[3] (Usmani 1998, 99). Among the most necessary reforms recommended by Usmani to the Deobandi curriculum are that "every madrasa [should] make Sufism and moral excellence (*ihsan*) part of the curriculum [and] … The teachers and administration of every madrasa should establish a spiritual link with a Sufi shaykh for the purpose of reform and training" (Usmani 1998, 94–95).

With the infusion of radical Salafi/Wahhabi ideologies into the curriculum of the greatly enlarged numbers of Deobandi *madaaris* in Pakistan, the image and character of God instilled in pupils has become almost the exact opposite of the images of God that Khorasani mystics such as Rumi, Sana'i, 'Attar, Jami, Ansari, Bidil, Sa'di, and others have depicted, as was briefly discussed earlier. That is, the images constructed of God in present-day Deobandi *madaaris* seems to be the epitome of harshness, vengefulness, and reprisal, and God's primary tasks are to proscribe, forbid, punish, and keep people accountable for every minor infraction. Such renderings of God are the complete opposite of how traditional Khorasani mystics depicted God—that is, as the absolute manifestation of love, justice, compassion, kindness, tolerance, generosity, and the ultimate source of forgiveness, blessings, and hope. The image of God that inspired respect for, and trust in, others promised peace, harmony, tolerance, and enduring friendship in society. The escalations of violence and brutality by the Taliban against the great majority of the peoples of Afghanistan since their capture of Kabul in September 1996 must be, at least in part, due to the kinds of education they have received within the highly politicized and radicalized Deobandi *madaaris* in Pakistan.

Many of the most notorious of both Afghan and Pakistani Taliban leaders, including Jalaluddin Haqqani, the founder of a notorious Afghan terrorist network operating from Pakistan, have attended *Darul Uloom Haqqania*, a major Deobandi *madrassa* near Peshawar, Pakistan. A former Pakistani ambassador to the United States, Hussain Haqqani, during a visit to the Haqqania *madrassa* at the time when the Afghan Taliban ruled in Kabul, asked a nine-year-old seminarian named Mohammad Tahir, what did the verse in the Qur'an which says, "of all communities raised among men, you are the best, enjoining the good, forbidding the wrong and believing in God," mean to him? Tahir's response, according to the ambassador, was radically different from the interpretations of virtually all authoritative commentators of this verse (Q 3:110). Tahir said: "The Muslim community of believers is the best in the eyes of God, and we must make it the same in the eyes of men by force . . . we must fight the unbelievers and that includes those who carry Muslim names but have adopted the ways of unbelievers" (Haqqani 2002, 60).

This shocking understanding by young students is replicated in numerous other instances, many of the students winding up in Taliban violence against those who do not agree with them. As stated before, the use of human intellect and reasoning is stressed by Hanafi scholars (rationalists/people of opinion) and is encouraged for proper understanding of foundational Islamic texts and in fulfillment of pious obligation. In prewar Afghanistan, the Hanafi school of jurisprudence was universally followed by the Sunni population of the country and alternative interpretations were not known or available. The recent arrival of Wahhabi/Salafi ideals through the highly politicized Deobandi *madaaris*, producing the Taliban, has added fuel to the fires of the societal conflict consuming Afghanistan.

To illustrate this key point, let us very briefly review the difference among the recognized *mazaahib* on how best to fulfill one important religiously mandated obligatory act, that of the payment of *zakatul fitr*, alms to be given to the poor, needy, and indigent, for purifying one's fast during the month of Ramadan.[4] That is, the head of Muslim households are obligated to pay a prescribed amount of various edible foodstuff per each and every member of their family, regardless of age, by or before the end of the month of fasting each year. The Maliki, Shafei'i, and Hanbali schools insist that the kinds of foodstuff which can be given as *zakatul fitr* (alms) are limited to dates, raisins, wheat, barley, and dry cottage cheese. The Hanafi School, on the other hand, permits paying the equivalent in value of any of the specified food items in cash or kind (Saabiq 1992, 349). Because, they argue, the purpose of paying this *zakat* (purification of one's act of fasting) is to help poor people and make them happy, and it can be paid in cash if cash is preferred by the recipients. In the past, locals dispensed their obligations by giving either food items or cash to the needy without anyone objecting.

It is important to point out that currently, in the Indian subcontinent, two different movements claim close association with the name of Deoband—that is, the older Tablighi Jamaat movement and the much more recent Taliban movement, each exhibiting diametrically opposed views and behaviors. The Tablighi Jamaat promotes values which are utterly nonviolent, conciliatory, peaceful, educational, discursive, and moderate. In contrast, the Taliban have adopted a harsh, violent, confrontational, and aggressive demeanor. Both movements are popular but in different communities within India and Pakistan; the question then is why? Even a cursory review of these movements show that the Tablighi Jamaat are active and widely influential in urban and densely populated nontribal or detribalized parts of India and Pakistan. But the Taliban seems to thrive in the heart of the rural, ecologically marginal Pashtun and Baloch tribal belt between Afghanistan and Pakistan. Indeed, the Taliban are almost exclusively members of the world's largest tribal society, famed for, and proud of, their combative and violent tribal culture.

The Afghan Taliban movement's adoption of the extremist Salafi ideology (whether for political convenience or not) has met with stiff resistance from the urban and detribalized non-Pashtun communities within Afghanistan— segments of the population who have retained their core values of traditional Khorasani "local knowledge of Islam" (see Shahrani 1991), the knowledge and practices of Islam preserved and perpetuated through various forms of vernacular literature in Afghanistan and Central Asia. This body of didactic Islamic literature, written in the local languages (Persian, Turki/Chaghatai Uzbek, and Pashtu) are produced, reproduced, and deployed orally and in written form as part of collective religious discourse throughout the area. That is, local knowledge of Islam in local languages was disseminated via popular instructional materials used in primary level mosque schools or read aloud in private or public Sufi gatherings. Some of the most important of such texts in wide circulation, especially in rural areas of Afghanistan, are: *Panj Ganj, Chahar Kitab,* Sa'di's *Gulistan, Bostan, Diwani Hafiz, Diwani Bidel, Ahamdi Jami,* and in some urban circles, even Rumi's *Mathnawi*. These sources of local or popular Islam consisted of "the knowledge of both Shari'a and Sufi tradition of Islam acquired, possessed, and utilized by the masses of Muslim believers in specific places and times" (Shahrani 1991, 185). The contents of these texts augmented by *wa'z* (preaching) and *khutbah* (homily/sermon) during Friday prayers helped shape the social behavior, values, and beliefs of the common people, and as such, are foundational to the lived everyday Islam in the region. The focus of these didactic texts is almost entirely on actualization of Islamic teachings (i.e., practices/praxis) which include dispensing normative principles, religious beliefs, and practices to the generally poorly educated or nonliterate Muslims. It is the strength of this traditional knowledge of Islam in Afghanistan which has mobilized, in particular, the non-Pashtun population of the country, to resist Taliban extremism during the past two decades, and this is likely to continue for decades to come.

Politicization and Instrumentalization of Islam in Afghanistan

With the exception of a group of young radical Islamist students, led by Gulbuddin Hekmatyar, who engaged in a failed rebellion in the summer of 1975 against the government of President Muhammad Daoud (r. 1973–1978), the Taliban have distinguished themselves for waging an armed jihad against the Islamic Republic of Afghanistan—that is, under President Burhanuddin Rabbani, whom they ousted and eventually assassinated in 2011—and since their defeat in 2001 by the US-led international coalition, against their client regimes in Kabul.[5] According to traditional understanding of Islamic principles and practices in Khorasan, acceptance of Muslim rulers is obligatory. In the absence of a legitimate cause—such as a publicly declared apostasy by the ruler or preventing their Muslim subjects from fulfilling their obligatory daily prayers and meeting their required religious obligations—the use of arms against the government is forbidden. Sunnis' view on this subject is supported by considerable textual evidence, especially authenticated hadith as well as other authoritative interpretive sources.

For example, a universally respected hadith scholar among his peers, the *ulama*, Imam An-Nawawi (1233–1277), says: "It is forbidden to rebel against them [Muslim rulers] and fight them by the consensus of the Muslims scholars even though [if] they were wrongdoers and oppressors" (An-Nawawi 1998, 540–41). One of the most important books on Islamic creed, from Hanafi perspective is, *al-Aqeedah at-tahaweyah* by Abu Ja'far at-Tahawi Al-Hanafi (852–933 AD). He has declared that: "We do not support any armed rebellion against our leader and governors even if they have committed injustice to us. We do not call nor revolt against them" (at-Tahawi 1995, 24). Similarly, Imam Abu Al Hassan Al-Ash'ari (873–935), an acknowledged grand Imam of the Sunnis (874–936 AD), says: "They (Sunnis) believe on praying for the leaders of the Muslims and they do not raise sword against them" (Al-Asha'ri 1950, 323). Imam al-Bazdawi (d. AH 483) one of the foremost theorists of the Hanafi school of thought, asserts: "If the head of the state committed a sin, we must pray for him to repent, and rebellion against them is unallowable because the revolution leads to chaos and corruption in the world." Imam al-Bazdawi further states: "If the head of the state tyrannized and did wrong, he cannot be impeached and this is the Fatwa of the school of Abu Hanifa in this regard" (Al-Bazdawi 2003, 198). It is important to note here that we are discussing the fatwa of *ahl al-sunnah* and Hanafis whom the Taliban claim to follow, yet in practice they are clearly deviating from its tenets.

The danger of insurgency and its drastic consequences for the community was not unknown or unanticipated by Prophet Muhammad (peace be upon him). In fact, the Prophet, even before his escape from the oppression of his own Meccan tribesmen, migration to Medina, and establishment of his incipient state, had insisted, during the pledge of al-Aqabah, that his companions obey him as their leader in all situations, whether in difficulty or ease, sadness or joy. He had also stressed that they should not revolt against their leaders unless they see a clear sign, with proof, of infidelity to the core values of Islam. Imam Ibn Hajar in his explanation of this hadith has said that the people should not rebel against the state unless they see an act of faithlessness that cannot be subject to other interpretations.

As it was anticipated by many extremely learned grand jurists, rebellions and insurgencies do not and cannot put an end to oppression. Instead, insurgencies can turn the situation from bad to worse. For example, the failed rebellion by a small number of young Islamists radicals in the summer of 1975, instead of removing the tyrannical government of Muhammad Daoud who had allied himself with a faction of the Communist party, fatally weakened his regime and made it possible for the communists to take control of the state power in Kabul only three years later. The devastating consequences of the past four decades of bloody warfare and violence in Afghanistan clearly indicates that diagnosis of political leaders as unfit to rule, by Islamic radicals' standards, is problematic, to say the least. In our complicated globalizing world full of political intrigues and proxy wars, getting rid of one set of undesirables does not guarantee the successful rise of a better group of elites to replace them. No seminary curriculum, including both old and new Deobandi Nizami curriculums, can offer a workable Islamic blueprint for political leadership. Such challenges are unlikely to ever be solved by studying two years of calligraphy and ten years of jurisprudence. Instead, the Taliban impetuosity, zealotry, and ignorant dependence on Pakistani opportunists peddling extremist ideologies has proved disastrous; it has perpetuated endless wars, vicious revenge killings, and continued instability and insecurity in the region.

Tragically, since the early 1980s, aside from considerable funds dedicated to the growth of Deobandi *madrassas* in Pakistan, substantial amounts of money and talent were wasted in the militarization of the school curriculum for Afghan refugees in Pakistan. Most of this aid was lavished by the United States to stimulate resistance against the Soviets. In addition to narratives of violence and images of combat and destruction, children were taught to count with pictures showing bullets, Kalashnikovs, mines, tanks, and missiles (Stephens and Ottaway 2002, A01). The Soviet Union imploded under the weight of its own revolutionary self-deception. But the Afghan youth, who have by now moved on with their lives, are still counting dead bodies killed by suicide bombers and bullets being fired by their own Afghan compatriots.

Legacies of Political Abuses of Islam in Afghanistan

The conservative, but caring embrace of political order to avert possible chaos and violence, even at the price of unjust rule, by the Sunni Hanafi religious scholars and political sages of Khorasan, have not been without their own legacies in the political history of countries such as Afghanistan. In fact, despotic rulers have consistently abused the cautionary stance of the Hanafi scholarly tradition in their own favor, causing mayhem and bloodshed by the rulers and their henchmen against their own Muslim subjects. For example, the creation of the modern Kingdom of Afghanistan during the final decades of nineteenth century is exemplary of such an instance.

Amir Abdur Rahman (r. 1880–1901), after his installation to the Kabul throne by the British occupation forces as the Amir, declared jihad against all his presumed or suspected domestic enemies, and slaughtered tens of thousands, so that his kingdom lived in peace! In order to emasculate the clerics who enjoyed some financial autonomy by relying on pious endowments (*awqaf*, plural of *waqf*), the Amir nationalized the charitable institution. This act alone effectively made the *ulama* utterly dependent on government support, thus rendering them as virtual instruments in the service of the rulers. He also established an examination system for the appointment of imams and other official functionaries to eliminate possible defiant clerics from his domain, a policy which continued not only by the Amir's successors during the twentieth century but also by all other Muslim majority countries with similar ill effects. The loss of educational and professional independence by the *ulama* led to further abuse of the Islamic tradition of humanism, tolerance, and peaceful coexistence in the region.

More importantly, following the rebellions and civil war of the 1920s, blamed on conservative clerics, which led to the removal of the reformist King Aman-Allah (1919–1929) from power, effecting a dynastic shift to the Muhammadzai clan, the Musahiban, control of Islamic education and functionaries became even more pervasive and detrimental. In addition to establishing state-run religious seminaries, the new Musahiban rulers established the *Jamiat-ul-Ulama* (council of religious scholars). In 1930, the first fatwa issued by the council was the necessity of allegiance by Mullahs and *Pirs* (Sufi leaders) to Nader Shah, the new king who formed the council. After Nader Shah's assassination (1933), his son Muhammad Zahir Shah (1933–1973) kept the Council of Ulama, but also established several national *madaaris* in various cities, such as Kabul, Herat, Jalalabad, Balkh, and Kunduz, to provide a more closely monitored Islamic education inside Afghanistan. Although the curriculum of these *madrassas* were different from the Deobandi system, it did not include the major text from the corpus of Khorasani mystical tradition.

When the communists took over government power, they also came to control the same religious institutions and relied on the use of sympathetic Mullahs as instruments for furthering their political agenda. They even created a new ministry, *Shuu'n Islami* or the Ministry of Islamic affairs. Dr. Najibullah, the last communist president of Afghanistan, also established *Shuray-e Sartasari Ulama wa Rohaneyooni Afghanistan* (the Grand Council of Afghanistan's Religious Scholars and Spiritual Leaders) as a means to appease many of them. The mujahideen government as well as Taliban Emirate, however, did not maintain the Council of Ulama, assuming that they personified religious legitimacy, and as such, they did not feel the need for it. Hamid Karzai, on assuming power in 2002, revived the communist era *Shora-ye Sartasari-ye Ulama-ye Afghanistan"* (the Grand Council of Afghanistan's Scholars and Spiritual Leaders [GCASSL]) once again. This religious body with its three thousand members on the payroll of the government, is deployed as its main source of political support and religious legitimacy in the post-Taliban environment.

To counter the Taliban claims that they are the authentic promoters of Islamic religious virtues, during the first four years of his rule, Karzai appointed one of the most conservative and obstructionist figures, Fazel Hadi Shinwari, who was one of Karzai's staunchest supporters, to the dual role of the chief justice of the Supreme Court (2002–2006) and the head of the *ulama* council (GCASSL). Despite the fact that the Council of Ulama is supposed to be an independent entity, this relationship has continued under Shinwari's successor, Qiamuddin Kashaf, who is the current leader of the council. For all intents and purposes, the council, a majority of whose members are drawn from among the Deobandi system seminaries, and many of whom are sympathetic to the Taliban ideology, are extracting rent for compliance, which the Kabul regimes are happy to accommodate. That is to say, all the institutions and processes for the government and its adversaries to deploy religion (Islam) instrumentally are present and ready to be utilized by the highest bidders.

The fate of the concept of jihad in Afghanistan's political culture has not been spared from abuse during the past decades of war and violence. The rulers of the country, starting with Amir Abdur Rahman, used jihad domestically to justify centralization of power. The concept of jihad, however, gained new significance in Afghanistan's political culture after the communist coup and Soviet intervention of 1979. Reminiscent of jihad resistance in connection with the Anglo-Afghan wars (1839–1842 and 1879–1880), this Islamic concept once again became the most powerful mobilizing force for popular resistance against Afghan communists and their Soviet patrons. Unfortunately, it was quickly and effectively appropriated by the Pakistani Inter-Services Intelligence (ISI) and the CIA to be deployed in furthering the Pakistani foreign policy interests as well as the larger Cold War objectives of the United States in the region. Pakistan used jihad to politicize ethnic identities and promote tensions, especially between the Pashtun and non-Pashtuns in Afghanistan, always siding with the Pashtuns with the hope of solving its border dispute over the Durand Line (see chap. 7 in this volume for details), and by controlling the political future of Afghanistan to gain "strategic depth" with India in the event of a nuclear war. Pakistan's strategy of support for the most radical elements of jihadi groups in Afghanistan during the 1980s, combined with the American policy of making the Soviets pay for their sins in the Vietnam War, culminated in globalization of jihad, by inviting large groups of Afghan-Arab and other international jihadists to fight America's Cold War enemy in Afghanistan. A policy, which also entailed support for funding Deobandi *madaaris* to educate the future Taliban and eventually lay the foundation for the rise of Al Qaeda (and the later Islamic State/Daesh) and the attacks against the United States and its allies. The transformation of notions of jihad from a struggle for self-defense by Muslims locally and nationally to a globalized terror network has followed torturous paths, but is always tied to machinations of local, and increasingly global, political powers.

Conclusions

Afghanistan's challenge for ending the four decades of war and violence and an end to the carnage are threefold: establishment of an effective, honest, and humane government in Kabul (which has not happened and is not likely to occur anytime soon); guarantees of economic and political liberties for the *ulama* and clerical establishments in the country (which is doable); and necessary investment in appropriate Islamic education reflective of the deeply rooted values of traditional Khorasani Islamic teachings. The experiences of the last sixteen years since American intervention, shows that war and expenditure of exorbitant amounts of money is unlikely to bring the desired outcomes. Over a trillion dollars have been wasted by the United States alone in waging war in Afghanistan since 2001. An additional one hundred billion dollars are spent on humanitarian and development programs with questionable results, to say the least.

It is clear that wars under whatever name—counterterrorism, counter insurgency, conventional war or remote war via drones—will not solve problems of insecurity in Afghanistan or anywhere. Attempts of rapprochement and inclusion of extremist militants in the kleptocratic governments, whether in the shape of Gulbuddin Hekmatyar, the Haqqani terrorists, or the Taliban and Daesh, are unlikely to produce any positive outcomes. Such undertakings are likely to address the symptoms while neglecting the deeper ideological roots of extremism having been introduced to the theological discourses of Muslims of this region and beyond. The Taliban are the latest manifestation of problematic and often opportunistic relations between rulers (recently including external or alien forces) and instrumental uses and abuses of religious elites for political ends in the country. Temporary economic and political arrangements of convenience between Afghan governments (whether monarchic, republican, communist, or Islamist and Islamic) have only aggravated the situation further. The self-serving governing elites empowered by the international community have chosen to recruit a selected number of *ulama* and Sufi leaders, mostly residing in the capital, Kabul, to claim a semblance of legitimacy. In return, these religious leaders or members of their family are paid in cash, real estate, and government offices.

Taliban radicals and most jihadi commanders and leaders have, however, tasted economic and political freedom by appropriating powers of the central government into their own hands. It is important to add that revising the curriculum in the seminaries, while critical for transformative positive change, will not be sufficient to effect the desired result. The deep roots of the curricular problem are essentially buried in the fertile soils of oppressive, corrupt, opportunistic, and extractive politics and economics which uses religion and the Muslim clergy instrumentally to insure their own hold onto power by any means. The Taliban extremists are also unlikely to change because of their likely future total dependence on the coffers of the corrupt government or their foreign patrons.

Therefore, an important incentive for political acquiescence could be the revival of the institution of *awqaf* by the Afghan government in order to promote economic self-reliance of the clerics, their Council of Ulama, and other religious establishments, including the *madaaris*. Establishing an independent Islamic Foundation, *waqf*, to help with the registration, supervision, and management of all mosques and *madrassas* as well as providing legislative advice to the government and performing religious functions could be a major step forward toward resolving the current chaos and instability in Afghanistan and the wider region.

Similarly, a concerted effort must be made to reform and upgrade Islamic educational institutions within the country. Currently, the higher education system in Afghanistan is in a state of crisis and is compounding problems of religious education in the country. That is, since the US-led NATO and non-NATO allies' intervention of 2001, dozens of public and private institutions of higher education have been established in Afghanistan. However, admission to private colleges and universities is not affordable to most rural youth in the country. While public institutions are free of charge, their quality is rather poor. The better ones demand high scores in the nationally administered college entrance examination (*Imtihani Konkoor*). Students graduating from provincial schools, due to the poor quality of instruction, have little chance of admission to better public universities. That leaves most rural youth without meaningful alternatives except by attending Pakistani *madrassas* which are free and open to any Afghan youth wishing to enter them. Indeed, Pakistani *madrassas*, via hordes of their former graduates populating rural mosques in Afghanistan, are actively recruiting across the country. But, thousands of their graduates return to Afghanistan each year where they cannot find employment, a situation which makes them resentful toward one of the most corrupt governments in the world, and ready to join the ranks of the Taliban.

The challenges facing Afghanistan are, then, establishing departments of Islamic studies within its universities as well as supporting the establishment of new *madaaris* by the independent *awqaf*-supported Islamic foundations mentioned earlier. This would also call for training appropriate faculty to staff them and, more importantly, adopting an effective and appropriate curriculum of instruction. Such an endeavor will also involve reeducating the large numbers of the graduates of Deobondi *madaaris* from Pakistan, if the root causes of extremism and Talibanism in Afghanistan and the region are to be addressed in the long haul.

The outdated Nizami curriculum of *madrassas* of the region, which has been in use for centuries, will need a critical and thorough review and revision. This cannot be done without a reliable, credible, and a politically independent entity, which, in turn, requires the establishment of appropriate inclusive and effective governance. Such a curriculum must be built on the firm foundations of Afghanistan's "local knowledge of Islam" with a strong presence among the rural Muslims of Afghanistan. A humanistic body of popular knowledge of Islam enshrined in the *adab* and *Akhlaq* literature of the region, literature that has guided masses of Muslims in Afghanistan and the wider Khorasan region to live their lives as pious Muslims for centuries. The revised and reformed *madrassa* curriculum must embody valued traditions of shari'a-based Khorasani ethical mysticism in line with the demands of modern life to enable the human soul and soil to meet and conjoin.

BASHIR AHMAD ANSARI is a former diplomat and a well-known writer from Afghanistan. He writes in Persian, Arabic, and English, and he has written over ten books on culture, religion, and politics in Persian.

NOTES

1. Avicenna's propensity toward rational mysticism becomes evident toward the end of his book, *"Al-Isharat wa Al-Tanbihat"* (The Signs and Admonitions/Warnings) as well as his later works. By suggesting ranks and levels for accomplished mystics, he curiously refers to

Salaman and Absal, two characters from Greek mythology, as possible ideal models for Sufi adepts to emulate (Avicenna, 1983 (4):49–50). Salaman and Absal also became two very well-known fictional characters in the didactic Persian literature, including in books under that title written by different authors in different time periods.

2. For a brief history of the establishment of Darul Uloom Deoband (1866), shortly after the fall of Muslim Empire in India (1857) in the hands of East India Company, see Qasmi (2011).

3. All the books included in Usmani's lists are on ethics, spirituality, and the purification of the heart. *Bidaya al-Hidaya* is one of Ghazali's (1058–1111) final works which covers the etiquette of everyday life for Sufi practitioners aspiring for companionship or closeness with the Creator and His creation. As such, the book embodies Ghazali's lifetime experience in the field of spirituality. The second book, *Arba'in*, is also authored by Imam Ghazali and focuses on reforming one's *baatin* (inner-self), spirituality, and purification of the heart. The book, *Ihya al-'Ulum* is considered the masterpiece of Ghazli's works, and is recognized as one of the greatest texts of Muslim spirituality. A book which is one of the most widely read since it has been available in many languages of the Muslim world for centuries. *Awarif al-Ma'arif* explains the philosopher Suhrawardi's mystical ideas and moral prescriptions for the conduct of Sufi adepts. The last suggested work, *Al-Takashshuf*, was written by Thanawi. This book or didactic training manual is divided into three levels offering guidance for the beginner, intermediate, and advanced trainees or practitioners of the Sufi order both in theory and practice.

4. *Mazaahib* refers to the four universally accepted Sunni (Hanafi, Shafi'i, Maliki, and Hanbali) schools and one Shi'a (Ja'fari) school of legal and ritual interpretations of the Islamic foundational texts dating back to eighth and ninth centuries.

5. An Islamist college student in early 1970, Hekmatyar became the head Hezbi Islami, one of the larger and better organized anti-Soviet mujahideen groups in Peshawar, Pakistan, during 1980 (for details see Shahrani and Canfield 1984). Favored by Pakistan before the rise of Taliban Movement in 1995, Hekmatyar refused to join the mujahideen government in Kabul, except nominally for a short period, and was fighting the American-led coalition during the last fifteen years before signing a peace agreement with the Ghani-Abdullah government on September 29, 2016.

Bibliography

Abdullah al-Ansari, Abdullah. 1966. *Manazil al-Sairin*. Cairo: Mustafa Al Babi Al Halabi.
Adamski, Michael J. 2009. "The Evolution of the Deoband Madrasa Network and U.S. Efforts to Combat Militant Ideology." Master's thesis, Georgetown University.
al-Asha'ri, Abul Hasan. 1950. *Maqalat Al-Islameyeen,*. Cairo: Maktaba An-Nahdah.
al-Bazdawi, Ali I. 2003. *Usool Ad-Deen*. Cairo: Al-Maktaba Al-Azharyah.
an-Nawawi, Yayha Bin Sharaf M. 1998. *Sharh Sahih Muslim*. Vol. 12. Damascus: Darul Khayr.
at-Tahawi, Abu Jafar. 1995. *Al-Aqeeda Al-Tahaweyah*. Bierut: Dar Ibn Hazm.
Avicenna, Abu Ali. 1983. *Al-Isharat wa Al-Tanbihat*. Cairo: Dar Al-Ma'arif.
Cohn, Bernard S. 1997. *Colonialism and Its Forms of Knowledge*. Princeton, NJ: Princeton University Press.
Deoband Online: The System of Education. 2014. Available at http://www.deoband.net/ or http://www.darululoom-deoband.com/english/. Accessed April 2014.

Gamm, Niki. 2011. "Mysticism in the Ottoman Empire. Turkey." *Hürriyet Daily News*, December 17.
Haqqani, Husain. 2002. "Islam's Medieval Outposts." *Foreign Policy* 133, November/December.
Ingram, Brannon D. 2011. "Deobandis Abroad: Sufism, Ethics and Polomics in a Global Islamic Movement." PhD Diss., University of North Carolina at Chapel Hill.
Interview with Dost Muhamad, an Afghan resident of Kabul. 2005. Summer.
Jalal, Ayesha. 2008. *Partisans of Allah: Jihad in South Asia*. Cambridge, MA: Harvard University Press.
Maybudi, A. F. Rashid-ud-Din. 2003. *Kashf ul Asrar wa Eddat ul Abrar*. Tehran: Amir Kabir.
Masroori, Cyrus. 2010. "An Islamic Language of Toleration: Rumi's Criticism of Religious Persecution." *Political Research Quarterly* 63 (2): 243–56.
Mayibudi, A. F. Rashid-ud-Din. 2003. *Kashful Asrar wa Eddatul Abrar*. Tehran: Amir Kabir.
Nawid, Senzil K. 1999. *Religious Response to Social Change in Afghanistan 1919–29: King Aman-Allah and the Afghan Ulama*. Costa Mesa, CA: Mazda.
Olesen, Asta. 1995. *Islam and Politics in Afghanistan*. London: Routledge Curzon.
Qasmi, Muhammadullah Khalili. 2011. "Darul Uloom Deoband, 1886–2010 = 1283–1431[H]." Comments at *Deoband Online*, May 7. Accessed September 30, 2016. http://www.deoband.net/blogs/darul-uloom-deoband-1866-2010-1283-143.
Roy, Olivier. 1990. *Islam and Resistance in Afghanistan*, 2nd ed., London: Cambridge University Press.
———. 1998. "Has Islam a Future in Afghanistan?" In *Fundamentalism Reborn? Afghanistan and the Taliban*, ed. William Maley. London: Hurst.
Rumi, Mawlana Jalaluddin Balkhi. 1379 H. *Masnavi*. Iran: Entesharat Dostan.
Saabiq, Sayyid. 1992. *Fiqh Al-Sunnah*. Vol. 1. Lebanon: Dar Al-Fikr.
Saa'di, Musleuddi. 1371 H. *Kulleyat Saadi*. Iran: Nashr Elm.
Shahrani, M. Nazif. 1991. "Local Knowledge of Islam and Social Discourse in Afghanistan and Turkistan in the Modern Period." In *Turko-Persia in Historical Perspective*, ed. Robert L. Canfield, 161–88. Cambridge, UK: Cambridge University Press.
———. 2005. "King Aman-Allah of Afghanistan's Failed Nation-Building Project and Its Aftermath" *Iranian Studies* 38 (4): 661–75.
———. 2013. "Islam and the State in Afghanistan." In *The Oxford Handbook of Islam and Politics*, ed. John L. Esposito and Emad El-Din Shahin, 453–74. Oxford: Oxford University Press.
Stephens, Joe, and David. B. Ottaway. 2002. "From U.S., the ABC's of Jihad." *Washington Post*, March 23.
Usmani, Muhammad Taqi. 1998. *Hamara Ta'limi Nizam (Our Nizami Educational System)*. Deoband: Maktaba-yi Dar al-'Ulum.
Wilber, Donald. 1949. "The Structure and Position of Islam in Afghanistan." *Middle East Journal* 6 (1): 41–48.

3

LANGUAGE, POETRY, AND IDENTITY IN AFGHANISTAN: POETIC TEXTS, CHANGING CONTEXTS

Mohammad Omar Sharifi

Introduction

In multilingual Afghan society, Persian poetry has held a notable place in the formation of national and subnational identities in the country's turbulent history. After Afghanistan's independence (1919) through the mid-1930s, concepts unique to the modern state, such as *citizenship*, *identity*, and *nationality* were crystallized around the notion of Muslim *umma* (nationhood) which was based on an existing textual tradition. By "textual" I am referring to both written texts as well as oral traditions. These traditions included primarily Islamic and customary codes of conduct and values. The texts were produced not only by religious scholars but also by highly influential Islamic philosophers and poets of the earlier centuries. Because of the strong historical influence of Persian (poetry) on the way of life and cultural traditions of Afghanistan, most of these texts, whether religious or nonreligious, were embodied and translated through poetry (predominantly Persian) and continued to be received, transmitted, and reconfigured, animating debates of the times.

Persian has served as the lingua franca in Afghanistan, first because Afghanistan's two major ethnic groups (the Tajiks and the Hazaras) are Persian speakers, and second, because a vast extant oral and written literature, especially poetic texts, produced and used by speakers of virtually all languages were and are in Persian (Tariq, Haqbeen, and Kakar 2012, 181–182). Despite government efforts to replace Persian with Pashto (from 1936–1964) as the official language of the country, the Persian language, especially its poetic texts, remained in wide circulation and use. Indeed, into the very present Persian poetry, as the measure of Afghanistan's cultural achievement, remains the most crucial element shaping and defining identity in ways that transcend its earlier formative periods. Understanding the language policies of successive Afghan governments and how and why Persian poetry has functioned and is influencing and shaping national discourse over the issue of identity, especially during the past several decades of invasions, wars of resistance, state failure, and proxy war is the main subject of this chapter.

The chapter is organized into three sections. First, I will discuss close relations between language policies and practices and cultural identity in Afghan society and polity. Second, I will examine, by way of a brief but broad history of the Persian language with a focus on Persian poetry, its production, perpetuation, and its critical role as a didactic socializing factor in Afghanistan and the region as a whole. Third, in order to understand why and how these literary texts continue to function and produce meaning under considerable societal upheaval—local, national, regional, and international—I will rely on various literary theories to elucidate the mechanisms and processes by which more context-dependent forms of meaning (i.e., at the indexical or "pragmatic" level) interact with more context-free and conventional kinds of meanings (i.e., at the symbolic or semantic level, focusing on language content and form). This part includes comparative analysis of poetic texts from different periods (including examples of poetry from the recent decades of turmoil) and analytical perspectives, with a focus on a semiotics of poetic texts within the Afghanistan social and cultural contexts.

Persian Poetry and Its Communicative Social Life in Afghanistan

Afghanistan as a nation, until recently, remained virtually unknown. It emerged from obscurity into international headlines in the 1980s when the Soviet Union invaded and occupied the country (1979–1989), sparking one of the longest and most tormented wars of resistance of the century. After the Soviet defeat and withdrawal, Afghanistan remained in international focus because of the onset of the civil war (1992–1996) and resistance to Taliban rule (1996–2001).

Unfortunately, information and media analysis generated by these events created a distorted and limited view of the country, its people, its culture, and history. There has been considerable emphasis on the impacts of tribalism and religious and ethnic differences in Afghanistan as impediments to the development of its sense of nationhood and national culture. A mere scanning of the literature produced in this era reveals that literature, especially poetry as a substantial category of literary production, has been simply ignored or treated at a superficial level, detached from the rich social, cultural, and political environment which nourished it. My aim is to argue against the treatment of poetry in Afghanistan as a decontextualized and museologized object of study. I will avoid treating poetry merely as embodiment of "literary knowledge," made for the exclusive admiration of it by the elite, as is often done.

Therefore, the purpose of this study is to examine all aspects of the poetic tradition in Afghanistan (which includes the writing, reading, recitation, performance, and knowledge of poetry) and its relation to social life and identity which requires an understanding of it in its own sociocultural and historical terms. While in most disciplines, material objects and commodity exchange determines social relations and cultural and national identities, I argue, in Afghanistan because of its unique cultural and historical circumstances, the country is relatively undercommoditized society. The reasons are: first, it was an isolated buffer state sandwiched between two great colonial empires, the British and tsarist Russian empires; second, its specific geography is characterized by remote and isolated valleys; and finally, because the governments of the postindependence era attempted to impose a single unified identity to replace the historic notions of nationhood inspired mostly by Persianate cultural and religious texts in favor of a new Aryan race-based identity (distinguishing Aryans from non-Aryans), interpreting identity from religious and ideological perspectives, and attempting to impose one national language (Pashto) on its people. My goal is to focus on the discussion of this last factor, the government's problematic policy of constructing and implementing a novel national identity in Afghanistan and its consequences for the society.

Persian poetry, despite its aesthetic brilliance, highly developed forms, and intricate composition of meter, rhythm, rhyme, sense, and sensibility, is ignored for the most part by Western scholars, primarily because of its embeddedness in and imbrications with social life. The following observation by Louis Dupree (1997, 75), however, is a significant exception when he says, "Many literate and nonliterate in Afghan society ... can recite Persian poetry by heart. Most have at least passing acquaintance with greater classical Persian poets: Rumi, Jami, and Ferdowsi. Poetry gives nonliterate the same general opportunities for expression as the literate in a society. Afghanistan, therefore, is fundamentally a nation of poets."

In Afghanistan poetry is not only a literary fact but also a social one. That is, a poem is produced within a context, which includes the life of the author, the audience for whom he or she writes, and the background relationship of various social, historical, moral, ethical, and valued cultural norms and practices. This short poem by Hanzala of Badghis, who lived in Nishapur during the first half of the ninth century AD in the court of Tahirid rulers (819–872), expresses a central theme which has persisted as an ideal in contemporary Afghan culture:

> If leadership rests inside the lion's jaws,
> Seize it. Go, snatch it from his jaws.
> Your lot shall be greatness, prestige, honor, and glory.
> Or else—face death like a man
>
> (Translated by S. Shpoon [1968, 50])

The public performance of poetry continues to serve as an important embodiment of social relations and self-identification, actualized by the performed poem's inherent power to objectify through its rhythm, rhyme, meter, and the play of words. Persian has established itself through its vast literary and religious texts, the main means of and medium for establishing and preserving relations across the country among various ethno-linguistic communities and between them and the state. Thus, poetry helps preserve and even celebrate differences—be they personal, cultural, ethical, or historic—as it helps unite the nation, including those of the ruling Pashtuns. This is because most Pashtun ruling elites have had great facility with Persian language and with Persian texts. Thus, where Pashto had failed to become the lingua franca, despite concerted efforts of the government as will be discussed further, Persian succeeded in retaining its role as the unifier and repository of Afghanistani identity and cultural heritage. Let us now turn to a brief look to the history of Persian poetry in general and its influence and role in Afghanistan.

Persian Poetry, Mirror of Reality

Persian literature and poetry in Afghanistan has a long illustrious history. Most of the great patrons of Persian literature such as the courts of Samanids (872–999 AD), Ghaznavids (961–1186 AD), and Timurids of Herat (1405–1508 AD) were located in this region, as were great poets, such as Rudaki (859–935 AD), Sanaei (d. 1131 AD), Ansari (1006–1088 AD), and Jami (1414–1492 AD), and philosophers and scholars, such as Ibn Sina (980–1037 AD) or Avicenna and Al Biruni (973–1048 AD). This rich literary and cultural heritage still survives and thrives in Afghanistan.

So strong is the aptitude for versifying everyday concerns, predicaments, aspirations, and desires that one can encounter poetry in almost every classical work and most modern works, whether history, biography, hagiography, literature, science, or metaphysics. The ability to write in verse form was and still is a prerequisite for any respectable scholar. For example, almost half of Avicenna's medical writings are in verse.

One of the main aspects of Persian poetry, as in other languages, is its abstract quality. These abstract and rather stylized ideas and images provide the conventional themes on which the poet composes his own variations on the literary canvas. The importance of Persian poetry in today's sociocultural situation of Afghanistan is also due to its ability to portray emotive, idealized images and expressive forms. This tendency to stylize and generalize individual forms is not, as sometimes presumed, a reflection of belief in the impermanence of all things except God. Rather, it is a positive leaning to discover and define the lasting and imperishable, and to portray the abiding features and formal essence of things. By means of the perpetuation of poetic form, the transitory, constructed, and ephemeral aspect of life and objects is, in actuality, disregarded. This notion is beautifully rendered in Ferdowsi's Shahnama (Book of Kings):

> Great buildings suffer destruction
> from the drop of rain and the ray of sunlight.
> Notwithstanding, I have created a great palace of verse (poetry)
> That is impervious to the wind and the rain
> (Translated by Prashant Keshavmurthy[1])

Persian poetry enjoys vast poetic license and maneuverability, both in religious and social issues, together with a liberal philosophical outlook and a mystical bent. As such, it is not just a means merely for expression of artistic sensibilities, but a sanctuary where a mind finds artistic and intellectual satisfaction and inspiration. Since Islamic laws and practices strictly forbid rendition of living forms through painting and sculpture, poetry has become the most important medium of expression in social, cultural, and religious life in Afghanistan and beyond. The following poem from Abdullah Ansari's *Munajat Nama* illustrates the point when he says:

> From the unmanifest I came,
> And pitched my tent, in the Forest of Material existence.
> I passed through
> Mineral and vegetable kingdoms,
> Then my mental equipment
> Carried me into animal kingdom;
> Having reached there I crossed beyond it;
> Then in the crystal clear shell of human heart
> I nursed the drop of self into a pearl,
> And in association with good men
> Wandered round the Prayer House,
> Having experienced that, crossed beyond it;
> Then I took the road that leads to Him,
> And became a slave at His gate;
> Then the duality disappeared
> And I became absorbed in Him.
> (Translated by Singh [1939])

Abdul Qahar Aasi (d. 1994), a contemporary poet, killed during the fratricidal wars destroying Kabul in early 1990s, demonstrates the versatility of Persian poetry as one of the main vehicles for self-definition, even for the constitution of identities and articulation of social reality in contemporary war-ravaged sociopolitical life in Afghanistan when he asserts:

> Neither the flower nor the moon, my heart's Persian.
> Persian is the ocean's quaver, sometimes a tumult
> From Syria to Kashghar, Sind to Khujand
> Persian holds a mirror up to the world above.
> To history, to fresh and grand covenants
> Persian is my blood and gilded speech.
> (Abdul Qahar 'Aasi, translated by Keshavmurthy [2008][2])

Poetics and Politics of Constructing an "Afghan" National Identity

Historically, the eastern dialects of Persian were known as "Dari." The name itself derives from "Parsi-e Darbari," meaning Persian language of the Royal Courts (Lazard 2006, 77–98). The ancient term *Dari* was adopted and enshrined into the Afghan constitution in 1964, to distinguish the Persian spoken in Afghanistan from the version spoken in Iran. In this way, the development of Persian Dari literature became politically linked with the national identity and political culture of modern Afghanistan.

Robert Canfield (1988, 185) has suggested that markers of social identities entail "cultural phenomena ... embodied in customs, emblems, institutions, lexical categories, etc., and they imply relationships among people. They are essentially normative constructs, entailing concepts of obligation, status, authority, and the like." The concepts of *identity*, *nationhood*, and *ethnicity* have remained contested topics in political as well as cultural discourse in Afghanistan, especially since the mid-1930s when Afghan nationalism, or more accurately, Pashtun nationalism, was adopted as the official policy of the government, a development which contributed to the growing crisis of social identity in Afghanistan, eventually leading to the war and chaos of the past four decades. The decades of war and violence has also added to crises of *social* identity in the country. Characterized often as a "fragmental" (Mousavi 1997, 23) society, the fragmentation is the outcome of many events linked to internal factors, including social, political, and economic underdevelopment as well as external forces, especially since the communist coup of 1978.

Throughout the eighteenth and nineteenth centuries, sociocultural identity, understood in the Afghan sociopolitical context, continued to be defined by the ideas, prescriptions, and proscriptions, transmitted via the authority of the Islamic "textual" tradition, produced by scholars of different origins in writing in Persian and Arabic. These "texts" defined and conveyed relations between the state and its people and the individual and community and provided codes of behavior. Poetry (both in Persian and Pashto) remained the most revered form of expression and communication.

Ahmad Shah Abdali (r. 1747–1773), the founder of Durrani Empire, the precursor to modern Afghanistan, himself was a poet. The following poem is attributed to him:

> Whatever countries I conquer in the world
> I will never forget your beautiful gardens.
> When I remember the summits of your beautiful mountains
> I forget the greatness of the Delhi throne.
>
> (Translated by Habibi [1968, 60])

King Amanullah (r. 1919–1929), not a poet but relatively liberal ruler, proclaimed equal rights for all his Afghan subjects (*ru'aya*), without regard to ethnic or racial origin, in the 1923 constitution (Kakar 1973, 9). It was, however, reversed by the mid-1930s when race- and language-based Afghan/Pashtun "nationalism" became the official policy of the Afghan nation-state. The policy asserted the racial supremacy of Pashtuns as the most "pure" of the Aryan race over all non-Pashtuns (who were not Aryan), a policy inspired by the Nazi ideology of the time (Mousavi 1997, 159). The country also witnessed the rise and enforcement of Afghan (Pashtun), nationalism under the reign of the Musahiban dynasty (r. 1929–1978) for decades to come.

Afghan/Pashtun racial supremacy was considered a "gift from God" by the ruling elite, and came to be seen by them as a basis for the establishment of social, political, cultural, and administrative structures to construct their desired "Afghan" nation-state. As Sayed Askar Mousavi (1997, 6) explains, "While all inhabitants of Afghanistan are referred to as 'Afghan' the Pashtun tribes [were] considered 'more Afghan' than others." The new government sought to subvert the prevailing systems of cultural meanings and alter notions of ethnicity, cultural identity, morality, and personhood mostly through its language cum racial policy, in order to redefine communities and establish a new identity based on the doctrine of racial supremacy. Language, and specifically poetry, continued to be at the center of all these cultural transformations and policies. Part of this newfound sense of nationalism was to transform the regional and colloquial language of Pashto into the national and official language of Afghanistan, displacing Persian. The Pashto language was presented as the national and official language of Afghanistan. Its teaching was made compulsory by government policy nationally (Gharghasht 1966, 44–45). In the educational system, the media, and the administration, Pashto replaced Persian. "The administration of Pashto courses, from now on, is carried out by the Ministry of Education. In Kabul alone, some 450 Pashto courses have been established; all government and other public officials are required to attend said courses in order to learn *their national language*" (Gharghasht 1966, 44; Pstrusińksa 1990, 33, emphasis added).

Afghan or Pashtun nationalism was a very new idea, introduced into Afghanistan by Mahmud Tarzi, the leading figure among educated modernists in favor of a constitutional monarchy, with influence in the court as his son-in-law was King Amanullah. He had a strong belief in the notion that Afghanistan must have its own unique language in order to preserve its independence and sovereignty especially from its neighbor, Iran. In 1914 he wrote:

> Now it becomes necessary to address ourselves, on the importance of *our national language Pashto* ... first, we should understand that every nation has a national language which gives it its life. A nation which loses its language also loses its life. The protection of the basic language of every country is as important as the protection of its life. We are called the Afghan Nation and our beloved homeland is called Afghanistan. We possess specific custom, ethics and a national language which we call Pashto. We must protect this language and attempt to develop and improve it. Every citizen of Afghanistan must learn this language even though they may not be Pashto speaker, and our schools must make the teaching of this language their most important vocation. (Tarzi 1918, emphasis added)

Perhaps the most consequential step taken as a result of this new policy was the total rewriting of the history of Afghanistan on the basis of this new ideology.[3] Aware of the preeminent position of poetry in Afghan society, the government initiated a massive effort in support of Pashto poetry by publishing newly "discovered" collections of Pashto "classical poems," contemporary poetic anthologies, and books, and by founding multiple Pashto literary societies.[4]

The Pashto classical poems were "reinterpreted" to match the new nationalist policies. The poem by Ahmad Shah Abdali, cited before, was recomposed as follows:

> By blood, we are immersed in love of you.
> The youth lose their heads for your sake.
> I come to you and my heart finds rest.
> Away from you, grief clings to my heart like a snake.
> I forget the throne of Delhi
> When I remember the mountain tops of my Pashtun land
> If I must choose between the world and you,
> I shall not hesitate to claim your barren deserts as my own.
> (Translated by Shpoon [1968, 55])

Multiple Pashto literary societies were established in order to encourage poetry writing and reading as the means of enhancing the favored national identity. "The Pashto speaking men and women were to be emulated by all the [other]

Afghan people as perfect examples of humanity. The Pashtun mode of dress, their code of conduct and literature were depicted and emphasized in every text" (Shorish 1985, 4–5). And Pstrusińksa (1990, 33, 36) have asserted that the zealous language policy in time overreached, creating far deeper sociopolitical fissures. "The country was divided into three groups: Pashto-speaking provinces, Both Dari [Persian] and Pashto-speaking provinces, and Dari speaking provinces. It was demanded that in the first group everything should function only in Pashto and this ideal should be achieved gradually in the mixed group. In the Dari group, communication in Pashto should be kept up ... Many years of communication of effort, however, had led the country to a kind of bilingualism" (Pstrusińksa 1990, 35).

Implementation of these policies resulted in ambivalence, ambiguity, and confusion, ultimately rendering any discussion of nationality, identity, and "ethnicity in Afghanistan" a taboo subject (Mousavi 1997, p. 5). Also, due to gradual marginalization of their language and culture, the non-Pashtuns compensated for being denied new publications with the increasing public recitations of existing literary texts, especially poetry, as a way of asserting and reclaiming their right in and share of the cultural heritage of Afghanistan. Thus, since the 1930s, contests in the recitation, reading, and the writing of poetry emerged as some of the most important sociopolitical events in Afghanistan.

Given the low literacy rate in Afghanistan, (45 percent for men and 17 percent for women according AMICS 2010/2011), poetry is an oral performance art rather than written art. Louis Dupree says, "[it] gives everyone, literate and nonliterate the same general opportunities for expression. Therefore, it is reasonable to claim that Afghanistan is fundamentally a nation of poets" (1997[1980], 75). Recitation, especially among people from rural Afghanistan where the level of literacy is extremely low, remained a central element of cultural reproduction and a highly reflexive mode of communication. Interjecting poetry is a specially marked, artful way of speaking that represents a special interpretive frame within which the act of speaking is to be understood. It heightens awareness of the act of speaking, establishes a connection between the audience and the speaker's understanding of past and present, connects oneself to his or her cultural heritage, and licenses the audience to evaluate the skill and effectiveness of both the reciter and the poet's accomplishment.

Poetry reading, both in family gatherings and at local and national events and festivals (especially poetry contests during Nauroz or the Afghan New Year) and through music and religious songs constitutes a major part of Afghanistan's social engagement and cultural identification. Nancy Hatch Dupree states "Love of poetry is pervasive throughout society. The ideal personality type in Afghanistan is the warrior-poet: brave in battle, eloquent in the village council ... While treasuring the poets of the past, a great many Afghans try their hand in writing poetry and poetry reading or *mushaira* (poetry contest) are popular forms of social interaction and entertainment" (N. Dupree 2002 [1989], 979). This "return" to poetry as a means of identity reclamation in Afghanistan lies in the nature of Persian poetry. Unlike the commonly held belief among contemporary western scholars of literature that poetry is a genre of exoteric or esoteric literature beyond the understanding of ordinary people, in Afghanistan poetry is not the exclusive province of the educated elite. Persian poetry, given its long history, has effectively established itself strongly among the masses due to its accessibility, simplicity and the wide range of social, cultural, moral, ethical, and religious subjects it covers (Shahrani 1991, 168).

Persian *charbaiti* (quatrain)—four verses of matching rhyme and meter, of which the first, second, and fourth lines must rhyme—is one of the most common and popular styles of poetic expression. The following is an example of a *charbaiti*:

Biya binshin avala az vatan goi
Do-vom az bulbul-e shirnin sokhan goi
Sokhan haye ke dilbar ba to gofta
Biya binshin yakayak to ba man goi
Come, sit by me and first tell me the news from homeland,
Then tell me of my sweet-talking nightingale
Everything my beloved has told you,
Come, come, tell it all word by word.

(Translated by the author)

Or:

Give me two things.
Then let the British come
A gun to fight with
That won't jam.
A girl to fight next to
Who will love.

(L. Dupree [1980, 75], translated by Shpoon)

When poems are recited in the native speaker's sociocultural context, it dialogically produces and reproduces knowledge and moral wisdom as a way of reinforcing social values and identities that shape their future conduct. The "return" to poetry as a means of establishing one's rights and negotiating one's sociocultural identity among mostly Persian-speaking non-Pashtuns in Afghanistan did not remain limited to poetry produced by local Afghan poets. The poems of Persian-speaking poets and Sufis, who lived outside present-day boundaries of Afghanistan, became popular and were widely recited. *Ghazals* or love poems of Hafiz Shirazi, poems of Bedil Dehlavi, and odes of Rumi are widely recited and revered, not only for their aesthetic beauty and moral teachings but also as means of connection to the cultural-historical heritage in a much wider Persianate cultural realm as rendered by Qahar 'Aasi in a poem mentioned above.[5]

The poetic texts, while pervasive in the cultural life of Afghan people and generative of more conscious ideological signs and symbols, cover a wide range of subjects and remain subject to change as circumstances alter. As such, poetic texts and their uses are situated, contextually grounded, and embodied, are dispositional and generative in character, and constitute a "habitus." "One of the fundamental effects of the orchestration of habitus is," according to Bourdieu, "the production of a commonsense world endowed with the objectivity secured by consensus on the meaning of practices and the world, in other words, the harmonization of agents' experiences and continuous reinforcement that each of them receives from expression, individual or collective [for example in Nauroz festival], improvised or programmed (commonplaces, sayings), of similar or identical experiences" (Bourdieu 1977, 79).

However, as Austin has suggested language not only says things in words, it also does things with and in words (in Berlin, et al. 1973, 125). That is, language has *real* effects on entities outside of language and its conventional aspects in the real world. In other words, certain forms of speech do something in addition to merely saying something. The following *charbaiti* (quatrain) by Daqiqi Balkhi (d. 980 AD) illustrates such indexicality.

Daqiqi Char cheez ra bargozida
Ze giti az hama khobi –wa zishti
Lab-e Yaqut rang-o nalayi chang
May-e khoonrang-o din-e zardohshti

Translation:

From all the good and bad in the world,
Daqiqi has chosen four:
Ruby-red lips, the sound of harp
Blood-colored wine, and the Zoroastrian religion

(Translated by the author)

For the reader or hearer of the poem to fully understand the poem, not only must he or she be acquainted with the referents that are objectively part of a shared cultural experience but also be sensitive to the objective fact that Persian, and not Pashto, is generally the language of choice in Afghanistan for expressing key sentiments. This is largely due to the existing vast literary and oral heritage produced in Persian, a very strong capacity for versifying everyday expressions of life, whether it is religious or science or metaphysics, and that Persian has been the lingua franca among various ethnic groups in Afghanistan for the last millennium.

The choice of Persian over Pashto in public discourse indicates something that lies well beyond what the poetic symbols in a verse stand for and stirs sentiments in the hearts of the knowing listener and reader. Forcing Pashto to replace Persian as a national language even among Pashto speakers have thus failed. Speaking of linguistic shifts among the Pashtun, Pstrusińksa states "A considerable number of Pashtun nomads in western Afghanistan lost their native tongue and began to use Dari [Persian]. One of the groups is the Nurzai from Adraskan. Another example of these Dari speaking Pashtun[s] are the Mohammadzai from Kabul and the Mohammadzai from Kandahar ... Most Pashto speakers living in urban areas learn Dari for practical reasons, business, education etc. and its role as *lingua franca*" (Pstrusińksa 1990, 30).

The lack of enthusiasm among most Pashtuns for the government's policy of racial superiority, along with the contradiction of these policies with their long-established Islamic and cultural beliefs forced policy makers to abandon their program of implementation "The Afghan royal family, in its self-identification with Pathans (Pashtuns), declared Pashto to be the official language of Afghans [all the peoples of Afghanistan], although even the king did not speak it, and had to take lessons. All official business and teaching were ordered to change to it. The people of Kabul were unable to read street and bus signs. Few of the students and faculty members in Kabul University understood Pashto, and chaos resulted in the classrooms. The educational system was set back even more until the order was cancelled" (Hunter 1959, 345).

Furthermore, the failure of the effort to establish Pashto as the official language proved very costly to the development of Afghanistan. For not only did this attempt at creating a new identity stunt the development of the Persian language and culture, along with those of the other peoples of Afghanistan, but also proved to be an obstacle to achieving a more inclusive political, economic, and social order in the country, and was a major source of opposition to the regime.

The situation began to change during the period from 1963 to 1973, the so called decade of democracy. In the new constitution that was ratified in 1964, the government modified its previous policy of establishing a new Pashtun based national identity and recognized Dari (Persian), alongside Pashto, as the second official language of Afghanistan. Relatively greater access was allowed for non-Pashtuns, especially Persian-speaking Hazaras, to institutions of higher education. The situation remained unchanged until the end of the monarchy era in 1978.

Afghanistan Poetry in the Last Three Decades

Communist takeover in 1978 and subsequent Soviet invasion had profound effects on the social, political, and linguistic landscape of Afghanistan. Literature and, especially, poetry has been the "domain as well as an instrument of cultural and political contention" in Afghanistan (Ghani 1998, 428). After the communist-led coup, the People's Democratic Party of Afghanistan's (PDPA) language policies can be divided into two phases: that of the Khalq faction (1978–1979) and of the Parcham faction (1979–1992). Khalqis were predominantly Ghilzais Pashtuns with a stronger tribal background than the old Durrani elite and were native Pashto speakers (Barfield 2010, 226).

During the first phase or Khaliqi period, the government was highly dominated by Ghilzai Pashtuns, which led to an abrupt displacement of the Pashtun elite associated with the monarchy. Meanwhile, the Parcham (flag) faction (1979–1992) included urban Persian-speaking Pashtuns as well as number of non-Pashtun intellectuals from other ethnic groups.

Initially, PDPA policy declared equal treatment of all language groups in Afghanistan, following the established Soviet system (Nawid 2011, 43). But conflict between Khalq and Parcham factions quickly reversed most of these reforms. Tarakai and other Khalq leaderships were mostly Pashtun nationalists and continued the policy of privileging Pashto over Persian.

According to Ahady "During their reign the Khalq faction, the communist authorities, in addition to Pashto and Dari (Persian), recognized Uzbeki, Turkmani, Baluchi as official languages. Although this seemed like an attempt by the Khalq faction to weaken the dominance of Pashtuns, in reality the policy was intended to weaken the status of Dari and eventually promote Pashto as the language of interethnic communication" (Ahady 1995, 622).

The Khalq faction continued heavily to use poetic traditions to disseminate their policies and ideas. Afghan literature in this period is characterized by highly revolutionary rhetoric and Marxist symbolism.

> This land requires revolution and nothing else
> This land desires bloodshed and nothing else
> Or
> In the trenches of defending the motherland
> People's army carries two torches
> One is Saur [month of communist coup in Afghan calendar] and the other is October
>
> (Nadery [2006], translated by the author)

Following the Soviet invasion and the rise of the Parcham faction, the communist government adopted a more systematic cultural policy. The government established a poets and writers association within the ministry of culture and information and a special committee was formed within the PDPA central committee to direct cultural policies and make the existing literature and traditions conform to the state's ideological lines. The policies were initially highly ideological but later adopted a nationalistic tone. Being the most highly prized and widely practiced art form among Afghans of all ethnicities, both literate and illiterate, poetry not only received official support and sponsorship but was also well incorporated in the educational system. A complete new curriculum for secondary and higher education was developed, using classic as well as contemporary poetry in order to contest the religious narrative of the jihadi opposition (Welch and Wahidyar 2013, 94, 96). National poetry contests were organized around the country and television and radio dedicated special programs to poetry and poetic traditions (including classic and contemporary Persian poetry). Several independent literary associations were established either directly by the government or by communities to organize poetry contests and poetry readings and celebrate famous classic and contemporary poets. According to official statistics, the communist government published 270 poetry books during the 1980s (Nadery 2006). In other words, poetry became a main medium of cultural and political contention and struggle between the regime and its mujahideen opposition.

At the same time, after the Soviet invasion, millions of Afghans immigrated to neighboring countries, especially to Iran and Pakistan, and formed exiled communities of poets and writers. The most significant feature of this period was the formation of political parties by mujahideen leaders in cooperation with the religious leadership. Each mujahideen party—there were seven parties in Pakistan and eight parties in Iran—established their own cultural committees (*Komita-e Farhangi*). Both oral and written poetry, due to its long traditions in Afghanistan, continued to be the most respected and widely practiced way of expression and propaganda.

Persian and Pashto poetry became the vehicle for political struggle and support of jihad against communists and their Soviet supporters. For many Afghans, literary activities became the central element in shaping understanding of the world and experience of themselves. In the politically repressive and economically harsh conditions of refugee camps, with their political discourse dominated by religion, Persian poetry remained one of the very few mediums available for public expression as well as social, cultural, and political mobility. It formed a conventional yet highly aesthetic space for expressing oneself and the environment. While the dominance of jihadi groups and parties in Iran and Pakistan and the religiously conservative atmosphere of refugee camps in the 1980s and 1990s shaped the self-perception of Afghan refugees, the potential for creative use of cultural and religious idioms allowed the continued use of poetry for self-expression on issues and topics that were otherwise considered taboo. In this context, Persian as well as Pashto poetry should be read in a broader context, for its content and form provides a space through which the contradictions between the existing traditions and new social and cultural realities and experiences in refugee camps could be addressed.

Meanwhile, independent Afghan poets and cultural associations continued to create a more visible and cohesive environment for mobilization through what is known as resistance poetry. This form of poetry is characterized by less symbolic language, a highly rhythmic tone, and clear types between good and evil (Nadery 2006, 4). This generation of resistance poets was a mix of those who were already established writers during the pre-Soviet period and young poets who were the product of religious seminaries in Iran, religious *madrassas* and mujahideen schools in refugee camps in Pakistan. The most famous resistance poets of this period are Khalilullah Khalili (1907–1987) and Abdul Rahman Pazhwak (1919–1995) in Pakistan and Abu Taleb Mozaffari, Asef Rahmani, and Kazem Kazemi in Iran. The following example by Khalili expresses a central theme of resistance poetry:

> *Mard namerad ba marg*
> *Marg az o nam jost*
> *Nam cho jawaid shod*
> *Mordanash asan kojast*
> Man does not die with death
> Death gets its name from Man
> When the name becomes eternal
> It's death, is never easy
>
> (Khalili [1989, 104, 106], translated by the author)

Civil War and Sociopolitical Fragmentation

The fall of the communist regime and brutal civil war between various mujahideen groups caused disillusionment among many Afghans. While some poets continued to support jihadi parties and write for their co-ethnics, many were disgusted with bloodshed and started to either question their role in supporting armed groups or openly criticize the destruction and warring factions.

The following poem by Asi (Lalaey braai Malima, 1994) illustrates the disillusionment that prevailed in Afghanistan during the civil war among various mujahideen groups:

> Ah Kabul,
> Covered with wounds, destroyed and forgotten…
> Your irreparable wounds radiate despair
> No one to alleviate your sorrow, grief is everywhere for you…

> Ah Kabul, how easily your sacred hopes and dreams shatter ...
> Ah Kabul, you and I both know, they all come from the same pot ...
> Remember that colorful sky, that in the past shone blue
> Was nothing but a facade, a disguise for destruction and deceit ...
> Through the ignorance of these supposed Muslims, the infidels appear righteous.
>
> (Qahar Asi, Lalaey Braai Malima, translated by the author, also see Chapter 4 in this volume)

The mujahideen government led by Jamiat e Islami, and a predominantly Tajik mujahideen party, presided over a shattered administration and lacked any financial resources to formulate a cohesive language policy. During this period, many cultural institutions and organizations were either looted or destroyed. Many prominent poets and writers were forced to leave the country. The only notable case of a language-related policy was the change of the national anthem from Pashto to Persian. This change, coupled with the non-Pashtun government in Kabul, furthered the Pashtun sense of resentment, anger and marginalization that later manifested itself in harsh Taliban policies of revenge.

Taliban Period

The Taliban takeover of Kabul in September 1996, while seen by some scholars a triumph for Pashtun nationalism (Nawid 2011, pp. 48), is a tragic phase of Afghan history and political culture. From the very beginning, Taliban closed all literary associations and cultural organizations, banned all media except the Shari'at Newspaper and radio, and imprisoned or forced many writers and poets to exile. Taliban did not announce an official language policy (Nawid 2011, 69), but Pashto gradually became the dominant language of the administration and government. Furthermore, the Taliban launched an unofficial, yet systematic, anti-Persian/Dari program by burning Persian books and manuscripts, including the burning of fifty-five thousand Persian manuscripts in the Pul-e Khomri Library (Nadery 2000, 3). This policy of banishing the Persian was, on the one hand, mostly attributed to the dominant role of Persian speakers and other non-Pashtun groups in the anti-Taliban movements and, on the other hand, reaffirmed the Pashtun identity of the Taliban in Afghanistan. Besides, it was a convenient policy to address concerns of Pashtun nationalists who felt marginalized after mujahideen takeover of power in 1992.

Meanwhile, the Taliban continued to capitalize on specific aspects of Pashto poetic traditions to bridge their political and ideological version of Islam and nationalism to a wider audience and as a tool for recruitment. While denouncing lyric Pashto poetry, Taliban poetry is highly rhythmic, with two-part structures and a heavy use of repetition. Their style is different from traditional

Pashto poetic styles such as *Masnavi* or *ghazal*.⁶ The poetic themes mostly focused on topics such as religious duties, nationalism, and glorification of martyrdom, Pashtun traditional cultural symbols, and political liberty.

> I who passed the test of love, I who awaken the world with the call for Jihad
> I bring fear in the eyes of all evil doers, as I carry the flower of freedom with me.
> I teach pride to the stormy waves of the sea, as I am the bravest of all braves.
> Angels, do not wait long, as I am heading to the fields of Jihad and martyrdom.
> I will make all crusaders fearful with nightmares, as I am a student of Jihad.
> (Kandahari [2014], translated by the author)

After the fall of the Taliban regime, and the retreat of their leadership in Pakistan, the Taliban continued to articulate their views and thoughts through poetry and *Taranas* (songs). In response to the establishment of a democratic system in Afghanistan after 9/11, Taliban poetry is increasingly incorporating symbols and cultural references from traditional Pashtun culture in addition to its religious themes in an attempt to present itself as a nationalistic force and challenge the modern notions of human rights, democracy, and liberty associated with the new Afghan constitution. Their poetry actively presents a narrative which denounces democracy as a threat to Islam and the unity of Afghanistan:

> Once my teacher told me of something called freedom.
> I respectfully asked my teacher, "What is it? An imported concept or an authentic truth?"
> My teacher, full of tears, replied,
> "We forgot our history, our values, we forgot real freedom.
> I worry that the time approaches,
> When we will neither have the pen nor be able to wield the sword.
> True freedom is in the Koran and in Sharia, not in laws made by Man."
> (Kandahari [2014], translated by the author)

Afghanistan Literature after 2001

After 2001, the opening of Afghanistan to the world, the effects of an international presence, and the return of millions of Afghan refugees have deeply affected the sense of identity among a new generation of Afghans. This is not only reflected in the Afghan constitution of 2004 where, beside Pashto and Persian Dari as official languages, Uzbeki, Turkmeni, and Baluchi are also recognized officially as national languages, but also in Afghan poetic traditions. With the collapse of Afghan ideologies and the opening of the space for expression, Afghanistan's poetry has largely moved away from being overtly political, ideological, or ethnic and has become subjective, with a strong emphasis on new concepts such as human rights and women's rights as well as social criticism, feminism, and love. The social criticism and questioning of many traditional Afghan cultural and linguistic norms pervades many current poetic productions. Despite the popularity of lyrical forms such as *ghazals* and quatrains, new forms or free verse poetry (*Sher-e Azad*) with no rhyme or meter, is becoming dominant among the new generation of Afghan poets. For them, the free verse form is seen as more appropriate for the expression of contemporary realities of life in Afghanistan.

Conclusion

Since the emergence of modern Afghanistan as a nation-state in late nineteenth century into the very present, language, and especially its poetic form as the measure of Afghanistan's cultural achievement, became, as if by reaction, the most crucial element in shaping and defining identity in ways that transcended its earlier formative context.

Until the early twentieth century, sociocultural identity, understood in the sociopolitical context of southwestern and Central Asia, was continuously defined by the authority of the Islamic "textual" tradition transmitted through writing in the Persian language. The rise of modern Afghan nation-state, or, more precisely, Pashtun nationalism, in the 1930s, challenged the existing cultural traditions and practices and tried to change the notions of identity, personhood, and ethnicity through its language policy. Thus, language, and specifically poetry, became the center of cultural as well as political transformation. Aware of the preeminent position of poetry, the efforts to raise Pashto, instead of Persian, as the national and official language of Afghanistan is characterized by attempts to develop Pashto poetry through state institutional support. This policy was based on the understanding that poetry is not only a literary fact but also a social one. Being sidelined, the non-Pashtuns started turning to existing literary texts, especially poetry, as means of asserting their identity. Therefore, writing and recitation of poetry and poetry contests, *Majles e Mush'ara*, became some of the most important sociopolitical events in Afghanistan. Because the poems are produced within a context reflective of complex background relationships entailing various social, historical, and cultural factors. Understanding the ways in which poetry functions is a mirror of the local discourse over the issue of identity and personhood in Afghanistan. The difference between poetic styles, themes, and forms highlights the transformation that has marked Afghan society for most of twentieth century and especially in the last four decades. In Afghanistan's political developments after the communist coup and the struggle between various ideologies during the Soviet invasion and Taliban era, poetry had a mutually defining relation with ethnic as well as national identity and the political as well as social nature of struggle and transformation that the country has endured. Being a poet or knowing poetry becomes the very fact of claiming one's heritage, establishing social position, and defining one's political and cultural life and future continuity. As Ferdowsi, in Shahnama has said:

> Much I have suffered in these thirty years,
> I have revived Ajam with my verse
> I will not die then alive in the world
> For I have spread the seed of the word

Ferdowsi (1995, 34)

Notes

1. Keshavmurthy Prashant, personal communication, March 15, 2008)
2. Abdul Qahar Aasi, Afghan poet (1955–1994), one of the leading contemporary poets, was killed during the mujahideen civil war.
3. *Anjuman e Adabye Kabul* (Kabul Literary Society) was renamed, *Pashto Tolana* (Pashto Academy), in the mid-1920s, to foster and encourage the rewriting of the history of the language and enriching it with new words and grammar.
4. In 1944, *Pata Khazana* was "discovered;" it was identified as a "hidden treasure," a book about ancient Pashto poetry. The authenticity of this book is disputed by philologists.
5. Hafiz Shirazi was a Persian Poet and Sufi, born 1310 or 1337; Abdul Qadir Bedil was a Persian poet and Sufi in India (1642–1720); Jalal ud Din Rumi Balkhi was a Persian poet and Sufi (1207–1273).
6. *Mathnavi* is a poetic form based on independent rhyming lines of five couplets; a *ghazal* is a poetic form with rhyming couplets and shared meter.

Bibliography

Aasi, Abdul Qahar. 1989. *Lalayee baraye Malima*. 105th ed. Series 351. Kabul: Ministry of Information and Culture.
"Abdul Qahar Aasi." 2011. Last modified November 16, 2011. Accessed February 2017.
Afghanistan Multiple Indicator Cluster Survey 2010–2011. Report. January 2013. Accessed August 10, 2017. http://cso.gov.af/Content/files/DAMICS.pdf.
Ahady, Anwar-ul-Haq. 1995. "The Decline of the Pashtuns in Afghanistan." *Asian Survey* 35 (7): 621–34.
Barfield, Thomas.2010. *Afghanistan: A cultural and political history*. Princeton, NJ: Princeton University Press.
Bauman, Richard, and Joel Sherzer, eds. 1989. *Explorations in the Ethnography of Speaking*. Cambridge, UK: Cambridge University Press.
Berlin, Isaiah, L. W. Forguson, D. F. Pears, G. Pitcher, J. R. Searle, P. F. Strawson, and G. J. Warnock. 1973. *Essays on J.L. Austin*. Oxford: Oxford University Press.

Besnier, Niko. 1990 "Language and Affect." *Annual Review of Anthropology* 19: 419–51.
Bourdieu, Pierre. 1977. *Outline of a Theory of Practice*. Cambridge, UK: Cambridge University Press.
Buchbinder, David, and Barbara H. Milech. 1991. *Contemporary Literary Theory and the Reading of Poetry*. New York: Macmillan.
Canfield, Robert L. 1988. "Afghanistan's Social Identities in Crisis." In *Le Fait Ethnique en Iran et Afghanistan*, 185–99. Paris: Centre National de la Recherche Scientifique.
Dupree, Louis. 1997 [1980]. *Afghanistan*. Karachi: Oxford University Press.
Dupree, Nancy Hatch. 2002. "Cultural Heritage and National Identity in Afghanistan." *Third World Quarterly* 23 (5): 977–89.
Ferdowsi, Abolghasem. 1995. *Shahnameh*. Tehran: Sepehr.
Ghani, Ashraf. 1988. "The Persian Literature of Afghanistan, 1911–78, in the Context of its Political and Intellectual History." *Persian Literature (Albany, NY, 1988)* 428.
Gharghasht, M. N. 1966. *Rahnomay-e Kabul*. Kabul: Government Press.
Ghobar, Mir G. M. 1981. *Afghanistan in the Course of History*. Qom, Iran: Kanoun-e Mohajir.
Habibi, Abdolhay. 1967. *History of Afghanistan after Islam*. Tehran: Dunyae Kitab.
———. 1968a. "Pashto Literature at a Glance." *Afghanistan* 20 (4): 51–64.
———. 1968b. "Pashto Literature at a Glance." *Afghanistan* 21 (1): 53–57.
Haley, Michael Cabot. 1988. *The Semeiosis of Poetic Metaphor*. Bloomington: Indiana University Press.
Hunter, Edward. 1959. *The Past Present: A Year in Afghanistan*. London: Hodder and Stoughton.
Kakar, M. Hasan. 1973. *The Pacification of the Hazaras of Afghanistan*. New York: Afghanistan Council, Asia Society.
Kandahari, Nizami. 2014. Taliban Poetry. *Shahmat Info*. Last modified July 27. Accessed August 24, 2014. http://www.shahamat.info.
Keshavmurthy Prashant. 2008. Personal communication, March 15.
Khalili, Khalilullah. 1989. *Selected Anthology of Khalilullah Khalili*. Kabul: Government Publishing.
Lazard, Gilbert. 1968. "La dialectologie du judéo-persan." *Studies in Bibliography and Booklore* 8 (2/4): 77–98.
Mousavi, Sayed Askar. 1997. *The Hazaras of Afghanistan: An Historical, Cultural, Economic, and Political Study*. London: St. Martin's Press.
Nadery, Partaw. 2000. "Book Burning by Taliban." *Khorasan Zameen*, July 11. Accessed August 19, 2014. http://www.khorasanzameen.net/php/read.php?id=1274.
———. 2006. "Political and Ideological Poetry in Afghanistan." *Khorasan Zameen*, September 21. Accessed August 19, 2014. http://www.khorasanzameen.net/php/read.php?id=209.
Nawid, Senzil. 2011. "Language policy in Afghanistan: Linguistic diversity and national unity." In *Language Policy and Language Conflict in Afghanistan and Its Neighbors: The Changing Politics of Language Choice*, ed. Harold Schiffman 31–52.
Pstrusińska, Jadwiga. 1985. *Pašto au dari: Selections for Studying the Official Languages of Afghanistan and Their Literature*. Kraków: Nakł. Uniwersytetu Jagiellońskiego.
———. 1990. *Afghanistan 1989 in Sociolinguistic Perspective*. Society for Central Asian Studies.

Rubin, Barnett R. 2002. *The Fragmentation of Afghanistan: State Formation and Collapse in the International System*. New Haven, CT: Yale University Press.

Shahrani, M. Nazif. 1991. "Local Knowledge of Islam and Social Discourse in Afghanistan and Turkistan in the Modern Period." In *Turko-Persia in Historical Perspective*, ed. Robert L. Canfield, 161–88. Cambridge, UK: Cambridge University Press.

Shorish, M. M. 1985. *Themes of Islam and Nationalism in the Textbooks of Afghan Children*. Paper presented at the World Seminar on the impact of Nationalism on Ummah, London.

Shpoon, Saduddin, Paxto Folklore and the Landey. 1968. *Afghanistan Journal* 20 (4): 40–50.

Singh, Jogendra. 1939. *The Persian Mystics: The Invocations of Sheikh Ābdullāh Ansarī of Herat, AD 1005–1090*. London: Dutton.

Tariq, Mohoammad Osman, Fazel Rabi Haqbeen, and Palwasha Lena Kakar. 2012. *Afghanistan in 2012: A Survey of the Afghan People*. Kabul: Asia Foundation.

Tarzi, Mahmud. 1918. "Afghan Language." In *Siraj al Akhbar*, January 23.

Welch, Anthony, and Attaullah Wahidyar. 2013. *Evolution, Revolution, Reconstruction: The Interrupted Development of Higher Education in Afghanistan*. New York: Peter Lang.

Yarshater, Ehsan. 1962. "Some Common Characteristics of Persian Poetry and Art." *Studia Islamica* 16: 61–71.

4

LINEAGES OF THE URBAN STATE: LOCATING CONTINUITY AND CHANGE IN POST-2001 KABUL

Khalid Homayun Nadiri and
M. Farshid Alemi Hakimyar

Introduction

The city of Kabul has been a site of continuity and change for much of its modern existence. Since its early establishment as a minor trading town and, subsequently, a center of political administration, Kabul has been regularly exposed to migrations of people, flows of resources, and cultural influences inside and beyond the modern borders of Afghanistan (Thackston 1996; Dupree 1974, 1975; Hanifi 1976; Daoud 1982; Planhol 1993; Grevemeyer 1987). While the circumstances of Kabul have changed over time, its geographic and political conditions have historically given rise to interactions between diverse social communities, including provincial groups, court personnel, skilled professionals, and political exiles.[1]

These diverse social interactions became more frequent during the early twentieth century. Successive Afghan governments, supported by foreign economic assistance and technical expertise, progressively consolidated political, economic, and military authority over much of modern Afghanistan, inducing the migration of new groups into the capital city. Diverse cross sections of provincial high school graduates mixed in Kabul University, where they sought work in the government ministries (Yousefzai 1974, 179–180) or postgraduate training abroad (Eberhard 1962); indigent economic migrants, faced with population pressure and increasingly limited land, began to regularly visit Kabul in search of various forms of manual employment (Jung 1974); and the Kabuli style of music, drawing on Hindustani, *ghazal*, and *kiliwali* (Pashtun folk music) influences, came into fuller form, eventually diffusing to other cities and towns in Afghanistan via *sazande* (musician) networks and radio broadcasting

(Baily 1994, 1981; Slobin 1970; Sakata 2002). Together, these patterns of social consociation and state consolidation became deeply ensconced by the latter half of the twentieth century, so much so that those who were born and raised in the capital became incrementally imbued with a distinctive Kabuli identity (Issa and Kohistani 2007). Ethnic and linguistic identities became subordinated to more quotidian familial, schooling, occupational, and neighborhood ties, generating a context in which bonding across social categories became unremarkable.[2]

Social consociation and state consolidation also made new forms of political conflict possible. While the intersection of diverse social communities within the capital and expansion of state power served to integrate Afghanistan's territory into a more defined unit, political divisions among the educated and professional classes of Kabul began to take shape along lines of ideology and proximity to power, first in the form of constitutionalism (Habibi 1984, 6–71; Ghobar 1967; Farhang 1988) and later in the shape of revolutionary politics (Roy 1988, 1984). Combined with Cold War competition, internal divisions provided the conditions for the political dislocations of the 1970s, particularly the People's Democratic Party of Afghanistan (PDPA) coup of April 1978, plunging rural Afghanistan into an extended period of political violence. While the city of Kabul was largely insulated from indiscriminate violence under the administration of the Soviet-sponsored PDPA, rural and remote areas in Afghanistan were afflicted by large-scale conflict and displacement (Shahrani and Canfield 1984).[3] It was only until the disintegration of the state apparatus in 1992 that the capital was directly exposed to widespread violence, made possible in part by external support and producing an unprecedented level of killing and physical destruction, particularly across the east-west axis of Jadi Maiwand (Maiwand Avenue). The contradictions of social heterogeneity and political competition in' Kabul was brought into sharp relief during this period, when *tanzim* (religion based political organization) and former communist factions fought for control of the capital city in pitched street battles, apportioning the city into different areas of control (Dorronsoro 2007).

Despite protracted bouts of conflict, displacement, and government turnover over the past three decades, the combination of social consociation and political competition have continued to characterize Kabul. In the post-2001 period, the capital has remained a distinctive site of social interaction among native Kabulis, Afghanistan-born expatriates, economic migrants, and internally displaced families. Relationships of friendship, marriage, and economic interdependence cut across the capital city, reviving Kabul's historical tradition of social consociation (Schetter 2005). Rural-to-urban migration has once again brought together diverse groups of people in the central bazaars and residential areas. And music has also reemerged as an important area of cross ethnic exchange in the postwar period (Dupree 1976; Boone 2010). As Kabul has reappeared as a site of social consocation in the post-2001 period, it has also returned to its position as political arena. Afghan personalities and factions have recurrently clashed over political and economic resources, employing both public platforms (television, parliamentary maneuvers, street demonstrations) and private mechanisms (personal relationships, access to foreign governments) to accumulate influence within the capital city (for details on the role of TV, see Chapter 8 in this volume).

Nonetheless, the current period of political development in Kabul can be distinguished from those of the past. While Kabul has undergone periods of political contraction and consolidation in the past, the scope, depth, and duration of violence preceding the post-2001 experience was unprecedented. Identities and personal relationships shaped during the course of the wars in Afghanistan became important in the process of reconstruction, permeating the government ministries, opposition groups, and much of the nongovernmental organization (NGO) sector. Former members of the anti-Soviet *tanzimat*, the *Parcham* (flag) and *Khalq* (masses) factions of the PDPA, the Maoist *Shola-ye Jawed* (eternal flame), and the Taliban movement, as well as monarchy-era elites, educated youth, and women's rights activists, interact with one another to attain influence within the Afghan system. The scale and complexity of external resourcing in Kabul have also been exceptional. Since the conclusion of the Bonn Conference in December 2001 marking a new period in Afghan political development, the capital city has been the site of exceptionally large and diverse flows of foreign aid and technical assistance, shaping the physical and social complexion of the capital city. These resources have been used to rehabilitate, functionally and symbolically, important physical structures of the prewar order, including Kabul International Airport, hospital facilities, government buildings, and the prominent Kabul lycées. But they have also largely neglected needs that are crucial for the functioning of a city of Kabul's present size, including residential housing, city roads, and the water and sewage systems. External resourcing has also indirectly financed new and relatively conspicuous forms of private consumption, evident in the shopping malls and homes found in Sherpur, Wazir Akbar Khan, and other areas near the city center. To an extent not seen in prior phases of modern Afghan history, the post-2001 period has exhibited the location of extremely powerful and marginal forces in close location to one another (Esser 2013).

This chapter assesses the effects of these circumstances on Kabul's politics and economy. Despite the physical accessibility of Kabul city, the social and political currents of change within the capital since 2001 have received very little academic attention. Over the past decade, social science studies of Afghanistan have centered on the rural dimensions of violence, foreign assistance, and development outcomes, but surprisingly little analysis has been devoted to the urban dynamics of Kabul and, in particular, their relation to provincial territories. The relative absence of such research is striking, given the large body of literature connecting historical developments in Kabul to social structural change (Allen 1974; Samady 2001; Gregorian 1969; Dupree 1974; Anderson 1978) and political violence (Shahrani 1979; Shahrani and Canfield 1984) in the provinces. This chapter aims to address this lacuna by studying three interrelated areas of urban life—social, political, and economic—to evaluate the broader patterns of change in Kabul. In the next section, the historical role of Kabul is described and explained with reference to changes in the estimated population of the capital city over time. Section 3 examines the social dynamics of the Soviet-built Mikroryan apartment blocks and Shahr-e Kuhna (Old City) neighborhood of Kabul. Patterns of elite-led political mobilization in Kabul are discussed in section 4, and section 5 studies the effects of external resourcing on the Kabul environment. A final conclusion summarizes the chapter.

Understanding Kabul in Historical Context

Since its incorporation into the Afghan political system of Ahmad Shah Abdali in the eighteenth century, Kabul has acquired multiple dimensions—as military enclave, as center of bureaucratic, commercial, and educational advancement, as site of social pluralism and contention, as civil war prize, as overcrowded city. Nonetheless, many of Kabul's various manifestations have remained deeply intertwined with the evolution of the state in Afghanistan. The importance of government administration in shaping the economy and society of the capital city and the diffusion of such changes to other areas of Afghanistan have made it impossible to separate developments in the city of Kabul and the wider Afghan state system.

By consequence, changes in Kabul have historically conveyed a great deal of information about the course of the Afghan political system. By the nineteenth and early twentieth centuries, these changes had incrementally begun to take shape. Despite the pattern of external wars and internal dislocations that characterized this period, the successive reigns of Dost Mohammad Khan (r. 1826–1839, 1845–1863) and his son, Sher Ali Khan (r. 1863–1879), saw the increased specialization of administration and the recruitment of nonfamilial relations in Kabul. These trends continued under the reign of Abdur Rahman Khan (r 1880–1901). Having established a regular army and a complex of state arms workshops (*mashin khanah*) in the capital city, Abdur Rahman led a series of highly coercive military campaigns into all of the areas that constitute modern Afghanistan, including Kunar, Maimana, the Shinwari and Ghilzai territory, the Hazarajat area, and the eastern territory then known by noninhabitants as Kafiristan (Kakar 1979). During the subsequent periods of rule by Habibullah Khan (r. 1901–1919) and, in particular, Amanullah Khan (r. 1919–1929), Kabul developed a more prominent

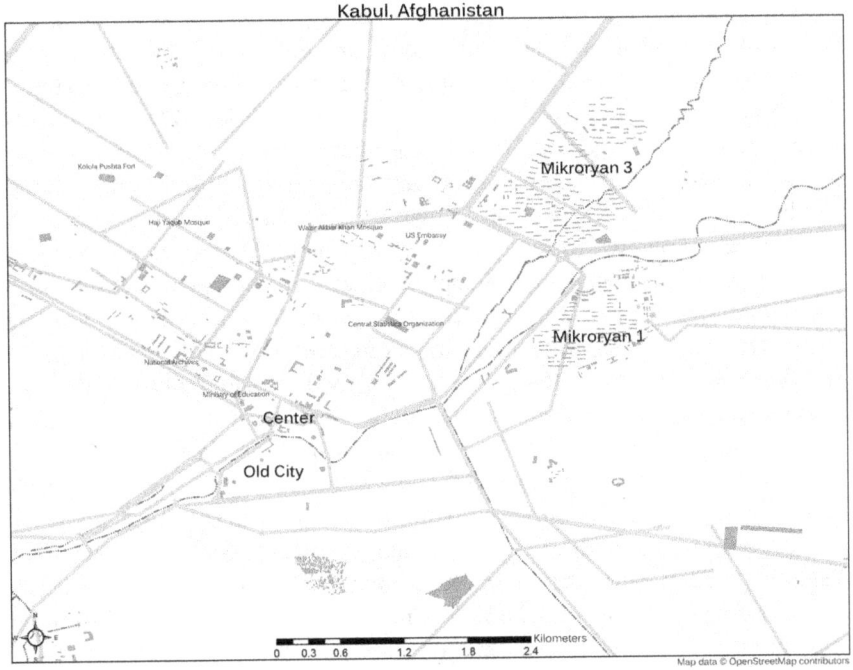

Map 4.1. Kabul city before 1978. © OpenStreetMap contributors, CC BY-SA 2.0.

role in shaping urban society through the establishment of state schooling, the *shirkat* (joint-stock company) system, and new social and ideational trends (Gregorian 1969; Poullada 1973; Nawid 1999). These changes could be seen in the estimated increases in the size of the Kabul population. Although efforts to estimate the Kabul population, particularly observational evaluations, are subject to a substantial level of uncertainty (Balland 1992), the temporal trend in the population size is informative. The estimated expansion in the Kabul population from 50,000 or 60,000 people in the 1830s to 120,000 people one century later constituted a large population increase, reflecting both the growth of the native population and the migration of peoples, motivated by state influence or coercion, to the capital city. This trend accelerated in the subsequent period of rule by Nadir Khan (r. 1929–1933) and his lineage, which took control over Kabul in 1929.[4] During this period of political development, Kabul achieved a dominant military position over the rural sector, while becoming the leading conduit of domestic and international capital (Nadiri 2017). The coincidence of military and economic power provided the conditions for large migrations of communities in Afghanistan to the capital city, increasing the population from 120,000 people at the beginning of Nadir's rule to an approximate 900,000 people four decades later. Successive governments also constructed new, architecturally modern quarters of garden houses and multiple-storied apartment buildings, including Shahr-e Naw (1935), Karta-e Char (1942), Karta-e Sey (1958), and later, Wazir Akbar Khan Mina (middle 1960s) (Hanifi 1976, 449). The Kabul population continued to grow rapidly in the years that immediately followed the PDPA coup, although many from the urban professional classes escaped or disappeared during this time.[5] Rural families displaced by violence or economic insecurity migrated in significant numbers to the relatively secure capital during the PDPA period, producing an increase in the city population of approximately 300,000 people between 1978 and the mid-1980s. This period also saw the development of residential housing inspired by the Soviet administration, including apartment blocks in Mikroryan and Koh-e Sher Darwaza. The demographic growth of Kabul under PDPA rule, however, was rapidly reversed after the fall of the government of Dr. Najibullah and the increasing intramujahideen violence throughout Kabul, during which some 500,000 people reportedly fled the city; this process of depopulation would eventually stabilize under the austere conditions of Taliban rule (1996–2001).

The post-2001 period has clearly corresponded with a rapid expansion of the Kabul population. Since the international intervention in Afghanistan, the city population has increased from an approximate 1.8 million people to an estimated size of between 3 million and 4.5 million people in 2008, and likely many thousand more people today. A leading source of this population growth has been the influx of internally and externally displaced refugees into the capital city, as well as economic migrants venturing to Kabul from different areas of Afghanistan and abroad. Out of the Kabul population in 2012, it has been estimated that approximately 360,000 people were born abroad and 1.9 million people were born elsewhere in Afghanistan, a figure that does not include children subsequently born within the capital city (Central Statistics Organization 2014). These estimates, although subject to a high degree of uncertainty, imply that the Kabul population has expanded by at least 70 percent in less than ten years, largely because of internal migration, making Kabul one of the fastest growing cities in the world.

The current environment of Kabul contains a more diverse set of social groups than ever before, including internally displaced communities, economic migrants, elite families, and professional classes, in addition to a relatively small section of native Kabulis. Yet, despite these developments in the size and complexion of the Kabul population, the contradictory pattern of both social consociation and political conflict in the capital has remained in place during the post-2001 period. Kabuli society has not exhibited significant levels of ethnic violence or polarization, particularly of the form and degree observed in other urban areas of Central Asia (for example, Osh) and South Asia (including Quetta, Karachi, Hyderabad), But its politics remain contentious, even if this contention the political divisions underlying this contention have been transitory in nature

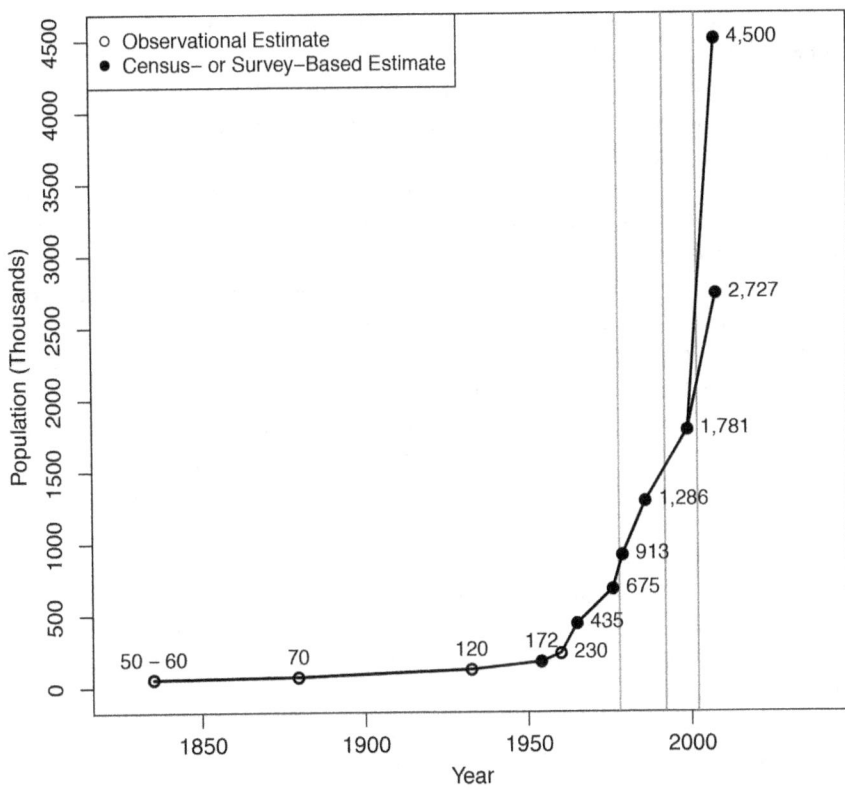

Figure 4.1. Population estimates of Kabul City. *Sources*: Burnes (1835); Masson (1842); MacGregor (1871); Hensman (1881); Ahmad and Aziz (1934); *Survey of Progress 1961–62* (1963); *Greater Kabul Census* (1965); *Fourth Public Census of Population and Housing* (1986); Grötzbach (1990); *Kabul City Population Survey* (2000); Central Statistics Organization (2008); Ahad (2010); Planhol (2012).

Note: Vertical markers indicate years in which Afghanistan experienced historical discontinuities, including the Saur Revolution (1978), the collapse of the PDPA government of Dr. Najibullah (1992), and the fall of the Taliban government of Mullah Mohammad Omar (2001).

and have enjoyed limited popular support. How does one make sense of these puzzling circumstances? A preliminary examination suggests that this contradiction between social consociation and political conflict can be found in the study of institutions. At the societal level, preexisting norms and crosscutting cleavages have served to enable cooperation. Kabul's diverse residents have historically evaluated one another along multiple dimensions—familial reputation, personal networks, wealth, physical appearance, personality, and morality, for example. These types of interaction have, in turn, frequently catalyzed mixing across ethnic and linguistic lines. Crosscutting cleavages have also served to constrain social antagonism (Dahl 1982; Lipset and Rokkan 1967; Coser 1956). Differences within social communities and commonalities across them have historically made ethnic or linguistic mobilization relatively unappealing for Kabul's population. Disparities in wealth, access to power, and religiosity, for example, frequently divide families or individuals that share the same ethnic or linguistic background. Furthermore, ties that cut across communities, particularly shared class and marriage, frequently connect families embedded in different communities.

At the political level, however, norms of behavior are much less defined, and institutions capable of regulating national political competition do not exist. Because the Afghan system does not possess strong political institutions or well-defined norms that can govern political competition, politicians can abruptly alternate between divisive and cooperative behavior. Resources, moreover, have become closely intertwined with access to political power, obstructing the development of capable and less personalized government institutions. In the post-2001 period, political elites belonging to every section of Afghan society have been able to translate political influence into economic wealth by securing contracts tied to the international presence. This has, in turn, increased the returns to personal relationships in the capital city, greatly inhibiting the initial development of merit- and rule-based government (also see Chapters 5 and 6 in this volume).

Social Kabul: Everyday Life in Two Neighborhoods

This section examines patterns of social interaction in two sections of Kabul—Mikroryan and Shahr-e-Kuhna, drawing on interviews conducted during the second half of 2013 and first half of 2014. These areas of Kabul differ from one another along multiple dimensions, but they both demonstrate the importance of shared social status and the physical environment as critical components of community stability. The Mikroryan area is not a close-knit neighborhood, but relative economic prosperity, liberal social views, and physical privacy make this community work. The Shahr-e-Kuhna neighborhood, by contrast, is a relatively cohesive community drawn together by longstanding interpersonal ties and traditional patterns of employment and social mores.

3.1 Diversity and Anonymity in Mikroryan

The Mikroryan residential complex is an upper middle-class section of Kabul located in the northeast region of the city and comprised of four multistoried, prefabricated concrete apartment blocks—First/Old Mikroryan, Mikroryan II, Mikroryan III, and Mikroryan IV.[6] These residential projects were built in stages—the construction of the Old Mikroryan apartment block was completed

Lineages of the Urban State | 85

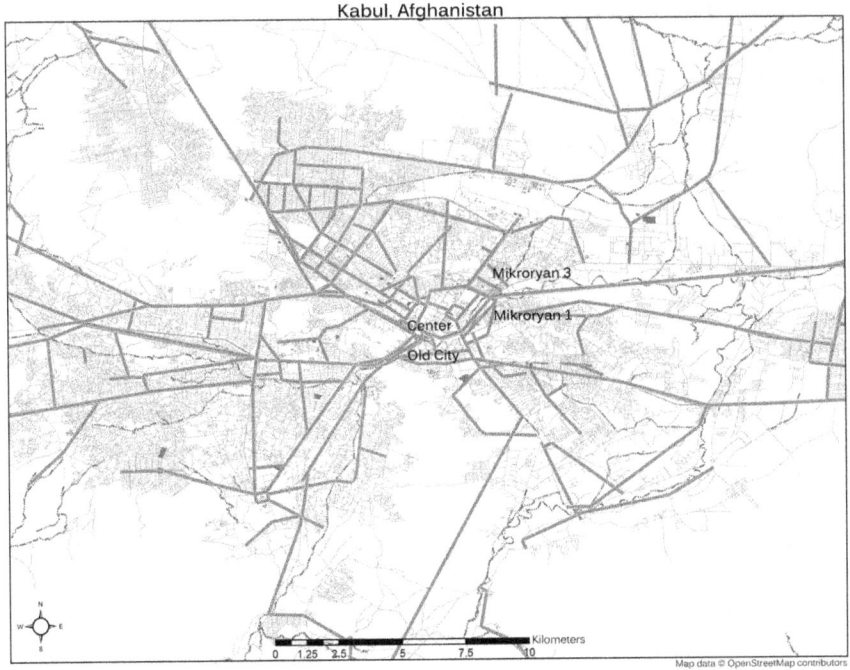

Map 4.2. Kabul since the US-NATO intervention of 2001. © OpenStreetMap contributors, CC BY-SA 2.0.

in 1964, and the remaining sections of the Mikroryan complex were sequentially built under the administration of the Soviet-supported PDPA. Designed as self-contained neighborhoods, the Mikroryan apartment blocks were organized in close proximity to essential functions, including schools, mosques, shops, and parks. This closed design corresponded with urban planning in the Soviet regions more generally (Liu 2012, 88), but it would also serve to seclude Soviet and PDPA officials from the rest of Kabul. Apartment units were initially distributed to PDPA cadres and Soviet officials, and were later made available for purchase to nonparty members of the Afghan government bureaucracy.[7] The present-day Mikroryan complex is comprised of nine thousand apartment units that house approximately 160,000 people of the middle- and upper-income classes. While apartment prices vary based on unit size, location, and upkeep, the Mikroryan residential units are in general expensive. Four-room apartments, for example, can be rented for $400 to $500 per month, and purchased for approximately $150,000 to $220,000.

Centrally located, relatively secure, and connected to the municipal electricity and water systems, the Mikroryan area is one of the more prosperous neighborhoods in Kabul. The Mikroryan apartment blocks rarely experience the extended electricity shortages that typify other parts of Kabul city. They are reliably heated by a central radiator system throughout the winter months. And water is accessed through an area-specific piped distribution system, although the antiquated nature of this water network leads to shortages during particularly hot summers.[8] A majority of Mikroryan apartments have access to cable television and cooking gas, and an increasing number of households are connected to the internet. The prosperity of the Mikroryan neighborhood can also be seen in its public spaces. Mikroryani stores attract both neighborhood patrons and window shoppers from other areas of Kabul, and command relatively high prices. Although small in size, these stores offer an especially wide selection of merchandise—traditional Afghan cooking ingredients, dry and fresh fruits, and imported foods. The Mikroryan park attracts large numbers of neighborhood residents and out-of-area Kabulis. Families visit the park for weekend walks and sweets, joggers wind down its paths, and groups of men and women can be seen trading the latest pieces of gossip. These public spaces are generally more secure than other parts of Kabul. The privacy and density of the apartment system, as well as the large numbers of elite Kabulis that live in Mikroryan, contribute to an environment relatively secure from the types of political violence commonly seen in other areas of Kabul city.

Residents of the Mikroryan area tend to be employed in the government, NGOs, and multilateral or technical professions (e.g., medicine or engineering), underscoring the proximity of Mikroryani households to the political establishment and civil society of Kabul. Interviews in the Mikroryan area show that many area residents speak English, and an even greater proportion is able to speak a regional language (Russian or Hindi/Urdu). Despite possessing similar economic backgrounds, Mikroryani households come from a diverse set of social backgrounds. A large share of interviewees self-identified as Tajik, with much of the remaining share of respondents identifying themselves as Pashtun. A very small share of the sample reported belonging to the Hazara or Uzbek ethnic groups. Despite a substantial degree of social diversity, almost all respondents are capable of speaking Dari (the most commonly spoken language in Kabul city), and the vast majority of respondents are multilingual (Dari and Pashto, in particular, also see Chapter 3 in this volume). A large proportion of interviewees, furthermore, were born outside of Kabul province, comprising a wide distribution of provinces and regions. Most of these individuals arrived in Kabul city during the PDPA period, prospectively for reasons of insecurity or employment, or settled in Mikroryan after the fall of the Taliban government.

Although the prosperity and privacy of the Mikroryan apartments provide for an absence of communal cohesion, a shared orientation toward more secular beliefs and practices can be observed in the Mikroryan area. Neighborhood mosques do not hold the status of communal center that they do in other areas of Kabul. Many residents of Mikroryan are not familiar with their neighborhood imam (mosque leader), and even fewer attend the neighborhood mosque with any regularity.[9] In some instances, residents have installed reinforced window systems in part to dampen the sound of the *azan-e fajr* (dawn call to prayer). Mikroryan residents, however, make sizable contributions to neighborhood mosques, particularly during charity ceremonies. As a consequence, while Mikroryani mosques tend to be smaller than those of other neighborhoods, and typically possess higher quality furniture and equipment. And whereas imams in other parts of Kabul are compensated with three meals each day, in Mikroryan they additionally receive cash payments of approximately 150 afghanis from each household per month. On the holy days of Eid-ul-Fetr and Eid-ul-Udha, religious observance takes place within the family household in Mikroryan. Residents typically arrange receptions exclusively for relatives and family friends in the courtyards of the apartment blocks.

3.2 Cohesive and Insulated Communities in Shahr-e Kuhna

Shahr-e Kuhna, or old city in Persian, is the original site of Kabul. Primarily comprised of traders and skilled workers with longstanding ties to Kabul or to their communities of origin, this area is more insulated from the international presence than other parts of Kabul. While Shahr-e Kuhna emerged from the civil war and Taliban periods with large expanses of severe physical destruction, it became repopulated by relatively dense communal networks, old and new, in the post-2001 period.

Shahr-e Kuhna has a substantially different composition than that of Mikroryan. Residents of the Shahr-e Kuhna neighborhood are primarily comprised of cohesive low- and middle-income communities of native Kabulis, many of whom did not possess the resources to flee the successive wars of the 1980s and 1990s. These communities vary from one neighborhood section to the next. In the Shor Bazaar area, Dari-speaking Sunni households descended from lineages of the Kabul and Shamali areas are a major constituency, along with *sadat* (plural of *sayyid*) families that historically have carried out religious functions for the community. In the historically Qizilbash quarter of Chendawul, a community of Hazaras has become the major constituency. Although a number of Qizilbash remain in Chendawul, the community is today dispersed throughout other areas of Kabul or has otherwise relocated abroad. While the neighborhood continues to be comprised of Kabulis, in recent years a large number of people from Parwan, Panjshir, and other northern provinces have settled in the upper hills of the Shahr-e Kuhna area.

Shahr-e Kuhna is significantly less prosperous than Mikroryan. Residents of Shahr-e Kuhna are primarily employed in trade and artisanal occupations. A much smaller proportion of area residents are engaged in unskilled work and homecare, and very few individuals obtain income from salaried professional positions. Only a small proportion of sampled residents speak English, and fewer are able to speak a regional language. Moreover, relatively few Shahr-e Kuhna residents are exclusively engaged in pursuing educational opportunities or are unemployed, suggesting that households in Shahr-e Kuhna have fewer resources with which to support members who do not earn an income. Because many of the households in Shahr-e Kuhna are relatively poor, like Mikroryan there is relatively modest economic differentiation within the neighborhood.

Shahr-e Kuhna has limited access to high-quality community services. Area residents access electricity through the public grid, although blackouts are a recurring phenomenon. Water is accessed more reliably through community hand pumps. The dry vault toilet systems used by Shahr-e Kuhna residents are occasionally cleaned through a traditional arrangement in Kabul—donkey-led carts that haul away waste for use as fertilizer. In this context, recent initiatives to introduce nonessential and costly services have attracted limited interest from the community. For example, the installation of digital telephone lines in 2011 that offer internet access has attracted very limited interest from the surrounding community. In contrast to areas of Kabul that have been subject to high levels of real estate speculation, Shahr-e Kuhna has seen a modest degree of physical change. Improvements in the physical environment have primarily come from household-initiated improvements of homes and storefronts, as well as a small number of public renovation projects sponsored by NGOs and development agencies. One of these projects includes the American financed improvement of Bagh-e Ghazi (Ghazi Garden), which serves as an athletic ground for soccer and other sports. During the prewar period, Bagh-e Ghazi was a site of traditional wrestling, notably the *zoorkhana* and *pahlawani* styles. However, like other areas of Kabul, Bagh-e Ghazi has not been maintained since its improvement. While the site was well maintained under one year of American stewardship, its condition has subsequently declined after the Kabul municipal government took control over it.

Social interaction in Shahr-e Kuhna also differs from that of Mikroryan. Most families in Shahr-e Kuhna have spent many years in the area, including both prewar and wartime eras, and consequently are closely acquainted with one another. Interpersonal ties, familial reputations, and gossip characterize this area of the capital city, providing for a relatively intimate social environment. Contributing to this dynamic is the geography and household economies of the area. The close quarters and narrow walkways of Shahr-e Kuhna make it difficult to avoid being noticed, particularly for the neighborhood shopkeepers who interact most frequently with the surrounding community. Consistent with the prospective relationship between income and social preferences observed in Mikroryan, the relatively less prosperous Shahr-e Kuhna sample has a substantial proportion of respondents who self-report as conservative. These respondents identified with a more literalist application of religious teaching and a suspicion of social change.

Political Kabul: From "Sons of the Soil" to Urban Cliques

While Kabuli society has been generally characterized by consociation in the post-2001 period, political interactions within the capital have been less accommodative. Since the conclusion of the Bonn Agreement in December 2001, Kabul has seen mob attacks, parliamentary fistfights, and street demonstrations in different quarters of the capital. In the television media, politicians, government officials, and commentators have traded accusations of corruption, incompetence, and in more extreme circumstances, ethnic inferiority or non-belonging. In contrast to the social dynamics of Kabul, capital city politics have almost always been public and fragmented, with constantly changing coalitions that do not neatly map onto group categories often used to describe politics in Afghanistan.

Many Afghanistan observers trace these patterns of political contention to the anti-Soviet jihad and ensuing civil war. But wartime differences, often inadequately characterized in strictly ethnic terms, do not make much sense of post-2001 politics in Kabul. A closer examination reveals just as significant contention *within* social categories as across them (Schetter 2005). Thus, the Panjshiris of *Jamiat-e Islami*, often labeled as an exemplar of the Tajiks, have ceased to operate as a cohesive group. Similarly, the Hazara leaders of *Hezb-e Wahdat* have further divided into competing factions and no longer exercise the authority over educated Hazara youth that they had in previous years (Ibrahimi 2009); similar divisions have taken shape between veteran and youth cadres in the predominantly Uzbek party of *Jonbesh-e Melli*;[10] and the Pashtuns that have emerged in the post-2001 environment have never constituted a single group, encompassing Pashto-speaking adherents of *Hezb-e Islami* originating in eastern Afghanistan, Kabuli members of Sayyaf's *Ittehad*, elite familial lineages with ties to Kandahar or Kabul, and former Marxist-Leninists.

In post-2001 Kabul, interpersonal connections and individual strategies have come to shape politics (for details see chapter 5 in this volume). Central government officials and legislators with rural bases of support choose to spend most of their unoccupied time in Kabul, where access to economic resources and new political opportunities often outweigh those in the provinces. In this respect, the present system exhibits patterns of intermediation similar to the prewar Afghan political system, in which Kabul incrementally became the focal point of politics in Afghanistan (Weinbaum 1977). At that time, provincial elites and educated youth increasingly contested for influence within the center, which had established greater authority over peripheral areas throughout the middle twentieth century by acquiring education or professional experience in central offices. While present-day Kabul does not enjoy the same form and degree of authority in the provinces that it had in the past, it nonetheless remains an object of intense competition among political entrepreneurs of different backgrounds.

Nonetheless, the present system does differ from the past. Whereas earlier political elites contended among one another with limited popular involvement, contemporary political actors employ public space to display their individual achievements, connections to the wartime past, or access to international actors. This change was a consequence of the wars in Afghanistan. Exposure to conflict widened the scope of popular involvement in political life, increasing the appeal of the kind of political entrepreneurship seen in post-2001 Kabul. Conspicuous areas of activity—city spaces, public holidays, the television media, and identity cards—have all attracted significant political partisanship because they provide the greatest exposure to ordinary Kabulis, and therefore to political influence within the country's largest population center. On the heavily trafficked streets of Kabul, political partisans conspicuously display their respective allegiances by decorating car dashboards with images of slain icons of Afghanistan's recent past, including Dr. Najibullah, Abdul Ali Mazari, Ahmad Shah Massoud, Abdul Haq, Haji Qadir, and Burhanuddin Rabbani. Politicians rename urban spaces after slain political leaders—Great Massoud Road (connecting Kabul International Airport with the city center, and intersecting Massoud Square), Martyr Abdul Haq Square (between the apartment blocks of Mikroryan One and Mikroryan Two), Martyr Baba Mazari Square (in the Karta-e Seh neighborhood)—to memorialize political struggles of the past and highlight their connection to the present. Private television stations owned or otherwise financed by politicians have served as barely concealed platforms for mobilizing votes, priming supporters, and targeting rivals (see Chapter 8 in this volume for details). And public holidays that commemorate assassinated political elites have become distinctly political rallies for changes in the Afghan political system.

Some of these political efforts have occasionally generated contention. The renaming of Kabul Education University to Ustad Burhanuddin Rabbani University set off a modestly sized but persistent series of student protests. Another series of demonstrations occurred on the fifteenth anniversary of the death of Dr. Najibullah, with supporters petitioning the government to rename Ariana Square in recognition of the former president. Political partisanship has also emerged in connection with the "week of martyrs," (*hafta-ye shuhada*) enacted in 2002 to recognize the annual anniversary of the death of Ahmad Shah Massoud. During the week of martyrs commemoration in 2012, a violent confrontation emerged in the Karta-e Seh area after a vehicle driven by a partisan of Ahmad Shah Massoud struck and seriously injured a young Hazara man. When the Kabul city police declined to intervene, the Hazara demonstrators engaged the nearby police officers in a street battle that left several dead. Most recently, partisanship in the television media and parliament has created significant controversy. In an interview in December 2013, retired general Abdul Wahid Taqat claimed that Afghanistan belongs to Pashtuns and that ethnic Tajiks and Uzbeks should move to Tajikistan and Uzbekistan, respectively. The inflammatory remarks led to large protests against Zhwandoon TV and resulted in the detainment of Taqat by the attorney general's office (AGO). These and other reactions also prompted Taqat to express regret for his remarks, in which he revealed that his private life apparently differs from his divisive political behavior—according to Taqat, his wife is an ethnic Tajik, he speaks Dari with his children, and his daughters are married to Panjshiri men. Taqat's arrest has since set off a round of protests by predominantly Pashtun supporters against the AGO.

Government identification offers yet another conspicuous and combustible area of politics. Since the announcement of plans to issue electronic *tazkira* (identity cards) in 2009, the issue of ethnic categorization has become a contentious issue, mirroring prior contestation surrounding demographic enumeration in Afghanistan as a whole (Balland 1992). Non-Pashtun political elites primarily belonging to the Tajik, Uzbek, and Hazara communities called for the electronic identity cards to specify ethnic or tribal ancestry as an expression of social origin, while predominantly Pashtun politicians supported the status quo designation of Afghan=Pashtun because it purportedly maintained national unity. Contention over the identity cards escalated throughout 2012 and 2013, culminating in a physical confrontation in the *Meshrano Jirga* (house of elders) in December 2013 and again in late December 2017 and early January 2018 in Wulusi Jirga or the Lower House. However, much of the debate surrounding the identity card issue was not solely rooted in expressions of social origin or appeals to national unity, but also in access to power. This is because the new identity cards could validate the demographic size of different ethnic categories in Afghanistan, influencing the composition of future government cabinets (Carberry 2013), even as it masks the prevalence of mixed ethnicity and other dimensions of social identity found in the contemporary population of Kabul.

In each of these instances, the political dynamics of the capital city have been much more contentious than the functioning of Kabuli society would suggest. Whereas social dynamics in Kabul are shaped by the diversity and multidimensionality of everyday life, politics has been characterized by reductionism and recurring conflict. As suggested earlier, one reason for this disjunction is the absence of norms or political institutions capable of constraining conflict, as evidenced in the contested presidential elections of 2014. Another contributor can be found in the economy of Kabul. During the post-2001 period, external resources have become deeply intertwined with the political system of Kabul, giving rise to patterns of cronyism and private gain that have increased the distance between ordinary and new elite Kabulis, even as foreign assistance has supported large sections of the city population.

Economic Kabul: Making Distribution Work

Kabul's society and politics possess their own logics, but both of these spheres of activity are deeply intertwined with the economic system of the capital city. Because of the unique position of Kabul in the Afghan political system—notably, its access to human and economic capital, as well as its extensive administrative offices—much of the city's present population derives income from economic assistance extended by international donors.

This is not a new phenomenon. For almost a century leading up to the PDPA coup, the city of Kabul had been the recipient of substantial flows of foreign assistance. Under the administration of Amir Abdur Rahman Khan, this assistance was almost entirely controlled by the Amir and narrowly employed in support of the Amir's project of "internal imperialism" (Dupree 1977). In Kabul, the Amir employed foreign assistance to establish arms workshops and introduced administrative education to court personnel (Kakar 1974).[11] During the subsequent administrations of Amir Habibullah Khan and Amir Amanullah Khan, government-channeled aid reached a wider set of elite Kabulis. Foreign assistance financed the establishment of new schools of general and military education, the introduction of communications and electrical infrastructure, and the preliminary construction of Kabul-e Jadid (modern Kabul), a southwestern expansion of Kabul city and the would-be seat of future governments (Guha 1967; Gregorian 1969, 183–201, 239–254). This trend of somewhat more widely distributed aid continued into the period of rule by Nadir Khan and his lineage. During the four decades of rule by members of the Nadir Khan family, successive governments continued to influence the allocation of aid and foreign expertise, but external resources reached an increasingly larger number of people in Kabul and other major cities (comparatively little foreign assistance reached the rural areas of Afghanistan). This strategy of predominantly urban and peri-urban development generated substantial employment and goods for export, a development that in turn contributed to some institutional upgrading.[12] Externally sponsored hospital, transportation, and school projects employed large sections of bureaucrats and professionals, spilling over into the music, food, and shop-keeping economies that supported Kabuli society.

Unlike the prewar circumstances of Kabul, the present political economy of the capital city differs in that the central government does not exercise primary control over the allocation of foreign assistance. Rather, a wide array of bilateral governments, multilateral bodies, and NGOs have operated autonomous aid programs in Kabul and the provinces. According to data collected by the

Organization for Economic Cooperation and Development (OECD), more than 71 percent of official development assistance (ODA) was allocated to external organizations operating within Afghanistan between 2002 and 2010. The present situation is also different in that external resources have largely financed net imports and key services such as transportation and logistics instead of investment in productive urban and rural enterprise. The end result has been a Kabul economy that is financed through multiple organizational channels with different objectives and practices, and that has primarily served to distribute resources instead of developing productive capabilities. This particular political economy has had far-reaching effects on the social fabric of the capital city, evidenced throughout the physical environment of Kabul. In the center of the city, upscale and expansive properties remain out of reach for the vast majority of Kabul residents. Shopping centers, grocery stores, and fast food restaurants served the large expatriate community and a small section of Afghan professionals employed in nearby private and public offices, but do not generate domestic demand for Afghan goods. And many educated Kabulis have established their own NGOs, although most are vaguely conceived and exist only on paper, in the hope of raising funds from donor organizations.

Foreign financing has also shaped patterns of politics in Afghanistan. Since the international intervention in 2001, prominent politicians and businessmen from a diverse array of backgrounds have been able to translate political connections into economic wealth by securing government-owned plots of land in Kabul or contracts in sectors tied to international military and development efforts in Afghanistan. The intertwined nature of national politics and external sponsorship are particularly visible in the capital, where many of the large Afghan business groups are based, including the Azizi Group, a diversified company active in the banking and real estate sectors and the Watan Group, a construction, security, and logistics company, both of which are politically connected to the family of President Hamid Karzai; the Gas Group, a fuel distribution firm owned by family members of former Vice President Marshal Fahim and a prominent recipient of Kabul Bank financing; and the Ghazanfar Group, a company involved in the oil and gas sector that is owned by the family of Husn Banu Ghazanfar, the present minister of women's affairs; the Gulbahar Group, an import-export business that owns the Gulbahar Towers and Gulbahar Center in Kabul; and the Dawi Group, a fuel storage and distribution business owned by Abdul Ghafar Dawi, the husband of parliament member Shukria Barakzai, who enjoys close personal ties with much of the power elite in Kabul.

The intertwined nature of external relationships and domestic politics in Afghanistan has, in turn, exerted differential effects on politics in the capital city. It has concentrated substantial pools of wealth among the political and economic elite, evident in the conspicuous forms of consumption in the wealthy sections of Kabul, notably the Sherpur and Wazir Akbar Khan, and Shahr-e Naw areas. The overt display of economic wealth, as well as the ways in which it has been acquired, have in turn generated alienation among ordinary sections of the Kabuli population. In the gated community of Sherpur, senior government officials and opposition figures live on large plots of land that were confiscated in 2003 from families that had moved into the area as early as the 1950s (Fontenot and Maiwandi 2007).[13] Other acquisitions of wealth occurred through politically connected contracting with international military forces and development agencies. In the years that immediately followed international intervention in Afghanistan, business groups with ties to both domestic politicians and external donors acquired leading positions in the emerging industries of fuel distribution, construction, and security provision in the economy of Afghanistan. Operating along the transportation corridors that connect Afghanistan to its surrounding region, these business groups acquired sizeable sums of wealth that were invested in the high-end property markets of the capital city, including large compound houses rented to international NGOs and shopping centers offering amenities that few residents of Kabul could ever afford. These investments, moreover, are not only exceptionally expensive but are also stylistically and physically detached from the surrounding city (Feenstra 2010). The residential areas of Sherpur and Wazir Akbar Khan, for example, are known as "Little Pakistan" or "Little Dubai" because these neighborhoods draw on architectural styles developed in parts of Peshawar or the UAE where their builders and buyers have previously lived. As a consequence, they depart functionally and aesthetically from the cement or clay-brick courtyard homes (*khana-ye hawilidar*, or household with courtyard) that characterize prewar architecture in Kabul and that are visible throughout the rest of the city. Contributing to the isolation of the Sherpur and Wazir Akbar Khan areas are the layers of heavy protection that separate these neighborhoods from the rest of the city. Surrounded by armed guards and blast walls, these houses paradoxically deter interaction with ordinary people while at the same drawing attention.

While external resourcing has exerted an isolating effect on political elites in Kabul, it has also facilitated cooperation between business groups. The most prominent partnership has included Kabul Bank and its principal beneficiary, the Afghan Investment Company, ventures that brought together members of the Karzai and Fahim families, the Dawi Oil Group, the Azizi Group, the Ghazanfar Group, the Gulbahar Group, and former minister of agriculture Obaidullah Ramin, together with cofounders Sherkhan Farnood and Khalilullah Ferozi. Capitalized in 2004, Kabul Bank expanded on the basis of winning a $1.5 billion annual contract to administer the salaries of approximately 80 percent of government employees, almost all of which was paid for with foreign assistance. With an increasingly large deposit base, the management and board drew on the bank's financial resources to finance investments in real estate property in Afghanistan and Dubai. Kabul Bank also drew on its resource base to make a substantial financial contribution—allegedly up to $14 million—to the 2009 election campaign of incumbent President Karzai. These and other illegal actions taken by Kabul Bank were clearly motivated by self-interest, but also demonstrated a logic of inclusive distribution that made it easier for its principals to maneuver Kabul's various political factions. Although business disputes did emerge between some of the participants in the Kabul Bank scandal, the diverse cross section of elites that ultimately joined the business venture is demonstrative of a wider pattern of economic cooperation in Kabul. By providing significant resources without downstream accountability, external sponsorship has incidentally enabled economic cooperation across political divisions.

While the distributive nature of the Kabuli economy has worked in the context of predictable and significant external sponsorship, it has become much more problematic as international aid has declined. This is because many of the external resources allocated to Afghanistan have been channeled by both international and domestic actors toward largely unsustainable economic activity, notably imported goods, transportation and logistics services, and real estate speculation. As a consequence, the decline in external aid precipitated by the drawdown of international combat forces, uncertainty over the future US-Afghanistan relationship, and the presidential election crisis of 2014 have resulted in a dramatic contraction in employment and property values in Kabul, and a reported increase in crime. This can be seen in the increasingly long lines of unskilled day laborers at Haji Yaqub Square and other pickup areas for temporary construction work, as well as the rising number of university graduates unable to find office-based administrative work. It can also be observed in the reported 40 percent decline in property values and gross investment in 2013 alone, the 40 percent depreciation of the afghani since 2011, and the withdrawal of deposits from large financial institutions in Kabul ("Uncertainty over Security Pact" 2013). In this context of economic contraction, one recent addition to Kabul's network of shopping centers, featuring a cinema designed for three-dimensional films, a swimming pool, and room for more than 160 shops, has unsurprisingly attracted little interest from potential tenants. With the expected decline in external resources in the coming years, distributive investments such as these will no longer be viable. What precisely will take their place, however, remains unclear.

Conclusion

This chapter has aimed to describe the changing position and role of Kabul in Afghan society, politics, and economy. Significant similarities connect the past and present. The contradictory coincidence of social consociation and political conflict has remained in place. In most Kabul neighborhoods, socially stable forms of everyday life prevail in spite of the legacy of war. However, political conflict remains a salient feature of the capital city, even if such contention does not correspond to the ethnic and linguistic categories often used to describe Afghan politics. External assistance also continues to play an important role in the Kabul economy, as it did in the past. Foreign aid has provided an important source of direct or indirect income for Kabul households, particularly for the salaried professionals that can be found in Mikroryan and other affluent neighborhoods.

Nonetheless, the present system does differ from the past. Whereas prewar political competition tended to occur among a small group of Kabuli elites, present-day politics has become much more contentious and spasmodic. Unconstrained by capable political institutions or well-defined norms that can govern political competition, politicians unpredictably alternate between divisive and cooperative behavior, standing in contrast to the more structured functioning of Kabuli society. The political economy of Kabul has also changed. While earlier governments were able to achieve significant economic and institutional gains through aid coordination, the present political system has been subject to a highly disorganized external resource base that has been allocated largely toward distribution instead of production.

These related patterns were brought into sharp relief by the presidential election of 2014, when a flawed voting process nearly escalated into a violent breakdown of order in Kabul. The electoral fraud that precipitated the crisis, the absence of credible electoral institutions that could resolve electoral irregularities, and the brinksmanship that persisted throughout the process were all signs of a political system that had not developed the conditions necessary to prevent or arbitrate a political transition. If Afghan government institutions do not become more capable, credible, and productive in the coming years of declining foreign assistance, future transitions will be even more difficult to peacefully attain.

Farshid Hakimyar is president and CEO of Snow Leopard Traders LLC, and has worked with international donor agencies and the Afghan government for over eleven years.

Khalid Homayun Nadiri is a management consultant at McKinsey & Company. He earned his PhD at the Johns Hopkins School of Advanced International Studies (SAIS) in 2017.

Notes

1. Territorial groups include, for example, the indigenous Persian-speaking Sunni population, the prominent lineages of the Abdali Pashtun tribes of Kandahar, and the Shia Qizilbash of Chendawul and Murad Khani, descended from soldiers commanded by Nadir Shah Afshar, and later, Ahmad Shah Abdali; Skilled artisans, trading families, and the *mashayekh* lineages representing the Naqshbandi and Chishti Sufi orders in Afghanistan (Edwards 1986; Nawid 1997) are some of the occupational networks; Notable court personnel include the *ghulam bachagan* (slave boys or court pages) of successive courts in Kabul during the nineteenth century, recruited from a variety of ethnic communities in Afghanistan (Kakar 1974; Shahrani 1984); Exile groups included Turkestani figures displaced by the Russian conquest of Central Asia, notably Amir of Bukhara Alim Khan and his brother Sidiq Khan Hashmet, Osman Khoja, Hashim Shayeq, and Mawlawi Amin Qurbat (Adamec 1975; Olcott 1981; Fraser 1988; Penati 2007), and Indian dissidents belonging to the anti-British Provisional Government of India, including Pratap Singh Mahendra, Maulana Barakatullah, and Maulana Obeidullah Sindhi (Adamec 1975; Ansari 1986).

2. A notable exception to this pattern was the Hazara community of Karta-ye Sakhi, many of whom descended from slaves captured and sold by the administration of Abdur Rahman Khan. This community constituted the most impoverished section of Kabuli Hazaras, deriving income mainly from *juwaligari* (porter) employment, and was excluded from much of Kabuli society.

3. Targeted assassinations were more regularly seen in Kabul. Government assassinations of PDPA opponents, and violence between PDPA factions occurred with some frequency in Kabul (Giustozzi 2000).

4. In doing so, the Nadir Khan and his brothers ousted Habibullah Kalakani (r. January 1929–October 1929), who had in turn displaced Amanullah Khan.

5. An investigation conducted by the International Crimes Unit of the Netherlands National Police documented over five thousand individuals targeted for death by Da Afghanistan da Gato da Satawulo Idara (Afghanistan Interests Protection Service, the successor organization to the pre-Saur intelligence services, Masuniyat-e-Melli and Zabt-e-Ahwalat) under the government of Nur Muhammad Taraki (r. 1978–1979). This list is almost exclusively comprised of urban-dwellers, and in particular residents of Kabul. See https://www.om.nl/onderwerpen/kopie-international/zie/afghanistan-death/death-lists/.

6. The name of this residential area derives from the Soviet term *mikroraion* (microregion) used to describe an urban administrative subunit (Planhol 2009).

7. At the time, Mikroryan apartments could be purchased by state employees for fifty thousand to one hundred thousand Afghanis. Once purchased, they were not permitted for sale.

8. Many Mikrorayon residents supplement access to the piped water system by installing private tankers of eight hundred to two thousand liters of water in the summer.

9. A small number of pious families are scattered throughout the Mikroryan blocks. Neighbors offer superficial Eid greetings to one another, understanding that these gestures will not be fulfilled.

10. In recent years, Adbul Rashid Dostum and the old guard leadership of Junbesh have increasingly come into conflict with a cadre of young and educated members who did not fight in Afghanistan's wars and want to develop a more positive, programmatically oriented party agenda (Peszkowski 2012).

11. The manufacture of arms and other military equipment were to become a significant area of employment in Kabul. Between 1901 and 1904, the government workshops retained approximately fifteen hundred men, and in 1919, the workshops employed five thousand men (Gregorian 1969).

12. This strategy had its own problems. As Maxwell Fry (1974) observes, government-sponsored investment resulted in the establishment of successful urban industrial projects, but artificially directed savings, and therefore potential production away from the rural sector.

13. At that time, these plots were valued by real estate specialists in Kabul at $70,000 to $170,000 (Calogero 2011), but increased rapidly in subsequent years as space inside of the city became increasingly scarce and larger numbers of expatriates flowed into the capital.

Bibliography

Adamec, Ludwig W. 1975. *Historical and Political Who's Who of Afghanistan*. Graz, AT: Akademische Druck-u. Verlagsanstalt.

Ahad, Wahid A. 2010. *Natural and Man Made Disaster Risks of Kabul City*. Kabul Municipality, Islamic Republic of Afghanistan.

Ahmad, Jamaluddin, and Muhammad Abdul Aziz. 1934. *Afghanistan: A Brief Survey*. Kabul: Durautalif.

Allen, Nigel. 1974. "The Modernization of Rural Afghanistan: A Case Study." In *Afghanistan in the 1970s*, ed. Louis Dupree and Linette Albert, 113–25. New York: Praeger.

Anderson, Jon W. 1978. "There Are No Khans Anymore: Economic Development and Social Change in Tribal Afghanistan." *Middle East Journal* 32 (2): 167–83.

Ansari, K. Humayun. 1986. "Pan-Islam and the Making of the Early Indian Muslim Socialists." *Modern Asian Studies* 20 (3): 509–37.

Baily, John. 1981. "A System of Modes Used in the Urban Music of Afghanistan." *Ethnomusicology* 25 (1): 1–39.

———. 1994. "The Role of Music in the Creation of an Afghan National Identity, 1923–73." In *Ethnicity, Identity and Music: The Musical Construction of Place*, ed. Martin Stokes, 45–60. New York: Berg.

Balland, Daniel. 1992. "CENSUS ii. In Afghanistan." In *Encyclopaedia Iranica* 5 (2):152–59.

Boone, Jon. 2010. "Kabul's Only Rock Band Pushes Afghanistan's Cultural Frontiers." *The Guardian*, March 31.

Burnes, Alexander. 1834. *Travels into Bokhara: Being the Account of a Journey from India to Cabool, Tartary and Persia*. London: J. Murray.

Calogero, Pietro Anders. 2011. "Planning Kabul: The Politics of Urbanization in Afghanistan." PhD diss., University of California, Berkeley.

Carberry, Sean. 2013. "Afghans Confront Sensitive Issue of Ethnicity." *Morning Edition*, National Public Radio, May 8.

Central Statistics Organization. 2008. *Statistical Yearbook*. Kabul: Central Statistics Organization.

———. 2013. *Statistical Yearbook*. Kabul: Central Statistics Organization.

———. 2014. *National Risk and Vulnerability Assessment: 2011-2012*. Kabul: Central Statistics Organization.

Coser, Lewis A. 1956. *The Functions of Social Conflict*. Glencoe, IL: The Free Press.
Dahl, Robert Alan. 1982. *Dilemmas of Pluralist Democracy: Autonomy vs. Control*. New Haven, CT: Yale University Press.
Daoud, Zemaray. 1982. *L'État Monarchique dans la Formation Sociale Afghane*. Berne-Francfort: M. P. Lang.
Dorronsoro, Gilles. 2007. "Kabul at War (1992–1996): State, Ethnicity and Social Classes." *South Asia Multidisciplinary Academic Journal*. Accessed January 26, 2014. http://samaj.revues.org/212.
Dupree, Louis. 1974. "The Emergence of Technocrats in Modern Afghanistan." New York: American Universities Field Staff.
———. 1975. "Settlement and Migration Patterns in Afghanistan: A Tentative Statement." *Modern Asian Studies* 9 (3): 397–413.
———. 1976. "It Wasn't Woodstock, But—:The First International Rock Festival in Kabul." New York: American Universities Field Staff.
———. 1977. "Afghanistan, 1880–1973." In *Commoners, Climbers and Notables: A Sampler of Studies on Social Ranking in the Middle East*, ed. C. A. O. van Nieuwenhuijze, 152–74. Leiden: Brill.
Eberhard, Wolfram. 1962. "Afghanistan's Young Elite." *Asian Survey* 1 (12): 3–22.
Edwards, David B. 1986. "Charismatic Leadership and Political Process in Afghanistan." *Central Asian Survey* 5 (3–4): 273–99.
Esser, Daniel. 2013. "The Political Economy of Post-Invasion Kabul, Afghanistan: Urban Restructuring beyond the North-South Divide." *Urban Studies* 50 (15): 1–15.
Farhang, Mir Mohammad Siddiq. 1988. *Afghanistan dar Panj Qarn-e-Akhir (Afghanistan in the Last Five Centuries)*. Peshawar: Derarsheh.
Feenstra, Anne. 2010. "Kabul's Kitschy Wedding Cake Architecture." Kabul: Afghanistan Analysts Network.
Fontenot, Anthony, and Ajmal Maiwandi. 2007. "Capital of Chaos: The New Kabul of Warlords and Infidels." In *Evil Paradises: Dreamworlds of Neoliberalism*, ed. Mike Davis and Daniel Bertrand Monk. New York: The New Press.
Fourth Public Census of Population and Housing. 1986. Central Statistics Organization, Democratic Republic of Afghanistan.
Fraser, Glenda. 1988. "Alim Khan and the Fall of the Bokharan Emirate in 1920." *Central Asian Survey* 7 (4): 47–61.
Fry, Maxwell J. 1974. *The Afghan Economy: Money, Finance, and the Critical Constraints to Economic Development*. Leiden: Brill.
Ghobar, Mir Ghulam Mohammad. 1967. *Afghanistan dar Masir-e-Tarikh (Afghanistan in the Course of History)*. Kabul: Dawlati Metbaeh.
Giustozzi, Antonio. 2000. *War, Politics and Society in Afghanistan, 1978–1992*. Washington, DC: Georgetown University Press.
Greater Kabul Census. 1965. Royal Government of Afghanistan.
Gregorian, Vartan. 1969. *The Emergence of Modern Afghanistan: Politics of Reform and Modernization, 1880–1946*. Stanford, CA: Stanford University Press.
Grevemeyer, Jan-Heeren. 1987. *Afghanistan: Sozialer Wandel und Staat im 20. Jahrhundert*. Berlin: Express.
Grötzbach, Erwin. 1990. *Afghanistan: Eine Geographische Landeskunde*. Darmstadt: Wissenschaftliche Buchgesellschaft.

Guha, Amalendu. 1967. "The Economy of Afghanistan during Amanullah's Reign, 1919–1929." *International Studies* 9 (2): 161–82.

Habibi, Abdul Hai. 1984. *Junbish-i Mashrutiyat dar Afghanistan*. Kabul: State Press.

Hanifi, M. Jamil. 1976. Preindustrial Kabul: Its Structure and Function in Transformational Processes in Afghanistan. In *The Mutual Interaction of People and Their Built Environment: A Cross-Cultural Perspective*, ed. Amos Rapoport, 441–51. The Hague: Mouton.

Hensman, Howard. 1881. *The Afghan War of 1879–80*. London: W. H. Allen.

Ibrahimi, Niamatullah. 2009. *The Dissipation of Political Capital among Afghanistan's Hazaras: 2001–2009*. Working paper no. 51. London: Crisis States Research Centre.

Issa, Christine, and Sardar M. Kohistani. 2007. "Kabul's Urban Identity: An Overview of the Socio Political Aspects of Development." *Asien* 104: 51–64.

Jung, Chris L. 1974. "Some Observations on the Patterns and Processes of Rural-Urban Migrations to Kabul." New York: Afghanistan Council of the Asia Society.

Kabul City Population Survey. 2000. Central Statistics Office, Islamic Emirate of Afghanistan.

Kakar, Hasan Kawun. 1979. *Government and Society in Afghanistan: The Reign of Amir Abd al-Rahman Khan*. Austin: University of Texas Press.

Kakar, M. Hassan. 1974. "Trends in Modern Afghan History." In *Afghanistan in the 1970s*, ed. Louis Dupree and Linette Albert, 13–33. New York: Praeger.

Lipset, Seymour M., and Stein Rokkan. 1967. "Cleavage Structures, Party Systems, and Voter Alignments: An Introduction." In *Party Systems and Voter Alignments: Cross-National Perspectives*, ed. Seymour M. Lipset and Stein Rokkan. New York: The Free Press.

Liu, Morgan Y. 2012. *Under Solomon's Throne: Uzbek Visions of Renewal in Osh*. Pittsburgh, PA: University of Pittsburgh Press.

MacGregor, C. M. 1995 [1871]. *Central Asia, Part II: A Contribution towards the Better Knowledge of the Topography, Ethnology, Resources and History of Afghanistan*. Petersfield, U.K.: Barbican.

Masson, Charles. 1842. *Narrative of Various Journeys in Balochistan, Afghanistan and the Panjab Including a Residence in those Countries from 1826 to 1838*. London: R. Bentley.

Nadiri, Khalid Homayun. 2017. "Brokers, Bureaucrats, and the Quality of Government: Understanding Development and Decay in Afghanistan and Beyond." PhD diss., The Johns Hopkins University.

Nawid, Senzil. 1997. "The State, the Clergy, and British Imperial Policy in Afghanistan during the 19th and Early 20th Centuries." *International Journal of Middle East Studies* 29 (4): 581–605.

———. 1999. *Religious Response to Social Change in Afghanistan, 1919–29: King Aman-Allah and the Afghan Ulama*. Costa Mesa, CA: Mazda.

Olcott, Martha B. 1981. "The Basmachi or Freemen's Revolt in Turkestan 1918–24." *Europe-Asia Studies* 33 (3): 352–69.

Penati, Beatrice. 2007. "The Reconquest of East Bukhara: The Struggle against the Basmachi as a Prelude to Sovietization." *Central Asian Survey* 26 (4): 521–38.

Peszkowski, Robert. 2012. "Reforming Jombesh: An Afghan Party on Its Winding Road to Internal Democracy." Kabul: Afghanistan Analysts Network.

Planhol, Xavier de. 1993. *Les Nations du Prophète: Manuel Gèographique de Politique Musulmane*. Paris: Fayard.

———. 2009. "Kabul ii. "Historical Geography," *Encyclopaedia Iranica* 15 (3): 282–303. Accessed December 30, 2012. http://www.iranicaonline.org/articles/kabul-ii-historical-geography.
Poullada, Leon B. 1973. *Reform and Rebellion in Afghanistan, 1919-1929: King Amanullah's Failure to Modernize a Tribal Society*. Ithaca, NY: Cornell University Press.
Roy, Olivier. 1984. "The Origins of the Islamist Movement in Afghanistan." *Central Asian Survey* 3 (2): 117–27.
———. 1988 "The Origins of the Afghan Communist Party." *Central Asian Survey* 7 (2–3): 41–57.
Samady, Saif R. 2001. "Modern Education in Afghanistan." *Prospects* 31 (4): 587–602.
Sakata, Lorraine Hiromi. 2002. *Music in the Mind: The Concepts of Music and Musician in Afghanistan*. Washington, DC: Smithsonian Institution Scholarly Press.
Schetter, Conrad. 2005. *Ethnicity and the Political Reconstruction in Afghanistan*. Working Paper No. 3, Zentrum für Entwicklungsforschung.
Shahrani, M. Nazif. 1979. *The Kirghiz and Wakhi of Afghanistan: Adaptation to Closed Frontiers and War*. Seattle: University of Washington Press.
———. 1984. "Introduction: Marxist 'Revolution' and Islamic Resistance in Afghanistan." In *Revolutions and Rebellions in Afghanistan: Anthropological Perspectives*, ed. M. Nazif Shahrani and Robert L. Canfield, 3–57. Berkeley: University of California Institute of International Studies.
Shahrani, M. Nazif, and Robert L. Canfield, eds. 1984. *Revolutions and Rebellions in Afghanistan: Anthropological Perspectives*. Berkeley: Institute of International Studies, University of California.
Sharan, Timor. n.d. *The Power Dynamics of Informal Political Networks and Statehood: Three Decades of Violence, Intervention and Conflict (1978-2014)*.
Slobin, Mark. 1970. "Music and the Structure of Town Life in Northern Afghanistan." *Ethnomusicology* 14 (3): 450–58.
Survey of Progress 1961-62. 1963. Royal Government of Afghanistan.
Thackston, Wheeler M. 1996. *The Baburnama: Memoirs of Babur, Prince and Emperor*. New York: Oxford University Press.
"Uncertainty over Security Pact Drives Final Nail into Afghan Bubble." 2013. Reuters, December 18.
Weinbaum, Marvin G. 1977. "The Legislator as Intermediary: Integration of the Center and Periphery in Afghanistan." In *Legislatures in Plural Societies: The Search for Cohesion in National Development*, ed. Albert F. Eldridge, 95–121. Durham, NC: Duke University Press.
Yousefzai, Baqui. 1974. "Kabul University Students: A Potential Political Force?" In *Afghanistan in the 1970s*, ed. Louis Dupree and Linette Albert, 167–82. New York: Praeger.

5

WEBS AND SPIDERS: FOUR DECADES OF VIOLENCE, INTERVENTION, AND STATEHOOD IN AFGHANISTAN (1978–2016)

Timor Sharan

Introduction

"More questions? Your team was here just three months ago. What benefit would your questions bring to me? The river is dry, and all our crops are destroyed. We have nothing to eat," Baba Kohisaaf uttered, looking straight into my eyes with suspicion but also, a longing for compassion. Baba Kohisaaf was a little over sixty but looked much older as years of war and poverty had left their mark.

The Yamchi village in the Sayyad district of the Sar-i-Pul province of northern Afghanistan is an ethnic Uzbek village, located on a dry, barren hilltop. The agricultural land around the village is predominately *Lalma* (rain-fed) and rises over a plain of stepped, terraced fields with a few irrigated plots of land on both sides of an ephemeral river-stream. The village is home to roughly one hundred families. The influence of the famous ethnic Uzbek strongman, Abdulrashid Dostum, is visible in the Sayyad district and in the village itself through the district governor and several commanders who occupy key positions. In 2008, Afghanistan experienced one of the most devastating droughts in the post-2001 period. My Afghan colleagues and I were sent by Afghanistan Research and Evaluation Unit (AREU), an independent policy research organization based in Kabul, to the Yamchi village to carry out field research for the "Livelihood and Food Insecurity" research project.

Baba Kohisaaf's household provided an excellent case study due to their never-ending battle with poverty, a backdrop to the struggle for his daughter's divorce approval. For this, he was required to maneuver around local district and provincial government procedures while exhausting every means, legal or illegal, to achieve his goal. On one hot Sunday afternoon, I found myself taken aback by Baba Kohisaaf's recent sufferings. It was mesmerizing to hear him articulate, in broken Dari-Persian dialect, the details of his struggle. He spoke of how he had regularly bribed provincial judges. He did not comprehend the complex bureaucratic rules and procedures and felt cheated by almost every official he had dealt with. Although he was defeated by the formal system, he was able to obtain a letter from the powerful ethnic Uzbek strongman, General Abdulrashid Dostum, using a distant informal kinship connection to a neighboring village commander. The letter, of which Baba Kohisaaf did not know the contents, as he could not read and write, terrified the provincial judge who instantly approved the case. He took the letter out from his pocket, proudly saying: "I carry this letter with me everywhere. This letter is my power."

Baba Kohisaaf's story reveals that Afghanistan's modern history of nation-statehood, including in its last four decades, is dominated by a complex web of informal relations and resource competition. The story also exposes an important puzzle: how could the post-2001 Afghan state survive and maintain a degree of political order when state institutions are corrupt, weak, and fragmented and struggles to provide basic functions.[1] With the 2014 international military withdrawal, the presence of coalition forces play a role as a guarantee for stability; but it does not explain how political stability and order is maintained in large parts of the country, such as the Sayyad district, where international military forces had little noticeable presence. The answer to this puzzle lies in how the Afghan state reassembled and transformed in post-2001 international intervention as the result of power dynamics between competing *political networks* over the control of the state, which is also rooted in Afghanistan's historical and sociological process of state formation. How have these political networks embedded in state institutions and how informal institutional rules locked them in a complex system of interdependencies.

This chapter is an attempt to address Baba Kohisaaf's puzzle. It begins by outlining the post-2001 literature on the Afghan state. Section 2 theorizes the relationship between political network forms of organizations (political networks) and the institutions of Afghan state. It offers a new explanation for the relationship between these networks and the state, one that is situated in the analysis of political networks constituting the state. It contends that Afghanistan's last four decades of violence, intervention, and statehood have been shaped by power struggles between competing jihadi political-military networks (known as *tanzims*) and new Western ones that emerged in the post-2001 period with the support of international state-building over the control of the state. In Afghanistan, political networks are a distinct *hybrid hierarchical structure whose members share power and resources through informal and constantly renegotiated deals and pacts*. Both the former jihadi political networks and those established after 2001 are hierarchically arranged around a charismatic leader (for example, Abdulrashid Dostum,

Gul Agha Shirzai, Commander Raziq, Mohammad Mohaqqeq, Hamid Karzai, Haji Zahir Qadir, Hanif Atmar, and Karim Khalili) while retaining network-like structures in terms of their institutional arrangements, patterns of exchange, and flows of resources. Political networks are dependent on each other's power and resources for political outcomes in an informally structured and continuously renegotiated arrangement. Section 3 shows how political networks maintain themselves within the post-2001 state by practicing three main institutional rules: (a) patron-client relations in expanding their political network, (b) opportunism and rent-seeking to pay off for their political networks, and (c) instrumentalization of identity-based divisions to maintain links with the constituencies they claim to represent and mobilize in moments of contestation like the parliamentary and presidential elections. It concludes that these institutional rules are important for political stability and order in post-2014 Afghanistan.

The State since the 1990s: Collapse, Fragmentation, and Reassembling

The collapse of the Soviet-backed Najibullah regime in 1992 resulted in the fragmentation of the Afghan state and society with each mujahideen *tanzim* leader and commander controlling different strategic regions of the country (Rubin 1995).[2] Once in Kabul, the power dynamics among *tanzims* interlocked them in a power struggle over the control of the state (Roy 1990; Shahrani 1998). None of the *tanzims* could keep military hegemony, and none was willing to compromise with its rival. The result was three years of intense civil war in Kabul between rival *tanzims* over the control of the city (Dorronsoro 1995).

While most analyses of the 1990s are rich in highlighting the nature and impact of Afghanistan's state collapse and fragmentation, the post-2001 literature has focused on the role and impact of international efforts to build formal state institutions (Ottoway and Lieven 2002; Ghani, Lockhart and Carnahan 2005; Rubin 2006). Maley (2002, 2006) and Goodson (2003) highlight the failure of the international community at Bonn to resolve elites' divisions and their impact on state rebuilding. Suhrke, examining the impact of the international peacebuilding effort, suggests that donors have created a "rentier state" because of their "tight embraced" approach to state building (2009, 243–44). She argues that the Afghan state has become closely tied to the power of foreign troops and capital, which essentially undermine the legitimacy of the state. Ghani, Lockhart and Carnahan (2005) assert that the Afghan state suffers from a "sovereignty gap" because of its primary dependence on donors, a condition characterized as "quasi-sovereignty" by Jackson and Rosberg (1982). Both of these studies condition the survival of the state to the continuation of international funds and military presence.

Many of the above analyses characterize the post-2001 Afghan state as "weak," "fragile," "corrupt," and even as a "narco-state." This characterization of the Afghan state is consistent with the dominant liberal peace evaluation, which measures success in terms of the state's formal institutional capacities to exercise autonomy and sovereignty. According to this institutionalist approach to statehood, it is hardly surprising that many of the above analysts are skeptical about the survival of the state in post-2014 Afghanistan, given their focus on the role of formal institutions in providing a structural framework to contain inter-elite competition. Evidently, the skeptics have few resources with which to explore the nature of statehood and stability of post-2001 Afghanistan when this does not conform to their liberal democratic statehood assumptions and criteria. These studies neglect the more important informal politics of state-building: the role and power dynamics of endogenous political networks and their informal institutional rules in use, such as patronage, illegality, and opportunism.

A number of studies have attempted to address these inadequacies by employing various micro-level analyses to explain the nature of statehood in Afghanistan. Giustozzi (2004 and 2007) and Mukhopadhyay (2009) highlight the role of warlord politics and strongman politics, which they argue have guaranteed stability. Bhatia and Sedra (2008) expose the central role of local commanders and power brokers in the constitution of the Afghan army. In a more insightful account, Goodhand (2010) underlines the role of a war economy in supporting the Afghan state. Recent policy studies have somewhat crudely positioned the Afghan state alongside the predatory elites and their corrupt practices (Cordesman 2010). A more comprehensive account of the post-2001 state and statehood is provided by Coburn (2011), who examines the dynamics of endogenous social groups in the small Afghan town of Estalif, north of Kabul, to explain how stability is maintained in that small region, where the state seems to be a mere "useful fiction."

This analysis draws on these studies but offers three important caveats. First, Afghanistan's three decades of conflict and development cannot be reductively framed in relation to the role of elites and their actions. It starts from the position that elites must be framed in relation to the political network forms of organizations (political networks) that they constitute and represent. This study considers political networks as a unit of analysis. The analysis presents the argument that political power is assembled and flows through political networks in the state. Second, the state in Afghanistan cannot be treated as a unitary entity, exhibiting an unproblematic and uniform organizational structure. We must concur with recent studies of the anthropology of the state in Central Asia, which view the state as a "contested field," subject to material and symbolic competition and conflict between rival political forces (Collins 2009; Schatz 2004; Reeves 2014; Rasanayagam 2011). The post-2001 state in Afghanistan is essentially a "complex strategic terrain," to use Jessop's (2000, 4–9) phrase, where competing local political networks occupy key strategic nodes, then attempt to expand their power and interests. Third, the post-2001 state reassembling cannot be reduced to the formal agreement in 2001 at the Bonn Conference only. Post-2001 statehood and governance must be understood by analyzing the continuities and changes in the power dynamics of mujahideen political-military networks (*tanzims*) since the 1980s. As such, the role and power dynamics of former mujahideen *tanzims* and their splintered branches and their informal institutional rules are fundamental to our understanding of statehood and governance in post-2001 Afghanistan.

By the mid-1980s, seven major Sunni *tanzims* in Pakistan and eight Shi'a *tanzims* in Iran were functional, financed by the United States, Pakistan, Iran, and other countries in the war against the Soviets. These former *tanzims* (except the Hizb-i-Islami) were essentially decentralized, political-military network forms of organizations (political networks) because of their open hierarchical structures and their operational mode (Sinno 2008). They were fragmented along ethnolinguistic, tribal, sectarian, and personality lines (Shahrani and Canfield 1984; Roy 1990). The mujahideen insurgency was essentially a "network insurgency" (Mendel 2010, 734). Arquilla and Ronfeldt used the term *netwars* to describe networks in conflict, because of their network organizational structure and their network operation mode and communication lines (1996, 33). Their command, coordination, and communication could only be implemented through the informal social structure of personal network ties. This meant that they had to build extensive webs of connections with tribal chiefs, village mullahs, commanders, and community leaders to coordinate actions and achieve military objectives (Roy 1990; Shahrani and Canfield 1984).

Baba Kohisaaf's case reveals how authority and power within the post-2001 state still flows through former mujahideen *tanzim* networks, in his case, through the powerful patronage network of Junbish *tanzims* in the North. In the post-2001 period, these *tanzims* have undergone a process of restructuring in terms of their organizational capacity, internal structure, and power relations. Subsequently, they have further splintered into smaller political networks, and new Western-educated networks, closely linked to the international community, have emerged.

The 2001 Bonn Conference provided an excellent opportunity for the *tanzims* to reach a political agreement, known as the Bonn Agreement, which enabled them to constitute, reassemble, and transform the post-2001 state in their favor.[3] Under the agreed political framework, they came to control strategic parts of the Afghan state. As I have shown elsewhere, *tanzims* and centers of power were able to fill in the state administrative apparatus and the bureaucracy through their use of state positions and the dependencies created within the state (Sharan 2011). Afghanistan's national army and police were also divided among key *tanzims* (Giustozzi 2008; Bhatia and Sedra 2008). As such, the post-2001 state institutions (i.e., constitution, parliament, elections, human rights commission) and arrangements (i.e., electoral law, financing arrangements) emerged as the result of contestation, negotiation, and bargain among competing political networks across multiple administrative levels. The state bureaucracy became a shadow to, and subordinate to, political networks because their allegiance is not to the state but to the political networks that had helped them secure the position.

Political Networks and the Post-2001 State: A Conceptualization

The post-2001 political networks are open hierarchical entities arranged around a charismatic leader while retaining network-like structures in terms of their institutional arrangements, patterns of exchange, interdependent flows of resources, and reciprocal lines of information. They are a hybrid of networks and hierarchies. While entry for new members is controlled by assessed loyalty to the leader and the network, exit is easier. They are self-organizing entities with their own modes of conflict resolution and bases of legitimacy. However, the leader plays an important role as the "central node," building critical linkages outside the network while simultaneously managing the network internally (explained below). In Afghanistan, a network leader typically enjoys a strong religious and/or political appeal to a particular ethno-regional or tribal constituency.

The Power Dynamics of Political Networks within the State

In post-2001 Afghanistan, political networks exhibit a three-level interaction, involving (1) the whole network, (2) the individual network, and (3) the local community level, as depicted in figure 5.1. Each level is mutually interdependent on the other for their ability to influence political outcomes. A whole network is comprised of several competing individual networks connected to one another by a complex set of resource-power dependencies. In post-2001 Afghanistan, the relationship between members in a network and among networks are shaped mainly by patterns of resource-power dependency relations. This political-economic dimension of political networks is best reflected in the Marsh and Rhodes (1992) and Rhodes (2007) model of power dependency. Within a network, relationships among members are shaped by an asymmetry of power dynamics between those who are resource rich (e.g., money, information, expertise, and constituency legitimacy) and those who are resource poor. As Rhodes points out, bargaining is key to the functioning of political networks because game-like interactions are rooted in trust and regulated by rules of the game, which are negotiated and agreed on by network participants (1997, 53). In post-2001 Afghanistan, where uncertainty is high and institutional rules of opportunism and rent-seeking are dominant, members within the individual network and political networks within the whole network constantly negotiate and bargain over influence, allegiance, state positions and resources.

Individual networks are embedded in communities they claim to represent. This is not to say that each community is tied to a single individual network; however, several individual networks might compete in the same community

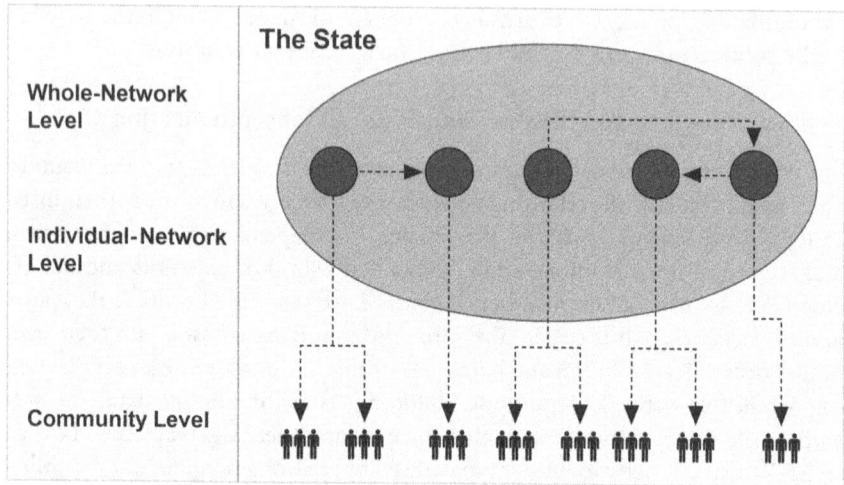

Figure 5.1. Dynamics of political networks and levels of interaction.

along identity lines for material and symbolic gain. Individual network leaders play the critical role of gluing the whole network together: ensuring internal cohesion within their network, maintaining ties with local communities, and providing connections across individual networks within the state are represented in figure 5.1 by vertical lines and horizontal arcs, respectively. In essence, network leaders function as a patron and a power broker, enabling the network to span across "structural holes" (Burt 1992) within the state and society, negotiating bargains and mobilizing support at the community level.

While individual networks tend to be relatively stable with the occasional potential for splintering, whole networks are often temporal, fluid, and spatial. Whole networks form and restructure as crises emerge and positions and resources shift. For instance, during the 2009 presidential elections, two main whole networks were established and centered around the incumbent President Karzai and his chief rival, Abdullah Abdullah. Similarly, a year later, when a Special Election Court was set up by Karzai and his clientele in the judiciary, ordering the removal of the sixty-two sitting Members of Parliament (MPs) from the *Wolesi Jirga* (lower house), two distinct whole networks were formed around the crisis, one centered around President Karzai and another around the ad hoc Support for Rule of Law grouping led by Haji Zahir (Sharan 2013). In both occasions, whole networks were composed of many individual networks, stretching from the center to the local community level.

The contingency that political networks must secure is the political network's control of safe positions within the state (i.e. the presidency, vice presidencies,

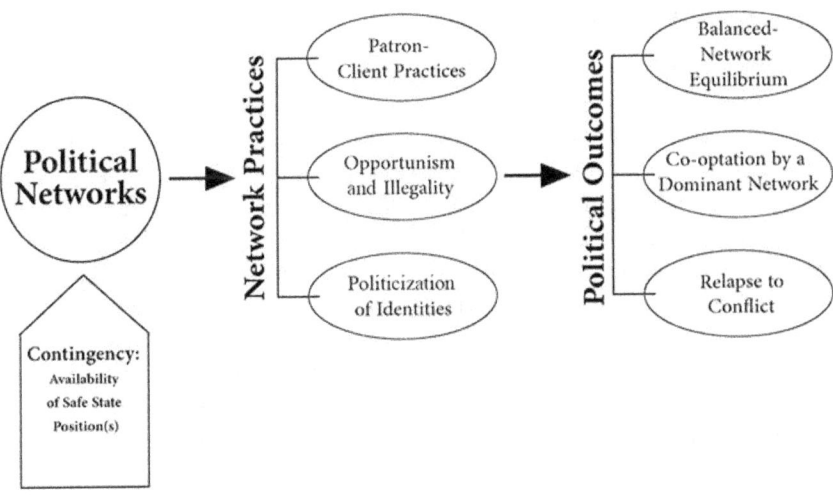

Figure 5.2. Political network practices and political outcomes framework.

ministerial positions, directorates, governors) from which it can materially and symbolically contest against potential rivals. A safe position gives the necessary legitimacy to political networks to make a claim to the state. As shown in the next section, within the state, political networks use state resources and the state's legitimacy to expand and consolidate their power and accumulate and safeguard their wealth. More importantly, their safe position gives them access to projects and contracts, helping them to shape policy in their favor. Safe positions are rarely safe for long because in a situation of a "contested field" dictated by the asymmetry of power and resources, competing political networks try their best to undermine their rival's safe position.

A political network is successful when it can (1) sustain and consolidate its political power within the state, (2) collect financial gains, and (3) maintain strong ties with their local communities. A political network must achieve at least two of the above functions to be successful. The ability of political networks to perform these functions is bound to vary. Some political networks might enjoy having financial wealth but have a low political power base (constituency mobilization power) while others might hold higher mobilization power but low financial wealth. As the next section shows, in post-2001 Afghanistan, a political network success is a function of the following three main network practices or institutional rules: (1) patron-client relations; (2) opportunism and illegality for rent redistribution; and (3) instrumentalization of identity-based divisions for political mobilization in moments of contestation.

Institutional Rules and Statehood in Post-2001 Afghanistan

In post-2001 Afghanistan, political networks operate within a somewhat defined institutional context and established institutional rules which are grounded in Afghanistan's historical political-economic and political-cultural developments, especially in its last three decades of war and violence.[4] However, these institutional rules, such as rent-seeking, corruption, and instrumentalization of identities, have become closely combined and interlinked with political networks and their power dynamics. Former *tanzims* in the post-Bonn period took measures to preserve these rules making them a feature of statehood and governance. Because, as noted by Owen-Smith and Powell (2007, 603), while institutions shape the strategies and intentions of political networks and help them coordinate complex interactions between them, networks generate the categories and hierarchies that help define institutions and contribute to their efficiency or make them vulnerable.

Patron-Client Relations

The patron-client relationship is not a new phenomenon in Afghanistan. The founder of the Durrani Kingdom in 1747 established the foundation of a *networked kingdom* that his successors built upon and further expanded. The Durrani Kingdom was essentially a "collective power-sharing enterprise" among a confederation of tribes and khanates rather than a centralized monarchy; in this confederation, a council of nine tribal and ethnic chiefs *Sardars* ("Amir-i-Lashkar," the head of army) ruled the country through an expansive system of patronage and rent (Gregorian 1969, 48). Patron-client relations among them were often reinforced through strategies of interfamilial marriage, partnership, and gifts. With the collapse of monarchy rule in 1973, the model of governance and the structure of patron-client relationships was significantly transformed from an alliance of a powerful class of Durrani monarchs, landed gentry (e.g. tribal chief and khans), and mullahs, to modern political organizations. In the last four decades of war and violence, patron-client relations have been driven by the complex dynamics of a war economy, social-cultural relations, and the economics of exchange and association (Goodhand 2004).

In the international intervention and state reassembling after 2001, patron-client relations became linked with the empowered political networks. As I have shown elsewhere, political networks have been able to maintain an extensive network by offering their clientele ministerial positions, licenses, government contracts, and development funds as patronage resources (Sharan 2011). President Karzai, as a whole network leader, was able to build an expansive patronage network stretching all the way to the provinces and districts. He relied on two types of patronage relations to keep himself in power: (1) individual network power brokers and (2) middle-ranking provincial and district officials, who had come

Figure 5.3. Individual networks and their governor clientele.

to power through political networks, but within the new political environment, their position had become more dependent on him. The findings of the Killid Group on the appointment of thirty-four governors in 2013 (figure 5.3) shed light on the complex system of patronage in post-2001 Afghanistan where each individual network was given a sphere of influence in the form of control over a territorial province for resource extraction and distribution, acting as partners of the state. The ties of loyalty and reciprocity between the political network and its clients within the network and across other political networks are conceived in interpersonal dyadic terms and subject to constant negotiation. The availability of numerous political networks and the clients' ability to defect provides the client considerable leverage within the political network.

Karzai was able to rely on powerful political networks and their leaders who acted as power brokers. These included Ahmad Zia Massoud, the brother of the famous anti-Taliban commander Ahmad Shah Massoud for the ethnic Tajik clientele, Karim Khalili, Mohammad Mohaqqeq, and Sadeq Modabber among the ethnic Hazara, and the former Hizb-i-Wahdat *tanzim* members, Haji Din Mohammad (of the powerful Eastern Arsala family) and Gul Agha Shirzai (his influence in the region was based on his appointment as governor only, unlike Din Mohammad who was locally rooted), for the Eastern Nangarhar Pashtun connections, Karzai's brother Ahmad Wali Karzai for Kandahar, and Akhundzada for the Helmand links. General Dostum, the ethnic Uzbek leader of the Junbish political network, also provided some links until his relations deteriorated with Karzai in 2008 after the Akbar Bay incident (Karzai also manufactured the incident to gain leverage within the Dostum network). Other political network leaders such as Abdur Rab Sayyaf, the former leader of Etihad-i-Islami and an influential member of parliament, Sebghatullah Mojaddadi, the former mujahideen interim president of Afghanistan in 1992 and the leader of the upper house, and Pir Gilani, the leader of the Mahaz-e-Millie tanzim, were utilized by Karzai for their networking abilities and their connections among the religious groups. These individual network leaders acted as mediators or power brokers, guaranteeing some level of political order and stability. This dynamic interlocked individual networks within a bargaining and reciprocity system where they are dependent on each other's resources and power.

With the National Unity Government's (NUG) and President Ghani's emergence to power and his strong anticorruption and good governance rhetoric, there was hope that the patronage system and the power of individual networks would gradually decline and the former political order would be dismantled. However, the author's recent study into the 183 appointments by the NUG since September 2015 suggests that, in fact, old patron-client practices still exist, but they have become transformed and sharpened, with a strong ethnic element, between the former jihadis on one hand and the Western-educated technocrats on the other (Sharan 2016). A look at the list of cabinet ministers and advisers to the leaders of NUG reveals that the role of individual networks remains strong (figure 5.4). First, and perhaps the most obvious trend, is that the balance of power shifted from Hamid Karzai's whole network to the networks of Ashraf Ghani and Abdullah Abdullah (figure 5.3). Despite the fact that some of Hamid Karzai's former clients were co-opted by Ghani, they did not enjoy the same degree of influence: powerful and influential figures, such as the liberal reformers Rangin Spanta and Omar Daudzai, and traditional religious authorities, such as Ishaq Gailani and

Figure 5.4. Individual networks and cabinet clientele.

Abd Rab Rasul Sayyaf, were no longer part of the politically influential circle. In fact, many of Karzai's clients and supporters were sidelined by technocrats (whose own networks were weak and limited); even prior to the 2014 elections, Ghani had sidelined the strongmen and warlords (such as Matiullah Khan) that the West and Karzai favored by elevating loyal technocrats to power. This was best seen in the appointment of Western-educated liberals as governors in Herat, Kandahar, Kunar, and Kunduz, most of whom were his allies during the election campaign.[5] Abdullah, on the other hand, tried to empower his former northern jihadis—whom Karzai had repressed (such as Mohammad Mohaqqeq, Mohammad Khan, and Abdul Hadi Arghandiwal)—and elevate their client-members to the posts of governor and senior officials within the NUG administration.

Moreover, an analysis of the nominations of cabinet ministers suggests that the power and influence of individual network leaders, such as Mohammad Mohaqqeq, Mohammad Khan, and Abdul Hadi Arghandiwal, increased significantly.

Illegality and Rent Seeking

Maintaining a political network is expensive, especially where there are multiple patrons and the exit for clients easy. Financial acquisition and then, distribution, plays an instrumental role in helping to remain competitive, otherwise members would be co-opted by the rival.

With increased international aid and the demand for logistical support to the NATO forces in Afghanistan, resource extraction through illegal means such as violence, extortion, and land grabs by members of individual networks have become an important institutional rule. Illegality and rent-seeking is achieved through various means such as state links (e.g., access to information, financial assets, and coercion), licit and illicit business links (e.g. Kabul Bank, drug trade, private security firms), and development aid and contracts.[6] Most of these individual networks and their clienteles, together, have established a monopoly over licit and illicit trades, government contracts, development aid, and extractive industries. According to a recent United States Institute of Peace (USIP) report, more than forty MPs are involved in illegal extraction from mines in Afghanistan. Interestingly, most of these profitable contracts were linked to the NATO-led coalition operation, which indirectly and unwittingly fueled illegality and illicit economic activities in Afghanistan.[7]

The crisis experienced by Kabul Bank, Afghanistan's largest bank until 2010, exposed the complexity and extensiveness of the connections across Afghanistan's political, financial, and administrative institutions and structures. According to the investigation into the corruption within the bank, the bank had become the "unofficial arm of the Karzai government," helping corrupt elites transfer money to offshore accounts (Bijlert 2011). On the list of 200 people involved in receiving irregular loans from Kabul Bank, there were 103 MPs, several governors, and some ministers (Bijlert 2011). Of the total amount of debt owed to Kabul Bank amounting to $982.6 million, $75 million in bribes paid by the bank, a substantial amount, had gone to MPs and other powerful officials, including the governor of Balkh province, Atta Mohammad Noor, and the former first vice president, Qaseem Faheem (*Unfinished Business* 2014).

Several recent studies have highlighted the increasing involvement of influential regional governors, such as the governor of Balkh province, Atta Mohammad Noor, and former governor of Nangarhar, Gul Agha Shirzai, in illegal activities (Mukhopadhyay 2009; Hakimi 2012). The US House of Representatives' 2010 report, one of the most comprehensive investigative studies into the contracting of US funds, found that Shirzai was directly and indirectly partnering with several logistics and security companies in Nangarhar which provided services to the host nation trucking (HNT) contract (Tierney 2010). The HNT was one of the most lucrative contracts in Afghanistan, worth $2.16 billion, split among eight Afghan, American, and Middle Eastern companies to provide logistics (e.g., food, supplies, fuel, and ammunition) for the NATO forces in the Eastern region. The report concluded that most of the money had gone into the pockets of warlords, including to Gul Agha Shirzai and criminal networks.

In post-2001 Afghanistan, illegal activity and rent seeking seems to be fundamental to the survival of the individual networks and key to the survival of the state. The combination of patron-client practices and illegal activity has interlocked political networks and their clientele into long-lasting interactions. However, these two institutional rules on their own are not enough to help political networks survive. Most political networks attempt to maintain a close tie with their local communities to secure a degree of legitimacy and cover their illegal practices. While rent might help buy loyalties, political networks still need communities as an additional bargaining card in political exchange, especially in moments of high contestation like the elections (also see, Chapter 6 in this volume).

Instrumentalization of Identity-Based Divisions

It is widely accepted that the three decades of violence and conflict had a major impact on the intensification of identity-based divisions in Afghanistan, especially on the basis of ethnicity (Dorronsoro 1995; Maley 1998, 2002; Wimmer and Schetter 2003; Simonsen 2004). The eruption of civil war in the 1990s, in part, had roots in the historical discriminatory policies of the former regimes who manipulated Afghanistan's religious, tribal, ethnic, and linguistic differences to expand their rule (Emadi 2010, 5). Historically, the Durani rulers had always attempted to retain a degree of legitimacy by repositioning themselves along identity lines (Shahrani

1986). However, the war strengthened the link between the former jihadi *tanzims* and specific ethnic and tribal communities, instrumentalizing ethnic markers.

In the international state building effort after 2001, ethnic divisions have become further sharpened (Wimmer and Schetter 2003). As I have shown elsewhere, politicization of identities provides a powerful mask for political networks to pursue their illegal and rent-seeking practices, whether it is to elect a new parliament speaker, subcontract a project, or grab land in a district (Sharan 2013; Sharan and Heathershaw 2011 2009). Moments of contestation like the 2009 and 2014 presidential elections shows ethnic divisions must be understood as a combination of political network competition over access to state resources and battles over primordial identities. Regular ethnic tension and conflict between the MPs in the *Wolesi Jirga* over vote of confidence for cabinet ministers or election of the speaker of the house has become a daily routine.

To sum up, in post-2001 Afghanistan, identity-based solidarity has offered an excellent cover for political networks and elites to hide their rent-seeking practices. These practices have been carried out within a state that provides a framework for interpolitical network competition, compromise, and accommodation. Political order and state survival is achieved through the mutually reinforced practices of patron-client relations, opportunism, and illegality as well as the politicization of identity-based divisions, which feeds into and feeds off the governance and state institutions at all levels. This is not to say that state institutions are irrelevant, but they are made meaningful as the result of competition for power and conflict and compromise between rival political networks in their day-to-day performances.

Conclusion

The post-2001 statehood and governance of Afghanistan is mainly rooted in its last four decades of conflict and violence. In post-2001 Afghanistan, political networks have come to play an important role in reassembling and transforming the state in their favor. Interactions over the past four decades among competing political networks has established a set of institutional rules which shape and guide their day-to-day practices. This chapter highlighted and discussed in detail the three main institutional rules of patron-client relations, illegality and rent seeking, and instrumentalization of identities as the key features of governance and statehood in post-2001 Afghanistan. The power dynamics of political networks and their established institutional rules have interlocked them into a complex system of resource and power interdependency. This has essentially produced a "networked state" which does not fit in the classic neoliberal categorization of the state as "weak," "strong," or "failed." The post-2001 Afghan state is somehow stable, and political order was mainly maintained during the Karzai era. In post-2014 National Unity Government, the carefully balanced power dynamics maintained by President Karzai has been undermined with a new Western reform dominated network around President Ghani actively sidelining the former Jihadi networks. President Ghani has tried to change the established rules of the game and weaken political networks.

Although the balance has been restructured slightly in favor of Ashraf Ghani's Western-educated technocrats, Ghani continues to encounter significant resistance from jihadi political networks. As shown elsewhere, these changes have intensified power struggle among these competing political groupings leading to further ethnicization of politics in post-2014 Afghanistan.[8] It appears that these political networks are deeply entrenched in the political system and any significant change at this stage seems a distant reality.

TIMOR SHARAN is the Deputy Minister of Policy and Program at Independent Directorate of Local Governance. He holds a PhD in Politics from the University of Exeter and an MPhil in Development Studies from University of Cambridge.

NOTES

1. The classic liberal peace choice theory expects states either to reform by pursuing shock-therapy democratization, principally through multiparty elections, or collapse following an intervention. It asserts that for the state to survive it must provide certain basic services to its citizens, exercise autonomy, and possess coercive capacities.

2. Ismail Khan, a Jamiat-i-Islami commander, occupied the West, Wahdat-i-Islami controlled the Central regions, and Hizbi-Islami dominated part of the South and Southeast. In Balkh province, Wahdat, Junbish and Jamiat *tanzim* commanders clashed with one another to control the provincial state before General Dostum emerged victorious.

3. At the Bonn conference, four main groups were invited by the international community. The first group was the Northern Alliance (NA) jihadis, a loose coalition of former mujahideen groups who had fought one another during the civil war (1992–1996) but had formed a united front to counter the Taliban offensive. Among them, the most dominant political network was Jamiat *tanzim* which, in turn, was dominated by its military wing, the Panjsheris of Shura-yi-Nizar. The Rome group was associated with the former King, Zahir Shah. The Peshawar group was linked to Gilani, supposedly representing the old seven Sunni mujahideen groups in Pakistan. The final group—known as the Cyprus group—was associated with Humayoun Jareer in Iran. The Rome group was selected to balance and represent the Western interests, and the NA were the winners against the Taliban, while the two smaller groups were arguably selected to please Afghanistan's neighbors, in particular, Iran and Pakistan.

4. This analysis employs Douglass North's definition of institutions as "humanly devised constraints that structure human interaction. They consist of both informal constraints (sanctions, taboos, customs, traditions, and codes of conduct), and formal constraints (constitutions, laws, property rights)," or simply, the "rules of the game" (1990, 1–2).

5. See for example, Matta (2015), "The Failed Pilot Test."

6. See Wissing (2012) for supportive data.

7. See Tierney (2010). The report was prepared by the majority staff of the Subcommittee on National Security and Foreign Affairs of the Committee on Oversight and Government Reform.

8. See Sharan and Bose. 2016.

Bibliography

Arquilla, John and David Ronfeldt. 2001. *Networks and Netwars: The Future of Terror, Crime, and Militancy*. Santa Monica, CA: RAND Corporation.

Bhatia, Michael, and Mark Sedra. 2008. *Afghanistan, Arms and Conflict*. London: Routledge.

Bijlert, M.V. 2011. "The Kabul Bank Investigations: Central Bank Gives Names and Figures", *Afghanistan Analyst Network*. May.

Burt, Ronald S. 1992. *Structural Holes: The Social Structure of Competition*. Cambridge, UK: Cambridge University Press.

Coburn, Noah. 2011. *Bazaar Politics: Power & Pottery in an Afghan Market Town*. Stanford, CA: Stanford University Press.

Collins, Kathleen. 2009. *Clan Politics and Regime Transition in Central Asia*. Cambridge: Cambridge University Press.

Cordesman, Anthony H. 2010. "How America Corrupted Afghanistan: Time to Look in the Mirror," *Centre for Strategic & International Studies*, September 8.

Dorronsoro, Gilles. 1995. "Afghanistan's Civil War," *Current History* 84, January.

———. 2012. "The Transformation of the Afghanistan-Pakistan Border," In *Under the Drones: Modern Lives in the Afghanistan-Pakistan Borderlands*, ed. Shahzad Bashir and Robert D. Crews, 30–44. Cambridge, MA: Harvard University Press.

Emadi, H. 2010. *Dynamics of Political Development in Afghanistan: The British, Russian and American Invasions*. New York: Palgrave MacMillan.

Ghani, Ashraf, Clare Lockhart, and Michael Carnahan. 2005. *Closing the Sovereignty Gap: An Approach to Statebuilding*. Working Paper 253. London: Overseas Development Institute.

Giustozzi, Antonio. 2004. *Good State vs. Bad Warlords? A Critique of State-Building Strategies in Afghanistan*. Working Paper, 1 (51). London: Crisis States Research Centre.

———. 2007. "War and Peace Economies of Afghanistan's Strongmen," *International Peacekeeping* 14 (1): 75–89.

———. 2008. "Bureaucratic Façade and Political Realities of Disarmament and Demobilisation in Afghanistan." *Conflict, Security and Development* 8 (2): 169–92.

Goodhand, Jonathan. 2004. "From War Economy to Peace Economy? Reconstruction and State Building in Afghanistan." *Journal of International Affairs* 58 (1): 155–74.

———. 2010. "Who Owns the Peace? Aid, Reconstruction, and Peacebuilding in Afghanistan." *Disaster* 34 (1): S78–102.

Goodson, Larry P. 2003. "Afghanistan's Long Road to Reconstruction." *Journal of Democracy* 14 (1): 82–99.

Gregorian, Vartan. 1969. *The Emergence of Modern Afghanistan: Politics of Reform and Modernization, 1880–1946*. Stanford, CA: Stanford University Press.

Hakimi, Aziz. 2012. *The Changing Nature of Power and Sovereignty in Afghanistan*. CIDOB Policy Research project, September 12.
Heathershaw, John. 2009. *Post-Conflict Tajikistan: The Politics of Peacebuilding and the Emergence of Legitimate Order*. London: Routledge.
Jackson, Robert H., and Carl G. Rosberg. 1982. "Why Africa's Weak States Persist: The Empirical and Juridical in Statehood." *World Politics* 35 (1): 1–24.
Jessop, B. 2000. *The Strategic Relational theory of the State*. Seoul: Han-ul Publishing.
Maley William. 1998. "Introduction: Interpreting the Taliban." In *Fundamentalism Reborn? Afghanistan and the Taliban*, ed. William Maley. London: Hurst.
———. 2002. *The Afghanistan Wars*. New York: Palgrave MacMillan.
———. 2006. *Rescuing Afghanistan*. London: Hurst&Company.
Marsh, David, and R. A. W. Rhodes. 1992. *Policy Networks in British Government*. Oxford: Clarendon Press.
Matta, Bethany. 2015. The Failed Pilot Test: Kunduz's Local Governance Crisis. Kabul:Afghanistan Analyst Network.
Mendel, Jonathan. 2010. "Afghanistan, Networks and Connectivity." *Geopolitics* 15 (4): 726–51.
Mukhopadhyay, Dipali. 2009. *Warlords as Bureaucrats: The Afghan Experience*. Washington, DC: Carnegie Endowment for International Peace.
North, Douglas. 1990. *Institutions, Institutional Change and Economic Performance*. Cambridge: Cambridge University Press.
Owen-Smith, Jason, and Walter W. Powell. 2007. *Networks and Institutions: The Sage Handbook of Organizational Institutionalism*. New York: Sage.
Ottoway, M. and Lieven, A. 2002. "Rebuilding Afghanistan: Fantasy versus Reality", Washinton DC: *Carnegie Endowment for International Peace Policy Brief 12*.
Rasanayagam, Johan. 2011. *Islam in Post-Soviet Uzbekistan: The Morality of Experience*. Cambridge and New York: Cambridge University Press.
Reeves, Madeleine. 2014. *Border Work: Spatial Lives of the State in Rural Central Asia (Culture and Society after Socialism)*. Ithaca and London: Cornell University Press.
Rhodes, R. A. W. 1997. *Understanding Governance: Policy Networks, Governance, Reflexivity and Accountability*. Buckingham, UK: Open University Press.
———. 2007. "The New Governance: Governing without Government." In *Public Governance*. Vol. 1: *Theories of Governance*, ed. Mark Bevir. London: Sage.
Roy, Olivier. 1990. *Islam and Resistance in Afghanistan*, 2nd ed. Cambridge, UK: Cambridge University Press.
Rubin, B. R. 1995. *The Fragmentation of Afghanistan: State Formation and Collapse in the International System*, New Haven: Yale University Press.
Rubin, Alissa J., and Rod Nordland. 2011. "Kabul Bank Is Portrayed as a Private A.T.M for Afghanistan's Elite." *The New York Times*, March 29.
Schatz, Edward. 2004. *Modern Clan Politics: The Power of "Blood" in Kazakhstan and Beyond*. Seattle and London: University of Washington Press.
Shahrani, M. Nazif. 1986. "State Building and Social Fragmentation in Afghanistan: A Historical Perspective." In *The State, Religion, and Ethnic Politics: Afghanistan, Iran, and Pakistan*, ed. Ali Banuazizi and Myron Weiner, 23–74. Syracuse, NY: Syracuse University Press.

———. 1998. "The Future of the State and the Structure of Community Governance in Afghanistan." In *Fundamentalism Reborn: Afghanistan and the Taliban*, ed. William Maley. London: Hurst and New York: Columbia University Press.

Shahrani, M. Nazif, and Robert Canfield, eds. 1984. *Revolutions and Rebellions in Afghanistan: Anthropological Perspectives*. Berkeley: Institute of International Studies, University of California.

Sharan, Timor. 2011. "The Dynamics of Elite Networks and Patron-Client Relations in Afghanistan." *Europe Asian Studies* 63 (3): 1109–27.

———. 2013. "The Dynamics of Informal Political Networks and Statehood in Post-2001 Afghanistan: A Case Study of the 2010–2011 Special Election Court Crisis." *Central Asian Survey* 32 (3): 336–52.

Sharan, Timor, and Srinjoy Bose. 2016. "Political Networks and the 2014 Afghan Presidential Elections: Power Restructuring, Ethnicity, and State Stability." *Conflict, Development and Democracy* 16 (6): 613–33.

Sharan, Timor, and John Heathershaw. 2011. "Identity Politics and Statebuilding in Post-Bonn Afghanistan: The 2009 Presidential Election." *Ethnopolitics* 10 (4): 297–319.

Simonsen, Sven Gunnar. 2004. "Ethicizing Afghanistan? Inclusion and Exclusion in Post-Bonn Institution Building." *Third World Quarterly* 25 (4): 707–39.

Sinno, Abduulkader H. 2008. *Organizations at War in Afghanistan and Beyond*. Ithaca, NY: Cornell University Press.

Suhrke, Astri. 2009. "The Danger of a Tight Embrace: Externally Assisted Statebuilding in Afghanistan." In *The Dilemmas of Statebuilding: Confronting the Contradictions of Postwar Peace Operations*, ed. Roland Paris and Timothy D. Sisk. London: Taylor & Francis.

Tierney, John F. 2010. *Warlord, Inc.: Extortion and Corruption along the U.S. Supply Chain in Afghanistan*. Washington, DC: US House of Representatives.

Unfinished Business: The Follow Up Report on Kabul Bank. 2014. Kabul: Independent Joint Anti-Corruption Monitoring and Evaluation Committee, October 2.

US House of Representative. 2010. *Warlord, Inc.: Extortion and Corruption Along the U.S. Supply Chain in Afghanistan* (2010), Report was prepared by the Majority staff of the Subcommittee on National Security and Foreign Affairs of the Committee on Oversight and Government Reform.

Wimmer, Andreas, and Conrad Schetter. 2003 "Putting State-Formation First: Some Recommendations for Reconstruction and Peace-Making in Afghanistan." *Journal of International Development* 15 (5): 525–39.

Wissing, Douglas A. 2012. *Funding the Enemy: How U.S. Taxpayers Bankroll the Taliban*. Amherst, NY: Prometheus Books.

6

MERCHANT-WARLORDS: CHANGING FORMS OF LEADERSHIP IN AFGHANISTAN'S UNSTABLE POLITICAL ECONOMY

Noah Coburn

IN A NEW building, not far from the gates of Bagram Airfield, are the offices of a recently established charitable foundation. This foundation, which also hosts a small local *shura* or council meeting of elders, does not at first brush seem different from many of the Afghan NGO (nongovernmental organization) or charitable foundation offices that have sprung up across the country in the past decade due largely to the influx of international funds. The charity distributes food to the poor and serves as a gathering point for several of the politically active residents of the area.

Discussions with Bagramis living nearby, however, reveal some of the unique qualities of the place. For example, there is a significant amount of tension between the foundation and another local *shura* that is made up primarily of former commanders and others who fought in the jihad against the Soviets. The new foundation also has a rather large number of young men who work for it or with it, and the head of the foundation, a merchant named Haji Zia, is in his thirties.[1] This is young for an area where politics have been historically dominated by patriarchal structures that reinforce respect for elders and limit the access of young people to power.

At the same time, however, Zia does not resemble some of the clean-shaven, laptop-carrying group of young, generally westernized Afghans who work for various NGOs in Kabul. As his name suggests, Haji Zia recently made the pilgrimage to Mecca an overt, public claim of piety, and while he has kinship ties to some of the area's most notorious families, he is not a commander himself. Often referred to simply as a contractor, *qarardadi*, Zia is part merchant, part commander, part philanthropist, and consummate politician, representing an emergent form of political power in Afghanistan.

This chapter asks why we have seen this seemingly new form of leadership emerging in the area around the airfield and what it says about both changes and continuities in local politics, institutions, and the relationship between state and society in Afghanistan over the past three decades. It argues that, while in many ways Zia is simply a new rendition of older patterns, he and other leaders like him represent a method of leadership that is particularly reliant on the current unstable political economy of the area.

Merchant-Warlords

With a figure like Haji Zia, it is sometimes difficult to separate fact from the stories that are now widely told about him, particularly by other young men in the area. Young men, in particular, give his story details that make it sound more like an epic tale than local history. In these tall tales and hyperboles, however, is a story about how people understand their local political economy and how they envision leadership evolving in this contested political setting.

People say that Zia comes from the poor side of a rather well-connected family. One of his paternal relatives is a well-known commander who had fought against the Soviets, but Zia's own immediate family had few resources and he was lucky to secure some work driving for several of the local Afghans who worked on the base. While working as a driver, one of these men employed on the base had inside information on the bidding process for a small construction project installing fencing. Working on the base, he could not bid on the contract himself. Instead, he partnered with Zia, who was to be the public face of the business for those on the base, while the other man fed him inside information. The strategy was effective and the two made a quick profit. Zia, however, saw this as an opportunity and quickly abandoned his initial partner. By nurturing his new contacts on the base, he hoped to win larger and larger contracts.

Now a rising businessman, it was said that he was using the influence of a relative who was a local commander to convince other Afghan businessmen to withdraw their bids through bribes and thinly veiled threats. Whether the threats were real or not, they were convincing enough for Zia to quickly pass most of his competitors for construction on the base. Eventually, he was contracted to build many of the walls that surround the base, as well as the complex road system inside and outside the base. In order to ensure that his deliveries were made on time, Zia also created arrangements with insurgents in surrounding districts, who would allow his trucks to pass through while preventing his competitors' trucks from passing. Such careful political arrangements meant that within a couple of years, Zia was one of the largest Afghan contractors on the base with many millions of dollars' worth of contracts. Around this time, however, with rumors of corruption rampant, several US military officials were arrested and sent back to the United States to face charges of collusion and accepting kickbacks from Zia and others during the bidding process.

Blacklisted by the military, Zia no longer had access to military contracts, but by this point, it was too late to stop his rise to power. He had diversified his company's work to include legitimate construction projects with other clients and well as a series of other "logistics" projects. By this point he was working on construction projects in the local bazaar, as well as further afield in Kabul, and had won other paving contracts from international funders that did not rely on the US military's list of banned contractors. As one young man whispered excitedly to me in the market, "His fame has now even reached cities like Herat and Mazar!"

Simultaneously, Zia worked to win the goodwill of the community by establishing his foundation, which distributes food to the poor on holidays and performs other charitable acts, such as helping families who had fallen on hard times with handouts. Some still speak of him as corrupt and not generous enough, but there is a grudging respect for him and a sense that at least he was giving some resources back to the community.

At his foundation, he also gathers together a *shura*, or group of about a dozen influential elders, to "advise" the foundation. These men meet regularly at the offices of the foundation and serve as a form of informal local governance, discussing local grievances against the base and resolving small-scale disputes. Most of the funding for the *shura* allegedly comes directly from Zia's various businesses, but much of the authority of the council comes from the local reputations of these men. Having this group of influential elders seems to be a direct response to criticism that Zia and his associates are too young to be so influential in local politics and that they are not respectful enough of the elders in the community, particularly those commanders who had been involved in the jihad against the Soviets.

As a result, this *shura* is also in direct competition with a local *shura* of low- to midlevel commanders in the area who were involved in the jihad. This group also meets regularly to resolve disputes and address community concerns. Members of this *shura* claimed to be the "real" representatives (*wakils*) of the area. In actuality, however, many in the community are also ambivalent about this group, which include several men associated with looting and killings during the civil war period. Perhaps feeling pressure from Zia's charity, which mobilized a good deal of the local youth, the commanders' *shura* recently established a youth branch and reached out to some young people not associated with Zia's businesses. At this point, very little remains resolved, particularly as both groups seem content to enjoy the large number of resources brought into the area by the base. It is likely, however, over the course of the next few years, that these resources will dwindle as international troops withdraw, perhaps forcing these groups to compete more fiercely for scarce resources.

In the meantime, Zia has cordial relations with some of the key government officials in the area. While he, himself, is not involved in formal state politics, his uncle did win a seat in the 2010 provincial council elections. It is also telling that when people in the area discuss this, many suggest that Zia had instructed him to run (with phrases like "they decided to campaign"). Other people think that Zia will run for office in the upcoming parliamentary elections, though he denies this. Regardless, it is clear that Zia, while perhaps not wanting to be directly associated with a national government that most in the area describe as corrupt, ineffective, and sometimes parasitical, he sees the importance of cultivating relationships with those in the state bureaucracy.

All these elements help explain why the anthropologist and the townspeople have trouble classifying Zia. He is simultaneously a merchant, contractor, and community activist with ties to the national government, the international military, local warlords, and, I was told, local insurgents. In other towns in the area further from the base, it is common to see a similar variety of different forms of political power (Coburn 2011), but it is less usual to see these different types converging into one person. By using both the individual politics of his strong personality and also the communal politics that respects local elders and suggests that he and his uncle are actually a single political unit, Zia has been able to maximize his grip on local power, and is now looking increasingly toward the national stage.

This chapter argues that while Zia's form of leadership appears new, it grows out of historical patterns reflecting the dynamism of forms of Afghan leadership. In part, the instability of Bagram's political economy has allowed a new generation of younger political leaders to arise that are taking advantage of the ongoing conflict, suggesting to some a potentially troubling future of political leadership in Afghanistan.

State, Tribe, Islam, and Other Moral Orders

Leadership, as the ability to amass various forms of social, economic, and political capital, mobilize resources, and represent a community within a certain moral framework, takes on series of guises in Afghanistan, most of which include various forms of social capital such as honor or reputation. The rich literature on political leadership in Afghanistan and neighboring areas was triggered in a large part by Fredrik Barth's study of leadership among the Pashtuns in the frontier area of Pakistan. In the area, he argued, the title *khan* "merely implies a claim to authority over others; it is a statement of a person's willingness to lead" (1959, 74). The attempts by various khans to assert this claim and the responses of men throughout the community to these claims then structured almost all political organization among the Pashtuns. This work then inspired numerous studies of the variety of ways that local political structures reinforced political positions of leadership.[2] Referred to variously as *khans, maliks, arbabs, pirs, mirabs, babas, bais, qommandons,* and *wakils*, the Afghan political landscape is dotted with various types of leaders that rely on a variety of forms of authority.

One is immediately struck both by the number of types of nonstate leadership positions in Afghanistan and the variance in the powers and shape that their authority takes. For example, the *mirab* is a leader who historically regulates the way in which water is distributed in an area. In certain areas, this is simply a mediation role between groups, in others, however, the *mirab* possesses influence and authority that reaches far beyond simply the allotment of hours of water for irrigation (Coburn 2011, 2013). Part of this is the way that different areas, even those very close to each other, experienced the past thirty years in very different manners, creating different political economies. For example, some villages in the Shomali near Bagram were razed by the Taliban while others were bypassed almost completely. More recently, development projects from the base have greatly favored certain areas over neighboring communities. This has shaped the way that resources are distributed and what potential leaders must do in order to gather them. More generally, however, there have always been multiple sources of political legitimacy in Afghanistan that are often in tension with each other.

The clearest divide, historically, is the divide between areas controlled by the national government and the areas left to "unruly" tribes, sometimes referred to as *Yagistan*. As Thomas Barfield argues, much of Afghan history is the push and pull between the state, based primarily in the cities, and the tribes in Yagistan over resources and autonomy (Barfield 2010, chap. 2).[3] This has created a "Swiss cheese style" of governance where the state controls certain pockets of populations, but other areas are largely autonomous. These divides, then, create opportunities for the leaders that are best able to manipulate them. In fact, the "pure" technocrat sitting in Kabul and the "pure" tribal leader who has no interaction with the state are not particularly strong or dynamic leaders in Afghanistan historically.[4] Instead, those that thrive can cross these borders and adapt to changes. Sometimes this is through raiding, other times it is it through simple trade, and occasionally it is a mixture of both. Zia is not of the state but takes advantage of its existence. He trades on his various forms of political capital and the blurred nature of sovereignty in Afghanistan.

Further blurring these boundaries are the various forms of political legitimacy found in Afghan political society. As David Edwards describes, historically in Afghanistan, Islam, honor and rule "represent moral orders that are in many respects incompatible with one another" (1996, 4). Indeed, in Istalif, the town where I previously conducted research, the leadership roles generated by these orders were in many ways distinct and difficult to combine. It was difficult, for example, for a religious man to defend his honor in certain moments, whereas an official associated with the state was likely to be thought of as both dishonorable and unlikely to be pious (see Coburn 2011, chap. 6).

The fact that these different moral orders exist give young men in the town a variety of ways of rising to a leadership position. Young men who studied religiously could eventually become mullahs, while those that worked to resolve disputes between associates might become *maliks*. There was a certain flexibility in the route that one chose based on individual preference, but once one became a mullah, it was difficult to have the same reputation for being honorable like a *malik*, and inversely, once one became a *malik*, it was difficult to be perceived as pious. Young men thus have the opportunity to navigate the incompatible moral orders described by Edwards in a way that older men do not.

In Istalif, however, the effects of the intervention were rather minimal. Some aid had entered the district, but not enough to seriously disrupt the political economy. This was in sharp contrast with the political and economic instability around Bagram that created more dynamic models of political leadership.

Dynamic Leadership in Afghanistan

Ethnographic debates over the precise definitions of leadership types in Afghanistan miss some of the political patterns that this variety reflects. By taking a longitudinal approach to the ethnographic data to understanding leadership, as suggested by Shahrani (1986), the first thing that one notices is the dynamism of leadership forms in Afghanistan, particularly, but not exclusively, in times of upheaval. Two cases suffice in suggesting that forms of political leadership in Afghanistan have never been entirely stable.

Among the Kirghiz of the Pamirs, studied extensively by Shahrani, the key leader, referred to as the *khan*, gained his influence through his control and manipulation of resources, and "tyranny and oppression have had little or no part in the process" (1986, 10). The way the khan has manipulated resources, however, has changed. In the 1930s and 1940s, the khan gained much of his influence by hosting government officials and extracting resources to "feed" them, as well as using the drafting of young men as another means of extracting resources from the community. Starting from the 1950s, after establishing direct contact with the Afghan king, the Kirghiz Khan was able to extract more and more aid from the government. This reversed the flow of resources, allowing him to extract less from other Kirghiz (Shahrani 1986). Following the communist coup, however, and a period in Pakistan, the khan used the ties of Turkic brotherhood to have the entire community relocated to eastern Turkey. Here, as representatives of the people to the Turkish government and media, the khans status shifted again, and tellingly, Kirghiz Khan became referred to using the Turkish term *Agha* instead of khan (Shahrani 2002, epilogue).

In the case of Uzbeks in the north of Afghanistan, khans build their reputation based on their ability to command resources and exercise their influence among potential followers. One of the places where this took place both metaphorically and in concrete form was during *toois*, of circumcision, or marriage festivals used as an excuse to hold *buzkashi* matches (studied extensively by

G. Whitney Azoy [2012]). As Azoy argues, khans demonstrate their strength in part by owning horses and riders who win on the *buzkashi* field, but on a higher level, real influence is demonstrated by the ability to host a *tooi* that is attended by a large number of followers. Conversely, holding a *tooi* that is poorly attended is then a great mark of shame.

The game changed, however, as leadership and resources changed during the jihad against the communist government. Forced into exile in Pakistan, khans now had access to different resources that reshaped how *toois* were held. For example, one khan that Azoy refers to as Aid Khan hosted *toois* aimed at the diplomats and relief workers living in Peshawar. Now these displays of influence were used to gain international resources, rather than local reputation.

There are numerous other examples of the ways in which Afghan leaders have adapted to changes in the political economy and shifts in the availability of resources, ranging from tribal leaders who led militias during the jihad, to the way in which these former commanders have more recently moved into a variety of businesses. In each of these cases, however, changes in the political economy have resulted in a shift in how leadership is established.

Bagram

Sitting outside the gates of Bagram, the flurry of activity on any given day is impressive. Indian and Pakistani businessmen sit in local teahouses. They negotiate the sale of a range of food stocks and supplies found in most Afghan bazaars but also deal in heavy construction equipment, barbed wire, and HESCO bags, canvas and wire mesh security barriers that are used in building military installations but which are increasingly being used by businesses and rich individuals. The men barely look up as a NATO convoy roars through town.

In such a setting, the skills necessary are less about the actual business of construction or logistics but become a complex game of arranging partnerships. In such a setting, particularly as spending increased with Obama's surge, local political brokers thrived. This is the setting that Haji Zia emerged from. With his businessman's approach to the base, he quickly learned the language of contracting and subcontracting. He made contacts on the base, both among higher ranking officers and among their subordinates, who he involved in manipulating the costs of various projects, allegedly paying them in cash.

At the same time, however, Zia has maintained his contacts in the community and among various commanders. Giving back to the local community has won him the respect of many, particularly in the face of a state that failed to provide its citizens with much development aid. Local commanders have provided him with the threat of violence in return for economic capital and access to base resources. Yet, he has kept enough distance between himself and these commanders that he was not involved in any of the human rights accusations against various leaders in the area. In an era when young people, in particular, no longer had the memory of the jihad against the Soviets, a time when many commanders earned their credentials, communities were weary of the role of these former commanders. As likely to be remembered for fighting the Soviets as they are for their role in the devastating civil war or in the inequitable distribution of resources following the initial US invasion, the commanders' *shura* at Bagram no longer had the monopoly on local authority that it had before.

In this setting Zia's youth actually works in his favor. It allows him to disassociate himself with the past crimes of many of the local commanders, even while he pays his respects to some of them through things like ritualized visits. His youth similarly appeals to the neoliberal business model of many of those internationals on the base or working for NGOs. Zia plays up his role as a young businessman looking to help his community through investment. In an intervention that relied increasingly on both private contracts, but also the desire to "Afghanize" the intervention, military officials find Zia appealing.

This unique political economy that emerged from the contracts generated by the base also helps explain the shift in leadership styles from Istalif, where young men had to work to earn rather set positions, to Bagram, where a young man like Zia can carve out what is a genuinely hybrid style of leadership.

The Political Economy of Instability

Over the past decades, Afghanistan has often been ruled by those who can best control and manipulate its political economy. Barnett Rubin argues convincingly that the rise of the Taliban was due in a large part to economic issues and their ability to bring stability to roads and allow for trade (2000). The implementation of their version of Islamic justice that took advantage of Pakistani concern over access to and control of Central Asian trade routes, something that warring mujahideen factions had failed to do. As the Taliban opened roads and brought some stability, particularly to the southern part of the country, many communities that did not agree with the Taliban's ideology tolerated Taliban governance in exchange for political and economic stability. By 2001, however, the Taliban's insular policies had destroyed the economy, and when the United States invaded in 2001, the promise of economic growth helped initially drive out the Taliban.

Michael Bhatia picks up on this theme during the American occupation where the political economy had become largely dominated by international contractors and the Afghan subcontractors who benefited from the flow of resources into the country (2005). With the American public's new low tolerance for soldier casualties, the international community quickly found itself contracting many aspects of the intervention. For the most part, international contractors such as DynCorp and Deloitte, won hefty contracts for things such as training the Afghan National Police and embedding public relations consultants in various government ministries. The vast bulk of this money was awarded to international firms, who were already well connected to the US military and the United States Agency for International Development (USAID) and had professional grant writers who knew the complex language of the bureaucracy of contracting. These contractors, however, were quick to contract much of the actual work out to third-country (often times Turkish) or local firms. Often, contracts could then get subcontracted out again, until the person actually implementing the project was several layers removed from the agency awarding the funds. In many instances, this has even aided in the reemergence of the Taliban (Wissing 2012).

In earlier political periods in Afghanistan, it was generally older men who gained prestige and influence by controlling political resources. On one hand, this was because it took time to acquire material resources, such as land, but gaining reputation took time as well. In the case of the Uzbeks studied by Azoy, a man had to host smaller successful *toois*, to demonstrate his strength, in order to eventually host larger and larger gatherings.

In exile in Pakistan during the communist era, many leaders found that instead of relying on internal forms of legitimacy, granted by their peers and the wider community, they could rely on external sources. Money and weapons from the Americans and Saudis, funneled through by the Pakistanis, allowed leaders to secure their positions while ignoring some of the historical rituals, such as feasting and visiting, that reaffirmed leadership in an early era. These rituals, however, did not die and continue to maintain cultural significance.

Following the American invasion, many refugees returned to their communities to rebuild their homes. Many of the rituals of leadership returned, but sources of external capital remained. In some cases, these had shifted, but men could still secure influence by looking outside their communities, whether it was by securing a grant from an NGO, trafficking weapons, or trading in opium. Those who were able to manipulate a variety of these sources—in the same way that, in previous eras, leaders played the state and tribes off of each other—were the ones who made the greatest advances during this period.

In the case of Haji Zia and others young men like him, younger men seem suddenly able to rise to leadership positions in a way that they had not before. In part, this is simply the amount of money flooding the country from the international intervention, allowing a young man to acquire funds rapidly. However, Zia's youth also allows him a flexibility that older leaders lack. Zia is able to, at the same time, speak the language of development and counterinsurgency to base officials while speaking to local leaders about honor and the well-being of the community.

On a national level, the older generation of leaders is attempting to make a similar transition. Former commanders who led militias during the jihad have been elected to parliament or have acquired ministries. At the same time, many have branched out, first turning militias into private security companies and later, setting up construction and logistics firms. Many of the former militia leaders of the 1980s, from Ismael Khan to Mohammad Atta Noor, are, like Zia, increasingly difficult to classify. They are now government officials *and* commanders *and* businessmen *and*, in some cases, religious leaders.

The shift, however, is that in the political world of the pre-Russian invasion Afghanistan, youth like Zia were at a serious disadvantage. In most instances, it would take them years to acquire the social, religious, or economic capital to rise in their communities. Now, however, in the shadow of the international military base at Bagram, it is those that can move most easily between these nodes that have the most influence.

Leadership and Instability

As these cases indicate, shifts in the dynamics and characteristics of leadership are far from a linear process. Instead of moving gradually toward an ordered, state-centric system, at certain moments, leadership has appeared more or less predictable, depending not on ideology or notions of development as much as the political and economic conditions of the day.

For those living around the base, questions remain, however, about what the long-term effects of instability and the resulting moral contradictions in local communities will have. One striking example that I heard several times during interviews around Bagram is the phrase "Haji Zia awal yak tarjuma aadi bud" or "Haji Zia was initially an ordinary translator." This phrase was used by various speakers either to heap scorn on Zia or to praise him. For some of the members of the older generation, reference to his humble origins was meant to be humiliating and to demonstrate that his reach had exceeded his grasp. At the same time, however, young men use this phrase to praise Zia's hard work and savvy business knowledge and to point to the hope that they could also rise using hard work and the careful cultivation of political alliances.

For now, these two opinions coexist in uneasy tension, but it remains to be seen in the long run, once international funds to the country decline, whether Zia is still seen as a hero to be emulated or as a momentary aberration. Will Haji Zia's foundation continue to coexist with the local mujahideen *shura* or will these local commanders attempt to reassert themselves as the number of international troops in the area dwindles?

The very ambiguity of the situation has helped young leaders like Zia to emerge. More stability, however, could either mean a return to more historically tribal mechanisms or, less likely, a more assertive and effective state. Either of these would damage Zia's empire, since more aggressive commanders would take back the roles that they have lost, and an effective state would cut into Zia's ability to make quasi-legal deals. Instead, his influence comes precisely from instability and the ambiguity that accompanies it. He can lead because few are sure of what will happen next.

Thus, many in this emerging generation of leaders has a genuine interest in seeing this ambiguity and instability continue. With the drawdown of international troops and the reduction of aid, however, we can be sure that leadership dynamics in Afghanistan will continue to shift.

NOAH COBURN is a political anthropologist at Bennington College. He is author of *Bazaar Politics* and *Losing Afghanistan: An Obituary for the Intervention*, as well as coauthor of *Derailing Democracy in Afghanistan* with Anna Larson.

Notes

The research for this chapter was conducted with support from grants from the United States Institute of Peace (in particular, see Coburn and Larson 2014) and Bennington College. The material has been further developed in Coburn 2016.

1. Names and some signifying details have been changed throughout the text.
2. See, for example, Jones (1974), Barfield (1981), Shahrani (1986 and 2002), Edwards (1996), and Coburn (2011), among others.
3. Many of the chapters in Shahrani and Canfield (1984) also focus on this push and pull.
4. This is seen perhaps most clearly in Mukhopadhyay (2014).

Bibliography

Azoy, G. Whitney. 2012. *Buzkashi: Game and Power in Afghanistan*. 3rd ed. Long Grove, IL: Waveland.
Barfield, Thomas. 1981. *The Central Asian Arabs of Afghanistan: Pastoral Nomadism in Transition*. Austin: University of Texas Press.
——. 2010. *Afghanistan: A Cultural and Political History*. Princeton, NJ: Princeton University Press.
Barth, Fredrik. 1959. *Political Leadership among Swat Pathans*. London: Athlone.
Bhatia, Michael. 2005. "Postconflict Profit: The Political Economy of Intervention." *Global Governance: A Review of Multilateralism and International Organizations* 11 (2): 205–24.
Brown, Wendy. 2010. *Walled States, Waning Sovereignty*. New York: Zone Books.
Coburn, Noah. 2011. *Bazaar Politics: Power and Pottery in an Afghan Bazaar Town*. Stanford, CA: Stanford University Press.
——. 2013. *Informal Justice and the International Community in Afghanistan*. Washington, DC: USIP.
——. 2016. *Losing Afghanistan: An Obituary for the Intervention*. Stanford, CA: Stanford University Press.
Coburn, Noah, and Anna Larson. 2014. *Derailing Democracy in Afghanistan: Elections in an Unstable Political Landscape*. New York: Columbia University Press.

Edwards, David B. 1996. *Heroes of the Age: Moral Fault Lines on the Afghan Frontier.* Berkeley: University of California Press.

Gregory, Derek. 2007. "Vanishing Points: Law, Violence, and Exception in the Global War Prison." In *Violent Geographies: Fear, Terror, and Political Violence,* ed. Derek Gregory and Allan Pred, 205–36. New York: Routledge.

Hansen, Thomas Blom, and Finn Stepputtat. 2006. "Sovereignty Revisited." *Annual Review of Anthropology* 35: 295–315.

Jones, Schuyler. 1974. *Men of Influence in Nuristan: A Study of Social Control and Dispute Settlement in Waigal Valley, Afghanistan.* London: Seminar.

Kaplan, Amy. 2005. "Why Is Guantanamo? Theme Issue, 'Legal Borderlands.'" *American Quarterly* 57 (3): 831–58.

Larson, Anna, and Noah Coburn. 2014. Youth *Mobilization and Political Constraints in Afghanistan.* Washington, DC: USIP.

Mukhopadhyay, Dipali. 2014. *Warlords, Strongmen Governors, and the State in Afghanistan.* New York: Cambridge University Press.

Rubin, Barnett. 2000. "The Political Economy of War and Peace in Afghanistan." *World Development* 28 (10): 1789–1803.

Scott, James C. 2009. *The Art of Not Being Governed.* New Haven, CT: Yale University Press.

Shahrani, M. Nazif. 1986. "The Kirghiz Khans: Styles and Substance of Traditional Local Leadership in Central Asia." *Central Asian Survey* 5 (3/4): 255–71.

———. 2002. *The Kirghiz and Wakhi of Afghanistan: Adaptation to Closed Frontiers and War.* Seattle: University of Washington Press.

Shahrani, M. Nazif, and Robert Canfield, eds. 1984. *Revolutions and Rebellions in Afghanistan: Anthropological Perspectives.* Research Series Number 57. Berkeley: Institute of International Studies, University of California.

Wissing, Douglas A. 2012. *Funding the Enemy: How US Taxpayers Bankroll the Taliban.* Amherst, NY: Prometheus Books.

7

BORDERS, ACCESS TO STRATEGIC RESOURCES, AND CHALLENGES TO STATE STABILITY

Ahmad Shayeq Qassem

IN 1947, AS British colonial rule was coming to an end and the largest concentrations of Muslim people in the northwest and northeast portions of British India were clamoring for a separate country, the monarchic regime in Afghanistan moved to challenge the territorial integrity and national sovereignty of the incipient Muslim majority nation to its southeast. The Afghan regime's challenge to the emergence of the new Muslim majority nation called *Pakistan* was in contrast to Afghanistan's historic image, which had long served as a source of hope and inspiration to the Muslim leaders of Hindustan and even some of the pioneer advocates of an independent Pakistan.[1]

Far from advocating the emergence of Pakistan, leaders of Afghanistan effectively staked claim on parts of its territory with the assertion of the "right of self-determination" for the Pashtun inhabitants of its northwestern region. Since then, Afghanistan has repudiated the legitimacy of the border with Pakistan known as the Durand Line (Qassem 2007, 65–80). The most recent expression of this policy came in March 2014 when President Hamid Karzai's cabinet rejected any mention of the word *border* or its equivalents in a cross border security cooperation document that the Pakistani authorities had proposed to the Afghan government. The cabinet also ordered all state institutions to avoid using the term *border* or its equivalents in official correspondence and instead use the term *Durand Line* to refer to the Afghan-Pakistan boundary (Bakhtar News Agency 2014).

Afghanistan's belligerent position on the status of its border with Pakistan bears the hallmarks of at least three of the nine common justificatory categories that states have historically advanced in territorial disputes. Although never presented as a cohesive case in a single official document, the constituent elements of Afghanistan's position on the status of this border arguably rest on the notion of cultural homogeneity, economic necessity of access to the Indian Ocean, and the historic claim of sovereignty over all Pashtun regions. By rejecting the original border treaty signed in 1893 and challenging Pakistan's authority to inherit the erstwhile legacy in the region from British India, the Afghan position, in effect, also rejects the principle of *uti possidetis juris* (literally meaning "as you possess under law") and the primacy of treaties in international law (Sumner 2004, 1779–1812).

In concrete terms, the Afghan government's official statements, state-run media, and popular opinion in the past, have questioned the indeterminacy of the original border agreement, validity of the agreement in the wake of the partition of the erstwhile British India, alleged arbitrary division of the Pashtun people, and the plebiscite and tribal jirga which the British India authorities conducted in consultation with the then Frontier Congress Party's provincial government to determine whether the people of the North-West Frontier Province (now Khyber Pakhtunkhwa) and Federally Administered Tribal Areas (FATA) wanted to join India or Pakistan in 1947 (Qassem 2007).

Cross Border Ties and Domestic Ethno-Politics

Aside from the legalistic aspects and the pros and cons of the official Afghan position on the status of the Durand Line, the issue cannot be fully grasped without reference to the relevant aspects of domestic ethno-politics in Afghanistan. In the context of power politics competition among the elites of the major ethnic groups, what one could probably term as the "dictatorship of the alleged numbers" has played an instrumental role to justify the empowerment of various "ethnic entrepreneurs" in Afghanistan. Even though the ethnic configuration of the country's population, in terms of percentages, were highly controversial, ethnic power stratification of the political system has traditionally followed the downward hierarchy of the Pashtun, Tajik, and interchangeably, Hazara and Uzbek communities.

A serious challenge to the century-old Pashtun dominance of the political and military power structures in Afghanistan came first, briefly, in 1929, under the leadership of Habibullah Kalakani—an ethnic Tajik from the Kohdaman plains north of Kabul—and the second time, it came in the wake of the victory of the Afghan mujahideen with the central role that the Tajik-dominated *Jamiat-e Islami* party took in the central government as well as the consolidation of the regionalization of political power along ethnic lines elsewhere across the country in the 1990s (a process which had begun in the early 1980s).

Pashtun nationalist elites and writers obviously did not look favorably on the seemingly drastic power shift during both episodes. But what is perhaps more instructive pertains to the manner in which the more conservative Pashtun forces and the nationalists forged a common cause and brought to bear the power of extraterritorial coethnic forces to restore Pashtun ascendance in the seat of power in Kabul.[2]

The mobilization of FATA manpower and resources by Mohammad Nader Khan in connivance with the British India authorities in 1929 had proven instrumental in dislodging Kalakani from the seat of power in Kabul. It came after the deposed King Amanullah had attempted but failed to mobilize the Pashtun populace in the southwestern region to such proportions that could wrest control of Kabul as the symbolic seat of power from Kalakani's forces (Ghobar 1999, 10–20).

A somewhat similar scenario unfolded in the wake of the victory of the Afghan mujahideen and the assumption of the symbolic seat of power in Kabul by the *Jamiat-e-Islami* leaders, particularly Burhanuddin Rabbani and Ahmad Shah Massoud. The leading Pashtun-dominated *Hezb-e Islami* party under the leadership of Gulbuddin Hekmatyar in various alliances launched a fierce military campaign and effectively imposed a blockade of the capital from the south and east between 1992 and 1994, but failed to dislodge the mujahideen government. Once again, it was the mobilization of what one could probably term as "*madrasa* manpower*,*" radicalized religious zealots and cross border coethnics in FATA and Baluchistan, as well the economic resources of the cross border trucking industry and narcotics mafia with dedicated support from the Pakistani military-intelligence establishment (particularly the Inter-Services Intelligence or ISI) that finally dislodged the Tajik-dominated Islamic State of Afghanistan and replaced it in 1996 with the Taliban's Islamic Emirate of Afghanistan in Kabul and many provinces. The inescapable conclusion drawn by ethno-nationalists from these extraordinary episodes in Afghanistan's modern history evokes the notion that the manpower and resources of coethnics from across the border can potentially serve as guarantor of Pashtun ascendance in the political system in Kabul.

Another element of domestic ethno-politics and its relevance to the Afghan state's official repudiation of the border with Pakistan pertains to the instrumentalization of the power and influence of the Kuchis in Afghanistan's state structures and policies. The term *Kuchi* derives from the Dari-Persian word *Kuch*, pronounced as in "coach" in English, which means "spatial movement/migration" in the standard translation and "load" or even "household" in colloquial Dari-Persian.

Anthropologists do not agree on whether the Kuchis collectively form an ethnic group, tribe, subtribe, clan, or kinfolk, as the tag of identity overlaps with members of multiple tribes and subtribes among the Pashtuns. For the purposes of this chapter, however, it may suffice to say that the Kuchis, in effect, form a multitribal subsection of the Pashtun population with an actual or historic claim of a pastoral lifestyle in Afghanistan or Pakistan. This is not to say that there are no other nomadic communities outside the Pashtun ethnic group. There are; but their limited mobility, small numbers, and location mainly in the mountainous regions of the north and northeast have rendered them politically marginalized or completely ignored (Tapper 2008, 97–116).

Although the Afghan constitution does not provide for a genealogical definition of the term, in practice, the political institutions that were designed to give agency to the Kuchis effectively facilitate additional Pashtun representation in the political system rather than representing the nomadic population defined in terms of adherence to a particular lifestyle and mode of subsistence. It is inconceivable that a non-Pashtun living or opting for a nomadic lifestyle could qualify for the benefits that state institutions are meant to afford to the Kuchis as a distinct Pashtun community.

The Afghan constitution provides for a reserved quota of ten parliamentary seats in the lower house and two more seats in the upper house of the National Assembly (parliament) for the Kuchis, drawn from the entire territory of Afghanistan as a single electoral constituency.[3] All the Kuchi lawmakers currently in the parliament are ethnic Pashtuns coming from generations with sedentary lifestyles and with records of educational qualifications and work in the public or private sector. The constitution also includes other specific provisions that ethnic entrepreneurs can use to push for favorable treatment of the Kuchis—for example, Articles 14 and 44, that obligate the state to undertake programs for the "settlement and improvement of the life" and education of the Kuchis.

Certainly, there has been a tradition of using the Kuchis for political and military purposes and to consolidate the power of various Pashtun rulers from Emir Abdul Rahman Khan in the late nineteenth century to Mosahiban family's monarchy from 1930 to the 1970s. The Pashtun-dominated governments in Kabul used the Kuchis instrumentally in the non-Pashtun center and north of the country to pursue their policies of "internal colonialism," expropriating huge areas of pasture and farmland from the local Hazara, Uzbek, and Tajik communities, causing interethnic tension in the country. Abdul Rahman Khan used the Kuchis to subjugate the Hazara and various other uprisings in Afghanistan, and the Mosahiban rulers resettled large numbers of the Kuchis in the north of the country and arguably even used the colossal Helmand Valley Project for the settlement of the Kuchis as a secure base of Pashtun support stretching southwest from Kabul to Herat (Cullather 2002, 512–37; Patterson 2004; Ferdinand 2006; Wily 2013).

The political value of the Kuchis is not lost on contemporary ethno-nationalists and ethnic entrepreneurs either. A treatise written by "Samsor Afghan" (a pseudonym, allegedly Mohammad Ismael Yun, a Pashto literary and media figure) advocates the settlement of Kuchis along the northern borders of Afghanistan and north of Kabul as a means of securing Pashtun power in Kabul. Separately, the former finance minister and current president (since 2014) Ashraf Ghani Ahmadzai—himself claiming Kuchi descent, but who may not necessarily qualify for the term "ethnic entrepreneur"—produced a policy proposal as part of his election manifesto for using state resources to help the Kuchis so as to address the recurrent conflicts with sedentary communities along their seasonal migration routes and pastures in Afghanistan (Ahmadzai 2014, 102–6). For a trained anthropologist, it is curious that Ahmadzai's policy proposal prescribes a standard state interventionist policy and is seemingly oblivious to more community-based alternative approaches to the resolution of what is essentially an intercommunity dispute on the right of ownership and the exploitation of allegedly "common" resources.[4]

As for the border policy and the question of nomads, the ambiguity in the definition of the term *Kuchi* in the constitution and the official disregard of the border with Pakistan together represent another example of the domestic ethnopolitical use of numbers in Afghanistan. It keeps the door open to any coethnics with an actual or historical claim of nomadism to assert, de facto, Afghan citizenship and enjoy related constitutional privileges regardless of whether they hail from Afghanistan or Pakistan. Research shows that large numbers of Kuchis hail from Pakistan, where they have long settled and invested in profitable industries. Others who still travel to Afghanistan as herders do so only during the summer, while they are mainly based in Pakistan during the rest of the year (Barfield 2004).

Finally, the notion of Pashtun victimhood in both countries serves not only to preserve effective bonds across the border but also to protect indigenous resources and appropriate a disproportionate number of state resources to the region with a concomitant positive effect on the empowerment of the ethnic entrepreneur in the country's power structures. Though no dedicated research has been undertaken to study the topic in relation to the region thus far, aspects of the narrative of continued instability in the Pashtun heartlands, as promoted by ethno-nationalists in both countries, evoke the political and social psychology concept of "competitive victimhood" (Sullivan et al. 2012, 778–95).

The conception of as ruthless a group as the Taliban as "disaffected brothers," presentation of the opium growers cartel as "poor farmers," portrayal of the nomads as a "desperate" category in need of help, and even the recast of the status of Pashto in the ethno-nationalists' contemporary political nomenclature as an "oppressed" language may present a good case study of the "high-status group members"—that is, the Pashtun power elites—engaging in a "competitive victimhood" perceptional process not only for "stigma reversal" but also for "reparative politics and policies." More broadly, the notion of "Pashtun alienation" due to recent dislocations in the traditional configuration of ethnic power structures in Afghanistan and the longtime ascendance and alleged oppressive practices of the loathed "Punjabis" in Pakistan have been almost a standard staple of the descriptive and analytic assessments of the region's woes in recent decades.[5]

Hence, the importance of potential coethnic manpower and resources in Pakistan for the perpetuation of the dominant Pashtun role in Afghanistan's political structures militates against the official recognition of the Durand Line as a legitimate international border. On the contrary, state institutions such as the Ministry of Borders, Tribes and Ethnic Affairs and a number of educational institutions are meant to channel state resources to maintain cross border patronage ties with the Pashtun coethnics in Pakistan. Similarly, the ethno-nationalists have long advocated the policy of accommodation and use incentives far more than coercive measures toward the Taliban and the opium growers, allocate state resources and use affirmative action for the settlement of the nomads, and empower ethnic entrepreneurs in order to alleviate the effects of Pashtun alienation in both countries.[6]

The Mining Sector in Landlocked Territory and Ethno-Politics

Afghanistan is said to be rich in mineral resources, but the key information usually used as reference points to valuate the country's mineral deposits seems blurred in the midst of a myriad of crosscutting interests involving both Afghan and US officials in order to project optimistic economic prospects for the country. There are also difficult technical, security, and international challenges to overcome if Afghanistan is to realize the benefits of its substantial natural resources.

In 2007, the US Geological Survey (USGS), in partnership with the US Department of Defense Task Force for Business and Stability Operations (TFBSO), used an advanced airborne sensing technique known as "hyperspectral imaging" over about 70 percent of the country's territory to map the availability of mineral deposits and other surface natural resources (USGS 2007). Over the course of forty-three days and twenty-eight flights, the USGS collected data that covered approximately 440,000 square kilometers, arguably showing the "enormous size and variety of Afghanistan's mineral wealth position[ing] the country to become a world leader in the minerals sector" ("Afghanistan the First Country Mapped" 2012).

Keen to highlight the "economic arm" of their "counterinsurgency strategy" at the time, Pentagon officials seized on the USGS's pioneering airborne imaging to estimate that Afghanistan possessed mineral deposits in excess of $1 trillion (Alexander 2010). President Karzai and his cabinet ministers, even keener to attract foreign investment and present the huge Afghan bureaucracy and security forces as economically viable in the long run, put the estimate as high as $3 trillion ("Railroad Could Unlock Afghanistan's Mineral Riches" 2014).

So far, the Afghan government has awarded three major mining contracts mainly with international investors, but they all suffer from numerous challenges that have delayed the start of extraction work on the deposits. In 2007, the Afghan government awarded a thirty-year lease of the Mes-e Aynak (literally meaning, in Dari, "little copper well") copper mine in Logar Province to the state-owned Metallurgical Corporation of China (MCC) ("Q&A" 2013). Based on this author's interviews with senior Afghan officials involved in the award of the contract, the Afghan government's decision to prefer the MCC over its Canadian and Kazakhstani competitors was partly influenced by the view that China's close ties and influence over Pakistan would help secure the implementation of the contract against Pakistan-sponsored terrorist attacks. The MCC undertook to build a power plant at the site and a railroad connecting it to Pakistan's border. However, ten years have passed, but extraction work has not yet started due to security challenges and the need to excavate and protect priceless cultural artifacts reflecting the region's rich Buddhist heritage. To add to these challenges, the MCC is now asking for a revision of the terms of the contract to free it from the obligation to build the power plant and the railroad (Shahid 2013).

The second major mining project, with an even bigger potential for the country's economy, is the contract for the development and extraction of iron ore deposits in the central province of Bamian. The Afghan government awarded the major part of the Hajigak iron ore contract to a consortium of seven Indian companies led by the state-owned Steel Authority of India Ltd. (SAIL) and another, relatively smaller part of it, to Canada's Kilo Goldmines Ltd. (Najafizada 2011; Kilo Goldmines 2011). The Indian consortium initially promised to invest $10.8 billion in two equal phases in the project, which also included the construction of a 400-megawatt power plant at the site. However, they later scaled down the ambitious plan to a $2.9 billion investment with the suggestion that the full investment would be done "eventually" in several "phases" (Mehdudia 2013). Although it is not clear whether it is part of commitments in the same contract, India had also expressed interest in building a 900-kilometer rail link to connect the Hajigak mine to the Iranian port of Chabahar, partly with Indian assistance. The proposed rail link bypasses Pakistan, which has made no secret of its opposition to growing Afghan-Indian relations (Jacob and Chatterji 2011).

Another important mining project has brought together Rateb Popal—President Karzai's cousin, a former Taliban official and convicted New York heroin smuggler—with China National Petroleum Corporation (CNPC) in a joint venture to extract and process crude oil from the northern Amu Darya Basin Oil Zone (ADBOZ) in Sar-e Pol Province. Although oil extraction and processing have continued in recent years, the partnership, envisaged to expand substantially and cover even larger hydrocarbon projects in the region, is threatened by disputes over financial issues (Donati 2014).

This particular project was also challenged early by the local community, where the reigning Uzbek leader General Abdurrashid Dostum and his supporters protested the early deployment of Popal's controversial private security company known as the Watan Group for the security of the project site. The Watan Group is widely accused of giving a share of its business proceeds to the Taliban to allow for the safe passage of the International Security Assistance Force (ISAF) supply convoys that it escorted into the southern region. Research indicates that such "protection money" forms a major part of the Taliban's one hundred million dollar plus annual revenues, and the symbiotic relations between the private security companies and the Taliban bind the two sides with vested interests in perpetual insecurity (Tierney 2010).

Dostum and his supporters demanded that local people should be given a share of employment opportunities in the project rather than bringing in others from outside the region, exactly in the same way that local people were initiated into official security structures to protect the Ainak copper mine project in Logar Province. As usual, Dostum's seemingly legitimate demands were smeared by the Kabul government and international media as yet another antic of the northern "warlord." Soon thereafter, Karzai visited China to participate in the 2012 summit of the Shanghai Cooperation Organization (SCO) where Afghanistan was awarded the "observer" status. On Karzai's return, Afghanistan's National Security Council (ANSC) accused Dostum of "undermining national interest" and instructed the country's attorney general to file a criminal case against him. Kabul also dispatched hundreds of additional security personnel to beef up security and intimidate Dostum's supporters in the province. Regardless of how the controversy finally died out, the episode once again showcased Karzai's willingness to employ Afghanistan's international ties and domestic resources in the service of his highly controversial kinfolk and patronage network (Bhadrakumar 2012).

Hence, of the three major mining projects that Afghanistan awarded to international investors, the first was influenced by the imperative of security insofar as it relates to perceived ability of China to exert influence over Pakistan; the second suffers from the constraints of a landlocked geography and the acrimonious nature of relations between India and Pakistan; and the third one is mired in the politics of ethnic patronage and corruption radiating out of Kabul to the provinces. Beyond the mining sector and other domestic natural resources, the country's cherished goal of leveraging its location to serve as a "land-bridge" or crossroad of transit trade between Central Asia and South Asia can hardly be realistic without Pakistan's genuine cooperation which, in good measure, depends on the amicable resolution of the border dispute (Qassem 2011, 191–206).[7] The importance of resolving the border dispute for the future of Afghanistan is perhaps best described in the words of Dr. Rangin Dadfar Spanta, who, after years of serving as Afghanistan's national security adviser, wrote in a local Dari/Persian newspaper: "I found Pakistan as the biggest enemy of my country. Unfortunately, I must say that Afghanistan has two [alternative] ways to stability: 1-[Either] It should be under the suzerainty of Pakistan; [or] 2-It should recognise the Durand border and promise that its territory will not be used against Pakistan" (Spanta 2014).

The Unsustainable Border Dispute

Notwithstanding the occasional statements and grandstanding by some Afghan politicians, the continuation of the irredentist policy against Pakistan seems increasingly untenable due to the developments of the past forty years and the need for Pakistan's genuine cooperation toward security in Afghanistan. The irony is perhaps best exemplified by the bellicose statement of General Sher Mohammad Karimi, Afghanistan's chief of staff of the National Army, staking a claim on Pashtun regions of Pakistan "up to Attock [District]," which is anathema to the Afghan government's expectation of Pakistani cooperation toward peace in Afghanistan.[8]

A major development of the past three decades pertains to what amounts to a shift in the gravitational center of Pashtun power patronage from Afghanistan to Pakistan. From the 1950s to the 1970s, the Afghan monarchy and Mohammad Daoud's republic patronized nationalist Pashtun tendencies in Pakistan through the active pursuit of a pro-Pashtunistan policy. The Afghan regime incited Pashtun separatism and sponsored tribal forces to fight the Pakistani security forces across the border. The call for the right of self-determination for the Pashtun regions of Pakistan arguably served as a cloak for the ambition to amalgamate those regions into Afghanistan at a later stage. The policy pushed Afghanistan into the orbit of the Soviet Union's influence and estranged it from the Muslim world and the West in the context of the Cold War rivalries.

By the late 1970s, and with the Soviet intervention in the 1980s, Pakistan was able to reverse this trend with its support of the Afghan Islamists. Chief among the beneficiaries of Pakistan's countermeasure was the Pashtun-dominated Hezab-e Islami Afghanistan. In the mid-1990s, however, it was replaced by the Taliban as a more potent Pashtun-dominated Islamist group, and which has continued its violent campaign with the Pakistani security establishment's strong support to this day. Pakistan's Pashtun-led religious parties, namely the Jamaat-e-Islami Pakistan and both factions of the Jamiat Ulema-e-Islam, effectively played the role of big brother patron for the Hezb-e Islami and the Taliban. The Pakistani military-intelligence establishment used these religious parties to project lethal and subversive power in Afghanistan (Qassem 2009b 45–88).

Thus, with a much larger Pashtun population and through the close cooperation of the far more resourceful Pashtun-dominated religious parties of their own, the Pakistani military-intelligence establishment effectively shifted the pivot of Pashtun power patronage from Afghanistan to Pakistan. The roles are now reversed and the landscape has changed in such a fundamental way that the erstwhile rival claimants of Pashtun leadership, Mohammad Daoud Khan of Afghanistan and Marshal Mohammad Ayub Khan of Pakistan, may have found the situation so far-fetched as to defy imagination. President Hamid Karzai's appeals and entreaties to Pakistani leaders, including the Pashtun religious leaders of Pakistan, to help restore peace in Afghanistan is a far cry from the heyday of Afghanistan's patronage and incitement of Pashtun ethno-nationalism and separatism in Pakistan.

Another aspect of the developments in the past four decades which may loosen the traditional and rigid Afghan position on the status of the border relates to what one could possibly describe as an ideational transformation of Afghan elites and people in general about the capabilities of Pakistan as a state and its political demographics as they relate to Afghanistan. In the past, Afghanistan's irredentist claims against Pakistan partly stood on the notion of Pashtun victimhood in the Pakistani body politic, fed by pioneering Pashtun nationalists such as Abdul Ghafar Khan and their political legacy as well as the state propaganda in Afghanistan.

With the exodus of millions of Afghan refugees, 85 percent of them Pashtun from across the borders of Pakistan, extensive people-to-people interactions, and the phenomenal growth of the national and international media in recent decades, the moral and effective elements of solidarity and justice to the allegedly oppressed coethnics in Pakistan seem no longer sustainable in Afghanistan. The Afghan elites and general public are far better informed about the commitment of Pakistani Pashtuns to their country and their significant influence in Pakistani power structures. Also, they are better informed about the superior economic, diplomatic, and military capabilities of Pakistan relative to Afghanistan, rendering any aspirations of a return of the so-called Afghan territory seem more of an illusion than a realistic prospect.

The matter was perhaps best exemplified in President Karzai's speech on November 11, 2013, at the inauguration of the Afghan National Army Officers Academy, established in Kabul with British support. Addressing an audience of new cadets and staff, Karzai held out the example of the Pakistani military as a strong and disciplined role model that the Afghan cadets could aspire to emulate. Such views present a total contrast to past portrayals of Pakistanis and their country as a weak and artificial nation that the Afghans could hope to chip away at. Unlike the pre-1980s era, which the more elderly and former and current Afghan officials often tend to speak about with an air of grandeur and strength vis-a-vis Pakistan, now it is widely acknowledged by Afghan leaders, politicians, and the media that Afghanistan is no match for Pakistan in terms of coercive and economic capabilities and diplomatic skill in the international arena.

The salience of identity politics as a result of years of turmoil, migration, and ethno-factional rivalries and tensions also seems to have reduced the dispute about the border to more of a Pashtun issue rather than a national cause that elites and members of all ethnic groups could affectively (emotionally) and effectively identify with. The proliferation and availability of research materials have helped to disabuse the Afghan elites of some of the more preposterous, but previously popular, notions about the status of the border. As late as 2005, it was a commonly held view, even among many educated Afghans, that the original border agreement signed in 1893 with the then British India was valid for only a century, and expired in 1993. Many educated Afghans would even draw parallels with the status of Hong Kong, which was finally returned to Chinese sovereignty in the 1990s. Media outlets in Kabul, though very limited in number under the mujahideen government, did raise the question of the agreement's expiration in 1993, and some very senior government leaders still held the view, as late as 2005, that the validity of the border agreement had since lapsed.[9]

A telling example of the fragmentation of previously common assertions about the status of the border among perceived political elites of various ethnic groups came in the context of presidential debates between the three leading contenders in March 2014. In response to a question about the topic, the two leading candidates, with primordial tribal affinities and an alleged power base among the Ghilzai and Durrani Pashtuns, respectively—Ashraf Ghani Ahmadzai and Zalmay Rasoul—asserted the traditional Afghan position by rejecting its legitimacy and invoking the long-worn ethno-nationalist cliché that only the people of Afghanistan and those affected on both sides of the border have the right to decide how to resolve the contentious issue. In contrast, the perceived Tajik candidate, Abdullah Abdullah, acknowledged that "there are different views" about the legitimacy of the border with Pakistan.[10]

The electoral politics in post-Taliban Afghanistan imposes additional imperatives for the resolution of the border dispute. Successive elections and representative politics in the past decade seem to have reinforced the importance of cross ethnic factional and party alliances for electoral success and governance. No aspiring or incumbent Afghan leader can realistically hope anymore to succeed on the back of ethno-nationalistic politics of which the irredentist policy against Pakistan is a natural outgrowth. The need to appeal to the widest possible cross section of ethnic groups for successful election and governance can potentially disincentivize ethno-nationalism and the appeal of belligerence against Pakistan.

Another relevant factor which is favorable for the early and amicable resolution of the border dispute ensues from the independence of Central Asia and its imperatives for better Afghan-Pakistan relations. With the breakup of the former Soviet Union as a largely opportunistic supporter of the Afghan irredentist policy in the context of the Cold War and Afghanistan's declared policy to serve as a crossroad of transit trade and commerce between independent Central Asia and South Asia, the continuation of the irredentist policy is hardly the right prescription for the realization of Afghanistan and the region's economic potential (Qassem 2011, 191–206).

Last but not least, it may well be argued—though with a good measure of caution—that the core Pakistani power structures may have finally come to better appreciate the blowback effects of their policy of supporting terrorism as an instrument of foreign policy in Afghanistan. One could argue that there is no strong reason to disbelieve the notion that the leaderships of both the Pakistan People's Party (PPP) government and the incumbent Muslim League (ML-N) government under Mohammad Nawaz Sharif's successor may well be genuinely interested in the return of peace and stability in Afghanistan, but even more importantly, it is pertinent to note that Pakistan's updated "Army Doctrine," for the first time in its history, in 2013, identified homegrown militancy as the "biggest threat" to the country's national security.

Though there is no empirical research yet to substantiate a direct connection, the Pakistani military has followed its new security threat conception with air strikes and an offensive against terrorist targets in the North Waziristan region for the first time in the past decade. In fact, the Pakistani military's reticence to take action against terrorist targets in North Waziristan has been a major irritant for the United States and ISAF in Afghanistan as the region is widely reported to harbor the so-called Haqqani Network, which the former US chairman of the Joint Chiefs of Staff, Admiral Mike Mullen, described as the "veritable arm of Pakistan's Inter-Services Intelligence." The Pakistani military's offensive is said to be aimed at Tehrik-i-Taliban Pakistan (TTP) as the Haqqani network leaders are reported to have been given safe passage out of the region or pushed to fight in Afghanistan, but in view of the close ties between the Afghan and Pakistani Taliban, the question remains as to how much longer the Pakistani military can afford to comfortably distinguish between the two in pursuit of its policy of security sabotage in Afghanistan.

Conclusion

The longstanding border dispute and related acrimonious relations with Pakistan have not only profoundly affected Afghanistan's security and stability but also its ability to make effective use of its natural resources and strategic location as a crossroad of overland commerce and interaction between Central Asia and South Asia. Afghanistan's long irredentist position against Pakistan presents an unseemly mismatch with the applicable principles and provisions of international law, but finds rationale in the dynamics of subnational identity politics and the need to draw on potential extraterritorial resources to buttress certain strings of ethnic power politics within Afghanistan.

The social, structural, and ideational transformation of Afghanistan, due to decades of invasions, proxy wars, and violence as well as the significant changes in the surrounding region in the wake of the fall of the former Soviet Union, has made the perpetuation of the belligerent status quo between Afghanistan and Pakistan less sustainable. If Afghanistan were to realize its potential as a resource-rich country located in a landlocked but important geography, it would need to initiate the necessary steps toward the eventual resolution of the border dispute with Pakistan. There is no doubt that years of state propaganda, the dynamics of "competitive victimhood," and the emotional dimensions of coethnic solidarity between sections of the populace in both countries have created a hard legacy for the resolution of the issue, but it is not necessarily as intractable as it seems due to what may well amount to a deliberate lack of innovative ideas proffered by the traditional ethno-nationalist Afghan leadership.

The International Court of Justice (ICJ), for example, has resolved numerous cases of other border and territorial disputes since its inception in 1945, but it defies belief that successive Afghan regimes have never considered using the ICJ to reach an amicable resolution of *their* border dispute. Of course, the advocates of the irredentist policy, particularly those who can appreciate the fragility of the Afghan case in relation to international law, will probably never agree to the principle of ICJ arbitration on the issue. In fact, this may well be part of the reason that they often defer to the authority of national tribal institutions such as the "Loya Jirga" in cases of a domestic nature that have no concern whatsoever with Pakistan.

Afghan politicians also refer the border resolution issue to abstract notions such as the "decision of the people of Afghanistan" or the "decision of people on both sides of the border" to evade responsibility for taking on what essentially is a highly emotional matter to a large section of the Afghan society. However, there may be ways to harness the zeal of even some of the most ardent advocates of the irredentist policy toward the resolution of the issue. As a matter of both principle and pragmatism, the most educated, influential and vocal advocates of Afghanistan's territorial claims against Pakistan could very well be initiated into a state-sanctioned expert body to build the strongest Afghan case for presentation to the ICJ.

The resolution of the border dispute is essential not only to inaugurate prospects of more cordial relations with Pakistan; it is also an imperative to reassure the myriad populations of multiethnic Afghan society that the country's potential and resources are meant to serve the interests and well-being of all Afghan citizens regardless of their real or attributed ethnic identities. The Afghan leaders cannot seriously expect the Pakistani power structures to help stabilize Afghanistan, while effectively staking claim on more than half of their territory and challenging their national sovereignty. Nor can Afghanistan afford to allow its meager resources and those donated by the international community to service the needs of a perpetual conflict in terms of military capabilities and a huge security infrastructure and personnel to continuously thwart the subversive designs of its more resourceful and powerful neighbor.

AHMAD SHAYEQ QASSEM, PhD, is an analyst of Afghanistan's affairs, and former Afghan diplomat in Britain and Australia. He is author of *Afghanistan's Political Stability: A Dream Unrealised* and several other publications on Afghanistan in refereed journals as well as in the international media.

Notes

1. For example, the renowned eighteenth century Muslim scholar Shah Waliullah Dehlawi (1703-1762) invited the Durrani Afghan King Ahmad Shah Abdali to invade India and crush the power of Hindu Marathas as an existential threat against the Muslim Mughal Empire (Nadwi 2004, 222–230). Another example of an iconic Indian Muslim leader somewhat romantically inspired by Afghanistan and the spirit of its peoples can be found in the person of Sir Mohammad Iqbal (1877–1938), who was a pioneer advocate for the creation of Pakistan. Iqbal's poetry and views in admiration of Afghanistan as a country free of direct colonial rule are well known.

2. For a Pashtun ethno-nationalist view of the power shift in the 1990s, see Ahady (1995, 621–34).

3. This figure likely overrepresents the Kuchis in the parliament. In the absence of a reliable census, one way of estimating the ratio of representation to population is to look at the figures of the "top-up" registered voters for the presidential and provincial council elections as recorded by Afghanistan's Independent Election Commission in 2014. During the 2013–2014 period, a total of 3,801,084 new voters were registered, out of which 29,431 were identified as Kuchis, which represents only about 0.8 percent of the total. However, the ten allocated seats for the Kuchis in the 249-member lower house constitutes over 4 percent of the total figure which indicates a five-fold overrepresentation.

4. For a discussion of community partnership in managing common resources, see Anderies and Janssen (2014).

5. For a contemporary narrative of Pashtun victimhood in Pakistan, see Siddique (2014). For a narrative of Pashtun victimhood by an Afghan ethno-nationalist, see Misdaq (2006).

6. For an analysis of how the narrative of Pashtun victimhood informed the post-Taliban political reconstruction of Afghanistan, see Qassem (2009b). For an analysis of how the narrative has influenced the Karzai government's reconciliation policy, see Qassem (2014).

7. For a discussion of the Afghan government's declared policy to transform the country into a crossroad of transit trade and its attendant challenges, see Qassem (2011).

8. General Karimi made the bellicose claim against Pakistan in a widely reported interview with the leading Afghan TV channel Tolonews in July 2011. The clip of the interview is available on *YouTube* under the title "Chief of the Afghan Army: We Don't Accept Durand Line," uploaded on July 18, 2011, accessed August 2, 2014, http://www.youtube.com/watch?v=aur33yVUyiA.

9. For example, the author interviewed the then first vice president Ahmad Zia Massoud in 2005, where the latter proffered the view that the validity of the border treaty had lapsed in 1993.

10. Abdullah is of mixed Pashtun-Tajik parentage, but his strongest power base is among the Tajiks.

Bibliography

"Afghanistan the First Country Mapped Using Broad Scale Hyperspectral Data." 2012. USGS, July 17. Accessed July 25, 2014. http://www.usgs.gov/newsroom/article.asp?ID=3280&from=rss_home#.U9TBgmK9KSM.

Ahady, Anwar-ul-Haq. 1995. "The Decline of the Pashtuns in Afghanistan." *Asian Survey* 35 (7): 621–34.

Ahmadzai, Ashraf Ghani. 2014. *The Charter of Change and Continuity* [Farsi-Dari version], 102–6.

Alexander, David. 2010. "Afghan Mineral Wealth Could Top $1 Trillion: Pentagon." *Reuters*, June 14.

Anderies, John M., and Marco Janssen. 2014. *Sustaining the Commons.* Tempe, AZ: Center for the Study of Institutional Diversity.

Bakhtar News Agency. 2014. "Session of the Cabinet of the Islamic Republic of Afghanistan Held". March 31.

Barfield, Thomas. 2004. *Nomadic Pastoralists in Afghanistan: Reconstruction of Pastoral Economy.* Washington, DC: Bank Information Center.

Bhadrakumar, M. K. 2012. "China's Afghan Oil Deal on the Skids." *Asia Times Online*, July 13. Accessed November 10, 2017. http://www.atimes.com/atimes/South_Asia/NF13Df01.html.

Constitution of Afghanistan [Dari and Pashto version]. 2004. *Official Gazette*, No. 818, January 28, Articles 14 and 44.

Cullather, Nick. 2002. "Damming Afghanistan: Modernization in a Buffer State." *Journal of American History* 89 (2): 512–37.

Donati, Jessica. 2014. "FEATURE-From New York Heroin Dealer to Afghanistan's Biggest Oil Man." *Reuters*, July 7.

Ferdinand, K. 2006. *Afghan Nomads—Caravans, Conflict and Trade in Afghanistan and British India 1800–1980.* Copenhagen: Rhodos International Science and Art.

Ghobar, Gholam Mohammad. 1999. *Afghanistan in the Course of History.* Vol. 2. Herndon, VA: American Speedy.

"Hyperspectral Data." 2012. USGS Projects in Afghanistan. Accessed July 27, 2014. http://afghanistan.cr.usgs.gov/hyperspectral-data.

Jacob, Jayanth, and Saubhadra Chatterji. 2011. "India's Track 3: Afghan-Iran Rail Link." *Hindustan Times*, November 1.

Kilo Goldmines. 2011. *The Hajigak Iron Ore Project.* June 8. Accessed August 9, 2014. http://www.kilogold.net/wp-content/uploads/2012/09/2012-Kilo-Investor-Presentation-Hajigak-Project-and-Afghanistan-Overview-.pdf.

"The 'King-Maker' General Drawn to the Scene Once Again" 2012. [Translation from Farsi/Dari by author]. junbesh.net. Official website for the National Islamic Movement of Afghanistan, June 11. Accessed August 2, 2014. http://www.junbesh.net/?p=728.

Mehdudia, Sujay. 2013. "Afghanistan Allows SAIL-led Team to Develop Hajigak Assets in Phases." *The Hindu*, August 22.

Misdaq, Nabi. 2006. *Afghanistan: Political Frailty and External Interference.* London: Routledge.

Nadwi, Syed Abul Hasan Ali. 2004. *Saviours of Islamic Spirit: Hakim-ul-Islam Shah Waliullah Dehlawi*, Vol. 4. Lucknow: Academy of Islamic Research and Publications.

Najafizada, Eltaf. 2011. "Afghanistan Awards Indian Group Hajigak Iron-Ore Mining Rights." *Bloomberg*, November 2. Accessed August 9, 2014. http://www.bloomberg.com/news/2011-11-28/afghanistan-awards-most-hajigak-iron-ore-mining-rights-to-indian-group.html.

Patterson, Mervyn. 2004. *The Shiwa Pastures, 1978–2003: Land Tenure Changes and Conflict in Northeastern Badakhshan*. Kabul: Afghanistan Research and Evaluation Unit.

"Q&A, Aynak and Mining in Afghanistan." 2013. *The World Bank*, April 2. Accessed July 27, 2014. http://www.worldbank.org/en/news/feature/2013/04/02/qa-aynak-mining-afghanistan.

Qassem, Ahmad Shayeq. 2007. "Afghan-Pakistan Relations: Border Controversies as Counter-Terrorist Impediments." *Australian Journal of International Affairs* 61 (1): 65–80.

———. 2009a. "Afghanistan: Imperatives of Stability Misperceived." *Iranian Studies* 2 (2): 247–74.

———. 2009b. *Afghanistan's Political Stability: A Dream Unrealised*. Farnham: Ashgate.

———. 2011. "The Afghanistan Conundrum: Regionalizing the Peace Effort." In *South Asia: Envisioning A Regional Future*, ed. Smruti S. Pattanaik, 191–206. New Delhi: Pentagon.

———. 2014. "Afghanistan's Political Reconciliation Policy: Ill Conceived and Self-Defeating." *Strategic Analysis* 38 (4): 476–92.

"Railroad Could Unlock Afghanistan's Mineral Riches." 2014. Bloomberg, February 28. Accessed July 27, 2014. http://www.bloomberg.com/infographics/2014-02-28/unlocking-afghanistan-s-mineral-riches.html.

Shahid, Anisa. 2013. "Chinese Company Seeks Amendment to Ainak Copper Mine Contract." Tolonews TV, August 22. Accessed August 9, 2014. http://www.tolonews.com/en/afghanistan/11650-chinese-company-seeks-amendments-to-ainak-copper-mine-contract.

Siddique, Abubakar. 2014. *The Pashtun Question: The Unresolved Key to the Future of Pakistan and Afghanistan*. London: Hurst.

Spanta, Rangin Dadfar. 2014. "Doctor Rangin Dadfar Spanta: Ba Wazeefa-e Moqaddasam Bar Megardam" ["Dr. Rangin Dadfar Spanta: I Return to My Sacred Mission"], *Etelaat-e Roz Daily*, July 21. Accessed August 3, 2014. http://www.etilaatroz.com/سپنتا-دادفر-رنگین-دکتور/.

Sullivan, Daniel, Mark J. Landau, Nyla R. Branscombe, and Zachary K. Rothschild. 2012. "Competitive Victimhood as a Response to Accusations of Ingroup Harm Doing." *Journal of Personality and Social Psychology* 102: 778–95.

Sumner, Brian Taylor. 2004. "Territorial Disputes at the International Court of Justice." *Duke Law Journal* 53 (6): 1779–1812.

Tapper, Richard. 2008. "Who Are the Kuchi? Nomad Self-Identities in Afghanistan." *Journal of the Royal Anthropological Institute* 14 (1): 97–116.

Tierney, John F. 2010. *Warlord, Inc: Extortion and Corruption Along the US Supply Chain in Afghanistan*. Washington, DC: US House of Representatives.

USGS. 2014. "USGS Projects in Afghanistan: Hyperspectral Data." Accessed November 10, 2017. https://afghanistan.cr.usgs.gov/.

Wily, Liz Alden. 2013. *Land, People, and the State in Afghanistan: 2002–2012*. Kabul: Afghanistan Research and Evaluation Unit (AREU).

8

BROUGHT TO YOU BY FOREIGNERS, WARLORDS, AND LOCAL ACTIVISTS: TV AND THE AFGHAN CULTURE WARS

Wazhmah Osman

WITH MORE SUICIDE bombs, attacks, and killings of civilians by official and unofficial Afghan and foreign forces, cases of rampant corruption and blatant disregard of the law by Afghans and foreigners, and a litany of other disasters associated with failed war-torn countries, everyone agrees that the situation in Afghanistan is becoming more dire. After the ouster of the Taliban and renewed promises by the international community to rebuild the country, many Afghans and non-Afghans wishfully imagined that the country was entering a postwar, postconflict, post-religious extremism era. A decade and a half into international and local efforts to build the nation and bring a semblance of peace to the site of the United States' longest running war, Afghanistan continues to plummet into lawlessness. The dream of a functioning democratic nation is moving further from reality. Yet the media are often extolled as the one "candle that burns in the darkness."[1] Of course, the media generally, and television more specifically, have also been described as "addictive like opium" and "uncontrollable like Satan" by their opponents.

After almost four decades of war, including a six-year blackout by the Taliban of all media except their own Shari'a Radio, post–9/11 Afghanistan is experiencing a surge in new media creation with dozens of new free broadcast television and radio stations, mobile telephone providers, and a fledgling but steadily growing internet infrastructure. The political economy that sustains this rapid proliferation of media is distinctively Afghan and rooted in long-standing relationships of patronage, development aid, and war economies that emerged during the Cold War and dramatically increased since 2002. Also, contrary to the uprisings that have fomented in the rest of the Middle East and Asia, the medium at the heart of the most public and politically charged social movements and activism in Afghanistan, instigating often violent cultural clashes, is television. In this chapter, based on a larger book project, I examine the role of media in the development of the public sphere in post–9/11 Afghanistan, the cultural contestations that it is producing, and the impact of the political economies that sustain it.

Via production and reception studies, along with content analysis of the most popular genres on Afghan television, I assess the everyday influence of new, radically increased media forms. I argue that despite operating in a dangerous arena—facing a range of constraints, threats, violence, and regimes of censorship—Afghan media producers are supported by the popularity of their work and provide a platform for local reform, activism, and indigenous modernities to challenge both local conservative groups and the international community that has Afghanistan in its purview of influence and discourse.

In other words, a fragile but vibrant public sphere has emerged. The development of a robust and free media as the key feature of a public sphere is important in all countries but especially in dystopic ones like Afghanistan. As a counterbalance to the government, warlords, and foreign interests in Afghanistan, the formation of a vibrant public sphere has the potential to underwrite democracy, national integration, and peace. After over thirty years of ethnic, racial, tribal, gender, and class violence, the media are providing a semblance of justice, debate, and healing.

However this comes at a high price. Like the wider public, Afghan media producers are caught between warring ideologies that range from Islamist to commercial to "developmentalist." Their secular, reformist, and nationalist visions are often at odds with powerful forces endogenous and exogenous to the government, sometimes including the owners and funders of the media institutions they work for. Their high profiles coupled with their low socioeconomic status leaves them vulnerable to all kinds of abuse and death. Hence the larger question for the future of Afghanistan is how much longer can a public sphere protect people or even exist in a country that has lost most of its previous state and civil infrastructure, where guns, local militias, foreign militaries, and physical force are the status quo?

Imperial Ambitions and Foreign Projects

In order to understand the complexities of Afghanistan's current media landscape, it is first imperative to understand its geopolitical history and ethnic and racial makeup.

Known as the "Gateway to Asia," Afghanistan has historically been at the crossroads of imperial ambitions. In what was called the Great Game, the colonial powers of England and Russia would often instigate trouble, pitting the various ethnic groups against one another. Part of their divide and conquer strategy also involved annexing parts of Afghanistan, thus redrawing the boundaries of the country in their own interest.² For Afghan rulers, maintaining the country's sovereignty involved a balancing act of minimizing foreign annexation while also appeasing the interests of a heterogeneous population consisting of autonomous ethnic groups such as the Pashtuns, Tajiks, Uzbeks, Hazaras, and Turkmans, among many others smaller groups.

Early on, as a result of these border uncertainties (see Qassem, in this volume), the state attempted to implement an isolationist policy. Likewise, as a result of constantly being under the threat of foreign invasions, the people of Afghanistan have always been suspicious of foreign involvement and interference. During British colonial rule of the region, the British tried to build railroad tracks to stretch their empire. Fearing foreign invasion and influence, Afghans in tribal areas repeatedly destroyed their "iron horse." As a result, whereas India and Pakistan have intricate national railroad systems, Afghanistan did not have any to speak of until this last decade (there are now two railway lines).³ Likewise, today the Taliban and other religio-tribal groups destroy telecommunication satellite towers that transmit and broadcast signals for wireless telephones, radios, and televisions (The Killid Group 2016).

Yet in actuality, the government's isolationist policy was largely a failure. These incidents aside, Afghans themselves have long bypassed scholarly, geographical, and political barriers through their own cultural and economic exchanges with Central Asia, China, India, Iran, and Pakistan as well as other countries. Yet in academia and popular culture, the myth of Afghanistan's "isolation" and "irredeemableness" continues to gain currency and has become a formidable paradigm (Barfield 2010; Crews 2015; Dupree 1973; Gregorian 2013).

In the age of globalization, Afghanistan is even less impervious to cultural influences and changes. Due to Afghanistan's distinctive post-9/11 economy, the vast majority of its media funding and actual media technologies and products comes from its regional neighbors as well as cross-regional interests. As media ethnographers who study transnational media and the effects of globalization have begun to explore, satellite television is rapidly transforming the mediascape in the Gulf countries from Syria to Iraq (Abu-Lughod 2004; Kraidy 2010; Salamandra 2016a,b). How is Afghanistan's distinctive geographic location in Central Asia and distinctive sociocultural position, dominated by Indian, Iranian, Turkish, and Western media products and at the margins of Arab and Russian influence shaping or impeding its development? Is this laying the foundations of cultural imperialism or fostering freedom of speech, debate, diversity, and democracy for the entire region? These are the questions I grapple with in this chapter.

As a result of the destruction of its cultural institutions such as its media, arts, education, and museums, contemporary Afghanistan is, culturally speaking, particularly vulnerable and unsettled. Also, after almost four decades of war and instability, there is serious concern that with the impending withdrawal of the the International Security Assistance Force (ISAF) and American troops, another civil war could break out. Indeed, security is deteriorating considerably, especially in the north. Taliban and Al Qaeda violence is now augmented by the appearance of Islamic State of Iraq and Syria (ISIS) in eastern border regions. Therefore, questions about cultural vulnerability, cultural imperialism, the role of empire, and civil unrest and more wars, are legitimate and take on a new urgency in a place and space that continues to be at the crossroads of imperial ambitions, where ethnic violence remains pervasive, and the possibilities of redefining national identity and allegiances are wide open. In Afghanistan, national television systems, and politics more generally, are shaped just as much by internal dynamics as they are by relationships with neighboring and more distant countries. While this is true of all nations, it is particularly the case in Afghanistan due to its geopolitical position and significant dependence on foreign aid.

Ethnography of the Televisual Village

Given this dystopic state of affairs, coupled with television's national and transnational reach and high illiteracy rates in Afghanistan, television is imagined as a particularly powerful medium by local and foreign officials for uniting or dividing the nation and the region by reconciling differences and promoting peace or aggravating tensions. While social media played a pivotal role in the Arab Spring and Green Movements, this is not the case everywhere. In Afghanistan and many of the former Soviet Republics, internet diffusion is low due to issues of state surveillance and barriers to access. Although internet infrastructure is slowly being built in middle-class neighborhoods of the capital Kabul, for the most part, internet use via computers and mobile devices is limited to social elites and some university students.

As I have argued elsewhere (Osman 2014a), technological determinism and the fetishism of digital and new media have precluded more nuanced understandings of social activism in the region and beyond. By focusing exclusively on the transformative or liberating aspects of new media, such studies erase the socioeconomic and political digital disparities that exist between and within nations. Television is still the dominant media form in many parts of the world and therefore one of the best means to study national politics, popular movements, and social activism across the Middle East, the Caucasus, and South and Central Asia (see Abu-Lughod 2004; Kraidy and Khalil 2009; Mandel 2002; Mankekar 1999; Oren 2004; Rollberg 2014; and Rajagopal 2001).

In order to understand how local agents and actors within diverse groups use the media to assert their political claims, we have to observe the on-ground cultural contestations that open up a space for collective action, social movements, and self-representation. Early and contemporary media scholars have been exploring the potential and problems of communication technologies in establishing the conditions for democracy in large-scale societies (Dewey 1927; Lippmann 1925; McLuhan 1952; Schudson 1998). The role of media in the formation of identity and subjectivity, both in the individual and collective sense, has been a central concern of media theorists. An integral part of this research is scholarship on the formation of publics, counterpublics, and split publics (Calhoun 1992; Dornfeld 1998; Rajagopal 2001; Robbins 1993).

Thus my goal with this research project became to redirect the global dialogue about Afghanistan to local Afghans themselves. In other words, how do Afghans' institutions "talk back" to discourses pertaining to Afghanistan that have been reverberating globally on an unprecedented volume and scale?

How do modern Afghans conceptualize and measure signifiers of cultural progress and regression outside of the developmentalist models? What do terms like *conservative* or *progressive* mean in contemporary Afghanistan? How are diverse belief systems, sensibilities, and understandings of themselves constituted and expressed on a daily basis? How are charged issues such as gender and sexuality, human rights, democracy, and religion contested, framed, and negotiated by local cultural producers?

Television has become the medium that is both a mirror and amplifier of Afghanistan, enabling Afghans to see themselves and speak to their own images and projections. The fact that television is broadcast nationally and simultaneously, viewed together within large household structures, and relatively accessible and popular has made television an important nationwide institution in Afghanistan—perhaps the medium that best provides a sense of Afghanistan as an "imagined community" (Anderson 1983)—as well as a site of social contestation. Arguably, television is a national barometer of the state of the nation, its heartbeat and pulse, the venue that is inciting and inspiring the most cultural contestations. It is the only medium in Afghanistan that reaches the masses and enables large-scale dialogue even though that dialogue sometimes takes violent forms as well. It also has the subversive and counter-hegemonic potential to help support broad reform and change. The larger questions as to whether television is elevating debate and creating a public sphere or refeudalizing the country by inciting sensationalism and polarizing public opinion are central to this thesis.

To fully grasp the rapidly transforming cultural dynamics and complexities of a place like Afghanistan requires a method that taps into and is tuned to the everyday lives of the local people over the course of a substantial amount of time. Thus my methods are largely ethnographic, drawing on media studies that have inspired my own, including the work of Lila Abu-Lughod (2004) and Faye Ginsburg (1995, 1999, 2002) among others.

In general, Afghanistan has been neglected as a serious site of ethnographic research with a few notable exceptions (Barfield 2010; Shahrani and Canfield 1984; Crews 2015; Dupree 1973; Gregorian 2013; Mills 1991; Tapper 1991; Saikal,

Nourzhanov, and Farhadi 2012). The media, in particular, have had almost no scholarly attention with the exception of a few influential scholars (Edwards 1995; Skuse, Gillespie, and Power 2011). My research is the first in-depth ethnography of the Afghan mediascape. I conducted a total of eighteen months of fieldwork in Tajikistan, Pakistan, India, and Turkey, including a full consecutive year, from 2009 to 2010, in Afghanistan. While there, I visited and conducted research in almost all the provinces and major cities, but the bulk of my time was in the capital city of Kabul.

While my research is primarily an ethnography of local television production and transnational media circulation in Afghanistan, in the absence of serious media scholarship on Afghanistan, I had to also engage with the reception side of the debates. In the absence of technologies that assess viewership, these interviews have become crucial for gauging the popularity of programming, specifically, what audiences across different demographics value about television programs and if they see a reflection of the issues that are important to their daily lives. On the production side, I interviewed international consultants, embassy officials, and media producers and distributors in order to understand their motivations and goals for funding, marketing, and circulating their own cultural products as well as "local" coproductions in Afghanistan. I also interviewed Afghan television producers to assess their own meaning-making processes. Thus, I carried out over one hundred formal interviews with high- and low-level media producers and government officials as well as a cross section of Afghans ranging from those living in slums to presidential candidates and religious leaders.

Political Economy of the Media Sector

In the decade and a half since 9/11, Afghanistan has experienced a rapid expansion of media outlets and an influx of media imports from the surrounding nations and beyond. Currently there are thirty-six free television stations and the numbers are growing. While most television station owners describe their networks as private enterprises that function solely on advertising revenue, some investigation made it clear that other sources of funding also come from a combination of activities and sources, both Afghan and foreign, clandestine and candid.

In the aftermath of 9/11, the United States government identified Afghanistan, Pakistan, and its northern Central Asian neighbors as particularly problematic due to the rise of Islamism in the form of extremist networks such as the Taliban and Al Qaeda. Thus, Western attention turned to the Central Asian Republics with promises to bring democratic policies and structures. With this mission, the United States military, in addition to providing arms through the Department of Defense and the State Department, identified the media as a central means of disseminating its messages. The British government followed suit with the Department for International Development (DFID) and the BBC. The explicit aim of BBC's overtly named Marshall Plan of the Mind, established in 1992 and later renamed BBC Media Action in 1999, was to "teach capitalism to the communists" (BBC Media Action 2017, Select Committee on Foreign Affairs 1999). The chairman of the organization explained, "The BBC-MPM is an educational, charitable trust … to transfer skills and knowledge of democratic principles and market economies via national radio and television to assist the transition process. It is the most significant project dedicated to mass knowledge transfer within the Former Soviet Union" (Mandel 2002, 213).

The framework for development aid originated in a series of discussions at the Bonn Conferences. Organized and spearheaded by the United Nations and the United States, Afghan and international civil society organizations and prominent individuals were invited to establish a new transitional government and were tasked with creating a new constitution, which would codify the terms of the new state, from the media to the justice system. In December of 2001, over ninety countries promised more than twenty billion dollars in the first Bonn Conference for the reconstruction of Afghanistan, including its media sector. In fact, the information and communication technologies (ICTs) sector, which includes everything from telecommunications infrastructure building to media training and literacy, was designated as a key target area for funding.

Although the numbers and figures are difficult to ascertain because not all the countries met their projected promises and, since the worldwide economic recession of 2008, international funding has significantly decreased, approximately 60 to 70 percent of Afghanistan's gross national income consists of international humanitarian aid. Likewise, although we know that the media and communication sector is one of the main areas targeted for aid by the United States and the United Kingdom and therefore heavily funded, the exact figures are also difficult to ascertain because there are many different branches of the governments that distribute the money to many different nongovernmental and governmental organizations and subcontractors, both local and from the donor countries.

Even though the US government is legally required to be transparent and make their expenditures public, following the money trail to find exactly which media projects are funded by which branches of the US government and for how much is nearly impossible—as they only provide piecemeal figures associated with some of their branches.

Despite the statistical and quantitative obfuscation, there is enough information to have a sense of media funding patterns, which I discuss in the next section. In this respect, whereas in the West, historically, television and television studies has been shaped by either the British public service broadcasting model of citizen "uplift" or the American commercial model in which advertising is crucial, Afghanistan's media system falls outside of this paradigm. Given our limited academic models, Afghanistan's mediascape can best be understood as "development realism" (Abu-Lughod 2004). The international donor community specifically funds two types of television programming: (1) they produce original programs in collaboration with local Afghan producers, and (2) they subsidize or provide, at no cost, their own programs dubbed in local languages (when necessary).[4]

Yet the development model is not adequate to fully understand the complexities of Afghanistan's political economy either. Unofficial sources of funding include arms smuggling and opium revenues. In fact, a number of television stations are owned by "warlords." In Afghanistan a third, distinctive economic model has emerged, an amalgam economy, rooted in longstanding relationships of patronage, development aid, and war profiteering. Since the media in Afghanistan are funded in ways that were never imagined by any media theorists, my research reveals the need to break out of Western media frameworks. Hence, the media proliferation that has happened in the decade and a half since 9/11 is sustained by a new and old configuration of resources from the international donor community, transnational media corporations, and local economies.

Sectarian Violence, Warlord TV, and Foreign Funding

In this competitive arena, most television producers vying for international donor aid use the rhetoric of development, including progress, education, and elevation of society. The resultant transnational productions have a progressive multicultural approach to nation building; they produce media messages aimed at uniting the nation by promoting human rights awareness, diversity, and plurality.

This is especially true with the most successful private stations, Tolo TV, Ariana Television Networks (ATN), and 1TV [Teliviziuni Yak] Afghanistan, which downplay their ethnic origins. The public is traumatized by years of sectarian violence. Therefore, TV stations that polarize public sphere debates with blatant ethno-religious messages or foreign allegiances and televisually attack other groups tend to be marginalized. To appear only to address their own group or, worse yet, foreign interests is akin to sociopolitical and economic suicide in the eyes of national advertisers and broad-based international donor campaigns that seek to reach wide audiences.

Nonetheless, some foreign funders and niche television stations owned by warlords with questionable histories continue their efforts to retribalize Afghanistan and polarize the region. It is important to note that, depending on a particular Afghan's ethnic affiliation, one person's warlord is another's hero. In the power vacuum left by the Soviet withdrawal from Afghanistan, most of the Soviet era commanders and leaders vying for control and a place at the table for their ethnic groups took part in the ethnically divisive and violent civil war (1992–1994). The line between protecting their own people, retaliation, and hate-motivated attacks and mass killings became blurry. The most notorious warlords are considered to have the most "blood on their hands," specifically carrying out large-scale acts of violence against other ethnic communities, but hardly any of them have clean hands. In the local languages, the term for warlords is *jung salarha*. Other common names for them are *zoor awarha* (Dari) and *tupaksalaran* (Pashtu), which can be translated literally as strongmen and gunslingers, but more generally, these are ruthless, powerful people, such as warlords and lesser known "mini-warlords" and their thugs who exercise brutal violence with impunity (see Chiovenda, chap. 9 in this volume).

Warlord television stations try sometimes to feed deep-seated ethnic, racial, tribal, and gender tensions by promoting their own blatant ethno-religious messages or foreign allegiances and televisually attack other ethnic groups and countries (for details, see Osman 2012). One common method that most warlord television stations employ is to produce promotional specials that glorify their leaders. These self-aggrandizing productions usually take the form of elaborate docudramas that feature their own television owners and financiers as natural heroes and saviors who guide their own ethnic groups and tribes through an epic journey and battle against ruthless and amoral foes to victory. In the process of presenting the greatness of their leaders, these pseudohistorical narratives conveniently distort history to erase their warlords' track records. Needless to say, people from other ethnic groups, especially those who have been directly impacted by the war crimes of the featured warlords and their militias, do not respond well to these productions.

For example the television stations Noor and Badakhshan, which are financed by the Tajik political party Jamiat-e Islami, have been one of the most prolific producers of such docudramas in homage to their late leaders Burhanuddin Rabbani and Ahmad Shah Mas'ud. As the Northern Alliance, Rabbani and Mas'ud's commanders joined and led the US coalition to oust the Taliban and Al Qaeda, which resulted in the assassination of both men by the Taliban and Al Qaeda. [Mas'ud's assassination occurred on September 9th 2001— i.., before the US intervention and partnership with the Northern Allaince and Rabbani's a decade later in 2011] Ever since then, they have achieved a venerable martyred status for fighting Islamic extremism and terrorism, which masks and makes mention of their tarnished human rights records dangerous (Sifton 2005, sec. 3.A. and 3.C.; Human Rights Watch 2006; Nordland 2012).[5]

While these promotional programs and specials are commonplace among ethnically affiliated television stations, some specific stations go further by engaging in direct televisual attacks. The epic battle between the secular Tajik television station Emrose and the religious Hazarah Tamadon television is one of the longest running and heated examples of ethno-religious mudslinging. Najibullah Kabuli, who is the owner of Emrose TV as well as a member of parliament (MP) and a businessman, claims that Tamadon TV, owned by the leader of the Shi'a Shura yee Ulama (Council of Shi'a Clerics), Ayatollah Mohseni or Shaikh Mohseni, "is a puppet of the Iranian government" since the Iranian government has built multiple mosques throughout the country for Mohseni. Mohseni, in turn, has accused Kabuli of using his television station as a platform for Tajik and

Pakistani agendas. To support their allegations, they both have provided ample but unsubstantiated televised evidence such as secret government documents showing financial backing from neighboring countries.

Yet none of the ethnically oriented stations are immune from trying to use their broadcasting powers to aggrandize their political base and influence national politics. During the last elections in 2014, many of the ethnic television stations were fined for biased coverage (Khitab 2014). Dawat Radio and Television Group, owned by Abdur Rabb Rasul Sayyaf, an ethnic Pashtun, was charged with one of the heftiest of the fines. Sayyaf who is also a current MP, has an illustrious record of warlordism (Sifton 2005, sec. 3.A. and 3.C.; Human Rights Watch 2006).

Additionally, while the international community publicly promotes democracy through public information campaigns (described below) as well as funding actual elections, it is no secret that the United States has its favorites too and uses various mechanisms to influence the results (Rohde and Gall 2004). There were widespread uprisings and public outcries during the last presidential election (in 2014) over what was deemed as US government manipulation of free and fair elections through mechanisms of public opinion management, namely, dubious polling and media campaigns (see Osman 2014b).

Overall, stations that blatantly incite ethnic bias tend to be marginalized by viewers and discredited in televised debates by the more reputable stations. According to my interviews, people are traumatized by years of ethnic, racial, gender, and religious violence. The culture has shifted, in large part due to television's influence, so that at least publicly, bias and racism are no longer tolerated.

In a highly saturated and inflated television market, television programmers need to fill the most air space with the cheapest programs that reach the widest audiences in order to attract either advertisers, donor money, or both. In the battle for establishing national and cultural legitimacy and authenticity, giving audiences what they want is as much a by-product of capitalism as it is of democracy. The less ethnically divisive stations, Tolo TV, 1TV Afghanistan, and Ariana Television Networks (ATN) happen to also be the most commercially successful ones and the ones funded most heavily by the United States. As such, the argument can be made that there is a direct correlation between being attuned to the democratic principles of diversity, inclusivity, and pluralism and the language of profit. In other words, having a progressive multicultural approach to nation building in order to attract potential audiences, donors, and advertisers, is not just a lofty social justice ideal but also, simply put, a good business practice.

Genres

Within this distinctive media economy, the most ubiquitous and popular genres are (1) jointly produced public service announcements (PSAs) and the news, (2) imported dramatic serials, and (3) foreign reality television formats. Through content analysis and reception studies, I analyzed the effects of these local and transnational productions.

The PSA, Political Satire, and News

The PSA has become the favorite launching pad for much needed educational and informational campaigns by the international community. Initially, PSAs were solely sponsored by various Afghan government offices in conjunction with international donor organizations; now, due to their popularity, even the few stations that are outside of the purview of international funding are producing PSAs independently. Their messages include topics like teaching democracy, women's rights, antiwar protest, and national, transnational, racial, and ethnic unity.

During the 2009 and 2014 presidential elections, the democracy PSAs ranged from procedural ones about voting rights and how to vote to expository ones on what voting and elections are and what it means. Others explained to people that it is not in their best interest to allow village or tribal elders to "buy" their votes. The women's rights PSAs addressed everything from street harassment to encouraging women to join the police to more complicated cultural phenomena such as honor killings and *baad* exchanges (offering girls in marriage to resolve blood feuds).

The news and PSAs also address the practical challenges of living in a war zone such as demonstrating how far civilians must stay away from passing US Army convoys and how to identify areas that have been cleared of mines and avoid areas that are still mined. Additionally, the news and special bulletins throughout the day inform people of where there are road closures due to military or insurgent activities. In Afghanistan, television literally helps Afghans navigate daily life and can mean the difference between living and dying.

The antiwar PSA messages are particularly powerful and popular with audiences. The *"Jung bas ast!"* or ("Enough War!") series has short vignettes that feature real newsreel footage of horrific acts of violence and its victims, dead and living, from the aftermath of suicide bombings and other types of violence inflicted on Afghans by other Afghans. The culprits of the violence remain ambiguous but the implication is that they are Afghan extremists or insurgents such as the Taliban and other groups that are motivated by racial, ethnic, gender, and religious xenophobia. The PSAs in the series always end with a male announcer stating sternly "enough war!" in either Dari or Pashto, with accompanying black text in the respective language and a blood red exclamation mark that slowly drips over a white background.

In the United States, due to the stratified nature of capitalism, news-based coverage of war, particularly of war-related deaths and violence, is censored by the overlapping interests of the advertising industry, television executives, and the government. Likewise, Afghan television stations predominantly funded by the US government are likely to be pressured and constrained. News producers complained that they were pressured by owners, directors, and managers not to air newsreel footage of violence perpetuated by the US military, especially when the violence resulted in civilian casualties.

However, despite the constraints, Afghan television producers manage to show a variety of newsreel violence and a lot of it. Media organizations also have taken on the very dangerous task of holding warlords accountable for present and past atrocities.

For example, the Killid Group, in conjunction with their extensive network of radio stations, Radio Killid, and multiple nationwide magazines, produced a 125-episode series on war crimes and war criminals. Saba TV, in conjunction with their newspaper, *Hashte Subh* (Eight in the Morning), Afghanistan's largest and longest running daily since the ouster of the Taliban, also regularly produces hard-hitting investigative reports on abuses of power. They partner with the Independent Human Rights Commission of Afghanistan, a UN-mandated independent body.

Programs such as *Zang Khatar* (Danger Bell) on Tolo TV and *Talak* (Trap) on Nooreen TV are part of a growing genre of political satire that combine investigative journalism and comedy sketches to confront abuses of power stemming from politicians and warlords within and outside of the government. During the 2009 and 2014 elections, I witnessed television's new prominent role in boldly staging the debates about democracy, capitalism, and "nation-building." Afghan broadcast television very openly critiqued and analyzed all aspects of the candidates' campaign platforms (including the campaign of the incumbent Hamid Karzai), addressed policy failures, and investigated accusations of corruption and wrongdoing. Operating in a fictitious world of humor and parody enables political satire programs to evade the censors to a degree, though their commentary, like the news, can be equally damaging and incisive. In one episode of *Talak*, which aired after the last elections, the hosts went to an animal market to interview sheep and goats about their thoughts on how democracy and nation building is working out in Afghanistan.

As I discuss later in this chapter, these brave media challenges to warlords and other ruthless political elites do not pass without reprisals and punishment. Yet for the media makers and their organizations who continue to produce such damning reports, their desire for justice outweighs their fears. Having been traumatized by decades of war, they, like the rest of the public, are avowedly and explicitly against war, which they hope to convey through PSAs, political satire, and the news. As seasoned antiwar activists know, showing the realities of war and war-related violence and producing well-researched reports that document war crimes, as opposed to the edited, sanitized, biased, and sensationalized Hollywood and US news-style violence, is a very effective means of perhaps not achieving peace but at least coalescing public opinion and the tide of change against war and, in the Afghan case, also against warlordism.

Dramatic Serials

Dramatic serials, or soap operas, from many countries, ranging from regional neighbors to Western countries, can also be found on most Afghan television stations. Yet, by far, the most ubiquitous and popular are from India, with Turkey and Iran trailing. Islamists and tribal leaders attack them for tainting an imagined pure Afghan Islamic culture and charge them with cultural imperialism, the dark side of globalization theory; they worry about the cultural influences of Hinduism, secular Sunni Islam, or Shiite Islam.

The common concern among media activists and cultural critics is that distinctive heterogeneous and local cultural ideas and practices are being erased, tainted, and diffused by the homogenizing force of Western capital expansion. Media studies scholars interested in the transnational political economy (Bagdikian 2000; McChesney 2004; Schiller 1976, 1989) have also analyzed the structural imbalances and capitalist expansionist strategies that enable global media to flow disproportionately one way in favor of Western nations. However, new media scholarship is also revealing that the tides of change are dissociating "global media" from the West, and that new global players are emerging from non-Western countries. For example, Indian media exports are finding avid consumers all over the world (Ganti 2004; Larkin 2008).

In Afghanistan, is there a reason to worry about cultural imperialism from its regional neighbors? The fact is that, as a result of four decades of war, Afghan television stations cannot compete with the established media industries of India, Iran, and Turkey.[6] Due to dispossession and displacement as well the destruction of media archives and the targeted killing of Afghan media stars, personalities, and producers during the different wars, the Afghan media industry lost tremendous talent and a well-honed tradition of production aesthetics and styles. However, in this case, Islamists use the rhetoric of cultural imperialism to promote and impose their own brand of "true" Islam. This is a direct attempt at erasing Afghanistan's diverse cultural history and varied experiences with Islam. Additionally, the large fan base of these imports find these dramatic serials valuable and liberating in many ways, particular in generating debates over domestic and gender issues both at home and in the public arena.[7] Likewise, it is important to distinguish between practices of Islam in everyday contexts and Islamism as a legal and political framework (Asad 1993; Göle and Ammann 2006; Mahmood 2005).

Reality TV

Reality television formats have also found an avid viewership in Afghanistan. Based on international formats, these serials are locally produced and tailored to Afghan audiences in collaboration with their Western sponsors. A few of the popular ones include: *Who Wants to be a Millionaire* (1TV); *Afghan Star* (Tolo), based on *Pop Idol* and *American Idol*; and *Dream and Achieve* (Tolo), which is a business entrepreneurship show similar to *The Apprentice*. These competition-based television shows, which identify winners by the votes of audiences via mobile phones or a panel of judges or both, are funded by Western media corporations and governments with the explicit goal of promoting both democracy and capitalism. Whether their mission is successful or not is difficult to determine. For example, in Ruth Mandel's 2002 article, "A Marshall Plan of the Mind: The Political Economy of a Kazakh Soap Opera," an influential work in transnational media studies, Mandel seizes on a serendipitous opportunity to examine how a mandate by the British Foreign Office to introduce Kazakhs to capitalism via the British format soap opera *Crossroads* plays out.

The British writers instructed the Kazakh writers to include in their scripts elements that positively represent free markets and entrepreneurship. However, Mandel explains, it is quite difficult to determine whether the "economic literacy" scenes in which people were writing checks and running shops at a bazaar (an outdoor market) actually encouraged any of the viewers to open bank accounts or small businesses or even shop, for that matter. Similarly, it is difficult to ascertain whether *Dream and Achieve*, *Afghan Star*, and *Who Wants to be a Millionaire* are converting Afghans into rabid consumers and capitalists. All we can say with certainty is that they are providing guidelines for a certain type of success, one that is based on both the accumulation of wealth and following your dreams. Some tend to be more overt in their messages and others are subtler. The commercials that air during these shows advertise new luxury housing suites, cars, appliances, banking, and telecommunications, promoting a capitalistic model of a materially lavish life, which is far outside of the means and reach of the vast majority of viewers.

The ideology that underpins and frames such media campaigns pairs capitalism and democracy to be mutually constitutive, one paving the path for the other. According to the award-winning documentary *Afghan Star*, made by the British filmmaker Havana Marking, which is based on the third season of the television serial *Afghan Star*, apparently a third of the country voted on short message service (SMS) for their favorite singers; for many audience members, this was the first time they have participated in voting. This is cited in the voice-over as demonstrative of the democraticizing effects of the program, as if voting for your favorite singers is akin to choosing an elected leader, whose decisions affect every facet of our lives. Lest we forget, the phone ompany that sponsors the program, Roshan, also makes money from the audience's SMS voting.

It is also important to note that *Afghan Star*, the documentary, like the television series, was produced by Tolo TV, the Afghan version of the popular western "Pop Idol" format. Tolo TV, which is arguably one of Afghanistan's most popular television stations, is also one of the largest recipients of USAID funding (Auletta 2010). Hence, if we follow the commodity funding trail, such assertions in the documentary are not independent observations but part of the larger US ideological mission. Conservative forces have also condemned these shows, especially the participation of the female contestants, for their Americanizing or westernizing effects. This is similar to their argument that Indian, Iranian, and Turkish dramatic serials are turning the public or public opinion in favor of adopting Hindu, Shiite, or secular Sunni codes of being.

The Pen or the Sword?

Continual attempts by religious authorities and the Afghan government to block some programming and commission others confirm that transnational television production and circulation in a place like Afghanistan has implications far beyond just entertainment. "Thus revealing the political significance of texts dismissed by many social scientists as fictive and therefore inconsequential, as 'mere' entertainment or, less charitably, as kitsch," Purnima Mankekar writes in her groundbreaking ethnography of the impact of television programming in uniting and dividing India (Mankekar 1999). This is not to underestimate the significance of providing entertainment and distraction in a dystopic country like Afghanistan. However, it is precisely for this reason, given Afghanistan's current dismal state of affairs, that the media offers the one counterbalance to the injustices of the government, warlords, and foreign interests in Afghanistan and hope for democracy, national integration, and peace.

Afghanistan is far from being free of conflict, war, and the Taliban. Today, Afghanistan is a barely functioning democracy on the verge of collapse. The government has to readily acquiesce to the power of religio-tribal warlords and drug traffickers at the expense of the many. The judicial and the electoral systems are fraught with corruption and fraud. The vast majority of people think that the presidential and parliamentary elections are a sham. The rule of law is virtually nonexistent.

People realize that dealing with such powerful, ruthless *zoorawarah* is beyond the means of tribal justice systems' practice of holding *loya jirgas*, or public assemblies of elders. And since the official justice system of Afghanistan is corrupt and international law has failed them, people want the media to be the judge, jury, and executioner of warlords, alleged war criminals and even corrupt government officials. They know that the American government is complicit in bringing many of these dubious characters, ranging from drug lords to genocidal mass murderers, and Western trained kleptocrats to power in the first place and are appalled that since 9/11, the Afghan government has given many of them official posts within the government. Like village *jirgas*, where familial or tribal justice is enacted on a small scale, they want a national forum and venue, whereby they can publicly bring their grievances against these national criminals and demand retribution. Afghan media producers and journalists frequently complain that people have unreasonable expectations, hoping and sometimes demanding that the media avenge them by publicly shaming every *zoorawar* who is still using their power as a stronghold or chokehold on the people.

Indeed after experiencing almost four decades of war and its brutalities, a traumatized Afghan public has very high expectations of media and journalism in general, and television in particular. My conclusion is that Afghan media producers are delivering and meeting those high demands. As we have seen thus far, with PSAs, the news, and political satire, media makers uncover, investigate, and expose everything from cases of corruption, abuses of power, and violence stemming from local officials to international warlords and government officials. With dramatic serials and reality television programs, Afghan media programmers are providing to the avid and large viewership of these programs glimpses into the world's diverse lifestyles and cultures and televisual representations of gender and sexuality practices of people from around the world, which opens up space crucial for private and public discussion around sensitive cultural issues of national importance.

Yet there is a huge cost to this emergence and quick expansion of the public sphere in Afghanistan. Just like most Afghans, media makers are not strangers to threats and violence; yet by virtue of their profession, Afghan media makers, the good ones at least, fall directly into the crosshairs of these dangerous individuals on a regular basis. In the examples previously mentioned, Najiba Ayubi, the manager of Killid group, who produced the 125-episode series on war crimes and war criminals, was repeatedly visited and threatened by a group of *zoorawarah*. Sanjar Sohail, the director of political affairs and news programming at Saba TV and their corresponding newspaper *Hashte Subh*, came under attack by the Kabul Shura yee Ulama (Council of Clerics) in June of 2011 with threats of heavy fines and closure for reporting on the finding of the Independent Human Rights Commission of Afghanistan (IHRCA).[8] Subsequently, in 2012, after a series of battles with the IHRCA, to international dismay and outrage, Hamid Karzai, who has often been extolled for enabling free speech in Afghanistan, illegally fired three of IHRCA's top commissioners, including Nadir Nadery, the top investigator on the human rights abuses report, and appointed new ones. Cases of *zoorawarah* thugs and their militias, endogenous and exogenous to the government, threatening, destroying equipment, and beating up media makers, is all too common. Some pay with their lives.

In this equation, where *zoorawarah* and *jung salarah*, have become the ultimate villains of the Afghan psyche, media makers and journalists are the ultimate protagonists and superheroes of the people. Media producers and programmers who have established themselves for their fearless reporting and programming have large followings of fans that revere them and perceive them as saviors, protectors, and an extension of their wills. Journalists who have built a reputation for fair, independent, and courageous reporting by virtue of their honorable work

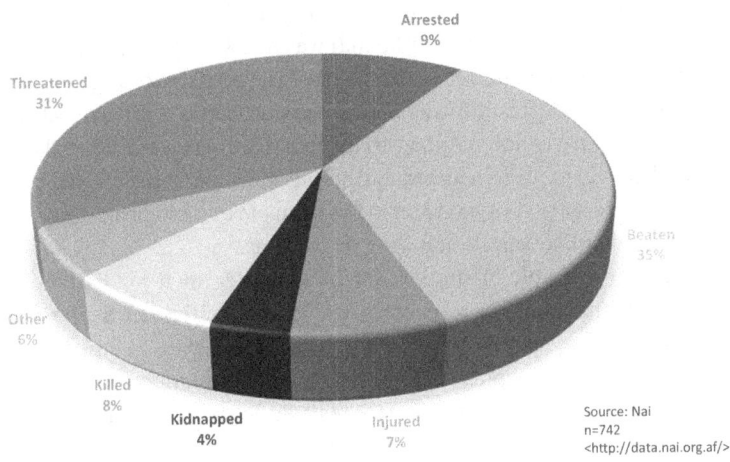

Figure 8.1.

move outside the bounds of ethnic, tribal, or religious sectarianism. They are applauded and celebrated as national heroes.

Thus, people are highly sensitive and become incensed when media makers and journalists are harmed in any way. In this reciprocal relationship, the media explosion in Afghanistan is providing audiences with a platform for issues that are crucial to them, and in return, people are voicing their support for the media. Audiences have coalesced to form a strong public, vociferously rising in opposition to conservative elites and in defense of the media. When respected media makers are harmed, people protest, hold vigils, and riot for weeks.

As I have argued elsewhere (Osman 2014a), while globally, governments are cracking down, often violently, on popular uprisings in public spaces, in Afghanistan, public protests are proving to be a powerful social force, mainly because the government is relatively weak and spaces for public gatherings, *maidaans*, or town centers, are plentiful. During my field trips, I witnessed a range of uprisings, riots, and protests over incidents of election fraud, Qur'an burning by US soldiers, the Shiite Marriage Law (otherwise known as the Rape Law), civilian casualties, government corruption, deaths of journalists, student tuition hikes at Kabul University, and the banning of popular television programs, among other issues. The outpouring of support and grief for fallen or slain media heroes also reverberates throughout the country.

The case of Ajmal Naqshbandi, a well-respected reporter, who also worked as a fixer and translator for foreign correspondents, is an example of this. In March of 2007, he was working with an Italian journalist on a dangerous assignment in Helmand when they were both captured by the Taliban. Subsequently, the release of the Italian journalist and Naqshbandi was negotiated in exchange for the release of five Taliban prisoners. Yet in the chaos of the actual exchange, while the Italian was recovered, Naqshbandi was accidently left behind and later beheaded by the Taliban. Their driver Sayed Agha was the first to be beheaded. Once the beheadings, captured on video, were released and televised in Afghanistan, the public clamor could be heard across Afghanistan in the form of riots and protests as well as peaceful vigils and public murals honoring the victims.

Another example of support for local homegrown media heroes is that of Sultan Munadi, another respected Afghan journalist. In September of 2009, while on assignment as a fixer for the *New York Times*, Sultan Munadi and his contact, journalist Stephen Farrell, were both kidnapped by the Taliban near Kunduz. British special forces safely rescued Farrell in a nighttime raid and in the process, shot and killed Munadi as he was attempting to board the rescue helicopter, mistaking him as the enemy. To add insult to injury, his body was left behind with no explanation. Widespread anger ensued as people protested for over a week in Kabul. Local news, echoing public opinion, expressed anger at a common sentiment that Afghan journalists are considered dispensable or worse yet disposable in the international news production circuit.[9]

The same sense of public outrage was expressed over the January 2011 acid attack on well-known and respected journalist Razaq Mamoon who was formerly a host of a popular weekly political commentary and interview program on Tolo TV. The gathering and outpouring of support outside of his hospital in Kabul was massive. Contrary to some news reports that he was targeted for personal reasons, most of the news outlets confirmed Mamoon's own account that the Iranian agents were responsible, since he had just published a book detailing and condemning the Iranian government's involvement in Afghanistan's affairs. He is a fierce critique of Afghanistan's neighbors' interference in Afghan affairs.

When media makers are targeted, attacked, and killed by *zoorawarah*, media outlets, in solidarity with one another, also advocate for themselves and pay homage to the victims by (1) providing in-depth news coverage of the attacks on media makers and media censorship more broadly, (2) televising the subsequent protests on the news, and (3) producing special programs that provide in-depth investigation of the incidents of censorship and violence as well as expository programs that address the role of media freedom in democratic societies. Between the large outpouring of people at these protests and the subsequent broadcasting of the protests on television and radio, in the majority of cases, government officials have been forced to address the public. In order to prevent public protests from

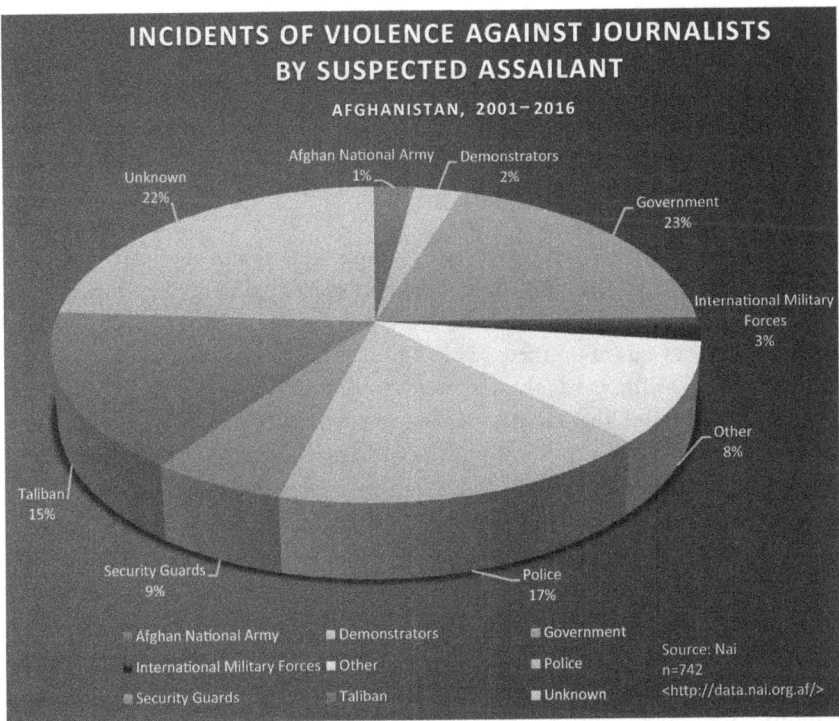

Figure 8.2.

devolving into riots, they have to at least make rhetorical gestures to appease the public and acknowledge collective grievances that have become sites for mass mobilization. It is hard to determine whether the media are capitalizing on people's protests or creating the conditions for protest in the first place.

In either case, it is a mutually beneficial phenomenon, whereby, each party amplifies one another's shared interests and messages, thereby creating larger and longer mass gatherings, which in turn require more news coverage.

One example of this is the ongoing battle between religious authorities within and outside of the government and Afghan television stations over censoring representations of women's bodies. The Afghan government has repeatedly issued decrees banning the televising of international dramatic serials, music video shows, and reality television for "indecency" and "inappropriate" expressions of gender and sexuality. Yet the television stations use their popular support continue to air them. For example, after Ariana Television Network (ATN) abruptly stopped airing the popular Indian serial *Kum Kum* in May of 2008 due to pressure from the Shura yee Ulama (Council of Clerics) via the Ministry of

Culture and Information, fans of the program held protests outside of both the ministry and the ATN headquarters in Kabul. Using the protests as evidence of the serial's popularity, ATN fought in the courts to reinstate the serials by arguing that the government does not have the right to ban entire programs, that blurring and fading exposed parts of women's bodies and Hindu religious idols should suffice. They succeeded in getting the programs reinstated and set a precedent for other stations as well.[10]

In a similar case, when a reporter and a cameraman were physically assaulted and their equipment damaged by the Afghan secret police in December 2009, Sepehr TV subsequently featured the event repeatedly on their news. They also aired a special program on media laws and free speech the following week and for several weeks afterward. The program showed the injuries of the victims who were brutally beaten and the destruction of their equipment along with interviews from media law experts about the illegality of the government's actions. Instead of evading responsibility and danger by brushing the incident under the proverbial Afghan rug, the owner of Sepehr, Dr. Najib Sepehr, and manager Elham Mohammadi made the brave decision to use their station to generate discussion around the violence.

Likewise, in January of 2016, when a Taliban suicide bomber attacked the staff bus of Kaboora Productions, an affiliate of Tolo TV, injuring dozens and killing seven people, Tolo TV took the incident, as did several other television stations, as an opportunity to both condemn the Taliban and produce multiple programs educating people about media freedom.

Conclusion

Without a doubt, the combined power of the public arena and broadcast media is a very effective social tool for collective action in Afghanistan. Yet there are serious limits to both the media's self-advocacy and the public's strong and unwavering support. The media-related crimes and murders mentioned in this chapter are a few of the many. Yet no arrests are made and no one is prosecuted in most of these cases.

Zoorawarah can continue to censor media makers with impunity and without fears of retribution. Broadcasting the incidents of violence and censorship against media personnel and the media writ large, as well as the subsequent protests and production of investigative and expository programs is indeed generative in creating dialogue and raising awareness about media rights and the important role of a free media in a society, but it is clearly not enough.

Thus far, we have seen examples of two types of potential cultural imperialism. By aggressively promoting and offering their own media products, programs, and formats, at little or no cost, the argument can be made that foreign countries are impeding the development of Afghanistan's own media industry, artistry, and media crafts. Additionally, we have seen examples of censorship, both from endogenous and exogenous forces, ranging from pressuring the government to ban programming or directly pressuring producers to do so.

In extreme cases, we have seen an egregious third form of censorship becoming prevalent in Afghanistan. High-level media personnel and wealthy media owners who are often prominent public figures, such as politicians, warlords, drug lords, religious leaders, and businessmen, hire body guards and live behind gated fortress mansions, while low-level television personalities and reporters are subjected to threats, physical attacks, and death for providing people with programming they want to watch and which gives them a platform to raise their voices. Hence, it is the mid- and low-level media professionals, not the owners of the television stations they work for nor the foreign governments that are the patrons of the stations, who bear the ultimate burden of media freedom and reform in Afghanistan. Caught between warring ideologies that range from Islamist to commercial to "developmentalist," as brave as these Afghan media personalities and journalists are, and despite their high media profile, their low socioeconomic status leaves them vulnerable to abuse and possible death.

Reporters Without Borders, the Committee to Protect Journalists, and Nai, an Afghanistan-based journalist watchdog group supported by Internews and USAID, have been documenting rising statistics in acts of violence and murders perpetuated against media makers including violence against news anchors, journalists, singers, and actors. In the Reporters Without Borders' "Deadliest Countries" section of its *Round-Up 2016 of Journalists Killed Worldwide* report, Afghanistan ranks second, with war-torn Syria leading in first place, and cartel-ridden Mexico trailing in the third spot. In the Committee to Protect Journalists' *2016 Global Impunity Index*, Afghanistan ranks seventh in having the most unresolved cases of journalists murdered. Since 2001, Nai's extensive online data mapping project has collected evidence of 742 incidences of violence against journalists in Afghanistan.[11] Their "Top Five Organizations Experiencing Violence" are, respectively, Tolo TV, Ariana Television Network, 1TV Afghanistan, Pajhwok Afghan News, and Civic Activists.

The extent and extremity of violence against media makers—some of whom I came to know during my research in Afghanistan—was one of the surprising findings of my fieldwork. The Ministry of Information and Culture, who oversees television broadcasting, has been repeatedly targeted by different groups. Almost every media institution I visited has a showcase of "Media Martyrs" displayed prominently either in their lobby or outside area. For women working on screen, visibility itself can be deadly. The semiotics of televisual representation have become highly volatile. A number of Afghan women, ranging from news broadcasters to hosts of music video programs, have been victims of alleged "honor killings."[12] Afghan media producers, writers, editors, reporters, engineers, and

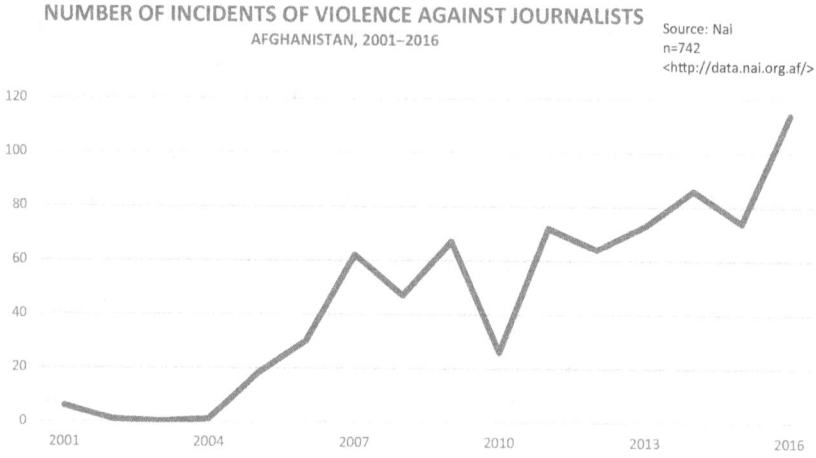

Figure 8.3.

fixers have been kidnapped, attacked, wounded, and killed by forces ranging from the Taliban and other extremists, to agents of surrounding countries, and international military units.

The *zoorawarah* of ruling elites and extremists like the Taliban and ISIS also destroy telecommunication towers that transmit and broadcast signals for wireless telephones, radios, and television. ISAF, NATO, and American forces try to protect telecommunication towers by either placing them within the compound walls of their military bases or by having soldiers guard them. The big difference between the "iron horse" of the British Raj and the internationally funded media of today is that the public almost unanimously supports today's media. It is time to also protect the flesh and blood of the people who run the one institution with the most democratic potential to protect people and restore peace and justice in the dystopian country. Television owners, the Afghan government, and the international community must be held accountable for the safety of Afghan journalists, presenters, singers, and actors. This is not just a problem of personal safety; the future of independent media in Afghanistan depends on it. While the violence directed at media makers is productive in generating debates, if violence continues to increase as it has without any real legal enforcement measures, it does not bode well for the future of Afghanistan.

Currently self-censorship is becoming more and more prevalent among media makers. Over the last decade, it has taken a Foucauldian turn to self-discipline as a means of appeasing the hegemonic powers of a few power elites. Once the venues for mass communication and mediation are controlled and censored by direct force or by fear and intimidation, cultural debates cease to be in the service of the public. The question, then, is how much longer will the media remain a viable institution reflexive of the peoples' voices, if the threat of internal and external *zoorawarha* or *zoormandha* goes unchallenged and if crimes committed against media professionals go unpunished? What will then happen to the lively, though often volatile, debates that the media are currently fostering? Will the public service and developmental programs disappear entirely? What new models of media, if any, will emerge?

My final cautionary point is that while the international community's funding of the Afghan media sector is problematic in certain ways, the impending military pull-out must not mean a corresponding pull-out of development assistance. Surprisingly, at least the media development model of a much grander national reconstruction project, long a source of critique from the Left, is proving successful in Afghanistan. This is contingent, of course, on the input and agency of local producers within media institutions, itself contingent on those same producers being protected and valued.

The saving grace for Afghanistan is that the model of media development that is being implemented is a multilateral development model, whereby resources and funding are dispersed from the international donor community, thus making it more akin to the public interest model. That is, there is a direct correlation between the amount and diversity of international resources that is being funneled into the Afghan media sector and the number and diversity of media outlets and programs that result. The fact that Afghanistan is not unilaterally dependent on US aid is precisely why Afghanistan has not yet fallen down into the slippery slope of commercialization and its media world remains vibrant and viable, albeit fragile. Furthermore, being under the gaze of international backers ensures that Afghan media institutions are more accountable to freedom of speech. There are many international media watchdog organizations, including some affiliated with the US government, who genuinely believe in their mission to create an independent media and diverse public sphere in Afghanistan.

At this critical juncture in the tangled history of US-Afghan relations, daunting though the task might seem, the US-led international community must not once again abandon the country's nation building and development projects, especially regarding the media. As globalization theory reminds us, just as media technologies cause global reverberations, so too do technologies of violence. No country can be deemed inconsequential to global peace and stability, especially one with a tumultuous recent history. Mending the "broken," "collapsed," and "failed" state of Afghanistan can only happen via a mass venue for healing and purging, via remembering and forgetting, debating and imagining.[13] For that to happen, there cannot be a better or worse medium than television.

WAZHMAH OSMAN is assistant professor of globalization and development communication in the school of media and communication at Temple University. She is the producer of the documentary film, *Postcards from Tora Bora*.

NOTES

1. Ramazon Bashardost, former presidential candidate and current parliamentarian, first coined the phrase. He is one of the few members of parliament who has not been involved or implicated in the numerous corruption scandals that has plagued other MPs.
2. For example, in 1893, more than a decade after the conclusion of the Second Anglo-Afghan War, the ethnic Pashtuns, whom the British deemed as particularly problematic due to their numerous uprisings, were divided between Afghanistan and modern-day Pakistan, then British India (see Saikal, chap. 1, and Qassem, chap. 7, in this volume for details).
3. Completed in 2010 and funded by the Asian Development Bank, one stretches from Termiz, Uzbekistan to the airport in Mazar-i-Sharif, and the other railway, funded by Turkmenistan, links Serhetabat, Turkmenistan with Toorghundi and has reportedly been halted due to security threats posed by the Taliban.
4. Iranians, Tajiks, and Afghans share dialects—Farsi, Tajik, and Dari, respectively—of the same language, Persian, which is one of the official languages of Afghanistan. Additionally, during the Soviet occupation, many Afghans became refugees in Iran and Pakistan. Subsequently, Afghans became more fluent in Farsi or learned Urdu, which is very similar to Hindi. In the north of Afghanistan, most of the tribes and ethnic groups, such as the Uzbeks and Turkmen, also understand Turkish. Thus, most Afghans can understand the imported programs without the common overdubbing in Dari or Pashto.
5. Aina Television, is owned by Abdul Rashid Dostum, an Uzbek leader and Afghanistan's current first vice president, has a history of alleged human rights abuses (Sifton 2005, sec. 3.A.; Human Rights Watch 2006), also produced and nationally aired at least three promotional specials glorifying Dostum during my fieldwork.
6. Although space constraints do not permit me to elaborate on this point, it should be noted that in contrast to India, Iran, and Turkey, the media flows between Afghanistan and its neighbors to the north such as Tajikistan and Uzbekistan, as well as to the east to Pakistan, are bilateral and multidirectional.
7. For more information see Osman (2011).
8. Sohail also explained that with *Hashte Subh*, their corresponding newspaper, they have more liberty to report on abuses of power because, due to high illiteracy rates, the information does not reach the masses.
9. For more information on the vital role of local frontline journalists in the international news production chain as well as the unjust structural disparities that favor international correspondents and embedded journalists and place local frontline journalists in grave danger, please see Osman (2017).
10. For more information on the role of international dramatic serials in the Afghan culture wars, please see Osman (2011).

11. The graphs and pie charts that illustrate the statistics on violence against media makers in this chapter are created by Christalyn Michaelle Steers McCrum for the author, based on Nai's reports at http://data.nai.org.af/.

12. For an in-depth analysis of gender and gender-related media attacks and killings, see Osman (2014a).

13. In development circles and in political science terminology, Afghanistan is frequently described as a "failed," "broken," "fragmented," or "collapsed" nation (Ghani and Lockhart 2008; MacMunn 1977; Rubin 2002), terms that have replaced the earlier classifications of "late state formation," "the rentier state," and "third world despotism," (Rubin 2002). This language of "failure" with its problematic colonial and neocolonial epistemological roots is frequently used as a teleological framework.

Bibliography

Abu-Lughod, Lila. 2004. *Dramas of Nationhood: The Politics of Television in Egypt*. 1st ed. Chicago: University of Chicago Press.
Anderson, Benedict. 1983. *Imagined Communities: Reflections of the Origin and Spread of Nationalism*. Rev. ed. London: Verso.
Asad, Talal. 1993. *Genealogies of Religion: Discipline and Reasons of Power in Christianity and Islam*. Baltimore, MD: John Hopkins University Press.
Auletta, Ken. 2010. "The Networker: Afghanistan's First Media Mogul." *The New Yorker*, July 5.
Bagdikian, Ben. 2000. *The Media Monopoly*. 6th ed. Boston: Beacon Press.
Barfield, Thomas. 2010. *Afghanistan: A Cultural and Political History*. Princeton, NJ: Princeton University Press.
BBC Media Action. 2017. "History and Links to the BBC". Accessed August 4, 2017. http://www.bbc.co.uk/mediaaction/about/history.
Calhoun, Craig. 1992. *Habermas and the Public Sphere*. Cambridge, MA: MIT Press.
Committee to Protect Journalists. 2016. *Getting Away with Murder: 2016 Global Impunity Index*. New York: Committee to Protect Journalists. https://www.cpj.org/reports/cpj_impunity_pages.pdf.
Crews, Robert. 2015. *Afghan Modern: The History of a Global Nation*. Cambridge, MA: Harvard University Press.
Dewey, John. 1927. *The Public and Its Problems*. New York: H. Holt.
Dornfeld, Barry. 1998. *Producing Public Television, Producing Public Culture*. New Haven: Princeton University Press.
Dupree, Louis. 1973. *Afghanistan*. Princeton, NJ: Princeton University Press.
Edwards, David B. 1995. "Print Islam: Media and Religious Revolution in Afghanistan." *Anthropological Quarterly* 68 (3): 171–84.
Ganti, Tejaswini. 2004. *Bollywood: A Guidebook to Popular Hindi Cinema*. Abingdon, UK: Routledge.
Ghani, Ashraf, and Clare Lockhart. 2008. *Fixing Failed States: A Framework for Rebuilding a Fractured World*. London: Oxford University Press.
Ginsburg, Faye D. 1995. "The Parallax Effect: The Impact of Aboriginal Media on Ethnographic Film," *Visual Anthropology Review* 11 (2).

———. 1999. *Visible Evidence*. Edited by Michael Renov and Jane Gaines. Minneapolis: University of Minnesota.
Ginsburg, Faye D. and Lorna Roth. 2002. "First Peoples Television." In *Television Studies*. Edited by Toby Miller. London: The British Film Institute.
Göle, Nilüfer, and Ludwig Ammann. 2006. *Islam in Public: Turkey, Iran, and Europe*. Istanbul: Istanbul Bilgi University Press.
Gregorian, Vartan. 2013. *The Emergence of Modern Afghanistan: Politics of Reform and Modernization, 1880–1946*. Stanford, CA: Stanford University Press.
Hirschkind, Charles, and Saba Mahmood. 2002. "Feminism, the Taliban, and Politics of Counter-Insurgency." *Anthropological Quarterly* 75 (2): 339–54.
Human Rights Watch. 2006. "Afghanistan: Justice for War Criminals Essential to Peace: Karzai Must Hold Officials Accountable for Past Crimes." Accessed September 17, 2016. https://www.hrw.org/news/2006/12/12/afghanistan-justice-war-criminals-essential-peace.
Internews.org and Nai. 2016. *Violence against Journalists in Afghanistan*. The Internews Violence against Journalists—Afghanistan Project. http://data.nai.org.af/.
Khitab, Muhammed Hasan. 2014. "14 Media Outlets Fined for Law Violation." *Pajhwok Afghan News*, April 23. Accessed September 23, 2016. http://beta.pajhwok.com/en/2014/04/23/14-media-outlets-fined-law-violation.
Kraidy, Marwan, and Joe F. Khalil. 2009. *Arab Television Industries*. London: British Film Institute.
Kraidy, Marwan. 2010. *Reality Television and Arab Politics: Contention in Public Life*. Cambridge, UK: Cambridge University Press.
Larkin, Brian. 2008. *Signal and Noise: Media, Infrastructure, and Urban Culture in Nigeria*. Durham, NC: Duke University Press.
Lippmann, Walter. 1925. *The Phantom Public*. New York: Transaction Press.
MacMunn, George F. 1977. *Afghanistan from Darius to Amanullah*. Quetta: Gosha-e-Adab.
Mahmood, Saba. 2005. *Politics of Piety: The Islamic Revival and the Feminist Subject*. Princeton, NJ: Princeton University Press.
Mandel, Ruth. 2002. "A Marshall Plan of the Mind: The Political Economy of Kazakh Soap Opera." In *Media Worlds: Anthropology of New Terrain*, ed. Faye D. Ginsburg, Lila Abu-Lughod, and Brian Larkin, 211–28. Berkeley: University of California Press.
Mankekar, Purnima. 1999. *Screening Culture, Viewing Politics: An Ethnography of Television, Womanhood, and Nation in Postcolonial India*. Durham, NC: Duke University Press.
McChesney, Robert. 2004. *The Problem of the Media: U.S. Communication Politics in the Twenty-First Century*. New York: Monthly Review Press.
McLuhan, Marshall. 1952. "Technology and Political Change." *International Journal* 7 (3): 189–95.
Mills, Margaret A. 1991. *Rhetorics and Politics in Afghan Traditional Storytelling*. Philadelphia: University of Pennsylvania Press.
Nordland, Rod. 2012. "Top Afghans Tied to '90s Carnage, Researchers Say." *The New York Times*, July 22. Accessed September 17, 2016. http://www.nytimes.com/2012/07/23/world/asia/key-afghans-tied-to-mass-killings-in-90s-civil-war.html?_r=0.
Oren, Tasha. 2004. *Demon in the Box: Jews, Arabs, Politics, and Culture in the Making of Israeli Television*. Newark, NJ: Rutgers University Press.
Osman, Wazhmah. 2011. "'Trashy Tastes' and Permeable Borders: Indian and Iranian Soap Operas on Afghan Television." *Soap Operas and Telenovelas in the Digital Age: Global*

Industries and New Audiences, ed. Diana I. Rios and Mari Castañeda, 237–56. New York: Peter Lang.
——. 2012. "Thinking Outside the Box: Television and the Afghan Culture Wars." Unpublished manuscript. New York: New York University.
——. 2014a. "On Media, Social Movements, and Uprisings: Lessons from Afghanistan, Its Neighbors and Beyond." *Signs: Journal of Women in Culture and Society* 39 (4): 874–87.
——. 2014b. US Exports Its Warped Democracy to Afghanistan. *Al Jazeera America*. July 14. Retrieved from http://america.aljazeera.com/opinions/2014/7/afghan-electionsusmedia abdullahabdullahashrafghani.html.
——. 2017. "Jamming the Simulacrum: On Drones, Virtual Reality, and Real Wars." In *Culture Jamming: Activism and the Art of Cultural Resistance*, ed. Marilyn Delaure and Moritz Fink, 348–64. New York: New York University Press.
Rajagopal, Arvind. 2001. *Politics after Television: Religious Nationalism and the Reshaping of the Indian Public*. London: Cambridge University Press.
Reporters without Borders. 2016. *Round-Up 2016 of Journalists Killed Worldwide*. Paris: Reporters without Borders. https://rsf.org/sites/default/files/rsf_2016-part_2-en.pdf.
Robbins, Bruce. 1993. *The Phantom Public Sphere*. Minneapolis, MN: University of Minnesota Press.
Rohde, David, and Carlotta Gall. 2004. "The U.S. Has a Favorite in Afghanistan. That's a Problem." *The New York Times*, September 26. http://www.nytimes.com/2004/09/26/weekinreview/the-us-has-a-favorite-in-afghanistan-thats-a-problem.html.
Rollberg, Peter. 2014. "Media Democratization in Russia and Eurasia." *Demokratizatsiya* 22 (2): 175–77.
Rubin, Barnett R. 2002. *The Fragmentation of Afghanistan: State Formation and Collapse in the International System*. 2nd ed. New Haven, CT: Yale University Press.
Saikal, Amin, Kirill Nourzhanov, and Raven Farhadi. 2012. *Modern Afghanistan: A History of Struggle and Survival*. London: I. B. Tauris.
Salamandra, Christa. 2016a. "Ambivalent Islam: Religion in Syrian Television Drama." In *Islam and Popular Culture*, eds. Karina van Nieuwkerk and Mark Levine. Austin: University of Texas Press.
——. 2016b. "Creative Compromise: Syrian Television Makers between Secularism and Islamism." In *Islam and the Media*, Vol. 1, ed. Anna Piela. London: Routledge.
Schiller, Herbert I. 1976. *Communication and Cultural Domination*. White Plains: International Arts and Sciences.
——. 1989. *Culture, Inc: The Corporate Takeover of Public Expression*. New York: Oxford University Press.
Schudson, Michael. 1998. *The Good Citizen: A History of American Civic Life*. New York: The Free Press.
Shahrani, M. Nazif, and Robert L. Canfield, eds. 1984. *Revolutions and Rebellions in Afghanistan: Anthropological Perspectives*. Berkeley: Institute of International Studies, University of California.
Sifton, John. 2005. *Blood-Stained Hands: Past Atrocities in Kabul and Afghanistan's Legacy of Impunity*. New York: Human Rights Watch, July 7. Accessed September 17, 2016. https://www.hrw.org/report/2005/07/07/blood-stained-hands/past-atrocities-kabul-and-afghanistans-legacy-impunity.

Skuse, Andrew, Marie Gillespie, and Gerry Power, eds. 2011. *Drama for Development: Cultural Translation and Social Change*. London: Sage.

Tapper, Nancy. 1991. *Bartered Brides: Politics, Gender and Marriage in an Afghan Tribal Society*. 1st ed. London: Cambridge University Press.

The Killid Group. 2016. "Silenced by Security Threats." Accessed August 1, 2016. http://tkg.af/english/2016/08/01/silenced-by-security-threats/.

United Kingdom Parliament. Select Committee on Foreign Affairs. *Minutes of Evidence: Memorandum Submitted by the BBC World Service*. London: Committee Publications, 1999. https://publications.parliament.uk/pa/cm199899/cmselect/cmfaff/815/9101206.htm.

PART II: PERSONAL AND COLLECTIVE IDENTITIES, GENDER RELATIONS, AND THE TRUST DEFICIT

9

"THE WAR DESTROYED OUR SOCIETY": MASCULINITY, VIOLENCE, AND SHIFTING CULTURAL IDIOMS AMONG AFGHAN PASHTUNS

Andrea Chiovenda

Introduction

Akbar Ahmed, in his first ethnography on the Pashtuns of Pakistan's Federally Administered Tribal Area (FATA), emphatically (and uncompromisingly) wrote that theirs was "strictly a man's world" (Ahmed 1976). Granted, his judgment was certainly skewed by his lack of access to women and by his institutional role as political agent for the Tribal Agency of Pakistan where he was conducting his fieldwork research (so that the private, "invisible" side of daily life gained no appreciation in his analysis). Indeed, subsequent female anthropologists, like Benedicte Grima, Nancy Lindisfarne-Tapper, Inger Boesen, and Niloufer Mahdi have since then shed light on the "dark side of the moon" in Pashtun society (Boesen 1983; Grima 1992; Mahdi 1986; Tapper 1991). They have shown that, far from being a silent, docile, and submissive element in a male-dominated social equation, Pashtun women maintain, in fact, a degree of leverage, if inconspicuous, in the political and public life of Pashtun society. Still, Ahmed's remarks do resonate as irrefutably familiar to the ethnographer of today. The Pashtun public sphere is still, by and large, the apparently exclusive domain of male members of communities, both urban and rural, albeit in different degrees. Pashtun social dynamics, at the same time, defy and corroborate the principles of practice theory that Pierre Bourdieu spelled out radically forty years ago. On the one hand, Bourdieu's model would prove inadequate in its strong emphasis on the individual's "learned ignorance," which makes him or her "ignorant both of the projective truth about his practical mastery ... and of the true principle of the knowledge his practical mastery contains" (Bourdieu 1977 [1972], 19). On the other hand, however, the presence of deviant behaviors vindicates Bourdieu's idea, whereby individuals continuously strategize and adapt their "unthought" principles to the infinite array of instances that real life presents them with. In this light, the later, and more inclusive, interpretations of practice theory, as laid out by Marshall Sahlins and Sherry Ortner, may help us better understand the psychosocial environment in which Pashtun male individuals fight their way out through daily life (Ortner 1984; Sahlins 1981).

I found in my informants a remarkable degree of awareness and consistency about the cultural schemata that should, in theory, lead their behaviors, and at the same time, I witnessed their conscious (and unconscious) choice to strategize those same behaviors in relation to specific everyday situations in order to maximize self-interest and personal well-being. I will argue in this chapter that such cultural schemata have not only changed in the last three decades (which is no surprise) but that it is precisely the thirty-plus years of continuous violent conflict that engulfed the country that was responsible for the modification of pragmatic behaviors at first and for the creation later of an alternative set of moral values legitimizing the new behaviors, both of which are today competing with preconflict ethics and morality, which survive among many individuals from the older generations and some from the newer ones.

A Pashtun Cultural Context

The cultural idioms which Pashtuns in my research area (Nangarhar province, southeast Afghanistan) and most Pashtun populations in Afghanistan and Pakistan think should be followed, in order to conduct a respectable and honorable life, are simply called, collectively, *pakhto*. Successfully abiding by these principles is defined as *pakhto paalal*, or "following pakhto." Choosing not to, or not being able to follow *pakhto* causes the "perpetrator" to incur moral reproach and costs him a loss in social capital. His and his family's reputation may remain tainted forever, in the most extreme cases. Yet, notwithstanding the fact that these principles exist in the imaginary of everyone, it is also true that they are negotiated daily and reworked and strategized through practical behavior, which, as Bourdieu argued, holds the last word in the real standings of social relationships and interactions. So, we can find the seeds of sociocultural change (including within the cultural idioms that everyone is aware of) in the behaviors and practical choices that each individual displays every day. *Pakhto* is not an immobile, static set of principles which everybody has professed to uphold since time immemorial, but rather is a malleable set of injunctions that individuals adjust, partly consciously, partly unconsciously, to the necessities of daily life. Daily life and its requirements, in turn, are the product of history and historical social conditions, and as such, produce individual and collective practices. The individual's daily practices, which are built upon cultural idioms, may well react to "an *objective event*, which exerts its action of conditional stimulation calling for or demanding a determinate response" (Bourdieu 1977

[1972], 83, emphasis mine). In such a case, change takes place, and this may happen both in the realm of pragmatic behavior, and in that of the cultural models, which emerge modified, and in changing, will call for different behavioral performances. As Fredrik Barth understood, when pragmatic behavior—praxis—becomes too far removed from the cultural idiom and too widely spread within a community (or when a new form of praxis is actively embraced by influential-enough members of the community), it will be the cultural model that will undergo a shift in significance and form. That is the feedback process (Barth 1966).[1]

There has not been an "objective event" in recent Afghan history as momentous and dramatic as the forty-years–long conflict that has characterized the country until now. According to the theoretical paradigm that I sketched above, we should expect to see equally momentous changes either in the cultural idioms, or in the pragmatic behavior of individuals, or in both. In fact, this is what I will argue here. The concepts of *nartob* (manliness) and of *ghairat* (readiness/courage and willingness to actively uphold the rules of *pakhto*) have undergone heavy modifications and adaptations in response to a protracted context of violence and armed conflict.

Pashtun society is generally definable as a strongly honor-based society, where the concept of public shame is present in equal strength. The segregation between sexes is heavily enforced, and any kind of relationship between two people of the opposite sex who are not closely related by blood is avoided—although, in recent years, there have been "amendments" to this rule, mostly out of expediency due to the intolerable economic condition of certain families, as well as to the fifteen plus years of close contact with the international community which lives and works in the country. As is the case with many ethnographic examples throughout the Mediterranean and Middle Eastern regions (see, among many examples, Bourdieu [1966], Giovannini [1981], and Herzfeld [1985]) as well as among Afghan Pashtuns, the behavior of women is taken as the yardstick for judgment on the respectability and honorability of a family as a whole. "The women of my family are my *namus*," you often hear men say, which means that their honor, and that of their family members, rests on the appropriate behavior of their women. If the family's women must, through their public performance, ensure the maintenance of the family's honor and public respectability, it is the men's responsibility to protect and restore such respectability when it becomes tainted by some faux pas on the part of the women or on the part of someone outside the family toward its women. Usually this entails some sort of violent retaliation, either against the family's woman, or the outside offender, or both, if they are deemed to have acted in accord with each other. A male family member who has *ghairat* (who is *ghairati*, or, alternatively, who is a *ghairatman*) must take action in these cases, lest he be publicly disgraced and considered *beghairata*, that is, unworthy of being a Pashtun, of being a *nar* (a "manly," virile man).

The equivalent of *namus* in the male realm is *izzat*. The family's honor and respectability also depends on its men's behaviors. A man's *izzat* gets hurt when the man sees his rights clamped down on (for instance, during an economic transaction), is publicly insulted, or is not accorded the respect, as a *nar*, that every Pashtun man, regardless of his social status, is entitled to. As it happens in the case of *namus*, also in the case of a hurt *izzat*, the way to restore integrity often entails a violent retaliation, which every man who calls himself *ghairati* is required to display. Failing to do so carries with it the stigma of being *beghairata* and the loss of personal respect within the community at large.

Nartob is the capacity to show publicly that a man is a (manly) man. Indeed, Micheal Herzfeld's felicitous definition for his Greek Cipriot context is here even more apt: "to be good at being a man" (Herzfeld 1985). More specifically, *nar* is not only an "ordinary man" (for which meaning another word is used—*saray*) but rather a virile man, a man with all his masculine prerogatives, which obviously have very much to do with certain characteristics that are often associated with virility in many other ethnographic contexts—courage, strength, fearlessness, assertiveness. Yet *nartob* has also a moral side to it, which is not only linked to idioms of aggressiveness and violence. Protecting the rights of the weak, supporting the poor, defending women and children, awareness and cognizance of one's *qawmi laar* (the ways and customs of one's tribal group of ascription), diplomatic skillfulness in managing instances of social friction and conflict, are all features that are expected in a *nar*. Obviously, a *nar* is also someone who possesses and displays *ghairat*, which is the capacity to act promptly and effectively in cases in which one's *namus* or *izzat* have been compromised by someone's less-than-appropriate public behavior. Most of the times, when the public display of *ghairat* comes into play, it is in situations of retaliatory action, which are usually violent to some degree. Still, violence and aggressiveness per se are not necessarily the blueprint of a *nar*. There exists, so to speak, a "good" violence, and a "bad" violence.

One of my informants, a twenty-six-year-old man from a rural village near Gardez, in Paktia province, told me:

> You know, there are two kinds of ghairat. There is good ghairat, and bad ghairat. For example, imagine you are walking in the street with your sister, and a strange man passes by and looks at your sister intensely, as if he knew her. If you start speculating that they are having an illicit relationship and kill them both without even inquiring with any of them, you are not a ghairati man, you are ignorant and stupid [*besauada aw kamaqal*]. On the contrary, if you discover that your wife has been the object of bad verbal or physical harassment against her will, and you kill the culprit, this is good ghairat, something obligatory [*majbur*].

In other words, a violent behavior which is carried out as expression of a man's ghairat, in defense of his namus or izzat is not only "good," but strictly necessary, lest one be branded as a beghairata (lacking manly attributes, in colloquial terms). On the contrary, free-wheeling acts of violence, which go against the principles upon which the idea of a nar rests, render the perpetrator beghairata in and of itself. Abuses, bullying, behaviors which purposely offend the namus or izzat of somebody else, are supposed to encounter social reproach, and to backfire against the perpetrator.

Whereas all of the above represents a concise (and deficient) portrait of the cultural models that are still strongly felt among many individuals of the communities within which I am working, still I want to reiterate that everyday life as I saw and experienced it among my Pashtun friends is, as Bourdieu correctly posited, lived through strategizing around these principles, adjusting and adapting these ideal models of behavior to one's daily necessities and real life social intricacies so that public perceptions and moral significances are continuously negotiated among individuals. In the background of this incessant work of smoothing edges and reconciling opposites lies self-interest.

Let me add here that these cultural models exert a different grip on individuals if they live in an urban setting as opposed to a rural one (and of course, in relation to personal idiosyncrasies; see Hollan 1992). As could be easily expected, the face-to-face small community that the village embodies, where often many of the villagers belong to the same lineage or related groups of lineages, represents an environment where these cultural idioms retain a larger grip on the individual than they do on people in a city like Jalalabad. The relative anonymity of the urban setting allows for somewhat freer behavioral expression, while the strict environment of the village requires a high degree of strategizing and adapting behaviors for pragmatic reasons. It is not surprising then, that among those who live in Jalalabad, a good percentage have either purposely moved to the city in order to escape a village context that they felt was smothering, or are so successfully adjusted to the life of the city that the regular visits they pay to their villages of origin, where many of their relatives still live, is often perceived as an unpleasant occasion.

The Shifting Meanings of a "Moral" Masculinity: Cultural Idioms and Pragmatic Behaviors

Now, how did forty years of protracted violent conflict (and massive displacement of the Pashtun as refugees) change some of these social dynamics, cultural idioms, and strategizing behaviors? Let me present some of the ethnographic material I gathered during my fieldwork.

In Jalalabad, where I lived for the last section of my field research from August 2012 to June 2013, I spent time regularly with the members of a self-described "civil society" organization, who independently got together after the demise of the Taliban regime in order to organize charitable activities and raise money to help the most disadvantaged in the community. Though such was the main objective of the organization, its members also used the room they rented to hold their meetings as a space where they could gather daily and see each other after work hours (for those who had a job), or in general, to spend time with each other whenever they could. The organization was made up of only men, who were mostly from an educated middle class, often holding college degrees. The man in charge of the group was a physician in his late forties, Baryalay Mumtaz, who for some time in the past had practiced privately, but who at the present was no longer practicing. Other prominent members were Rahmatullah, a man in his early fifties who worked in Kabul at the Academy of Sciences in the Pashto literature and culture department, and Farid, a civil engineer in his early forties who worked as an adviser to the Nangarhar provincial governor Gul Agha Shirzai. All of them self-identified as pious Muslims, though to various degrees (among the occasional participants in their communal afternoons and evenings were also a couple of more religiously oriented individuals, trained in shari'a law and Islamic studies). I found them to be an interested and patient group of people, willing to share with me part of their time and conversation. Rahmatullah, in particular, was deemed by the others as most suited to talk to me about the state of Pashtun society in Nangarhar. In spite of their high level of education, almost none of the members of the organization was able to speak sufficiently good English, and our conversations were all held in Pashto.

Rahmatullah was born and raised in Jalalabad well before the communist takeover in 1978. We spent time talking about the idea of *saritob* (moral appropriateness, humane behavior), and *nartob* (manliness) within Pashtun culture.

> You know, the pillars of Pashtun culture used to be Islam and customs [*pakhto*]. Today customs trump religion. It was not like this before the war. I remember, society was more free in the past ... women were not only holed up in the homes, boys and girls alike went to school, there were even romantic involvements between boys and girls ... Today things have changed, there is no authority anymore to enforce security ... the worst instincts of people can just be expressed, there is no restraint ... certain things are inside everyone, if there is no structure to keep things in order ... well, you see how Afghanistan is today. This is why we have all these *zurawaraan* [abusive individuals, bullies], all these *kumandanaan* [militia commanders], all this violence, all this aggressiveness ... This is not pakhto, this is not nartob ... These people take advantage of their power to oppress the poor and the weak ... today many have very little, and few have a lot ... The powerful take advantage of the weak ... this is not pakhto, this is not Islam ...

While Rahmatullah was speaking in this manner, the four or five same-aged peers who were listening nodded and uttered a few words of agreement, while other younger members of the organization kept following the speaker, fascinated by the possibility to learn something about a past they never experienced personally. In this passage, Rahmatullah was, in essence, arguing a couple of main points. First, he implicitly asserted that a proper (from his own standpoint) implementation of Islamic norms and values led in the past to more balanced and "modern" social arrangements and cultural idioms. Women did not live in what other informants have described as "prisons" ("Do you see these houses all aligned here by the canal? These are all prisons for women," the male director of an Afghan NGO [nongovernmental organization] in Jalalabad said to me one day, pointing his finger at the houses of his neighborhood); schools were available for both girls and boys, who, furthermore, apparently managed to have also some sort of emotional mutual engagement. In a cultural milieu where the "correct" form of Islam is implemented and kept above traditional customs (*pakhto*, or more generally, *rawaaj*), Rahmatullah stated, such a state of things becomes possible. As he did several times during our conversations, Rahmatullah showed he considered the religious fundamentalism of the mujahideens first, and of the Taliban later, as a distortion of a "correct" way of interpreting Islamic tenets.

Secondly, Rahmatullah strongly believes that a deterioration of the conditions of *saritob* (social collaboration and ethical behavior) has characterized the Pashtun social environment during the Soviet occupation, and the civil war (and the Taliban regime as well, in all likelihood). The embodiment of such deterioration in his opinion is represented by the *kumandanaan*, the militia commanders, both big and small, who emerged during the Soviet occupation, and who also maintained their power and following during the civil war. Although the excesses and ever-more violent behavior of the commanders were among the main reasons that officially justified the creation and successfulness of a militant religious group such as the Taliban in the mid-1990s, during the latter's regime, the commanders did not disappear altogether (or at least those who survived), but rather kept a very low profile and a disguised position in society, only to take advantage of the post-2001 new political and strategic context to reemerge and gain new visibility and clout (see Giustozzi 2000, 2003, 2009; Giustozzi and Ullah 2006). The kind of unethical activities which, in Rahmatullah's view, the commanders carried out before the Taliban and which they resumed after their demise, are, for him, not only contrary to Islam but also to *pakhto*. Excessive violence, the use of one's own position of power and military capabilities to appropriate resources from those who could not wield an equal power, and disregard for the honor of one's own peers, are all characteristics that, in Rahmatullah's opinion, make a man not a *nar*—a manly, virile man—but rather a *beghairata*—a man without manly attributes, a coward. It is interesting, however, that he sees in the lack of a superordinate structure—the state's coercive apparatus—the main root of the problem with deteriorating social relationships. The absence of a structural deterrent to the emergence of people's worst instincts seems to Rahmatullah to be the source of those pernicious developments in moral social standards that currently engulf Pashtun society.

In a later conversation, he clarified his views further:

> What these people [the kumandanaan] do is not nartob, it's *zulm* [cruelty, abuse, oppression, injustice]. These people are not *narina* [plural of nar, manly men], they are *zalim* [he who does zulm]. All this stealing [of land, public and private], this using of their guns and armies to fight, this abducting of children [of both sexes, for sexual purposes], this is being beghairata.

ANDREA: So, if they are beghairata, why do so many young men follow them, work for them, keep them in great esteem?

RAHMATULLAH: Well, I think a lot has to do with opportunities ... there are no jobs here at the moment. The kumandanaan give our young men a salary, they pay them, and the youth are attracted to the only thing that gives them some money ...

ANDREA: I am sure this is important, yet from what I could see it also seems that a lot of people treat these guys [the kumandanaan] with great respect, a lot of young people seem to think that they are strong men [*qawi narina*], and wish to be like them ...

RAHMATULLAH: Well, in part you are right ... it is true that moral values [*akhlaqi arzakhtuna*] have changed among us since the war started. Before the war, a nar had to demonstrate that he was able to help the poor and weak people, and not only do things for himself. If somebody had done then what the kumandanaan and zurawaraan do today, people would have called them beghairata, and not respected them. Today people do give them respect [*ihtiram*], this is true ... maybe also because they are afraid of them [*de kumandanaanu na yerigi*] ... After all the violence that there has been during the war, certain bad behaviors have become normal ... children are not educated in the previous values anymore, they copy what they see around them. This is why I think that school is important ... you need somebody to tell you that what you see around you is wrong ... otherwise it becomes right ... If the son of a *zurawar* goes to school and gets a good education [in the previous values], he will be able to say to his father: "What you are doing is wrong, and I will not do as you are doing." We don't have this now ...

Coincidentally, this conversation happened the day when a member of the civil society organization came to the room that served at its headquarters to discuss a problem he was having in his family, and to receive advice about it.

Ahmad Khogiany, a young man of about twenty-seven years of age, working for a UN organization in Jalalabad but originally from the troubled rural district of Khogiany, presented the case of his father-in-law, back in the village where his family and his wife's family are from. Two years earlier, a former mujahideen commander from their area appropriated a plot of cultivable land that belonged to Ahmad's father-in-law. One day the commander showed up on his land, kicked out the farmers that had been hired to farm it, declared that the field was his, and that he would start working it for himself. Proper documentation from king Zahir Shah's time, proving that the plot of land belonged to Ahmad's father-in-law, was presented to the *woliswal* (the district governor), but nobody took action to dislodge the commander from Ahmad's father-in-law's land. Now Ahmad was thinking of appealing to a *jirga* (a council of ad hoc appointed elders in charge of solving intracommunity conflicts; see Baryalay 2006), and was asking the other members of the organization whom they thought would be best to involve as *jirgamaraan* (the *jirga* members). I asked:

> ANDREA: You did not think of confronting him to have him give you back the land. Why?
>
> AHMAD: We are less powerful than he is. If we tried to fight with him, he would defeat us, and then he would keep all the land. If I go to the jirga, at least I can keep some of the land.
>
> ANDREA: The jirga would not decide to give you back the whole plot of land? After all you have the right documentation...
>
> AHMAD: No, that commander is powerful, the jirgamaraan do not have the power to force him to do anything... they will decide in a way that is best to keep him happy, and not start a fight... They will tell him that what he is doing is wrong, so he will respect their opinion, and will accept to keep only half of our plot of land... that's the best that can happen...
>
> RAHMATULLAH: [interjecting, and addressing me] You see how things work here now? The *zurawar* [sing. of zurawaraan] wants a piece of land, he takes it, and he knows that the jirga will only decide to have him give back half of it... in the end he got half of a land that was not his, and the legitimate [*mashroo*] owner lost half of a land that was his... this is how it goes now...
>
> ANDREA: Why did the woliswal not do anything about it?
>
> RAHMATULLAH: But they are all the same! Why would he do anything about it? They are all the same people! The woliswal also is a kumandan, he has his own fighters... they are all the same kind of people... he does the same things to other weak people as this man did to Ahmad's father-in-law...

Such opinions about the state of facts in Pashtun areas of the Southeast have been reported to me by many other informants, in roughly the same terms. Eamal, an old former communist party (PDPA) member in Jalalabad, to this day professing to me (in private) his faith in socialism, aired the same grievances when he complained about the backwardness of the Pashtun cultural environment, still clinging to practices such as the *jirga* which, in his opinion, only serves the interests of the powerful against the weak. Commenting on the reach of the PDPA members within the pre–Saur Revolution state apparatuses, and recalling the first years of the Soviet-backed governments, he said to me once: "The war destroyed our society. Before the war there was a strong state, a strong police and army. There were strong people in the government, with good values [*arzakhtuna*] ... you could not do just whatever you wanted to do ... they would put you in jail forever ... we were civilized [*mutamaddan*] ... Today it's only chaos [*gad wad*]. There is violence [*tashadod*] and abuse everywhere."

Similarly, a former KhAD member (intelligence services) under presidents Babrak Karmal and Mohammed Najibullah, now working for a (different) civil society organization in Jalalabad, once used his blackboard to draw a dense chart, and explain to me, with an hour-long monologue full of disdain, how it had happened that in all executive positions of authority in Afghanistan, from the local to the national ones, now sat only former mujahideen commanders of the war against the Soviets, and their younger cronies.

All these informants, and many others alongside them, perceive that there has been a steep increase in the use (and abuse) of violence in the Pashtun sociocultural context since the beginning of the long period of conflict in 1979. Some, like the former KhAD member, stress structural problems, like the number of political positions that the US-backed Afghan government has given to ex-mujahideen commanders. Others, like Rahmatullah and Eamal, feel that something has changed deeply within the moral fabric of today's Pashtun men. They talk of moral values (*akhlaqi arzakhtuna*) that have supposedly lost the meaning they used to have and acquired new registers of significance, which they not only now do not recognize and feel comfortable with but altogether reject as aberrant. Rahmatullah is adamant in saying that he thinks many of those who are now powerful *kumandanaan*, in his eyes are little more than dishonorable bandits and thugs. Worse still, they do not represent a *nar* for him, but rather a *beghairata*—possibly the worst insult one might proffer against a Pashtun man. He was also somehow forced to admit that, in the end, many young men today join the commanders' private armies not only, or exclusively, because of the good and sure salary the commanders provide. The "easy" money they get is certainly part of the equation, yet there are several other factors involved. One of these factors is that a good number of the young men who join any commander's militia seem to do so out of a sentiment of admiration and emulation. In other words, at least some among the youths likely see the commanders as a role model and an example to follow, not only because of their accomplishments in life (power, riches, status) but also because of the image that they give of themselves to the external world as men—that is, the model of masculinity they publicly project and embody.

As an ethnographer who started working in Afghanistan in 2009, I obviously cannot fully appreciate how much of my informants' impressions about the changes that they feel occurred over the decades is the outcome of objective conditions or of their subjective experience and interpretation of what happened in the past thirty years. Certainly, the fact that so many middle-aged informants, from different geographic, class, and educational backgrounds, seem mostly in agreement when reporting a steady deterioration of the overall condition of social relations would make me think that there is more than a kernel of truth in their interpretation of the recent past in their area. What I was able to acknowledge personally, though, is the ubiquity of cases of abuse and violence by powerful individuals (the *kumandanaan*, in most cases), as well as less conspicuous cases of daily, petty acts of abuse between neighbors, fellow villagers, sometimes relatives, which index the same pattern (only applied to a smaller scale), and which have just as much the capability of easily escalating and morphing into much larger scale interfamily feuds. During the four years in which I worked in the country, I had the chance to record countless cases of ongoing conflict and outright abuse.

What also emerges from my interactions with young and old Pashtuns, rural and urban, educated and not, is the further perception of a shift in the visibility, role, and overall influence that certain social categories hold within today's sociocultural milieu. Though I can only make a quick reference here to such phenomena, let me say that the shift seems to have operated at a "systemic" level, although its causes and sources are to be found in the same processes I am highlighting in this essay, initiated by the perpetual state of conflict that the country suffered since 1978. Ethnographic literature on Pashtun populations, both from Pakistan and Afghanistan (particularly Ahmed 1976, 1980; Anderson 1978. 1983; Barth 1959; Edwards 1996; 2002), had emphasized two aspects of Pashtun society that seemed to be quite consistent throughout the geographical areas occupied by Pashtun people. These two aspects are: (1) the high degree of authoritativeness and consequent informal authority maintained by those individuals within society who went under the name of malik, or khan (mostly in Afghanistan, and Pakistan, respectively), and (2) the secondary role that local religious figures held vis-à-vis the *malikaan* and *khanaan* (plural of *malik* and *khan*). The exact definitions of *malik* and *khan* change in relation to the areas taken into consideration. Yet, in general terms, both *malikaan* and *khanaan* can be described as figures who have reached maturity, own a reasonable amount of landed property, command respect of the people for possessing, and correctly managing, certain cardinal attributes that respectable male members of society should display (e.g., *ghairat*, wisdom, piety, "fluency" in the cultural language of *pakhto* , as well as in the religious language of Islam), and descend from a lineage which produced in the past other similar figures.

Local religious characters, usually called *mullayaan* (singular, mullah), were, by and large, individuals with a limited formal education (both in secular and religious subjects), who mostly performed certain ritual roles within any given community (like male circumcision ceremonies, wedding blessings, ratification of *jirga* decisions, leading daily prayers in the mosque), and who traditionally held a less influential position as opposed to the *khanaan* and *malikaan*. Fredrik Barth (1959) and Jon Anderson (1978, 1983), for example, give interesting accounts of the "unequal" relationship that characterized *malikaan/khanaan* and *mullayaan*. David Edwards (1996), on the other hand, describes, fascinatingly, the exceptional contingencies that, mostly in a colonial historical past, brought the most charismatic among these religious figures to temporarily attain a position of leadership, in the context of a religiously-inspired violent rebellion (a jihad). Given this background, the "systemic" phenomenon that seems to have taken place over the past decades in Afghanistan concerns the emergence of a new category of religious figure—armed with a more thorough training in religious subjects from Pakistani and Indian *madrassas*, or even Middle Eastern ones, in some cases—to the detriment of the category of *malikaan* and *khanaan*, which, over time, was overshadowed by the new, upcoming military "heroes" that the war created—the *kumandanaan*. If, in some cases, there might have been an identity difference between a prewar *malik/khan* and a wartime *kumandan*, in the majority of the cases, the average *kumandan* seems to have sprung from younger individuals who had not yet reached the "rank" of *malik* or *khan*, and who created a fresh pedigree for themselves through brave behavior in battle and leadership abilities in military contexts (along the lines I have already underlined above). Furthermore, the higher reputation that the foreign-trained (or outright foreign) *mullayaan* held in comparison with the traditional local ones within the broader context of the religious character that the anti-Soviet struggle first, and the civil war and Taliban conquest, later, attained, was pivotal in the overshadowing of the social "class" of *malikaan* and *khanaan*.[2]

Recurring Patterns

During my fieldwork research, a good half of the incidents that I was made aware of, and could partially follow personally, regarding perceived abuse, exploitation, and harassment, as well as actual cases of perpetrated violence and conflictive interpersonal and interfamilial relationships, did not fall into the category of the many familiar cases of honor-driven disputes and feuds that I had become used to from the previous ethnographic literature (Ahmed 1976; 1980; Barth 1959; Lindholm 1982; Zadran 1977). Rather, they were characterized by a marked differential in power between the two parties involved. The more powerful party was usually an individual who had made a name for himself during either the anti-Soviet struggle or the subsequent civil war. This individual had often acquired landed property, set up a business of some sort, and possibly obtained a political position of authority at some level, either within the local or regional structures of governance. He had furthermore maintained a close number of younger followers who guaranteed for him armed support in cases in which he wanted to affirm his power, achieve specific goals, or simply present a deterrence force against his adversaries. The weaker party was usually the member of a family with modest economic wealth, and little or no political influence. Cases of abuse that presented these characteristics were fairly common and widespread. The case that Ahmad was presenting about his father-in-law's land is one example in point. I have collected additional cases about commanders who, for example, forced another individual into a disadvantageous economic transaction, or who "stole" a child (of either sex) from his or her destitute family to keep as a bride, or a sexual toy (if male).[3]

The prestige and respect that the commanders largely enjoy among the population must be seen as an overdetermined phenomenon. It is certain that the ruthlessness these men demonstrated during the years of conflict, coupled with the availability of armed forces at their command today, instills fear into the average person. Fear brings an outward display of respect from others. In the Pashtun cultural context, wherein power and the personal ability to exert force is seen as an intrinsic feature of manliness, the boundary between respect deriving from fear and respect deriving from admiration of one's moral virtues becomes necessarily blurred. Furthermore, as most of my informants stated, and as far as I could confirm, most institutional positions of authority are, in fact, at the moment, in the hands of these same individuals who made a name for themselves during the conflicts (the only exception I am aware of in my geographical research area is the current director of the Directorate of Education of Nangarhar province, who was a psychology professor at Nangarhar University, and does not have a past as a militia leader). They have become influential political figures who act as powerful patrons for many and to whom many appeal in order to "get things done" when they have to deal with the public administration or have personal issues with their peers. This objective position of power (objective because it is institutionalized and sanctioned by the state apparatus) renders these characters, as a whole, as a catalyst for admiration and envy and a model of moral masculinity for new generations of men who might wish to attain any degree of power and authority whatsoever. In such cases, the aberrant behaviors (aberrant, that is, from the standpoint of the previous ethical standards prevalent in Pashtun society before the conflicts) that these commanders display and maintain to this day, may usher in a new moral paradigm for public action in the eyes of the youths who, as Rahmatullah noticed with regret, were exposed only to a sociocultural context of violence and war while growing up.[4]

As for the remaining half of the cases I had the chance to discuss with my informants, the fact that the model heralded by the many influential former (and current) commanders may have "seduced" a good share of today's twenty- and thirty-year-old men was brought home for me slowly during my fieldwork, by listening to a plethora of petty cases of abuse that saw as protagonists not the commanders, but rather unassuming, inconspicuous villagers across several rural districts in Nangarhar province. Irfan, a twenty-nine-year-old man from a village in the highly volatile district of Pachir-wa-Agam, with a college degree in agronomy and a temporary job in a development organization, described to me one of these cases that involved his family in the village.

> I told you, the people in the village fight all the time … it's like they enjoy fighting. For example, four or five months ago, the farmer who is our neighbor, and who has a field which borders one of our fields, started cultivating a field which had been left abandoned for many years, and which borders both our fields. We don't know who owns it, it has been left to itself for a long time. Anyway, in order to reach other fields that we own, we had to pass through this abandoned field. It's a common thing, there is often a right of passage into the fields of other people [very often cultivated fields are intersected by narrow strips of elevated, noncultivated ground, in order to give the possibility to others to pass through one's fields freely]. One day, this neighbor of ours started working the land of the abandoned field, and did not allow us anymore to pass through. We had to go a long way to get to the other fields we owned, beyond the abandoned field. We went several times to this farmer to ask why he was appropriating something that was not his, and to try to make him change his behavior. He did not care, he just said that he wanted to cultivate that field, and that he did not give us the right to pass through. He was arrogant [*mughror*], and acted like a bully [*zurawar*]. At that point, many other families would have gathered their men and would have ended up fighting with the men of the other family to solve the thing. Our neighbor was disrespecting us [*ihtiram na kawalo*] and our honor [*izzat*] was at stake. But we chose not to fight. We went to some elders in the village, and we called up a jirga to solve the problem without fighting. The guy accepted the jirga, and now we are in negotiations. The family of this neighbor is a powerful family … this is why he thought that he could do this abuse [*zulm*] without problems. But we have influence too [*nufuz*] … people in the office of the district governor know us, they know we are *pachayaan* [descendants of the Prophet Mohammed] and that we are good Muslims … the guy had to accept the jirga … The elders have already

told him that the right of passage is something that he must give to other people, he can't just do as he pleases ... We have yet to reach an agreement.

ANDREA: So, he accepted the jirga just because you were also an influential family [*ghat famil way*]?

IRFAN: Yes, I am sure that if we had been a weak family [*zaif*], he would have not accepted the jirga. You see, abusive people [*zurawaraan*], if they are powerful, they can do whatever they want, they can even not accept a jirga. Who is going to force them? The elders do not have the power to implement their decisions [*faisala*] ... And even when a powerful person accepts the jirga, after he has taken away a piece of land that did not belong to him from a weak family, a jirga will only be able to settle things by leaving half of the stolen land to the zurawar ... the legitimate owner will lose half of his land anyway ... it's not fair ... it's really wrong ...

ANDREA: Does it happen often?

IRFAN: Yes, at least more than it did before. Old people say that it got worse in the past years ... It's crazy [*da liwantob de*] ... one day you go to your field and you might find somebody that is working your land ... they start working a little bit of your land across the boundary. You confront them, and they might say "Oh, I am sorry, I did not realize," or even "I don't care, I work this land as mine now" ... What can you do? ... It's bad [*da kharab de*] ... There are a lot of zurawaraan now ...

Irfan's neighbor, who works his own land, unlike many others who hire seasonal laborers, is not a former commander or "war hero," nor is he connected to any of these individuals. He is Irfan's peer, of the same age, and lives in the same village; like Irfan, he was born during the Soviet occupation, was raised during the conflict(s), and never left Afghanistan as a refugee. His personal "army" is composed only of his own male relatives. Note also that the words chosen by Irfan to explain the pitfalls of the *jirga* system, of which the *zurawaraan* apparently take regular advantage, replicates almost verbatim those that Rahmatullah chose to describe the same problem (also, my conversations with Irfan were held only in Pashto). Such similarity lends credibility to the interpretation of the phenomenon as both informants acknowledge it.

I interpret the numerous such occurrences that were reported by my informants as an index of the shift in meaning that moral values (particularly about masculinity) have undergone during the three decades of conflict in the Pashtun areas where I have been working. The "state of exception" (in the sense in which Giorgio Agamben uses this expression, after Carl Schmitt's similar concept in *Political Theology*; see Agamben 2005 and Schmitt 2006 [1922]) that was ushered in by the anti-Soviet struggle opened the way for the justification of aberrant actions carried out by the militia commanders of the time, commanders who broke many of the erstwhile culturally accepted norms in dealing with violence and abusive behaviors. The militia leaders increasingly characterized their own public figures through a disproportionate and, at times, gratuitous use of violence as well as openly self-aggrandizing goals. Such deviant behaviors were rationalized by acknowledging the exceptional necessities of the conflict context. From the same standpoint, these mujahideen militia leaders were seen as righteously displaying their *nartob* (manliness) and *ghairat* (courage, fearlessness) by joining and actively engaging in the holy war (jihad) launched against the anti-Islamic Soviet occupation forces, and Soviet-backed Afghan government. Over time, however, and despite the changed political and strategic landscape following the Soviet withdrawal, and the collapse of Najibullah's procommunist government, these aberrant models for personal and communal action evidently lingered within the sociocultural environment, remained the main schemata for the activities of powerful individuals, and slowly became routinized and institutionalized. This Weberian paradigm for the rationalization, routinization, and institutionalization of personal charisma, that seems to have worked in the context of recent Afghan historical events, dovetails nicely with Fredrik Barth's transactional interpretation of social and cultural change (Barth 1966). From this viewpoint, the state of exception that the war context created, which justified and rationalized the suspension of some of the main behavioral requirements for *pakhto paalal* (follow pak *pakhto* hto, i.e., Pashtun customs), morphed into a permanent vacuum in which the aberrant actions of the *kumandanaan* began to enter into the social feedback cycle, so that widespread deviant behaviors set new principles (and hence new moral values) on which shifting cultural schemata and idioms became premised. Previous ethically aberrant and unacceptable comportments became normalized and even, at least for some, normative.[5]

Indeed, for those who were not seduced by the feedback result of the commanders' aberrant behaviors (like many among my middle-aged informants, as Rahmatullah and Eamal), those actions and misdeeds continue to this day to be considered as reproachable and dishonorable. The abusive, violent, and oppressive comportments of these "warlords" (as they are now known in Western parlance) remain, for the people who did not buy into their charisma, not a proof of their *nartob*, or manliness, but rather, a demonstration of their being no more than odious *zurawaraan* (bullies), who have furthermore become *beghairata* because of their misdeeds. In this view, the commander who abusively appropriates the land of another man, or kidnaps the young daughter of a less powerful family, or forces someone, through violence, into an unwanted economic transaction, is using his might to operate outside the cardinal moral standards of *pakhto*, and by doing so does not earn for himself the name of *nar*, but rather that of *beghairata*.

The problem, however, lies in the fact that today the kind of behaviors that would make a commander a *beghairata*, at least in the eyes of some, have become extremely common in the Pashtun Southeast. The figure of the *kumandaan*, still proliferates in spite of everything else. These individuals, furthermore, have a sizable following of well-armed young men, who form de facto private armies at their orders. The moral example that they set in the collective imaginary flies very far and can make profound inroads into the consciousness (and the unconscious) of many young men. The hundreds who enlist in the commanders' private armies do so, certainly, for diverse reasons, including to have a stable income, which in today's Afghanistan is a scarce and precious resource. Nevertheless, it is very likely that a sizable number of Pashtun young people (at least in the area I have worked in) now see in the commander a figure to emulate, admire, and even envy. This is an aspect of my research that I have yet to fully investigate, but the material I gathered so far makes me suspect that the charisma and institutionalized behavior embodied by the new "social class" of militia commanders has had a deep impact on the general (un)consciousness of the post–Saur Revolution generations. It seems at this point likely that the "culture of violence" that the war institutionalized over the years spilled over onto the civilian population, beyond the individuals who are, or were, directly involved in war activities, as the commanders and their followers. All the people I interacted with, both in Jalalabad and in the rural districts, have been consistent in their perception of a highly conflictive social environment, to a higher degree than the prewar situation presented, and with an increased proneness to use aggression and violence to gain an edge over one's peers, covillagers or neighbors. (This aggression is apparently coupled with a consequent perception of helplessness on the part of the "victims" and of impunity on the part of the "perpetrators," particularly, it seems, when compared with the pre-1978 situation, when, as my informants report, the population could rely at least on a modicum of state-managed policing activity.) It is certainly true that ethnographic literature from the past has shown how Pashtun society, as a whole, was far from being a peaceful and free-from-frictions environment, even before the collapse following the Saur Revolution. Yet, the people who are able to recall the times before the last thirty years concur in perceiving today to have a harsher social context, where local conflicts (*lanjay*) and abusiveness (*zulm*) are increasingly present.

Conclusion

In this chapter, I have argued that the abnormal and exceptional necessities stemming from a war context, which for years unleashed and justified equally aberrant behaviors, had a momentous feedback effect on the generations that were born and raised during the decades of war (and, implicitly, on the form and character that the Afghan state has acquired since 2001). For some among those individuals who were more exposed to the ugliness of the conflict, the concepts of *nartob* and *ghairat* have been renegotiated to reconcile those aberrant behaviors they witnessed, and these renegotiated concepts have become more and more institutionalized. It seems likely that, for these subjects, *nartob* and *ghairat* today are more closely linked to the expression of sheer power (*qowat*) and military prowess (*zur*) and to the capacity of affirming one's own interests through aggressive behavior (*zulm*) than to the moral standards that my middle-aged friends have always associated with the ideas of *nartob* and *ghairat*. The functions of social control that the principles of *pakhto* had carried out in the past suffered a breakdown which, in some cases, seems to be irreversible. A new *pakhto*, based on sheer power and force, seems today to be competing against the "pre-war *pakhto*," which was, by and large, based on ethical behavior and social censorship.

ANDREA CHIOVENDA is a postdoctoral fellow in the Department of Global Health and Social Medicine, Harvard Medical School, and an affiliated faculty member in the Institute for Liberal Arts and Interdisciplinary Studies at Emerson College, Boston.

Notes

1. In 1954, Raymond Firth, during his presidential address to the Royal Anthropological Institute (Firth 1954), had laid the foundations of the concepts that Fredrik Barth would develop and refine later, to which I am referring here. Firth's emphasis on the difference between social organization (a process) and social structure (a systemic abstraction for heuristic purposes) as well as his acknowledgment of the secondary role attributed in anthropological thought (of his time) to the individual's psychological motives and private meanings as constituents of social action and social change, represent a preface to the development of Fredrik Barth's transactional theory.
2. It should be kept in mind, in this regard, that particularly the Pashtun areas of Afghanistan, during the anti-Soviet conflict, saw a sizable influx of both fighters and religious preachers from the Arabian peninsula and the Middle East, in addition to those returning Afghan and Pakistani Pashtuns who had received religious training in Deobandi and Wahhabi *madrassas* in Pakistan and India during the 1970s and 1980s (see Fair 2008). Arabic-speaking Middle Eastern preachers came to hold significant prestige within Pashtun society during the Soviet occupation, and were crucial for the balance shift in social capital between *malikaan/khanaan* and religious figures, both local and foreign.
3. The exploitation by adult males of male minors as "sex toys" (in Dari, referred to as *bacha bazi*), is a phenomenon found all over Afghanistan, apparently regardless of ethnic group or religious affiliation. The extent to which the practice is carried out in specific areas of the country is hard to quantify, given the reluctance of the population to speak out about such an inherently problematic issue. I have not gathered enough information about *bacha bazi* while talking with my informants to be able to discuss exhaustively the way in which

the practice is interpreted, judged, and, more importantly, justified by community members in a Pashtun milieu. What seems certain, however, is that the existence of the phenomenon predates the beginning of the conflict period (1978). Whether the war increased the instances in which the practice was carried out is difficult to gauge. The phenomenon of *bacha bazi* finds itself at the center of a complex and delicate interplay between social constraints, cultural idioms, erotic desire, power differentials, and public display of dominance. Anthropologist Afsaneh Najmabadi has recently analyzed some of these elements in her work on sexuality in modern Iran, and the Persian cultural world as a whole (of which Afghanistan is also part; Najmabadi 2005). However, her book relies only on literary and iconographic evidence, while a thorough ethnographic investigation is needed to shed more light on the contemporary and experiential aspects of the phenomenon. At the time of this writing (June 2016), the Afghan Independent Commission for Human Rights released the executive summary of a detailed report on *bacha bazi*, based on 2200 interviews carried out in seventeen Afghan provinces. The analysis of the full report will hopefully give a useful starting point for ethnographers to conduct in-depth research on the issue in the future.

4. It is worth noticing here how the state can play a powerful role as enabler or inhibitor of certain dynamics, even in the case of a "weak state," or outright "failed state," as Afghanistan is often referred to in common Western policy-making parlance. Within the hypercentralized model of governance after which the post-2001 Afghan state has been shaped, the appointment of former *kumandanaan*, militia leaders, and "warlords," to institutional positions of authority, has occurred often intentionally and instrumentally (through decisions originated either in Kabul or Washington) in order to satisfy short-term strategic and military necessities in the protracted campaign against the Taliban movement (for the most conspicuous cases, see Giustozzi [2009]). Whether intended or unintended, the social and cultural consequences of such course of action, which had its source in the core apparatuses of the state, are what informants like Rahmatullah and Eamal are regretting today.

5. It is important to point out, however, that such Weberian trajectory through routinization and institutionalization may be considered to have continued unabated after the vacuum I refer to here was (at least officially) "filled" by a state structure, after 2001. The appointment (*not* election) of many *kumandanaan* to positions of authority within state apparatuses (either local, regional, or national), helped consolidate and reaffirm the sociocultural processes that had taken place during the years of the Soviet occupation, the civil war, and the Taliban regime, which I am discussing.

Bibliography

Agamben Giorgio. 2005. *State of Exception*. Translated by Kevin Attell. Chicago: University of Chicago Press.

Ahmed, Akbar. 1976. *Millennium and Charisma among Pathans: A Critical Essay in Social Anthropology*. London: Routledge and Kegan Paul.

———. 1980. *Pukhtun Economy and Society: Traditional Structure and Economic Development in a Tribal Society*. London: Routledge and Kegan Paul.

Anderson, Jon W. 1978. "There Are No Khans Anymore: Economic Development and Social Change in Tribal Afghanistan." *Middle East Journal* 32 (2): 167–83.

———. 1983. "Khan and Khel: Dialectics of Pashtun Tribalism." In *The Conflict of Tribe and State in Iran and Afghanistan*, ed. Richard Tapper. New York: St. Martin's Press.

Barth, Fredrik. 1959. *Political Leadership among Swat Pathans*. Oxford: Oxford University Press.

———. 1966. *Models of Social Organization*. RAI Occasional Paper no. 23. London: Royal Anthropological Institute.

Baryalay, Haroon J. 2006. *Jirga Theory and Reform Proposal*. LLM Research Paper. Cambridge, MA: Harvard University Law School.

Boesen, Inger. 1983. "Conflicts of Solidarity in Pakhtun Women's Lives." In *Women and Islamic Societies: Social Attitudes and Historical Perspectives*, ed. Bo Utas. London: Curzon Press.

Bourdieu, Pierre. 1966. "The Sentiment of Honor in Kabyle Society." In *Honor and Shame: The Values of Mediterranean Society*, ed. John Peristiany. Chicago: Chicago University Press.

———. 1977. [1972]. *Outline of a Theory of Practice*. Cambridge, UK: Cambridge University Press.

Edwards, David. 1996. *Heroes of the Age: Moral Fault Lines on the Afghan Frontier*. Berkeley: University of California Press.

———. 2002. *Before Taliban: Genealogies of the Afghan Jihad*. Berkeley: University of California Press.

Fair, Christine. 2008. *The Madrassah Challenge: Militancy and Religious Education in Pakistan*. Washington, DC: United States Institute of Peace.

Firth, Raymond. 1954. "Social Organization and Social Change." *Journal of the Royal Anthropological Institute of Great Britain and Ireland* 84 (1/2): 1–20.

Giovannini, Maureen. 1981. "Woman: A Dominant Symbol within the Cultural System of a Sicilian Town." *Man* 16 (3): 408–26.

Giustozzi, Antonio. 2000. *War, Politics and Society in Afghanistan, 1978–1992*. Washington, DC: Georgetown University Press.

———. 2003. *Respectable Warlords? The Politics of State-Building in Post-Taleban Afghanistan*. Working Papers series 1, 33. London: Crisis States Research Centre.

———. 2009. *Empires of Mud: Wars and Warlords in Afghanistan*. New York: Columbia University Press.

Giustozzi, Antonio, and Noor Ullah. 2006. *"Tribes" and Warlords in Southern Afghanistan, 1980–2005*. Working Paper no. 7. London: Crisis States Research Centre.

Grima, Benedicte. 1992. *The Performance of Emotions among Puxtun Women*. Austin: University of Texas Press.

Herzfeld, Michael. 1985. *The Poetics of Manhood: Contest and Identity in a Cretan Mountain Village*. Princeton, NJ: Princeton University Press.

Hollan, Douglas. 1992. "Cross-cultural Differences in the Self." *Journal of Anthropological Research* 48 (4): 283–300.

Lindholm, Charles. 1982. *Generosity and Jealousy: The Swat Pukhtun of Northern Pakistan*. New York: Columbia University Press.

Mahdi, N. Q. 1986. "Pukhtunwali: Ostracism and Honor among the Pathan Hill Tribes." *Ethology and Sociobiology* 7 (3–4): 295–304.

Najmabadi, Afsaneh. 2005. *Women with Mustaches and Men without Beards: Gender and Sexual Anxieties of Iranian Modernity*. Berkeley: University of California Press.

Ortner, Sherry B. 1984. "Theory in Anthropology since the Sixties." *Comparative Studies in Society and History* 26 (1): 126–66.
Sahlins, Marshall D. 1981. *Historical Metaphors and Mythical Realities: Structure in the Early History of the Sandwich Islands Kingdom*. Ann Arbor: University of Michigan Press.
Schmitt, Carl. 2006. [1922]. *Political Theology: Four Chapters on the Concept of Sovereignty*. Chicago: University of Chicago Press.
Tapper, Nancy. 1991. *Bartered Brides: Politics, Gender, and Marriage in an Afghan Tribal Society*. Cambridge, UK: Cambridge University Press.
Zadran, Alef S. 1977. "Socio-Economic and Legal-Political Processes in a Pukhtun Village, Southeastern Afghanistan." PhD diss. SUNY, Buffalo.

10

ENGENDERING THE TALIBAN

Sonia Ahsan

Introduction

On September 27, 1996, in a Toyota pickup truck, a relatively unrecognized group entered the United Nations compound in Kabul where former president Mohammad Najibullah Ahmadzai was living in exile awaiting his trial. This group castrated the former Afghan president and dragged his mutilated body out onto the Kabul streets. The castrated and bloodied corpse of this former Afghan president was hung on a pole in the center of the city (Rashid 2000, 49). Through these brazenly irreverent acts, this group, which would eventually become known to the world as the Taliban, sent out a formidable message to potential adversaries that they too could face the same brutal fate.

This chapter interrogates the changes and continuities in the relationship between Islam and gendered politics as expressed through the significance of moral policing in the Taliban movement. It begins by outlining the institutional arrangements related to family and marriage at the urban and rural levels of the community before the Taliban movement and asks if and how these arrangements reconfigured themselves with the advent of the Taliban. While Islam has long been central to the social and moral worlds of Afghans, this chapter argues that the lived experiences and everyday practices of ordinary Afghans sustained significant changes during the Taliban regime. Since one of the primary modalities of Taliban governance concerned the everyday lives of ordinary women, it is within these life worlds that one may find traces of the violence perpetrated by the Taliban state. As the relationship between Islam and politics shifted in the Taliban regime, characterized specifically by reprioritizing *Amr Bil-Ma'roof Wa Nahi 'Anil-Munkar* [commanding the lawful and forbidding the sinful acts in Islam], and in *Pukhtunwali* [honorable codes of conduct in Pashtun/Pukhtun society], the ways in which ordinary Afghan women constructed their moral worlds experienced corresponding changes.[1] Through my ethnographic fieldwork at a *khaana-yi aman* (home of peace or secure home) in Kabul, this chapter highlights the far-reaching effects that persist to this day on the life worlds of women as a consequence of integrating the Taliban version of Islam into the body politic of Afghanistan.[2] The chapter concludes with an analysis of the effectiveness of the Taliban methodology pertaining to gender and sexuality on state building processes.

Gender and Sexuality before the Taliban

A family legal code for Afghanistan has always been embedded within various interpretations of Islamic law, and thus any reform efforts are viewed with suspicion and even hostility (Tapper 1984, 296). While Nur M. Taraki (1978–1979) is famous in recent history for introducing Decree Number 7 (see below), the coerced modernization efforts preceded Taraki and fit into the reforms promulgated by Amir Abdur Rahman (1880–1901), who, for instance, posed restrictions on cousin marriages which are allowed under Islam. Paradoxically, Abdur Rahman also introduced the death penalty for adulterous women, which is a contentious interpretation of a Qur'anic verse (Dupree 1984, 306–40). Regarding his other gender laws, Abdur Rahman mandated an upper limit of thirty rupees for a bride price, but this measure had little practical applicability.[3] Other Afghan leaders charted alternative trajectories for women's rights in Afghanistan, which were controversial at the time. For example, the essays of Amir Habibullah (1901–1919), which emphasized the centrality of women to modern nation building projects, found their resistance in the religious leaders of the time. Dupree writes, "They contended that education for women would lead to the breakdown of the family, sexual anarchy, and ultimately degrade women. The honor of the nation would be lost." Despite similar opposition from conservative elements, King Amanullah (1919–1929) advocated the removal of the *chadari* (a form of veiling in contemporary Afghanistan) and *purdah* (gender segregation) and introduced education reform for women (Dupree 1984, 307).

Decree Number 7 was introduced in 1978 by Nur Muhammad Taraki to elevate the status of women in Afghanistan by establishing limitations on monetary exchanges in the marital institution. The other goals of this decree were to allow freedom with respect to choosing marital partners and mandating minimum age requirements for marriage (Beattie 1984, 190). Such reforms may be read within the larger framework of colonialism and the universalization of a Western configuration of marriage embedded within uniquely Western historical processes, which were not necessarily experienced in Afghanistan (Tapper 1984, 294–95). Mapping Western historical changes onto Afghanistan created incommensurable ambivalences and contradictions. Thus, some measures, such as a ban on cousin marriage, were introduced that were wholly extraneous to the local contexts and even contrary to an Islamic value system.

Such legal restructurings were accompanied by institutional developments motivated to further women's rights reforms. Today the primary institution concerning gender is the Ministry of Women's Affairs (MOWA), which unlike the Ministry of Justice, has no legislative capacity, but plays a significant role in the production of vocabulary concerning women's rights in Afghanistan. One may locate the historical precedence of MOWA in institutions like the Ministry of Social Affairs (MOSA), which was assigned to Dr. Anahita Ratebzad, given her services to the People's Democratic Party of Afghanistan (PDPA). The PDPA played a significant role in establishing the Republic of Afghanistan under the aegis of Mohammad Daoud Khan (1973–1978) as a consequence of the April 1978 Saur Revolution. MOSA was short-lived, however, and was abolished two months later, and the affairs related to women were consigned to the Ministry of Education. The Democratic Organization of Afghan Women (DOAW), established by Dr. Anahita Ratebzab in 1965, was reorganized under the title Khalq Organization of Afghan Women (KOAW) in 1978, and Dil Ara Mehak was appointed as its president (Beattie 1984, 184–208). This organization instituted substantial measures for female literacy, which were viewed by some factions in Afghanistan as invasive.

Thus, most governments before the Taliban strategically deployed women's rights rhetoric to further their political goals and provide the façade of a progressive politics. While women were afforded rights within some legal statutes, the necessary political organizations needed to compel practical implementation of these ideal standards did not exist. The Women's Institute, which was established in 1975, previously known as Women Welfare Association, was viewed with mistrust by ordinary Afghan women, who considered their concerns not represented by the elite women of this institution. While this institute had at one point, by some accounts, more than eight thousand members and field offices in ten cities, it did not gain everyday relevance in the lives of ordinary Afghan women. Similarly, other institutions like the Revolutionary Association of the Women of Afghanistan (RAWA) are rendered irrelevant based on their appeals for a secular Afghanistan, armed resistance for women, and their operating base in Quetta, outside Afghanistan. Given these social impediments, political organization for women faced massive challenges.

Taliban Instrumentalization of Islam for Political Ends

The Taliban state preferred designating and dealing with total populations rather than with individual cases. Instead of targeting particular individuals who provoke trouble, women were targeted as total and homogenous populations. Immediately after the Taliban captured Kabul, they began targeting the private realm, which has historically been a world of women. While administrative measures against the private realm of women have a long precedence in Afghan history, the Taliban governance created significant ruptures and historical changes. Juan Cole has noted that the public sphere of the Taliban rendered both men and women formless and invisible as heterogeneity was eliminated and penalized any semblance of difference (Cole 2003, 771–808). The Taliban succumbed to a totalizing homogeneity as they became more and more obsessed with redesigning engendering the public and private realms. Before the Taliban, the *chadari* was not the mandatory form of dress in Afghanistan, even if some women chose to wear it. Now, the *chadari* wearers were borne with the burden of depicting legitimate culture, symbolizing forced piety, and disseminating official purity in the public, roles that had historically been relegated to males. By wearing the *chadari*, and becoming faceless and formless, the women could enter the realm of the responsible.[4]

Restricting female mobilization in the public is not limited to Afghanistan as a temporal or spatial formation. These traditions, some of which preceded the Taliban, are, of course, evident in state-sanctioned public movements in other countries as well. For example, a woman may not go in an all-female group to perform Hajj in Saudi Arabia and must be accompanied by a state recognized male *mahram* (a next of kin with whom marriage is not possible and sexual intercourse would be considered incestuous). As Ahmed Rashid notes, for the most part, Afghan women before the Taliban, especially in non-Pashtun (non-Pukhtun) areas, enjoyed relative freedom of public movement and sartorial expression (Rashid 2000). Afghans had a long tradition of women dancing in weddings and festive occasions, social activities that were entirely banned by the Taliban. The Taliban expanded their rules to all spheres of life and decreed that a male *mahram* must be present in a woman's proximity if she was to venture out in public *for any reason*. These decrees achieved what they were designed to do, that is, to seriously restrict female mobility in the public. Images of pious and modest daughters and wives, bearers of the family's honor and respectability, saturated the Taliban imaginary, and these representations solidified through oral stories and folklore narratives that were deliberately circulated as part of a didactic state campaign to educate the masses on issues of sexual propriety. The Taliban banned female education by closing sixty-three schools, a measure that, while targeted for girls, also affected male education (Cole 2003; Rashid 2000). Cole cites several narratives of women who were banned from public movement through a variety of justifications. One incident involved women being beaten for wearing white socks, as that color desecrated the Taliban flag. Another woman notes that women were banned from leaving their homes during Ramadan, a measure that was circulated entirely through folklore narratives, as it has no basis in Islam. Girl's schools were called the "gateway to Hell, the first step on the road to prostitution" (Cole 2003, 797). Historically, the male members of the family would make decisions concerning female education, marriage, or entry into the public realm. The Taliban wrested these decision-making capacities out of the hands of the male members, as they considered themselves better suited to chart the futures of the women of Afghanistan.

Reading gender segregation as mandatory in Islam was nothing new in Afghanistan. The continuity is evident in the centrality of Islamic principles to the Taliban regime. Even before the Taliban, the primary institution through which honor functioned was the Islamic form of marriage, as Tapper notes, "Both equality and competition are confirmed or denied through the complex institution of marriage and expressed in the language of honor" (1984, 300). The shift however is in the *methods* of interpreting Islamic laws, the primacy of moral policing, the engendering of administrative regulations, and the reinforced surveillance for potential sexual transgressions. The Taliban rhetoric makes manifest their aversion to a secular state where the role of *ulama* [religious intellectuals] is relegated to the margins. Although some of these anxieties of the Taliban may be explained by the measures taken by previous governments to limit the religious authority of *ulama*, they are also concerned with the increasing Westernization in the contemporary moment of the Afghan public. The changes that the Taliban instituted may become intelligible when one compares them to the era of Abdur Rahman. The measures introduced by Abdur Rahman greatly limited the authority of the *ulama*, relegating them to the sphere of bureaucracy. Since *ulama* have had a traditional influence on the politics in Afghanistan, this measure was unprecedented and greatly resented in conservative arenas.

The entwinement, between modernity and tradition, triggered by a distrust of the modernized Pashtun man, seen by the Taliban state as incapable of handling matters of dishonor, is demonstrated in vivid ways when the Taliban state boldly intervenes in the previously private realms of the family. Taliban laws and policies, apparently focused on protecting women, have had significant influence in humiliating and shaming the fathers, husbands, and brothers whose daughters, wives, and sisters are extricated by the Afghan state from the family in the name of shelter and security. When the runaway woman turns to the newly formed family courts for mediation and negotiation with her relatives, the Afghan state inevitably enters into the intimate matters of the family. The family courts have an interest in such kind of intimate intervention as this solidifies the legitimacy of the state and renders it indispensable to the previously private realm of the *khaanawaada* (family).

Ethnographic Fieldwork on the Effects of Talibanization

Taliban violence was directed toward both public and private realms, and in this way, both revealed and concealed their power mechanisms. Despite initial claims that they would not enter the private realm of the home and were more concerned with moral crime in the public realm, the Taliban invaded the privacy of the home in multiple ways. For instance, they would regularly monitor private phone calls, and their radio pronouncements punctuated the everyday lives of Afghans by calling on them to propagate proper sexual behavior. The radio transmissions were key in reaching out to the Afghan people, conditioning the interiority of their homes and fashioning ethical landscapes within the inner sections of historically private spaces. Executions amassed a radio audience as the Taliban publicly advertised them through this medium during their reign (Rosenberg and Rahimi 2012). Maulana Fazillulah, of Swat Taliban, favored radio broadcasts so much that he was dubbed "Maulana Radio" by the Swatis (Mujtaba and Ahmed 2013). Modern media has been used for ethical self-fashioning and creating modern publics and counterpublics in a variety of ways in other places (Hirschkind 2013). The Taliban's use of Radio Shari'at had an Afghan particularity as, in addition to didactic propagations of proper moral behavior, their radio fatwa (religious ordinances or edicts) were part of the public spectacle of power by inciting fear into the population.[5] By announcing the names of those who were *about* to be killed, the Taliban created a modern public built around fear and apprehension of what was *about to come*. Radio Shari'at both publicized the events and shaped ethical soundscapes while it also concealed the actual workings of the state apparatus (Hirschkind 2013). Discernibly, the Taliban were well aware of the power of radio and modern media and utilized it for their governance. A number of women I met told me that during the Taliban era, because of the sanctions in place on their public movement, radio was a favored source of engaging with the public domain without the necessity of face-to-face interaction. This kind of faceless public engagement created a uniquely modern Afghan public. The ethical architecture of the home was not only made publicly accessible but also reconfigured in significant ways through these radio fatwa.

In 2010, a video was released in which the Taliban purportedly fired nine shots, killing an allegedly adulterous woman (Roberts 2012). It showed cheering crowds at this execution. The people I interviewed told me that these spectacles had the tacit support of the Afghan government, who was seeking to appease conservative elements of society. It may seem that the most religious and puritanical are the ones in favor of the Taliban negotiations for moral transgressions, but even those who fancy themselves as modern or secular in the Taliban government may succumb to some of the same ideological assumptions as the most devout. Thus, Islam has been instrumentalized for unfortunate ends by almost all governing modalities in Afghanistan. Rarely do Afghan officials, even those outside the supporters of the Taliban, reject Islamic honor outright. I was told time and again that there was no contradiction, or rather should not be any, in being honorable and modern and that being honorable did not preclude the possibility of accepting modern notions of women's rights and emancipation. This kind of coerced amalgamation of two polarized dichotomies—that which was perceived as modern and that which was traditional—was evident in the feminist narratives that sought to challenge punitive aspects of honor codes, and yet appealed to some sort of honorable and chivalrous national image to seek justice and retribution. So for instance, feminists would often say that oppressing women was dishonorable and contrary to Islam, and thus, women's rights should be supported for Islamic reasons. In other words, Islam was instrumentalized by the Taliban, the Karzai government, and the feminists, all for varying ends. In this sense, Islamic honor was always at the center of negotiations between the local feminists and the Taliban, the Taliban and the Karzai government, and the Karzai government and the feminists. Thus collusions between Islamic fundamentalists and Afghan state apparatuses may be the most ostensible example; however, progressive feminist movements and neoliberal projects also, perhaps not unintentionally, participated in reappropriating Islamic honor codes.

In my interview with a high-ranking official of the Ministry of Women's Affairs, her struggle between historical notions of honor and modern questions of women's emancipation became apparent and her positions vis-à-vis these issues seemed ambiguous at times and flatly contradictory at others. She noted, for example, "We must move forward with the Taliban. I do not anticipate any serious consequences for women's rights as a result of the negotiations with the Taliban."[6] Given her association of sexual transgression with the economically disenfranchised and her personal goals of ascending the political hierarchy, she clearly saw herself as separate from the lower classes, unadulterated by wanton debauchery of the masses. Other powerful women towed a similar line. Nazima, a very intelligent and impressive woman who ran a successful organization, told me that it was not good politics to link yourself too much with secular feminism. In other words, to further personal professional goals, it was better not to be seen as critical of the Taliban or appear too modern. Trapped between the two positions of modernity and tradition, this placement enables a disavowal of nonnormative behavior by honorable subjects vying to gain national recognition as well as by honorable subjects seeking to embrace the degenerate and improper sexualities ascribed to adulterous bodies (that is to say, sexual promiscuousness is almost too illegitimate even for those who seek to disrupt). To say it directly, political ends justify the instrumentalization of Islam in the service of status quo.

A Look at the Contemporary Feminist Movements in Afghanistan

The feminist movements, such as the Afghan Women's Network (AWN), have sought to embed the language of women's rights into the reconciliatory projects of transition. "No rights, no peace" is one of the slogans of the contemporary feminists. There is a pronounced tension between the activists and the female politicians on the future of women's rights in Afghanistan. The female politicians are often accused of abandoning women's rights causes, despite the help from the activists in their election campaigns. Notwithstanding these accusations, at the *khaana-yi aman*, I witnessed strategic partnerships between the activists and the politicians as they relied on each other for support: the activists to get their agendas to parliament and the politicians to get elected. Despite these partnerships, there was a palpable lack of trust among the activists, who viewed the politicians as adhering to a different class, and not being conversant in the issues of everyday Afghan women.

At the Bonn Conference in 2011, AWN brought together various feminist organizations inside Afghanistan to give a joint statement on the status of women in Afghanistan. It included a call to Islamic countries in addition to the Western countries. "Afghan Women further appeal to Islamic countries to promote improvements in Afghan women's skills and expertise in Islamic law and jurisprudence in their development and diplomatic engagements in Afghanistan. These skills and qualifications are necessary for Afghan women to work in high level positions in the judiciary" (Afghan Women's Network 2011). This statement asks that the participation of women be read as integral to good governance. In an interview with the head of the Open Society in Afghanistan, she stressed the importance of women to all sectors of society. In my travels across Afghanistan with women's rights organizations as they established their bases in the provinces, I saw female parliamentarians receiving training for not only gender advocacy but also other economic and political issues facing Afghanistan. A friend who worked as the gender director for the Civil Service Commission told me that she was no longer interested in the gender department as she thought Afghan women needed to move beyond gender dialogue into mainstream social arenas. Many women, who had previously been active for women's rights, told me that they did not want to talk about gender rights anymore, but about political and economic reform. This would enable them to contribute more to Afghan society. The "gender talk" was passé, and women wanted to be seen as contributors to all aspects of social life.

Changing Conceptions of the Afghan State

The Taliban state is not a stagnant group, but a social relation or social arrangement, produced by a uniquely Afghan history. It conditions and mystifies a transcendental essence made manifest in honorable and dishonorable states of being. The Taliban state then vacillates between two poles of piety and of promiscuity, and this movement produces the honorable state. The responsibility for killings and other violent acts are rendered intelligible by explicating the banality of the ordinary lives of the Taliban rather than focusing on the remarkable domain of their extraordinary rule. Granted that the Taliban ruled by spectacles of fear, but these spectacular displays of violence were grounded in the recesses of the everyday. The militarization of public spaces was achieved by squelching the routine activities characteristic of the everyday life of Kabul: music, dancing, singing, kite flying, and even laughing (Cole 2003). Quotidian practices such as walking down the street or taking public transportation elicited suspicion and violence. Natasha, the wife of a Talib fighter at the *khaana-yi aman*, told me that she had a heightened awareness of her surroundings during the Taliban years and always felt fearful and vulnerable when she ventured outside the home.

Those who had themselves once constituted the margins established the Taliban state. Yet the Taliban were never passive objects that let themselves be simplistically manipulated by the Afghan state. They maneuvered and reconfigured the state in significant ways. The Taliban themselves fomented a large-scale rebellion, bringing revolutionary changes to the Afghan governing modalities. Thus, their state represented an always unfinished and unfolding project, which was constituted by its marginality and was best observed within the spaces that it marginalized like the *khaana-yi aman*.[7] In this Taliban world, there are no simple oppositions between fragility and power or honor and dishonor, as these concepts are complexly entwined for the purposes of state governance. The *madrassas* had spatially isolated the Taliban from Afghan society and now they deployed the same kinds of spatial isolation to others. Although the Taliban ostracized some social actors, they kept them within the parameters of the city for close observation. The Taliban state project, always incomplete and insufficiently imagined, constantly invoked images of wildness, butchery, and debauchery. This state was inherently unstable as there was always a threat of explosion from within.

The Taliban movement reconfigured the Islamic fundamentalist imaginary as it engaged directly with the Afghan state and its ideological assumptions that situated feminist movements at its margins. For Olivier Roy, any movement that is not directed toward the state is apolitical or a rejection of modernity. By this definition, of course, the Taliban movement is inherently modern as its main engagement and preoccupation has always been directly with the state. If post-Islamism is concerned with, as Olivier Roy would have us believe, the realm of the political over the religious, then the Taliban movement is a post-Islamic movement. Roy's observation that the political precedes the religious in Muslim countries is applicable in Afghanistan (Roy 2004, 5). Insofar as Islamic fundamentalist governance posits an ostensive and deliberate synthesis between religious morality and politics, the work of critical analysis is to delineate, as much as possible, an ideological separation between morality, religion, and politics through careful scrutiny.

Attending to the interstices and microcapillaries of the everyday lives of the Taliban and their wives, we can discern how they make and inhabit their worlds and encounter conflicts and incongruities that unsettle and unmake their worlds. The Taliban state exerted power that was simultaneously distant and imminent, visible and invisible, orderly and chaotic, spectacular and mundane, rational and magical. In this world, the women became "a subliminal and precarious world of individuals" who could not admit to their own existence (Puar 2007, 150). Following Veena Das, who calls the local practices through which the state inscribes itself into the ordinary life of communities "magical," the Taliban's spectacular displays can be grounded in the everyday routines of daily life (2007, 163). Mahmood Mamdani has noted that, when violence is so woven into the social fabric that it becomes indistinguishable from everyday life, victims may eventually become killers, who can then be understood in everyday lives of those who commit "street murder[s] rather than the bureaucratic efficiency of a mass extermination" (Mamdani 2001, 219). Mamdani's work describes a political configuration in which victims are not easily demarcated from the killers. In other words, his work renders the Taliban violence against its own population *thinkable* by situating the political formations produced during colonial rule into their proper historical context. The freedom fighters of yesterday are the oppressors of today. Those who resisted the state have now become its personification par excellence. In making the other vulnerable, the Taliban themselves are rendered vulnerable. Precariousness of the "other" presupposes my own precariousness. The women are sometimes friend, sometimes enemy, sometimes a cure, and sometimes a poison that shifts from the center to the margins and coerces the state to change its corresponding definitions of who is categorized as what and when. The Taliban violence is rendered intelligible once it is historicized within the legacy of women's rights reform in Afghanistan. The focus of the Taliban movement has been to restructure the everyday lives of Afghans as a response to the anxieties of secularism and Westernization that they view as threatening.

Conclusion: Effectiveness of the Taliban Methodology

The Taliban primarily saw themselves as protectors of the traditional Afghan family, especially its most integral component, the women. This self-perception led to massive interventions in the intimate spheres of the private, resulting in radically publicizing the private realm of the family, precisely the opposite of what they perhaps intended. The *chadari* was important for the Taliban to cultivate female honor in public, but sartorial expressions of honor were not limited to female bodies alone. Deviant acts, depending on the degree of presumed transgression, were not morally neutral for men and they too were held culpable, although to a lesser extent, by the same religious edicts. The Taliban impeded some life possibilities for men and encouraged others. For men, mandatory beards became an important marker of religious identity and one that separated honorable male bodies from dishonorable ones. The *chadari* and the beard, tangible embodiments of metaphysical substances, the noticeable lack of which, induced reactionary violence, renders ostensible that these are not merely exterior appendages but define an existential core. The bearding undertaken by large numbers of Afghan men was one manifestation of the prescriptive demonstrative piety of honor codes, where growing a beard functions as a reorientation into masculine honorable identity

Today, the Taliban continue to negotiate with the Afghan government as the evermore violent influential social actors. Their social influence can partly be attributed to the awe they instigate in the masses as religious authoritarians. As exemplified in the "reconciliation" and "reintegration" rhetoric of the Provincial Reconstruction Team (PRT), the Americans have not been able to deny this influence. The contemporary wisdom seems to be that working with the Taliban and not angering them would be the path of least resistance. However, this strategy, while politically astute, causes tremendous anxiety in feminist groups given their past experiences with the Taliban movement. While I was told by some feminists that even the most conservative Taliban members are realizing that it may be in their interest to reprioritize the significance they have attached to women's rights in the past in order to establish a strong presence inside Afghanistan and to win international recognition, the anxiety across the political spectrum regarding the reconciliation of the Taliban is palpable. I saw these fears voiced on several occasions in conversations between local feminists and Western officials. At a United Nations–hosted conference, a vocal feminist confronted an official from the German embassy about a conference in Germany, which, according to her, did not include significant representation from the feminist lobby. Such suspicions and anxieties abound in local level politics as well among feminists, politicians, the Taliban, and Western actors.

An analysis of the Taliban state demonstrates some continuity and some change as they have tried to negotiate with kleptocratic modernization efforts of the Afghan government. Their anxieties surrounding women's rights can be read in opposition to contemporary Westernization projects as well as the secularizing projects of the past governments. The Taliban have allegedly tried to purify Islam by eradicating all foreign influences from it. History has shown that this strategy has not been effective. This is a realization that is not lost on the Taliban. I was told by a number of feminists that the Taliban, in their negotiations with the Afghan government, are prioritizing issues of economic and political reform, rather than gender rights. They realize that in order to continue their authority as influential social actors, they, not unlike the feminists, must become conversant with the everyday problems of ordinary Afghans.

SONIA AHSAN obtained her PhD in anthropology from Columbia University in 2015. She researches and publishes on feminism in Afghanistan.

Notes

1. For a comprehensive historical account of *Amr Bil-Ma'roof Wa Nahi Anil-Munkar* in Islamic jurisprudence, please see Cook [2000]. I use the term *Pukhtunwali* to describe the prescriptive and descriptive rules and laws that have historically governed Pashtun societies. *Pukhtunwali* circulates both as an unwritten code of tribal law, and a written set of rules that have been taken into account when writing the constitutions of Afghanistan and Northern Pakistan.

2. I conducted fieldwork at a *khana-yi aman* (home of peace or secure home) in Afghanistan in the years 2008 and 2010–2012 with funding from the Wenner Gren Foundation, the American Institute of Afghan Studies, the A. M. Foundation, and the Scheps Foundation of Columbia University. The *khana-yi aman* , administered by the Ministry of Women's Affairs (MOWA), emerged as a modern phenomenon in Afghanistan. While they may be read as marginal to mainstream Afghan social worlds, I witnessed a significant impact of these institutions on many Afghan families in which marital disputes and runaway cases were being negotiated at the family courts in Kabul; these family courts often worked with the *khana-yi aman* to arbitrate family settlements and resolve gender conflicts.

3. Hugh Beattie cites Hasan Kakar who calls the thirty rupees as a maximum bride price an insignificant amount.

4. This and other portions of the chapter have appeared in my 2015 doctoral dissertation submitted to Columbia University, "Sexual Ethics and the Politics of Promiscuity in Afghanistan."

5. Fatwa are defined as legal opinions in response to queries concerning Islamic jurisprudence.

6. I have withheld the identities and names of my interlocutors out of concern for their safety.

7. While the *khana-yi aman*, as an institution in its current formation, officially materialized after the Taliban regime fell, it faces staunch opposition from the contemporary post-Taliban movements and other conservative elements. By some accounts, the post-Taliban Afghan governments have participated in the polemic against these institutions to appease the Taliban. Thus, these spaces are marginal to the contemporary formation of the Afghan government and its entwinement with the Taliban.

Bibliography

Afghan Women's Network. 2011. *Afghan Women's Declaration: International Conference on Afghanistan in Bonn*. December 5. Afghan Women's Network.

Ahsan, Sonia. 2015. "States of Honor: Sexual Ethics and the Politics of Promiscuity in Afghanistan." PhD diss., Columbia University.

Beattie, Hugh. 1984. "Effects of the Saur Revolution in the Nahrin Area of Northern Afghanistan." In *Revolutions and Rebellions in Afghanistan*, ed. M. Nazif Shahrani and Robert L. Canfield, 184–208. Berkeley: Institute of International Studies, University of California.

Cole, Juan. 2003. "The Taliban, Women, and the Hegelian Private Sphere." In *Social Research* 70 (3): 771–808.

Cook, Michael. 2000. *Commanding Right and Forbidding Wrong in Islamic Thought.* Cambridge, UK: Cambridge University Press.

Das, Veena. 2007. *Life and Words: Violence and Descent into the Ordinary.* Berkeley: University of California Press.

Dupree, Nancy. 1984. "Revolutionary Rhetoric and Afghan Women." In *Revolutions and Rebellions in Afghanistan*, ed. M. Nazif Shahrani and Robert L. Canfield, 306–40. Berkeley: Institute of International Studies, University of California.

Hirschkind, Charles. 2006. *The Ethical Soundscape: Cassette Sermons and Islamic Counterpublics.* New York: Columbia University Press.

Mamdani, Mahmood. 2001. *When Victims Become Killers: Colonialism, Nativism, and the Genocide in Rwanda.* Princeton, NJ: Princeton University Press.

Mujtaba, Haji, and Jibran Ahmed. 2013. "No More Peace Talks, 'Mullah Radio' tells Pakistan." November 7. http://www.reuters.com/article/us-pakistan-taliban-idUSBRE9A60OR20131107.

Puar, Jasbir K. 2007. *Terrorist Assemblages: Homonationalism in Queer Times.* Durham, NC: Duke University Press.

Rashid, Ahmed. 2000. *Taliban: Islam, Oil, and the New Great Game in Central Asia.* London: I. B. Tauris.

Roberts, Christine. 2012. "Woman Brutally Executed by Taliban While Crowd Cheers." *Daily News*, July 8. Accessed October 1, 2016. http://www.nydailynews.com/news/world/woman-brutally-executed-taliban-crowd-cheers-video-article-1.1110068.

Rosenberg, Matthew, and Sangar Rahimi. 2012. "In Video of Execution, Reign of Taliban Recalled." *New York Times*, July 8. http://www.nytimes.com/2012/07/09/world/asia/roadside-bombs-kill-at-least-18-in-afghanistan.html?_r=0.

Roy, Olivier. 2006 *Globalized Islam: The Search for a New Ummah.* New York: Columbia University Press.

Shahrani, M. Nazif, and Robert Canfield, eds. 1984. *Revolutions and Rebellions in Afghanistan: Anthropological Perspectives.* Berkeley: Institute of International Studies, University of California.

Tapper, Nancy. 1984. "Causes and Consequences of the Abolition of Bride Price in Afghanistan." In *Revolutions and Rebellions in Afghanistan*, ed. M. Nazif Shahrani and Robert L. Canfield, 291–305. Berkeley: Institute of International Studies, University of California.

11

ANTICIPATING DISCONTINUOUS CHANGE: AFGHANISTAN IN RETROSPECT AND PROSPECT

Robert L. Canfield and Fahim Masoud

"A riot is the language of the unheard."
—Martin Luther King Jr.

"There is nothing that man fears more than the touch of the unknown."
—Elias Canetti, *Crowds and Power.*

The Event

On September 7, 2013, Fahim Masoud encountered a demonstration in Herat, Afghanistan, that became a riot and eventuated in one death and several injuries. He was on his way to give a lecture in an early morning university class that was located on "Saraki-Wolayat" (Provincial Governorate Street), a street where a number of significant buildings were located. The Iranian Consulate lay across the street, as well as the Afghan-Turk high school. United Nations offices and the Herat Hospital were nearby. Directly across the street from the Iranian Consulate were photographic shops where folks could get their pictures made when applying for visas at the consulate.

As Masoud's car was turning into the university compound, he and his host noticed hundreds of people gathering in front of the consulate. This was unusual. The crowds were loud and noisy; clumps of individuals were conversing in the middle of the street, impeding traffic. A cluster of them was moving toward the governor's office. They seemed to have a complaint, perhaps against the Iranian Consulate. To Masoud, visiting the city after a three-year absence, the scene seemed ominous, but his companion reassured him, "This is Afghanistan. Don't worry, we see these things every day. Activities like this are common here." But to his friend's surprise the crowd was not just waiting for the consulate to open: they were beginning to protest. They threw rocks at the consulate gate and its security guards. They attacked the entrance, trying to break in. They became threatening. Some of them were saying they were ready to die to protest against the consulate. Fahim texted a friend, "The situation is very grave here."*

The security guards at the consulate tried to restrain the crowd. One guard fired a few shots in the air to scare them away, and the crowd backed off, at least for a few minutes. Soon the crowd came back. More shots were fired in the air. Someone lunged for the AK-47 of one of the guards, but the guard, faced now with personal danger, wrestled the gun away and fired several shots. The attacker was hit three times in the rear and three bystanders were wounded. A few minutes later, someone else attacked a guard who was trying to hide in his booth. The two of them wrestled for control of his gun. Once the guard broke loose he shot the attacker in the neck and head, killing him instantly.

Now the crowd became aggressive. The consulate had been the original target but, shut out of that building, they turned their rage against the photo shops across the street, whose owners, according to rumor, were part of the notorious extortions of the consulate. The only way to get a visa, it is said, is to pay a huge bribe, reputedly a thousand or even two thousand dollars. So only the rich and well connected can get a visa. The photo shops took the brunt of the mob's wrath. They smashed windows, carried off computers and other valuables, and vandalized whatever else they found.

As Masoud and the students next door watched, some of the protestors began to scale the walls of the university compound. At just that moment police and security forces of several kinds filled the square—members of the army's quick reaction force, special forces of the police, even officers from the intelligence division. The riot was over.

In the aftermath of the riot, various explanations for it were proffered among the Afghans. The security officials who shut down the riot regarded the rioters as foolish people duped by the propaganda of the Taliban living among them.

---

* Statements in the chapter referring to Masoud's communications come from emails and texts sent from Afghanistan to Canfield over a period of weeks after the riot took place. The first note was written on the day of the event, and in the next few days the two exchanged comments on what had happened. Another burst of email transactions took place a few weeks later when we decided to write up the event as a problem in cultural analysis. This required that Masoud describe in several notes the wider social setting of Afghanistan at the time. It was in these notes that he wrote some of his personal assessments of the situation that appear in the chapter. Altogether, the email communications on which this chapter is based were written between September 7, 2013 and February 21, 2014.

Many Afghans regarded the rioters as driven to desperation. "To my university friend," Masoud wrote, the rioters "were people who *az zendagi deli shan ser shoda* ('people who have been fed up with life') and just wanted to do something."

Foreign powers have intruded so often in Afghan affairs that it was easy for Afghans to believe that outsiders had instigated the affair. Iran, India, China, and other Central Asian countries have a stake in what goes on in Afghanistan, with Herat being the center of political and economic activity in the country's western flank, and a place where Central Asian and Middle Eastern interests converge. So any of those countries, people reasoned, could have been behind the riot.

Pakistan, for instance. Afghans are ready to blame everything untoward that happens in the country on Pakistan. The connection between the Taliban and the Pakistani intelligence agency (the ISI) has been well established. Masoud wrote:

> One of my friends who remained at the scene [of the riot] and gave a TV interview said that, as he was watching the situation being neutralized, a police officer from the intelligence section of Herat, checked a guy's pocket and found a phone. Earlier, this policeman had heard the guy speak in Pashto giving reports to someone. The police officer dialed the number the suspect had just dialed and discovered that the people on the other end of line were from a Taliban group. He handcuffed the guy and put him into the back of a police wagon to take him to the police station for interrogation. Whether this was a Taliban organized protest, I don't know. The police certainly thought that elements of the Taliban were there and wanted to exploit the situation and create instability and violence throughout the city of Herat.

What about Iran? Iran has a long history of meddling in Afghanistan affairs. Afghans take that for granted. The officials of the consulate, of course, deflected their accusations away from their own country, accusing the Americans and Israelis as fostering "destructive forces" that could have induced the riot, but Masoud knows that Iran is no friend of Afghanistan:

> Lord Palmerstone used to say that countries have neither permanent enemies nor permanent friends; they have permanent national interests … By engineering [unemployment in Afghanistan] Iran can have some leverage over Herat's politics and security. It also wants to send a message to the Americans, saying, 'Look, we are capable of creating chaos and thus tarnishing your image, so play nicely with us in Syria and elsewhere … ' The Iranian Consulate in Herat is tasked with a special mission: establishing an [Iranian] foothold in Herat city and providing security and protection to whatever Afghan groups are advancing Iran's interests in Afghanistan.

The Problem

Here is our problem. A gathering became a demonstration and the demonstration became a riotous mob, and in the process, someone was killed, several people were injured, and thousands of dollars of property was destroyed. It was a transformation among a diverse assembly of individuals, few of whom knew each other, each with his own set of issues, who for a few minutes converged in a common cause against the consulate. Their behavior seemed to reveal that the consulate had betrayed them and prompted their outrage. And from the consensus that they developed as they talked about their problems with the consulate, a narrative developed that provided the justification for their collective rage.

Common feelings of outrage could develop among this adventitious collectivity of strangers because they shared conventions of behavior—speech and gesture—that make social interaction and coordination possible. Durkheim (1982) found in the behavior of crowds evidence that "society" was an objective reality, worthy of disciplinary inquiry, distinguishable from other fields of study such as psychology, economics, political science, and biology. In social interaction, we see culture in practice. Every event, as Marshall Sahlins puts it, has "a distinctive cultural signature" (1985, xiii). The meanings applied to an event are never the only ones possible; from a repertoire of possibilities, particular interpretations are applied in the instant, endowing every instant, every situation, with a unique configuration of meanings.[1]

Our Approach

To grasp why a group of strangers should act this way, that is, how they could join in a spontaneous attack on the consulate, we would need to know what their visit to the consulate that morning meant to them and how their individual concerns converged into a sense of commonality that could justify their aggressive behavior. That, we confess, is impossible for anyone at our remove from the situation to discover. None of the participants could be interviewed after the riot as they quickly dispersed. We therefore cannot pretend to provide a full account of all the issues involved in the riot. Masoud, however, was able to find out some of the common problems that the Afghans had with the consulate. And in a six-week visit with his family in the fall of 2013, he was immersed in the society and gained a sense of what the people around him felt about the national situation, which we believe had something to do with the riot. Thus, on the basis of what information we can obtain and what we can surmise, we believe we can say something useful about the causes of the riot, and in the process say something about the meaningful analysis of events.

The limitations are all too obvious, but they are not unlike the problems we have in developing social science explanations for almost any event. We can propose broad claims about social affairs but the evidentiary materials we adduce in support of them are often founded on opportunistic contacts with people. So our impressions for what took place in a specific setting depends on what people choose to tell us, on the comments of witnesses who may differ among themselves, on fortuitous encounters, even on off-hand comments. Moreover, our subjects are human beings whose agendas are sometimes elusive and complex, and their motives sometimes concealed. So we present a construction of what seems to have taken place, based on the resources available.

Our Claim

Masoud was positioned to discover some of the circumstances of the affair that can help us imagine what induced the behavior of those who came to the consulate on that fateful morning. We treat as authoritative his communiqués from Herat and his interpretive notes on what was going on in the country at that time. We also draw from comments of other observers of the situation at that time. What all of them emphasize is the widespread sense of unease about the future that dominated public discussion at that time, due to a recent announcement: the American and NATO forces that had been fighting the Taliban and Al Qaeda for more than a decade were planning to withdraw from Afghanistan by December of 2014. This news generated discussion among the public about what the absence of these troops would mean for Afghanistan. Would civil war again break out, as it had several times in the previous three decades? What could keep the Taliban from returning to power?

The prospect of another period of societal conflict awakened memories of what many people had gone through in the recent past—that is, during the civil wars of the 1980s and 1990s, and the subsequent period of Taliban dominance (especially from 1996 to 2001 when they occupied Kabul), when rustic young men brandished weapons in the streets and capriciously enforced unnatural and odious regulations in the name of Islam, beating offenders and sometimes publicly executing them. Memories of a nightmarish past were combining with fears of a conflicted future.[2]

The implications of the American/NATO withdrawal were not the only unresolved issue of importance on the horizon. Two other issues added to the sense of an ominous future. One was whether President Karzai would finally sign an agreement with the Americans and NATO for their relationship with Afghanistan after December 2014. He was temporizing even though the agreement had been worked out by his administration and approved by the parliament. As long as he delayed, the question remained unsettled of how firmly foreign powers would be committed to the country. The other important unresolved issue was the upcoming national elections, especially the crucial question of who would become president.

An Explanation for the Event

We believe this sense of dread about the future affected the behavior of those who came to the Iranian Consulate on September 7, 2013. The strains created by anticipations of trouble ahead were a factor in the way the visitors to the consulate behaved on that morning. The riot was but one affair that displayed the pervasive anxiety about what was coming, albeit one of the more dramatic of those displays.

Our Evidence

Masoud's Impressions in Afghanistan

Masoud's report on the attitudes he encountered when he visited his family in the fall of 2013 reveals how strongly worries about the future colored the popular sensibility about the present. "Before going on to Herat [after arriving in Kabul]," he wrote:

> I was able to stay at Kabul airport for a full day. To pass time, I confabulated with many Kabulis about Afghanistan, to know where things stood from their perspective. They seemed worried, desperate, and helpless. They told me how Afghanistan was losing its last chance of transforming itself and becoming a modern country with a developed economy. They attributed the insecurity and the depressed economy to their corrupt politicians ... These people in Kabul were mad at their leaders for not honoring their promises to make things better for the country.
>
> On landing at Herat airport, I was greeted by my family. Although they were excited to see me, they seemed too rushed to the extent that it made me uneasy. As he was driving, my father, a former military officer, was registering a number of complaints about the increase in criminal activities (kidnappings) and other major problems plaguing Herat. We arrived home and everyone's first message was: don't go outside alone and don't ever stay outside late.
>
> The entire city seemed empty. It looked as if the city was mourning something. But mourning precisely what? As I inquired I sensed that they were mourning the repetition of history in Afghanistan. They were seeing signs that Afghanistan was going back to its days of internecine wars, daily violence, and widespread poverty.
>
> That attitude pervaded affairs in the city of Herat. Once known for its high employment rate, stability, and ongoing infrastructure projects, Herat had now become a large fortress, only with more guns and less food for the population. At 9 pm, the entire city shut down, and no one dared to go out of their residences. Three years earlier (2010) this wasn't the case. People loved to go to entertainment parks with their families and walk

around late at night with no worry of being kidnapped or killed. Now, at every city entrance and exit throughout the city military and police units were standing guard.

It had become impossible to travel around the peripheral areas of Herat because the Taliban or the [other] anti-government elements were in control. A week after my arrival, the Taliban killed three engineers in a brutal manner. A week after that, they beheaded nine construction workers in Karokh district, only an hour from the city. These acts of violence demonstrated not only the inability of the Afghan security forces to provide stability but also the commitment of the Taliban to seize power.

Moreover, in another note, Masoud wrote:

Intense rivalries over power have already begun. This is manifested in an increased number of kidnappings and political assassinations. A week after I arrived in Herat, two armed men killed the leader of an ethnic Hazara district. According to several newspapers, the killing was due to his growing political popularity. Assassinations from motorcycles are the most fashionable way of killing one's opponent.

Terror and fear are dominant in the city of Herat. No one travels to the outskirts of the city any longer. The rich and those with prestige and power are responding differently. For one, they have stopped their investments and are securing their liquid assets by stashing them away in foreign banks and are leaving the country for the Gulf and other stable neighboring countries.

Days after I arrived in Herat province, a seventeen-year-old girl, while on a trip to the bazaar, got shot in the head by two armed men. The story I got was that she had declined a marriage proposal from one of them. The case went cold and nobody prosecuted the perpetrators.

Yesterday, the Taliban killed 4 engineers and two aid-workers in a nearby district known as Golran. I don't know what is happening, but people in Herat are telling me that the security situation has never been so bad in the last 10 years.

In this setting the American and NATO troops that had been bearing the burden of fighting the Taliban announced that they would be leaving Afghanistan permanently. The question on the minds of many Heratis and Afghans in general was: in light of the American troops' exodus, can their government provide jobs and a sense of security? The answer, I'm sad to report, they knew, was "No." And that's the reason why many Afghans feel so uncertain about the future of their country and why so many are desperately trying to leave for other places.

Masoud's estimate of the prospects for the country was, of course, not sanguine. "It is really hard to predict the future of Afghanistan. I had tea with a good friend yesterday, and during our conversation, I learned that his brother works in the office of Marshal Fahim—Karzai's first vice-president. I asked him how his brother assessed the security situation. He said his brother was more confused than ordinary citizens, and that he couldn't tell at all what would happen tomorrow, let alone next year. Confusion is what is going on in Afghanistan."

The General Sense of Insecurity

The fundamental issue was, of course, security. Karim Amini in Tolo News writes that "2013 was full of ups and downs for Afghanistan, but Afghans appear most concerned about the future, not the past. Most acutely, it is the fear of a security vacuum in the wake of the NATO withdrawal that wracks them."[3] Amini quotes individuals from various parts of the country. A Kandahari resident said, "We are just asking for security and stability in 2014." A Nimrozi resident: "Security must be provided, because there is no development without security." A man in Mazar-e-Sharif: "We ask the international community to support the Afghan government in 2014, and after 2014, because Afghanistan needs support" (Amini 2014).

In reply to a blog by Masoud in the Center on Public Diplomacy, a commenter ("Nasrat") wrote, "Despite some progress in establishing relatively well functioning security forces, the government failed to deliver services to people on the basis of good governance. Inequity, lack of justice and most importantly the widespread corruption in government is devastating the newly built institutions and the government as a whole" (*CPD Blog* 2013).

The notable individuals in the community, of course, worried about what would happen to them, as they were more likely to be targeted by the Taliban. The women likewise recognized a special threat from the Taliban. Sociologist Baryalai Fetrat points out that "As foreign troops pull back, traditionalists who have been largely silent for the past decade—and who still have strong backing in society—are reappearing to attack the gains that Afghan women have achieved ... working in offices, becoming artists, or getting higher education. The women who have been pioneers in the fight for their rights are now facing more and more pressure and are fearful for their future. Artists like Aryana and Fereshta are the primary targets" (quoted in "Afghan Female Celebrities" 2013).

Unsurprisingly, the prospect of civil conflict ahead was having a devastating effect on Afghanistan's economy. According to Sayed Sharif Amiry of Tolo News, "Investments have stopped. Foreigners are closing their nongovernmental organizations (NGOs), and Americans are no longer endowed with bags of dollars starting big projects which used to employ thousands of Afghans" (Amiry 2013). The economy was weakening and the general order of affairs was becoming less secure. The Afghan business community had also halted its projects; panic seemed to be taking over. "What we have now," said Masoud, "is *haraj wa maraj* (chaos)." Prospects for living safely and comfortably were dimming as the time of the final exodus of the American/NATO forces approached.

Masoud summarized the situation as he saw it in fall 2013. "Afghanistan is in disarray. Corruption is pervasive, making Afghanistan the second most corrupt country in the world. Mass poverty is plaguing people ... Most professionals have been laid off and there are no jobs available. The common man is living in extreme poverty. Theft, kidnappings, assassinations, burglaries, and other heinous crimes emanate from unemployment. Unemployment is the mother of all social troubles."

Long-time observer of Afghanistan, Pamela Constable, in an interview on the PBS NewsHour summed up the situation similarly: [I know] "many Afghans who have already left the country or are planning or trying to leave the country, people who have good jobs, people who were in good positions, not just poor people, but people who had some very strong prospects for success in that country, who are now so genuinely worried about things falling apart . . ."; indeed the sense that things were falling apart "has infected us all" ("How Does Political Uncertainty Affect Afghanistan Security" 2014). The country, she said, was "on edge."

Strategic Preparations for an Ominous Future

The edginess that Constable saw in the mood of the Afghans was manifest in the measures they were taking to prepare for the worst, in case their world would again be ripped asunder. They were renewing ties with distant relatives and old friends, strengthening strategic alliances, affirming old loyalties. According to the BBC, in September of 2013 a former Afghan senator and district governor in the northern province of Sar-e-Pol changed sides, defecting to the Taliban. It also reported that "Low-level defections to the Taliban, mostly by Afghan policemen, have happened in several parts of the country" ("Afghan Politician Defects" 2013). Masoud knows of mullahs who have changed their views in anticipation of the expected return of the Taliban.

At the same time, according to Masoud,

> Warlords are arming themselves, reconstituting their militias. For example, Ismael Khan, who is presently the Minister of Water and Energy, is arming [his militia]. Khan, originally from Herat, was the governor of the province until President Karzai removed him in 2005. Even though Mr. Khan no longer holds power in Herat, he still maintains more control over the affairs of this province than the current governor. Mr. Khan, along with other warlords around the country, is gearing up for the American troops' exodus. These warlords believe that the US has already accomplished its mission: killing of Osama bin Laden and breaking down Al Qaeda's leadership structure—and thus has no interest in staying in Afghanistan.

The Situation in Herat

As Constable said, even well-positioned Afghans were trying to move to other countries, or at least to establish beachheads elsewhere to which they could move their families in case of a crisis. Iran has historically been among the most frequently visited countries by Afghans, usually to find work. Masoud notes that "Afghans seeking work in Iran have historically been just crossing the border into the country [to get jobs]. And Iran was okay with this because it needed workers to rebuild itself after its devastation in the hands of Sadam. But once the Americans came to Afghanistan in 2001 there were many more opportunities for work inside the country, so fewer Afghans have sought jobs in Iran. Lots of cash flowed [inside Afghanistan] and many people became busy making money in all kinds of ways. But then events took a turn for the worse ... because the international community, especially the US, announced their troops' withdrawal in 2014." In that event, in summer and fall of 2013, Iran again became an important place to visit, only this time to establish a route of escape and a place of refuge. Now access to Iran was critical.

It was common for Afghan visa applicants at the consulate to have problems with the consular officials because the officials often made onerous extra demands. They demanded bribes, sometimes for as much as one thousand dollars. Moreover, according to government rules, visitors going in and out of Iran had to leave a deposit with the consulate to ensure that they would return. In practice, the rule became an issue because when Afghans appeared to claim their deposit, the officials found excuses to delay repayment.

A Model of the Riot as an Event

At this point we can construct a scenario of what happened on the morning of September 7, 2013. The folks who arrived at the consulate—many of them—were not unaware of the ways of the consulate and some, on the basis of previous encounters, were already chafing and irate. And of course, these folks were now worried about the trajectory of their country. Some of them had come to the consulate specifically to establish connections in Iran for their families in view of the expected troubles ahead. For them, the transactions they sought were important, even urgent. A lot was at stake in their business with the consulate.

Masoud described the situation this way:

> These people came to the Consulate to get a visa or get their visa money back ... Given the current unstable situation in the western part of the country (Herat, Farah, Badghis, and Chaghcharan) and the dire economic climate, these individuals wanted to get out of the country or die trying (most of the educated Afghans and those with some money travel to Iran

and from there go to Turkey to then go to Germany or any country they can enter in Western Europe). That's why they were there pounding at the gates of the Iranian Consulate that day.

Common feelings of urgency, outrage, and betrayal congealed outside the building and adventitiously formed into an incendiary situation. What happened at that instant did not have to happen. It obviously was unplanned. But the shared fury of the crowd combusted into a rampage. The event was spontaneous, but its aleatory form revealed a structure broadly in place in the country. In that sense, the behavior of this out-of-control crowd objectified frustrations and fears that pervaded Afghan society. The riot expressed the feelings of a people helplessly trapped in an ineluctable trajectory of change that was both ambiguous and horrifying. Anticipation was here a social fact, shaping the perspectives and the actions that were coming to dominate life in Afghanistan. It was a change that Douglass North (1989, 89) called "discontinuous," a radical shift in "the formal rules" that the denizens of the country were going to have to live by.

On Events as Cultural Moments

An assortment of issues converged in the moment of September 7, 2013, to create the distinctive affair at the Iranian Consulate. Already, ahead of schedule, the Afghanistan peoples were seeing ahead and recognizing that they had to be rearranging their affairs. Their strategies differed according to the options available to each individual and group, but they all reflected the general sense that the world they had known was passing away, and in its place lay a social order as yet inchoate but ominous. They were responding to a future that, at least in the fall of 2013, was both menacing and unclear. So the measures they were taking were defensive, protective. It was in that setting that a gathering at the consulate could explode in riotous behavior. What actually happened was not the only possible way that the sentiments of the moment could have been expressed, but the event as it transpired displayed a sentiment commonly felt by many at the time.

Riots will occur again in Herat, if past is prelude, but none of them will be freighted with the particular constellation of associations that congealed into this one. Each will be informed by, and in some way express, a distinctive set of meanings apt for that moment, for every event is a unique cultural instant, never to be replicated.[4]

On Theoretical Approaches

Our approach here, on the topic of rioting as a social problem, differs markedly from the work of Mark Granovetter (1978). Granovetter's interest in rioting as a social activity is to define what it takes for a person to join in a riot. His focus is on individual behavior, individual incentives, and individual thresholds of participation in a social situation. We address our rioting event as a problem in how a group of people (in our case, individuals who scarcely knew each other) could come to agreement on the definition of the situation—agreeing that the objects of their wrath were so deserving of punishment that they agreed to wreak vengeance with their own hands. We seek to identify the social and historical conditions of the riotous moment. Granovetter assumes that even when individuals agree on the definition of the situation they may not necessarily join in when riotous behavior is potential or actually taking place, because individuals vary in the degree to which they can be influenced by the social pressures of the moment. Because thresholds of susceptibility differ, individuals will participate in riotous behavior differentially according to how strongly the social conditions push them beyond an internal resistance threshold. His argument is not incompatible with our analysis but it focuses on the conditions of individual participation whereas our argument focuses on how individuals come to agree on the nature of a situation.

ROBERT L. CANFIELD is Professor Emeritus in anthropology at Washington University in St. Louis. He is author of a number of books and articles on social and political affairs in Afghanistan and Central Asia, and his most recent is the coedited volume, *Ethnicity, Authority, and Power in Central Asia: New Games Great and Small.*

FAHIM MASOUD is working as a threat analyst at Prescient, a premier risk management and technology firm that provides intelligence-based services to federal, domestic, and international clients.

NOTES

1. This is the way anthropologists think about social situations, but the occasion of this conference, sponsored by the Vincent and Elinor Ostrom Workshop in Political Theory and Policy Analysis, provides an opportunity to recognize the contribution to the study of culture in relation to economic analysis by economists like the Ostroms of this university and our colleague at Washington University Professor Douglass C. North. The work of these economists seems to us to match well to the concepts of culture that anthropologists take as fundamental. The Ostroms and Douglass North, have been interested in the way social practices and institutions influence markets and economies generally, how folks in social interaction create rules and social conventions that allow a community to cooperate in the management of shared resources (the Ostroms), and the way institutions influence market processes, structuring political, economic, and social interactions. North's recognition that "institutions" can include informal social conventions brings his perspective into close alignment with anthropological concepts of culture.

2. See Martin Heidegger's discussion in *Being and Time*, which stresses that human beings act in fields of time—past, present, future—as part of a larger social and historical collectivity, as part of a people, a "Volk." Human collectivities possess a collective heritage in terms of which they act. When they make decisions, they actualize salient elements of their collective past. Yet, at the same time humans are future oriented: they respond to the past, in present contexts, for the sake of the future. See also the article on Heidegger in the *Encyclopedia Brittanica* (Naess and Wolin, 2017).

3. Karim Amini (2014) asserts that "Whether or not the international community continues to support Afghanistan in the coming years is likely to come down to whether or not President Hamid Karzai signs the Bilateral Security Agreement (BSA) with the United States, which would ensure a contingency of foreign troops stays behind after 2014."

4. This paper was completed in 2015. Subsequent events demonstrated how powerful the urge to escape had become in Afghanistan.

Bibliography

"Afghan Female Celebrities Defy Fundamentalists." 2013. *Newsweek*, August 16. Accessed January 25. http://newsweekpakistan.com/afghan-female-celebrities-defy-fundamentalists/.

"Afghan Politician Defects to Taliban." 2013. BBC News, September 19. Accessed January 25, 2014. http://www.bbc.co.uk/news/world-asia-24159810.

Amini, Karim. 2014. "Local Afghan Voices on 2014." TOLOnews.com, January 1.

Amiry, Sayed Sharif. 2013. "Afghanistan Put to the Test in 2014." TOLOnews.com, December 31.

Bennett, John W. 1976. "Anticipation, Adaptation, and the Concept of Culture in Anthropology." *Science* 192 (4242): 847–53.

CPD Blog. 2013. "Afghanistan: A State of Fear (Part I)." blog entry by Fahim Masoud, December 20, 2013. http://uscpublicdiplomacy.org/blog/afghanistan-state-fear-part-i.

Durkheim, Emile. 1982. [1895]. *The Rules of Sociological Method*. Edited with an Introduction by Steven Lukes. Translated by W. D. Halls. New York: Free Press.

Granovetter, Mark. 1978. "Threshold Models of Collective Behavior." *American Journal of Sociology* 83 (6): 1420–43.

Heidegger, Martin. 2010. *Being and Time*. Translated by Joan Stambaugh. Revised and with a foreword by Dennis J. Schmidt. Albany: SUNY Press.

"How Does Political Uncertainty Affect Afghanistan Security?." 2014. *PBS NewsHour*, January 20. Accessed January 21, 2014. http://www.pbs.org/newshour/bb/world/jan-june14/afghan_01-20.html.

Naess, Arne D., and Richard Wolin. 2017. "Martin Heidegger." In *Encyclopedia Brittanica*. Encyclopedia Brittanica. Accessed January 24, 2014. http://www.britannica.com/EBchecked/topic/259513/Martin-Heidegger.

North, Douglass C. 1982. *Structure and Change in Economic History*. W. W. Norton.

———. 1990. *Institutions, Institutional Change and Economic Performance*. New York: Cambridge University Press.

———. 1991. "Institutions." *Journal of Economic Perspectives* 5 (1): 97–112.

Sahlins, Marshall. 1985. *Islands of History*. Chicago: University of Chicago Press.

PART III: ADAPTING TO A NEW POLITICAL ECOLOGY OF UNCERTAINTIES AT THE MARGINS

12

BADAKHSHANIS SINCE THE SAUR REVOLUTION: STRUGGLE, TRIUMPH, HOPE, AND UNCERTAINTY

M. Nazif Shahrani

"*Khush Darakhsheed, waley doulat musta'jal bud..* خوش درخشید، ولی دولت مستعجل بود
Shone well, but [Rabbani's control] of state was too short/hasty"
(Haafiz of Shiraz, *cited by Zuhurrullah Zuhuri*)

Introduction

More than three decades ago I had attempted to assess the "Causes and Context of Responses to the Saur [Communist] Revolution in Badakhshan" (Shahrani 1984). A range of actions and reactions to the Saur Revolution (April 27, 1978) were underway then by different ethno-linguistic and sectarian actors belonging to different age, education, and ideological groups inhabiting cities, towns, and villages of this remote and extremely mountainous northeastern province as well as Badakhshanis living in Kabul and other cities of Afghanistan. The range of responses of various Badakhshani actors at the time, motivated by different sets of shared normative principles and institutional practices constrained by the realities of the province's physical geography and extant power structures, included the following:

First, small numbers of educated Badakhshanis, many of them members of the oppressed, minority Shi'a Ismaili sectarian communities living just south of the Tajikistan border of the former Soviet Union, especially the district of Shughnan, actively supported the Khalq-Parcham Marxist regime in Kabul. Included among the ardent supporters of the communist regime were also a few educated Badakhshanis from the provincial capital, Faizabad, and the central district of Jurm who worked for the government and lived in Kabul or other provincial towns.

Second, a great many in the province, both rural and urban, did not take much notice of government change in Kabul, which they had always considered an alien extractive body imposing itself on them. Indeed, many regarded it as another *paadshah gardeshi* (dynasty succession event) which, as in the past, did not concern them. Therefore, they passively went on about their lives, as long as they were not subjected to direct repressive demands by the new regime.

Third, a relatively small, but influential and knowledgeable group of individuals and their families who could afford to, chose to leave the province and the country in search of safe refuge, mostly to Chitral and Peshawar, in Pakistan. For many poorer and less connected people, who may have wanted to leave, this option was not viable due to the great distance over very rough terrain, the cost, and road hazards, so they remained in the province against their own wishes.

Finally, a small group of educated young Badakhshanis in government boarding schools in Kabul, and many traditionally trained religious scholars, most of them in the Deobandi *madrassas* of the Indo-Pakistan subcontinent, helped organize armed resistance against the communist regime in Kabul (Shahrani 1984, 139-169). Historically, while there had been little or no active support for the old monarchy, Badakhshanis had not taken up arms against their Pashtun rulers from the time of the subjugation and annexation of the province by Amir Abdur Rahman Khan (r. 1880–1901) to the modern buffer state of Afghanistan, created for him by British India and tsarist Russia.

The range of reactions among the peoples of Badakhshan province, I have argued, could not be explained only in terms of the event of Marxist revolution and their intentions and claims to rapidly modernize the country through radical land and social reforms; or by the wishes of the provincial periphery to retain local autonomy, protect their meager personal wealth, or defend their faith (Islam); or even by the desire to establish an "Islamic" government as a few Islamist youth were advocating at the time. Expectations of success against the communist regime and their Soviet patrons then seemed in vain, but the seriousness of the peoples' reactions demanded a closer examination of a century-long history of state-periphery relations. That is, the "basic political processes [i.e., regularities of actions by the state institutions/impersonators and their subjects in situations structured by rules, norms and shared strategies], social power balance, and contest for control [or capture of the institutions of the extractive] state," especially among the emergent young, educated contestants in Afghanistan had to be considered to fully understand the reasons behind the strong resistance to the communist regime in Kabul and its aftermath (Aya 1979, 40; also see Crawford and Ostrom 1995, 582; Reeves 2014, 195–99).

The factors motivating opposition to the Marxist Revolution of 1978 in Badakhshan, both by leftists and Islamists alike, did not radically differ. Some of the key grievances by the supporters and opponents of the Marxist coup were:

Badakhshan's dead end, distant geographic location, its inhospitable terrain without roads and access to services (with the minor exception of some schools), and the total absence of any kind of modern industry or agricultural development enterprises due to the alleged willful neglect of the Pashtun-dominated central governments in Kabul.[1] Another factor aggravating the situation in Badakhshan was the historical legacies of iniquitous spatial distribution of ethno-linguistic and sectarian communities with differential access to power and meager strategic resources (arable land, pastures, services, and opportunities) within the province. That is, the larger Sunni Tajik and Uzbek groups occupied the more fertile valleys in the central districts of the province while smaller "mountain" or Pamir Tajik groups (the Sheghni, Zebaki, Wakhi, Sanglechi, Yumgi, and Kurani wa Munjani), adherents of the Ismaili Shi'a sect and followers of the Agha Khan, occupied the less productive, harsher, and higher-elevation river valleys in the peripheries to the north and northeast along the Panj River and its tributaries. These later groups suffered from even greater isolation, discrimination, and exploitation by the Sunni Badakhshanis. All ethnic and sectarian groups, in turn, experienced collective abuse in the hands of oppressive and extractive government officials lording over them in equal measure. Furthermore, unlike the eastern, southern, and western frontiers of Afghanistan with Pakistan and Iran, the entire province of Badakhshan was rimmed in by the "iron curtain" of the former Soviet Union and People's Republic of China bordering the province on the north and northeast, denying the peoples of this province access to their own kinsmen across the borders as well as to the outside world. In addition, since the 1930s, the Kandahari Pashtun nomads (*kuchi* or *maldaar*) were given exclusive rights by the Kabul regimes to pasture their herds in the vast summer pasture grounds of the province in Dashti Shiwa and Dashti Riwat areas in the central high plateau areas of the province. This was a government act which denied the Badakhshani herders access to their own traditional pasture grounds.

Thus, for Badakhshanis, the Marxist coup was not only an important cause but also a critical trigger event for armed resistance against the Kabul regime— that is, it was not simply a "religious/Islamic" reaction to communism alone. Badakhshanis actively opposed the communist regimes and have been active in subsequent internecine bloodletting in Afghanistan. The aim of this chapter is to address the following key questions at this juncture in the turbulent history of the country: What has been the impact of nearly forty years of war and violence on the historic grievances of inhabitants of this province? Are they alleviated or exacerbated? What has been the impact of the war on Badakhshan's geostrategic role in national, regional, and international politics? How has state failure affected communal power realignments within the province? Has the role of Badakhshani power elites in provincial, regional, and national politics been significantly changed, and how? What have been and are likely to be the consequences of the re-imposition of centralized state power since 2001 on the current and future power dynamics within the province and beyond? More significantly, what could be the geostrategic consequences of the relocation of Taliban and Central Asian Islamist extremist fighters to Badakhshan and other northern provinces of Afghanistan following the eventual withdrawal of US-NATO troops from the country in 2014, 2015, or later? It is to the discussion of some of these critical issues at various phases of the conflict that I wish to turn.

Resisting the Marxist Regimes and Its Policies and Practices, 1980–1992

The initial armed rebellion in Badakhshan broke out in early 1979, carried out by members of the local leftist group known as the Sitami Melli, primarily in response to the purges conducted by the Peoples' Democratic Party of Afghanistan (PDPA or Khalq Party) against the members of the Parcham faction of the Communist Party and their allies the Sitami Melli, led by Tahir Badakhshi, a prominent leftist intellectual from the provincial capital, Faizabad.[2] These purges were spearheaded by Hafizullah Amin, the ultra-Pashtun nationalist leader of the Khalq Party whose henchmen executed Badakhshi sometime in 1979.

In retaliation, members of the Sitami Melli from Badakhshan, together with their allies from the adjacent provinces in the north, staged an armed uprising and took control of Baharak, a key district close to Faizabad in central Badakhshan, in April 1979. This leftist rebellion, however, was quickly crushed, decimating most of the young Badakhshani communists from Central Badakhshan. Hafizullah Amin then unleashed his wrath on the peoples of the province by appointing a Badakhshani communist ally, Mansur Hashimi, a high-ranking member of the PDPA, to identify and severely punish suspected local enemies from his own home province. This vicious campaign, led by Hashimi and reportedly assisted by communists from the district of Shughnan near the Tajikistan border, resulted in the mass murder of countless innocent Badakhshani religious and political dignitaries, many of them teachers, pious individuals, and religious scholars.[3] This bloody suppression, triggered by the Sitami Melli's armed rebellion against the Kabul regime, was broadened against all their suspected enemies. Hashimi's atrocities angered the people, paving the way for a much larger and sustained jihad movement and further bloodshed in the province and beyond.[4] The communist regime, however, continued to enjoy the support of peripheral districts such as Sughnan, Ishkashim, Zebak, and Wakhan, located next to the Soviet Tajikistan border.[5] This was due primarily to local Ismaili populations' sympathies for the Kabul regime but also due to their geographical proximity and vulnerability to Soviet firepower across the border.[6]

The first successful Islamist armed uprising in Badakhshan was launched in June 1979 in the remote district of Kuran and Munjan where the lapis lazuli mines are located, adjacent to Panjsher valley and to Nuristan near the Pakistani frontiers. The mujahideen launching the resistance were members of Jami'ati Islami Afghanistan led by Burhanuddin Rabbani, an Egyptian trained Islamic theologian and former professor at Kabul University from Faizabad, the capital of Badakhshan province. Rabbani had sought refuge in Pakistan in the 1970s for fear of persecution by Muhammad Daoud's republican regime (1973–1978), so in 1978, his Jami'ati Islami party was headquartered in Peshawar, Pakistan.

Following the Soviet military intervention of December 24, 1979, Rabbani's Jami'at became one of seven Afghan mujahideen resistance organizations recognized by the government of Pakistan who were entitled to receive US and international support distributed by the Pakistani InterServices Intelligence, the ISI. Thus, multiple long and tortuous supply routes for the Jami'ati Islami mujahideen were established from the cities of Chitral and Peshawar in Pakistan to Badakhshan. With the help of a new supply of weapons and money from Jami'at in Peshawar, most of the central districts in the province were liberated from the PDPA during the early 1980s. Jami'at's initial monopoly, controlling key districts in central Badakhshan, however, was soon challenged when Rabbani began to follow the well-established institutional practices of favoring his own relatives, individuals from his place of origin (Yaftal area near Faizabad), and Tajiks in general, for access to weapons and financial resources.

Therefore, seeds for politicization of local and national ethnic identities within the resistance movements were firmly planted, and new cleavages and tensions gradually grew in the province and the larger region. Rabbani's competitors, Hizbe Islami, of Gulbuddin Hekmatyar, recruited some of the Uzbeks from the Argo region and some Tajiks and Baluch from the Kishm area while Sayyaf found sympathizers among disgruntled Tajiks from the valleys of Zardew, Sarghelan, and Warduj to challenge Rabbani's hegemony in the province. Competition by local commanders for access to multiple sites of new external resources (that is, they were collecting rent from the new centers) in return for pledges of support to eager aspiring national Islamist leaders in Peshawar fueled the tensions locally, resulting in bloody fights for control of turf and territory within Badakhshan. These feuds resulted in the deaths of many local commanders and innocent people in the province and created unprecedented communal tensions.

Competition for the control of lapis lazuli mines in the southeastern part of the province close to the Panjsher valley, one of the most lucrative resources in the province aside from opium trafficking, led to factionalism within Rabbani's Jami'ati Islami. That is, since the early 1980s, Rabbani's Panjsheri allies, the late Ahmad Shah Massoud and his lieutenants, garnered the support of Badakhshani commanders from the Kuran and Munjan area where the lapis mines are located to secure the control, extraction, smuggling, and sale of this rare semiprecious gemstone, via Pakistan, to international markets, a development which resulted in permanent and unresolved tension between some Badakhshani and Panjsheri factions of the Jami'ati Islami organization until now.[7] Since the spring of 2015, this district, together with the adjacent districts of Yumgon and Warduj, have become new strongholds for the relocated Taliban and Central Asia Islamist extremists from Pakistan, allegedly by Pakistan's ISI. Therefore, creating a serious security concern for the province as well as for the former Central Asian Soviet republics and China to the north and northeast.

Triumph, Hope and Tragedies, 1992–2001

A year after the implosion of the former Soviet Union, Rabbani's commander Ahmad Shah Massoud, in collaboration with Rashid Dostum, who defected from the ranks of the Kabul regime, took control of the capital, Kabul, in 1992. Two months later Rabbani assumed the presidency of Afghanistan, the first Badakhshani and second Tajik ever to become head of state in recent history of the country. Badakhshanis, who had contributed significantly to the mujahideen victory over the Kabul regimes and their Soviet patrons, were jubilant and expected vigorous attention to the needs of the impoverished and widely neglected peoples of the north in general and of Badakhshanis in particular. Such hopes and expectations were in line with past institutional practices of the rulers of Afghanistan who favored their own kinsmen and place of origin.

They were, however, quickly disappointed as the various mujahideen factions, especially Gulbuddin Hekmatyar, turned their guns against Rabbani's government. Tragically, the ethnically motivated opposition soon became the proxy wars of all against all, destroying Kabul, the capital, and eventually paving the way for the rise of Taliban extremist movement. In September 1996, the Taliban dislodged Rabbani and his government from Kabul, first to Mazari Sharif, then to Taliqan in northeastern Takhar province, and eventually to Faizabad as the seat of his beleaguered government, as the Taliban conquered most of the provinces in the north. By the time of the American military intervention (October 7, 2011) against the Taliban, the only areas completely under the control of Rabbani's government and the Northern Alliance was the Badakhshan province plus the Panjsher valley and the northeastern flanks of Takhar province. Four years of a Badakhshani presiding over the Afghan state, preoccupied with brutal proxy wars and violence, denied the possibility of any kind of development and reconstruction efforts in the country, especially in Badakhshan. Indeed, the jihadi triumph and the hopes of the nation dissipated into a global tragedy following the September 11, 2001, attacks against the twin towers and Pentagon in the United States.

These tragic wars and violence were not without significant consequences for the Badakhshanis as well as Afghanistan. That is, the collapse of the Soviet Union in 1991 and declaration of independence by Tajikistan the same year renewed the possibility of Badakhshan's historic and strategic role on the ancient Silk Road which had been denied since the imposition of tightly sealed Soviet closed-border policies dating back to the 1920s. This new opportunity for Badakhshanis was unfortunately complicated by the breakout of the Tajik civil war (1993–1997) and the arrival of tens of thousands of refugees to be cared for by the beleaguered Rabbani government in Badakhshan and other northern provinces. The loosening of Tajik border control opened a new route for drug running as well as the smuggling of gemstones, guns, alcohol, and other contraband to and from Central Asian republics (see Reeves 2014; Heathershaw 2009). Access to, and control of, this new strategic resource during the 1990s became another source of contention within the province among local commanders and their patrons in the Rabbani government.

Not surprisingly, the person-centered extractive politics and economics with all its attendant rules, norms, and shared strategies, and a powerful and lasting legacy of Afghanistan's past remained operative during Rabbani's rule in Kabul as well as in Badakhshan. His family members and close associates, mostly from his native Yaftal or from Faizabad, held key government offices and used available state resources to enrich themselves. Competition for control of the drug trade and smuggling routes to the Tajikistan border added new tensions and violence within the province. The violence for control of lucrative opium and drug-running routes within the province and beyond however worsened after the ouster of the Taliban and the establishment of the Karzai regime in 2002 (Foschini 2010). On the whole, the mujahideen triumph against the Marxist regime and a Badakhshan favorite son, Burhanuddin Rabbani, becoming president of Afghanistan, albeit for a short time (1992–1996/2001), ended in great disillusionment for the vast majority of Badakhshanis as well as the rest of the country.

During more than twenty years of war (1978–2001) in Badakhshan, the relatively extensive network of schools (first through twelfth grades) established before the communist revolution—that is, the only meaningful state-provided service in the province—were totally destroyed by the mujahideen in the central districts of Badakhshan. Because the PDPA used the schools as bases for their government and party operations, especially in the villages, the schools were targets for destruction by the mujahideen. Many Badakhshani youth who could afford to reach Pakistan in search of education enrolled in Pakistani *madrassas* as *talibs*. The only areas in the province where schools continued to operate and education improved were in the Ismaili-inhabited areas, especially the Shughnan district. Indeed, two teacher-training junior colleges had been established in Shughnan by the Marxist regime with aid from the former Soviet Union, and the Agha Khan Foundation had also begun to provide support to the Ismaili communities on both sides of the upper Amu Darya after the collapse of the Soviet Union. Hence, after two decades of war and violence, the minimal infrastructure in the province—roads, bridges, hospital, clinics, irrigation canals, and so on— had been further damaged, leaving the people trapped, more isolated, impoverished, and desperate.

Last, but not least, thousands of Kandahari Pashtun *kuchi/maldars* who had been granted grazing rights to the vast highland pastures of Shiwa and Dashi Rewat in Badakhshan by the Durrani monarchs, had been largely denied free access to these pastures during the 1980s and 1990s. Many local large herd owners had begun to use these valuable grazing resources on a regular basis. The few Pashtun *kuchis* who ventured into the areas became important sources of extracting rent for passage or usage by the commanders, whose territories they passed through during their migrations or who controlled the pasture grounds. After the establishment of the Karzai regime, however, the Pashtun nomads returned in full force with their deeds of ownership in hand, issued by the pre-1978 governments, to reclaim their pasture. Most of them have now returned with their herds, reclaiming most, but not all, of the pastures they formerly utilized (for details, see Patterson 2004).

Disillusionment and Uncertainty, 2001–2017

The Bonn agreements midwifed by the United Nations and the United States, called for Burhanuddin Rabbani to step down from the presidency which he had held, at least nominally, since 1992-2001, so that their hand-picked man, Hamid Karzai could step in as the chairman of the interim government in December 2001. Rabbani stepped down without resistance. However, as has been the case in Afghanistan politics, no leader imposed by outsiders as temporary ever remains so. Hence, Karzai morphed into becoming the transitional head of state and then twice "elected" president, thus ruling the country "temporarily" from 2001 until 2014.

The Panjsheri faction of Jami'ati Islami (the late Marshall Fahim, Yunus Qanuni, and Dr. Abdullah Abdullah) emerged as the most powerful block, occupying key ministries in Karzai's initial cabinet. Rabbani, although marginalized, remained an important player and a significant political deal maker until his violent death in the politics and economics of extraction and exclusion that was taking shape under the aegis of the United States and her NATO coalition allies in post-Taliban Afghanistan.[8] Rabbani had always preferred person-centered politics over normative, institutional, and procedure-based management, both in his Jami'ati Islami party and while presiding over the government institutions. He ran for a parliamentary seat from Badakhshan in 2005 and was easily elected, using it to protect his own considerable personal real estate and other economic assets in Kabul, Badakhshan, and other sites both inside and outside Afghanistan. He also lobbied to protect the interests of all mujahideen commanders against any and all suspected threats from Karzai and Western-educated English-speaking technocratic minions.

While Badakhshan governors changed at an alarming rate, one of Rabbani's maternal first cousins (Shamsur Rahman Shams) held onto the post of deputy governor of the province through 2013. His close allies from

Yaftal also filled many of the key police, army, and security posts critical to drug- and gun-running and smuggling contraband. His power and control in the province was gradually challenged, however subtly, by Karzai and the late Marshal Fahim who empowered and protected former jihadi commanders, such as Zalmai Mujadidi from the Jurm district, to maintain the control of lapis lazuli mines in the hands of the Panjsheri cartel and to control some smuggling routes to the Tajik border. Indeed, a number of other Badakhshan parliamentary delegates began to rival Rabbani and Mojadidi for the control of strategic drug trade routes and the appointment of border guards and district officers (*Wuluswals*) and other officials who controlled the routes to border crossings in different parts of the province (see Foschini [2010], and Hansen, Dennys, and Zaman [2009]). Hence, the Badakhshanis' control of state power may have momentarily "shone well, but was too short/hasty" (see the epigraph). After two decades of war and violence (1978–2001) and another decade and a half of so-called reconstruction and development (2001–2017), most recent reports about Badakhshan begins with these facts:

> [Badakhshan is] the most remote and impoverished province in Afghanistan. It is 89.9% mountainous and its population 96% rural.... Food security is a major problem and maternal mortality rate is one of the highest in the world. Winter snowfall and spring floods cause annual road closures from December to April for 10–15 of the province's 27 districts ... bordering Tajikistan, China, ... and Pakistan, the province holds several transit points for Afghan opium and heroin on its way to Central Asia, Russia and Europe.... There are few employment opportunities, roads or linkages to the rest of the country. As a result of political and economic changes [since 2002] in Afghanistan the cultivation and transportation of narcotics have become major economic activities in recent years.
> (Hansen, Dennys, and Zaman 2009, 5; see also Afghanistan Research and Evaluation Unit and World Bank 2004)

While these reports clearly point to the continuity of some of the sources of Badakhshanis' discontent, they leave out considerable changes in the social institutional fabric of Badakhshani society and significant continuities and changes in Badakhshan's relationship with the center in Kabul as well as its altered relationship within the region beyond the borders of Afghanistan. In the remainder of this chapter, I will limit the field of this examination to a brief discussion of the of the outcomes of action situations (decisions and choices) and shared strategic behaviors by key Badakhshani leaders within the context of specific opportunities and constraints and at critical moments during the past four decades for the peoples of this province, the country, and for themselves.

Post-Taliban Badakhshan: Lost Hope and Uncertainty

Unlike what Will Durant (2002) asserts, that "politics is not life, but a graft on life," for the peoples of Badakhshan and Afghanistan, during the past forty years, politics, war, and violence has been their life and not simply a graft on their lives. More importantly, the institutions of state, unlike in Max Weber's theory of the state, as claiming, successfully and legitimately, a monopoly on the legitimate use of physical force within a given territory (1946, also see Mitropolitski 2011), the institutions of state in Afghanistan, in general, and Badakhshan, in particular, have been what Madeleine Reeves describes as the "products of situated practices," entailing universal uncertainty of borders and of local commanders "impersonating" the state and its laws (Reeves 2014, 195–99). This current reality on the ground is, without a doubt, a significant consequence of the wars and violence of the past decades as are a number of other novel experiences in this province as well as the country in general. It is to the brief discussion of some of these major continuities and changes that I wish to turn now.

Badakhshan's Changing Geostrategic Position

Let me begin with the dramatic changes of territoriality and borders. Before 1978, Badakhshan's borders with the former Soviet Union and China were effectively closed, sealed by barbed wire and watch towers maintained in virtually all accessible parts by the Soviet and Chinese governments. Travel for education, trade, and commerce commonly undertaken by Badakhshanis to the cities of Bukhara, Samarkand, Khiva, Kokand, to Russia and Europe, to the Eastern Turkistani urban centers of Yarkand, Kashghar, Turfan, Urumchi, and beyond to China along the ancient Silk routes were completely cut off. Before 1978 and for many decades, any and all unauthorized border crossings had serious consequences for the perpetrators, and smuggling across the Soviet and Chinese borders were nonexistent. The only exceptions may have been minor cross border trading expeditions by the Kyrgyz and Wakhi across the high passes into the remote Pakistani towns of Eshkomen, Gilgit, and Chitral (for details, see Shahrani 2002).

The Saur Revolution and subsequent collapse of the Soviet Union effected unprecedented change to border enforcement and resulted in the establishment of new traffic in goods (both licit and illicit) across borders, especially through Tajikistan and Kyrgyzstan to Central Asia, Russia, and Europe. The first major collective exodus of the Afghan Kyrgyz from Badakhshan to the Gilgit areas of Pakistan occurred in August of 1978, only months after the communist coup. This was followed by the continuing exodus of small numbers of Badakhshani refugees across the borders to Chitral and Peshawar, Pakistan, and the flow of arms and materials from Pakistan to Badakhshan, both by mujahideen fighters and small numbers of international nongovernmental organizations (NGOs) that provided health, educational, agricultural, and minor road construction assistance in the province.⁹

The more dramatic changes, as indicated earlier, were the developments across the Tajikistan border immediately after the Saur Revolution of 1978 and then following the independence of Tajikistan and the onset of Tajik civil war. The former Soviet Union, due to the close proximity of the Afghan Badakhshani territories south of the Oxus and the inability and later loss of control of most of Badakhshan by their clients in Kabul, began offering direct assistance to their Islamili sectarian supporters in the border districts of Shughnan, Eshkashem, Zebak, and Wakhan shortly after the coup, continuing to do so until the fall of the Soviet Union in 1991. This cross border traffic to the Shughnan, Eshkashem, and Wakhan regions intensified after Tajikistan's independence and the inauguration of assistance from the Agha Khan Development Network (AKDN), which targeted the Ismaili communities on both sides of the border. Indeed, since the US-ISAF-NATO intervention of 2001, the AKDN has built five bridges across the Amu River, connecting Ismaili communities on both sides of the river and establishing trade and commerce between them.¹⁰ Major beneficiaries of these efforts have been the historically marginalized, discriminated, exploited, and ignored Ismaili communities. Agha Khan Foundation (AKF) has provided considerable educational and agricultural support, and has built health clinics with the specific goal of eradicating or at least alleviating opium addiction which has been extremely common among the Ismaili communities of these border districts. The Shughnan district, in particular, has benefited the most from these developments and has become instrumental in providing well-trained school teachers for the rest of the province, whose schools were largely destroyed and their teachers scattered or killed during the years of war.¹¹ The improvement in the lives of these underserved and abused groups in the province since the Saur Revolution has been one of the more dramatic changes in Badakhshan. Even a small community of Afghan Kyrgyz in the Pamirs, who were unable or unwilling to join the 1978 exodus led by their leader, Haji Rahmanqul Khan Kutlu, to Pakistan and eastern Turkey in 1982, have benefited from the loosening of the border controls across Tajikistan (although it has been reported that opium addiction and other forms of exploitation by the Badakhshani and outside traders among the Kyrgyz and some Wakhis has increased considerably).

Furthermore, as indicated earlier, cross border access from Afghan Badakhshan to Tajikistan has also resulted in numerous "commanders wars," both armed and political, within the province, often encouraged and protected by their patrons in Kabul, both inside and outside the ruling cliques. The result has been new and increasing politicization of identities and interethnic and intervalley tensions within the province which were minimal to nonexistent before 1978. That is, prior to the communist coup and collapse of the Pashtun-dominated central government, Badakhshanis felt equally subjugated by the powers of an alien state. The ongoing "commanders wars" of the 1980s, especially in 1990 and after 2001, have produced multiple state impersonators resulting in an increased number of local grievances and recriminations against other alleged Badakhshani perpetrators of violence and abuse. These cumulative tensions in the province have now acquired a new ideological coloring with the rise of the indigenous and local Taliban and Daesh groups within the province that protect Al Qaeda, Uzbekistani, Tajikistani, Chechen, and Uyghur fighters in the area—that is, a novel condition has been established in the province with lasting and potentially serious consequences to communal harmony for decades to come.

The principal source of new hope, however, is the province's newly found potential strategic importance to what Secretary Hillary Clinton has dubbed the "New Silk Road Initiative" (see Fedorenko 2013) and what has become known more recently as China's "One Belt, One Road" (Kennedy 2015) initiative.

The provincial capital, Faizabad, is now connected to Kabul by a two-lane, all-season asphalt road. Plans for extending it to Eshkashem and linking it to the network of roads in Tajikistan and ultimately to Kyrgyzstan and China is frequently mentioned, including by a number of 2014 presidential candidates who, thanks to the new highway, took their campaigns to Faizabad during that infamously fraudulent election. Some improvements to the roads connecting Faizabad to the province's twenty-seven district centers are also in evidence, but many district centers are still cut off during the winter months from the rest of the country. Road improvements are also complemented by the network of cell phone towers which covers most of the central Badakhshan districts, including this author's village. The potentially positive role of the wars and violence in improving the strategic position of Badakhshan within Afghanistan and Central Asia remains unrealized but is pregnant with possibilities.

Power Realignments and Identity Politics

The wars and violence of the past decades have had a considerable impact on redistribution of power and influence as well as increased politicization of identities, both on the individual and collective levels. On the whole, the shift of power, wealth and influence has been away from the older, traditional nonreligious dignitaries to the religious scholars—both old and young, traditionally *madrassa*-educated, including those attending the government-run *madrassas*. Many older local leaders were killed by the communists by 1981, except for a few who joined the resistance or collaborated with younger educated teachers and who became commanders. Major losers were the leftist youth, with some exceptions for those who were in Kabul working in the upper echelons of the PDPA government and were able to leave the country after 1992 for safe refuge in former Soviet republics, Europe, or India. The only ones spared that fate were the Ismaili-educated youth, who were protected in their own communities by geography, distance, and proximity to the Soviet Union. As indicated above, they and their communities have improved their relative power relations in the province considerably at this time. Relatives of a few high-ranking communist Badakhshanis who gained access to export-import trade to the former Soviet Union and China in the 1980s and 1990s, especially from central Badakhshan, have become quite wealthy, although now they have left the province permanently, either for Kabul or other countries.

It is important to note that in pre-1978 Badakhshan, the size and extent of local wealth and power were rather limited, since the real source of all power and wealth customarily was in the clutches of the officials of the state institutions, and very few Badakhshanis had any access to them. The collapse of the Kabul regime coincided with the appearance of multiple centers of power, guns, and money in the form of jihadi political party organizations in Peshawar. Their eagerness to dispense them to willing clients opened new and vastly larger possibilities and opportunities. Therefore, securing patronage and connections directly or indirectly to such resources, especially to one of the controlling masters in Peshawar such as Rabbani, became critical for Badakhshanis to gain access to such windfalls. The greatest beneficiaries of these newly abundant resources were Burhanuddin Rabbani, his close relatives and cronies, people of Yaftal to some extent, and Sunni Tajiks from central Badakhshan.[12] That is, the bulk of guns and money reached those favored by the norms of the patronage system in the province. As a result, very few local Uzbek commanders were favored by Rabbani in the 1980s. Some non-Yaftali Tajiks from the old district of Baharak and Mowlawi Abdulaziz from the Ragh districts, when felt left out by Rabbani's Jami'ati Islami, sought guns and money from his Pashtun rivals, Hekmatyar and Sayyaf. Most of the more powerful Uzbek commanders in the Argo region, feeling left out by Rabbani, also joined Hekmatyar's camp to receive weapons and money for their operations. Competition for control of local commanders in Badakhshan by Peshawar-based jihadi parties led to serious conflicts for control of turf and territory to please their respective patrons in Pakistan. These feuds led to the death of many local commanders, who pitched one valley against the next, and of Uzbeks who fought against Tajiks within central Badakhshan before 1992 (see Hansen, Dennys, and Zaman 2009).

After the fall of the communist regime in Kabul and the assumption of the presidency and government of Afghanistan by Burhanuddin Rabbani and his Panjsheri allies, his supporters in Badakhshan became utterly triumphant, at least for a while. His family, relatives, and close allies claimed properties belonging to the state and began to divvy them up among themselves. For instance, when taking over the small modern military compound built by the Soviet army for their own use in Dashti Qoregh, on the northern bank of Kukcha River across from the Faizabad Airport, the buildings were reportedly ordered dismantled by

Rabbani's Yaftali commanders for the wooden walls, doors, and windows, which were then looted and carried out to their villages for reuse!

Rabbani's commanders established almost total control over the newly opened smuggling routes to Tajikistan. These and other indulgent and self-serving practices by elements of the Jami'ati Islami close to Rabbani led to an internecine "commanders war" within the province by 1995. A factional division arose between those supporting the Ahmad Shah Masoud led Shura-ye Nazar (Northern Alliance), who occupied the eastern parts of the province, and the Tang Bala that was formed against those controlling the Tang Payan, lower or western Badakhshan and who were not willing to join the Northern Alliance.[13] The Tang Bala faction was led by Najmuddin Khan of Baharak and Zalmai Mujadidi of Jurm while the opposing Tang Payani commanders included Basir Khalid and Nazeer Mad, both of Yaftal. These internecine Badakhshan commanders wars continued unabated despite the ominous threat from rampaging Taliban across northern Afghanistan. These feuds resulted in the killing of Najmuddin Khan and the expulsion of Zalmai Mujadidi to Kabul as well as several other deaths in the Kishm district. The reason for these struggles, at least in part, revolved around the control of revenues from the lapis lazuli mines, which were primarily controlled by the Panjsheris with their Tang Bala allies, in whose domain, in Kuran and Munajn, the mines are located (see Foschini 2010).

Rabbani's control of power and politics in Badakhshan continued during Karzai's thirteen years in power, only with minor adjustments. He and his Yaftali commanders, especially Nazeer Mad, currently mayor of Faizabad, appropriated much land belonging to the state and sold it in plots for construction of shops and businesses both in the old city of Faizabad (*Shahri Kuhna*) as well as in the new city (*Shahri Now*). Commander Nazeer Mad also cornered much of the revenue from the German Provincial Reconstruction Team (PRT) in the province. Rabbani, members of his family and close associates are now the wealthiest in the entire province, owning considerable real estate and many businesses.

Most of the commanders with close ties to Rabbani or to Karzai or Marshal Fahim have become tremendously wealthy. Zalmai Mujadidi, who was forced out of Badakhshan in 1995, allied himself with Karzai on his arrival in Kabul. Mujadidi became Karzai's chief of security for the presidential palace (the Arg) from 2001 to 2005. He then ran for parliament from Badakhshan on Karzai's urging and has been elected twice to the Wolusi Jirgah. As a result, Mujadidi has gained control of the lapis mines for his Kabul patrons as well as segments of the access routes through the Warduj valley for smuggling opium, heroin, guns, and alcohol via Eshkashem to and from Tajikistan and other Central Asian regions.

Indeed, most jihadi commanders from Badakhshan, great and small, are among the new rich in the province, and most have retained lucrative posts in the security forces or district administration or elected themselves to the parliament from the province. Election to the parliament has also become a major source for extraction of wealth and accumulation of power in this and other provinces (for details see Foschini 2010; also see, Coburn, chapter 6 in this volume and Sharan, chapter 5 in this volume). A few individuals with close ties to Rabbani and his allies from Badakhshan have also found important posts in the government ministries in Kabul, including foreign service posts overseas. Uzbeks, although they make up a substantial part of central Badakhshan's population, were not able to elect a single deputy to the Afghan parliament in 2005, and only one was elected in 2010. Very few Uzbeks from Badakhshan (those who were able to attach themselves to the kleptocratic regime of Karzai) have done well in amassing fortunes. As such, the Weberian theory of state has degenerated to a reliance on the old norms of "capturing" any institutions by whatever means and impersonating them with force and violence has proven to be the most secure and assured way to wealth and power in post-Taliban Afghanistan. This is so, despite the shedding of alligator tears by many of these same power elites while publicly advocating for social justice, reform, and revolution in the name of Marx and Lenin, Islamism or free market capitalist liberalism.

Recentralization of Governance and Future Prospects

Many among the Badakhshan-educated youth from the 1970s onward favored decentralization of governance and adoption of local self-governance as a strategy for the empowerment of various peoples of the province. This, however, was not the wish of Ustad (professor) Burhanuddin Rabbani, who remained a vocal advocate of strong centralized regime.[14] At the constitutional Loya Jirga of 2003, in which he played an active role, Rabbani did not support the call for a federal executive structure advocated by the non-Pashtun delegates from the northern provinces. His aim was to remedy Badakhshan's underrepresentation in the national parliament, to attract a fair share of development funds for the province, and to broaden Badakhshanis' participation in the government bureaucracy, in general, and by appointing them to administrative posts within the province itself. His achievements before his death in 2011, even with these modest goals, were at best minimal.

Before 1978, all governors and most high-ranking officials in Badakhshan were appointed from Kabul, a great majority of them Pashtun. The first indigenous governor of Badakhshan, Amir Bek, a Shughnani, was appointed by the communist regime. After Rabbani became president in 1992, Badakhshanis for the first time came to assume most of the administrative positions in the province, qualified or not. Most local commanders were already running a rump local government of their own in the absence of a central one. Hence, Rabbani's government simply anointed them by officially confirming their appointments and started paying them salaries in addition to what they were extracting on their own. In order to remedy the chronic underrepresentation of Badakhshanis in the Afghan national parliament (the Wolusi Jirga) in Kabul, whose divisions also used to be used as the electoral units in each province, he increased the number of districts (Wuluswali) in Badakhshan from seven to twenty-seven.[15] Karzai's regime, cognizant of this fact, however, cleverly changed the electoral units from the traditional districts to the provinces, allocating a specific number of deputies for each province to be elected using the single nontransferable vote (SNTV) system. Under the new electoral laws, Badakhshan has been allocated nine deputies based, allegedly, on a "guestimated" total population of about one million. Hence Rabbani's attempted resolution of the old grievance of underrepresentation has not worked, at least not until now.

Since the assumption of power by Hamid Karzai, governors of Badakhshan have been non-Badakhshanis except for Shah Waliullah Adeeb, a man from Darwaz and a Jami'ati Islami activist who was appointed in 2010 and was initially an "acting governor" under the Ghani and Abdullah administration, but lost his post to a non-Badakhshani. As indicated earlier, the deputy governor, a first cousin of Rabbani, was a fixture guarding the family's captured prize at least until 2013. New Badakhshani power elites have joined networks of patron-client ties within Badakhshan and the national capital, vying to keep control of offices and assets they possess. Rabbani's sudden death certainly has introduced a serious element of uncertainty about the ability of his eldest son, Salahuddin Rabbani, now appointed minister of foreign affairs in Ashraf Ghani's cabinet, who has stepped into his father's rather large political and economic shoes. A relatively small amount of development funding has reached the province compared with Kandahar, Helmand, Zabul, and other Pashtun-dominated provinces in the east and south where Taliban resurgence has been active. According to the US Government Accounting Office (GAO n.d., also see Cordesman 2010) the poverty rate in the province is between 55 and 76 percent; this makes Badakhshan among the very poorest in the country.[16] Major investment in the province through National Solidarity block grants has reportedly covered some 711 villages, and total spending of $16.7 million. These projects have included micro-hydropower stations (sixty-two of them), solar panels for electric lights, and safe drinking water, among other things. As a result, it is claimed that 20 percent of the people have access to clean drinking water (including my own village) and 37 percent of the population have electricity, which seems highly optimistic. Although rich in minerals and many rivers, the natural resources of the Badakhshan province and the country and its potential for large scale hydropower remains untapped. Unemployment, especially among high school graduates, is extremely high, pushing most of the working-age males to seek work in Iran under extremely dangerous and illegal conditions, should they be able to enter Iran.[17]

Many other young Badakhshanis have enrolled in Pakistani *madrassas* and are recruited by the Taliban. During the past two to three years, bands of them have launched attacks in the Warduj and Yumgan valleys against the government in an otherwise peaceful province. The Pakistani-trained local Taliban apparently have an easy time attracting many idle and disillusioned young men who feel left out to join their ranks. A large number of Badakhshani youth have also joined the volunteer Afghan National Army (ANA) for the monthly salary they receive. They are often sent into the volatile, Taliban-infested areas where many of them are returned weekly to the province in coffins. These are developments which do not bode well for the future of Badakhshanis.

Nearly three decades of polycentricism and local self-governance, however, has emboldened many communities to govern themselves and, if need be, defend their own newly acquired power and resources. On April 8, 2014, Tolo Television News International reported that the peoples of the Kuran and Munjan district ejected the mining company authorized by the Kabul regime to extract lapis lazuli from the area, and the locals strongmen have taken control of the mines themselves (see O'Donnell 2016). The chances for ordinary Badakhshanis to resist the return to the status quo prior to 1978 has, without a doubt, become much improved. This is despite the fact that their leaders, especially Burhanuddin Rabbani and his network in the Jami'ati Islami party, because of their falling into the same common vicious circle of extractive and exclusionary politics and the economics of the past, have once again failed them miserably. Worse yet, the international community, since 2001, has complacently buttressed the newly emergent commander-based provincial and national power structures, rather than encourage genuine reform and improvement of the local, provincial, and national governance institutions.

Conclusion

Unlike Ramazan Bashardost, a deputy from Kabul in the Afghan parliament who also ran for president in previous elections against Karzai, I do not believe that "our people are desensitized ... [that] the Afghan people have had their willpower stolen from them; [and] the society has become numb" (Bashardost 2014, 3). It is true that resistance is not possible from a situation of complete impotence and sheer poverty. Rather, as Eric Wolf has asserted, "its [i.e., resistance] possibility is contingent on the fields of power surrounding them" (1969, 290). There is no doubt that decades of war has traumatized the peoples of Badakhshan and Afghanistan, but they are survivors who are striving and yearning to reject the kleptocratic practices of the post-Taliban regimes and their policies of appeasement toward the Taliban as they demonstrated in the first round of presidential elections on April 5, 2014, by casting their votes in huge numbers despite real tangible threats against them.

Will their new, fraudulently elected leaders fail them again? Yes, the likelihood of another disappointment is very high indeed, in Badakhshan as well as in the country. Because peaceful, legally mandated changes in person-centered extractive centralized polities can be volatile and unpredictable, as was the case with the 2014 presidential elections in Afghanistan. The ordinary peoples in Badakhshan and in Afghanistan as a whole have always done their best; it is their elites and their foreign patrons, with their choices of inappropriate and self-serving clients and institutional structures of governance, who have let them down time and again. It is indeed the choice of *political institutions that are the key determinants of all nations' efforts toward prosperity or poverty, and stability or fragility* (Acemoglu and Robinson 2012). The choices for the Afghan elites are clear. Are they, as Bashardost describes them "ready to push their people to the precipice" (2014) as they have done so often in the past, or will they try to save them from falling into the precipice for once? Uncertainty about their actions, it seems, is the only certain thing.

M. Nazif Shahrani is Professor of Anthropology, Central Eurasian Studies, and Near Eastern Languages and Culture at Indiana University. He is author of *The Kirghiz and Wakhi of Afghanistan: Adaptation to Closed Frontiers and War* and editor (with Robert L. Canfield) of *Revolutions and Rebellions in Afghanistan: Anthropological Perspectives*.

Notes

1. This neglect is attributed to the events following the public hanging of Muhammad Wali Khan Darwazi—a Badkhshani courtesan of reformist king Shah Amnullah (r. 1919–1929) who also served as Amanullah's minister of foreign affairs—by Nadir Shah (r. 1929–1933), the founder of the Musahiban or Muhammadzai dynasty in 1929. Because of the Musahiban rulers' suspicion of Badakhshani elites' loyalty to Shah Amanullah, it is said that the peoples of the province have suffered fifty years of deliberate neglect by the Musahiban rulers of Afghanistan (see Roostayee 2009, 3); for more details on how the province has fared during much of the twentieth century, see Shahrani 1984, 148–159). Supporters of the Marxist regime saw the revolutionary regime as the remedy for this long neglect of the province, but their opponents rejected Marxism as the appropriate corrective to the longstanding problem between the center and the province of Badakhshan.

2. "Sitami Melli" is a popularized misnomer appended by the detractors of this leftist movement with the intention to defame them. The real name of this political movement, which was found and led by Tahir Badakhshi, an intellectual from Faizabad, the provincial capital, has changed over the decades, according to devotee Latif Pedram (currently member of the Afghan parliament from Badakhshan), these names have been: initially (1960s), Mahfili Entizar (Party of Reckoning), then Sazmani Inqilabeyee Zahmatkashani Afghanistan (SAZA—Revolutionary Organization of the Toilers of Afghanistan), then Sazmani Fedayeyee Zahmatkahshani Afghanistan (SAFZA or Organization of the Devotees

of the Toilers of Afghanistan), and most recently as Kongarayee Melli Afghanistan (National Congress Party of Afghanistan), which is now headed by Pedram. From its inception, this party has advocated for social justice and has alleged that the Pashtun-dominated governments of Afghanistan have consistently favored the Pashtun and thus committed injustice and oppression against the non-Pashtun groups in Afghanistan (Pedram 2007). Hence, they have stood against national oppression or in Persian, Sitami Melli (for more detail about the Badakhshi, see Shahrani 1984).

3. In 2007 a mass grave of over five hundred people was unearthed in Dashti Qoregh, near the provincial capital, Faizabad (visited by the author, see Hansen, Dennys, and Zaman 2009, 6). Many more were said to have been thrown into the rapids of Kukcha River from the helicopters and perished without a trace.

4. An unknown assailant, most likely a victim of Mansur Hashimi's repression from this period in Badakhshan, shot him dead in front of his house in Kabul, only a few weeks after the mujahideen victory in 1992.

5. Olivier Roy (2000, 139) reports that the Soviets also made use of large numbers of their own Shughni Islamilis from Soviet Tajikistan as KGB agents during their war and occupation of Afghanistan in the 1980s.

6. Their sympathies are apparently still there as it is reported that Shahnawaz Tanai, a well-known Pashtun member of the PDPA from Khost, who ran as a presidential candidate of the Hezb-e Ghorzangi Melli (National Movement Party), got 4704 votes from Badakhshan, and 3587 of those were cast for him in Sheghnan (see Foschini 2010, 6).

7. It is also important to note that Rabbani married one of his daughters to Ahmad Zia Massoud, the elder brother of Ahmad Shah Massoud, the legendary Jamiati Islami commander, in the 1980s to cement his political alliance with that family. This was a tactic commonly used by Afghan elites during the decades and centuries past.

8. Rabbani, serving as the president of the High Peace Council, was the victim of a Taliban suicide bomber (on September 20, 2014, at his home in Kabul); the bomber was pretending to deliver a message of "peace" from the Taliban Shura council in Quetta, Pakistan.

9. The number of Badakhshani refugees in Pakistan were relatively small, as by 2009, only 13,619 were reported to have returned to the province (see Hansen, Dennys, and Zaman 2009, 16).

10. Some envious people in central Badakhshan have been spreading rumors about the Agha Khan's plans to create a separate state for his Ismaili disciples inhabiting the Pamir and Qaraqoram mountain ramparts located in Afghanistan, Tajikistan, northern Pakistan, and western China.

11. A report issued by the Afghanistan Research and Evaluation Unit (AREU) and the World Bank in 2004, using United Nations International Children's Emergency Fund (UNICEF) data, states that by 2001, some 139 schools in the province (102 of them for boys and 37 for girls) were either completely, mostly, or partially destroyed and were in need of repair (see Afghanistan Research and Evaluation Unit and World Bank 2004, 15). The elementary school, called Ma'rufi Khash, located in the village of Shahran and which this author had attended, was among those completely destroyed to the last stone.

12. It is important here to note that Rabbani came from a fairly poor but pious family, and his father kept a very modestly stocked shop selling general merchandize in the bazaar in Faizabad, the provincial capital.

13. This geographical division of the province into two areas is used regularly by the Badakhshanis: first, an East-West geographical division of the province called Tangi, which is marked by the narrow gorge on the Kukcha River valley half way between the town of Baharak and the provincial capital, Faizabad; and second, the colder, more marginal, and narrower valley to the east of Tangi (versus the warmer and wider valleys west of it). Indeed, there was a move by some Tang Bala leaders, such as Zalmai Mujadidi from Jurm district, to divide the province into two separate provinces, but Rabbani is alleged to have prevented it.

14. In 1979, when on sabbatical leave from UCLA where I taught, I spent six months doing research, partly serving as an adviser to then minister for reconstruction of the mujahideen government in exile, Burhanuddin Rabbani, in Pakistan. I remember more than once talking to Ustad Rabbani about urging the mujahideen leadership to consider allowing decentralization of the administration when establishing their Islamic government. His answer was consistently no, adding that "the country after this prolonged war needs a strong centralized government." He also thought decentralization of power would lead to secessionism and civil war. I warned him that not considering decentralization would be more likely to drag the government and the country into civil war, but he was not moved. Years later, when I mentioned to him our conversations in Peshawar, he conceded only slightly, blaming the internecine wars on the unreasonableness of his opponents and that they had been imposed on him by the enemies of Afghanistan, both near and far.

15. Before 1978, by increasing the numbers of Woluswalis representing Pashtun-dominated southern and eastern provinces, and lowering the number of such units in the non-Pashtun north, central, and western portions of Afghanistan which held much larger populations, the government assured disproportionately larger Pashtun representation in the national parliament. Rabbani assumed that this scheme could continue, so he increased the number of districts in his own province and some of the other provinces in the north as well.

16. The rate is calculated on the basis of a per capita consumption threshold of 1,255 afghanis (approximately $US25) for monthly consumption, an expenditure representing the typical cost of attaining 2,100 calories per person per day and of meeting some basic nonfood needs. Data is from the US Government Accounting Office (n.d.).

17. In December of 2015, I was told that at least sixty young males from my own village were currently in Iran as migrant workers, and many more were seeking to join the Taliban, Daesh/Islamic State, and other armed groups in the province for lack of any other options.

Bibliography

Acemoglu, Daron, and James A. Robinson. 2012. *Why Nations Fail: The Origins of Power, Prosperity, and Poverty*. New York: Crown.

Afghanistan Research and Evaluation Unit and World Bank. 2004. *A Guide to Government in Afghanistan: Case Study: Badakhshan Province*, March. Accessed April 12, 2014. http://www.areu.org.af/Uploads/EditionPdfs/405E-A%20Guide%20to%20 Government-Badakhshan-CS-print.pdf.

Aya, Rod. 1979. "Theories of Revolutions Reconsidered." *Theory and Society* 8 (1): 39–99.

Bashardost, Ramazan. 2014. "Dr. Ramazan Bashardost: 'Our Leaders Push Their People over the Cliff.'" Interview by Armanshar Foundation, March 17. *Unveiling Afghanistan*. http://openasia.org/en/?p=3799.

Cordesman, Anthony H. 2010. *Agriculture, Food, and Poverty in Afghanistan: Is a "Population-centric" Strategy Possible?* Washington, DC: Center for Strategic and International Studies (SCIS). Accessed October 14, 2017. https://www.csis.org/analysis/building-china%E2%80%99s-%E2%80%9Cone-belt-one-road%E2%80%9D.

Crawford, Sue E. S., and Elinor Ostrom. 1995. "A Grammar of Institutions." *American Political Science Review* 89 (3): 582–600.

Durant, Will. 2002. *The Greatest Minds and Ideas of All Time*. New York: Simon & Schuste.

Fedorenko, Vladimir. 2013. *The New Silk Road Initiatives in Central Asia*. Rethink Paper 10. Washington, DC: Rethink Institute. http://www.rethinkinstitute.org/wp-content/uploads/2013/11/Fedorenko-The-New-Silk-Road.pdf.

Foschini, Fabrizio. 2010. "Campaign Trail 2010 (1): Badakhshan—Drugs, Border Crossings and Parliamentary Seats." AAN (Afghanistan Analysts Network), June 19. https://www.afghanistan-analysts.org/campaign-trail-2010-1-badakhshan-drugs-border-crossings-and-parliamentary-seats/.

Hansen, Cole, Christian Dennys, and Idrees Zaman. 2009. Conflict Analysis: Baharak District, Badakhshan Province. London: Cooperation for Peace and Unity. http://cpau.org.af/manimages/publications/Baharak_Conflict_Analysis_Feb_09.pdf.

Heathershaw, John. 2009. *Post-Conflict Tajikistan: The Politics of Peacebuilding and the Emergence of Legitimate Order*. London: Routledge.

Islamic State of Afghanistan. 2005. *Legislative Elections of 9 October 2005: Elections to the House of the People (Wolesi Jirga), Voting by Province*. Joint Election Management Board. http://psephos.adam-carr.net/countries/a/afghanistan/afghanistan2005.txt.

Kennedy, Scott. 2015. "Building China's 'One Belt, One Road'". Washington, DC.: Center for Strategic and International Studies (SCIS). https://www.csis.org/analysis/building-china%E2%80%99s-%E2%80%9Cone-belt-one-road%E2%80%9D. Accessed 10/14/2017.

Mitropolitski, Simeon. 2011. Weber's Definition of the State as an Ethnographic Tool for Understanding the Contemporary Political Science State of the Discipline. Canadian Political Science Association, April 26. http://ssrn.com/abstract=1823401.

Münch, Phillip. 2013. *Local Afghan Power Structures and the International Military Intervention: A Review of Developments in Badakhshan and Kunduz Provinces*. Afghanistan Analysts Network. http://www.afghanistan-analysts.org/wp-content/uploads/2013/11/20131110_PMunch_Kunduz-final.pdf.

O'Donnell, Lynne. 2016. "Afghan mineral wealth being looted by strongmen, experts say". *The San Diego Union-Tribune*. April 13, 2016. http://www.sandiegouniontribune.com/sdut-afghan-mineral-wealth-being-looted-by-strongmen-2016apr13-story.html. Accessed 10/14/2017.

Patterson, Mervyn. 2004. *The Shiwa Pastures 1978–2003: Land Tenure Changes and Conflict in Northeastern Badakhshan*. Kabul: Afghanistan Research and Evaluation Unit.

Pedram. Latif. 2007. *Man Setami Budam, Hastam wa Khawham Bud: Pashekhi Dr. Abdulatif Pedram … Bar Sukhan Farsayee hayee Marshall Muhammad Qasim Fahim* (I was a Setami, am one will always be one: Response of Dr. Abdulatif Pedram to the Rhetorical Charges of Marshall Muhammad Qasim Fahim, First VP of the Islamic Republic of Afghanistan). *Sukhangahyee Faratar Az Marzaha*. Accessed January 18, 2013. Faratarazmarzha.org.

Reeves, Madeleine. 2014. *Border Works: Spatial Lives of the State in Rural Central Asia*. Ithaca, NY: Cornell University Press.

Roostayee, Abdul Hanan. 2009. *Imkanati Enkishafi Eqtesadi Badakhshan, (Bakhshi Duwum) Ahwali Tarikhi wa Awza'yee Ijtima'i* (Badakhshan's Economic Development Potentials, (Part Two), Historical Preview and Social Conditions). Australia, January 3. http://www.afgazad.com.

Roy, Olivier. 2009. *The New Central Asia: The Creation of Nations*. New York: New York University Press.

Shahrani, M. Nazif. 1984. "Causes and Context of Responses to the Saur Revolution in Badakhshan." In *Revolutions and Rebellions in Afghanistan: Anthropological Perspectives*, ed. M. Nazif Shahrani and Robert Canfield, 139–69. Berkeley: Institute of International Studies, University of California.

Shahrani, M. Nazif. 2002. *The Kirghiz and Wakhi of Afghanistan: Adaptation to Closed Frontiers and War*. Seattle and London: University of Washington Press.

Shahrani, M. Nazif, and Robert Canfield, eds. 1984. *Revolutions and Rebellions in Afghanistan: Anthropological Perspectives*. Berkeley: Institute of International Studies, University of California.

US Government Accounting Office. n.d. *Afghanistan Development: Poverty and Major Crop Production*. GAO-10-756SP, an E-supplement to GAO-10-368. Washington, DC: Government Accounting Office.

Wolf, Eric. 1969. *Peasant Wars of the Twentieth Century*. New York and London: Harper & Row.

13

HAZARA CIVIL SOCIETY ACTIVISTS AND LOCAL, NATIONAL, AND INTERNATIONAL POLITICAL INSTITUTIONS

Melissa Kerr Chiovenda

ON AN EARLY spring day in Bamyan in 2013, I was sitting with a group of civil society activists who were preparing to travel to the neighboring province of Daikundi, the only other Hazara-majority province, to visit civil society organizations there. The meeting was a chance for the core group of civil society activists living in Bamyan to discuss what they believed were the most important tasks to be completed and subjects discussed with the activists in Daikundi. It was being held in the sunny meeting room of one of the main civil society organizations in Bamyan, on the second floor of a business center located in the main bazaar. Only a few of those in attendance were officially affiliated with this organization, though. Others worked full time at various civil society organizations, although most of the attendees held some other job, often in education, development, and journalism, or were students and dedicated their free time to civil society activities. We sat around a long conference table in the bright sunlight that streamed through the window, drinking tea and listening to everyone's thoughts. One man quickly put forth what he believed was the main problem which needed to be addressed. "These civil society activists in Daikundi simply are not as advanced as we are in Bamyan," he stated. "We need to teach them to work more like we do. We have more experience here in Bamyan, there is a lot they can learn from us." Everyone around the table, about fifteen men and five women, most in their twenties and thirties, agreed. "In Daikundi," the speaker continued, "civil society activists don't understand how necessary it is to remain independent, separate from political activities." Seeking elaboration, I later questioned him further. "Melissa, the whole point of civil society, is that it remain independent, from the government, from the political parties, and if possible, even from outside donors. We try to fund as much as we can ourselves. Well," he qualified, "most of us do. But even this organization, where we have met today, they rely too much on outside donors. It means that they lose control of their actions. Of course, they have the best intentions, but they are not doing the right thing completely, as those of us who are more independent do. And in Daikundi, they really have ties to the government, to outside donors."[1]

Unfortunately, due to a late-season snowstorm, the roads and passes we would have crossed in the journey to Daikundi were closed, and the trip was canceled, to my disappointment. It was not rescheduled due to the busy schedules of the activists. This discussion, however, led me to consider more deeply, and question more specifically, what the activists believed were better practices for civil society and what practices should be avoided. It led me to realize that Hazaras as a whole, and particularly civil society activists, have an ambiguous relationship with the various institutions—state, aid and international organizations, foreign governments, and others—they promote, denounce, and use to redress problems, both those specific to Hazaras and those which affect Afghans more broadly. In general, I found that there is a tendency among these informants to classify certain ideals as positive—education, democracy, human rights. Yet when these ideals are promoted through state institutions—elections, state-run schools, political parties—they come to be seen as corruptible, and often, discussions about Afghan state discrimination arise. When they are promoted through international organizations—the United Nations, the United States' various projects through various funding in Afghanistan, international human rights organizations—they are seen as being promoted in much purer form, uncorrupted by internal Afghan politics, whether at a very local or a national level.

This tendency to question such desirable institutions such as education, elections, and formal justice systems because they are affiliated with the state, which is viewed as corrupt, can be understood through Alexander's proposal that the civil sphere can be understood in terms of a binary, in which civil and democratic values such as cooperation and rationality are found on one side and noncivil and nondemocratic values such as aggression and irrationality are on the other. The civil side of the binary is viewed as the legitimate side, and the noncivil side is not only illegitimate but polluting (Alexander 2006). The civil society activists have placed the Afghan government squarely in the noncivil side, and as such, they reject institutions administered by the government as polluted. One might even take this argument a step further, and say that international organizations, such as the United Nations, and even the United States government, are in line with civil values and hence might even be considered purifying.[2]

Hazara marginalization and social exclusion by the state has a long history, while most Hazaras see international intervention in Afghanistan starting in 2001–2002 with the defeat of the Taliban as a clear turning point. From the point of view of the Hazara activists with whom I worked, the Afghan state is the institution, in its different manifestations, which has consistently betrayed Hazaras, while international organizations promote ideals such as equality and human rights which benefit Hazaras.

Hazaras, during the conflict period which started in the 1970s and continues today, initially fought fiercely among themselves only to later achieve a fairly unified political bloc and political ideology based on ethnicity. While a unified Hazara political bloc has not survived the creation of the current government, that awareness of the need to counter and act against the historically-rooted social exclusion faced by Hazaras seems to be one of the most important legacies Hazaras carry with them from the years of war. The international intervention after 2001 is, by many Hazaras and other Afghans, viewed as a turning point for Hazaras, when real opportunity and real integration into greater society, became a possibility, particularly as educational and employment opportunities relating to an influx of foreign nongovernmental organizations (NGOs) and funds benefited them. Yet many Hazaras continue to distrust their own state while adhering to the goals and ideals of the international community in Afghanistan, which, they believe, without interference from the Afghan state, will result in real inclusion for Hazaras. In spite of this, Hazaras work in and for state institutions, promoting ideals championed by the international community that they see as universal and that are clearly placed in the "civil" side of Alexander's binary, and yet that they also believe are not held by the state itself.[3] Universal ideals which are pure when promoted by outside organizations and institutions are polluted when touched by the corrupt Afghan state. And yet, Hazara activists continue to work toward these ideals, ideally independently but through state institutions when necessary, with the hope that somehow this state of affairs will change—and that their dedication to civil values might have a purifying effect. This chapter considers Hazara experiences with the Afghan state in the justice system, education, and electoral system, to try to shed light upon this ambiguity and understand the points of view of young Hazaras concerned with overcoming ethnic exclusion. A counterpoint is provided by a Hazara appeal to UNAMA (United Nations Assistance Mission to Afghanistan) on the part of activists seeking to bring attention and provoke a response to mass killings of Hazaras in Pakistan.

Research for this chapter is based on eighteen months of fieldwork, most of which was conducted in Bamyan Province. I mainly worked with a group of educated civil society activists (people who had at least completed high school, and often college) who are serving as a sort of "vanguard" in mobilizing Hazaras toward a nation building project. This loosely knit group was responsible for organizing protests, seminars, speeches, and other activities geared toward bringing attention to issues of perceived (and often very real) injustice and discussing just what it means to be Hazara in Afghanistan today, with importance placed on Hazaras' historical—and current—marginal position in society. This group of activists did not solely represent a political or socioeconomic elite, however. As access to education for most Hazaras is a relatively recent opportunity, many of the activists were from villages in Bamyan or neighboring provinces with a large Hazara population, while many others are returned refugees from neighboring countries Iran, and to a lesser extent, Pakistan. Strong ties are maintained with home villages. At the same time, there is a constant back-and-forth of the activists to Kabul, mainly West Kabul, which has an extremely large Hazara population. Those who might be considered elite, coming from families of a higher socioeconomic background and with more education, mix with those who might be the first high school graduates in their families and from a poor background. People from both backgrounds were able to achieve leadership positions among the activists.

Hazaras and the Afghan State

Since Hazara distrust of Afghan state institutions is due largely to historical experiences, a brief understanding of Hazara-state interactions is necessary. For Hazaras, this is a history of Pashtun-controlled state dominance. Since 1747, when the Pashtun military leader Ahmad Shah Durrani took control of a vast swath of territory extending from Mashhad in today's Iran to Lahore and Karachi in today's Pakistan, all the land that later became Afghanistan has been passed down from one Pashtun monarch to the next along several lineages from among a loose Durrani ethno-political confederation (Ewans 2002). Until the end of the nineteenth century, the various ethnic groups living as subjects under the Durrani rulers enjoyed a decentralized model of governance. Alongside Pashtuns (albeit largely within ethnically homogeneous geographical areas) lived Uzbeks, Turkmen, Tajiks, Kyrgyz, Baluch, Sunni and Shi'a Hazaras, Ismaili Tajiks, non-Muslim "Kafirs" (renamed Nuristanis), and many other smaller groups.

When Abdur Rahman Khan ascended the throne in 1880, he strove to bring all his subjects under the strict control of a centralized state apparatus. Not surprisingly, much of his twenty-year-long reign was devoted to suppressing the numerous revolts that his new approach provoked. Until then, the Hazaras, who lived in and along the fringes of the central nine-thousand-feet-high plateau, remained a quasi-autonomous substate entity within Afghan state territory. They maintained a mode of production and political leadership that relied on an aristocracy of *begs* and *mirs*, landowners who employed peasants in a quasi-feudal relationship featuring extensive networks of patronage (Mousavi 1997). The attempt by the Amir to enact strict control over the Hazara highlands was met with opposition, resulting in a campaign of suppression. It must be pointed out that he launched similar campaigns among other groups, including the political rival Ghilzai Pashtuns. However, the campaign against the Hazaras was tinged by sectarian concerns. Most Hazaras were Shi'as, that is to say, the "wrong" kind of Muslim (Poladi 1989; Mousavi 1997). The onslaught on Hazara lands and people took place amidst a degree of sectarian fervor and violence that all but obliterated traditional Hazara social and cultural structure. It is estimated that nearly 60 percent of the Hazara indigenous population was either enslaved, killed, fled Afghanistan, or deported elsewhere in Afghanistan. *Begs* and *mirs* were stripped of their position of authority and their lands either redistributed among their previous clients or appropriated altogether by non-Hazaras. The Hazara lands along the southern fringes of the central highlands (the most agriculturally productive) were used to relocate part of the southeastern Ghilzai Pashtuns, who had previously revolted against the Amir, or were allotted to Pashtun nomads as grazing pastures to be used during their summer movements from winter locations in the hot Pashtun southeast. Those Hazaras who survived the suppression of the revolt, and who were not sold into slavery, ended up being the most heavily taxed among all Abdur Rahman's subjects, reduced to pariah individuals within the realm, forced to perform only menial jobs, and virtually denied access to avenues for higher education (Mousavi 1997; Ferdinand, 1962).

Hazaras benefited from King Amanullah's reforms in the 1920s as they were recognized as an equal nationality to other citizens in the 1923 constitution, while Hazara slavery was outlawed in 1921 (Mousavi 1997). Hazaras do not seem to have been specifically excluded from government positions by law after this time. However, these reforms, and particularly the 1923 constitution, did not include an elected national assembly, to which the government should be held accountable, and provincial councils were only partly chosen through election. As such, systematic social exclusion continued against Hazaras. In 1931, Nadir Shah made further constitutional changes; an elected assembly was provided for, but candidates were preselected by the government. The 1964 constitution did allow for the direct election of national and provincial consultative assemblies (not legislative), marking an improvement over those previously implemented (*Encyclopaedia Iranica* 2011). For Hazaras, these changes certainly were a step in the right direction. However, years of social exclusion, lack of education, and economic problems meant that Hazaras were not fully able to take advantage of this new constitution, although in some ways their situation began to gradually improve, as some gained government and elected positions, and a middle class started to form. Real changes for Hazaras occurred in conjunction with the conflict that was soon to come.

The Soviet occupation of Afghanistan (1979–1989), following the 1978 communist Saur Revolution by the PDPA (People's Democratic Party of Afghanistan), spared the central highlands, the Hazara homeland, from the worst of the war. Political developments during the Soviet invasion and withdrawal resulted in a brief period during which Hazara parties, until that point divided into divisive factions, united under Abdul Ali Mazari and the Hizb-e-Wahdat party (Ibrahimi 2009). The subsequent civil war (1992–1996) following the collapse of Mohammad

Najibullah's communist government, which had remained in control of Kabul for several years following Soviet withdrawal, saw a resurgence of Hazara political activism centered around ethnicity and religiosity (Ibrahimi 2012), although it also saw the worst massacre of Hazaras in recent history. During an assault on the Hazara-majority Afshar neighborhood in Kabul between seven hundred and four thousand Hazara civilians were executed or disappeared at the hands of the Wahhabi-oriented Pashtun warlord Abdur Rabb Rasul Sayyaf. Hazaras also implicate the Tajik Ahmad Shah Massoud, then minister of defense, as bearing responsibility. The regime of the Taliban continued to discriminate against and oppress this ethno-religious group. Beyond destroying the Buddha statues in Bamyan, the Taliban purposely conducted several military operations against the Hazara "heretics" throughout their regime.

Support and protection from the Western powers that have, since 2001, controlled Afghanistan have meant for the Hazaras a quick and conscious renaissance.[4] Their young intellectual elites, some of whom received training in Iran as refugees and some of whom were part of a similar intellectual renaissance among Quettan Hazaras (Ibrahimi 2012), have enthusiastically embraced those values and ideals of equality and democracy that the private and institutional foreign organizations promote. While Hazara students still claim discrimination in Afghan public educational institutions, many have found the opportunity to start their own private schools and universities.[5] The percentage of children, both girls and boys, attending schools and universities among Hazaras is much higher now than among other ethnicities. The reason for this seems to be not only their experiences while living abroad as refugees but also, and perhaps more important, the fact that Hazaras perceive they have a very limited time to improve their situation, as they anticipate that after international troops withdraw, they may face a return to the difficulties they faced in their historical past. The possibility of the continuation of conflict, as well as the current brief break of intense conflict, drives current Hazara educational attainment.

In the several parliamentary, local, and presidential elections that took place since 2001, Hazara turnout at the polls has been proportionally much higher than that of other ethnic groups. Under the watch of foreign advisers who work alongside Afghans in the state apparatus, positions for Hazara bureaucrats and administrators have increased exponentially. And yet, this does not mean that Hazaras have completely escaped the oppressions and prejudices of the past. Karimi (2011), in his master's thesis on West Kabul, describes the many ways that social exclusion can be experienced by a people such as the Hazaras, and furthermore, how social exclusion has a cumulative effect. It is related to many factors, for example, in the Hazaras' case, loss of land which historically belonged to them, high taxation policies, restriction to manual labor or even slavery (in the past), little access to education, and less government representation. All of these factors create and feed an ongoing social exclusion, which continues even after one of the factors seems to have been "solved." The structure of society ensures that exclusion continues, so that even when gains are made, as a whole, people continue to experience detrimental effects of exclusion.

Election Process and Political Parties

Before the 2014 presidential elections in Afghanistan, ethnic Hazaras were featured prominently in multiple international media outlets, whose reports stressed the important role they would play. Hazaras, deeply invested in the democratic system, voted in higher percentages than other ethnic groups, such articles stated. A reading of such media suggests that Hazaras are possibly the Afghan group most invested in by the state. In fact, leading up to the 2014 elections, many of my Hazara friends posted declarations on Facebook (a key way civil society activists spread their ideas) emphasizing their commitment to democracy and to elections.[6] Hazara turnout in elections has been consistently high in past elections as well. Votes received by ethnic Hazara candidate Ramazan Bashardost, who achieved third position in the previous presidential elections (ahead of Ashraf Ghani, current president) also indicated Hazaras' ability to influence elections and influenced the amount of attention they received in 2014. At first glance, this does not seem to be a group totally disillusioned by the state itself.

Yet an examination of Hazara attitudes toward these elections demonstrated that Hazaras can believe fully in an ideal while distrusting the way this ideal (here, democracy) is implemented by the state apparatus. Several Hazara civil society activists contacted me after the 2014 election and expressed concern that nearly every Hazara-majority area had run out of ballots, including Bamyan, Daikundi, West Kabul, and Hazara-majority districts of Maidan Wardak, Uruzgan, and Ghazni. This was interpreted as a systematic attempt to marginalize the Hazara vote.[7] But Hazara, especially civil society, distrust concerning elections and politics runs much deeper. Bashardost was not affiliated with a political party when he achieved third place, and many stated this was part of his attraction. He was considered clean, unsullied by affiliation with the main Hazara political parties, which are considered problematic.

The creation of Hizb-e-Wahdat is considered by Hazaras in Bamyan today as the first time Hazaras displayed political and military strength by uniting most of the population under its umbrella. Hizb-e-Wahdat was formed in 1989, after founder Abdul Ali Mazari, a cleric trained in Iran, decided to open the party to Islamist and secular Hazaras, with a focus on ethnic affiliation rather than religious sectarian affiliation. Mazari would come to be known among Hazaras as the driving force behind their unification and the development of their ethno-political consciousness, particularly as he chose to include leftist politically active Hazaras as well as those with Islamist tendencies in the new party (Ibrahimi 2009).

Actual unity was short-lived. Mohammad Akbari, a key leader under Mazari and ethnic Kizilbosh, was not comfortable with the ethnic, rather than sectarian, nature of the party. Animosity between the two led Akbari to leave Mazari's Wahdat and join Ahmad Shah Massoud. Today Akbari leads Hizb-e-Wahdat Milli Islami Afghanistan. After Mazari was killed by the Taliban in 1995, Karim Khalili took over as leader, and yet, due largely to personality politics that flourished after 2001, the party split into two further groups, Hizb-e-Wahdat Islami Afghanistan led by Khalili, and Hizb-e-Wahdat Islami Mardom Afghanistan, led by Mohammad Mohaqeq, who had maintained a large degree of influence in the north. A fourth split is Hizb-e-Wahdat Islami Millat e Afghanistan, led by Qurban Ali Erfani. All four parties now operate largely by personality of leadership rather than a party platform.

For Hazara activists, who see the original Hizb-e-Wahdat as something pure, describing it and its leader Mazari as not only interested in bettering the situation of Hazaras but also in promoting the same universals the activists now espouse—democracy, human rights, gender rights, education, equality for all Afghan citizens, the dissolution of the party into something based on personality and patronage networks is especially painful. Few of the self-proclaimed civil society activists associate openly with any of these parties. Furthermore, in Markaz Bamyan, among youth, association is often kept a secret, as if it was something to be ashamed of. I tried to find youth who did affiliate with the parties to interview, but since so few would come forward, I had to abandon this approach for research. As I tried to arrange interviews, one of my main informants explained, "No one *wants* to be associated with one of these parties, they are corrupt, unjust, not really working for democracy." Perhaps had I not already worked so extensively with the civil society activists this would not have been such a problem. One especially prominent activist asked my advice as he had been pegged to lead a youth group of Mohaqeq's party. He was clearly torn as on the one hand, this would give him access to patronage networks and the chance to influence the youth. But, he was also distressed as he told me it was "wrong" for an activist to accept such a position (in the end he did accept). I believe he was afraid that he, or at least his image, would become polluted by this affiliation. Civil society activists believed that it was *they* who had inherited the party of Mazari and they who inherited his ideals. From the activists' point of view, the original Wahdat ideals have been destroyed by those who broke up the party in order to enhance their own personal position, and they are being kept alive by the activists and by the very nature of Hazaras in general, who they claim display a rare open-mindedness as a group.[8] The general population of Bamyan was wary of parties, and activists seemed more able to mobilize the population as a whole. I attended Mazari's birthday celebration at the headquarters of Khalili's Wahdat compound, where a quite modest crowd turned out. I later attended a celebration staged by the civil society activists. Hundreds of people packed into Mazari Square and the surrounding fields to listen to a several-hours-long program of speeches, singing, and poetry. It was clear in which setting they preferred to remember their martyred leader.

An Unjust Justice System

When I first arrived in Bamyan to conduct the main part of my research in summer 2012, many of my informants were eager to tell me about an event that had happened several months earlier. A sixteen-year-old Hazara girl, Shakila, was shot while staying with her brother-in-law. Their house was within the compound of a provincial council member, who happened to be a Sayed (a person descended from the Prophet Mohammad and hence considered to be of Arab, not Hazara, descent). Authorities initially suspected Shakila's brother-in-law, although he had an alibi. The provincial council member, who was at home, claimed he was alone praying when the murder occurred. When the investigation shifted away from Shakila's brother-in-law, the crime scene was no longer viable. The case was closed, and although later reopened under a new prosecutor with pressure from civil society groups, no real headway had been made at the time of writing.

For many, Shakila's case represented an ethnic divide that was opening between Sayeds and Hazaras, although a number of civil society activists denied that this was an ethnic issue. That summer, I met with three activists in the living room of the house where I was staying to discuss this and other issues. Fereshta, an activist in her thirties, stated clearly when asked if ethnicity impacted the activists' response, "No. This is an issue in which a young girl has been killed, and has not received justice. This is a crime against women, against humanity in general. This issue must be understood in this context." But a colleague, Hamid, who was in his twenties, quickly jumped in. "Sayeds think they can get away with anything. The first prosecutor, he was Sayed. How many working in the criminal justice system are Sayed? This case should have received attention nationally, but all of the Sayeds throughout the country mobilized against us." Informants were ambivalent when interpreting cases such as Shakila's. Some blamed a generally corrupt judicial system, targeting weak strata of Afghan society cross ethnically, while others emphasized what they perceived as malice against Hazaras in particular.

The power and influence of the Sayeds is somewhat ambiguous, and has changed throughout the years of conflict. Before the conflict, Sayeds maintained leadership influence from the social capital they gain from their ascriptive position. Kopecky (1982) wrote that, in the 1970s and before, Sayeds were able to unite divisive Hazara groups. Recent Hazara political mobilization was led by Sayeds in 1989, through the Shura e Inqelab e Ettifaq e Islami, the Council of the Islamic Revolutionary Alliance, an early manifestation of Hazara political consolidation which functioned as a political party and para-state. The *Shura* and its Sayed leadership lost power because the population felt that *Shura* demands for taxation and conscription were burdensome (Harpviken 1998, 185). Today, relying upon their status as descendants of the Prophet, Sayeds retain enough power for many Hazaras to resent them, although many Hazaras do support them for reasons of religion and tradition (and these two feelings are not always mutually exclusive). During my fieldwork, it became clear that there is an ambivalence among Hazaras as to whether Sayeds are actually a "special" holy group deserving respect or a group that plays upon the superstitions of the people to reap benefits for their own profit. While Sayeds seemed to have peaked in terms of political power in the 1980s, they certainly still retain the ability to mobilize enough supporters to remain important political players, while not monopolizing the very top echelons.

I did not find any activists who were satisfied with the justice system, whether citing the Shakila case or in more general discussions, although I did find certain individuals working within the justice system were acknowledged for their integrity. And yet, these activists stressed the importance of the rule of law, emphasizing that conflicts must be resolved within the state apparatus and not through community-based conflict resolution. Informants explained that traditional dispute resolution systems might restore harmony but would not provide justice. In order for these traditional, extrastate institutions to work, both sides in a disagreement needed to feel some satisfaction, meaning also, the one who was seen to be at fault in the dispute would receive benefits, especially should he be the more powerful party. To my informants, such a system is not justice; justice, they said, comes from a strong rule of law implemented impartially (also see Chapter 9 in this volume). Hazaras, having historically lived under a feudal system, and after integration into the Afghan state, ostensibly occupying the lowest rungs of society, explained they did not see any benefit in a system that continued to favor the actor with more power, espcially if he should be in the wrong. They saw themselves as the underdogs most likely to lose in a dispute resolution system aiming to restore harmony. It would be better, they told me, to work toward a more just state system, something that, if it does work as it should (even as it still does not now), will provide a better outcome for less powerful groups like Hazaras given enough time and reform. Before the current conflict, Hazaras might try to stay away from the state system because they knew it would be, in many if not most cases, prejudicial against them. In today's setting, state justice systems on paper should act fairly toward all groups, and ostensibly have the backing of the international community. Hazaras consider their best possibility to support justice within the state and to criticize the justice system when it clearly is not living up to the standards set for it by supralocal authorities. Such authorities, in the Hazara activists' eyes, clearly included international actors and trainers that they knew were working to reform the system and could hence be counted on more than the Kabul government.

Still, they reckoned that any practical attempt at redressing a fundamentally discriminatory condition for Hazaras had, to this day, obtained mostly disappointing outcomes. And although Hazara activists stress that they are not ethno-nationalist, most cases of intracommunity conflict seem to be interpreted through the lens of ethnic politics (for example, Sayeds who supposedly use their privileged position to escape criminal prosecution).[9]

Hazara activists I worked with use their marginality as a sort of tool, in hopes that it will further their political goals. And yet, there is a sense among them that politics is inherently unclean, impure, and that in seeking to adhere to values of human rights, gender rights, and democratic values, politics must be avoided, and rather, means such as development and civil society must be utilized, with the paradox remaining, although overlooked by the activists, that these groups are also, in some fashion, politically involved. This makes it difficult for those activists who are also clearly of an ethno-nationalist mindset. They must work to reconcile these two issues and demonstrate that they, in their activities, are not contaminated by the political institutions which they feel are repressing them. This tightrope seemed to me to be one of appearances, because going beyond the fact that activists' activities often seemed inherently political, activists would, on occasion, ally with certain members of the establishment. Maintaining their purity meant, then, keeping these sorts of alliances to a minimum and being sure to openly criticize established political leaders when necessary. At the same time, ideals such as justice, as interpreted through the training and messages given by foreign (often American) contractors who work with developing the justice sector in Afghanistan, make it clear that justice must be delivered through the state apparatus. But it is not only those working in the justice system who receive this training. Activists, development workers, and some university students are also invited to attend (I myself observed five such training sessions). The tendency of Hazara activists to accept what international and foreign organizations teach them, almost without question, means that these ideals are internalized, but the actual institutions, that is to say, the Afghan judicial system, police, and so on, are still seen as corrupt, whether more generally or more specifically relating to Hazaras. The belief that such institutions are still corrupt clearly relates to the past experiences of Hazaras, prior to and during the war (in addition to real corruption that certainly currently exists). Informants often spoke of their almost complete social exclusion because of exclusion from or lack of fair participation in such institutions.

Hazara trepidations about and desire to improve the justice system does not stem solely from the conflict years in Afghanistan. However, the political movement of Hizb-e-Wahdat not only galvanized unified ethnic action but was a result of the necessities that the conflict placed on Hazaras. Furthermore, the current conception of justice and of rule of law that Hazara activists promote is, if not an import accompanying international involvement and state-building efforts after 2001, promoted by international actors working in Afghanistan today. Hazaras' own political trajectory, combined with these outside influences, results in a situation whereby activists repeatedly demand justice be served in the face of power and patronage politics and a corrupted justice system.

Educational Institutions

When activists talk about their history within that of the Afghan state, they almost always begin with the wars undertaken by Abdur Rahman. Hazaras were included in the state, but, they point out, institutions were used as weapons against them. Abdur Rahman appointed his own rulers to Hazara lands, replacing Hazara leaders, and taxation was heavy (Gawecki 1980, 167). Gawecki further reports that in the 1970s (likely with the influence of communism), more Hazaras were afforded some access to institutions, such as elementary and secondary education, although there were few schools in rural Hazara regions and although higher education would have been more difficult to obtain. Several of my own informants told me that while Hazaras, according to the law, during these periods, did have a right to education, they were often denied admittance on the basis of their names or place of birth or residence, from which admissions might guess them to be Shi'a or Hazara. Since 2001, many more Hazaras receive education, although many also claim that, especially within state universities, a high degree of discrimination still exists.

Hazaras have received much attention as the ethnic group in Afghanistan with the highest attendance rates among both male and female schoolchildren (Oppel 2010; Larson and Hazelton 2008). Before the conflicts, Hazaras in the rural areas had very little access to schools because few existed. According to Mousavi, during times when a Pashtun-dominated state was promoting language and educational opportunities in Pashtun regions, Hazaras were left isolated (Mousavi 1997). In the 1970s, during the rule of Mohammad Daoud and Zahir Shah, as well as during the communist period, some few schools were created, but they served a very small percentage of the population. Many Hazaras relied on religious *madrassas* should they desire an education, but a secular education was much more difficult to obtain. This changed drastically with the push to bring schools to all rural areas after 2001. Schools are now present in all parts of Afghanistan, but Hazara regions are significant in that they face less insurgent activity and less social-cultural pressure that could discourage attendance. Rather, many Hazaras now consider it a key aspect of their identity that they support education for boys and girls.

One of the most common refrains I heard from Hazaras in Bamyan was "Pashtuns have stolen our history." When asked to elaborate, I was told that most (although not all) historians from Afghanistan had been Pashtun, and they had, according to my informants, written histories that entirely left out the Hazara point of view. Worse, they said, was that non-Afghan scholars relied heavily upon these historians when writing their own histories of Afghanistan, and the result has been that Hazaras are often left out of the story or possibly shown in a negative light. Of course, there have been Hazara scholars in more recent years who try to fill this gap by writing a history of Hazaras, for example, Hassan Poladi (1989), Sayed Askar Mousavi (1997), Mohamad Isa Gharjistani (1988), and Hussein Ali Yazdani (1989). Many Hazaras in Bamyan told me that with access to schooling, members of the community are becoming much more interested in finding out about these histories for themselves and are reading these works and others.

I spoke with teachers, school officials, and students in Bamyan after I began to hear about the frustration many Hazaras harbor about their history. I wanted to understand what was taught in Afghan schools regarding history and ethnic issues. The answer was very clear-cut. The Ministry of Education made a determination that bringing up any issue relating to ethnicity would potentially give rise to greater ethnic problems. As a result, within the official curriculum and textbooks, no mention of ethnic issues is made. In fact, I was given the chance to inspect history textbooks from several grades, and I did not find mention of ethnicity in any case, even when it seemed necessary to understand historical events. The fact that Abdur Rahman played up the Shi'a aspect of Hazara identity is left unsaid, as is the fact that ethnic Hazaras were one of several groups singled out. The war is rather described as a legitimate suppression of revolt against the state, and ethnicity and religious affiliation of any of those revolting is absent. Hazaras are at least one ethnic group that resent this policy. They see their history being overlooked, not told, in favor of a history that focuses on kings and the development of the Afghan state. To them, Afghan history is in fact a history of a Pashtun elite. As a result, Hazara activists and students in Bamyan are setting out to teach themselves their own history. Several people in the community are considered "historical experts" as they have (usually independently) studied those historical works that have been written by Hazara historians. They meld and interpret these histories and then retell them orally. When I first arrived in Bamyan, these retellings seemed informal, taking place in dorm rooms and around bazaars, listened to by whatever students happened to be present. However, it soon became apparent that they were becoming more formalized. The history experts were called upon to speak at such events as the birthday and anniversary of the death of deceased Hazara leader Abdul Ali Mazari, at Hazara Unity Day, and even in conjunction with the presidential elections in the United States. Several programs were held at educational institutions in Bamyan to show how democracy worked in America (usually with US Embassy sponsorship), and at most of them, one of the "historical experts" would give a speech, often relating Hazaras, the formerly enslaved people of Afghanistan, to formerly enslaved African Americans. If the United States could come to have a black president, went a narrative I heard several times at these talks, then the same could happen for a Hazara in Afghanistan one day.

Hazara concerns about educational institutions in Afghanistan also extended to more concrete issues. In Bamyan, I was often told, there were not the same opportunities for augmenting one's schooling with private classes that people in other areas found (of course, in any rural area, such opportunities will be limited). Schools themselves were of lesser quality, especially in the districts and areas located even a slight distance from the Bamyan center. Teachers often had little training, schools were horribly overcrowded, and there were not enough supplies provided for either students or teachers. Furthermore, in the more high-altitude areas, schools were forced to close for six months out of the year because of the intense cold (the schools are not heated and many students walk two hours or more to rural schools, impossible in the winter in these areas because of roads blocked by snow). Several school directors I interviewed told me they simply had to do their best, cramming a nine-month curriculum into six months. They expressed regret that their students then had to compete with students all over the country on the standardized *konkur* university entrance exam, believing that they could not prepare their students sufficiently. Again, it is certainly true that this is not simply an ethnic issue, as Hazaras in Bamyan are not the only Afghan citizens to live in high-altitude locales or extremely rural areas. Yet, Hazaras in Bamyan strongly believe they are more affected by this problem than others. Furthermore, Pashtuns are believed, by many Hazaras I interviewed, to live mainly in warm areas where this is not an issue. Other problems that prevent Pashtuns from attending school, such as societal pressure and pressure from insurgents, are seen to be a problem within Pashtun society and earn little sympathy.

During my last summer in Bamyan, in 2013, allegations of discrimination against Hazaras at Kabul University flared. Hazaras claimed that they were systematically given lower grades by professors in certain faculties. The professors claimed that Hazara students were simply not performing up to standard. Hazaras held protests in response, demanding that the professors in question be removed. Eventually a resolution was reached. At the same time, a large number of Hazaras study in private universities and schools, where they are less constrained by state curriculum. Many of these universities, such as Ibn Sina and Kateb University in Kabul, employ mainly Hazara professors trained in Iran. In these environments, both students and professors feel they are better able to reach their goal. To sum up, education, believed to be a right and a way to achieve success honorably, is implemented by the state in such a corrupted way, from the Hazara point of view, that most believe reliance on state educational institutions exclusively will never result in their advancement. Hazaras, hence, take it on themselves to remedy this situation—by writing, learning, and retelling a Hazara-centric history and by opening, promoting, and supporting private institutions. These histories are accepted as "true," in particular as they are promoted outside the auspices of the polluting state, which has, in their eyes, proved unable to present knowledge that might work against its own interests. When state educational institutions are necessary, Hazaras pride themselves on their performance, even if they do not believe them to be ideal, and protest what discrimination they believe still exists.

Appeals to UNAMA

In winter 2013, I met with a number of my informants who were protesting the killing of around one hundred Hazaras in a market in Quetta, Pakistan, that January. The activists had decided that the best way to approach the problem was to go straight to the United Nations, or, the Bamyan headquarters of UNAMA (United Nations Assistance Mission in Afghanistan). My friends set up tents outside of UNAMA headquarters in Bamyan and several went on a hunger strike. I visited them throughout their protest, both to give moral support and to continue my research. During the day, we sat outside in the sun on carpets, talking for long periods of time about the reasons for their protest. During the night, they set up *bukharis*, or wood-burning stoves, inside the tents and huddled under sleeping bags.

One young man became quite emotional as we spoke outside on the carpets. He kept repeating, "We have been the victims of a systematic genocide for over one hundred years. They have to listen to us!" Initially, wanting to help, I decided to point out what I considered weak points of their campaign. I tried to highlight those problems that in my opinion were inherent in trying to get the United Nations to recognize much greater mass killings than this as genocide, because it would require some sort of action on the part of the United Nations, an action they were especially not willing to take if it meant becoming entangled with the internal problems in Pakistan. I was met with disbelieving stares. "We have been killed since the time of Abdur Rahman....." the young man trailed off. I agreed, but pointed out that from the dry, bureaucratic standpoint of the United Nations, the century-long predicament of Hazaras in Afghanistan and Pakistan would probably not gain the same consideration and acknowledgment that other historical traumatic events have received (such as the Jewish Shoah, the Rwandan genocide, and the mass killings during former Yugoslavia's civil war). Several people asked "Why does that matter? We are being killed, even today . . . we are killed in Pakistan, we are killed in Afghanistan, and there has never been a stop to this killing!"

It was clear that my informants did not consider the United Nations to be prey to the same internal problems that they believed plagued Afghan state institutions. When I tried to explain that the United Nations was also concerned with political issues, and that it was unlikely to rock the boat by focusing on investigating a Hazara genocide (or mass killing, as one might rather call this incident), I was met with what seemed to be quite genuine shock. Almost all Hazara civil society activists, at least those that I spoke to, believe that the United Nations is primarily concerned with humanitarian issues and do not recognize the political wrangling that goes on within the organization. I was met with either a complete lack of understanding, or an unwillingness to understand, how the Security Council works, for example, and what it would take to actually have the United Nations make any concrete steps concerning the situation of Hazaras. After having their situation improve after UNAMA arrived, Hazara activists have come to believe that the United Nations will surely help them if the organization can only be made to understand what is happening and how it is part of a larger pattern of oppression and mass killing. Activists have read the declaration of human rights, and they have read the definition of genocide, and they believe that if they are given the chance to explain themselves, then the United Nations will respond to them. These are believed to be pure, civil ideas, and, under the auspices of an organization also believed to be pure, the activists did not accept that there was any room for pragmatism outside of such ideals on the part of the United Nations. Unfortunately, when a UNAMA representative came to meet them, they were told they did not have any concrete demands that UNAMA could address, and they should just go home. The hunger strike, which was a dry strike, meaning they also abstained from liquids as well as solid food, ended quickly and the activists went home after several more days.

The complete trust in the intentions of the United States is another area where Hazara activists seemed unable, or unwilling, to acknowledge the factors (political, economic, and strategic, among others) that shape policy. Many, when speaking of the United States, focused on civil rights issues, on the importance of having a black president today and how that directly related to Hazaras in Afghanistan, and the good work done by the United States in Afghanistan. Of course, there is a good amount of propaganda put out by the United States on these issues, and Hazara activists work closely with such embassy outreach programs as the Lincoln Learning Center to promote these ideas. And yet, they are not happy with their rate of progress, even as they attribute what progress they have made to international intervention. They often complain that they know Pashtun areas receive more development funds and attention, and they believe Pashtuns are being unfairly rewarded for participating in an insurgency while Hazaras have worked hard to help the nation building projects. The blame is never placed upon the United States or the United Nations, however, but on Pashtuns who work with these organizations and "spread lies" about Hazaras, such as the rumor that "they are all Iranian agents." The United States, in its efforts to promote civil ideas, has managed to place itself, in the eyes of the activists, if not in the eyes of the population at large, on the "pure" side of the binary.

Conclusions

Many Hazaras have long viewed the Afghan state as a Pashtun-run enemy that is corrupt and oppresses Hazaras even today, despite the fact that they see themselves as one of the groups most invested in the state-building project. Why

Hazaras decide to invest in a state that they believe is corrupt, even polluting, largely stems from the fact that they see no other choice. Independence is clearly not an option for a people who are concentrated in the isolated central highlands, in the capital, and the rest scattered throughout the country. To try to change the state, as insurgents from other groups do, is also not an option. For ideological reasons, Hazaras and the insurgents want something quite different from a new state. Furthermore, the current state, corrupted as it is, was put in place by the international benefactors that Hazaras align themselves with. Generally, they believe the international community does care about Hazaras and their difficulties, and that it is actors who are opposed to Hazaras from within the state that ensure the state remains corrupt. Hence the paradox. The state is corrupt, because many staffing it are corrupt, but it symbolizes the efforts of those outside benefactors who do have their best interest at heart. Perhaps, then, it is better to say that the state itself is not polluting, but rather those noncivil actors working within it have so completely polluted it that, at this point in time, it is rotten. Hazaras, particularly activists and those sympathetic to activists, hence continue to try to reform the state from within, to purify it, while at the same time remaining mistrustful in their dealings with it. And yet those who do work within the state, even in the name of civil ideals, risk pollution. Hazara activists in Bamyan are equally distrustful of the locally elected provincial council. A Hazara who becomes affiliated with state institutions is in some way sullied, and most of the provincial council members are considered to have achieved their positions based on patronage networks, or as one informant told me, "through the means of the mafia." They do not believe the provincial council has changed over the past fourteen years either, except with the loss of one member, Jawad Zuhak, who was considered to have worked hard for the development of Hazara areas and who was murdered by the Taliban, although rumors circulate that a Hazara rival was behind the event, in 2011. Zuhak appears to have been able to maintain civil ideals during his time in office, although another possibility is that he was "purified" by his martyrdom in the memories of the activists.

Hazaras, then, are contributing to the state-building project, because the ideals of such a project are in line with the democratic ideals they have come to embrace, and because at this point they see no other way to improve their situation than to seek education and work to improve things for themselves from inside the very apparatus they distrust. Indeed, they also believe a federal, rather than the current centralized, system, would better serve their needs. But in addition, Hazara activists are spreading the message that human rights, civil rights, the pursuit of knowledge through education, justice, and even gender equality are universal ideals and rights owed every human being. They believe that these ideals have been brought and promoted by foreign actors such as the United States, UNAMA, and other various international organizations working in Afghanistan. However, they also somewhat paradoxically believe that these ideals are somehow culturally inherent to Hazaras, a belief promoted by the civil society activists that tend to have an ethno-national point of view and that was promoted by Mazari himself. Currently, their only strategy is to work through, or in cooperation with, the corrupted Afghan state, the very institution that has been responsible for their historical suffering, to achieve these ideals, particularly as the supposed foreign benefactors of the Hazaras are insisting upon this. Therefore, even as they exercise their right to protest, their right to civil disobedience against this state, they also wholly work for its betterment from within while paradoxically believing that these ideals can only be polluted when administered by the state.

MELISSA KERR CHIOVENDA is a research fellow at Harvard Medical School's Department of Global Health and Social Medicine and an affiliated faculty member of anthropology at Emerson College, Boston.

NOTES

1. The independent nature of this particular civil society organization meant that it existed almost completely on the funds which members were able to donate. It had to borrow office space from other organizations. Most of its projects were focused on awareness building, such as protests, marches, speeches, and sometimes publications of newspapers. Therefore, the group itself did not intend to address community problems directly but rather, intended to mobilize community members to demand rights and improvements in Bamyan. Once a year the group did take up a collection to buy firewood for people being held in the local jail.

2. In May 2016, this sort of frustration with the state came to a head when massive, peaceful Hazara-led protests erupted throughout Afghanistan due to the decision to reroute a new electricity line (TUTAP, named for the countries in would pass through—Turkmenistan, Uzbekistan, Tajikistan, Afghanistan, Pakistan, although Pakistan was since dropped) originating from Turkmenistan through the Salang pass, bypassing the original planned route that would have passed nearby Bamyan and provided electricity. This was seen as a betrayal by Hazaras and not only became a rallying point for activists but also mobilized Hazaras from all backgrounds as well as people from other ethnicities. The Hazara maintained that the decision was once again evidence of prejudice against them, while the government maintained that, in fact, electricity would, via both routes, eventually bring electricity to Bamyan. Hazaras, not only activists but also leading politicians such as Mohaqiq, Khalili, Danish, and the governor of Bamyan, also claimed that electricity would come, but only after more than a decade more of waiting. Distrust for the government was shown by Hazara protests that repeatedly called Ashraf Ghani a liar; such charge gained traction when it was announced by a government official that, contrary to what Ghani had been saying, the decision to change the route was made under his own administration and not under that of previous president Hamid Karzai. Hazara activists rely on a German report

for validation which, in its executive summary, claims that while the Bamyan route would cost more, take slightly longer to build, and require some integration with coal-powered stations, the Salang route was treacherous, would prove difficult to repair, and, as electricity through the country is already following this route, would cut much power to the regions south, including Kabul, should there be an avalanche or some other disaster. Furthermore, it would make impossible the building of a third line that had been planned through the Salang Pass. Activists saw this as one more example of a corrupt government working against Hazaras and relied on their interpretation of the German report, prepared by the Fichtner group, to provide the reality they believed the state was trying to conceal (Fichtner 2013).

3. Whether they actually are universal is questionable. They may be classified as similar to the "North Atlantic Universals" described by Jean Rolph Trouillot (2002).

4. This "Hazara Rennaissance" did not emerge from nowhere after 2001, but was rather part of a trajectory that began with the stirring of Hazara ethnic identity when Wahdat was formed. It continued through the establishment of a small Hazara-educated middle class in Kabul which was then also largely incorporated into Wahdat. All the same, the post-2001 period marks a turning point because of greatly increased access to education and work opportunities, government structures that are much more inclusive of Hazaras, and less fear of persecution (although sectarian and ethnic incidents do continue from time to time).

5. Many of the private Hazara universities get start-up money from politicians; however, ongoing expenses are then paid for by university fees. The Marefat School, the most famous Hazara high school in West Kabul, also operates on donations and school fees collected from children, with scholarships given to children from lower socioeconomic backgrounds. I am not aware of other funding sources.

6. Many non-Hazara friends also issued such declarations, and turnout in the election was high across Afghanistan.

7. Hazaras were well represented in the electoral commission, but despite this, many of my informants believed that it was not enough to prevent this particular type of voting fraud.

8. Hazara activists claim that their "open-mindedness" stems from several sources. First, they maintain that their heritage is mixed, inclusive of a pre-Islamic Iranic group, early Turkic groups, and later Mongol interlopers. The result of this mixing, of being a place where further mixing happened on the Silk Road, and possibly of a Buddhist background, are all given as reasons some activists say Hazaras are naturally more open. Second, Hazaras often say that because they have been an oppressed group for so long, they have no reason to remain closed off to ideas that might benefit them and that their "traditional" way of thinking and doing things has been largely destroyed by Afghan cultural imperialism, so they must seek new, open ideas. Finally, many cite Mazari as a strong influence, quoting speeches and writings in which he stressed equality and justice for all peoples of Afghanistan. Certainly, Mazari was most concerned with the situation of the Hazaras and his own political situation, but in achieving his goals, there are plenty of sound bites and excerpts where he speaks of equality, women's rights, education, and justice for all peoples, alongside calls that Hazaras no longer be discriminated against.

9. In political bodies from the national parliamentary level to the local provincial council level, Sayeds have been, and are often still, counted as Hazaras, despite the fact that they both consider themselves distinct groups. Sayed abuse of power, or the implementing of a "ruler's law" (in Nazif Shahrani's words (2009)) rather than the rule of law is seen by many Hazaras to be a patently discriminatory practice, although this is not obvious from the outside.

Bibliography

Alexander, Jeffrey C. 2006. *The Civil Sphere.* Oxford: Oxford University Press.
Canfield, Robert L. 1972. *Hazara Integration into the Afghan Nation.* Occasional Paper No. 3. New York: Afghan Council for the Asia Society.
———. 1973. *Faction and Conversion in a Plural Society: Religious Alignments of the Hindu Kush.* Ann Arbor: University of Michigan Museum.
Encyclopaedia Iranica. 2011. "Constitutional History of Afghanistan." Accessed August 15, 2014. http://www.iranicaonline.org/articles/constitutional-history-of-afghanistan.
Ewans, Martin. 2002. *Afghanistan: A Short History of Its Peoples and Politics.* New York: HarperCollins.
Ferdinand, Klaus. 1962. "Nomad Expansion and Commerce in Central Afghanistan." *Folk* 4: 123–59.
Fichtner GmbH & Co. 2013. "Islamic Republic of Afghanistan Power Sector Master Plan." Technical Assistance Consultant's Report prepared for Asian Development Bank. https://www.adb.org/sites/default/files/project-document/76570/43497-012-afg-tacr.pdf. Accessed October 12, 2017.
Gawecki, Marek. 1980. "The Hazara Farmers of Central Afghanistan: Some Historical and Contemporary Problems." *Ethnologia Polona* 6: 163–75.
Gharjistani, Esa.1988. *Tarikh-e Nawin-e Hazarajat* (New History of Hazarajat). Quetta: Shuray-e Farhangi Islami.
Harpviken, Kristian Berg. 1998. "The Hazara of Afghanistan: The Thorny Path towards Political Unity, 1978–1992." In *Post Soviet Central Asia*, ed. Touraj Atabaki and John O'Kane. London: I. B. Tauris.
Ibrahimi, Niamatullah. 2009. *The Dissipation of Political Capital among Afghanistan's Hazaras: 2001–2009.* Working Paper Series 2, No. 51. London: Crisis States Research Centre.
———. 2012. *Shift and Drift in Hazara Ethnic Consciousness: The Impact of Conflict and Migration.* Working Paper Series, No. 5, September 27. Bonn: Crossroads Asia.
Karimi, Mohammad Ali. 2011. "'The West Side Story:' Urban Communication and the Social Exclusion of the Hazara People of West Kabul." Master's thesis, University of Ottawa.
Kopecky, Lucas Michael. 1982. "The Imami Sayed of the Hazarajat: The Maintenance of Their Elite Position." *Folk* 24 (1): 89–110.
Larson, Marisa, and Laura Hazelton. 2008. "Hazara People." *National Geographic.* Accessed August 13, 2014. http://ngm.nationalgeographic.com/geopedia/Hazara_People.
Mousavi, Sayed Askar. 1997. *The Hazaras of Afghanistan: An Historical, Cultural, Economic, and Political Study.* New York: St. Martin's Press.
Oppel, Richard A., and Abdul Waheed Wafa. 2010. "Hazaras Hustle to Head of Class in Afghanistan." *New York Times*, January 3. Accessed August 13, 2014. http://www.nytimes.com/2010/01/04/world/asia/04hazaras.html?pagewanted=all.
Poladi, Hassan. 1989. *The Hazaras.* Stockton, CA: Mughal Publishing Company.
Shahrani, M. Nazif. 2009. *Afghanistan's Alternatives for Peace, Governance and Development: Transforming Subjects to Citizens& Rulers to Civil Servants.* Afghanistan *Papers No. 2.* Ottawa & Montreal: A Co-Publication of Center for International Policy Studies (CIPS) and The Center for International Governance Innovations (CIGI) cigionline.org.
Trouillot, Michel-Rolph. 2002. "North Atlantic Universals: Analytical Fictions, 1492–1945." *The South Atlantic Quarterly* 101 (4): 839–858.
Yazdani, Hussain Ali. 1989. *Pozhohishi Dar Tarikh-e Hazara-ha.* Mashad: Mahtab.

14

ADAPTING TO THREE DECADES OF UNCERTAINTY: THE FLEXIBILITY OF SOCIAL INSTITUTIONS AMONG BALOCH GROUPS IN AFGHANISTAN

Just Boedeker

Introduction

The Afghan state has been characterized either as an "ethnic state" (Orywal 1986, 82) or in opposition to tribal groups (Tapper 1983). Both ideas of Afghanistan that were brought up in the 1980s—whether the "ethnic state" or the "conflict of tribe and state" in Afghanistan that Richard Tapper proclaimed in his famous edited volume—presume the existence of an Afghan state. However, due to its distinct geographic and social particularism, the strong dichotomy between urban and rural spaces and the cultural diversity of its people as well as the constant interferences of external political powers since the nineteenth century (Schetter 2004, 11–13), the Afghan state has hardly established institutions that carry distinctive authority beyond a few urban centers. In rural and remote areas—especially in the proximity of political borders—the social upheavals that took place in Afghanistan had multifaceted and indirect impacts on the social institutions that were likewise shaped by political concepts held by local groups and their interrelations with groups and political institutions in the bordering countries. Therefore, the question arises whether the "state" is the right frame to grasp the complex Afghan polity. Instead of the state, local ethnic and tribal groups that have real or imagined common descent, language, culture, common socioeconomic practices, or religious orientation, certainly constitute the core institutions in the various Afghan communities and "have repeatedly exerted a decisive influence on public affairs" (Canfield 1988, 75) in Afghanistan. But ethnic and tribal identities are likewise hard to grasp and mark rather flexible, segmented entities. Since the invasion of NATO and other Western troops, *ethnic group* has become the key concept in describing Afghan society. The classification of

Afghan communities as *ethnic* or *tribal* serves mainly to underline the "backwardness" of the society, since they are contrasted with concepts of the *modern state* without the benefit of an analytical framework whereby the flexibility of these concepts can be grasped.

Based on extensive multisited field research in Afghanistan, Iran, and Pakistan, this chapter discusses some of the processes of adaptation and transformation that Baloch social institutions experienced in response to the changing conditions in Afghanistan and at its political borders. It explores how, in changing action arenas in southwest Afghanistan, ethnic and tribal institutions adapted to different political conditions that interfered with local social practices as exogenous variables, including the nationality policy of the Soviets, the rise of the mujahideen and the imposition of Taliban rule. To illustrate the flexibility of Baloch group affiliation, the chapter takes the concept of *kaum* [*qawm*] as its starting point. This concept can refer simultaneously to the Baloch nation, ethnicity, tribal affiliation or even smaller entities of social cohesion, depending on the context in which it is used. It will emerge that because of the flexibility of their social institutions and the practiced spatial mobility, Baloch groups and individuals were able to relatively easily adapt to or elude the uncertainties the Afghan state has undergone.

The first section briefly introduces Elinor Ostrom's analytical tool, the institutional analysis and development (IAD) framework, that serves to scrutinize my ethnographic data on Baloch groups. The simplified version of this approach that will be applied to three case studies will conduce to exemplify what affected and shaped the social institutions in the southwestern province and how these institutions facilitated spatial mobility and social change. Then the concept of *kaum* that reflects social belonging among Baloch groups will be discussed to illustrate the fluidity with which social groups change. In the subsequent three sections, different case studies that shed light on the changing exogenous variables that impacted the Baloch social institutions and the resulting interactions and outcomes will be presented. After each case study, the different aspects of the respective case will be integrated and analyzed in the framework of institutional analysis. Finally, the results of these analyses will be summarized.

Making Use of Institutional Analysis and Development

This chapter will utilize a simplified version of the framework of institutional analysis and development (IAD) developed by Elinor Ostrom to discuss the context of some social institutions in southwestern Afghanistan. Elinor Ostrom in *Understanding Institutional Diversity* gives the following broad definition of institutions: "institutions are the prescriptions that humans use to organize all forms of repetitive and structured interactions including those within families, neighborhoods, markets, firms, sports leagues, churches, private associations, and governments at all scales" (Ostrom 2005, 3).

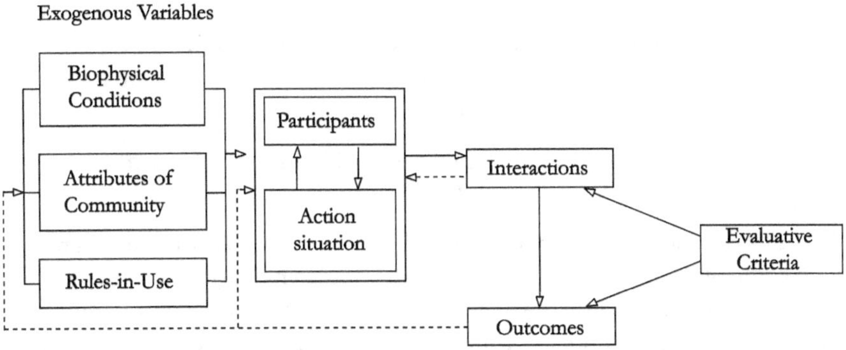

Fig. 14.1. A framework for institutional analysis (Anderies and Janssen 2013, 20; Ostrom 2005, 15).

In the southwestern Afghan province of Nimruz, the institutions that fit this definition are lineage groups, clans, or ethnic groups. These groups reflect the principles of mutual solidarity and cooperation that are the prescriptions that structure and determine large portions of social interaction in this region. Using this context, the impacts of the three decades of political unrest in Afghanistan on these social institutions will be assessed on the basis of three case studies.

As of IAD, the "grammar of institutions"(Ostrom 2005, 137–74) that becomes apparent in certain shared strategies, norms, and rules should be analyzed in action arenas. The context of these action arenas is defined by three clusters: "(1) the *rules* used by participants to order their relationships, (2) the *biophysical* world acted upon these arenas, and (3) the structure of the more general *community* within which any particular arena is placed." (Anderies and Janssen 2013, 21) The broad framework of an action arena is depicted in the following way:

In the following case studies, the action arenas are chiefly located in the southwestern Afghan province of Nimruz. The participants are a number of Baloch groups that are confronted with action situations that are influenced by exogenous variables like the Soviet invasion of Afghanistan, the Afghan civil war, interferences by Western forces, and also—due to the vicinity of two international borderlines—by the sociopolitical circumstances in neighboring countries like Iran and Pakistan. Biophysical conditions as exogenous variables will be omitted, even though a severe drought during Taliban rule strongly contributed to the depopulation of the province in this period (Rzehak 2003, 260; Pahwal 2004, xxi–xxiin14). However, the following will be generally focused on the impacts of the major political upheavals on the central social institutions on a local level—namely the respective reference groups. The resulting interactions and outcomes of a number of action situations and the underlying "grammar" of the social institutions will be discussed in the case studies. But first of all, the constitution of these social institutions that is determined by the concept of Baloch *kaum* groups should be introduced.

Kaum—A Flexible Social Concept That Enabled Baloch Groups to Adapt to Four Decades of Revolution

The differentiation between ethnic and tribal group as well as tribal and clan affiliation among Baloch groups in Afghanistan is far from clear-cut and differs from interlocutor to interlocutor. Variations in group affiliation even occur among the same interlocutors in different contexts. Shahrani and Canfield have alluded to the problem of applying the term *tribe* for Afghan groups in general since only some of these groups can be considered as "tribalized" societies (whereas others are "peasantized" or form local or political coalitions uniting people from different ethnolinguistic types) and even the social units suggested by the term *tribe* vary considerable in size among the largest tribalized groups (like Pashtuns, Turkomans, Baloch, and others) (Shahrani 1984; Canfield 1988). Canfield therefore remarks, with regard to Pashtun groups, "Because the Pashtuns are segmentary, sometimes broken into smaller localized agnatic groups, and sometimes drawn together on a larger scale, depending on issues and circumstances, the 'tribe' that is extant at a certain time can be a larger or smaller unit, a higher or lower level of agnatic coalition. Circumstances in different areas can favor the persistence of larger units than in others" (Canfield 1988, 80).

Among Baloch groups this phenomenon becomes comparably apparent in the concept of *kaum*. This concept is derived from the Persian term *qaum/qawm* but is formed in the Baloch context with a slightly different meaning. The Persian term *qaum* is not exclusively applied to Baloch groups but to various groups of the area symbolizing certain notions of group affiliation (Orywal 1986, 78–80). The general meanings of the term in (Iranian) Persian are: people; tribe; relative; family; sect; group; mass of people.[1] In the Balochi dictionary (Balochi Gâlband) written by Abdurrahman Pahwal and edited by Rzehak and Naruyi (Pahwal 2007) that focuses on the Balochi language of Afghanistan, different Balochi employments of the term are listed and translated into Pashto, Dari, and English. The single word *kaum* (Persian/Pashto: *qaum*) is translated into (1) tribe; (2) nationality; and (3) people without any elaboration on its genealogical meaning. According to Pahwal, the term is also used to describe "national" categories, which might be traced back to the influence of the nationality policy of the 1980s in Afghanistan and making its way to the Balochi dictionary as: *kaumîgirî* (Pashto: *qaumwalî*; Persian: *qaumîyat*): nationality; ethnicity; nationalism.

My observances point to the preferred usage of the term *kaum* (usually it is pronounced as *kôm*) by my Baloch interlocutors in Afghanistan and Iran.

Baloch individuals will usually ask a new acquaintance to which *kaum* he belongs. The respondent then decides which ascription might be the most feasible in a respective situation. If the counterpart belongs to a close group he would, for example, rather be precise and mention his lineage or clan, if the counterpart appears to be alien he would choose a superordinate ascription like of large groups or just "Baloch." Therefore, the term *kaum* should be considered as the central emic concept of group affiliation on different levels. In interviews and everyday communication, it turned out to be a decisive category for marking the boundaries and differences between groups. For this reason the social concept of *kaum* will be regarded as the main institution deployed in the action arena of Nimruz.

At the same time, *kaum* is an extremely polysemic term that reflects the flexibility of social structures in the Baloch settlement areas.[2] The fluidity of its content is an important precondition for the shifting parameters of group cohesion. The term *kaum* marks interchangeable reference groups that must depend on and adapt to various contexts. The social entities subsumed under this concept change over time and geography, while remaining important points of reference. So, the concept of *kaum* represents the flexible translocal figurations many Baloch and also members of other ethno-linguistic locality-based or religious communities in Afghanistan maintain across regional and national boundaries, resulting in the creation of various translocal spaces (Boedeker 2012b, 81–82).

The term *tribe* has a problematic connotation with regard to Baloch groups as the following citation from a recently published paper by Spooner (2013, 2) exemplifies:

> In the Islamic world, 'tribe' is not the same social formation as the other non-literate peoples we call tribes outside the world's historical civilizations, who (unlike the Baloch) before the colonial period had no dealings with markets or administrations based on literacy, that maintain a written record of the past, providing a control for living memory and extending the cultural sense of time. That extension of the same analytical term for non-literate communities into the Islamic situation, where people who do not read or write are nevertheless aware of the larger society which is governed by literacy, has misled us into ignoring the larger social history of the Baloch. The Baloch may have written no history of their own (at least until the 1950s), but they know they have a place in other people's history, if only because of their awareness of Islam. They are not the same category of social formation as those who were recently given a place in the literature as "The People without History".

I therefore generally refrain from this term and use terms like *group* or *kaum-group* instead that are even closer to the various meanings of these ascriptions.

In the following, I will describe three different cases to illustrate the flexibility of this social institution and how it was an important precondition for adapting to the "three decades of wars, violence and revolutions" in Afghanistan.

Case One: Mobility during Soviet Occupation

While the German anthropologist Erwin Orywal (Orywal 1982, 67–68) described the Baloch Sanjerani *kaum* as the predominant landowning group of Nimruz, especially in the southern areas, today this group seems to have left the province almost completely.[3] According to one of the members of the group's leading (Sardar) family whom I met in Pakistan in 2012, the reason for abandoning the settlements in southern Nimruz was that the Sanjerani landowners (*Khans*) were threatened by the "communist regime" in Afghanistan in the 1980s.[4] So the Sanjerani moved almost completely to Baloch areas in Pakistan and Iran. At the same time the Brahui, Baloch groups of pastoral nomads, established the main local mujahideen faction, the *Jabhe-ye Nimruz* and took over most of the former property of the Sanjerani (see below).[5] In contrast to the Brahui groups that had, due to their mobile lifestyle, the advantage of belligerence and experience with hit-and-run attacks on their enemies, the Sanjerani were, as a result of their centuries-long sedentary lifestyle in Afghanistan, not as capable of resisting.[6] In addition, both groups appear to have maintained no pronounced relations with each other over centuries.[7]

Under the Najibullah government (1987–1992) the situation for the Sanjerani changed again. According to the same interlocutor, the then provincial governor, who was deployed by the Soviets, tried to retrieve the Sanjerani to Afghanistan, as he belonged to one of their brotherly *kaum*-groups.[8] The local mujahideen faction that was opposed to the then governor, was—as the interlocutor underlined—more engaged in fighting the Sanjerani than the "communist" provincial government and, by this means, pocketed the property of the former Sanjerani landlords. The governor of Nimruz intended to support the Sanjerani against the *Jabhe-ye Nimruz* and promised to provide the Sanjerani with weapons. But since a notable portion of their members were living in Pakistani districts along the border with Afghanistan from where the Pakistani secret service ISI (Inter-Services Intelligence) was organizing the resistance against the Soviets, they were not in a position to risk a coalition with the governor who was deployed by ISI's enemy. So they had to stay in Pakistan.

During the Afghan civil war in the first half of the 1990s, the mujahideen faction ruled the province of Nimruz and their main commander (Abdulkarim Brahui) became the governor of the province. So once again, it was impossible for the Sanjerani to return to their former settlements in the province due to the rule of the hostile mujahideen faction. After the Taliban conquered the province, according to my interlocutor, the commander of the mujahideen faction asked the Sanjerani to support his resistance against the Taliban rule. But they rejected him with the announcement "Everybody fights for himself!" because of their experiences with the hostility of this group against their *kaum* group. In this way, the Sanjerani, who never composed the majority of the Baloch in southern Nimruz, lost most of their property and influence in this area.

The fading of the Sanjerani must be seen as symptomatic and representative for many of the Baloch *kaum* groups in Afghanistan, since the province was largely depopulated during the three decades of revolution. According to my interlocutor, most of the livestock of about twelve thousand sheep of this formerly settled group had been sold or died from hunger at the beginning of the communist rule. Most of my interlocutors in Quetta perceived the Sanjerani that resettled in Pakistan as a rather well-off group, mainly active in private business. The Sanjerani obviously had managed to take along some of their moveable goods or capitalized portions of their property. Similar to other rather well-off Baloch groups from Nimruz that went in this period to Iran, the Sanjerani preferred cross border migration over mujahideen resistance.[9]

The Sanjerani retreated to their *kaum* brothers in their ancestral lands as a consequence of the disturbances in Afghanistan during the three decades of political unrest since the Saur Revolution. Corresponding to the narrative of the Sanjerani, the colonization of the lower Hilmand started in the seventeenth or eighteenth century under their tribal leader Jahanbeg and his sons from today's Pakistani district of Chagai.[10] According to the narrative that was told to me, Jahanbeg, who lived during the reign of one of the grandsons of the Safavid king Shah Ismail, pursued, with his men, a gang of robbers that had abducted his daughter and a herd of camels from the region of Chagai. Jahanbeg and his Sanjerani supporters captured the robbers, who were deployed by the governor of Kerman to collect tributes, in Charburjak (in today's Nimruz). The castle where this group, after a siege, was purportedly captured carries to the present day the name *Qale-ye Jahanbeg*. It is said that after this incident, Jahanbeg and three of his sons settled along the banks of the lower Hilmand. According to this, his youngest son, Pasundkhan, remained in Chagai where he founded the Sanjerani lineage of the *Pasundkhanzi*. Two other sons, Nawabkhan and Eslamkhan, went to Rudbar where they expelled the local Pashtun groups and founded their lineages of the *Nawabkhanzi* and *Eslamkhanzi*; his oldest son Jahankhan even crossed the desert of Dasht-e Margo and settled in Chakhansur where he founded the lineage of the *Jahankhanzi*, and Jahanbeg himself founded the settlement of Khwajali where his tomb is still located. To that effect, the Sanjerani remained in their historic distribution area after their retreat to the starting point of their colonization of southwest Afghanistan, in Pakistani Chagai.

At the same time, as a consequence of the various Baloch insurgencies in Pakistan and the counterstrikes by the Pakistani army, Baloch groups from

Pakistan have continuously taken shelter in southern Afghanistan (Harrison 1981, 38–39; Rzehak 2003, 260). Accordingly, the Baloch settlement areas of Afghanistan served as an area of retreat for some Baloch groups from Pakistan while many of the local Baloch groups left the province for Pakistan and Iran.[11]

In contrast with the Sanjerani of Nimruz, the groups that identify with this appellation in the neighboring Afghan province of Hilmand apparently did not migrate completely to Pakistan. A Sanjerani interlocutor from Hilmand who did not speak Balochi but Dari and Pashto told me that the Sanjerani still play an important role among the Baloch landowning groups in this province.[12] According to him, Baloch groups like the Sanjerani, Rakhshani, and Brahui settled primarily in the southern districts of Hilmand (Dishu, Khanashin [Rigistan] and Garmsir). Also according to him, half of the population of the district of Garmsir are Baloch, both agriculturists and pastoral nomads. Beside Baloch groups, he enumerated a number of Pashtun groups that dwell in these provinces.

He described the relations between Baloch and Pashtun groups in Hilmand as rather close. And indeed, his mother was Pashtun while his father was Sanjerani. His siblings were married to both groups as well. The interlocutor reported, moreover, that some of the Pashtun groups like the Barech and Ishakzai speak primarily Balochi while only half of the Baloch individuals in Hilmand know this language. In his characterization of the group relations, he was hardly able to tell any differences between Baloch and Pashtun groups so blurred were the boundaries of the groups, and even the sympathy for the Taliban movement was, according to him, common among both groups.[13] According to him the *"war between Islam* [sic!] *and NATO and Taliban and* [Afghan] *government"* eclipsed the enmity between certain Baloch groups although he admitted that the Sanjerani have a certain hostility with the Brahui and Rakhshani. Obviously, the Sanjerani of Hilmand managed to come out of the political disturbances in Afghanistan easier than their relatives in Nimruz, probably as a consequence of their strong marital ties with the neighboring Pashtuns. However, the relations with their kinsmen in Pakistan, especially in the districts of Chagai and Nushki, were close, according to my interlocutor, and mobility across the border was very common. He underlined that most of the important elders (*Sardars*) of the Sanjerani are based in Pakistan.

In the IAD framework the action situation of the Sanjerani group was triggered by the Soviet land reform that forced the group to leave for the neighboring countries. This situation has persisted through the subsequent volatile periods until the present day. The main exogenous variables were the Soviet invasion, the interference of the Pakistani intelligence, the Afghan civil war, and the Taliban rule. The main interactions that followed the action situation were that the Sanjerani made use of their alliances with members of the *kaum* group to resettle in Pakistan. The outcome is their retreat to Pakistan. The primordial "grammar" of the social institution of the Sanjerani was their settled way of life and their strong relations with group members in Pakistan. Initially, they had to change this strategy in the described action situation by opting for mobility and reestablishing themselves in Pakistan. The frame of the Sanjerani in Hilmand was slightly different. They came out of the volatile times, impacted by the same exogenous variables by dint of their marital alliances with neighboring Pashtun groups. The outcome of this strategy was that they were able to remain in the region. Although the Sanjerani in Hilmand had a similarly sedentary lifestyle, the difference in their social institutions was basically due to a different set of rules that ordered their relationships: strong group alliances with the local Pashtuns and blurred group boundaries.

Case Two: Adaptability across Mujahideen and Taliban Rule

Contemporaneous with the exodus of the Sanjerani from Afghanistan, the *kaum* groups of the Brahui were gaining a decisive role in the political and economic affairs in Nimruz (Boedeker 2012b, 79–80). The members of these groups either speak Brahui (as well as Balochi) or claim to have Brahui-speaking ancestry. In contrast to Balochi, that is among the Iranian languages, Brahui is assigned to the Dravidian languages. Brahui groups are evenly spread over all the Baloch areas in Pakistan, Iran, and Afghanistan, but are most concentrated in the district of Kalat in Pakistani Balochistan. From this region the semi-independent government of the Ahmadzai Khans (Ahmadzai is the name of one of the Brahui groups) ruled the khanate of Kalat between 1666 and 1947 which, even today, many Baloch nationalists refer to as the prototype of an independent Balochistan (Axmann 2009; Baloch 1987).

While Orywal, during his research in the 1970s, hardly came across any Brahui in his description of the local groups—probably due to their mobility as pastoral nomads in those days—Brahui groups are dominant players in the province today.[14] The importance of these *kaum*-groups can be traced back to the role that some of their members played in the mujahideen resistance as well as during the rule of the Taliban (Pahwal 2004, 11–21; Rzehak 2008, 184–87).

Abdulkarim Brahui epitomizes the advancement of these groups. He became a mujahid during the Soviet occupation of Afghanistan. During his rebellion against the provincial government deployed by the Soviets, he and some of the members of his *kaum*-group established the dominant mujahideen faction *Jabhe-ye Nimruz* together with some of the local ethnic Pashtuns. Due to prerevolution military training he completed in Kabul and a period of service as a commander in the Afghan national army, Abdulkarim Brahui was predestined for a leading position in armed anti-Soviet resistance. Even today he is still known for his abilities and power in strategic and security affairs in Nimruz.[15] The *Jabhe-ye Nimruz* had a strong connection to Iran as its members used to retreat to Iran during their resistance. Whereas several interlocutors in Afghanistan who were not part of this movement insinuated a Maoist ideology to the leading elite of the *Jabhe-ye Nimruz*, Abdulkarim Brahui did not admit this ideological stance in interviews. Likewise, connections to the Iranian intelligence, the Jamiat-e Islami, Hekmatiar's Hezb-e Islami, or the Muslim Brotherhood that were suggested by Baloch outsiders in Afghanistan and Pakistan were not confirmed by the statements of Abdulkarim Brahui in interviews. Certainly, in these turbulent times, any accessible support with financial, logistic, or military resources was thankfully seized in the mujahideen's struggle for power. The *Jabhe-ye Nimruz* fought using all means against the provincial government that was headed by a governor who was himself a Baloch. As mentioned above, Brahui and his men helped to expel the Sanjerani from his own birthplace in southern Nimruz where his *kaum* group formerly had been in an inferior position.

After the withdrawal of the Soviets (1989) and the decline of the Najibullah government in Kabul (1992), Abdulkarim Brahui became the new governor of Nimruz. In 1995, the Taliban were advancing in Afghanistan. In a first attempt, the Taliban captured the provincial center Zaranj without any struggle and nominated a Pakistani Brahui (Hamidullah Niyazmand) for the office of the first province governor (Pahwal 2004, 16–18). Shortly afterward, Abdulkarim Brahui and the *Jabhe-ye Nimruz* managed once again to recapture the province for a few months. But after the second Taliban invasion, Brahui took refuge with some of his Brahui comrades in Iran until his return to Afghanistan after the withdrawal of the Taliban regime as a result of the Western intervention in Afghanistan.

Since the intervention of Western troops in 2001, Abdulkarim Brahui has become an important political player in Afghanistan again. He was the governor of the province of Nimruz after the Western invasion into Afghanistan in 2001. From January 2005 to February 2009, he was the minister for borders and tribal affairs, and from February 2009 to August 2010, he was the minister for refugees in the Afghan cabinet. After a short, intermediate period without political function, he was appointed to the governorship of Nimruz again in 2010. He remained in this post until September 2012 when president Karzai appointed new governors for ten provinces of Afghanistan including the province of Nimruz. Abdulkarim Brahui represents the advancement of the Brahui *kaum* in an exemplary way. In contrast to the rise and decline of the idea of Baloch nationalism in Afghanistan based on an imagined homogeneous Baloch ethnicity that will be discussed below, Abdulkarim's concept of Brahui *kaumîgirî* does not refuse the affiliation with any of the genealogical or political Baloch subdivisions. Although he generally defines the Brahui as a Baloch group, he keeps the option open to establish a discrete Brahui identity. According to this, the Brahui are even mentioned in the present Afghan constitution as a separate ethnic group of Afghanistan, separate from the Baloch (Rzehak 2012, 137).

During the civil war and the Taliban rule, according to a frequently told narrative, another member of the same Brahui *kaum*-group, Hajji Jum'a Khan, worked his way up from a "camel driver" to one of the leading figures in the opium trade of the Taliban and stayed in this position even until 2008 when he was lured to Indonesia and extradited to the United States (Boedeker 2012a, 52–53). Hajji Jum'a Khan was also notorious for his engagement in illicit trade with opium in the neighboring Pakistani district of Nushki.[16] According to an elder in Iranian Zahedan, who affiliated with the same Brahui subgroup as Abdulkarim Brahui and Hajji Jum'a Khan, Hajji Jum'a Khan was the main contact person in Afghanistan beside Abdulkarim Brahui and was considered as the group's *Sardar* (leading figure) in Afghanistan.[17] He kept in constant telephone contact with both individuals. The common engagement of Brahui groups in cross border trade was explained by their mobile and nomadic lifestyle.[18] A similar explanation for the rise of Brahui groups in Afghanistan was given to me by a Narui interlocutor in Iran who claimed that the groups succeeded in Nimruz due to their mobile lifestyle that resembled the lifestyle of the Pashtun activists of the Taliban movement.[19]

After more than thirty years of war in Afghanistan, the Brahui and their Pashtun allies became the dominant players in the province. As former pastoral nomads and one of the Baloch *kaum*-groups that is most widespread in Pakistan, Iran, and Afghanistan, Brahui groups were predestined for a dominant role in politics and cross border trade due to their mobility and translocal networks.

This case's action situation was also triggered by the Soviet intervention. However, it did not mark the retreat of the participants but led indirectly and circuitously to the advancement of the Brahui to become one of the dominant Baloch groups in Nimruz, perhaps due to their distinctive ethnic awareness. The exogenous variables were the Soviet invasion, the Afghan civil war, Iran (as an area of temporal retreat and a probable supporter of the mujahideen movement), the Taliban rule, and the Western intervention. The interactions of Brahui groups during these periods, in particular, those of Abdulkarim Brahui, were manifold. During Soviet occupation and the subsequent civil war, Abdulkarim Brahui and his *kaum* group built interrelations with the local Pashtuns. During Taliban rule, he reestablished strong relations with members of the Brahui *kaum*-group in Iran, certainly not without the knowledge of the Iranian intelligence that was worried about the hostile Taliban government in Afghanistan. Another branch of the Brahui, actually members of the same Brahui subgroup as Abdulkarim Brahui, maintained strong relations with the Taliban movement and received an important share in the profits of the cross border trade in opium. The action situation resulted in the social, political, and economic success of the Brahui groups that had been untraceable to Orywal in the 1970s. Brahui groups established and settled in the interstices where the Sanjerani used to live and were even represented in Afghan national politics by Abdulkarim Brahui.

What is the "grammar" of the Brahui *kaum*-group? In Afghanistan, his group managed to transform its spatial mobility into social mobility and capital. Most of the interactions of Brahui groups were based on spatial mobility, changing and diversifying group alliances with different groups and translocal connectivity. Because Brahui groups are equally spread across the tripartite border areas, they were able to make use of their cross border ties and establish themselves in new contexts relatively easily.[20]

Case Three: The Birth of a Baloch Nation under Soviet Rule?

Another important change in the social institutions of the province during the turbulent four decades was an emerging Baloch national movement based on an ethnic awareness negating the (sub)group affiliations of many Baloch individuals (Rzehak 2012, 149–51; Boedeker 2009, 360–63; Boedeker 2012b).

Two of my interlocutors were central figures in a Baloch national movement in Afghanistan (Boedeker 2012b, 78–79). One was the aforementioned former province governor during the Najibullah presidency during the period of the final stage of Soviet occupation until the beginning of mujahideen rule in the province in 1992. After the fall of the Taliban, this former province governor was elected unexpectedly into the national parliament and remained there until he was defeated in the elections of 2010. The other interlocutor ran a Balochi cultural center in Nimruz, called the "Balochi Academy." He is a relative of one of the masterminds of a Baloch national movement in Afghanistan, Abdurrahman Pahwal, who led the "department of languages and literatures of the brotherly nationalities" of the Academy of Science in Kabul in the 1980s (Pahwal 2004, xv).

The Balochi academy in Nimruz has a library and computer workstations and was meant to serve as a base for the promotion of Balochi language and culture and as well as a center for English language education.[21] Its foundation was certainly inspired by the Balochi academy in Quetta where a large number of the donated books originated. The construction of the building was supported by the Baloch diaspora in Europe and the Gulf region while the provincial government provided the ground on which it was built. With the help of the Ministry of Education, Baloch textbooks were compiled for primary education in local schools. Apart from the daily TV and radio programs broadcast by the state-run *Radio-o Televizion-e Afghanistan*, production of a private Balochi TV program in the province was also planned. All these activities were largely coordinated by these two individuals who supported and complemented each other—one from Kabul and the other from Nimruz.

To increase the number of Baloch inhabitants in Nimruz, they aspired to resettle Baloch groups from other parts of Afghanistan, and even from Turkmenistan, in Nimruz. But other than the idea of being of Baloch origin, some of these groups had hardly any linguistic or cultural patterns that point to this origin. This premise did not contradict the basic ideas of this Baloch national movement, since its initiators already neglected one of the central institutions of Balochi culture, the belonging to *kaum*-groups based on real, constructed, or imagined descent beneath the level of "Baloch." Because the initiators of the movement perceived belonging to smaller *kaum* groups was subversive for a Baloch national movement, they aimed for a static ethnic awareness, referring only to Balochness without the various groups' elaborated and complex interior differentiation.

This movement is rooted mainly in the nationality policy during Soviet occupation and the efforts made in support of the Balochi culture and language by a number of Baloch intellectuals during these times (Rzehak 2003, 268–73; Rzehak 2004, 28–29). After the policy of the so-called republican era of Mohammad Daoud (1973–1978) that aimed for the unification of all Afghans based upon the rejection of ethnic differences, after the Saur Revolution, the idea of nationality policy by the means of language planning, as in the Soviet Republics in Central Asia, came up. Therefore, since 1980, five languages, including Balochi, were promoted officially as "national languages" (Persian: *zabân-i millî*).[22] These languages were introduced into primary education, broadcast in radio and TV programs and published in periodicals.[23]

In 2010, during my second stay, relations between my Baloch acquaintances had changed considerably. In the interim, both key figures in the Baloch national movement had competed against each other for a seat in parliament and each accused the other of playing the "tribal" card. The parliamentarian in Kabul had lost his main supporter in the province. He had not visited the province for years because he thought that the area's security situation would not allow this. In Nimruz, it was mainly members of a related *kaum* group that supported him. His opponent in Nimruz was also backed by members of his own *kaum* group. As a consequence of the new figurations providing a basis of support for the competitors, *kaum* affairs were gaining renewed importance.

Ultimately, neither of the two candidates succeeded in the election, and Nimruz became the only province of Afghanistan to be represented in parliament by two women. Many people, including my interlocutors and other male candidates, were displeased with this election result. They even tried unsuccessfully to convince the Independent Election Commission of Afghanistan to accept at least one male candidate. The Baloch national movement had been noticeably weakened, while Abdulkarim Brahui became the province governor shortly after my stay. In a period of two years, the reference groups in Nimruz had changed considerably, at least on a political level.

This action situation deals with the rise and disintegration of a Baloch national movement. The main exogenous variables that provoked this movement were the implementation of Soviet nationality concepts by the Khalq-Parcham regimes, the Pakistani Baloch national movement, and the Baloch diaspora. The initial Soviet support of the Baloch national movement might have served its strategic aims to gain influence with the Baloch populations in Pakistan and Iran and its potential access to a "warm sea." However, similar claims were also pushed with regard to other Afghan "nationalities." The main exogenous variables that undermined this movement were certainly the strong relations of Baloch *kaum* groups in Nimruz across the border to those in Iran. These *kaum* relations that are primarily based on descent or marital alliance promised far more access to social and economic resources than an Afghanistan-based national movement could provide. The main interactions that were relevant to this action arena was the promotion of the idea of a Baloch nation to different groups spread all over Afghanistan that only vaguely identified with Baloch *kaumîgirî*. In addition, enormous efforts were made to spread the Balochi language and script, although a large proportion of the Afghan Baloch individuals are still generally illiterate. The outcomes regarding language and culture are remarkable, as becomes apparent in the composed textbooks and the Balochi academy. On the political level, the project of a Baloch national movement in Afghanistan failed in the short term. The reason was presumably in the "grammar" of the institution that pronounced Baloch ethnicity and negated Baloch heterogeneity and particularism. The structure of the movement was inclusive, static and homogenizing. Moreover, this movement was primarily Afghanistan-centered while the affiliation with Baloch *kaum* groups transcended this bordered space.

Conclusion

In all three cases, networks based on social institutions that refer to different levels of *kaum* groups played a major role in allowing people to adapt to the four decades of revolutions, war and violence. The flexible figurations based on the concept of *kaum* served as a precondition for reestablishing it in new contexts. The concept adverts to different reference groups like a Baloch nation—a group concept that was considerably increased by the nationality policy of the Soviets—, the ethnic group of the Baloch, or tribal groups like the Sanjerani. In the case of the Brahui, the perceived reference group might even change from case to case between ethnic group, like in the Afghan constitution, a Baloch group, or a confederation of various groups. The flexible concept *kaum* reflects the flexibility of the Baloch social institutions and the mobility of Baloch groups that enabled the national movement in the Soviet period, the reestablishment of the Sanjerani in their former settlement area in Pakistan, and the adaptation of Brahui groups and individuals to the political conditions during the civil war, Taliban rule, and after the invasion of Western troops.

It is remarkable—as the Sanjerani and the Brahui cases show—that mobile groups like the Brahui were obviously more successful in adapting to different action arenas during the decades of revolution than the settled, formerly dominant groups like the Sanjerani. While settled groups left the province, mobile groups established themselves in the nascent interstices. According to this, spatial mobility was a strategy of coping with insecurity in Afghanistan. In addition, the access to external resources, like the support of Iranian or Pakistani intelligence or the mujahideen *tanzims* that were mainly based in Pakistan, played an important role for the success or failure of Baloch *kaum*-groups in Afghanistan. This aspect was preeminent due to the proximity of Nimruz to the tripartite borders with Iran and Pakistan.

The increased accentuation of a Baloch nation and the importance in ethnic awareness in Afghanistan can be traced back to the Soviet nationality policy and the strong Baloch national movement in Pakistan. But after the Western intervention in Afghanistan the idea of a Baloch national movement flourished just for a short period of time. While in this context the meaning of the former flexible concept of *kaum* was reduced to a static denominator of ethnic group or nation, the concept regained its fluidity with the disintegration of this movement.

Baloch *kaum* identities are segmented, situational, influenced by certain interests, and not easy to grasp. The ability of adapting their social institutions to changing political conditions is a distinctive feature of Baloch groups because these groups have been exposed to political uncertainty for centuries and not only in Afghanistan but in the neighboring countries as well. The flexibility of these groups is derived from the historic and geographic context. Changing patterns of social institutions emanated from the heterogeneity of Baloch groups, the limited influence of political centers, and the locality of the Baloch dwelling zones in the frontiers of the former empires and at the borders of today's states, where different political ideas converge. Even today, the borders and the different political contexts that are framed by the borders facilitate protection from political persecution as well as access to social and political resources.

Due to their living conditions in a border context, spatial mobility and flexible social institutions are important premises for Baloch groups' viability. The "grammar" of the diverse social institutions of Baloch individuals might therefore change in rather short periods of time. Since the concept of change is an inherent feature of their social institutions, the political changes regarding Baloch groups appear less revolutionary than in other regions of Afghanistan.

JUST BOEDEKER is an associate of the Crossroads Asia Network (www.crossroads-asia.de) and is working with Afghan refugees in Berlin. He defended his PhD dissertation at Humboldt Universität zu Berlin in 2016.

Notes

I would like to thank the state of Berlin for the Elsa-Neumann-Stipendium I received between July 2008 and April 2011; the German Academic Exchange Service (DAAD), which contributed funding to my travels; and the German Federal Ministry of Education and Research, which has financed my employment between May 2011 and December 2014 in the competence network, Crossroads Asia, at Zentrum Moderner Orient (ZMO) in Berlin. Without this support, working in such a complex region would have been impossible.

1. Steingass gives the following translations for the term *qaum*: people, nation; tribe, family, kindred; a sect; some; a certain person; a company of men (exclusive of women) (Steingass 1957, 995); and translations of Junker and Alavi include: *Volk; Volksstamm; Verwandte pl; Familie; Sekte; Gruppe* (Junker und Alavi 2002, 582). An often-applied compound of the term is *qaum-o-xwīš*, used for: people and kin, friends and relations (Steingass 1957, 995) or *Verwandte, Verwandtschaft* (Junker und Alavi 2002, 582).

2. For a more detailed discussion on this term, see Rzehak (2012, 145).

3. Several interlocutors that belonged to other groups in Afghanistan were telling me that hardly any household of the Sanjerani remained in Nimruz. According to these interviewees, Sanjerani households either left for Iran or Pakistan. Different Sanjerani interlocutors I interviewed in Quetta confirmed this. Unfortunately, I had no opportunity to interview Sanjerani in Iran.

4. I conducted two interviews with this interlocutor on May 1 and 3, 2012, in Quetta. By "communist regime," he surely meant both: the Khalqi governments after the Saur Revolution in April 1978 (under the presidencies of Nur Mohammad Taraki and Hafizullah Amin) and the Parchami governments (1979–1989) installed after the Soviet invasion under the presidencies of Babrak Karmal (1979–1987) and Mohammad Najibullah (1987–1992).

5. *Jabhe-ye Nimruz* denotes "Front of Nimruz."

6. Abdulkarim Brahui, the former leader of the mujahideen group, accordingly underlined in an interview (Kabul, July 10, 2010) that the Sanjerani did not join his mujahideen faction because they were unable to fight the jihad against Soviet occupation due to their landownership and their settled way of life.

7. In his description of the colonization of Iranian and Afghan Sistan (today's Nimruz) by the Baloch Narui groups, al-Dhakerin notes that the Narui were able to defeat hostile Brahui groups by dint of a coalition with the Sanjerani that was consolidated through matrimonial alliances (al-Ḍākerīn 1370, 277–78). Furthermore, none of the Brahui groups range among the groups of common marriage partners of the Sanjerani that are according to my main interlocutor: the Baloch groups of the Narui, Nosherwani, Jamaldini, Zahrozi, Bilarani, Sargolzi, and the Sistani group of the Mir.

8. The then governor belonged to the Zahrozi. Beside the characterization of this group as a brotherly *kaum-group* by my main Sanjerani interlocutor, the Baloch intellectual Abdurrahman Pahwal, in an unpublished manuscript of a dictionary of Baloch groups in Afghanistan (and beyond), describes that the progenitors of the Sanjerani (Sanjer) and Zahrozi (Zahro) were two of the sons of Alikhan (Pahwal 1999, 135–36). His other sons, Bilar and Sargol, founded *kōm*-groups as well: the Bilarani and the Sargolzi.

9. Another well-off group were the Gorgej who formerly owned large properties in Hilmand, upstream from Zaranj (the provincial capital of Nimruz). Most members of this group went to neighboring Iran after the Saur Revolution and desisted from rebellion.

10. Whereas the information of my main interlocutor points to the colonization of the lower Hilmand in the seventeenth or eighteenth century, Orywal's information emanates from an immigration in the eighteenth or nineteenth century (Orywal 1982, 223).

11. According to my knowledge, no reliable demographic data on Baloch migration to Pakistan and Iran exists, particularly since the Baloch migrants were not regarded as refugees in the neighboring countries since they resembled the local population in the migration contexts that consisted to a large part of Baloch groups. However a large proportion of my interlocutors in Nimruz spent parts of the period between the Soviet invasion until the end of Taliban rule in Iran. I was even told that some of the settlements in Nimruz were almost completely depopulated in this period.

12. I conducted interviews with him in the campus of Kabul University on July 10 and 24, 2010.

13. The main difference between the two groups that he gave was that the trousers of the Pashtuns are sewn with less fabric than the ones of the Baloch.

14. Since Orywal, from his own research, could not prove Dupree had any personal contacts with Brahui individuals, he questions the information given by Dupree (Dupree 1973, 62) that there were about two hundred thousand Brahui in southwestern Afghanistan (Orywal 1982, 48–49). Orywal's interlocutors neglected the existence of Brahui groups. But elsewhere, Orywal mentions the Mamasani as one of the Baloch clans that settled in northern Nimruz (Zaranj) (Orywal 1982, 97). During my stays in Afghanistan, various interlocutors, among them Abdulkarim Brahui, who affiliated with exactly this group, perceived this group as a Brahui *kaum*. Presumably the self-conception of the Brahui changed over time. As Dupree explained in the 1960s and 1970s, most of today's Brahui groups declared themselves as Baloch. Therefore, Orywal argues that there hardly exist any Brahui groups and mentions the Mamasani as a Baloch group. Furthermore, Orywal focused on agriculturalists and thus he might not have been aware of the often mobile, pastoral, and camel-breeding Brahui groups.

15. During my second stay in Afghanistan in 2010, my host in Kabul always underlined, in regard to my planned short visit to Nimruz, that the only person who could safeguard my security there was Abdulkarim Brahui. Finally, Brahui facilitated my short and intense stay there during which my movements were fairly limited due to security concerns. Most of the time I had to stay in the governor's compound and the well-secured area around it. But Abdulkarim's power, in terms of security, also had its limits. During his governorship, in early 2011, he barely escaped an attempted attack with a remote-controlled bomb (Ramin 2016).

16. This became apparent in an interview on April 13, 2012, in Nushki.

17. I conducted this interview on May 20, 2012, in Zahedan (Iran).

18. This was told to me during the interview on April 13, 2012, in Nushki.

19. He related this in an interview I conducted on August 31, 2010, close to Zabol (Iran). Narui are a non-Brahui Baloch *kaum* group that prevails in Afghan and Iranian Sistan, and which also maintain strong group relations across the border.

20. In contrast with the Brahui groups in Pakistan and Afghanistan that are usually at least bilingual in Brahui and Balochi, members of these groups in Iran usually only speak Balochi (and Persian).

21. This center was founded in 2005 and transformed into a Balochi Academy in 2008 (Rzehak 2012, 149–50).

22. These languages were Uzbek, Turkmen, Nuristani, and Pashai, as well as Balochi.
23. Important periodicals were the *millliyat-hayi baradar* ("fraternal nationalities") of the Ministry of Tribal Affairs or the Balochi weekly newspaper called *Sob* that appeared since 1981.

Bibliography

Anderies, John M., and Marco A. Janssen. 2013. *Sustaining the Commons*. Tempe, AZ: Center for the Study of Institutional Diversity. http://sustainingthecommons.asu.edu /wp-content/uploads/2013/07/Sustaining-the-Commons-v101.pdf.

Axmann, Martin. 2009. *Back to the Future: The Khanate of Kalat and the Genesis of Baloch Nationalism, 1915–1955*. 2nd impr. Oxford: Oxford University Press.

Baloch, Inayatullah. 1987. *The Problem of 'Greater Baluchistan:' A Study of Baluch Nationalism*. Stuttgart: Steiner-Verlag Wiesbaden.

Boedeker, Just. 2009. "An Inter-Ethnic Conflict in the Cultural Environment of the Baloch National Movement in Present-Day Afghanistan." *Iran and the Caucasus* 13 (2): 357–64.

———. 2012a. "Cross-Border Trade and Identity in the Afghan-Iranian Border Region." In *Subverting Borders: Doing Research on Smuggling and Small-Scale Trade*, ed. Bettina Bruns and Judith Miggelbrink, 39–58. Wiesbaden: VS Verlag für Sozialwissenschaften.

———. 2012b. "Nation or Tribe? Some Observances about Baloch Group Affiliations in 2008 and 2010." *Orient: deutsche Zeitschrift für Politik, Wirtschaft und Kultur des Orients* 53 (2): 77–83.

Canfield, Robert L. 1988. "Ethnic, Regional, and Sectarian Alignments in Afghanistan." In *The State, Religion, and Ethnic Politics: Afghanistan, Iran, and Pakistan*, ed. Ali Banuazizi and Myron Weiner, 75–103. Syracuse, NY: Syracuse University Press.

al-Ḍākerīn (Dehbānī), Ġolām'alī Ra'īs. 1370. *Zādsarwān-e Sīstān: Šarḥ-e Mansūr-o Manẓūm-e Aḥwāl-e Ṭawāyef-e Sīstān*. Mašhad.

Dupree, Louis. 1973. *Afghanistan*. Princeton, NJ: Princeton University Press.

Harrison, Selig S. 1981. *In Afghanistan's Shadow: Baluch Nationalism and Soviet Temptations*. New York: Carnegie Endowment for International Peace.

Junker, Heinrich F. J., and Bozorg Alavi. 2002. *Persisch-Deutsch: Wörterbuch*. 9th ed. Harrassowitz.

Orywal, Erwin. 1982. *Die Balūč in Afghanisch-Sīstān: Wirtschaft und sozio-politische Organisation in Nīmrūz, SW-Afghanistan*. Berlin: Reimer.

———. 1987. "Ethnische Identität – Konzept und Methode." In *Die Ethnischen Gruppen Afghanistans: Fallstudien zu Gruppenidentität und Intergruppenbeziehungen*, ed. Erwin Orywal, 73–86. Wiesbaden: L. Reichert.

Ostrom, Elinor. 2005. *Understanding Institutional Diversity*. Princeton, NJ: Princeton University Press.

Pahwal, Abdurrahman. 1999. *Qāmūs-e qabāyel-e Baloč*. Zaranj: Unpublished manuscript.

———. 2004. *Die Taliban im Land der Mittagssonne: Geschichten aus der afghanischen Provinz : Erinnerungen und Notizen*. Wiesbaden: Reichert.

———. 2007. *Balochi Gālband: Balochi-Pashto-Dari-English Dictionary*. ed. Bedollah Naruyi and Lutz Rzehak. Peshawar: Al-Azhar.

Ramin. 2016. "Nimroz Governor Survives Bomb Attack." *Pajhwok Afghan News*, January 15. http://archive.pajhwok.com/en/2011/01/15/nimroz-governor-survives-bomb-attack.

Rzehak, Lutz. 2003. "Some Thoughts and Material on Balochi in Afghanistan." In *The Baloch and Their Neighbours: Ethnic and Linguistic Contact in Balochistan in Historical and Modern Times*, ed. Carina Jahani and Agnes Korn, 259–76. Weisbaden: Reichert.

———. 2008. "Remembering the Taliban." In *The Taliban and the Crisis of Afghanistan*, ed. Robert D. Crews and Amin Tarzi, 182–211. Cambridge, MA: Harvard University Press.

———. 2012. "Ethnic Minorities in Search of Political Consolidation." In *Under the Drones: Modern Lives in the Afghanistan-Pakistan Borderlands*, ed. Shahzad Bashir and Robert D. Crews, 136–52. Cambridge, MA: Harvard University Press.

Schetter, Conrad J. 2004. *Kleine Geschichte Afghanistans*. Munich: Beck.

Shahrani, M. Nazif. 1984. "Introduction: Marxist 'Revolution' and Islamic Resistance in Afghanistan." In *Revolutions and Rebellions in Afghanistan: Anthropological Perspectives*, ed. M. Nazif Shahrani and Robert L. Canfield, 3–57. Berkeley: Institute of International Studies, University of California.

Spooner, Brian. 2013. *Investment and Translocality: Recontextualizing the Baloch in Islamic and Global History*. Working Paper Series, No. 14. Bonn: Crossroads Asia.

Steingass, Francis Joseph. 1957. *A Comprehensive Persian-English Dictionary: Including the Arabic Words and Phrases to Be Met With in Persian Literature; Being Johnson's and Richardson's Persian, Arabic, and English Dictionary*. 4th impr. Edited by Francis Johnson and John Richardson. London: Routledge and Kegan Paul.

Tapper, Richard, ed. 1983. *The Conflict of Tribe and State in Iran and Afghanistan*. London: St. Martin's Press.

15

PARTY INSTITUTIONALIZATION MEETS WOMEN'S EMPOWERMENT? ACQUIRING POWER AND INFLUENCE IN AFGHANISTAN

Anna Larson

Introduction

Without having ever occupied a political role in government, political parties in Afghanistan have been repeatedly pushed to the fringes by successive rulers and regimes. As a result, they have acquired a reputation for extremism and violence among many Afghans. Indeed, as analysts have noted, using the term "parties" to describe these organizations as they currently exist is perhaps inaccurate, as they do not conform to the institutional and political characteristics that define political parties in western and/or "established" democracies (Ruttig 2006, 1). While numerous parties exist with different historical backgrounds, rough ideological stances, and reasons for forming, similarities can be drawn.[1] Few of them have established, publicly known policy agendas (reacting to issues as they happen rather than anticipating them and developing corresponding policy stances), most if not all claim to represent all Afghans (in spite of some having support bases that are clearly distinguishable on ethnic grounds, for example), and all have very similar internal structures based on a Soviet-style committee model with myriad second- and third-tier leadership positions used by the party leader as a means to reward loyal members. In addition, most derive their party identity from the personality and patronage of the party leader.

Since 2001, however, rebranded in the new "era of democracy," a number of parties have been attempting to exert greater influence in Afghan politics.[2] Part of this effort has involved increasing engagement with and participation in elections, which has seen parties mobilizing strategically around the single nontransferable vote (SNTV) system rewarded with greater numbers of seats in provincial council and parliamentary elections. This, in turn, has encouraged further organization and discipline in terms of selecting candidates for election, applying different strategies in different regions according to the size of the party's support base therein, and in the ways in which parties choose to engage with constituents, although this has not resulted in the development of policy platforms through which to persuade voters or in greater consolidation of elected party members as blocs within elected bodies (Larson 2015, 12). Other means through which parties have attempted to extend political influence have included providing services for constituents (such as literacy courses, dispute resolution mechanisms, financial assistance), pushing for greater public visibility through the leadership's engagement in key political events and processes (such as reconciliation with insurgents through the High Peace Council), through the purchase of television and radio stations—and through the greater engagement with female party members.

Women have played a relatively marginal role within parties and, indeed, in the political sphere more generally over the last century, although the extent and character of their involvement has varied from regime to regime. Women stood for office in the parliamentary elections in the 1960s, for example (Dupree 1971, 6), and during the mujahideen resistance to Soviet rule, women assisted the military efforts of the Islamist "parties" fighting the invaders, with stories of their carrying weapons in saucepans to the frontlines still commonly heard in local communities.[3] Nevertheless, the space that a number of women now occupy in positions of leadership within parties and in elected office as party members is unprecedented, and to date, remains undocumented.

Based on interviews conducted with party members and leaders over the last eight years, and drawing on data collected in January 2014, this chapter assesses the nature of party institutionalization in Afghanistan since 2001. It considers, in particular, the way in which this has coincided with women's political empowerment—but in doing so questions the meaning of the terms *institutionalization* and *empowerment* in a context of increasing insecurity. Combining these two subject areas in one short essay runs the risk of doing justice to neither, and there is certainly more to say about each. Nevertheless, I believe that the way in which these subjects complement one another adds value to the analysis. Using the institutional analysis and development (IAD) framework as a point of reference and exploring this approach briefly as a potential basis for future research, it attempts to ask why some aspects of party institutionalization have occurred, and why others have not. It also questions the extent to which the gains made by parties in 2014 were indicative of greater prospects for continued, sustainable political influence going forward.

Parties in Afghanistan 1904–2014

Political parties have a checkered history in Afghanistan, and there are differing opinions as to when that history began. Ruttig attributes the origins of political organization to the *mashrutiat* (constitutionalist) movement in the early 1900s, under the reign of Habibullah Khan (r. 1901–1919) and inspired by reformist journalist and statesman Mahmud Beg Tarzi, although he does not claim that formal parties had consolidated at this point (2006, 1). The Afghanan-e Jawan group that pushed for constitutional reform during this period, however, as documented by Dupree, would go on to inspire later groups of mobilized youth including the Wesh Dzalmian, noted for its Pashtunist roots but later more general opposition to the ruling elite and active in the 1940s (Dupree 1980, chap. 19). Although opposition to government was more systematically quashed in the 1950s under Daoud's premiership, underground movements continued to produce clandestine publications and met to discuss ideological alternatives for systems of government in Afghanistan.

At the same time, funding to higher education increased, and while this was seen largely as a technocratic and developmental step by ruling powers, including by the king, it was not intended as a means to build a new generation of leaders (Giustozzi 2010, 1–2; Larson and Coburn 2014, 6). Inevitably, however, the new intelligentsia used the relative political freedom that the universities provided to mobilize politically, and, during the 1960s, Islamist and leftist groups both flourished on campuses across the country, only to be sidelined by the king's refusal to sign the Parties Law and later by Daoud's systematic removal of opposition to his own rule (Shahrani 1984, 41).

Exiled to Pakistan and Iran, groups that had formed during this period consolidated as armed jihadi organizations (Shahrani 1984, 44, 55; Rashid 2008, 10) that also took on a social role, providing aid and services for increasing numbers of refugees coming across the borders. From the sidelines, then, these groups mobilized and organized opposition to the invading Soviet forces that would, with foreign support, eventually contribute to the ousting of those forces and the subsequent outbreak of civil war. With the notable exception of the People's Democratic Party of Afghanistan (PDPA) that, in several manifestations, became the ruling governmental force in the communist and later Najibullah regimes, political groups were not permitted to function as such, and had no space to develop as organizations. While some newer, anti-Taliban groups were able to function in secret under that regime's brutal authority, it was not until 2001 that parties reemerged, registering and rebranding themselves as official organizations in the new era of democracy that was anticipated.

This is not to say, however, that more political space was available for parties at this point. More space, in terms of the freedom to organize and speak publicly, was certainly granted and welcomed along with the official recognition provided by the 2003 Party Law—although as compared to the suppression imposed on parties since Daoud's reign, any kind of freedom to mobilize would have signified a dramatic change. What is notable, however, is that the new law did not establish parties as political entities with the potential to compete in elections and join with or oppose the government (Coburn and Larson 2014, 72). Instead, the law simply classified them together with civil society organizations and omitted any reference to the political structure with which they might potentially engage.[4]

As Larson and Coburn have argued, the political space in which opposition groups have been able to mobilize against government policy appears to have decreased over the last century, with executive control from one regime to the next becoming ever more overbearing (2014, 7). This control has also shifted from the forms of overt single party authoritarian measures as enforced by Daoud (he had attempted to organize a ruling party before his overthrow), to a more subtle manipulation of parliamentarians and party leaders through government patronage, and the persistent, persuasive narrative, presented by Karzai to enhance his own control over disorganized factions, that parties represent division and conflict.

In spite of these obstacles, and perhaps in some ways because of them, parties have made gains in increasing the extent of their political influence since 2001. These gains vary from party to party, but include the consolidation of parliamentary seats held by party members into relatively reliable voting blocs (for example by Hezb-i Islami, Junbesh-e Milli Islami, Wahdat-e Islami, Jam'iati Islami and Ensejam-e Milli); the willingness of more parliamentarians to align themselves publicly with parties; greater numbers of party-held provincial council seats; better and earlier preparation for elections in 2014 than for any previous election since 2001; extended service provision to constituents in the form of literacy or computer courses or hostels for university students, for example; greater visibility of party leaders in local and national media; greater awareness of and participation in national-level debates on issues such as the US-Afghan Bilateral Security Agreement (BSA); the hiring of paid staff to undertake administrative duties which remain separate from political positions within the party; internal elections to fill some positions; and greater numbers of women joining their ranks at a variety of levels of seniority (and most notably, as provincial council candidates and members). Combined, these gains have bought parties greater bargaining space in different political arenas, both at the local and national levels, and have helped to change some public perceptions about the potential utility of parties more generally. What has not occurred, however, includes: reform to party financing, which remains largely determined by the wealth and generosity of the party leader (and is often simply allocated to party activities from a personal bank account); an increase in the willingness of parliamentary candidates to register their party affiliation formally on electoral ballots; greater levels of member participation in decision making—again usually the preserve of the top leadership; proactive policy making undertaken in advance of issues occurring as a means to differentiate the party from others; and communication to the public of party decisions taken.

In this way, then, the gains that parties have made, both administratively and politically, have been substantial, especially given the baseline against which they can be compared—but they are coupled with caveats that render them slightly askew from what might traditionally be called "party development". Indeed, the increasing influence of parties in Afghanistan has taken place in ways that at once reflect and evade common, western understandings of institutionalization.

Institutions, Institutionalization, and Women's Empowerment

Before addressing issues of institutional analysis and change, the term *institution* demands brief clarification. The word is used here to denote a set of rules or norms that determine and regulate social behavior: "Institutions are the rules of the game of a society or more formally are the humanly-devised constraints that structure human interaction. They are composed of formal rules (statute law, common law, regulations), informal constraints (conventions, norms of behavior, and self-imposed codes of conduct), and the enforcement characteristics of both" (North 1993, 5).

This perspective is shared, to a large degree, by McGinnis and the IAD intellectual community, who also contend that institutions are "human-constructed constraints or opportunities within which individual choices take place and which shape the consequences of their choices" (McGinnis 2011, 170). North then distinguishes between institutions as sets of rules, from organizations as the actors or groups of individuals following those rules. Organizations, according to North, "are the players: groups of individuals bound by a common purpose to achieve objectives. They include political bodies (political parties, the senate, a city council, a regulatory agency); economic bodies (firms, trade unions, family farms, cooperatives); social bodies (churches, clubs, athletic associations); and educational bodies (schools, colleges, vocational training centers)" (North 1993, 5).

Parties, then, are organizations within which institutional norms (formal and pragmatic) exist to shape and regulate the interactions within them. This definition draws on the language of institutionalism and game theory, in which social interactions (or transactions) are considered to take place according to a complex set of rules or institutions. If parties are organizations in which institutions play out, then they may still continue to institutionalize changes and transformations—and by the term *institutionalization* this chapter will refer to a particular kind of change within organizations that results in the greater consolidation, "knowability," and stability of the institutional rules of the game that determine policy and practice.

Drawing on game theory, stability can be defined as the extent to which individuals and communities can trust in the dependability and continuity of the methods of transactions within political and social life. *Stability* is used here to denote a context in which the rules of the game—whether in political bargains, marriage practices, purchases of goods, or expectations of the behavior of police officers are broadly known and perceived to be constant (Larson 2010, 4). Thus, increased stability and institutionalization often go hand in hand. Instability, then, signifies the unpredictability of the rules in use (means) for social transaction and the space in which the rules of the game can be determined by the strongest player. This can be distinguished from security, which is used here to refer primarily to the lack of violent activity in a given context. While the term *security* has been used in many different ways across and within academic disciplines (in terms of personal security, human security, employment security, security from, security to), the narrowing of the term in this context allows for greater analytical clarity when applied to a context in which both instability and insecurity affect a significant proportion of the population.

According to Ostrom et al., the IAD (and previous Social Ecological System or SES) framework provides a way in which to analyze "how institutions operate and change over time" (McGinnis 2011, 169)—and thus, applied to this context, to look at the ways in which the constraints and opportunities that govern party behavior in Afghanistan have changed since 2001.The framework (see figure 14.1.) helpfully compartmentalizes different influences that affect party decision making and outcomes.

Applying these categories to the case, the "exogenous variables" become the various sociopolitical conditions and contextual constraints in which organizations such as parties function and in which institutions are established. These will be discussed in more detail below when considering how to contextualize party institutionalization in Afghanistan. The "action situations" become the locus of decision making—as McGinnis and Ostrom describe, these are the places "in which individuals (acting on their own or as agents of formal organizations) interact with each other and thereby jointly affect outcomes that are differentially valued by those actors" (2012, 6). In other words, these are the spaces in which decisions are made about how parties should function (very much affected by the exogenous variables). The "evaluative criteria" are the ways in which participants (e.g., party members) assess outputs, outcomes, and actions (McGinnis 2011, 172), which then feedback in to the process of institutional change—and the outcomes represent the resulting change that actually occurs.

Having outlined somewhat crudely the latest iteration of the IAD framework, the question that this chapter seeks to explore is whether it is possible to use this model to assess why some aspects of party institutionalization have taken place within parties in Afghanistan but others have not. More simply, what is it about the particular context in which Afghan parties find themselves, and the ways in which individuals within them respond to that context, that shapes the kind of organizational development that occurs?

Before attempting to answer this question, it is necessary to consider what we mean by *party institutionalization*, as this could shed light on the kinds of institutional changes that might be expected as parties develop over time. As Randall and Svåsand note, party institutionalization is often identified as a prerequisite to the strengthening of nascent democracies and the party systems within them, and yet oftentimes the term is not elaborated on or defined and remains largely west-centric in its usage (2002, 6). Indeed, according to these authors, "The notion of institutionalization that is employed has been developed largely in the context of western industrialized democracies and is, indeed, in a sense a distillation of their distinctive experience. It has not always sufficiently disentangled what is essential to party institutionalization from features that have historically or contingently been associated with it" (2002, 6).

By extension, the term is primarily used to describe a discrete set of processes that happen to parties irrespective of place or time. This is particularly pertinent to the Afghan case where, as noted above, it is clear that the historical trajectories and contexts that have influenced party development (and indeed the formation of the nation-state) are quite dissimilar in many ways to those affecting the emergence of parties in Western countries.

What, then, do we mean by the term? Randall and Svåsand elaborate on the contradictions in the existing literature on party institutionalization before suggesting that parties, as organizations, become institutionalized both through structural and attitudinal conditions, which are both internal and external to the party itself: "[W]e suggest that institutionalization should be understood as the process by which the party becomes established in terms both of integrated patterns of behavior and of attitudes, or culture. We suggest further that it is helpful to distinguish between internal and externally related aspects of this process. Internal aspects refer to developments within the party itself; external aspects have to do with the party's relationship with the society in which it is embedded, including other institutions" (2002, 12).

This way of conceptualizing party institutionalization fits comfortably within the IAD framework, as its emphasis on social context is reflected in Ostrom's "exogenous variables" category. These variables shape the ways in which parties as organizations and the institutions within them develop and change, affecting, in turn, which aspects of institutionalization occur, and which do not. Returning briefly to the list of changes that have occurred within parties over the last sixteen years in Afghanistan, as noted above, it is possible to hypothesize that while some structural aspects of institutionalization (such as the employment of administrative staff) have taken place within some parties, others—such as the devolution of control of party finances—are directly hindered by a lack of attitudinal change which, in turn, is a consequence of the current sociopolitical context. Another example of a kind of institutionalization that has occurred to some degree but which also requires further analysis is that of women's involvement within parties—or to put it more formally, the greater inclusivity that appears to be characterizing some party attitudes. The extent to which this is a sustainable change affecting women's empowerment requires careful attention.

Women's Empowerment

Empowerment is a peculiar term that has been used and critiqued across a number of contexts, with its relationship to feminist thought only one of multifarious applications in the study of social change (Cornwall and Brock 2005, 5). Bisnath and Elson describe how women's empowerment came to be used in the 1980s in conjunction with a radical equality agenda, which "was explicitly used to frame and facilitate the struggle for social justice and women's equality through a transformation of economic, social and political structures at national and international levels" (1999, 1). Since this time, it has become a key buzzword in development policy, and many scholars have argued that this co-optation of a once radical concept has helped to water down its meaning (Batliwala 1994; Cornwall and Brock 2005; Cornwall and Edwards 2014). In many development projects, empowerment has been reduced to simply another box to check to secure donor funding.

In Afghanistan the term *women's empowerment* has been used by international donors and Afghan women themselves in a particularly complex set of circumstances. On the one hand, one of the commonly assumed justifications for the 2001 intervention was the need to emancipate and empower women against the confinement of Taliban rule and use technical measures, such as the constitutionally guaranteed reserved seats system for women in parliament and the establishment of the Ministry of Women's Affairs, established through Afghan and donor efforts, to help redress the shortage of women engaging in the public sphere. On the other hand, donors have been reticent to push for transformational change. The following quotation from the World Bank's Interim Strategy Note for Afghanistan in 2007–2008 is indicative of general approaches toward gender equality measures: "The Bank's strategy is to lend support to the government's policy of gender mainstreaming, *continuing to pursue the least confrontational lines* and build opportunities into the Bank's portfolio where tangible gains can be made. This will involve strengthening women's involvement *in the sectors where they already have an acceptable presence* including health, education and the civil service" (Wordsworth 2008, 14, emphasis in original).

At the level of development practice, Afghan nongovernmental organizations (NGOs) and Civil Society Organizations (CSOs) have incorporated the language of empowerment into proposals for projects as diverse as microcredit initiatives, women's tailoring classes, and girls' education, all with the assumption that it is possible "to empower" others through these programs and with little emphasis on the way in which empowerment in its radical sense denotes a largely self-motivated process that is at once personal but also has wider social implications for groups of women acting collectively. Research conducted by the Institute of Development Studies in the United Kingdom suggests that women themselves find different "pathways" to empowerment—some of which are hidden, some individual, some collective—and that these are often distinct from the development policies designed to empower them from above (Cornwall and Edwards 2014).

This concept of *empowerment pathways* is interesting as it defies what have become conventional, diluted meanings of the term and provides space for women to determine what they consider to be empowering on their own terms. This is particularly important when considering how empowerment might occur in non-western contexts, as all too often in development policy, western ideals of what empowerment should look like are projected on to women whose social and political realities are very different from those of their would-be empowerers. It is with this approach in mind that women's roles in Afghan political parties can usefully be considered.

In 2005, women competed in parliamentary and provincial council elections across Afghanistan by the hundreds, taking advantage of the new reserved seats system and marking a stance of defiance against the prevailing political winds that had kept them from the public sphere for the last thirty years (see Staudt 1998, 179; Wordsworth 2007a; Larson 2011; Larson 2012). However, as one study on the winning female candidates from Mazar-i Sharif highlighted, many of the women who won seats had connections to influential male power holders and political parties, and had used the patronage networks and resources that these connections provided to their advantage in the elections (Wordsworth 2006). At the same time, as a result of the system, women needed far fewer votes to win a seat than their male counterparts and so were approached by some parties with offers of financial and logistical assistance in a bid by these parties to gain valuable seats. The question then became: would the ways in which women had won their seats detract from their ability to represent "women in general" in the legislature? And by extension, then, would these reserved seats in fact do anything to empower women? Or would they simply enrich certain women who already had influential connections? As will be discussed below, however, these may have been the wrong questions to ask.

In 2006, I interviewed one of the female parliamentary candidates for Balkh province, who was widely considered to be an affiliate of Mahaz-e Milli, in part due to the presence in the top right hand corner of her campaign posters of an image of that party's leader, Pir Gailani. When asked about this connection, however, she said she had no substantive connection with the party but had accepted the party's offer to pay for her posters. She went on to describe how, once a sitting Member of Parliament (MP), she had paid the money back in a straightforward cash transaction and refuted all further claims that she was a member of the party. During the course of the interview she also brought out a copy of an amended poster, cut in half to remove the picture of the party leader (Coburn and Larson 2014, 77).

Table 15.1. Women candidates in Afghan elections since 2001.

Election	Number of seats (reserved for women)	Women candidates/total (percentage)	Women winners/total (percentage)	Declared women party candidates/ total declared party candidates
Wolesi Jirga (WJ, parliamentary lower house) 2005	249 (68)	344/2835 (12%)	68 (27%)	No information*
Provincial Council (PC)2005	420 (105)	285/2854 (10%)	113 (27%)	No information*
PC 2009	420 (105)	328/3195 (10%)	117 (28%)	24/83**
WJ 2010	249 (68)	406/2556 (16%)	69 (28%)	6/32
PC 2014	458 (92)	308/2704 (11%)	96 (21%)	36/275

SOURCE: Independent Electoral Commission (compiled by the author).
*Space for party affiliation was not included on the official ballots in 2005.
**Data for this entry was sourced from the National Democratic Institute's *2009 Presidential and Provincial Council Elections in Afghanistan* report (National Democratic Institute 2010, 48).

Clearly then, at this point, while parties were using women as a means to gather "easy seats" in parliament, women were also using parties as vehicles for self-promotion, accepting resources in return for a promise of support, but later reneging on those promises in favor of the far more lucrative strategy of keeping their political alliances in parliament ambiguous (Larson 2010). In this way, women candidates were acting as economic entrepreneurs, using political office to their advantage, a strategy employed almost universally by their male counterparts.

Data collected between 2011 and 2014, however, indicates that the relationship between women candidates and parties may have changed somewhat, in that women are using parties not only as providers of campaign resources but as sources of political backing and capacity building. When interviewing women party members (many of whom were also provincial council [PC] members) in 2014 as part of a study conducted for the National Democratic Institute (NDI), women were keen to talk about their party affiliations and role when introducing themselves:[5]

> I am a PC member for Balkh province and a member of Hezb-e Wahdat Islami. I'm responsible for women's affairs in the party in Balkh province (Hezb-e Wahdat Islami, Balkh).

> I am a PC member for Balkh, and a member of the international relations committee within the PC. I am also a party member and in the party I am the head of women's affairs for Balkh province. (Hezb-e Wahdat-e Islami-e Mardum, Balkh).
>
> I am the head of the women's committee for Junbesh in Helmand province. (Hezb-e Junbesh-e Milli, Helmand).
>
> I am a PC member for Logar province and have been in this role for the last 4 years. I'm a member of Mahaz-e Milli and also a Peace Council Representative for Logar. (Hezb-e Mahaz-e Milli, Logar).
>
> I am a PC member for Bamiyan, and also the secretary of Paiwand-e Milli and the head of the women's committee . . . I am also an active member of the PC for Bamiyan. There are 9 seats in the PC for Bamiyan. I was a party candidate. (Hezb-e Paiwand-e Milli, Bamiyan).
>
> I am in charge of the Hezb-e Islami Women's committee in Badakshan. (Hezb-e Islami, Badakshan).
>
> I am a teacher in Balkh, in the teacher training institute. I'm also the head of the women's council for Junbesh in Balkh and a PC candidate for the party. (Hezb-e Junbesh-e Milli, Balkh).

As these examples demonstrate, women party members were not only keen to talk about their party connections in interviews but also to explain the levels of responsibility they held within the parties. Other party members interviewed, who did not hold positions of authority within the party, often talked about aspiring to them, with the prospects of becoming a provincial council or parliamentary candidate often cited as a personal goal. As one representative of Hezb-e Islami stated, "Now I am a member of the women's committee, but maybe I will be a candidate in five years' time." Perhaps of greater importance here, however, was the way in which women party members described their reasons for joining a party:

> I joined four years ago because I wanted to reach my own objectives through using the power of the party. This party tries to achieve peace and stability and there is no ethnic discrimination. In this sense the party also matched my own goals. (PC member, Hezb-e Wahdat-e Islami, Northern Afghanistan)
>
> It is five years since I joined the party. The reason was that I was an influential woman and hardworking but it didn't matter how hard I worked, I couldn't really achieve much. I worked for UN habitat for 16 years but I didn't get many personal benefits from this, I was always working to help other people. I decided to join a party because an individual can't do a lot without a cause, or a group behind them . . . So the main reason was that I wanted to receive the benefits of my hard work. I was elected to the PC as a result. (PC member, Hezb-e Wahdat-e Islami-e Mardum, Northern Afghanistan)

> I joined the party 4 years ago. The reason was that being a woman here in Afghanistan it is difficult to work without having political support. I decided to join in order to run for office. I got full support from the party and won the election. (PC member, Hezb-e Paiwand-e Milli, Central Afghanistan)
>
> I joined the party for several reasons—firstly for my own capacity building, and secondly because this was a young party with no ethnic discrimination (Hezb-e Jamhori-e Khwahan, Central Afghanistan).
>
> The National Coalition of Afghanistan is made up of different parties. When I studied their plans and leadership, I decided to join. Before this I had a foundation for women in one of the provinces with the support of UN HABITAT but I felt that we needed political support (Ettehad-e Milli member Kabul).

Almost without exception, women interviewed as part of this study described joining parties as a way in which to advance their own interests—whether through using parties as means to gain a seat in the PC, or for the capacity building opportunities they provide through their connections with organizations like the United States' National Democratic Institute, or, as in the last quotation cited, for the political support they could potentially give to existing charitable causes. These interviews need to be understood in context; all of those cited above were conducted two months before presidential and provincial council elections in 2014, and thus, it is unsurprising in some ways that women were choosing to emphasize their connections to parties and influential coalitions. This willingness to align politically can but does not always wane after an election cycle (and thus after party resources have been utilized for campaigns). Also, as demonstrated in table 15.1, even stronger public affiliation with the party does not always translate into formal affiliation on the ballot—and less so in parliamentary elections than PC elections. For all candidates, men and women alike, there is an overwhelming tendency to formally classify oneself as "independent." But the way in which many of these women talked about the work they do for the party suggests that, in contrast to the example given from 2006, many are finding pathways to empowerment by remaining publicly affiliated with parties, within their communities if not on the ballot, as opposed to simply using them for their resources in the run-up to elections.

These pathways may be seen by outside observers as used for women's personal benefit only, as they often involve running for office and acquiring significant resources and connections as a result. But the story is more complicated than this; as some of the quotations above indicate, this is also about acquiring political backing for women's organizations, charity work, and capacity building. And while these activities undoubtedly benefit the individual, they can also be appreciated more broadly by local communities, as suggested by the example of Sharifa Zourmati, a former parliamentarian for Paktia province whose contributions to community development appear to have afforded her safe passage through many otherwise insecure parts of the province (Coburn and Larson 2011,11; 2014, 172). Assuming that women in politics can represent women-in-general, even if they are inclined to do so, sets them up with a number of unrealistic expectations. After all, it is rarely expected that male politicians will do likewise. But this is not to say they cannot represent and work for their communities, including for women, while simultaneously promoting their own, personal interests. Indeed, drawing a stark distinction between the two is misleading, particularly when, as is often the case in Afghanistan, individual identity is comprised primarily of affiliations to several kinds of community (family, village, clan, ethnic group). While person-centered politics is prevalent in today's Afghanistan, communities can benefit from the increased connection to central resources that their representative indirectly provides—though of course this is not always the case (see also Chapter 6 in this volume).

How, then, does this relate to issues of party institutionalization discussed above? To return to Randall and Svåsand's framework (2002), it is possible to conceptualize the changes that may be occurring in women's relationships with parties in terms of structural and attitudinal factors both internal and external to the party itself. Internally, allocating space for women to compete as party candidates in elections and to take positions of leadership within the party (albeit most commonly as head of women's affairs departments) comprises both a structural and an attitudinal change. Externally, the growing cohesiveness of some parties, these parties' connections to international organizations and the technical resources they provide, and their increasing influence in public affairs and connection to influential players have combined to present an organizational image in some provinces that is now considered more attractive to potential members than has been the case for a long time, and perhaps this image is particularly attractive to educated women. Based on interviews conducted with party women, these parties notably include the Wahdats, Junbesh, and Ettehad-Milli. However, regional differentiation is also important. From these and earlier interviews, it appears that women are more likely to be involved in party activities either in urban areas or areas in which parties have a relatively strong support base already and in areas in which levels of security, on the one hand, allow women to pursue public positions in relative safety and, on the other, allow parties to capitalize on women's involvement. Thus, in Balkh, Bamiyan, Herat, Kabul, and Nangarhar, for example, women's involvement in parties appeared, in 2014, to be on the increase—and more so than in Paktika and Kunduz, for example. Additionally, the timing of interviews—just before an historic presidential election in which the incumbent Hamid Karzai was not constitutionally permitted to stand, having already served two terms—may well have had an impact on parties' cohesion, providing an extraordinary incentive to mobilize around campaigns.

This, along with the potential dividends that associating actively with the winning team could pay in the future, may also have encouraged women's increased involvement with parties between 2012-2014 in particular.

Contextualizing the Issues

Having explored some of the issues surrounding party institutionalization and women's role within parties in Afghanistan, it is necessary to return to the central question of this chapter: what is it about the particular context in which Afghan parties find themselves, and the ways in which individuals within them respond to that context, that shapes the kind of organizational development that is taking place? Is it possible to use the IAD framework to answer this and assess why some aspects of party institutionalization have taken place within parties in Afghanistan but others have not? This section looks at the a few examples of the exogenous variables that the Afghan context presents, through the three distinct but overlapping categories that Ostrom sets out in the IAD framework, and attempts to answer these questions in relation to parties in general in Afghanistan.[6]

Biophysical Conditions and the Immediate Environment

How does the immediate environment in which parties function affect the decisions that individuals make within them, and the way the organization develops as a result? Insecurity affects different parties in different ways across the country but generally means that in rural areas, open party activities are confined to existing support bases. Beyond the physical threat to party activists and the communication problems that insecurity causes, the instability it contributes to has arguably an even greater impact on the ways in which decisions are made and actions are taken by party members and leaders. Often, this takes the form of keeping key political alliances, decisions, and party positions on certain issues ambiguous in order that they may be changed at the last minute, with the effect that concrete, issues-based platforms are not made. As one midlevel official within a party stated in an interview in 2014, when describing how he deliberated over whether to join in 2007, "I liked the party, but the leader was supporting Karzai and also the idea of a free market. I was concerned about these issues and discussed them a lot with the leader, but I found out that to be a politician in Afghanistan you need to be flexible on these things."[7] In an unstable political environment, it makes sense to "be flexible" in order to minimize the opportunity costs of chosen interactions by keeping a range of options open.

A highly centralized political system also contributes to the way in which most party activity occurs in Kabul and other urban centers where resources are concentrated. Positions within patronage networks that connect directly to central government resources are valuable, meaning that party leaders will rarely stray too far from an accommodated, negotiated relationship with the president in order to maintain their connection to these resources (especially given that resources from other, perhaps more conventional sources, such as membership fees, are minimal). This being the case, very little sustained opposition to government has developed, and presidential powers have steadily increased since the Bonn Process. In the past, with fewer and smaller government patronage payouts, opposition groups formed and radicalized at the fringes—but between 2001-2014t, according to parliamentarians interviewed during these years, incentives to retain buy-in to the system as it stands increased dramatically with the disbursement of aid funds in the form of these payouts (also see Chapter 5 in this volume).[8]

Attributes of Community

The ways in which sociocultural and demographic aspects of the Afghan context affect party and party member decisions and the subsequent institutions and norms they create are numerous, and thus only some examples will be given here. The first, perhaps, should include the low levels of literacy in the country (and particularly in rural areas) that affect the ways in which parties can advertise their activities and encourage voters, for example. Although many do have publications, these have a very limited, urban readership, and thus, the costs of producing them are often too great for the little gain they bring. Still, the communities in which parties conduct their activities are changing rapidly, with a youth bulge and greater government emphasis on education resulting in many more educated young people looking to parties as potential vehicles for patronage and assistance—a change which most parties are proving slow to embrace. Providing hostels for university students—as larger parties with significant resources, including the Wahdats, Jami'at and Junbesh are known to do in Kabul and Balkh, for example—is a token measure of support to youth, but if they are really to take advantage of the computer literacy and language skills that young people have to offer, parties will need to restructure so as to provide training and leadership opportunities for enthusiastic youth wanting to move up the ranks (Giustozzi 2010, 6–7). A culture of deference to older, wiser, and more experienced party members persists, however, and often acts as a block to youth who attempt to challenge the status quo. In comparison, newer, Saudi-funded antidemocracy movements, such as Jamiyat Islah and Hezb-ul Tahrir, are competing successfully for young talent by providing internet access and even English classes, without a required deference to older leaders (Larson 2015, 5).

Other attributes of community that affect the way parties function include the legacy of parties' reputation for violence, which is still cited by a number of Afghans as reason enough not to associate with them. Also, the politicization of traditional identities—such as tribe, language, sect, and region—remains a central strategy of party leaders to mobilize large groups of people, which is particularly successful in times of upheaval, insecurity, or potential political change. The 2014 elections provide a case in point, with party leaders often justifying their chosen candidate affiliation to supporters in terms of the potential for the central-level representation of these identities. At other junctures, party leaders have been criticized by midranking members for emphasizing interethnic conflict, for example, between Hazaras and Kuchis over longstanding land disputes, to their own political advantage. This strategy could be otherwise described as political racketeering, where an outside threat is exaggerated in order to boost a leader's political and economic capital (for more details, also see Chapter 7 in this volume).[9]

In addition to this, community attributes include the lack of precedent for parties to charge a membership fee, with members expecting service provision and assistance from parties instead. This makes gathering resources (inside Afghanistan) very difficult, and adds to the way in which parties often rely on the personal bank accounts of leaders to bankroll their activities, which, in turn, solidifies the way in which leaders have absolute authority within parties.

Rules In Use

As McGinnis and Ostrom explain, the category *rules in use* is intended to bring the analyst's attention to the actual way in which rules are interpreted and enforced, as opposed to the rules on paper that formally set out how operations should function (2012, 6). This is very helpful in application to the Afghan context, in which informal norms or rules of the game often overlap with and trump formal rules on paper. This is particularly the case with the power of patronage networks to determine how a party is run—a party leader may well hold internal elections for the positions of heads of different committees, for example, but will persuade voters beforehand to align with his own, previously made decisions. This is not only true of the older parties, such as Hezb-e Jami'at Islami or Hezb-e Islami, but pervades the way in which newer ones are run also. Right and Justice, a movement recently formed ahead of the 2014 elections, has rotating leadership—on the surface, an apparently democratic characteristic—and yet there is no limit to the term that an elected leader can potentially hold office. These informal norms contribute to what is often a cult of personality in which a leader is given the highest possible status, cannot be questioned by other members, and has the final decision over all party activities.

These factors help explain why parties have institutionalized in some ways and not others, and how norms and rules of the game have become established and have changed in some ways but not others. They also point to the ways in which members respond and provide feedback to the system, which in turn affects the kinds of outputs and outcomes that party activities produce.

While I have argued above that, to some degree, structural and attitudinal change has taken place both within and outside of parties, in terms of their relationship with women members, it appears that general attitudinal change lags behind the few structural amendments (such as systematization of choosing candidates for election) that have been introduced. This, then, begs further questions: to what degree will parties be able and willing to support women's empowerment beyond these early shifts? What needs to change further and how might these changes occur given current exogenous variables? What incentive structures need to be in place? More detailed study is needed to examine these questions.

Finally, it is important to note that while the IAD framework appears to provide a useful means of conceptualizing institutional change within parties in Afghanistan, there are some elements of analysis that merit greater attention than they are given by the model outlined above. One such element is a historical component. As outlined in the early pages of this chapter, the history of party development in Afghanistan sheds a great deal of light on the way in which they operate today and on the barriers to institutional change that have existed and still exist. While this can be incorporated into the exogenous variables, it is arguable that more explicit reference is necessary. A second element to consider further is a temporal one: the way in which some changes may be short term in nature and not sustainable. When assessing the extent to which party members are willing to associate themselves publicly with a party—reflected in the feedback they provide into the action situations that then determine how the party works—it is important to consider their reasons for doing so. In the run-up to an election, candidates may be much more willing to align themselves politically and take the risk of losing other resources as a consequence because of the potential patronage gains of aligning with a winning party candidate or leader, which outweigh the advantages of remaining ambiguous in alliances. Thus, the gains that the party might make in terms of solidifying support blocs and appearing a cohesive, active entity may only be ephemeral in nature. When applying the IAD framework and toolkit to party institutionalization in Afghanistan, then, it is important to emphasize the element of the framework that accommodates the impact of individual actors' choices in changing contexts, and the ways in which these choices either facilitate or prevent long-term, transformative institutional change. In this way, the framework has the potential to capture the political nuances of institutional change in an insecure context with an uncertain political future.

Conclusions

This chapter has attempted to combine an analysis of party institutionalization in Afghanistan with a study of the changing nature of women's relationships with Afghan political parties. In doing so, it has perhaps overreached its capacity and has not delved into the finer details of each—which could be the subject of further papers. What it has tried to demonstrate is that the combination of these two issues is complementary and adds value to the study of both individually.

Attempting to explore the IAD approach to institutional analysis, the chapter has applied a recent iteration of the IAD framework to the analysis of institutional change within Afghan parties. In doing so, it has found this approach to be a useful one, particularly in its ability to help discover why some changes have occurred in parties and others have not. Combining this with Randall and Svåsand's (2002) conceptualization of party institutionalization, it is possible to conclude that while some degree of structural and attitudinal change has occurred within parties since 2001, a lack of attitudinal change remains a key obstacle to the greater institutionalization of parties and the extent to which rules and norms are publicly knowable and fixed. This, in turn, has been affected by exogenous variables, and, most particularly, continued and/or increasing insecurity, a centralized system of government hostile to the role of political parties, and the rules in use within parties that continue to uphold the primacy of leaders at the expense of moving the party forward.

There is little doubt that women's relationships with parties have changed since the first post-2001 parliamentary and provincial council elections were held—indeed, women (or at least, some women) have a great deal more leverage when it comes to negotiating their positions within parties and expect more in terms of self-development and progression from associating with parties than they did previously. Their interactions with parties not only have the potential to provide pathways to their own, personal empowerment but also provide platforms from which women party members and PC councilors can potentially promote the interests of their communities and, within these, groups of women. This should not be confused with their ability and willingness to represent women-in-general, which is an elusive prospect and a different issue entirely, but it nevertheless indicates the possibility for collective mobilization that fits more closely with earlier definitions of empowerment than with the watered-down development clichés so commonly heard today. It should be noted, however, that unless greater levels of attitudinal and structural change take place within parties, for example, by allocating women's positions in committees other than those of women's affairs and education, the extent to which women might truly influence party activities, outputs, and outcomes will plateau at the level of mutually beneficial participation.

ANNA LARSON is a research associate and senior teaching fellow at SOAS, University of London. She is coauthor of *Derailing Democracy in Afghanistan: Elections in an Unstable Political Landscape* with Noah Coburn.

Notes

1. Thomas Ruttig (2006) divides Afghan parties into four distinct categories or "waves": Islamist, ethno-nationalist, leftist and new Democrats.
2. This chapter focuses specifically on parties that have proven representation in parliament and provincial councils (i.e. parties for whom representatives in these bodies have been interviewed by the author and have confirmed their party membership).
3. I heard this from an interview I conducted with community members in Mazar-I Sharif, Northern Afghanistan, in 2006.
4. According to some observers this continued sidelining of parties was a deliberate attempt on the part of Hamid Karzai and Lakhdar Brahimi to "preserve stability" by de-emphasizing the social divisions that parties represented. (See Rashid 2008, 258).
5. Semistructured interviews were conducted by the author with twenty-seven party members, eleven of which were women. Interviews were conducted according to strict principles of academic rigor and research ethics. Data is cited here with the kind permission of the respondents and the National Democratic Institute (NDI).
6. A more detailed study could consider each party individually as many differences exist between them.
7. Interview with a Hezb-e Jamhori-e Khwahan (Republican party) member, conducted by the author on January 27, 2014. This relatively small, new party is now led by Adela Bahram, and was formed in 2003 by presidential adviser Sebghatullah Sanjar [now deceased] primarily in support of the Hamid Karzai administration. Its support base is largely confined to Kabul and Herat and for the most part, comprises youth who have benefited from the party's provision of free English and computer courses.
8. It is important to highlight here the role of outside funding to parties and political movements, more generally, in Afghanistan's recent history. The PDPA's reliance on Soviet funding became starkly apparent, for example, after 1989, with Najibullah's iteration of the party lasting only three years beyond this (for a detailed exposition, see Rubin 2002, chaps. 5, 6, and 7). Jihadi *tanzims*, initially receiving financial support from the United States via the Pakistani Inter-Services Intelligence (ISI), in line with Cold War priorities, to support their anticommunist campaign, have benefited greatly from Pakistan-ISI and Iranian funds, with the 1995–2001 Taliban movement also drawing significant resources from Pakistan.
9. This is not to undermine the significance of these disputes, nor their impact on local people. I do not wish to argue that the threat to either group is entirely fabricated by leaders—but instead to highlight the way in which leaders have nonetheless gained from promoting difference between ethnic groups. Charles Tilly writes at length on a similar, if more extreme, strategy, as deployed by national governments, in creating or exaggerating outside threats and then charging citizens for protection against them (Tilly 1985).

Bibliography

Batliwala, Srilatha. 1994. "The Meanings of Women's Empowerment: New Concepts from Action." In *Population Policies Reconsidered: Health, Empowerment and Rights*, ed. Gita Sen, Adrienne Germain, Lincoln C. Chen, 127–38. Boston, MA: Harvard University Press.

Bisnath, Savitri, and Diane Elson. 1999. *Women's Empowerment Revisited*. Background Paper for *Progress of the World's Women 2000: A UNIFEM Report*. New York: UNIFEM.

Coburn, Noah, and Anna Larson. 2011. *Undermining Representative Governance: Afghanistan's 2010 Parliamentary Election and Its Alienating Impact*. Kabul: Afghanistan Research and Evaluation Unit.

———. 2014. *Derailing Democracy in Afghanistan: Elections in an Unstable Political Landscape*. New York: Columbia University Press.

Cornwall, Andrea, and Karen Brock. 2005. "Beyond Buzzwords: 'Poverty Reduction,' 'Participation' and 'Empowerment' in Development Policy." Overarching Concerns Programme Paper No. 10. Geneva: UN Research Institute for Social Development.

Cornwall, Andrea, and Jenny Edwards. 2014. *Feminisms, Empowerment and Development: Changing Women's Lives*. London: Zed Books.

Dupree, Louis. 1971. "Afghanistan Continues Its Experiment in Democracy: The Thirteenth Parliament Is Elected." American Universities Field Staff Reports, 15 (3), South Asia Series.

———. 1980. *Afghanistan*. Princeton, NJ: Princeton University Press.

Giustozzi, Antonio. 2010. *Between Patronage and Rebellion: Student Politics in Afghanistan*. AREU Briefing Paper. Kabul: Afghanistan Research and Evaluation Unit.

Larson, Anna. 2010. *The Wolesi Jirga in Flux, 2010: Elections and Instability I*. Kabul: Afghanistan Research and Evaluation Unit.

———. 2011. "Women's Political Presence: A Path to Promoting Gender Interests?" In *Land of the Unconquerable: Lives of Contemporary Afghan Women*, ed. Jennifer Heath and Ashraf Zahedi, 119–27. Berkeley: University of California Press.

———. 2012. "Collective Identities, Institutions, Security, and State Building in Afghanistan." In *The Impact of Gender Quotas*, ed. Susan Franceschet, Mona Lena Krook, and Jennifer Piscopo, 136–56. Oxford: Oxford University Press.

———. 2015. *Political Parties in Afghanistan*. Washington, DC: United States Institute for Peace.

Larson, Anna, and Noah Coburn. 2014. *Youth Mobilization in Afghanistan: The Y Factor*. Special Report No. 341. Washington, DC: United States Institute for Peace.

McGinnis, Michael D. 2011. "An Introduction to IAD and the Language of the Ostrom Workshop: A Simple Guide to a Complex Framework." *The Policy Studies Journal* 39 (1): 169–83.

McGinnis, Michael D., and Elinor Ostrom. 2012. *SES Framework: Initial Changes and Continuing Challenges*. W11-6. Workshop in Political Theory and Policy Analysis, Department of Political Science, and School of Public and Environmental Affairs. Bloomington: Indiana University.

National Democratic Institute. 2010. *The 2009 Presidential and Provincial Council Elections in Afghanistan*. Washington DC: National Democratic Institute.

North, Douglass. 1993. "The New Institutional Economics and Development." Paper drawn from the John R. Commons lecture, American Economic Association, January 1992.

Randall, Vicky, and Lars Svåsand. 2002. "Party Institutionalization in New Democracies." *Party Politics* 8 (1): 5–29.

Rashid, Ahmed. 2008. *Descent into Chaos: Pakistan, Afghanistan and the Threat to Global Security*. New York: Penguin.

Rubin, Barnett R. 2002. *The Fragmentation of Afghanistan: State Formation and Collapse in the International System*. 2nd ed. New Haven, CT: Yale University Press.

Ruttig, Thomas. 2006. *Islamists, Leftists—and a Void in the Center: Afghanistan's Political Parties and Where They Come from (1902-2006)*. Berlin: Konrad Adenauer Stiftung.

Shahrani, M. Nazif, and Robert Canfield. 1984. *Revolutions & Rebellions in Afghanistan: Anthropological Perspectives*. Berkeley: Institute of International Studies, University of California.

Staudt, Kathleen. 1998. "Bringing Politics Back in: Institutional Contexts for Mainstreaming." In *Policy, Politics and Gender: Women Gaining Ground*, ed. Kathleen Staudt, 177–90. West Hartford, CT: Kumarian.

Tilly, Charles. 1985. "War Making and State Making as Organized Crime." In *Bringing the State Back In*, ed. Peter B. Evans, Dietrich Rueschemeyer, and Theda Skocpol, 169–91. Cambridge, UK: Cambridge University Press.

Wordsworth, Anna. 2006. "The Politics of Patronage: An Exploration of Women's Acquisition of Power in Afghanistan: Case Study: Legislative Elections in Balkh Province, 2005." Unpublished Master's thesis, University of London.

———. 2007a. *A Matter of Interests: Gender and the Politics of Presence in Afghanistan's Wolesi Jirga*. AREU Issues Paper. Kabul: Afghanistan Research and Evaluation Unit.

———. 2008 *Moving to the Mainstream: Integrating Gender in Afghanistan's National Policy*. AREU Working Paper. Kabul: Afghanistan Research and Evaluation Unit.

# PART IV:
VIOLENCE, SOCIAL SERVICES DELIVERY, AND THE RISING TRUST DEFICIT

16

CHILDBIRTH AND SOCIAL CHANGE IN AFGHANISTAN

Kylea Laina Liese

THE MIDWIVES AT CURE International Hospital in Kabul chose pink as the color for their department, and as a consequence, the entire maternity ward—the walls, curtains, scrubs—was awash in femininity. One afternoon, Hamida, a midwife, was assigned a sixteen-year-old patient in preterm labor with twins. The contrast between midwife and mother was obvious. Hamida had pale powdered skin, eyes carefully lined with khol, and wore her hair neatly pinned underneath a loose pink headscarf. Her uniform was hand sewn and well-tailored beneath a crisp, long white lab coat. Meanwhile, Farida, the patient from Nuristan, was a small girl who arrived with her sister, both pulling dusty blue chodars over their mouths while they spoke. She wore her hair in long beaded braids, and her skin was dark and freckled. Her dress was ornate, but worn and tattered, and it clashed with the printed pants she wore beneath. During contractions, she tensed and leaned against her sister, whimpering. Communication was difficult. Farida spoke very little Farsi, though her sister was more fluent, and we learned she was a little over six months pregnant. Hamida used an ultrasound to check the babies, who both had normal heart rates, before taking her back to the labor room for an exam. Farida was dilated to four to five centimeters, and her bag of waters was bulging from her vagina. "Inevitable abortion," Hamida explained, shaking her head sadly but also not addressing Farida. Her labor was too advanced to stop, and given the hospital's neonatal resources, these babies would be too preterm to survive outside the womb. Farida's sister had been asked to wait outside of the room because, according to Hamida, she was "dirty" and would transmit an infection to the other patients. Hamida tried explaining the situation to Farida but the language barrier was clear. Frustrated, Hamida stood with her arms folded until the head midwife came into the room. Upon hearing the report, the head midwife sighed and "tsked" in sympathy. "You know, these women from the villages, they have nothing. It is so sad. They have no education. Her husband is an old man and she is just a baby. She could have died," she said, taking Farida's hand. Farida's sister was eventually allowed in to translate while a third midwife escorted another woman to an empty exam table against the wall just a few feet away. The new patient was in active labor, making high-pitched moans and calls to Allah during contractions. Sweating in the summer heat, she removed her pants and was helped onto the delivery table, her IV bag hanging from the windowpane beside her. The midwife removed her white coat, placed a long rubber apron over her long pink scrubs, and a mask over her face. She placed sterile gloves on her hands, unwrapped her "delivery kit" of sterile instruments, and checked the mother's cervix. "Not yet, auntie, don't push yet. Just breathe. Good work." The mother moaned, gripping the edge of the bed with her toes, while a black plastic garbage bag was placed beneath her bottom. The head midwife left Farida and pulled the curtain between Farida and the new laboring mother. "Good work, auntie," the midwife coached, "Okay, now you can push. Push, auntie." Sounds drifted from the other side of the curtain: pushy grunts, soft coaching, several screams, instruments clanking, and finally the cries of the newborn baby. Meanwhile, Farida lay with her knees bent and pressed together, her head turned to the wall, her headscarf pulled to her nose. She was sobbing softly. Hamida returned and started an IV with Pitocin. That evening, Farida delivered small twin boys, both of whom survived for just minutes before passing.

Introduction

Despite the painstaking work of historians, journalists, humanitarian groups, and various sectors of the international community, the impact of the violence in Afghanistan remains unknown. Tallies of direct civilian casualties vary between organizations and by year. They pale in comparison to the number of individuals, families, and communities who endure the reverberations of war: displacement, food insecurity, drug trade and addiction, collapsed infrastructure, trauma, grief, and loss.

Local histories of violence describe how violence has been perpetrated and then interpreted by Afghan communities in ways that continue to mark daily lives. Common narratives, social norms, and shared understandings and expectations are reflections of these histories and their shared memories. This "violence of everyday life" (Scheper-Hughes 1993) inherently links the political violence and repression of the past several decades and the long-term structural violence embedded in class, gender, tribal, ethnic, and sectarian relations. Health care access and delivery is a social service system that lies at the nexus of these historical forces and the reconstruction policies and efforts employed by state and local actors to shape Afghanistan's future.

Afghanistan has ranked among the worst in the world for several basic health indexes, including child, infant, and maternal mortality. The removal of the Taliban regime in 2001–2002 and establishment of the Karzai administration led to a liberal influx of international monies to (re)build a public health system that tackles these issues. However, after nearly forty years of conflict, Afghanistan struggled with a lack of infrastructure, organization, and technical expertise to provide basic health services, especially given the challenges of geography, climate, ongoing insurgencies, and political instabilities. A consortium of donors along with the Ministry of Public Health (MoPH) proposed that nongovernmental organizations (NGOs) be primarily responsible for developing and executing basic public health care throughout Afghanistan, as they had before 2002. Both new and established NGOs bid for contracts from the Ministry of Public Health worth over $140 million (Palmer et al. 2006). These contracts form the backbone of the Basic Package of Health Services (BPHS), intended to coordinate primary health care and health systems reconstruction efforts.

The rebuilding of Afghanistan's health sector offers a lens into how society understands, prioritizes, and addresses local determinants of health and disease. I focus on maternal health as a cornerstone of family and social health. The plights of Afghan women have captured the attention of donor communities in the post-Taliban era. How do the local realities of Afghanistan's programs to reduce maternal mortality reflect the ways in which Afghan women are seen within their communities and by their government? Efforts to reduce maternal risk in Afghanistan provide a theoretical site to explore the entanglements of gender dynamics, health policies, communities, and local histories of violence. This chapter asks how local and international political economies shape women's reproductive choices and experiences.

Maternal Mortality in Afghanistan

In 2005, Afghanistan had one of the highest rates of maternal mortality in the world—1,600 maternal deaths per 100,000 live births (Bartlett et al. 2005). In many analyses of maternal mortality, socioeconomic variables play key roles and cut across national boundaries: lack of public infrastructure, poor access to reproductive health care, gender inequality, the compounding effects of war, malnutrition, disease, and poverty. In Afghanistan, attention has been paid to particular sociocultural and religious variables as well—child marriage, seclusion, veiling, interpretations of Islam (Liese 2009). However, BPHS maternal mortality programs focus primarily on providing biomedical care to women at the time of birth.

Acknowledging social underpinnings of poor health, yet implementing technical solutions that lend themselves to post-intervention "measurables" reflects a larger conflict in the global health paradigm (Biehl and Petryna 2013). Maternal mortality is the leading cause of death for women worldwide, killing more than eight hundred women per day (Buttah and Black 2013). Ninety-nine percent of these deaths occur in poor countries. In 1987, the World Bank and World Health Organization (WHO) designated the Safe Motherhood Initiative

(SMI) to develop and implement policies and interventions to decrease maternal mortality worldwide (AbouZahr 2003). Initially, the SMI strategy focused on general poverty reduction and programs to empower women. When these yielded limited success, the scope of SMI programming narrowed to address the proximate medical causes of maternal mortality (e.g., postpartum bleeding, infection, high blood pressure, unsafe abortion). Since obstetric treatments for these biological causes of maternal mortality have been successful in wealthy countries since the 1950s, the conventional way to understand maternal mortality is to think that most maternal deaths are medically preventable by improving women's access to lifesaving obstetric care in poor countries. In other words, if women in poor countries like Afghanistan had the same access to lifesaving medical care as women in wealthy countries, where less than 1 per cent of maternal deaths occur, then maternal mortality could be all but eradicated (Liese 2009). Several variables are missing from this analysis.

Maternal risk in poor countries is not equivalent to that in wealthy countries. Afghanistan provides a telling example. Women in Afghanistan's Badakhshan province have the highest recorded maternal mortality ratio in the world (6,507 maternal deaths per 100,000 live births, or a one in three lifetime risk of dying in childbirth; Bartlett et al. 2005). The leading cause of maternal death in Badakhshan is obstructed labor. Obstructed labor results when the head of the fetus cannot fit through the maternal pelvis, leading to uterine rupture. Although conventionally associated with very young, first-time mothers, the women who are dying in Badakhshan are in their late twenties and have previously had several successful vaginal births (Bartlett et al. 2005). I suggest (Liese 2009) that the pelvises of these women may be contracting later in their reproductive lives due to chronic vitamin D and calcium deficiencies, eventually preventing the passage of a fetus, resulting in maternal and fetal death. Early marriage, repeated childbearing and breastfeeding, seclusion, veiling, and malnutrition are prominent biosocial institutions in Badakhshan which may deplete these essential micronutrients. In this scenario, a "perfect storm" of complex social, historical, and environmental variables is at the source of the world's highest maternal mortality rate.

Between 2005 and 2008, I conducted ethnographic research in the mountainous Badakhshan province, in a small cluster of mountain villages along the Amu Daria River that divides Afghanistan and Tajikistan. Since the end of the Tajik civil war in 1997, this remote area has seen little imminent threat of outside violence. However, shared memories of armed raids and bride kidnapping and the fear of their reoccurrence reinforced behaviors contributing to maternal risk. Families reported that they preferred their daughters to be married young since men on horseback had once come through the villages, taking unmarried girls. Although these instances of violence have ceased in recent decades, husbands and wives explained that they have kept the restrictive norms of veiling and wife seclusion to protect women from neighbors who might one day report them to the mujahideen, should they return. How can people with local histories of recurrent violence be assured that the current peace is lasting, and not simply a pause before more violence (Goldstein 2003, also see Chapter 11 in this volume)? Women in wealthy countries are exempt from these combined conditions and the subsequent reproductive risks they pose. Likewise, although access to an emergency cesarean section may save the life of an individual woman with obstructed labor, it cannot address the underlying causes, nor is it feasible at a population level where the prevalence of obstructed labor is endemically high.

Access to Care

Global health experts have long identified access to skilled birth attendants as fundamental to reducing maternal risk. The assumption is that birth is safest with access to biomedical interventions and, in countries such as Afghanistan, "barriers" to accessing advanced obstetrical care in the event of an emergency should be addressed to ensure safe motherhood. In this section, I discuss one of the Ministry of Public Health's flagship programs to change the context in which women give birth based on an understanding of birth as a primarily physiological process and the challenges to this initiative. I provide an anthropological explanation for what global health experts describe as "barriers to care" by examining the nonmedical nature of birth in Afghan communities.

For most Afghan women, access to a trained midwife at the time of delivery, much less access to the surgeon, anesthesiologist, operating theater, medication, and equipment necessary for a safe cesarean section, is geographically out of reach. In rolling out the BPHS, the Ministry of Public Health encouraged both Afghan and foreign NGOs to compete for bids to quickly and efficiently provide access to comprehensive and basic health care to over 80 percent of the country. They defined "access" as falling within a two-hour walk to a health facility. Prior to 2002, there was one health care center per forty thousand people in the central and eastern regions and one per two hundred thousand people in the southern regions (Waldman and Hanif 2002). The MoPH often reports that more than 82 percent of the population live in districts with resources for the BPHS; however, this figure is misleading. In reality, the MoPH has awarded contracts that may cover parts of the country in which 82 percent of the population lives, but the people who live in the rural areas do not necessarily have real access to or actually seek care from BPHS facilities (Waldman and Hanif 2002).

One barrier for women in particular is access to female health care workers, especially in remote regions. In June 2004, 40 percent of health facilities in Afghanistan had no female providers and only 21 percent of facilities had a midwife. Only 10 percent of births were attended by a trained provider (Palmer et al. 2006). Some NGOs have used incentive packages to recruit female doctors and nurses from Tajikistan, contributing to a shortage of health care workers in that country as well. Another strategy has been to establish community midwifery (CM) education centers to meet the reproductive health needs of Afghan women in remote areas. These programs were designed to be successful where strong sociocultural norms often inhibit women from advancing in their education and then serving their communities. In order to be selected for the eighteen-month training program in a provincial capital, a woman had to both demonstrate that she was supported by the leadership (*shura*, or council) in her community and sign a contract promising to return to her village to serve as a midwife for three years following her graduation. The process of acquiring the agreement of community leaders involves many hours of negotiation and discussion. However, community support is a vital component to the anticipated success of the CM education program in Afghanistan. The endorsement by community leaders for young woman to become midwives signals their approval and paves the way for families to take advantage of her services. In many Afghan villages, the community midwife is one of few opportunities for women to participate as professionals in the formal sector of *their own* communities. The community buy-in of these prerequisites were intended to increase women's access to midwifery services by lending support from the male community.

The training for community midwives provides skills in clinic-based antenatal, labor, and postpartum care. The objective is to train experts in basic, normal childbirth, reducing iatrogenic complications. An important skill is their ability to promptly identify a problem that requires referral to a tertiary care center, thereby reducing delays that often prove critical to maternal survival. Since 2002, this project has been extended to twenty provinces throughout Afghanistan.

In 2010, I conducted a qualitative study funded by the international NGO Medical Emergency Relief International (MERLIN) in which I examined the roles, practices, and utilization of community midwives in their villages in rural Takhar, Badakhshan, and Kunduz provinces.[1] I was interested in the degree to which CMs are accepted as health professionals within their community and how women value and make use of the services they offer. I was also interested in the experiences of the CMs themselves. In the context of Afghanistan's conservative and patriarchal rural society, their training and employment is unique.

By and large, CMs have improved access to aspects of reproductive health care in the villages where they work. In particular, in addition to accessing CM care for contraceptive services, women also went to CMS for childhood vaccinations, primary care complaints, and occasional antenatal visits. These are important achievements considering that birth control reduces maternal mortality and improves both maternal and child health. However, only a small percentage of women went to the CMs when in labor, despite describing clinic births as preferable, in terms of safety, to home births.

Several intertwined sociocultural and structural barriers kept women from delivering with the community midwife. Bibigul, a forty-five-year-old mother of six, ties a set of keys to the base of her two long braids. She lives with her husband, father-in-law, and children in a small clay-straw home surrounded by a mud fence. She gave birth to each of her babies at home and had twice helped her sister-in-law with her births as well. She felt that home was more private and, although she felt the clinic was perhaps safer and better stocked, she had concerns about strange men being in the clinic while she was in labor. The path between her home and the new clinic winds along a narrow ridge and across two small streams that flood in the springtime. It is often muddy and slippery when not frozen or packed with snow. Bibigul has made the two-hour trip to the clinic three times since the community midwife arrived there. Twice she wanted her youngest child to be seen for his breathing problems, and once she accompanied her sister-in-law who was pregnant and bleeding. Each time she arrived at the women's entrance in the back, she found a line of women standing against the white plaster wall, waiting to be seen. "The midwife is only there for three hours in a day. Sometimes she does not come at all," Bibigul complained.

Bibigul was among several women who complained about the inconsistent hours kept by their CMs, as well as the long lines they lacked the time to wait in. However, the CMs reported that they were expected to be available twenty-four hours a day in the case of a delivery or postpartum emergency. Traveling to the clinic at night was often difficult for CMs, as they required an escort. Moreover, they were often called to women's homes despite that they were not trained for home births but for clinic-based births. Meanwhile, older, traditional midwives were willing to attend women at home and generally had more years of experience with deliveries. For all these reasons, CMs were not regularly used as skilled birth attendants. In essence, although more has been done to make the CM more culturally acceptable to the communities, the sociocultural context of their work is mismatched. Although the *shura* approves of women receiving care from their community midwife, the CM herself is still a young female, subject to the norms and expectations of her community. One woman asked, "Why should I go to her? Yesterday she was just my neighbor. She goes away and now she is a midwife? What does she know? I think she is still just my neighbor."

As Bridgette Jordan (1977, 1) argues, birth around the world must be understood as a social event that serves various purposes within families and communities. In Guatemala, another country which suffered decades of violence and repression, women and their families have long resisted giving birth in hospital settings. Although their reasons are both social as well as economic, Berry (2010) argues that the birth setting is one where kinship ties are reaffirmed as ultimate safety nets in times of conflict and instability. A similar argument can be made with birth and CM programs in Afghanistan.

Decades of violence reinforced protective social norms. Especially during the Taliban era, families had reason to be mistrustful of those who were not part of their kin network. Marriages are still preferred between close relatives, usually first cousins, in part to maintain the social safety that close clan ties provide. Men described their duty as to protect the women entrusted to their care: their mothers, sisters, wives, daughters. Women's movements and visibility were restricted and these restrictions were cloaked with religious notions of modesty, shame, and piety. To remove a woman from her home during labor is to take her out of the protection of the family. Walking dangerous paths from the home, in a vulnerable state, to a clinic where a woman may be undressed and seen by strangers is to relinquish control and encounter risk.

Robbie Davis-Floyd and Carolyn Sargent (1997) demonstrated how the technocratic model of Western obstetrics maintains authoritative knowledge when women enter the hospital. Women submit their bodies, privacy, relationships, decisions, and instincts to a model of care that depicts birth as dangerous and relies on intervention to ensure safety. This hegemonic system infuses fear and risk into our shared understandings of childbirth. We depend on medicine and technology to (physically and socially) "deliver" us from the dangerous liminal state brought about by pregnancy and childbirth.

Afghan families similarly described pregnancy as a liminal state and childbirth as inherently laden with risks for mothers and babies. As one husband poignantly described it, "A woman in labor is a woman between birth and death." Yet, fears of violence and transgression superseded the medical risks. Those fears were founded in common experience through decades of war, insecurity, and instability. However, even in Afghan communities with unusually high rates of maternal mortality, families did expect that access to biomedicine would be the solution. When weighing the risks of transportation, vulnerability, exposure, shame, and so on against the perceived benefits conveyed by a clinic-based birth with a community midwife, most families chose the devil they knew over the devil they did not.

When families did seek care and the outcomes were bad, anger was directed not at biomedicine but to the individuals who had presumably taken over responsibility for the safety of that woman. There has been only one maternal death in CURE International Hospital in Kabul in the last several years. A perfectly healthy thirty-two-year-old woman gave birth to a perfectly healthy baby girl. When the woman stood up from the delivery bed, an amniotic fluid embolism developed. An amniotic fluid embolism occurs when some of the amniotic fluid or fetal cells enter the mother's blood stream and cause an allergic reaction that results in heart and lung failure. It is extremely rare and often fatal. Several physicians were present and administered CPR (cardiopulmonary resuscitation) without success.

The family of the deceased woman was grief-stricken and angry. The night following her death, they came to the hospital and threw rocks, shattering the windows in several wards, including the maternity and pediatrics wards. They also filed legal complaints with both the police and Ministry of Health. The police responded by arresting several male physicians who were present when the woman coded. They were detained and reportedly tortured for a week, while midwives who had been involved with her care were repeatedly called in for interrogation. The family demanded a payout for the tragedy and anticipated that the international hospital would pay it. The doctors were eventually released and the interrogations stopped when several high-ranking officials aligned with the hospital became involved.

To anyone familiar with malpractice litigation in American obstetrics, this story will sound like a terrifying parable. However, it will also rid us of the assumption that high maternal mortality ratios somehow translate into complacency or sense of inevitability when women die. The family's anger was directed at the hospital and the doctors, whom they had trusted and paid to care for their relative. Threats and demand for payment in restitution for life highlight the vulnerability of all obstetric providers, including community midwives, in taking responsibility for caring for women in childbirth. Failure to meet that responsibility (however determined) can have dire personal consequences for providers.

And what would be accomplished if CMs were regularly present at births? Part of their mission is to reduce maternal mortality, presumably by keeping those women who would have normal births from developing complications. This presumes that the high rates of maternal risk among Afghan women are episodic to the birth event, and not part of a more complicated social, political, economic, and environmental history. This is not to say that women could not benefit from a skilled provider at birth. Certainly, the ability to administer Pitocin, a medication that prevents and treats uterine atony, may save the lives of women with postpartum hemorrhage. Likewise, sterile practices reduce complications from infection. However, we may be missing the larger picture of accountability by focusing on individual risk factors. Afghanistan's maternal mortality ratio cannot be exclusively explained by access to treatment. First, we must understand why so many more women in Afghanistan are presenting with these complications to begin with. The answer to this lies beyond the birth event. To focus on access to care as the defining difference between rich and poor women's reproductive health is to be sorely shortsighted.

Normal Birth in the Context of Conflict

When we view childbirth and reproduction through the lens of maternal mortality, we find it is inherently pathological, risk-oriented, and an experience of suffering or survival. Anthropologists such as Robbie Davis-Floyd and Carolyn Sargent (1997) demonstrate that childbirth itself is a normal process, often complicated by the iatrogenic practices of a technocratic health care system. But what relevance is that when birth appears to be, in fact, pathological, at least at the population level? The anthropological literature on maternal mortality in the poor countries focuses on the issues of subjectivity, power, and violence that establish and feed structural inequalities. What of the normal, safe, and healthy births? What does normal birth look like in Afghanistan, a place with such (statistically) extraordinary maternal risk? Focusing on maternal mortality and maternal risk exclusively is akin to ignoring the ethnographic importance of the vast majority of Afghan births as the event where society, culture, and families are reproduced.

Tsipy Ivry (2009) depicts how pregnancy embodies many of the cultural conflicts in Israeli society. How does childbirth reflect the larger social picture in Afghanistan? How can an exploration of childbirth be a lens for understanding broader contradictions and subtleties of the current conflict in Afghanistan? By exploring women's labors and births, we can connect impersonal figures associated with maternal mortality through the remarkably normal context in which they occur.

The midwives at CURE, a private hospital in Kabul, spanned seventeen-year-old unmarried novices to sixty-five-year-old widowed sage femmes. Hamida, at twenty-nine, was fairly typical. When Hamida was fifteen, she knew whom she would marry. He was a cousin and in school to be an engineer. She had seen his picture and knew he was handsome. She was especially happy that she would be able to continue living in Kabul, not far from her parents and brothers. "He was modern," she told me. "His family was like ours. His sisters didn't wear the *chodar*, and one of them was a doctor. He agreed that I should finish midwife school before we would get married." That was before the war, before moving to Iran, before losing her parents, before giving birth to two daughters in exile, before taking a job as a midwife in an Iranian hospital, and before her marriage became tense and then violent. When the family returned to Kabul, Hamida was depressed. She resented her husband and did not want more children. Although she felt she was treated poorly in Iran because she was Afghan, Afghanistan felt backward to her. She took a job at CURE International Hospital in Kabul because it was the most advanced and run by foreigners. Hamida liked working at CURE and admitted she was happy to get away from her family, particularly her husband and mother-in-law. The night shifts were long (fourteen hours), but they allowed her to come and go during daylight, which served to appease her family. She got along well with the other midwives and liked working with the patients. She explained that she preferred to work with patients who were from Kabul because they were more likely to be "educated and clean."

Hamida's personal narrative and participation in Farida's birth illustrate the integration and negotiation of various historical and social resources present in contemporary Afghanistan. Although she once suffered class and ethnic discrimination while in exile in Iran, Hamida looked down upon her patient as unclean, uneducated, undernourished, and uncommunicative. And yet, both women have shared histories of everyday violence related to war, migration, loss, and marriage. Farida's story reflects the more commonly depicted narrative of Afghan women as child brides, living on the edges of abject poverty, powerlessness, and oppression. Her birth story juxtaposes the unexplained death of twin sons with another woman's birth to a healthy child just a few feet away. For the midwives, the poor outcome of her pregnancy is "explained" by her social circumstances. Although medical training validates the midwives' "authoritative knowledge," there is little medical evaluation into the causality of Farida's "inevitable abortion." Poverty, violence, and gender oppression explain how the fetuses became unhealthy, emphasizing it is not just the pregnant body but the social body as well that are the primary determinants of health. When we orient causality to the ecosystem of social, historical, and environmental determinants, then the pregnant body becomes meaningful in respect to maternal and fetal health, not in and of itself.

How then do these experiences of pathological pregnancies relate to the normalcy of childbirth? After all, despite impressions derived from the media and scholarship, most Afghan women and babies do, in fact, survive childbirth. The woman beside Farida, who, while lying on a black plastic garbage bag, safely delivered her baby into the hands of a seventeen-year-old midwife, was one of two dozen who had done so that day. In any given birth setting, be it in a remote home in Badakhshan or a maternity ward in Kabul, the patients and providers embody social risk factors based on shared experiences of historical and everyday violence. Essentially, the participants of the birth carry the context of conflict into the normal birth environment. In doing so, they rely on each other for support. This is another way the context of childbirth is constantly reflecting and reproducing social relations. The relationships between midwives and laboring women are distinct from the more formal provider-patient relationship common in Western medical practice. They are fluid but organized by class, kinship, and hierarchy. The younger midwife deferred to the older patient, whom she called "auntie." Meanwhile, Farida's ethnic and social background determined her relationship with her midwives and the staff. When the midwives, obstetricians (all female), and patients were not actively involved with medical care, they interacted according to established social norms for female-only spaces.

Despite the insistence that hospital-based obstetric or midwifery care is designed to meet the physiologic needs of a safe birth, I argue it is far from neutral and merely shifts the cultural framing. Many of the practices of hospital midwives could be described as benign rituals, at best, and iatrogenic, at worst. As noted in Hamida's story, midwives deny family members access to the delivery room if they appear "dirty," explaining this would risk infection. This explanation defies germ theory but reflects discrimination against the women from rural villages.

Meanwhile, before each woman gave birth, midwives cleansed the patient's pubic region with iodine in order to "keep it sterile and prevent infection." Since birth is far from a sterile process, there is no science to support the practice. However, it does reinforce notions of female sex organs as inherently "dirty" and in need of cleansing that are prevalent in a larger global historical context as well is within the local Afghan cultural framework.

One of the most invasive practices is the use of routine episiotomies on first-time mothers who were presumptively diagnosed with "rigid perineum(s)."[2] The midwife injected lidocaine into the perineum shortly before the baby's head delivered, and then used scissors to make a three- to five-centimeter incision. Midwives insisted that performing this cut during a contraction made it less painful for the mothers. Nevertheless, the mothers would cry out in pain as the incision was made. Furthermore, after the baby was born and initially placed on the mother's belly, the baby would be removed to a warmer so that the midwife could sew the incision closed. The shoddy suturing of the incision often resulted in women returning to the hospital with painful infected sutures that required restitching.

Although couched in an outdated medical rationale, the cutting of episiotomies is an unnecessary intervention that reaffirms the authority of the midwife. When I first spoke with the midwives about the practice, they would insist that without it women would have "terrible fourth degree tears" that extended to the rectum. Therefore, women *needed* to have their bodies cut "for their own good." In reality, however, episiotomies are used to expedite the birth process. Instead of letting the perineum stretch over several pushes, possibly avoiding a tear altogether, the cut removes this final barrier to birth. When I suggested midwives withhold their scissors and see what would happen, they were initially resistant.[3]

In one instance, I was observing the labor and birth of a small young sixteen-year-old mother, shortly before lunch time. The midwife attending the mother was in her early fifties. The mother had been pushing for over an hour and it was clear in her tone that the midwife was growing impatient. When she reached for her scissors, she said, "She is exhausted. She cannot push anymore. And also, she will tear." As we spoke the head obstetrician came into the room and observed from behind our backs. The mother pushed with great effort as the baby's head made incremental progress into the world. With each push, we saw first the forehead, then the eyebrows, then the eyelids. She cried out with exhaustion and release when the head fully emerged. The rest of the baby was delivered in a single push and placed on his mother's belly. When we examined the new mother's vagina, it was sore, and swollen, and completely intact. Afterward, the head obstetrician commented to me, "I can see that episiotomy may not be necessary for the perineum, but who is to say it is not better for the mother's strength." Interestingly, the perceived weakness of women has justified unnecessary and iatrogenic interventions for Western women in hospitals for decades. As such, we should ask how the *culture* of biomedicine, as the dominant paradigm informing public health reform in Afghanistan, will affect the meanings and relationships inherent in the way women give birth.

Conclusion

The statistics of maternal mortality are insufficient to reflect the macro-level trends of women's bodies, much less the micro-level causality of maternal risk. And yet, the culture of pregnancy in Afghanistan has organized around "social suffering" as one way to make sense of tragic outcomes. This may be a matter of emotional pragmatism, and it does serve to draw attention to the plight of women. However, it is important to ask how this hegemonic discourse speaks to pregnant women and their birth attendants. Where does "normal childbirth" fit in a body politic of risk and suffering? Do we risk normalizing violence in shifting the critical gaze from the pathologies of pregnancy to a more neutral anthropology of pregnancy?

The question may be extended to more general anthropological work in Afghanistan. What are the boundaries of inquiry for "normal" in a place experiencing conflict?

There are no men allowed in the maternity ward of the hospital. This is women's space and, *kori zanon* (women's work). In that space, birth happens and death happens, sometimes side by side. Events on the maternity ward revolve around the spaces between birth and death—the labors of life. Understanding the roles of the women in the birth environment highlight how "local histories of violence" and "the violence of everyday life" can converge and create what a "normal" childbirth is in Afghanistan.

KYLEA LAINA LIESE, PhD, CNM, MSN, is a clinical assistant professor of nursing at the University of Illinois, Chicago.

NOTES

1. MERLIN is a United Kingdom-based international NGO who has partnered with an Afghan NGO, Care of Afghan Families (CAF) to implement midwifery-training programs in the Takhar (the city of Taloqan is its capital), and Badakhshan provinces.

2. An episiotomy is an incision made into the mother's perineum before the baby's head is born. It was once thought that if an incision was made, then the mother would heal more quickly than if she tore on her own. It was also thought this might prevent truly severe tears that extend to the rectum and can result in lasting damage. However, both of these ideas have been disproven since the incision only weakens the integrity of the skin and can cause a more severe laceration than might naturally develop.

3. While in midwifery school at Yale, CURE invited me to assess and advise their midwives for three months in 2010.

Bibliography

AbouZahr, Carla. 2003. "Safe Motherhood: A Brief History of the Global Movement 1947–2002." *British Medical Bulletin* 67 (1):13–25.

Bartlett, Linda A., Shairose Mawji, Sara Whitehead, Chadd Crouse, Suraya Dalil, Denisa Ionete, Peter Salama, and the Afghan Maternal Mortality Study Team. 2005. "Where Giving Birth Is a Forecast of Death: Maternal Mortality in Four Districts of Afghanistan, 1999–2000." *Lancet* 365 (9462): 864–70.

Berry, Nicole. 2010. *Unsafe Motherhood: Mayan Maternal Mortality and Subjectivity in Post-War Guatemala.* New York: Berghahn Books.

Bhutta, Zulfiqar A., and Robert E. Black. 2013. "Global Maternal, Newborn, and Child Health: So Near and Yet So Far." *New England Journal of Medicine* 369 (23): 2226–35.

Bielh, João, and Adriana Petryna, eds. 2013. *When People Come First: Critical Studies in Global Health.* Princeton, NJ: Princeton University Press.

Davis-Floyd, Robbie E., and Carolyn Sargent. 1997. *Childbirth and Authoritative Knowledge: Cross-Cultural Perspectives.* Berkeley: University of California Press.

Goldstein, Donna M. 2003. *Laughter Out of Place: Race, Class, Violence, and Sexuality in a Rio Shantytown.* Berkeley: University of California Press.

Ivry, Tsipy. 2009. *Embodying Culture: Pregnancy in Japan and Israel.* New Brunswick, NJ: Rutgers University Press.

Jordan, Brigitte. 1997. "Authoritative Knowledge and Its Construction." In *Childbirth and Authoritative Knowledge*, ed. Robbie E. Davis-Floyd and Carolyn Sargent, 55–79. Berkeley: University of California Press.

Liese, Kylea Laina. 2009. "Motherdeath in Childbirth: Explaining Maternal Mortality on the Roof of the World." PhD diss., Stanford University.

Palmer, Natasha, Lesley Strong, Abdul Wali, and Egbert Sondorp. 2006. "Contracting Out Health Services in Fragile States." *British Medical Journal* 332 (7543): 718–21.

Scheper-Hughes, Nancy. 1993. *Death without Weeping: The Violence of Everyday Life in Brazil.* Berkeley: University of California Press.

Waldman, Ronald, and Homaira Hanif. 2002. *The Public Health System in Afghanistan.* Kabul: Afghan Research and Evaluation Unit.

17

SIGNATURES OF DISTRUST IN CONTEMPORARY AFGHANISTAN: MORE THAN A DECADE OF DEVELOPMENT EFFORT FOR VULNERABLE GROUPS: THE CASE OF DISABILITY

Parul Bakhshi and Jean-Francois Trani

Background: Afghanistan—Past, Current, and Future Uncertainties

As Afghanistan enters the era following US involvement and its military presence, there is high degree of speculation about what the security situation will entail for the local population. The current pattern of dependency on international aid is similar to the one observed in Afghanistan in the second half of the twentieth century. To promote economic development through social and economic reforms, the government of King Mohammed Zahir Shah heavily relied on the technical and financial aid of the Soviet Union and the United States, receiving $552 million from the former and about $300 million from the latter between 1955 and 1965. Among other contributions, the Soviet Union built the Kabul airport, the Kushka Herat Kandahar road, the Salang road and several industrial projects. The United States provided considerable economic and technical assistance in the areas of agriculture, transportation, education, industry, mining, and training. The urban elite benefited widely from the development process and, as a result, participated more heavily in the political arena. Yet, the large majority of the rural population did not see any major improvement during the decades before the communist coup of 1978, except for opening of schools, elementary and middle levels.

For the most destitute sections of Afghans, the everyday demands of coping with poverty and relying on social networks has been a stark reality for decades, even up to today. Kantor and Pain show how the poorest households rely on powerful local elites for "credit, sharecrop land, employment or other needed services" (Kantor and Pain 2010, 2). Poverty in Afghanistan is characterized by a continual lack of resources but also by the unequal access to these resources based on gender, social, ethnic, and political characteristics. Authors have suggested reducing inequalities by targeting development efforts toward the needs of the poor, particularly by promoting small-scale agriculture through access to land and support to unskilled labor in the less developed regions of the country.

Although the presence of development actors is diminishing with the military pullout, it is a good time to review what has (and has not) been achieved over a decade of programs, policies, and interventions and decipher the glaring loopholes in initiatives that were designed to fight poverty and vulnerability in Afghanistan. In the present chapter, we aim to decipher some aspects of the complex dynamics that need to be understood in order to ensure that the achievements of over a decade of development efforts are not lost in the coming years. In the first section, we will discuss some of what has been accomplished and gauge the missed opportunities that have not been seized in the various efforts to 'reconstruct' Afghanistan. In the second section, we will present findings from surveys on poverty and vulnerability in Afghanistan that provide nuanced evidence that can be relevant in rethinking policies and for strengthening accountability mechanisms. Finally, we discuss at some length the various barriers and conditions that impede or encourage the use of evidence in political decision making and why this has not been done in the past fifteen years of intensive development.

Proclaimed Progress in Various Areas

Some claim that significant improvement has been made in living conditions of the population. Although statistics cited within the literature are widely contradictory, there is however a general consensus that basic health indexes have improved since 2001 (see for instance Alonge et al., 2015). Yet, approximately 80 percent of Afghans live in rural areas and access to healthcare remains a challenge due to inaccessible roads, violence, and a lack of transport facilities. Extreme weather conditions create further constraints for health delivery, as half of the country is inaccessible during the winter. Prolonged conflict, combined with few employment opportunities, have resulted in shortages of healthcare workers, which has severely impeded healthcare delivery Vaccine-preventable diseases, including acute respiratory infections such as pneumonia, meningitis, typhoid, and particularly diarrhea for children, continue to constitute an important part of the burden of disease (Wagner et al., 2017). In addition, frequent seasonal hazards, a lack of arable land, and subsequent rises in food prices have heightened food insecurity and chronic malnutrition (*AnnaD'Souza & Jollife, 2012*). Access to primary healthcare has improved, as the Ministry of Public Health (MoPH), in 2002, implemented a Basic Package of Health Services (BPHS) to address the country's major health problems. By the end of 2008, the BPHS expanded to reach approximately 85 percent of the general population (Edward et al., 2011). In addition to healthcare, considerable resources have been poured into education. School enrollment in grades one to twelve increased from 3.9 million in 2004 to 9.2 million in 2017, of which 39% are girls. The push to increase primary school enrollment has particularly benefited girls; their enrollments have increased from approximately 839,000 to over 3.5 million (Ministry of Education, 2017, also see Chapter 16 in this volume).

Political rights have been advanced as the national constitution came into force in 2004, recognizing the state's obligation to abide by international conventions and the Universal Declaration of Human Rights (UDHR). Under the constitution, sixty-eight seats are reserved for women in the lower house of the National Assembly. To further secure women's rights, the country has also ratified several international conventions, including the Convention on the Elimination of all Discrimination against Women (CEDAW). Although these developments are encouraging, numerous challenges remain and progress to date has failed to live up to the aspirations of the population. Furthermore, reforms promoting women's rights that fail to acknowledge Afghan cultural values have been shown to be counterproductive; previous attempts by the Soviet Union in the 1980s provoked huge civilian unrest followed by indiscriminate bombings of villages and mass migrations. In refugees camps, Afghan women became even more constrained in their movements than they were in their "mostly kin related villages" where they benefited from community support (for further details see, Chapter 15 in this volume).

The Vicious Cycle of Pervading Violence and Political Turmoil

Currently, three years into the Ghani administration and after the US reduced considerably their military presence in Afghanistan, the situation in the country is marked by uncertainty and anxiety among Afghans about losing the limited achievements observed in fifteen years of international community development efforts. The perpetuation of violence and political turmoil associated with the lack of vision by both national and international actors and with bad governance has prevented communities from substantially improving their livelihoods. The decades of past violence resulted in thousands of dead and disabled people, forced migration, destruction of physical and social infrastructure, disruption of education and health systems, and violation of human rights. Although the limited success or admitted failure of programs has constantly been attributed to the usual suspects—namely a rise in violence and lack of security and widespread corruption at all levels of bureaucracy—the inherent co-occurring factors that sustain the lack of success have not been sufficiently analyzed (also see Chapter 11 in this volume).

Fifteen years of reconstruction effort have taken place in a context of enduring instability. Security has rapidly declined since 2006, which has had a detrimental impact on reconstruction and development efforts. Suicide attacks have increased sixfold; bomb attacks have approximately doubled since 2005. The United Nations Assistance Mission in Afghanistan and the Office of the High Commissioner for Human Rights (2017) estimate that more than 8,531 civilian casualties (2,616 deaths and 5,915 injured) occurred in 2016 alone, marking a 80 percent increase compared to 2009 (UNAMA, 2017). Schools have increasingly become targets of attacks. Local jihadi commanders maintain strong influence in parts of the country while it is estimated that one third of the country is under Taliban control. Furthermore, three million Afghans are either internally displaced or are still refugees in neighboring countries. There are fifty-three camps in Kabul alone for internal refugees.

The assassination in 2011 of former president Rabbani, who was negotiating with the Taliban movement on behalf of the government of Afghanistan, was considered by political analysts to be a major blow to the peace process. Afghan forces have faced almost daily attacks by Taliban militants since then. Taliban militants have even conducted bold attacks in Kabul against the international community, demonstrating the difficulty to maintain security in the capital city itself. They control vast parts of the territory, particularly in the southern crescent from Farah to Nangarhar provinces, including Nimroz, Helmand, Kandahar, Zabul, Paktika, and Paktia. Large areas in other provinces are also under Taliban administration. Despite President Ghani's signature on the controversial Bilateral Security Agreement (BSA) with the United States, the limited presence of US troops in the country leaves a partially prepared Afghan army facing the threat of both Taliban militants and various regional warlords' militias. The current government has kept away several strongmen—such as Abdul Rasul Sayyaf, the governor of Balkh province, Mohammad Atta Noor, the former vice president, Yunus Qanooni, and the former Nangarhar provincial governor Gul Agha Sherzai, who are all a potential threat to stability in the country. Only Uzbek warlord Rashid Dostum has been included, as an ineffectual first vice president in the Ghani and Abdullah Abdullah government.

In 2015, two-thirds of Afghans reported they feared for their own security. Encounters with the Taliban represent the greatest source of experienced fear, and the risk of civil war is higher than ever. In the summer of 2015, the Taliban were able to briefly occupy Kunduz, and the Afghan National Army was able to retake the town only with the help of US troops (also see Chapter 11 in this volume).

Drug production is another significant concern, as Afghanistan's opium production level is rising: 4,800 tons produced in 2016, a 43% increase compared to 2015. Not only does the large availability of drugs increase the risk of intravenous drug use but in addition, it continues to fuel corruption and offers an alternative livelihood for the vast number of unemployed (UNODC, 2016).

However, recent reports have suggested that the extremely complex social and political situation has been made worse by the way development has been conceived and implemented. One factor that has been clearly stated is the loss of trust of local populations in development actors and foreign aid. This distrust is a direct result of a lack of understanding and consideration of the social and cultural realities that imbue every aspect of everyday lives of Afghans. Some argue that the democracy model being implemented in Afghanistan is a foreign import with little resonance to local norms and beliefs. This disconnect constitutes one of the main factors that explains why, despite considerable financial commitments to Afghanistan, the tangible evidence of improvement in equity and well-being remain elusive. However, there has been little introspection on the part of the international community to date on opportunities lost and drastic mistakes that have been made. Aarya Nijat presents the idea that international actors have addressed "technical problems, which can be addressed with the existing knowledge, systems, skills and expertise of Afghans and international partners" but have not been able to deal with more complex "adaptive problems which require long-term, sustained and consistent processes of adaptive change involving culture, value systems, religion, customs, habits and behaviours" as well as a third set of issues qualified as " combined sets of technical and adaptive challenges that require both for sustained durations over more than a mere 12 years" (2014, 7).

The current development effort has not been sufficient to address the needs of the population so far, and this is also due to the cost of enforcing security. The pattern of government expenditures shows the importance given to security over investment in health, education, and employment support programs in particular. The *Poverty Reduction Strategy Paper*, elaborated in 2008, proclaims that security is the first development priority. The priority to date remains security sector reform with five leading nations contributing to five central pillars: "military reform (US), police reform (Germany), demilitarisation (Japan), judicial reform (Italy), and counter-narcotics (United Kingdom)" (International Monetary Fund 2008, 585). In 2011, government expenditures for security represented an estimated $8.6 billion (24 percent of the GDP) and will represent an estimated 25 percent of the annual development effort through 2017. Compare that to security spending of 3.8 percent of the GDP by the United States, the country with the largest military budget in the world. Focusing on security also translated in funding "short term projects designed to meet tactical military objectives" and not genuinely addressing structural development needs (p. 11). By contrast, the effort to promote basic capabilities such as healthcare for all, education for girls, and employment for young men is much more limited, as shown by the following examples. The most preeminent development intervention, the National Solidarity Program (NSP), is expected to have cumulatively spent a significant $2.5 billion between 2003 and 2015 on village infrastructure. Despite its recognized success, the NSP is not sufficient to address decades with no rural development interventions. The national budget allocated $707 million to education (3.4 percent of the GDP) in 2010 and 2011 and $201 million to health (0.97 percent of the GDP) in 2011 and 2012. This last amount, provided mainly for the Basic Package of Health Services, a major public program, represents $6 per capita (for a population estimated at thirty million inhabitants). This is far less that the $34 per capita recommended in 2001 by the World Health Organization (WHO) Commission on Macroeconomics and Health to meet the health-related Millennium Development Goals in 2015 (Commission on Macroeconomics and Health 2015). Furthermore, 88 percent of the international aid is channeled outside the government budget, or the "core" budget, with a large volume leaving Afghanistan through imports, contractor benefits, and outward remittances (Hogg et al., 2013)(3). The situation is similar to the one observed in the 1950s and 1960s when foreign aid became the first source of income for the state, which allocated the resources without any democratic process to control it, increasing the risk of corruption and mismanagement. This state of affairs put a lot of strain on the relations between the state and society, with the open competition between citizens for resources.

We argue that this context has been particularly detrimental to vulnerable groups, particularly persons with disabilities. Our recent estimates indicate that 7.6 percent of Afghanistan's population is disabled, of which 1.8 percent have severe limitations. For the total disabled population, mobility and other physical disabilities represent 59 percent, while sensory disabilities (visual, hearing, and speech difficulties), learning and intellectual disabilities, mental and neurological disabilities, and associated disabilities (more than one type, such as physical and sensory or mental) represent, respectively, 19 percent, 7 percent, 10 percent, and 5 percent.

In this chapter, we attempt to decipher the dynamics that sustain the inherent inequalities that over fifteen years of development efforts have not been curbed in a significant manner. Moving beyond the traditional views of seeing poverty through one-dimensional indicators, we argue that there is an urgent need to focus on the multidimensional nature of poverty. In order to do this, we need to devise methods that allow for a gauging of poverty based on dynamic and pluralistic definitions. This will constitute the first steps towards mending the distrust that has resulted from the inefficiency of programs designed for the most destitute.

Outstanding Development Challenges: Looking at the Numbers

The dominant discourse claims that, in the absence of peace and security and due to corruption and heavy bureaucracy, economic development has been elusive. Despite the considerable funding from various donors, Afghanistan still faces innumerable challenges, as shown by main development indicators. Afghanistan's Human Development Index—a composite indicator including a measure of life expectancy at birth, expected years of schooling, mean years of schooling, and gross national income per capita—reached 0.479 in 2016 (compared to 0.236 in 2000 and 0.066 in 1993), placing the country at 169th out of 187 countries and territories (171st out of 173 countries in 1993) and in the low human development category (UNDP, 2017). Life expectancy at birth was forty-nine years in 2012; the mean years of schooling was 3.1 years. It is indisputable that the claimed milestones achieved are not on par with the level of funding pledged or even allocated. Moreover, the lack of an overarching accountability system for gauging progress (rather than sporadic or localized efforts) that presents a more comprehensive picture, is missing from the development process. In the following section, through evidence from surveys carried out on the field, we attempt to analyze the factors that sustain the inherent inequalities that have persisted despite fifteen years of development effort. Moving beyond viewing poverty one-dimensionally, we argue that there is an urgent need to focus on the multidimensional nature of poverty. In order to do this, we need to devise methods that allow for a gauging of poverty based on dynamic and pluralistic definitions. We strongly argue that looking at nuanced views that unpack complex realities constitutes the first step toward rebuilding the populations' trust in programs designed for the most destitute.

Education: The Mechanisms That Maintain Inequalities

Progress in access to primary school has been made since 2001, particularly for girls. Despite tremendous increases in gross school enrollment, Afghanistan's educational indicators are still among the lowest in the world, and significant gender and geographical disparities persist. The educational system faces significant constraints, including a shortage of teachers and equipment. Notably, girls' enrollment in school has made little progress. The estimated literacy rate for girls (fifteen to twenty-four years old) was 32 percent in 1993. A 2010–2011 UNICEF multi-indicators cluster survey (MICS) established the literacy rate at 22.2 percent (Central Statistics Organization and UNICEF, 2013).

However, findings from recent studies argue that blanket numbers hide the more complex question of vulnerability and inequality. Girls, as well as children with disabilities, are still disproportionately absent from the learning environment. Violence, threats, and intimidation against teachers and pupils by opponents of girls' education help explain the lower participation of girls, particularly in Pashtun-dominated areas. Yet, when enrolled, because of school proximity to their home, girls are more successful than boys in learning and score better in tests. This, in turn, suggests that, if current trends persist, instead of constituting a pathway toward fighting poverty and contributing to a peaceful society, education systems may just become another space where social exclusion processes are perpetuated. A public expenditure tracking study (PETS) of the education sector showed that the nature of issues faced need to be analyzed according to the

Table 17.1. Access to school among disabled girls and boys participating in the Afghan with Disabilities Community Based Rehabilitation Program of the Swedish Committee for Afghanistan (2013).

	Boys	Girls
Not literate	354	223
Literate without formal schooling	14	5
No school	368	228
Primary education not complete	66	25
Primary school	10	6
Middle school	6	1
Secondary school	2	1
Post-secondary school	0	0
Total attended/attending school	84	33
Total children, ages six to fifteen	452	261
Proportion who attended school	18.58	12.64

SOURCE: Authors study.

geographic, security, and political specificities of various provinces (Bamiyan, Balkh, and Laghman in the study) (Bakhshi 2011).

Furthermore, recent research conducted by the authors in thirteen provinces of Afghanistan shows that children with disabilities, who are particularly vulnerable and at risk of social exclusion, are not accessing school (table 17.1). These results show no improvement since our previous research in 2005.

Poverty: Simplistic Analyses of Complex Realities

One of the greatest challenges facing the government today is the eradication of extreme poverty. Inequality, vulnerability, and poverty continue to be exacerbated by reoccurring natural disasters, chronic instability, weak governance and democracy, corruption, and the intensification of violence in the absence of a clear political agenda of the United Nations and the US-led military coalition. Afghanistan remains the poorest country in the world outside Sub-Saharan Africa. Life expectancy is among the lowest in the world at 60 years, and infant and maternal mortality rates are among the highest globally at 257 per 1,000 births and 1,291 per 100,000 live births, respectively (Viswanathan et al., 2010; Britten, 2017). Gross national income was $528 per capita in 2011. Recently, poverty actually increased and 39.1 percent - 43.6 percent in rural areas and 26 percent in urban areas - of the population lived below the poverty line in 2014. Despite political commitment, growing insecurity, reduction in foreign military presence and international aid have impaired economic growth (World Bank 2017).

The World Bank estimates that 8 percent economic growth per year is required to employ all Afghan labor force, while the rate was of 1.5 percent in 2015. To overcome poverty, the country has been relying essentially on overseas assistance: 90 percent of all public spending is still financed by international aid (Waldman 2008). The literature has reported that international aid money has been wasted and international assistance ineffective, as approximately 40 percent of funding has been returned back to donor countries in the form of corporate profits or remuneration. Between 2002 and 2012, the United States has spent $100 billion in nonmilitary funds for very limited results in terms of delivering basic services, providing good governance, and guaranteeing human security (Brinkley 2013; ICG 2016). Furthermore, donors have provided only a little more than half of the aid pledged, and as a result, there are shortfalls in the funding for poverty reduction. As a consequence, a vast proportion of aid has failed to reach the poorest people (Waldman 2008). Without significant improvements in aid effectiveness, poverty reduction efforts will fail to yield sustainable results. The recently observed trend is toward a reduction in aid: between 2011 and 2013 aid funding for Afghanistan was reduced by 43 percent, from $894 million to $508 million. The most disturbing fact is that the majority of the population has poorly benefited from recent reconstruction and development efforts (Stockton 2002; Donini 2007; Trani et al. 2009; International Crisis Group 2016; Brinkley 2013). More than one in three Afghans still live in extreme poverty, which is, above all, a travesty of social justice (World Bank, 2017). Experts revealed that unemployment and poverty are source of further grievance against the Government of National Unity and a major driver of conflict (ICG, 2016). The link between the poverty of nations and the future threat of civil war is well documented. It has been argued that poverty reduction is also a necessary precondition for the creation of a secure and stable country (DFID, 2010). The 2015 edition of *Afghanistan in 2015* published by the Asia Foundation (2015) highlights Afghans' continuing dissatisfaction with the progress made. Fifty-seven percent of Afghans think that the country is heading in the wrong direction (compared to 40 percent in 2014 and 21 percent in 2006). The main reasons cited to explain this unfavorable assessment are the following: insecurity (45 percent), unemployment (25 percent), corruption (13 percent), bad economy (12 percent), and bad government (11 percent). Afghans have increasingly considered unemployment to be a reason for their difficulties since 2007. At the local level, problems identified included lack of infrastructure and basic services, particularly electricity (20.5 percent), roads (17.8 percent), drinking water (16.8 percent), education (11 percent), and paucity of healthcare facilities (9.6 percent). Unemployment (31.2 percent) and insecurity (22 percent) are also mentioned as major problems. Despite the criticism of this annual round of surveys, particularly their poor design, findings reveal that Afghan's perception of their country has not improved drastically since 2006.

Understanding poverty is considerably constrained by the paucity of available data. The Afghanistan Living Conditions Survey (2016/17) (CSO, 2017) is the most recent sources of information. According to the Afghanistan Living Conditions Survey, the unemployment rate rose from 9.3 per cent in 2011-12 to 19.4 per cent in 2017, but 34.3 percent if under-employment is included (not gainfully employed population). Half of women are not gainfully employed. In 2014, 33% of Afghans were reporting chronic and transitory food insecurity. Burning solid fuels for cooking (76 percent) and heating (95 percent) remains the rule despite its negative impact on health. Yet, some progress has been made. Furthermore, the report documented that only 35.4 percent of the population are literate (24% in 2007; 20.3 percent females, 50.1 percent males), 56.4 percent of child deliveries are attended by a skilled birth attendant (24% in 2007), 64% percent of people have access to safe drinking water (30% in 2007), 51% percent have access to adequate sanitation (10% in 2007), 90 percent have access to electricity (20% in 2007). The World bank recent report indicates that the key drivers of poverty remain vulnerability to shocks (including natural disasters and conflict). Other studies show the impact of winterization and seasonality, ineffective institutions and corruption, unemployment, forced marriage, high levels for expenditures on health, and ethnic, political, religious, and tribal prejudices (Brinkley, 2013, Dossa, 2013, Trani, 2017). Poverty is often described in terms of limited or no access to basic services and assets. Poverty was further understood in terms of insecurity, powerlessness, helplessness, inadequate education, lack of respect from others, and marginalization from services (Kabeer & Khan, 2014). Women often refer in interview to poverty as the inability to participate actively or be visible in everyday life (Schutte, 2014).

Exploring Multidimensional Poverty: Inequality in Development Progress

Methodology

Traditionally, poverty is defined through one indicator of household consumption or income. The poverty line in Afghanistan is based on the cost of basic needs (CBN) approach, which assembles a basket of goods and services that are deemed necessary to meet a minimum standard of living. Those falling short of the poverty line are identified as poor. The poverty line consists of (1) the food poverty line and (2) an allowance for basic nonfood needs. The food component is defined by caloric intake. Aggregating expenditure on goods and services composes the nonfood items.

This approach has been criticized by Amartya Sen (1976), who argued that it does not take into account the relative situation of the poor: individuals defined as poor remain poor even if they benefit from an increase in income as long as they remain below the poverty line. Sen's (1976) seminal work aiming at a multidimensional measure of poverty has addressed the issue of identifying the poor and has aggregated their characteristics in a unique index. The multidimensional approach draws on Sen's capability approach and focuses on various factors that impede an individual's well-being. Sen gives preeminence to the individual's well-being, which does not only depend on income but on capabilities and agency, the individual freedom to achieve goals the person values. Poverty, defined as deprivation of capabilities, refers to the absence of choice for a person to lead a life that she values. Multidimensional poverty measurement and analysis enables a greater understanding of how the inclusion of dimensions other than income can modify the appraisal of poverty. Multidimensional measures provide an accurate, easy to comprehend, and in-depth, and yet integrated, view of poverty that allows variation over time to be identified. Furthermore, multidimensional measures enable researchers to view not only how many deprivations people experience at the same time but also how these deprivations overlap.

Our approach is based on the method used to identify the poor called the "dual cutoff." This method involves two different forms of cutoffs, one pertaining to each single dimension of deprivation and the other relating to crosscutting dimensions. It also comprises a series of desirable properties including "decomposability," that allows overall poverty to be calculated as a weighted average of subgroups' poverty levels, and "dimensional monotonicity," which allows to capture the effect of an increase in experienced deprivations.

We identified fourteen dimensions of poverty based on discussion with experts in Afghanistan (table 17.2). We then tested the relevance of these dimensions through focus group discussions with Afghans.

The present chapter analyses the multidimensional poverty of 1544 individual respondents to a national survey carried out in 2005 with people from fifteen to sixty-five years old (table 17.3).

Vulnerable Groups Are Multidimensionally Poorer

Despite widespread poverty, the circumstances of Afghans vary considerably depending on their vulnerability status, as is shown below. Unfortunately, people with disabilities are often the poorest of the poor.

The first column in table 17.4 reports the second cutoff (k) followed by the multidimensional headcount ratio of poverty (H), the average deprivation share across the poor (A), and the adjusted headcount ratio of poverty (Mo) for different cutoffs across dimensions (k=1–14). Results show that all adults are deprived in one dimension and, for k=1, they are deprived, on average, in 5.87 dimensions, as indicated by (A). Very few people are deprived in twelve dimensions and no one is deprived in thirteen or more dimensions.

To be considered multidimensionally poor, an aggregate cutoff point is required. This cutoff point (k) serves as the poverty line. The union and intersection identification methods are commonly used by researchers although they are of

Table 17.2. Dimensions, indicators, and cutoffs for analysis.

Dimension	Questions	Cutoff
1. Health status	How often does your household get enough to eat? (always enough; sometimes not enough; frequently not enough; always not enough; always enough but with poor quality)	Frequently not enough Always not enough
2. Access to healthcare	How long does it take to get to the closest available health care facility?	More than thirty minutes
3. Education	What kind of education did you receive or are you receiving?	No education
4. Employment	Do you have any income-generating activities inside the house? Do you currently have work (regular or irregular)? Did you work or have a job for at least one hour per day during the last week? Did you work or have a job for at least one day during the month?	No to all questions
5. Material deprivation	Does any member of your household own any of the following? (radio, tape recorder; television; pressure cooker; oven, hotplate; refrigerator; bukhari; bicycle; motorbike; car; tractor; generator; kerosene lamp; sewing machine; house or apartment	Less than 6 assets If family own a tractor or a car, they are automatically classified as nondeprived
6. Living standards	How many people per room are there in your household?	More than three people per room
7. Access to clean water	What are the main sources of drinking water for your household? (piped into residence, compound, or plot; public tap or tap in the neighborhood; ground water; hand pump in residence, compound, or plot; public hand pump;	Well in residence, compound, or plot; covered well, open well and kariz; spring; river or stream; pond or lake; still water; rain water; tanker or truck

	well in residence, compound, or plot; covered well; open well and kariz; spring; river or stream; pond or lake; still water: dam; rain water; tanker or truck.	
8. Access to sanitation	What kind of toilet facility does your household have? (private flush inside, private flush outside, shared flush, traditional pit, open backed, open defecation field outside the house	Open backed Open defecation field outside house
9. Air quality	What is mainly used in your household for cooking? (Gas, stove with kerosene or petrol, firewood, dung, charcoal, electricity)	Charcoal, dung, firewood
10. Social participation	Did you take part in any ceremony during the past years?	No
11. Care	Who takes care of you in everyday life?	No one
12. Subjective well-being	Choose three adjectives from a list of ten. Different lists for male and female. Males disappointed; normal; happy; useless; brave; willing; proud; oppressed; poor; deprived Females tactful; independent; poor; normal; distrusting; unworthy; hopeful; excluded; strong; weak	Rather negative Very negative (when one to three negative adjectives are selected).
13. Psychological well-being	Mental distress is identified by a twenty-two-items tool, which takes into account Afghan culture and beliefs. The twenty-two items incorporate four conceptual dimensions of mental distress: social interaction difficulties,	Severe distress (if the respondent gave an answer of "yes" to more than eleven items.

(continued)

Table 17.2. Dimensions, indicators, and cutoffs for analysis *(continued)*.

Dimension	Questions	Cutoff
	learning difficulties, behavioral disorders, and anxiety and depression.	
14. Physical safety	Male Has anyone ever ill-treated you? Female Has anyone ill-treated you in the house? Has anyone ill-treated you outside in the street or the bazaar?	Yes

Table 17.3. Distribution of respondents according to disability status.

	n	%
Nondisabled	803	57.36
Physical	238	17.00
Sensory	114	8.14
Mental and associated	245	17.50

little use to policy makers. The union method considers a person multidimensionally poor if she is deprived on at least one dimension. Following this approach, all adults would be considered multidimensionally poor in Afghanistan. On the other hand, the intersection approach considers a person multidimensionally poor if they are deprived in all dimensions, although no adults are deprived in all fourteen dimensions. In order to aid policy makers and identify and target the poor more effectively, a cutoff which lies between these two extremes would be more appropriate. It is important to note that the chosen cutoff depends on the aim of the exercise.

Table 17.4 shows that if k=6, the level of poverty is very high at 60.9 percent of the total population, and on average, adults are deprived in 7.1 dimensions. If k=7, 40.2 percent of the adult population is poor, and, on average, they are deprived in 7.6 dimensions. However, targeting 40 percent of the population maybe overly ambitious given current shortfalls in aid. When k=8, 17 percent of the population is identified as poor, and, on average, adults are deprived in 8.5 dimensions. This cutoff is deemed the most appropriate, as when the cutoff is set at k=9, too few adults are identified as poor (6.8 percent) which would be of little use to policy makers. To feasibly target the poorest of the poor, a cutoff of k=8 has therefore been selected for the remaining analysis.

Table 17.4. Level (H), depth (A) and breadth (Mo) of poverty for all cutoffs.

dimensional cuttoff k (k=14)	Level H (%)	Depth A	Breadth Mo = A x H
1	99.8	0.419	0.418
2	98.5	0.423	0.417
3	95.1	0.434	0.413
4	89.2	0.448	0.400
5	75.9	0.476	0.361
6	60.9	0.505	0.308
7	40.2	0.545	0.219
8	17.0	0.607	0.103
9	6.8	0.662	0.045
10	1.9	0.715	0.014
11	0.1	0.791	0.001
12	0.0	0.857	0.000
13	0.0	NA	0.000
14	0.0	NA	0.000

Note: k: number of dimensions—Nobody is poor in twelve dimensions or more; H, headcount ratio; A: the average deprivation share across the poor (A) and; Mo the adjusted headcount ratio.

The following table (table 17.5) illustrates the adjusted headcount ratio (Mo) according to gender, disability, cause and type of disability, location, and ethnicity for a cutoff of k=8. Results show that some groups face a higher intensity of multidimensional poverty than others: females are more deprived than males. Women are more visible than ever before; however, discriminatory practices, domestic violence, and early forced marriages, all fueled by poverty, persist. It is reported that at least one in three women are physically beaten, forced into sex, or otherwise abused (Global Rights 2008). In response to these conditions, an increasing number of self-immolation cases have been recorded (Human Rights Watch, 2009).

A higher proportion of Afghans with mental impairment are deprived in eight dimensions compared to Afghans with physical or sensory disabilities and nondisabled Afghans. Similarly, the adjusted headcount ratio is higher for *ma'yub* (physically impaired) compared to *ma'lul* (sensory or mentally impaired, further discussed below); those living in rural areas more than those living in urban areas; and Uzbek and Hazara more than Pashtun and Tajik overall. Social and cultural norms continue to exclude groups of individuals from integrating into social and economic activities. In Afghanistan, the most vulnerable groups include: persons with disabilities, particularly women and children disabled at birth or people having a learning, intellectual, or mental disability. It has been shown elsewhere

Table 17.5. Adjusted headcount ratio (Mo) according to gender, disability, cause and type of disability, location, and ethnicity for a cutoff of k=8.

Male	Female	Disabled persons	Nondisabled persons	Physical disability	Sensory disability	Mental disability	Disabled with an identified cause	Disabled at birth	Urban	Rural	Pashto	Tajik	Uzbek	Hazara	Minority groups
0.070	0.139	0.243	0.097	0.171	0.288	0.338	0.223	0.270	0.048	0.133	0.107	0.085	0.147	0.113	0.090

Table 17.6. Adjusted headcount ratio (Mo) according to gender and types and causes of disability for a cutoff of k=8.

	Nondisabled persons	Physical disability	Sensory disability	Mental disability	Disabled with an identified cause	Disabled at birth
Male	.064	.158	.196	.309	.186	.243
Female	.132	.211	.236	.357	.305	.293

that these groups experience higher levels of poverty, as they are excluded and, therefore, are often denied access to basic services and resources (Trani, 2010, 2016). Public stigma is particularly high for those called *Dewana*, persons with various types of mental condition, explaining high multidimensional poverty linked to social exclusion. This difference in perception, based on the cause of disability, explains why, at the end of the war with the Soviet Union, people disabled from war benefited from advantages provided by the state that were refused to those disabled at birth or those having learning disabilities or mental illness. Miles (1990) explains that the allocation of financial and human resources was, at the time, already a political process in which the influence of the mujahideen was considerable.

Table 17.6 shows that the situation is systematically worse for women from these vulnerable groups, whatever the type or the cause of disability. Males and, particularly, females with mental disabilities experience a greater intensity of poverty. We argue that this is an original finding that demonstrates that women with disabilities are always multidimensionally poorer than men with disabilities, even if they are *ma'lul*—disabled due to an identified cause. In other words, women with disabilities do not benefit on a par with men with disabilities in terms of social recognition and inclusion, even when there is a clear cause explaining their disability. This is in line with previous research documenting that women with disabilities, in particular, are poor and discriminated against.

Thousands of Afghans have been, and continue to be, disabled by war and conflict, and in addition, many more have acquired impairments from birth due to inadequate health services, widespread disease, and malnutrition. In some cases, people with disabilities are considered to bring shame on the family. Our results show that people with disabilities are more or less marginalized depending on the type of disability and how it is perceived. *Ma'lul* and *ma'yub* are common terms used in Afghanistan to describe disability: *ma'lul* often refers to those disabled by an accident or other identifiable cause and *ma'yub* generally refers to those disabled by birth. In most instances these terms may be used interchangeably. *Ma'yub* also refers to individuals who do not function well and to those with unexplained or unclear causes. *Dewana* which refers to people with mental and intellectual disabilities are particularly stigmatized, as they are considered incurable, however individuals wounded by war are viewed in a positive light, as they are considered martyrs who fought for their country. How disability is perceived affects family status, marriage, employment, and educational and social opportunities. In Afghan culture, responsibilities widely differ for men and women. Men are the breadwinners and women are confined to the roles of daughter, sister, mother, and wife. Motherhood in Afghan culture is extremely valued and is the basis for a woman's self-worth. Women with disabilities experience a double dose of exclusion, as they are perceived as reproductively challenged and face considerable difficulties in marriage.

The Urgent Need to Look at the Knowledge and Devise Truly Evidence-Based Policies

So where do we go from here? The answer to this question is extremely complex. However, in view of the daunting challenges that the country will face in the post-2014 years, we present the idea that the main task will be to rebuild the eroded trust that the population has lost in development efforts. The ways and means to achieve this can be devised by looking more closely at existing knowledge about the country and use it to build accountability mechanisms.

Using Knowledge for Evidence-Based Policy and Accountability: The Process

It might seem cliché to reiterate this much-used phrase—*evidence-based policy and accountability*—that is made up of some of development workers' most cherished buzzwords. We argue strongly that this represents a strong impetus toward regaining some of the trust that has been lost due to ignorance and the arrogance of "experts" doing "development." Why the various actors have failed to maintain trust with the Afghans, to date, despite the existence of number of studies (large-scale surveys or qualitative analyses), reflects a certain level of disconnect between the various actors as well as a serious lack of coordination. This disconnect is a result of the nature of development efforts from the very onset that have been based on various implementation actors competing for funds from donors who have defined their own priorities. Research (large-scale surveys or more targeted analyses) has been viewed as having the descriptive role of documenting processes and the achievements and failures of programs and policies. The dual use of knowledge in order to provide evidence for policy as well as to build accountability mechanisms has not been promoted in practice by donors, despite their claims. One of the examples of this is the set of social policies that have been created to tackle the issues related to disability; they have been constructed more in line with political considerations than with the aim of tackling the problems of the most vulnerable populations. Finally, donors did not sufficiently fund the bottom-up accountability mechanisms that were required to build momentum for this specific use of knowledge. However, it is clear that this need to stress synergies between evidence and policy orientation and decisions as well as the imperative to better use evidence as a tool for strengthening bottom-up accountability mechanisms, in turn, requires an in-depth questioning of programmatic strategies and policy orientations and also their ability to not merely understand the specificities of the Afghan context but also to make these a central tenet of all initiatives that claim to help the most vulnerable groups.

Resistance to Reconciliation between Traditional Belief Systems and Proposals for New Mechanisms of Good Governance

Aarya Nijat states, "The international decision-making machinery has been characterized by a serious lack of coordination and is a prime example of an operationally dysfunctional situation that has become destructive overtime due to deeper problems that are often unacknowledged" (2014, 11). The author attributed failures of programs to two opposing views of development—the American and the European—that have divergent goals, funding levels, and implementation strategies. However, we argue that neither of these two worldviews have inherently understood the requirement to reconcile all levels of decisions and implementation with "traditional" views and thus repair the perceived disconnect between "foreign" intervention and everyday realities. One of the central components of this process of bridging the gap is to understand the deeply collective nature of life and interactions in Afghanistan. At the national level, authors have stated that it is urgent to understand "the hybridity—of formal and informal governance institutions—of the Afghan political order had to be at the heart of any governance reform intervention" (10). We argue that this hybridity needs to be incorporated into all development interventions by thinking of means and ways to pursue respect of individual rights through initiatives that do not isolate the person from the collective. To a large extent, donors, development actors, and experts are resistant to this pursuit. Donor priorities and assessment measures are, first and foremost, focused on individual perspectives. However, studies have shown (Trani et al. 2011) that aspirations and priorities are often constructed in the collective realm. This inability to grasp questions of social identity and interactions as well as local specificities, or their disregard, has largely contributed to the distrust that Afghans hold toward international intervention and will hinder the sustainability of programs that are currently implemented.

Thinking of Policies for the Most Destitute Groups in Terms of Multidimensional Vulnerability

The evidence that we have discussed in this chapter argues for a better understanding of the questions pertaining to poverty and vulnerability. Poverty has very often been viewed in terms of certain predominant factors (income and nutrition, primarily). The assessment of poverty has followed suit by measuring indicators in isolation without unifying frameworks for analysis of the process in its complexity. Similarly, understanding what constitutes the vulnerability of the person has also been viewed in silos by labeling the so-called vulnerable groups through the identification of one attribute, be it disability, women, Internally Displaced Persons, or some other attribute. The National Vulnerability Programme (NVP), implemented in 2005 in Afghanistan, was based on this siloed view and was unable to achieve any tangible impact during its year of existence. This perception of groups at risk, as isolated from others and unifiable under an arbitrarily chosen characteristic, cannot form the basis for effective policies and programs as it denies the inherent multidimensional nature of elements that constitute the vulnerability of a person or collective. We strongly argue that the policy network needs to be reflective of this. Finally, focusing on the multiple facets of vulnerability will also allow development actors to move beyond blanket policies that deal with large groups of persons and are unsuccessful, since these blanket policies have failed to decipher the hierarchy created by the underlying factors of vulnerability. This has been evident in the way disability concerns have been addressed in Afghanistan. The government body that deals with issues linked to disability as well as number of programs have focused primarily on concerns of the physically disabled (due to war or landmines) have largely ignored the situation and needs of those who are at the other end of the hierarchy: girls living with intellectual and mental disabilities. The policies that are being implemented for the promotion of women by the Ministry of Women's Affairs have not achieved the goals that were set. In the pursuit of laudable goals of equality, policies that are based solely on a single aspect of what constitutes the vulnerability of a person to adverse events are doomed to be inefficient as they analyze the situation through a unifocal lens. As a result, the hierarchy is maintained under a certain label such as *women* or *persons with disabilities* and the benefits of the initiatives are hijacked by the socially dominant, and accepted sections, such as men with physical disabilities. Finally, the success and achievements of policies that aim to be equitable need to be gauged by focusing on the most destitute subgroups as a benchmark.

Conclusions and Considerations

In this chapter, we have attempted to make a strong case for understanding the dynamics that have led to the widespread mistrust that Afghans have for the various interventions led by the international community. Since 2002, reconstruction and development efforts have been inadequate to improve the lives of millions of Afghans. Progress has failed to live up to the expectations of the population.

As the pullout of foreign troops is now a reality, the various actors in development efforts are revising various existing strategies as well as trying to ensure that programs become sustainable by relying on local ownership. The dominant discourse blames the lack of efficiency of development efforts on rampant corruption as well as on an increase in insecurity and insurgencies. We have argued that the various decision makers and donors need to reflect on the way development has been planned for Afghanistan and how it has consistently failed to create resonance with local specificities and cultural and social norms. By using the evidence from various studies carried out over the past years, it would be timely to now identify opportunities that take into account not just individual perspectives but also collective perspectives, and tailor policies to target the needs of the most vulnerable. As a result, we argue for a shift in the current approach to the development effort.

Some of the results presented in the present chapter indicate that greater attention needs to be directed towards women and people with disabilities. However, how can social integration and empowerment be promoted when segregation is the norm? Gender and power relations continue to restrict women's mobility, impeding access to healthcare and economic and social opportunities. Discriminatory attitudes persist toward Afghans disabled at birth due to a lack of awareness and knowledge, which significantly impacts psychological and subjective well-being. These are the most crucial issues to tackle, and policy makers face a difficult challenge here. Increasing knowledge and awareness is a fundamental step in challenging attitudes and improving access. The use of communication tools via the media has increased significantly and might constitute a solution in the current context of violence, which limits aid workers' movements. It is one of the most powerful and feasible ways to sensitize the population, making those who are most excluded more visible. Imposing views from outside communities has proven ineffective in Afghanistan, and conservative groups argue for cultural relativism. Challenging beliefs and improving access to services must involve religious and community leaders as they are highly influential and powerful actors.

In Afghanistan, poverty reduction policies and programs continue to be based on narrow understandings of poverty. In order to drive reconstruction and development efforts, we suggest the adoption of a multidimensional approach to poverty. To successfully alleviate poverty, it must not be assumed that all social groups face the same hurdle. Policy makers must take into account social norms, cultural values, and beliefs that strongly influence who gets access to what and when. Furthermore, it is crucial that public policies became truly participatory. There is a huge gap between the way foreigners perceive Afghans' situation and the reality of their lived experience.

Afghanistan is experiencing high levels of population growth, which will place even more pressure on existing resources and services in the near future. Substantial shortfalls in aid continue to hinder sustainable poverty reduction programs. It is imperative that donors' interest be renewed and that pledges are recommitted. Expectations must be realistic in Afghanistan and priorities have to be made. The literature paints a complex picture describing multiple agencies with contradictory agendas. Thus, coordinating efforts, reinforcing effective accountability mechanisms, and improving financial management is paramount in order to track expenditures and identify problems. Whether this is feasible in the new context where the international military force is departed and a new president, just elected, is struggling to establish his authority remains to be verified.

PARUL BAKHSHI is assistant professor of occupational therapy and surgery at Washington University in St. Louis. She is coauthor with Jean-Francois Trani of *Towards Inclusion and Equality in Education? From Assumptions to Facts.*

JEAN-FRANCOIS TRANI is associate professor at the Brown School, Washington University in St. Louis. He is coauthor with Parul Bakhshi of *Towards Inclusion and Equality in Education? From Assumptions to Facts.*

Bibliography

Alkire, Sabina, and James Foster. 2011a. "Counting and Multidimensional Poverty Measurement." *Journal of Public Economics* 95 (7–8): 476–87.
Alonge, O., S. Gupta, C. Engineer, A. S. Salehi, and D. H. Peters. 2015. "Assessing the Pro-Poor Effect of Different Contracting Schemes for Health Services on Health Facilities in Rural Afghanistan." *Health Policy and Planning* 30 (10): 1229–42.
———. 2011b. "Understandings and Misunderstandings of Multidimensional Poverty Measurement." *Journal of Economic Inequality* 9 (2): 289–314.
Arar, Nedal H., Polly H. Noel, Luci Leykum, John E. Zeber, Raquel Romero, and Michael L. Parchman. 2011. "Implementing Quality Improvement in Small, Autonomous Primary Care Practices: Implications for the Patient-Centred Medical Home." *Quality in Primary Care* 19 (5): 289–300.
Azarbaijani-Moghaddam, Sippi, Mirweis Wardak, Idrees Zaman, and Annabel Taylor. 2008. *Afghan Hearts, Afghan Minds: Exploring Afghan Perceptions of Civil-Military Relations.* London: European Interagency Security Forum.
Bakhshi, Parul. 2011. *Public Expenditure Tracking Study.* Kabul: ALTAI.
Bakhshi, Parul, and Jean-Francois Trani. 2006. *Towards Inclusion and Equality in Education? From Assumptions to Facts.* Lyon: Handicap International.
———. 2011. "A Gender Analysis of Disability, Vulnerability and Empowerment in Afghanistan." In *Development Efforts in Afghanistan: Is There a Will and a Way? The Case of Disability and Vulnerability,* ed. Jean-Francois Trani, 123–60. Ethique Economique. Paris: L'Harmattan.
Beath, Andrew, Fotini Christia, and Ruben Enikolopov. 2013. *Randomized Impact Evaluation of Afghanistan's National Solidarity Programme: Final Report.* Washington, DC: World Bank.
Blankenship, Erin. 2014. *Delivering Aid in Contested Spaces: Afghanistan.* Oxfam America Research Backgrounder Series. Washington, DC: Oxfam America.
Bourguignon, François, and Satya R. Chakravarty. 2003. "The Measurement of Multidimensional Poverty." *Journal of Economic Inequality* 1 (1): 25–49.
Boyce, William, Shoba Raja, Rima G. Patranabish, Truelove Bekoe, Dominic Deme-der, and Owen Gallupe. 2009. "Occupation, Poverty and Mental Health Improvement in Ghana." *ALTER: European Journal of Disability Research* 3 (3): 233–44.
Brinkley, J. 2013. "Money Pit: The Monstrous Failure of Us Aid to Afghanistan." *Worlds Affairs.*

Britten, N. 1998. "Psychiatry, Stigma, and Resistance." *British Medical Journal* 317 (7164): 963–64.
Britten, Stewart. 2017. "Maternal Mortality in Afghanistan: Setting Achievable Targets." *The Lancet* 389 (10083): 1960–62.
Burde, Dana, and Leigh L. Linden. 2013. "Bringing Education to Afghan Girls: A Randomized Controlled Trial of Village-Based Schools." *American Economic Journal: Applied Economics* 5 (3): 27–40.
Central Statistics Organization. 2017. *Afghanistan - Living Conditions Survey 2016-2017. Mid Terms Results Highlights*. Kabul: Islamic Republic of Afghanistan.
Central Statistics Organization, and UNICEF. 2012. *Afghanistan Multiple Indicator Cluster Survey 2010-2011: Final Report*. Kabul: Central Statistics Organization and UNICEF.
Central Statistics Organization, and the World Bank. 2010. *Setting the Official Poverty Line for Afghanistan: Technical Report*. Accessed July 2, 2011. http://cso.gov.af/Content/Media/Documents/CSO-WB_Tech-Report-Pov_v4(2)1162011121045651553325325.pdf.
Cerveau, Térésa. "Deconstructing Myths; Facing Reality: Understanding Social Representations of Disability in Afghanistan." 2011. In *Development Efforts in Afghanistan: Is There a Will and a Way? The Case of Disability and Vulnerability*, ed. Jean-Francois Trani, 103–122. Ethique Economique. Paris: L'Harmattan.
Commission on Macroeconomics and Health. 2001. *Macroeconomics and Health: Investing in Health for Economic Development*. Geneva: World Health Organization.
D'Souza, Anna, and Dean Jolliffe. 2012. "Rising Food Prices and Coping Strategies: Household-Level Evidence from Afghanistan." *Journal of Development Studies* 48 (2): 282–99.
Department for International Development. 2010. "The Politics of Poverty: Elites, Citizens and States. Findings from Ten Years of Dfid-Funded Research on Governance and Fragile States 2001–2010." 247. London.
Donini, A. 2007. "Local Perceptions of Assistance to Afghanistan." *International Peacekeeping* 14 (1): 158–72.
Dossa, P. 2013. "Structural Violence in Afghanistan: Gendered Memory, Narratives, and Food." *Medical Anthropology: Cross Cultural Studies in Health and Illness* 32 (5): 433–47.
Dupree, Nancy H. 1992. "Afghanistan: Women, Society and Development." *Journal of Developing Societies* 8: 30–43.
———. 2011. "The Historical and Cultural Context of Disability in Afghanistan." In *Development Effort in Afghanistan: Is There a Will and a Way? The Case of Disability and Vulnerability*, ed. Jean-Francois Trani, 47–74. Ethique Economique. Paris: L'Harmattan.
Edward, A., B. Kumar, F. Kakar, A. S. Salehi, G. Burnham, and D. H. Peters. 2011. "Configuring Balanced Scorecards for Measuring Health System Performance: Evidence from 5 Years' Evaluation in Afghanistan." *PLoS Medicine* 8 (7): x-x.
Ghani, Ashraf. 1990. "Impact of Foreign Aid on Relations between State and Society: Some Lessons from the Past and Some Thoughts on the Future." Paper presented at the Seminar on Social and Cultural Prospects of Afghanistan, Peshawar, Pakistan, March 20–21.
Ghobadi, Negar, Johannes Koettl, and Renos Vakis. 2005. *Moving out of Poverty: Migration Insights from Rural Afghanistan*. Kabul: Afghanistan Research and Evaluation Unit.

Ghobarah, Hazem A., Paul Huth, and Bruce Russett. 2004. "The Post-War Public Health Effects of Civil Conflict." *Social Science and Medicine* 59 (4): 869–84.

Global Rights. 2008. "Living with Violence: A National Report on Domestic Abuse in Afghanistan." 60.

Goodhand, Jonathan, and Mark Sedra. 2010. "Who Owns the Peace? Aid, Reconstruction, and Peacebuilding in Afghanistan." *Disasters* 34 (S1): S78–S102.

Hogg, Richard, Claudia Nassif, Camilo Gomez Osorio, William Byrd, and Andrew Beath. 2013. "Afghanistan in Transition: Looking Beyond 2014." Stockholm: Stockholm International Peace Research Institute.

Hogg, Richard, Claudia Nassif, Camilo Gomez Osorio, William Byrd, and Andrew Beath. 2013. *Afghanistan in Transition: Looking Beyond 2014*. Washington, DC: World Bank.

Human Rights Watch. 2009. "Afghanistan: Ending Child Marriage and Domestic Violence." 15. Kabul: Human Rights Watch.

International Crisis Group. "The Economic Disaster Behind Afghanistan's Mounting Human Crisis." https://www.crisisgroup.org/asia/south-asia/afghanistan/economic-disaster -behind-afghanistan-s-mounting-human-crisis.

International Monetary Fund. 2008. *Islamic Republic of Afghanistan: Poverty Reduction Strategy Paper*. Washington, DC: International Monetary Fund.

———. 2014. *Islamic Republic of Afghanistan: National Development Strategy. Executive Summary 1387–1391*. Kabul: International Monetary Fund.

Islamic Relief of Afghanistan. 2014. *Afghanistan in Limbo: New Aid Priorities and the Funding Crisis Putting Future Progress at Risk*. Kabul: Islamic Relief of Afghanistan.

Kabeer, N., and A. Khan. 2014. "Cultural Values or Universal Rights? Women's Narratives of Compliance and Contestation in Urban Afghanistan." *Feminist Economics* 20 (3): 1–24.

Kantor, Paul, and Adam Pain. 2010. *Poverty in Afghan Policy: Enhancing Solutions through Better Defining the Problem*. Briefing Paper Series. Kabul: Afghan Research and Evaluation Unit.

Kemeny, Cat. 2012. "Sustainable Health Care, Afghan Style." *Medicine, Conflict and Survival* 28 (2): 133–39.

Masannat, G. S. 1969. "Development and Diplomacy in Afghanistan." *Journal of Asian and African Studies* 4 (1): 51–60.

Michael, Markus, Enrico Pavignani, and Peter S. Hill. 2013. "Too Good to Be True? An Assessment of Health System Progress in Afghanistan, 2002–2012." *Medicine, Conflict and Survival* 29 (4): 322–45.

Miles, M. 1990. "Disability and Afghan Reconstruction: Some Policy Issues." *Disability, Handicap and Society* 5 (3): 257–67.

Military Expenditure Database. 2014. Stockholm International Peace Research Institute.

Ministry of Education, and Islamic Republic of Afghanistan. 2017. "National Education Strategic Plan (2017–2021)." 120. Kabul: Ministry of Education.

Nijat, Aarya. 2014. *Governance in Afghanistan: An Introduction*. Kabul: Afghanistan Research and Evaluation Unit.

Poole, Lydia. 2011. *Afghanistan. Tracking Major Resources Flows: 2002–2010*. Global Humanitarian Assistance Briefing Paper. Wells, UK: Global Humanitarian Assistance.

Rolland, Cécile. 2011. "'Today I Feel That I'm a Person . . .': Impact of Community Education on Disability Issues in Afghanistan." In *Development Efforts in Afghanistan: Is There*

a Will and a Way? The Case of Disability and Vulnerability, ed. Jean-Francois Trani, 243–68. Ethique Economique. Paris: L'Harmattan.
Saba, Daud S., Omar Zakhilwal, Abi Masefield, and Michael Schoiswohl. 2004. *Security with a Human Face*. Afghanistan National Development Report 2004. Kabul: UNDP Afghanistan.
Saikal, Amin. 2012. "The UN and Afghanistan: Contentions in Democratization and Statebuilding." *International Peacekeeping* 19 (2): 217–34.
Schütte, S. 2014. "Living with Patriarchy and Poverty: Women's Agency and the Spatialities of Gender Relations in Afghanistan." *Gender, Place and Culture* 21 (9): 1176–92.
Sen, Amartya. 1976. "Poverty: An Ordinal Approach to Measurement." *Econometrica* 44 (2): 219–31.
———. 1999. *Development as Freedom*. Oxford: Oxford University Press.
Serour, Gamal I. 2009. "Healthcare Workers and the Brain Drain." *International Journal of Gynecology and Obstetrics* 106 (2): 175–78.
Shalinsky, Audrey. 1989. "Women's Relationships in Traditional Northern Afghanistan." *Central Asian Survey* 8 (1): 117–29.
Skovdal, Morten, S. Emmott, and R. Maranto. 2014. "The Need for Schools in Afghanistan to Be Declared as Zones of Peace and Neutrality: NGOs and Communities Can Work Together to Promote Humane Schools." *Child Abuse and Neglect* 38 (2): 170–79.
Stockton, N. J. 2002. "The Failure of International Humanitarian Action in Afghanistan." *Global Governance* 8 (3): 265–71.
Trani, Jean F., Parul Bakhshi, Ayan A. Noor, and Ashraf Mashkoor. 2009. "Lack of a Will or of a Way? Taking a Capability Approach for Analysing Disability Policy Shortcomings and Ensuring Programme Impact in Afghanistan." *European Journal of Development Research* 21(2): 297–319.
Trani, Jean-Francois, Parul Bakhshi, Ayan A. Noor, Dominique Lopez, and Ashraf Mashkoor. 2010. "Poverty, Vulnerability, and Provision of Healthcare in Afghanistan." *Social Science & Medicine* 70 (11): 1745–55.
Trani, Jean-Francois, Parul Bakhshi, and Cécile Rolland. 2011. "Capabilities, Perception of Well-Being and Development Effort: Some Evidence from Afghanistan." *Oxford Development Studies* 39 (4): 403–26.
Trani, Jean-Francois, Parul Bakhshi, and Anand Nandipati. 2012. "'Delivering' Education; Maintaining Inequality: The Case of Children with Disabilities in Afghanistan." *Cambridge Journal of Education* 42 (3): 345–65.
Trani, Jean-Francois, and Cecile Barbou-des-Courieres. 2012. "Measuring Equity in Disability and Healthcare Utilization in Afghanistan." *Medicine, Conflict and Survival* 28 (3): 219–46.
Trani, Jean-Francois, Ellis Ballard, and J. B. Peña. 2016. "Stigma of Persons with Disabilities in Afghanistan: Examining the Pathways from Stereotyping to Mental Distress." *Social Science and Medicine* 153: 258–65.
Trani, Jean-Francois, Praveen Kumar, Ellis Ballard, and Tarani Chandola. 2017. "Assessment of Progress Towards Universal Health Coverage for People with Disabilities in Afghanistan: A Multilevel Analysis of Repeated Cross-Sectional Surveys." *The Lancet Global Health* 5 (8): e828–e37.
Tsui, Kai-yuen. 2002. "Multidimensional Poverty Indices." *Social Choice and Welfare* 19 (1): 69–93.

Viswanathan, K., S. Becker, P. M. Hansen, D. Kumar, B. Kumar, H. Niayesh, D. H. Peters, and G. Burnham. 2010. "Infant and under-Five Mortality in Afghanistan: Current Estimates and Limitations." *Bulletin of the World Health Organization* 88 (8): 576–83.

United Nations Assistance Mission in Afghanistan. 2017. "Afghanistan Protection of Civilians in Armed Conflict Quarterly Report." 5. Kabul: United Nations Assistance Mission in Afghanistan.

United Nations Development Programme. 1993. *Human Development Report*. New York: United Nations Development Programme.

———. 2013. *The Rise of the South: Human Progress in a Diverse World*. Human Development Report. New York: United Nations Development Programme.

United Nations Development Programme.2017. Human Development Index. http://hdr.undp.org/en/data.

United Nations Office on Drugs and Crime. 2016. "Afghanistan Opium Survey 2016: Cultivation and Production." 65. Kabul: UNODC.

Wagner, A. L., M. Y. Mubarak, L. E. Johnson, J. M. Porth, J. E. Yousif, and M. L. Boulton. 2017. "Trends of Vaccine-Preventable Diseases in Afghanistan from the Disease Early Warning System, 2009±2015." *PLoS ONE* 12 (6): x-x.

Waldman, Matt. 2008. *Falling Short: Aid Effectiveness in Afghanistan*. Kabul: Agency Coordinating Body for Afghan Relief.

World Bank. 2017. "Afghanistan Poverty Status Update: Progress at Risk." 47. Kabul: The World Bank.

Zand, Sogol. 2011. *Describing Life to Outsider (or: The Man Behind the Curtain)*. Research Project on Women's Participation in Development. Technical Report. Kabul: Afghanistan Research and Evaluation Unit.

INDEX

1TV, 156, 158, 169

Aasi, Abdul Qahar, 60–61, 66; *Lalae baraai Malima* (a poem), 70
Academy of Science, Kabul, 184
Abdali, Ahmad Shah, 63, 97n1, 146n1 (*See also* Durrani)
Abdali, Pashtun tribe of Kandahar, 97n1
Abdullah Abdullah, 25, 33, 108, 236, 244, 330; views on Durand Line, 143, 146n10
Abdur Rahman Khan (*See* Rahman, Abdur)
Adab, 53
Adeeb, Shah Waliullah, 244
"Afghan Arabs," 43, 51; influx into Pakistan, 196n2
Afghan: child brides, 323; Communist parties, 51; culture wars via media since 2001, 149–73; elites' views on Durand Line, 142; ethnolinguistic communities, 271; governments, 52; political order, 345; families, 320; Independent Human Rights Commission, 197n3; insurgents, 30; Kirghiz, 239; media landscape, 150; National Police (ANP), 128; Nationalism, 63; refugees in Iran and Pakistan, 31; Star (*TV show*), 162; women, 32; Women's Network (AWN), 206
Afghan-Turk Highschool, 213
Afghan-US Bilateral Security Agreement (BSA), 29
Afghanistan: 38, 48; access to health care, 317–12; Afghanan-e Jawan movement, 291; Baloch adapting to uncertainty in, 272–85; basic health index ranking of, 314; Bilateral Security Agreement with the US, 225; Birth of the Kingdom of, 2–3; border dispute with Pakistan, 140–44; business groups, 93–94; civil war, 58; child birth and social change in, 313, 323–25; conceptualizing institutional change in, 306–07; conspicuous consumption, 93–95; concept of *citizenship, identity and nationality in*, 57; challenges facing, 53; claimed health and educational improvements, 328–29; consequences of war, 90; Constitutions, 254; corruption rate, 31; creation as buffer nation-state, 3; crossroads, 21; culture of pregnancy in, 325; demographic growth, 347; dependency on international aid, 227; destruction of cultural institutions, 151; development challenges in, 332–36; "dictatorship of the alleged number" in, 134; discontinuous change in, 213–25; disillusionment with US and the West, 29; drug production in, 330; dynamics of leadership in, 126–31; economic exchange regionally, 151; educational institutions and the Hazaras in, 262–65; education and inequality in, 333–34; ethnic groups, 57; failure to establish modern state, 3, 5; future of, 33–34; family legal code for, 201; feminist movements in, 206–07; foreign subsidies given to, 1, 77, 93; "Gateway to Asia," 150;

353

GDP percentage spent on security and other sectors, 331; governments' language policy, 57–74; Hazaras in, 253–54, 257; High Peace Council, 247n8; Human Development Index, 332–33; identity politics in, 114–16; impact of Durand Line on state stability, 133–46; interventions and statehood in, 102–18; institutionalization of parties in, 290–308; Independent Election Commission, 145n3; India's military assistance, 30; instrumentalization of religion/Islam in, 8; Intelligences services of, 97n5; "internal colonialism" in, 136; intrusion of outside powers in, 213; Kingdom of, 49; as land bridge, 140; language policies, 61–73, 283; lingua franca of, 8; literacy rate, 64; literature after 2001, 72–73; location as asset and a curse, 22; Living Conditions Survey 2016/17, 336; *madrassa* system in, 38; Marxist Revolution in, 230; maternal mortality in, 314–17, 321–22; media development challenges, 171–72; military ties with former USSR, 4; mining sector resources, 138; motherhood in, 343; National Security Council, 140; *National identity* in, 64; National Solidarity Program, 244, 331; *National Vulnerability Programme implemented*, 345; natural resources value, 22; non-aligned, 5; non-Pashtuns in, 46, 51; nouveau riche's role in, 31; object of global attention since 2002, 6; Pakistan's relations with, 142–45; PDPA killings in, 97n5; poetry and identity, 56; political culture of, 3, 59; political parties of, 291–308; popular piety, 37; post 9/11 economy, 151; Post-Taliban trajectories, 7, 9; poorest country, 334; progress has failed in, 346; *Poverty Reduction Strategy Paper*, 331, 334; reassembling the state in post 2001, 110; reconstruction efforts, 329–30; refugees in Pakistan 142; relations between Kabul and provinces, 1; rise of extremism in, 41–43; Role of Kabul in history of, 77–96; safe haven for terrorists, 2; security sector reforms in, 331; socio-cultural identity in, 9; state institutions, 1, 13; Soviet Invasion and withdrawal from, 2; strategic location, 7; suicide attacks increased against, 330; Taliban rule in, 58; Taliban Pashtun nationalism in, 71; television's role in, 153; *terms of women's empowerment*, 297–303; unjust justice system, 259–62; vicious cycle of violence in, 329; village community midwives, 318; warlords in, 9; warlords' tv in, 156–59; *Wesh Dzalmian*, 292; women's predicaments, 31; women's empowerment, 290–308; writing Hazaras out the history of, 262–63

Afghanistan's National Security Council, 140

Afghanistan Research and Evaluation Unit (AREU), 102

Afshar, Nadir Shah, 97n1

Aghan Khan Development Network (AKDN), building bridges across Amu Darya, 239

Agha Khan Foundation (AKF), help to Badakhshan's Ismaili communities, 235, 239

Agha, Sayed, 166

Ahl al Sunna, 48

Ahli-Hadith, school of, 43

Ahli-Ray', school of rationalism of Khorasani mysticism, 43

Ahmadi Jami, 46

Ahmadzai, Muhammad Ashraf Ghani (See Ghani, Muhammad Ashraf)

Ahmadzai, Muhammad Najibulla (See Ghani, Ashraf, Dr. Muhammad Najibullah, and PDPA)

Akhlaq (etiquette), 44

Akhlaqi Arzakhtuna (ethical values), 188

Al-Ansari, Khwaja Abdullah, 38, 45, 59; *Munajat Nama* of, 60

Al-Aqabah, pledge of, 48

Al-Ash'ari, Imam Abu Al Hassan, 47

Al-Bazdawi, Imam, 47

Ai-Hanafi, Abu Ja'far at-Tahawi, 47

Al-Isharat wa Al-Tanbihat, 53n1

Allah, calls to during contractions, 314

Akbar Bay, incident manufactured by Hamid Karzai, 112

Akbari, Mohammad, tensions with Mazari, 258

Akhlaq, 53
Akhundzada, of Helmand, 112
Al Qaeda: 157, 221; attack against the US, 23–24; in Badakhshan, 240; birth of, 2, 51; global jihadist led by Osama Bin Laden, 6; resurgent, 7; violence in Afghanistan, 152
Alim Khan, Amir of Bukhara, 97n1
Amanullah (Amir/Shah): 80, 92; centralization and Pashtunization program, 4, 63; reforms helping Hazaras, 255; removal of 49; removal of veil (*chadari/purdah*) by, 201
America, 15 (*See* United States)
Amin, Hafizullah, 28, 232, 286n4
American, Empire: of trust, 4; and NATO forces, 217, 219–20. *See also* United States
Amir, 4. *See also* Amanullah, Habibullah and Rahman, Abdur
Amir Bek, 243
Amr bil Ma'roof Wa Nahyi 'Anil-Munkar (commanding the lawful and forbidding the sinful act in Islam), 200, 211n1
Amu Darya, 15, 235, 316
Amu Darya Basin Oil Zone (ADBOZ), 139
Anjuman e Adabye Kabul (Kabul Literary Society), 74n3
An-Nawawi, Imam, 47
Anglo-Afghan Wars, 51, 172n2
Anit-Brtish Provisional Government of India, 97n1
Akhlaqi arzakhtuna (moral values), 186, 188
Arabs, support of mujahideen, 30
Arabian Gulf, 41
Arbab, 124
Arab Spring, 152
Arbaki (local militia forces), 26
Arghandiwal, Abdul Hadi, 114
Ariana Television Network (ATN), 156, 158, 168
Army: Afghan National (ANA); casualties 26; recruits from Badakhshan, 245; retaking Kunduz, 330
Aryan, based identity, 58
Arzakhtuna (good values), 188
Asian Development Bank (ADB), 172n3
Atmar, Hanif, 104
'Attar, 39, 45

Attorney General's Office (AGO), 91
Avicenna. *See* Ibn Sina, Abu Ali al-Hussein
Awaqaf. *See* Waqf
Ayubi, Najiba, 164
Azan-e fajr (call to morning prayer), 87
Azizi Group (financial), 93
Azzam, Seikh Abdullah, 43
Ayub Khan, Marshal Muhammd (of Pakistan), 141

Baba, 124
Baba Kohisaf, 102–03, 105
Bach bazi (boy "sex toys"), 191, 196–97n3
Badakhshan(is): 12–13, 14, 229–48, 300, 318, 325n1; Baluch of, 233; borders, 237–38; capital city of, 229; causes of high maternal death in, 316–17; changing geostrategic position, 238–40; child birth in, 323–24; "commanders wars," 239; CM (Community Midwifery) Program in, 318–19; conditions in, 237; control of drug routes in, 237; deputy governor of, 236; disillusionment of, 236–37; effects of sates recentralization in, 243–45; geographical division of, 248n13; identity politics in, 240; increased number of Wuluswali/Districts in, 244, 248n15; Jurm district, 229; impact of the fall of Soviet Union on, 234; initial armed rebellion, 232; Ismaili's living in, 229; living in Kabul, 229; end of polycentrism and self-government in, 245; power realignment, 240–43; politicization of identities in, 233; Post-Taliban, 238; power elites, 230; refugees in Pakistan, 247n9; since the Saur Revolution, 229–48; resisting the Marxist regimes 23, 230–34; relocation of Taliban and Central Asian terrorist in, 231; rise of local Taliban and ISIS, 240, 248n17; Shughnan district's support for PDPA, 229; Uzbek commanders in, 241; women's health in, 316
Badakhshi, Tahir (leftist intellectual), 232
Bagram Airfield/base, 10, 121, 125; Haji Zia's activities in, 127–28; security regime in, 127–28
Bagramis (people of Bagram), 121

Baharak (District in Badakhshan), 232
Bai/Bay, 124
Balkh (province), 50, 298, 302, 304
Bamiyan (city), 300
Baraktulla, Mowlana, 97n1
Baloch/Baluch (i), 13, 68, 72, 254; Academy, 282; adaptability of *kaum* among, 279–82; adapting to uncertainty in Afghanistan, 271–85; Barahui *kaum*, 276; becoming a "nation" under Soviet rule, 282–84; concept of *kaum/qawm* among 274–75, 284–85; *Jabhe-ye Nimruz Mujahideen*, 276; mobility during Soviet occupation, 275–79; national movement, 283; Pakistani, 283; tribal group names, 271, 286n7; Sanjerani *kaum*, 276–85; TV program, 282; Zahruzi, 286n8
Baluchistan, 42, 135
Bamyan (Bamian), 13, 139, 251, 257, 259, 302
Barakzai, Durrani Pashtun, 4. See also Durrani, and Pashtun
Barakzai, Shukria (member of parliament), 93
Bashardost, Ramazan, 172n1, 245–46, as Hazara candidate for President, 257
Basic Health Package of Health Services (BPHS), 315, 328–29
Basir Khalid, 242
Bedel (Dehlawi), 45, 66, 74n5; *Diwan* (collection of poems) of, 46
Beg (chief), 254
Beghairata (unmanly), 181–82, 185, 188, 194–96
Besauada aw kamaql (illiterate and stupid), 182
Bibigul, 319
Bilateral Security Agreement (between Afghanistan and the US), 225
Bin Laden, Osama, 24, 43; killing of, 221
BPHS. See Basic Health
Biruni, 59
British India, 230
Bonn (Conference & Declarations), 24, 79, 89, 105; AWN and feminist organizations at, 207; calling Rabbani to step down, 236; offering opportunities to *tanzim* networks, 106
Borders, and stability, 133–46 (See Durand Line, and Ministry of Border, Tribes and Ethnic Affairs, 138); cabinet rejection of mentioning border with Pakistan 133
Bostan (of Sa'di), 46
Brahui (Baloch *kaum*), 279; "grammar" of, 282; Haji Juma'a Khan of, 281; inferior position of, 280; *kaumigiri*, 280–81
Brahui, Abdulkarim: governor of Nimruz, 280; leader of *Jabhe-ye Nimruz* of mujahideen, 279–80
British/Britain (Government): expedition to Afghanistan, 22; colonial rule 133; Department for International Development (DFID) and BBC support of media in Afghanistan, 154–56
British India: 133, 169; attempt to build railroads, 151; subsidies to Amir Abdur Rahman 3–4; 134
Buddha statues in Bamyan, 13
Buddhist heritage, 139
Burhanuddin Rabbani (See Rabbani)
Bukhara, 40, 238
Bukharan Soviet Socialist Republic, 40
Bnuria Masjid, Karachi Pakistan, 43
Bush, George W: global war on terror, 2; overthrow of Taliban, 2; regime change in Iraq 2, 6, 24; promises for Afghanistan, 2
Bush, Laura, 31
Buzkashi (game of), 126–27

Canada's Kilo Goldmines Ltd., 139
Canetti, Elias, 213
Capitalism, declaration of victory of, 2
Care of Afghan Families (CAF) NGO, 325n1
Carter, President Jimmy, 43
Central Asia(n) (post-Soviet republics): 13, 15, 22, 38, 73, 213; centers of religious learning, 40; city of Osh in, 82; colonized, 2–3; Daesh threat to, 6; trade, 128; relations with South Asia, 144
Chabahar (Iranian Port), 139
Chadari (veil), 202–03, 209
Chagai region (in Pakistan), 277–78
Chagcharan (city of), 222
Chakhansur (capital of Farah province), 277
charbaiti (quatrain), 66 (See Persian Poetry)
Charburjak, 277

Chendawul (in Kabul city), 87
Center on Public Diplomacy (CDP), 220
Central Asian Soviet Republics, 234
    (See USSR, and Soviet Union)
China, 12, 29, 138, 213, 234, 237–38; National Petroleum Corporation, 139; One belt, One Road, 240
Chishti (Sufi order), 97n1
Chitral, Pakistan, 230, 238
CIA: and Pakistan's ISI, 43 (See United States and Pakistan)
Citizenship, 57
Civil Service Commission, 207
Civil society (organization), 297; in Jalalabad, 183
Civil War: and social fragmentation 70 (See War)
Clinton, Secretary of State Hillary, 240
Cold War: 41, 149; effect on global power ecology, 2
Colonized non-Western world, 3
Comita-e Farhangi (Cultural Committee), 69
CM (Community Midwifery) education, 318–19, 321
Communist, coup of April 1978, 1; collapse of regime, 5; party, 48; takeover, 68
Conscription. See Military
Constable, Pamela, 221
Constitution, of 1964 leading to instability, 5
Convention on the Elimination of all Discrimination against Women (CEDAW), 329
CPR (cardiopulmonary resuscitation), 320
Culture(al): of biomedicine, 325; impact of war on, 3; idiom, 183; moment, 223; political, 3; of Violence, 194
Crimea, Russian annexation of, 29
CURE International Hospital in Kabul, midwives at, 313, 320, 322

Da Afghanistan da Gato da Satawulu Idara (Afghanistan Interest Protection Services), 97n5
Daesh. See Islamic State
Daikundi, 251–52, 257
Da liwantob de (It's crazy), 193

Danish, Sarwar, 268n2
Daoud, Muhammad: 47–48, 262, 283, 292; pro-Pashtunistan policy of 141–42; relations with Parcham leftists, 201; removal of opponents, 292
Daqiqi (Balkhi), 66. See Persian poetry
Dari/Persian: 86, 87; Lingua franca, 67; literary heritage, 8, 61; second official language of Afghanistan, 67; speaking Pashtun, 67
Darwazi, Muhammad Wali Khan, 246n1
Dashti Qoregh, 241, 247n3
Dasht-e Margo, 277
Daudzai, Omar, 112
Dawi, Abdul Ghafar, 93
Dawi Group, 93
Dehlawi, Shah Waliullah, 146n1
Deloitte, 128
Democratic Organization of Women (DOAW), 201
Deoband(i) madrassas/movement, 42–46, 50–53, 54n2; curriculum and preparer, 43–47; in Pakistan, 45, 48
Development(al): challenges, 332; economic development, 5; models, 150, 152
Diem, Ngo Dinh, 27
Directorate of National Intelligence-DNI (Afghan), 26
Disabilty, 317–47
Distrust, signature of, 327
Diwana (mentally ill person), 343
Dost Muhammad Khan (Amir of Afghanistan), 80
Dostum, General Abduilrashid, 97n10, 172n5, 330; challenging Watan Groups security project in Sar-e Pul, 139–40; collaboration with Rabbani, 234; local influence of, 102–03, 112
Durand Line, 4, 10, 51, 134; impact on stability in Afghanistan, 133–46. See Borders
Durrani, Ahmad Shah 3, 254; de-centralized rule, 254; Kingdom as networked polity, 110
DynCorp, 128

Economic: development, 5; elites' conspicuous consumption, 94

358 | Index

Education, boarding vocational schools in Kabul, 5
Eamal, 188, 197n4
Egypt, 2
Eid-ul-Udha, 87
Eid-ul-Fetr, 87
Elections: 2014, 7
Elite: jihadi and technocratic, 6; changing power, 7; decimation of, 7; ruling cliques, 8; ruling royal, 7, 23
Empire, of trust/by invitation, 4
Empowerment, pathway to, 298; of women, 297–03
Ensijam-e Milli (party), 293
Episiotomy, defined, 325n2
Erfani, Qurban Ali, founder Hizb-e-Wahdadi Islamic Millat e Afghanistan, 258
Eshkashem, 239–40
Eslamkhanzi, Lineage of Sanjerani Bloch, 277
Estalif, town north of Kabul, 105
"Ethnic entrepreneurs," 134
Ethnicity, 61; hierarchy of in Afghanistan, 134
Ethnolinguistic and tribal cleavages, 1; discrimination against, 5; groups, 7, 151; impact of NATO and Western troops' invasion on, 271
Ethno-politics: 134–46; and the mining sectors, 138–40
Etihad-i-Islami. See Party
Ettehad-e Milli. See Party
Europe, 238, 240; war in, 1, 10, 15; Eastern, 38; Western, 223
European Union (EU), refugee problems, 12
Evidence-Based Policy and Accountability, mechanisms for, 344–47

Fahim, Vice President Marshal Qaseem, 93, 115, 236
Faisala (decision), 193
Faizabad, 12, 240; airport, 241; capital city of Badakhshan, 229; *Shahri Kuhan* and *Shari Now*, 242. See Badakhshan
Faizullah, Maulana, (of Swat Taliban), 205
Far East, 22
Farah (province), 222
Farid, 184
Farida, 313–14, 322–23

Farnood, Sherkhan, 94
Fatwa, 49
Federally Administered Tribal Areas (FATA), 134, 179; and Baluchistan, 145; lack of access to women, 179; mobilization by Nader Khan, 135
Ferdowsi, 58; *Shahnama* of 60, 74
Ferozi, Khalilullah, 94
Fiqh (jurisprudence), 42, 44
Food insecurity, 102
Foreign aid/assistance, 5, 92
Foreign policy (US), militarization of, 2
Frontier Congress Party, 134

Gailani, Ishaq, 112
Gas Group, 93
Gate, Secretary of Defense Robert, 27
GDP (Gross Domestic Products-Afghanistan), 331
Gender, and power, 347; relations, 10
Ghafar Khan, Abdul, political legacy of 142
Ghani, Ashraf, 25, 28, 30, 33, 112, 117, 136, 244, 257; administration, 329; sidelining strongmen, 114; stance on Durand Line, 143; signing of BSA (Bilateral Security Agreement), 330
Ghairat(man) (upholding rules of *pakhto*), 181, 190, 196
Ghairati (honorable), 182
Ghat family way (an influential family), 193
Ghazals, 66, 72–73, 77. See Persian Poetry
Ghazali, Imam, 44, 54n3
Ghaznavids, 59
Ghazanfar Groups, 93
Ghazanfar, Husn Banu, 93
Ghazni, 257
Germany, 30
Gilani, Pir Sayyed Ahmad (Chief of Mahaz-e-Milli Tanzim), 112, 117, 298
Ghilzai, 4, 68; given Hazara pasturelands to, 254–55; territory, 80, 254–55. See Pashtun
Gilgit, 238
Good Governance, new mechanisms of, 345
Government: Afghan national, 12; favoring the Pashtun, 5; Pashtun dominated, 8; occasion for discrimination, 5
Great Britain, 21

Great Game, the, 3, 22, 150
Green Movement, 152
Glistan (of Sa'di), 46
Ghulaman bachagan (court pages), 97n1
Gulbahar Center, 93
Gulbahar Group, 93
Gulbahar Tower, 93
Gulf, region, 41; Sheikhdoms, 43; war in 1991, 2, 8, 16n1

Habibullah (Amir 1901–1919): 4, 80, 92; essay on centrality of women in modern society, 201; and *mashrutiat* (constitutionalist) movement, 292
Hafiz Shirazi (*Diwan* of), 46, 66, 74n5
Hafta-ye Shuhada (martyrs' week), 90
Hajar, Imam Ibn, 48
Haji Juma'a Khan (Brahui Baloch), drugsmugler, 281
Hajj (pilgrimage to Mecca), 203
High Peace Council, 291
Hijigak (iron mine in Bamyan), 139
Haji Din Muhammad, member of Arsala family, 112
Haji Yaqub (square), 95
Haji Zia (of Bagram), a *qarardadi* (contractor), 121–31
Hamida, 313–14, 322–23
Hanbali, 38, 46
Hanafi, 45, 47–49. See also Sunni
Hanifa, Imam Abu (699-767), 38; Fatwa of, 48
Hanzala of Badghis, 58
Haqq, Abdul, 90
Haqqani, Hussain, 45
Haqqani, Jalaluddin (network), 27, 30, 45, 51
Haqqania, Darul Uloom, 45
Haqqani Network, 144
Hashimi, Mansur (ranking member of PDPA from Badakhshan), 232, assassination of, 247n4
Hashte Subh, 8am newspaper, 164
Hazara (Shi'as), 4, 12, 57, 86, 87, 89, 112, 136, 151, 251–52; Abdu Rahman's campaign of suppression against, 254–68; Afghan state as a Pashtun-run enemy state, 266–67; Ballots running out majority district, 257; Bashardost as candidate for President, 257; *begs*, 254; benefiting from Amanullah's reforms, 255; civil society activism, 251–69; demonstrations in Kabul, 91; and educational institutions, 262–65; engagement with international institutions, 251; lack of access to education, 262; of Karta-ye Sakhi, 97n2; massacre in Afshar, Kabul, 256; *mirs*, 254–55; participation in elections, 257; pastures given to Ghilzai Pashtuns, 255; Persian speaking, 67; political parties, 257–59; positive views of international organizations and the US, 252; protests regarding electricity lines (TUTAP), 268n1; reasons for the claim of being "open-minded," 269n8; "Renaissance" 269n4; social exclusion and marginalization, 252–53, 256; Quetta, 256; traditional social structure, 255; in Western Kabul, 254; Unity Day, 263; written out of history of Afghanistan, 262–63
Hazarajat, 80
Hekmatyar, Gulduddin, 47, 51, 135, 280; recruitment of disgruntled Badakhshanis by, 233
Helmand (province), 244
Helmand Valley Project, 136
Herat, 114, 213, 215, 222, 302; fear in the city of, 219; situation in Herat in 2014, 222; Taliban killing of engineers in Karokh district, 219
Hezb-e Ghozangi Melli. See Party(ies), Political
Hezb-e Ittehadi Islami (Sayyaf). See Party(ies), Political
Hezb-e Jamhori-e Khawhan, Central Afghanistan. See Party(ies), Political
Hezb-e Junbushe-e Milli. See Party(ies)
Hezb-e Isami. See Party(ies), Political
Hezb-e Mahaz-e Milli. See Party(ies)
Hezb-e Paiwand-e Milli, central Afghanistan. See Party(ies), Political
Hezb-ul Tahrir. See Party(ies), Political
Hezbe-e Wahdat Islami (Hazara political organization). See Party(ies), Political
Hezbe-e Wahdat Islami-e Mardom, Balkh. See Party(ies), Political

High Peace Council, 247n8
Helmand (province), 278
Hindustan, 77; Muslim leaders of, 133
Herat (i), 11, 38, 50; Iranian Consulate in, 2013; rioters, 12
Hindi/Urdu, 86
Hindu Marthas, 146n1
Hizb-e-Wahdati Islami (of Akabari). See Party(ies), Political, 258
Hong Kong, 142
Hussein, Saddam: invasion of Kuwait, 2; removal of by US and coalition war, 6, 24
Hyderabad, 82

IAD (Institutional Analysis and Development) approach to institutional analysis, 307; framework, 278, 291, 297, 303; and conceptualizing institutional change, 306. *See also* Ostrom
Ibn Sina, Abu Ali al-Hussein (Avicenna), 38, 59
Identity: electronic cards, 91; ethnic tensions about, 91; instrumentalization of, 115–16; personal and collective, 7, 10, 57, 61; politicization of, 239
Ihsan (moral excellence), 44
Ihteram (respect), 186
Ihteram na kawul (disrespect), 192
Independent Human Rights Commission of Afghanistan (IHRCA), 164
India(n): 30, 38, 213, 240; Ocean, 133
Indonesia, 281
Improvised Explosive Devise (IED), 31
Institute of Development Studies (UK), 298
Institutions, definition of, 294; formal and pragmatic norms, 294; stability of, 294–95
Imtihani Konkoor, 52
International Court of Justice (ICJ), 145
International Crimes Unit of Netherland National Police: documentation of PDPA killings, 97n
Intelligence services, names of, 97n5
Intelligentsia, 23 (*See also* Elites)
Internally Displaced Person, 345
International Monetary Fund (IMF), 31
International Security Assistance Force (ISAF), 139, 152, 169

Inter Service Intelligence (ISI), Pakistan, 16n3, 27, 51, 213
Iqbal, Sir Muhammad, 145n1
Irfan, 192–93
"Iron Amir" (*See* Rahman, Abdur)
Iran (ian): 13, 38, 70, 213, 254; duplicity in the Taliban war in Afghanistan, 6; consulate in Herat, 11–12, 213, 218, 222–23; Islamic Revolution, 41; Port of Chahbahar, 139; US enmity, 30
Iraq, 2, 24, 38; "bad war or war of choice," 29
Ishkashim (district in Badkhshan), 232
Ismail Khan (Jamiat-i-Islami commander in Herat), 117n2, 129, 221
Islam: 124; and gender segregation, 204
Isma'ili Shi'is, 12; in Tajikistan 254
Islam: 124; gendered politics, 200, 204; honor and rule, 125; legacies of political abuse, 49; local knowledge of, 46–47, 53; *mazaahib* (schools of shari'a), 45, 54n4; piety-based traditional, 8; political, 41; politicization and instrumental uses of, 37, 41, 47; radical ideologies of Mujahideen, 8; "traditional," 7; in transition, 37. *See* Religion
Islamabad, 30
Islamic: blue print for leadership, 48; education, 38, 41; government, 230; literature distributed in Soviet Central Asia, 43; militancy & extremism, 37; resistance of the 1980s, 1; Revolution in Iran, 41; textual tradition, 61; theological discourse, 8; values, 40. *See also* Jihad
Islamic State: of Afghanistan, 135; of Iraq and Syria (ISIS), 152; of Khurasan (IS/ISK/Daesh); 33, 51; presence in northern Afghanistan, 6; regional threat, 6, 7
Islamists, 47; armed uprising in Badakhshan; 232 radicals, 48
Izzat (honor), 182–83, 192

Jabhe-ye Nimruz, 276–80
Jahankhanzi, 277
Jalalabad (city of), 50, 183, 187–88, 194
Jadi Maiwand (Maiwand Avenue, Kabul), 78
Jahanbeg, 277
Jamaat-e Islami Pakistan, 141

Jami, 45, 58–59
Jamiyati Islah, 304
Jamiati Islami Afghanistan: 12, 71, 89, 134, 245, 280, 304; launching the resistance to Communism in Badakhshan, 233; internecine commanders war, 242; triumph of Panjhseri faction, 236. *See also* Party(ies), Political
Jamiat-ul-Ulama (Council of Religious Scholars), 49
Jareer, Humayun, 117n3
Jihad: 190; against the Islamic Republic of Afghanistan by Taliban, 47; against the Red Army, 1, 42; globalization of, 2, 5, 8; ethnic groups participation in, 1
Jihadi groups: receipts of weapons and cash, 1; in Pakistan, 292
Jihadist movements, 8
Jirga (council) system, 187, 192; pitfalls of, 193
Jirgamaran (members of a jirga), 187
Jonbesh-e Melli (Uzbek political organization heard by Rashid Dostum), 89, 112, 293, 302, 304. *See* Part(ies), Political
Journalists, violence against, 166
Juwaligari (porter), 97n2

Kaboora Production (of Tolo tv), 168
Kabul (the capital city): 11, 14, 47–48, 50, 197n4, 200, 239–40, 256, 302–03; Badakhshanis in, 230–49; Bank, 93; Bank scandal 94–95, 114–15; continuity and change in post 2001, 77–97; destruction of, 5, 60, 70; during PDPA rule, 86; economic dynamics, 92–96; Education University in, 90; ethnic tensions, 90–91; Hazaras in Western, 254, 257; in historical context, 80–84; International Airport, 79; internet use, 152; music, 77; massacre of Hazaras in, 256; maternity ward in, 323; NGO operations, 92; population in 1800s, 81; political dynamics of, 89–92; revolutionary politics in, 78; rural to urban migration, 78; *Shur yee Ulama* (council of clerics), 164; social dynamics of, 84–97; shifting demographics, 9, 82–84; Taliban attacks in, 330; University, 67, 77, 165

Kabuli (from Kabul), 78, 82, 218; society, 92
Kabuli, Najibullah: owner of Emros tv, 157; quarrel on the air with shi'a owned Tamadon TV, 157
"Kafirs" (*See* Nuristanis)
Kalakani, Amir Habibullah (r. 1929): 134–35; claiming the throne of, 4; ouster 97n4
Kalashnikovs, 49
Kandahar, 114, 244, 330
Karachi, 82, 254
Karimi, General Sher Mohammad (Chief of Staff of the ANA), bellicose statement of, 141, 146n8
Karmal, Babrak: 286n4, lessons learned, 15, 188; replacement of, 28
Karzai, Hamid: 11, 14, 31, 50, 93, 104, 116–17, 164, 236, 244, 268n2, 302; appeals to Pakistan Pashtun leaders, 141; and Bilateral Security Agreement with US, 225n3; cabinet estimate of values of minerals, 138; cabinet rejection of mentioning border with Pakistan 133; cartel, 29; clients of, 112–14; family, 31; government and feminist, 206; leadership style with neighbors and allies, 24–29; Kabul Bank scandal, 94–95; political network, 112; reluctance to act, 32–34; removal of parliamentary members, 108; return of Pashtun *maldars* (mobile herder) to Badakhshan during, 236; at Shanghai Cooperation Organization (SCO) meetings, 140; speech at Afghan National Officers Academy, 142; and technocrats, 236
Karzai, Ahmad Wali, 112
Karta-e Char (Kabul neighborhood), 82
Karta-ye Sakhi (Kabul neighborhood), 97n2
Karta-e Sey (Kabul Neighborhood), 82, 90
Kashaf, Qiamuddin, 50
Kashmir, 2, 93
Kashghar, 238
Kazakhstani, 138
Kazemi, Kazem (poet), 70
Kaum/qawm, among Baloch, 272; adaptive dynamics, 274–85; definition of, 286n1
Kerry, John (US Secretary of State): intervention after fraudulent election, 7, 25

Khalili, Karim, 104, 112, 268n2
KhAD (PDPA intelligence service), 188
Khalili, Khalilullah (poet laureate of Afghanistan), 70
Khalq (Masses, political party), 79. See Party(ies), and Peoples Democratic Party of Afghanistan
Khalq Organization of Afghan Women, 201
Khans/khanaan pl. (local leaders): 7, 124, 190, 196n2; among Pashtun 124, 189; of the Kirghiz of Afghan Pamirs, 126, of Uzbeks in northern Afghanistan, 126
Khanawada (Family), 204
Khana-yi Amn (safe house), 11, 200, 207–08, 211n2, 211n7
Khana-ye hawlidar (house with compound), 94
Khiva, 238
Khogiany, Ahmad, 187
Khomeini, Ayatullah, 41
Khorasan(i): 37, 41, 50–53,; Sufi mystical ideals of, 8, 37–43
Khutbah (homily/sermon), 47
Khyber Pukhtunkhaw (See Northwest Frontier Province-NWFP)
Kilid Group, findings of, 111, 164
Kiliwali (Pashtun folk music), 77
King, Martin Luther Jr., 213
Kipling, Rudyard, 22
Kirghiz/Kyrgyz (of the Afghan Pamirs), 126, 238
Kishm (Badakhshan district), 233
Kizilbosh, 258
Koh-e Sherdarwaza, 82
Kokand, 238
Kongrayee Melli Afghanistan (National Congress Party of Afghanistan. See Paty(ies), and Sitami Melli)
Kori zanon (women's work), 325
Kuchi (Pashtun mobile herders), description of, 135; Ashraf Ghani as a, 136; constitutional privileges given, 136, 145n3
Kukcha River, 241
Kum Kum, Indian tv serial, 167
Kumandanaan (militia commanders), 184–86, 188–90, 194–95; 197nn4–5
Kunar, 80, 114

Kunduz, 14, 50, 114, 166, 302, 318
Kuran and Munjan (district in Badakhshan), 232, 233, 242
Kutlu, Haji Rahmanqul, flight to Pakistan and Turkey, 239
Kuwait, invasion of, 2
Ky, Nguyen Cao, 27
Kyrgyz, 254 (See also Kirghiz)

Lahore, 254
Lanjay (local conflict), 195
Lalma (rain-fed farming), 102
Lapis lazuli mines (in Badakhshan), control of, 233, 242
Leadership,instability of, 130–31
Liberalism's triumph over Communism, 22
Libya, 2
Lincoln Learning Center (US Embassy outreach program), 266
Literature, vernacular 8; Persian, 39
"Little Dubai," 94
"Little Pakistan," 94
Logar (province), 138, 300
Loya Jirga, 145, 163

Madrassa (Madaris, pl), 38, 43, 50, 52–53, 190, 209, 240; in Central Asia, 40; Deobandi, 230; in Pakistan 70, 235; "manpower," 135; Wahhabi, 196n2
Mahendra, Pratab Singh, 97n1
Maidan-Wardak (province), 257
Maimana, 80
Mahaz-e Milli (party), 298; in Logar, 300 (See also Party)
Mahram (next of kin with the threshold of incest), 203
Majbur (obligatory), 182
Majles e Musha'ara (poetry contest), 73
Malik (malikaan pl), 124, 126, 189–90; 196n2
Maliki, 46
M'alul (mentally impaired), 341, 343
Mamoon, Razaq, 166
Mansour, Mullah Akhtar, 27
Maoist ideology, 280
Marriage, preferences, 320
Marefat School (in West Kabul), 269n5

Marking, Havana (British film maker), producer of *Afghan Star after Pop Idol*, 162
Marthas, 146n1
Marxist-Leninist, 89
Masculinity: among Pashtuns, 179–97; of new generation, 1991–95; shifting meaning of moral, 183–90
Mashhad, 254
Mashin Khana (arms workshop), 80
Massoud, Ahmad Shah, 16, 90, 112, 135, 157, 233, 242, 247n7, 256; road and places named for, 90
Massoud, Ahmad Zia, 112, 146n9, 247n7
Mashayekh lineage, 97n1
Mas'uniyat-e-Melli. *See* Security
Maternal Death, 320 (*See also* Badakhshan)
Mathnawi/Masnawi, 39, 47, 71, 74n6
Matiullah Khan, 114
Mazaahib (schools of shiri'a). *See* Islam
Mazaamin (curricular subjects), 44
Mazari, Abdul Ali (Hazara leader), 90, 263, 269n8; Birthday celebrations, 259; and Hizb-e-Wahdat party, 255, 257; killed by Taliban, 258; Square, in Bamyan, 259. *See also* Harzara
Mazar-i Sharif, 15, 172n3, 234, 298
Ma'yub (injured person), 343
Mecca, 48
Media funding, 10
Medical Emergency Relief International (MERLIN-NGO), 318, 325n1
Medina, 48
Mediterranean, 181
Merchant-Warlords, 121–31
Mes-e Aynak (coper mine), 138
Meshrano Jirga (house of elder), 91
Merchant-warlords, 9
Metallurgical Corporation of China (MCC), award of Mes-e Aynak copper mines, 138
Middle East (Muslim): 181; social activism, 152; uprisings, 149; US policies during Cold War, 2; wars in, 15
Midwives, 313–14; community (CM), 318
Militia Commanders: as social class, 194
Mikroryan (Soviet built apartments in Kabul), 80, 82, 84, 87, 96, 97n5; design and construction, 84; diversity and anonymity in, 84–87; ethnic composition of residents, 86; language competency of residents, 86; religious holidays in, 87
Mines: Mes-e Aynak copper mines, 138
Mineral, cabinet estimate of values 138
Ministry of: Borders, Tribes and Ethnic Affairs, 138; Information and Culture, 167–69; Justice, 201; Public Health (MoPH), 315, 317, 321, 328; Social Affairs (MSA), 11, 201; Women's Affairs (MOWA), 11, 201, 206, 211n2, 297
Military, conscription, 5; intervention, 8
Mir (local ruler), 254
Mirab (water manager), 124–25
Modabber, Sadeq, 112
Moghul dynasty, 40
Mohaqiq, Mohammad, 104, 112, 114, 268n2; leader of Hizb-e-Wahdati Islami Mardom Afghanistan, 258
Mohamad Khan, 114
Mohammad, the Prophet, 259
Mohseni, Ayatullah or Shaikh, 157
Mojaddadi, Sibghatullah, 112
MP (Member of Parliament), 298
Mujahideen: *jabhe-ye Nimruz* of Baloch, 276
Monarchies (Afghanistan): British subsidies to, 1
Mongol invaders, 13; 269n8
Movements, political, Afghanan-e Jawan, 291
Mozaffari, Abu Talib (poet), 70
Mujadidi, Zalmay, 237, 242; as Karzai's chief of security, 242
Mughror (arrogant), 192
Muhammad, the Prophet, 39, 48
Muhammadzai, clan of Durrani Pashtun, 3, 49; 67, 246n1 (*See also* Musahiban)
Mujahideen (Afghan): 22, 104, 285; Arab support for, 30; defeating the Red Army, 2; parties triumph, 5; wrecking Kabul, 5; *tanzims*, 285; US and Allies support of, 30
Mullah Nizam Uddin Sehalvi (1677–1748), 44. *See* Deobandi
Mullayan (Mullah sing.), 190
Mullen, Admiral Mike (US Joint Chief of Staff), 144
Music, 77
Mumtaz, Baryalay, 184

Munadi, Sultan 166
Munajat Nama (*See* Al Ansari)
Musahiban, Dynasty, 4, 49, 246n1; control of Islamic education, 49; policies of "internal colonialism," 136 (*See* Nader Khan/Shah)
Musharraf, General Parvez, 24, 30
Muslim Brotherhood, 280
Muslim League (of Pakistan), 143
Muslim, World, 40–42, 49, *umma*, 57
Mysticism. *See Tariqa*, Sufism
Mutamaddan (civilized), 188

Nader, General/Khan/Shah, 4, 49, Constitutional changes, 255; Kabul during the rule of, 81–82, 92, 97n4
Nadery, Nadir, 164
Nai (Afghanistan-based journalist watch group), 169
Najibullah, Dr. Mohammad: 1, 28, 50, 90, 188, 194, 255–56, 276, 280, 286n4; government of, 82, 104; killing of in the UN compound, Kabul, 200
Najmuddin khan of Baharak, 242
Namus (family honor), 181–82
NDI (National Democratic Institute), 299
Nangarhar province, 11, 180, 184, 191–92, 330
Nangarhar University, 191
Naqshbandi, Sufi, 97n1
Naqshbandi, Ajamal (murdered New York Time fixer), 166
Nar/Narina, pl. (manly), 181–82, 185, 188
Natasha, the wife of Taliban member, 208
Nartob (manliness), 181–82, 184, 196
National Coalition of Afghanistan. *See* Parties
National identity, in Afghanistan, 64
National language, 63
National Solidarity Program, block grants, 244
National Unity Government (NUG): 6, 21, 25, 32–33, 112, 116
National unity, inhibitors of, 7
Nationalism, Afghan, 9 (*See also* Tarzi, Mahumud, Amanullah, Amir/Shah)
Nationality (*nationhood*), 57, 61
NATO, 169
Nawabkhanzi Lineage of Sanjerani Bloch, 277

Nazeer Mad of Yaftal, 242
Nazima, 206
Nazism, 8
Nimroz, residents, 220, 273, 278, 330
Nishapur, 58
Nizamia *Nisab* (curriculum), 44, 48, 53 (*See* Deobandi movement)
NGOs (Non-Governmental Organization), 10, 79, 121, 127, 220, 297, 315, 317; and the Hazaras, 253; in Jalalabad, 185
Non-Pashtun, communities within Afghanistan, 46
Noor, Atta Muhammad (Governor of Balkh), 115, 129, 330
North Korea, 31
North Waziristan, 144
North West Frontier Province (Pakistan), 42, 134
Northern Alliance, 12, 16n3, 117, 157, 234
"North Atlantic Universals," 269n3
Nouroz (Afgan New Year), 64; festival, 66
Nufuz (influence), 192
Nuristan (province), 232, 254, 313
Nushki, 278

Obama, President Barak: "good war"/"war of necessity," 29; troop surge of 2009 and "Afghanizing" the war, 6, 26; military surge, 25
Official Development Assistance (ODA), 93
"Objective event," 180–81
Omar, Mullah Muhammad: death in Pakistan 27; meeting Bin Laden, 43
Opium, growers of, 138
Open Society, head of, 207
Organization for Economic Cooperation and Development (OECD), 93
Osama Bin Laden, 6
Osman Khowja, 97n1
Osh, Kyrgyzstan, 82
Ostrom, Elinor and Vincent Workshop in Political Theory and Policy Analysis, Indiana University, 224n1; Institutional Analysis and Development (IAD), 272–73, 295; SES (Social Ecological System), 295
Ottoman, Empire, 40

Pachayaan (descendants of the Prophet Muhammad), 192
Padshah Gradeshi (dynastic succession event), 230
Pahlawani, 88
Panjsher (valley): 12, 89, 91, 232, 233
Pakistan: 2, 13, 41, 133; backing Taliban & radicals, 5, 51; border dispute with Afghanistan, 10; creeping invasion of Afghanistan, 23; duplicity in the Taliban war in Afghanistan, 6; foreign policy interests, 51; *madrassa* system in, 38; Military Inter-service Intelligence (ISI), 51, 135, 144, 234, 276; opportunists, 48; Pashtun-led religious parties, 141; relations with Baloch, 276; Saudi & Iranian strategic ties, 30; sponsored terrorist, 139; support for the Afghan Islamists, 141–46; Tribal Agency, 179
Pakhtunwali/Pukhtunwali (male code of honor), 11, 200, 211n1
Pakhto, 180, 184–85, 196
Pakhto paalal (following *pakhto*), 180, 194
Paktia, 11, 301, 330
Pakitika, 302, 330
Palestine/Palestinian, 2, 43
Pamir, 247n10
Panj Ganj (didactic Islamic text), 46
Panjsher Valley, 232
Parcham (Flag, branch of Communist Party). *See* Party(ies), 7
Parliament, "easy seats" to win, 299
Party(ies), Political: attitudinal change about, 306; "development," 294; Etihad-i-Islami, 112; Ettehad-e Milli, 301–302; Hezb-e Ghorzangi Melli, 247n6; Hezb-e Ittehadi Islami (Sayyaf), 89; Hezb-e Jamhori-e Khawhan Afghanistan, 301; Hezb-e Isami, 89, 135, 293, 300; Hezb-e Mahaz-e Milli, 298; Hezb-e Paiwand-e Milli, 301; Hezb-e Mahaz-e Milli recruitment services, 304; Hezb-ul Tahrir, 304; *Hezbe-e Wahdat Islami* (Hazara political organization), 89, 112, 117, 261 (in Balkh), 299; Hezb-e-Wahdati Islami (of Akabari), 258; *Hezbe-e Wahdat Islami-e Mardom, Balkh*, 300; impact or environmental context, 303–307; Jamiati Islami Afghanistan: 12, 71, 89, 134, 245, 280, 304; institutionalization of, 294–97; *Jonbesh-e Melli* (Uzbek led by Rashid Dostum), 89, 112, 293, 300, 302, 304; *Khalq* (Masses, political party), 79; Kongrayee Melli Afghanistan (National Congress Party of Afghanistan), 246n2; Law, 292; National Coalition of Afghanistan (parties), 301; *Parcham* (Flag, branch of Communist Party), 7; reputation for violence, 304–305; Shura e Enqelab e Ettifaq e Islami (the Council of the Islamic Revolutionary Alliance, 259; *Wesh Dzalmian*, 292
Pashto/Pashtu/Pukhtu (official language of Afghanistan), 8–9, 46, 67, 86; literary societies, 63; poetry, 59–73
Pashto Tolana (Pashto Academy), 74n3
Pashtun/Pathan/Pakhtun, 4, 16n3, 25; Army Doctrine, 144; ascendance to power, 134; backwardness of, 188; Badakhshanis taking arms against rulers since 1880s, 230; co-ethnic in Pakistan, 138; cultural context, 180–83; cross border ethnic ties, 30; girls education among, 333; inhabitants in Pakistan, 133; *kiliwali* music, 77; Kandahari *maldar/kuchis* in Badakhshan, 236; masculinity, 179–97; Muslim League of, 143; nationalism, 61–73; nomads losing their language, 67; of the southeast, 87; Peoples Party (PPP), 143; rule in Afghanistan, 58; sex segregated, 11; social dynamics, 179–80; Teherik-i-Taliban, 144; tribal belt, 43; women, 179; women and family honor, 181
Pashtun victimhood, for analysis of, 146nn5–6
Pata Khazana (hidden treasures), 74n4
Pasunkhan (Sanjerani khan), 277; sons Nawabkhan and Eslamkhan, 277
Patron-Client relations, 110–14
Pazhwak, Abdurahman (poet), 70
Pazhwak Afghan News, 169
PBS News Hour, 221

Pentagon, 26
Peoples Democratic Party of Afghanistan (PDPA), 15, 68, 78, 92, 187, 201, 232, 240; assassination of opponents, 97n3; Badakhshanis responses to, 230; Decree #7 on women, 201; factional fighting, 27–28; forming government, 292; increase in Kabul's population during rule, 82; language policies, 68; Khalq & Parcham factions, 68; Shughnan district of Badakhshan support for, 229; use of schools as military and party bases, 235
Pakistan Peoples Party (PPP), 143
Palmerstone, Lord, 215
PC (Provincial Council), 300; elections, 301, 307
Persian/Dari/Tajik), 41; dialectical difference, 172n4; history of, 58; *lingua franca* in Afghanistan, 57; poetry and cultural identity, 57–73 (*See also* Dari/Persian)
Peshawar (Pakistan), 43, 45, 94, 230; Islamist leaders in, 233
PETS (public expenditure tracking study), 333
Pitocin, 321
Poetry: resistance, 8; *charbaiti* (quatrain), 64; didactic, 8; mirror of political culture, 8
Pir (Sufi leader): 7, 49, 124
Politics, of rage, 2; networked 9; local 122
Political: religions of twentieth century, 8; Afghanan-e Jawan movement, 291; parties 13–14; structures, 124. *See* Party(ies)
Political: culture, 8; ecology of uncertainty, 12; economy, 121–131; instability, 127–30; support of media sector, 149, 154–59;
Political Networks: definition of, 103, composition of, 104; power dynamics within the state, 107–10; role of, 102–18; rent seeking illegality, 114–15; successful when, 109
Political party/parties: 291–308; ethnic basis of, 290; history of in Afghanistan, 291–94; institutionalization of, 290–308; law, 292; marginalization of by ruler, 290; *mashrutiat* (constitutionalist movement), 291; means of increasing influence, 291; mobilizing, 290; personality & patronage of leaders, 290; public visibility of, 291; and SNTV vote system, 290; relationship between women and, 299; reputation of, 290; women's empowerment, 290–308. *See also* Party(ies)
Political Theology, 193
Politicization of identities, 8
Popal, Rateb (Karzai's cousin and heroin smuggler to NY), 139
Post-colonial Central Asia and the Middle East, 3
Poverty, eradication of, 334; multidimensional 336–44
Power (state): articulation of, 1; monopoly of, 1; structure of in Afghanistan, 1; technologies of, 7, 9
Provincial Council. *See* PC
Provincial Reconstruction Team (PRT), rhetoric of, 210
Proxy wars: consequences for Afghanistan, 1; support for 8
Public Service Announcements (PSA), 10; *jung bas ast* (Enough War), 159
Purdah (*See* chadari)

Qadir, Haji Zahir, 90, 104; leading Rule of Law group in parliament, 108
Qale-ye Jahanbeg, 277
Qanuni, Yunus, 236, 330
Qaraqoram (mountains), 247n10
Qarardadi (contractor), 121
Qawi narina (strong man), 186
Qizilbash, 87; of Chendawul and Murad Khani, 97n1
Qowat (power), 196
Quetta, Pakistan, 202
Quetta, 82
Qumandans (jihadi): 124; participation in civil war, 1–2; opposing the Taliban, 2; role in criminal activities, 2
Qur'an, 38; burning of, 165
Qurbat, Mawlawi Amin, 97n1

Rabb (Sustainer), 39
Rabbani, Burhanuddin: 12, 47, 90, 135, 157, 229, 233, 241; assassination by Taliban,

247n8, 330; assuming Presidency in 1992, 234; collaboration with Dostum, 234; conflict with Hekmatyar, 234, 241; disinterest in decentralized government, 248n14; nepotistic practice, 233, 235; Panjsheri allies, 233; sudden death of, 244
Rahman, Abdur (Amir of Afghanistan, 1880–1901): 80, 97n2, 136, 230, 265; allotting Hazara pastures to Pashtun nomads, 255; British support for, 4, 92; controlling Hazaras 262; centralization of state, 254; cruelty, 4; declaring jihad against enemies, 49; "internal imperialism," 92; limiting the role of *ulama*, 204; legal edict on gender and family relations, 201; military campaigns, 80; policies of, 49–50; self-exile to Samarkand, 3; use of jihad domestically, 50
Rahmani, Asef (poet), 70
Ramadan, 46, 203
Rahmatullah, 184–88; 192–93; 197n4
Ramin, Obaidullah, 94
Rasul, Zalmay, views on Durand Line, 143
Ratebzad, Dr. Anahita, 201 (*See* PDPA)
Rawaaj (customary practice), 185
Raziq, Commander, 104
Red Army (USSR), jihad against, 1, 8
Refugees (Afghan), in Iran and Pakistan, 6; influx of Pashtuns, 196n2
Religion (Islam): politicization and nationalization of, 8; and politics, 37. *See* Islam
Reporters Without Borders, 169
Research: ethnographic, 1; interdisciplinary, 1
Revolutionary Association of Women of Afghanistan (RAWA), 201
Riot, a model of, 222–23
Rewat, Dashti (pastureland in Badakhshan), 236
Rome Group, 117
"Rules in Use," 305. *See* Ostrom
Rumi (Balkhi), Muhammad Jalaluddin (1207–1273), 39, 45, 58, 66, 74n5; *Mathnawi* of, 47
Russia, tsarist, 3, 230; conquest of Tashkent, 3, 97n1

Sadat (pl of Sayyed), 87
Saddam (*See* Hussein, Saddam)
Sa'di Shirazi, 39, 45
Safe Motherhood Initiative (SMI), 315–16
Salafi, ideologies, 41, 44
Salaman and Absal, 54n2
Salang pass, 268n1
Shamali plain (north of Kabul), 87, 125
Samanids, 59
Samarkand, 3, 40
"Samsori Afghan" (*See* Yun, Muhammad Ismael)
Sanaie, 39, 45, 59
Sangriev, Vladimir, 15
Sanjerani (Baloch *kaum* in Farah, Hilmand and Nimruz): 275–78; during Soviet occupation, 276; hostility with Barhui and Rakhshani, 278; *Sardars* (elders) of, 278
Sardars, ethnic chiefs (Amiri Lashkar), 110
Saraki-Wolayat (Governor's Mansion Street), 213
Saray (ordinary man, in Pashto), 182
Sar-e-Pol (province), defection to Taliban, 139, 221
Sarghelan, 233
Saritob (moral appropriateness, in Pashtu), 184–85
Saudi Arabia, 2, 41–42
Saur Revolution: 229–48; actions and reaction to in Badakhshan, 229–38; impact on border of Badakhshan, 238; generation after, 194; impact on Hazaras, 255; nationalities policy effect on Baloch, 283
Sayed (persons claiming descent from the Prophet Mohammad), political mobilizers, 259–61; role challenged, 260–61
Sayyaf, Abdur Rabb Rasul: 16n3, 89, 112, 114, 158, 256, 330; sympathizers in Badakhshan, 233; role in Hazara massacre in Afshar, Kabul, 256
Sazande (musician), 77
Security, Afghan: capabilities of, 21; five pillars of sector reforms, 331, increased suicide attacks against in Afghanistan, 330; forces, 7, 26–27; percentage of GDP spent on, 331; *Mas'uniayt-e-Melli* (national

368 | Index

security), 97n5; size and cost, 26; threats (regional and global), 1; Watan Group, 139–40
September 11 attacks in the US, 234
Serhetabat, Turkmenist, 172n3
Shahnama (*See* Ferdowsi)
Shahr-e Kuhna (old City of Kabul), 80, 84; access to service, 88; Bagh-e Ghazi garden in, 88; cohesive and insulated, 87–89; demographic composition, 87–89; NGO presence in, 88; Zoorkhana/pahlawani, 88
Shah Ismail Safavi, 277
Shahri-e Now (New City): 94; founding of, 82
Shafi'i, 46
Shakila, 259
Shamali plain, 10
Shams, Shamur Rahman (Rabbani's cousin), 236
Shariat: Taliban Newspaper, 71; Taliban Radio, 149, 205
Sharif, Muhammad Nawaz, 30, 143
Shari'a, (Islamic law and ethics), 40
Sher-e Azad (free verse poetry), 73
Sher Ali Khan (Amir), 80
Sherpur (a Neighborhood in Kabul), 79, 94
Sherzai, Gul Agha, 104, 112, 115, 184, 330
Shiite Marriage Law, 165
Shi'a, 41–42; Shura yee Ulama (Council of Shi'a clerics), 157
Silk Route, 238, 269n8
Sindhi, Moulana Obaidullah, 97n1
Shinwari, Fazl Hadi, 50
Shinwari, territory, 80
Shiwa, Dashti (pastures in Badakhshan), 236
Sitami Melli (leftist group): 232, 246n2
Shor Bazaar, 87
Shughnan (District in Badakhshan), 230–32, 239, 247n5
Shura e Enqelab e Ettifaq e Islami (the Council of the Islamic Revolutionary Alliance), Hazara political group known as *Shura*, 259
Shura (council): local, 121–24, 318–19
Shura-yi Nizar, 117, 242
Shuray-e-sartasari Ulama wa Rohaneyooni Afghnaistan (Grand Council of

Afghanistan's Religious Scholars and Spiritual Leaders), 50
Shura yee Ulama, opposition to Indian tv serials *Kum Kum*, 167
Sidiq Khan Hashmat, (brother of Alim Khan, Amir of Bukhara), 97n1
Silk Road, 234; initiative for New, 240
Sistan, Afghan and Iranian, 286n7
SNTV (single nontransferable vote), 244, 290
Shuu'n Islami, Ministry of, 50
Social: institutions, 224n1; Organization, 180–81, 196n1; process, 180–81, 19n1; Services (basic delivery of), 14; Structure, 180–81, 196n1
SES (Social Ecological System), 295 (*See also* Ostrom)
Society (multi-ethnic/divided): fighting civil wars, 2
Somalia, 31
Southwest Asia, 73
Spanta, Rangin Dadfar, 112, 140
State: post-2001 Afghan, 103; changing conception of, 207–209; character of since 2001, 195; as "ethnic state," 271; conflict of tribe and, 271; fragmentation and reassembling of, 104–107; Hazara distrust of, 254; Hazaras and the, 254–57; sovereignty gap, 104
Sufi, 52
South Asia, 22, 82
Soviet: 40; Baloch becoming a "nation" under occupation, 281, 282–84; empire of trust, 4, inspired *coup de tat*, 5; Invasion of Afghanistan, 2; occupation of Afghanistan, 22, 33, 255; struggle against, 193–94; Tajikistan, 232; troop withdrawal of 189, 5; withdrawal from, 2
Soviet Union (USSR): 21, 29, 327; Afghanistan being pushed to the orbit of, 141; building Kabul Airport & Kushk-Herat-Kandahar road, 327; collapse of the, 2, 28, 49; Communist allies, 7; direct assistance to border district of Badakhshan, 239; implosion of, 234; invasion of Afghanistan, 2, 5, 41; Republics, 240; shattering of Afghan

institutions, 7; subsidies to Afghan Communists (1978-1992), 1
Special Inspector General for Afghanistan Reconstruction (SIGAR), 16n4
Spehr, Dr, Najibulla, Spehr tv, 168
Stalin, Joseph, 9
State(s) & statehood (Afghanistan): 124; anthropology of in Central Asia 105; categorization of, 116; challenges to stability of, 133-46; institutional rule of, 110; multi-ethnic Muslim, 8; "networked" 116; relations between center-periphery, 7; post-colonial, 15; Urban lineages of, 77-97; "weak," "failed," 197n4
Steel Authority of India Ltd (SAIL), 139
Subsidies: British to Afghan monarchs, 1; Soviet Union to Communists, 1
Suicide bombings, 149
Sufi(sm): *pirs* and their networks, 7; Khorasani, 38, 44, 46
Suhrawardi, 44
Supreme Court, Chief Justice of, 50
Syria, 2, 12

Tablighi Jamat, 46
Tahirids, rule of, 58
Tajiks: 57, 136, 151, 233, 254; of Kohdaman, 134; of northern Afghanistan 4
Tajikistan: 12; civil war, 234; cross border smuggling, 235; fighter in Badakhshan, 240; health workers in Badakhshan, 318; independence of, 234
Takhar (province), 14, 234, 318, 325n1
Taliban/*Taliban* (seminary students): 21, 23, 28, 30, 45-46, 51, 157, 200, 213-15, 274, 320; attacks in provinces, 330; anti-, 9; in Bamyan 13; beheading journalist, 166; 138; capture of Kabul, 11, 202; connection with Pakistan & ISI, 213; conquest of Nimruz, 276; deep root of extremism, 37; destroying telecom towers, 151; domination of Afghanistan, 2; effectiveness of gender policies, 201, 209-10; gender and sexuality before, 201; impetuosity, 48; imaginary regarding women, 202; instrumentalization of Islam, 202-206; insurgency, 7; Islamic Emirate of Afghanistan, 50, 128, 135; media blackout, 149; moral policing of, 200; and moral transgression, 205-206; and opium growers; ouster of, 14; opposition to, 1; as protectors of traditional Afghan family, 209-10; Pakistani, 45; Pashtun nationalist policies, 70-71; policies on women, 201; relocated in Badakhshan, 234; radical ideologies of, 8, 46; Sanjerani resistance against, 277; status of women, 31; Swat, 205; *taranas* (songs), 72; US-NATO dislodging of, 6, 9; use of modern media, 205
Talibanization, 204
Taliqan, 234
Tanai, Shahnawaz, 247n6
Tang Bala, 242, 248n13
Tanzim (Jihadi political organizations): 78, 285; identity politics of, 116; leaders 104; political military networks, 105, 110
Taqat, General Abdu Wahid, inflammatory remarks about non-Pashtuns, 91
Taraki, Nur Muhammad (Communist Part First Secretary 1978-1979), 286n4; Decrees on women's status, 201
Tariqa (mysticism), Khorasani, 38
Tarzi, Mahmud, 63; constitutionalist movement, 292
Tashadod (violence), 188
Technologies of power (See Power)
Teherik-i-Taliban Pakistan (TTP), 144
Television and media: Afghan producers, 161; *Afghan Star after Pop Idol*, 162; Badakhshan tv, 157; dramatic serials, 161; ethnography of, 152; Noor tv, 157; promotion of owners and supporter, 157; private stations, 156; popular genres, 158-60; political satire 159, Public Service Announcement (PAS), 158-60; reality tv, 161-63; role of government, warlords and foreign interests, 150; unofficial sources of funding, 156-59; Zhwandoon TV, 91
Television Stations: ATN (Ariana Television Network), 156, 158, 168; Emros tv, 157;

Noor tv, 157; Tamadon TV, 157; Tolo tv, 156, 158, 169
Thanawi, 44
Thieu, Nguyen Van, 27
Timurids rule, 59
Termiz, 15
Terrorism: 9/11 attacks, 6
Third World, 5
Tolo tv, 156, 158, 169. *See* Television
Tooi, 127
Tradition, textual, 57
Transparency International, annual list, 31
Tribes, 124; Durrani and Ghilzai, 28
Tribal belt, Pashtun and Baloch, 46
Tribal leaders, 127
Trump, President Donald, 21, 30
Trust deficit, 10, 12
Tooghundi, 172n3
Tunisia, 2
Turfan, 238
Turki (Chaghatai Uzbek), 46
Turkey, 2, 38, 172n6; refugees in, 12, 223
Turkistan, 40, 97n1; Eastern, 238
Turkman, 68, 72, 151, 254
Turkmanistan, 172n3
TUTAP (electricity pylons passing through Turkmenistan, Uzbekistan, Tajikistan, Afghanistan) project, 268n1

UAE (United Arab Emirates), 94
Ulama, 47, 49–50; council of, 50–52
Umma, 57, 204
United Nations, 24, 200, 210, 267; Assistance Mission in Afghanistan (UNAMA), 252, 330; HABITAT, 303; Hazaras appeal to UNAMA, 265–66; Office of for Coordination of Humanitarian Affairs, 31; Security Council, 30
US-NATO: invasions/intervention in Afghanistan, 9, 11–12, 26, 47, 52; initial goals of, 21; withdrawal of troops, 232
United States: 21, 28–30, 236, 267, 281; Afghan Bilateral Security Agreement (BSA), 25, 225n3, 293; Afghan trap, 25; Afghanistan relations, 95; Agency for International Development (USAID), 48, 129; Al Qaeda attacking interests, 2; Cold War objectives, 51; costs of war and reconstruction, 24, 51; Department of Defense Task Force for Business Stability Operations (TFBSO), value of mineral deposits in Afghanistan, 138; drone attacks, 26; Embassy support for Hazaras, 263; experience in Afghanistan, 21, 29; enmity with Iran 30; Government Accounting Office, 244; identification of Afghanistan as problematic due to Islamism, 154; involvement in Vietnam, 21–22, 29; militarization of foreign policy 2; NDI (national Democratic Institute), 301; non-military aid, 14; NATO Allies invasion of Afghanistan, 1, 6, 12, 23–24, 33; promotion of globalized jihad, 2; reduced military presence, 329; role in development and reconstruction of Afghanistan, 2, 6; September 11 attacks, 9; soldiers killed, 24; State Department choice of media for messaging, 154; supporting jihad against Red Army, 8; and UN, 236, 252, 327; withdrawal from Afghanistan, 11, 14
Urfan, 41
Universal Declarations of Human Rights (UDHR), 329
Urumchi, 238
Uruzgan, 257
Usmani, Taqi Uddin, 44 (*See* Deobandi movement)
USSR (*See also* Soviet Union): collapse of, 2; role in development and reconstruction of Afghanistan, 2; militarized foreign policy, 2; 1989 withdrawal from Afghanistan, 2
Uyghur, fighters in Badakhshan, 240
Uzbek: 46, 112, 136, 151, 254, 330; of Argu, 233; commanders in Badakhshan, 241; of northern Afghanistan 4, 102; of Badakhshan, 12, 233
Uzbeki (language) 68, 72
Uzbekistani: fighter in Badakhshan, 240

Vietnam, 27, 33, 51
Vietnam, North, 29
Viet Cong, 29
Village jirgas, 163
Violence, in the Middle East, Southeast and Central Asia, 2
Vulnerable groups with disabilities (in Afghanistan), 332; higher numbers and poorer among Hazara and Uzbek, 341; multidimensionally poor, 337–44; *m'alul* (mentally impaired), 341, 343; public stigma for *Diwana* person, 343
Vulnerability, multidimensional, 345

Wahdat-I-Islami, 293, 302 (*See also* Hezb-e Wahdat, and Party9ies)
Wahhabi, ideology, 44–45, 256
Wakhan (district in Badakhshan), 232, 239
Wakhi, 238
Wakil, 124
Waqf (awqaf pl.), 49, 52
War, 10–12, 15; anti-colonial, 8; between Islam and NATO and Taliban, 278; civil, 70; comparison of Vietnam and Afghanistan wars, 27; consequences of, 90; devastation of infrastructure and resources in Afghanistan, 6, 15; dividend of, 1, 15; during 1990s, 5, 41; "humanitarian," 7; impact on identity and political culture, 1–2, 8; proxy, 1, 5, 15, 234; producers of, 7, 8; role of *Qumandans* in, 2; on global terrorism, 2; technologies of, 4; state formation, 7; on Terror, 2, torn countries, 149
Warduj, 233–34, 245
Warlords, 149, 197n4; *jung salaran, zoor awara and tupaksalan*, 157
Washington, 197n4
Watan Group (financial and security), 93, 139–40. *See also* Security
Wa'z (preaching), 47
Wazir Akbar Khan Mena (Neighborhood in Kabul), 79, 82, 94
Wesh Dzalmian, 292
West Asia, 22
Western, great powers, 5, 15

Wolesi Jerga (lower house of parliament), 32, 108, 116
Woleswal (district governor), 187
Women: empowerment of, 297–303; Institute, 201; poor treatment of, 185; political party participation of, 291; and military resistance, 291; reserved seat in parliament, 329; Welfare Association, 202
WHO (World Health Organization), 315, 332
World Bank, estimates of economic growth, 334
World War II, 4, 9, 41; post war empires, 16n2

Xinjiang (China), 38

Yaftal, 233, 237; commanders, 242
Yaghistan (land of rebels), 125
Yakawlang, 13
Yale (University), 325n3
Yamchi village (in Sayyad District of Sar-i Pul province), 102
Yarkand, 238
Yemen, 2
Yumgan, 234, 245
Yun, Muhammad Ismael, 136

Zabt-e-Ahwalat (Recording of Security Conditions), 97n5
Zabul, 244, 330
Zahedan (Iran), 286n17
Zahir Shah, King Muhammad (r. 1933–1973), 187, 262; reliance on foreign aid, 227; Rome Group of, 117
Zaif (weak), 193
Zakat, 46
Zakatul fitr, 45–46
Zalim (Oppressor), 186
Zaranj, 280
Zardari, Asef, 30
Zardew (district in Badakhshan), 233
Zebak (district in Badakhshan), 232, 239
Zhwandoon TV, 91

Zia-ulHaqq, 41–42
Zia (*See* Haji Zia)
Zoorawar(ha/an pl.), 163–64, 168–72, 187, 193
Zoorkhana/pahlawani, 88
Zourmati, Sharifa (former parliamentarian-Paktia), 301

Zuhak, Jawad, 267
Zuhuri, Zuhurrullah, 229
Zulm (Oppression), 186, 192, 195–96
Zur (force), 196
Zurawaraan (bullies), 184, 194

www.ingramcontent.com/pod-product-compliance
Lightning Source LLC
Chambersburg PA
CBHW071357300426
44114CB00016B/2093